SECOND EDITION

THE COMMERCIAL OFFICE LEASE HANDBOOK

New York Model Clauses and Commentary

Lawrence D. Eisenberg, Jonathan L. Mechanic, David Alan Richards, and Michael Werner

Litigation notes researched and prepared by Asher R. Fried

ABA
AMERICAN BAR ASSOCIATION
Real Property, Trust and Estate Law Section

Cover design by Andrew Alcala

Printed in the United States of America.

26 25 24 23 5 4 3 2

A catalog record for this book is available from the Library of Congress.

CONTENTS

ACKNOWLEDGMENTS

The authors would like to thank Asher R. Fried of Lawyers Title Insurance Company, who prepared the litigation summaries for each chapter.

Messrs Mechanic and Werner would like to thank Jonathan Bash, Ansel Bencze, Cadine Bramwell, Michael Celler, Hunter Chamberlain, Emilie Cooper, Sana Gupta, Brian Helweil, Neil Hood, Valerie Kelly, Meyer Last, Austin Leist, Eric Marlowe, Tess Rowley, Katherine Skipper, Michael Stahr, Brian Stuart, Melanie Taylor, and Kendall Torpey, all of whom helped enormously in the writing of this treatise.

INTRODUCTION

A lease is not merely the grant of an interest in property but the embodiment of all of the rights and obligations of the parties to it and of the rules that will govern their relationship to each other and to the property demised over a period of time—more often than not, a long period of time. Hence, while at first blush one might imagine that a lease is a less significant agreement than, say, a contract of sale because while the latter deals with an anticipated conveyance of the entire bundle of property rights, the former deals with only a portion of those rights, nothing could be further from the truth. It is the lease that remains a vital, often consulted, and not infrequently litigated living document that likely will be relied upon by the parties to it on a regular basis over a long period of time.

This updated book, however, is not a treatise on the origins or nature of the lease. In it you will find no mention of "livery of seisin," the conveyance of an estate for years, or the distinction between the lease as a conveyance to which the law of real property would apply and the lease as a contract to which the law of contract would apply. Rather, this is a practical guide to commercial leasing practice designed for the practitioner, whether experienced or inexperienced, seeking a fuller understanding of why each provision of a lease is included in it, why it is important to the landlord and/or the tenant, and why and how to negotiate it.

A lawyer inexperienced in leasing matters gets a call from his or her client—"I'm sending over a lease for some new office space I'm taking. There shouldn't be much to talk about because it's on a standard form." Or a young associate at a law firm is asked by a partner to "prepare a lease reflecting the terms set forth in this term sheet." Alternatively, an experienced practitioner is struggling with one of the more arcane or trap-laden lease provisions—whether in the context of having to draft one that responds to the peculiarities of a highly negotiated term sheet or having to comment on one that just seems inappropriate. What to do?

This book combines, side by side, clause by clause, useful organized commentary on the ubiquitous "Standard Form of Office Lease" promulgated by the Real Estate Board of New York, Inc., and a sophisticated, but not uncommon, model form of manuscript lease that might be prepared for any office building landlord. Because the section headings used in both forms are almost identical, the book will aid any practitioner by providing easy-to-find, helpful examples and practice commentary for any lease form, provision by provision.

This Second Edition also contains additional chapters that were not included in the First Edition addressing expansion options, rights of first offer, and leasehold condominiums.

To provide a user-friendly practice guide, the book is organized into 54 chapters, each chapter corresponding to a single article of the model lease form and containing seven sections. The sections of each chapter are entitled, respectively:

- **General Purpose** (which explains the need met by the Article and how it functions);
- **Sample Clause** (which sets forth the applicable Article of the model form);
- **Landlord Concerns** (which explains why the Article is important to the landlord and distinguishes among those portions that are vital to the landlord's concerns and those portions that the landlord would like to have, but should be able to get by without);
- **Tenant Concerns** (which explains the pitfalls of the Article from the tenant's perspective (and where applicable, why the Article is important to the tenant) and distinguishes among those portions that the tenant must negotiate (and how to negotiate them) and those portions that the tenant should find tolerable if not desirable);
- **Standard Real Estate Board of New York Clause** (which sets forth the parallel Article from the REBNY "Standard Form");
- **Comments on the Standard Real Estate Board of New York Clause** (which explains how the model Article differs from the REBNY "Standard Form" Article and why, in this context, "Standard" is not a term to be confused with "Reasonable" or, for that matter, "Balanced"); and
- **Litigation Issues** (which, with citations, discusses the case law applicable to the Article).

Finally, the book, in an appendix, sets forth in full the REBNY Standard Form.

The authors hope that this book will prove to be a valuable and practical hands-on aid to lawyers navigating the sometimes difficult waters of commercial leasing.

—David Alan Richards

CHAPTER 1

Demise

1.1 General Purpose

The general purpose of the demising clause is to describe the space, including the square footage, leased to the tenant. Typically, the square footage is expressed as a "rentable" number, which includes an arbitrarily determined add-on factor to the usable square footage. Accordingly, the usable square footage is based on applying a so-called loss factor to the rentable square footage. The loss factor is also larger for partial floors than for full floors because of the allocation of the public corridors among the tenants on the floor. This loss factor varies from time to time, building to building, and even with respect to a particular building.

The Real Estate Board of New York (REBNY) recommends that the usable area be calculated generally as follows:

1. *Single tenant floors*, by measuring the floor to the outside surface of the building and subtracting therefrom the finished enclosing walls, public elevator shafts and stairs and their enclosing walls, and HVAC and telephone facilities not serving the floor in question.
2. *Multi-tenant floors*, by first calculating the usable area of the entire floor as if single-tenanted, then deducting corridor areas, including common toilets (but not enclosing walls), then calculating the usable area of each tenant's space by measuring each exterior building wall to its outside surface and demising walls to their center and walls which abut corridors to the corridor side, and finally, adding to each tenant's space its pro rata portion of the corridor area deducted as aforesaid.

Note that not all landlords follow the Real Estate Board formula.

In comparing various potential spaces, a tenant should not focus solely on the loss factor. The efficiency and suitability of space is affected by many other items, such as the mullion spacing of the perimeter wall and columns, and the extent to which a space with a materially higher loss factor may actually be a better value than a space with a smaller loss factor.

1.2 Sample Clause

1.01 Demise. Subject to the terms and conditions of this Lease, Landlord hereby leases for the Term [the entire] [a portion of] the [_____] floor[s] of the Building (the "Premises"), substantially as shown hatched on the plan annexed as Exhibit [_____]. Landlord and Tenant agree that the Premises is conclusively deemed to contain [__________] rentable square feet.

1.3 Landlord Concerns

The landlord wants the premises to be located and configured "substantially" as shown on attached plans, because, particularly if the premises' demising walls have not yet been constructed, the final, as-built location and, perhaps, configuration may vary from the plans because of field conditions and errors in construction. In addition, the landlord wants the plan to exclude mechanical and electrical closets, common hallways, and other areas that are reserved to the landlord.

The landlord wants the rentable square footage of the premises agreed upon in advance and set forth in the lease to provide certainty regarding the fixed rent, tenant's proportionate share of escalations, and electric charges (if charged on a rent inclusion basis), that is, the material economic terms. Note, though, that the space, as actually configured, may have a greater rentable square footage than the predetermined number.

1.4 Tenant Concerns

The tenant would prefer to have the plans be as precise as possible, to ensure that its tenant's expectations regarding the layout and location of conduits and tie-ins to building systems are fulfilled. Regarding the rentable square footage, since the exact location of the demising walls may not have been established, the tenant would prefer to measure the area after the walls are constructed, to ensure it is paying only for space actually demised (as grossed up to reflect any agreed-upon loss factor), and to have its own architect involved in making this determination. In any case, the tenant wants an agreement that its proportionate share will be calculated using the same standards of measurement for the balance of the building as used for the premises. It is in this manner that the tenant can be assured that it is truly charged its "proportionate" share.

In addition, the tenant may want to specify that the demise includes the nonexclusive right to use the common hallways, stairways, loading docks, and public areas of the building.

1.5 Standard Real Estate Board of New York Clause

Witnesseth [*top page 1*] Owner hereby leases to Tenant and Tenant hereby hires from Owner ______________ in the building known as ______________ in the Borough of ______________, City of New York.

1.6 Comments on Standard Real Estate Board of New York Clause

The board form provides for the specific rentable area and plan reference to be inserted into the lease; however, as discussed earlier, the parties may desire to measure the space after it is constructed.

1.7 Litigation Issues

The purpose of a lease is to "manifest [the] intent of identified parties to transfer control and possession of specified space, for a specified term, at an agreed-upon rental."[1] This purpose is expressed in the demising clause. Failure to specify the area to be leased will result in a determination that no lease was created. In *Davis v. Dinkins*,[2] an agreement by New York City providing for occupancy by homeless families of at most 150 of 189 rooms in a motel was held not to be a lease of any particular portion of the premises.

Failure to manifest an intent to transfer control and possession can result in the characterization of the agreement as a license, resulting in the inability to enforce the agreement against a subsequent owner. The description of the instrument as a "lease" or a licensee as "tenant," or payment of the consideration as "rent," will not convert a license to a lease where control over a specified space was not created. In *Linro Equipment Corp. v. Westage Tower Associates*,[3] an operator of laundry equipment could not enforce an agreement, deemed to be a license, entered into with a condominium sponsor when the project was converted to condominium ownership. The agreement (1) required the plaintiff to install and maintain laundry machines; (2) was for a renewable seven-year term; and (3) provided for the payment of "rent" by the plaintiff. The agreement was held to be a license because "the essential element of sole and exclusive dominion and control over the designated space was lacking."[4] The "tenant" was to keep its equipment in good working order, and had limited access to the building and laundry area. By failing as a lease, the agreement was personal to the sponsor and revocable by the condominium board.

If the intention is not to grant exclusive control, as in the usual laundry "lease" (where the "tenant" provides and maintains equipment, and has access for servicing the equipment and collecting proceeds), designating the agreement as a "lease" and stating that the laundry room is "leased exclusively" will not create a leasehold demise.[5] However, the fact that a tenant may install and maintain laundry equipment does not mean that a "laundry lease" must fail as a lease. If there has been a grant of exclusive possession of the premises, and the description of the premises can be proven by evidence,

1. *In re* Island Helicopters, Inc., 211 B.R. 453, 465 (Bankr. E.D.N.Y. 1997).
2. 206 A.D.2d 365, 613 N.Y.S.2d 933 (2d Dep't 1994).
3. 233 A.D.2d 824, 650 N.Y.S.2d 399 (3d Dep't 1996).
4. 233 A.D.2d 824 at 826.
5. Dime Laundry Serv. v. 230 Apts. Corp., 120 Misc. 2d 399, 466 N.Y.S.2d 117 (Sup. Ct. N.Y. Cnty. 1983).

even outside of the four corners of the lease, a lease may be established.[6] Note that the courts have upheld an agreement termed a license as a lease of a theater,[7] and a restaurant management agreement was held to be a sublease.[8]

Although the failure to specifically describe premises may result in a non-enforceable lease,[9] premises not described in a lease may be deemed included in the lease if it can be proven that the undescribed premises were intended for use with the described premises, or were essential for such use. Conduct of the parties, subsequent to the delivery of possession to the tenant, may further define the specifically demised premises as including additional premises or appurtenant rights. In the condemnation case *T.D. Golf, Inc. v. State of New York*,[10] the claimant was a subtenant of a golf course that was described in the sublease as being the same premises leased to the sublessor by the city of Hancock, New York. The court held that certain other land, actually owed in fee by the sublessor, was part of the subleased premises although never specifically described in the sublease. The sublessee's occupancy of the added land, used for parking and a practice tee, was deemed essential to the use of the specifically demised premises. Further, the use of the additional land was known and not objected to by the sublessor. This decision may be contrasted to the ruling that parking spaces and basement storage, used by a tenant without objection from the landlord for several years, were not essential to the operation of tenant's insurance agency, and thus not deemed part of the premises.[11] Mere convenience is insufficient to create an implication resulting in the addition of space, or an appurtenant easement, to a leasehold.

KRU Inc. v. 1000 Massapequa, Inc.[12] further illustrates the concept of inclusion by necessity. The premises did not specifically include an easement over a service road, owned by an adjacent owner, required by the tenant in order to have access to its loading dock. The adjacent owner erected a fence blocking the tenant's use of the service road, which was the sole means of access to the loading dock. The lease required that all deliveries be received at the loading dock. The court held that the access was in fact guaranteed, and thus the inability of the tenant to use the loading dock constituted an actual partial eviction.

Similarly, the tenant in *Broadway-Spring Street Corp. v. Jack Berens Export Corp.*[13] was partially evicted when the landlord altered a freight elevator in a manner that prevented the tenant from using it. Although the lease contained no express right of

---

6. Solon Automated Servs., Inc. v. Eastwood, 94 A.D.2d 961, 464 N.Y.S.2d 89 (4th Dep't 1983).

7. Am. Jewish Theatre, Inc. v. Roundabout Theatre Co., Inc., 203 A.D.2d 155, 610 N.Y.S.2d 256 (1st Dep't 1994).

8. The Statement, Inc. v. Pilgrim's Landing, Inc., 49 A.D.2d 28, 370 N.Y.S.2d 970 (4th Dep't 1975).

9. Davis v. Dinkins, 206 A.D.2d 365, 613 N.Y.S.2d 933 (2d Dep't 1994).

10. 32 A.D.2d 719, 304 N.Y.S.2d 454 (3d Dep't 1969).

11. Telesca v. M.L. Bruenn Co., Inc., 71 Misc. 2d 208, 335 N.Y.S.2d 875 (City Ct. New Rochelle 1972).

12. 238 A.D.2d 314, 656 N.Y.S.2d 47 (2d Dep't 1997).

13. 12 Misc. 2d 460, 171 N.Y.S.2d 342 (Mun. Ct. N.Y. Cnty. 1958).

the tenant to use the elevator, the court held such use to be a reasonably necessary and essential appurtenance. This decision was based on the tenant's use of the elevator with the knowledge of the landlord prior to the alteration, and on the fact that the conduct of the tenant's business included hauling 500-pound bales of textile remnants from the ground floor to the mezzanine.

Properly drafted lease provisions may permit alterations to a tenant's premises. In *Arrathoon v. Pergament Oceanside Corp.*[14] the premises were described at the beginning of the lease as a store and basement approximately 50 feet by 80 feet in a shopping center to be constructed. Paragraph 34 of the lease stated that the store "shall be the last store on the easterly end of the shopping center." After completion of the center and commencement of the defendant's lease, the landlord sought to extend the shopping center. As a consequence of the proposed extension, the defendant's premises would no longer be the last store on the easterly end of the shopping center. The court permitted the extension based on a reservation in paragraph 2 of the lease, providing that "there shall be no allowance to Tenant for a diminution of rental value and no liability on the part of landlord by reason of inconvenience, annoyance or injury to business arising from Landlord . . . making any repairs, alterations or improvements in or to any portion of the building or demised premises, or in . . . appurtenances . . . thereof." The court held paragraph 34 to be descriptive of where the demised premises would be upon completion, but not restrictive of the landlord's rights under paragraph 2. Furthermore, the tenant could not assert that it would be deprived of beneficial parking adjacent to its store, upon which the extension would be located, since the parking area was shown on a plot plan that was not included as an exhibit to the lease, and thus was not part of the premises.

Inclusion of a map or plan assists in defining the premises and appurtenant rights such as parking, but such drawings are interpreted within the context of the language of the body of the lease. In *Bayside Federal Savings and Loan Association v. Cord Meyer Development Corp.*,[15] a landlord was permitted to vary the configuration of a parking lot from that shown on an annexed map, where the lease covenant provided for a parking area of such size not less than that shown on the map. However, if a landlord covenanted to provide parking "substantially" as indicated on an annexed map, the tenant could prevent part of the parking lot as shown on the map from being used by another tenant for the sale of merchandise.[16]

---

14. 53 Misc. 2d 959, 281 N.Y.S.2d 263 (Sup. Ct. Nassau Cnty. 1965).
15. 28 A.D.2d 866, 281 N.Y.S.2d 893 (2d Dep't 1967).
16. 125 Hempstead Turnpike Corp. v. Tracco Hempstead, Inc., 14 Misc. 2d 554, 177 N.Y.S.2d 778 (Sup. Ct. Nassau Cnty. 1958).

CHAPTER 2

Premises; Condition; Landlord's Work

2.1 General Purpose

The twofold purpose of this provision or series of provisions[1] is (1) to describe (for the landlord) the premises' state or condition as basically acceptable to the tenant, subject to any required landlord's work; and (2) to describe (for the tenant) any work that the landlord is to perform prior to the tenant's occupancy. In the REBNY form, and in many manuscript leases, the components of these concerns may be separated.

The so-called "as is" standard of condition often constitutes a stand-alone provision and aims to forestall any later tenant complaint by the landlord's assertion that the premises, in its "as is" condition, is acknowledged by the tenant to be satisfactory or at least satisfactory subject to the completion of "Landlord's Work."

Since this last item will vary substantially from tenant to tenant, "Landlord's Work," if any, is the subject of a cross-referenced separate provision or, in the REBNY form, a rider. In buildings leasing up for the first time, where raw space must be built out (often for full-floor tenants), a detailed "Work Letter" may be attached, setting forth the standards for the tenant's plans and specifications to be submitted for the landlord's review, and strict timetables for tenant construction apportioning the risk of any delay. Where a lease is being negotiated for a building that is not yet constructed, the parties may enter into a separate "design and construction agreement" to cover the provisions typically seen in a "Work Letter" as well as standards for base building design and construction, strict timetables for landlord construction apportioning the risk of delay, and the coordination of landlord and tenant work. The discussion of work letters and design and construction agreements is beyond the scope of this book, but the more typical work provisions will be examined.

1. See Sample Clause in section 2.2, *infra*.

2.2 Sample Clause

2.01 Condition of the Premises.

(a) On the Commencement Date, Tenant shall accept the Premises in its "as is" condition on such date, subject only to Landlord's performance of Landlord's Work[, the Premises being in "broom clean" condition, the base Building mechanical systems serving the Premises being in good working order and condition and the common areas of the Building servicing the Premises being in material compliance with all applicable Laws.] All initial improvements that do not constitute Landlord's Work shall constitute Alterations and shall be performed by Tenant, at Tenant's expense, in accordance with Section [___].

(b) The taking of occupancy of the whole or any part of the Premises by Tenant shall be conclusive evidence, as against Tenant, that Tenant accepts possession of the same and that the Premises so occupied were in a good and satisfactory condition and as otherwise required by this Lease at the time such occupancy was taken.

(c) After the occurrence of the Commencement Date, Landlord and Tenant shall promptly confirm the Commencement Date, the Rent Commencement Date and the Expiration Date by a separate instrument; provided, that the failure to execute and deliver such instrument shall not affect the determination of such dates in accordance with the provisions of this Lease. Pending the resolution of any dispute as to the Commencement Date and/or the Rent Commencement Date, Tenant shall pay Rent based upon Landlord's determination.

2.02 Landlord's Work.

(a) Landlord, at Landlord's expense (except as otherwise set forth in Exhibit [___]), shall perform or cause to be performed the work described on Exhibit [___] ("Landlord's Work") in accordance with the provisions thereof. Landlord shall, at Landlord's expense, remedy latent defects with respect to Landlord's Work; provided that, Tenant gives Landlord notice of such defects within 12 months after the Commencement Date.

(b) [Except as set forth in Sections 2.02(c) and (d), i][I]f for any reason Landlord shall be unable to deliver possession of the Premises to Tenant on any date specified in this Lease for such delivery, Landlord shall have no liability to Tenant therefor and the validity of this Lease shall not be impaired, nor shall the Term be extended, by reason thereof. This Section 2.02(b) shall be an express provision to the contrary for purposes of Section 223-a of the New York Real Property Law and any other law of like import now or hereafter in effect.

[Sections 2.02(c)–(g) are examples of negotiated provisions]

(c) [If Landlord fails to Substantially Complete Landlord's Work on or before [__________] (such date, as the same may be postponed day-for-day by reason of Tenant Delays and/or Unavoidable Delays [subject to a cap of [___] days of Unavoidable Delays], the "Outside Date"), then, as Tenant's sole and exclusive remedy therefor (except as set forth in Section 2.02(d)), the Rent Commencement Date shall be postponed beyond the date the Rent Commencement Date would otherwise have occurred by [___] day for each day in the period commencing on the day after the Outside Date until the date that Landlord's Work is Substantially Complete.]

(d) [If Landlord fails to Substantially Complete Landlord's Work on or before [__________] (such date, as the same may be postponed day-for-day by reason of Tenant Delays and/or Unavoidable Delays [subject to a cap of [___] days of Unavoidable Delays], the "Outside Termination Date"), then Tenant may as Tenant's sole and exclusive remedy therefor (except as set forth in Section 2.02(c)), terminate this Lease by notice given to Landlord within 30 days after the Outside Termination Date. If Tenant timely gives such notice pursuant to the immediately preceding sentence, then this Lease shall terminate on the date such notice is given and neither Tenant nor Landlord shall have any further obligation or liability to the other under this Lease, except for any provision herein that expressly survives the expiration or earlier termination of this Lease. If Tenant fails to give such notice within 30 days after the Outside Termination Date then Tenant shall be deemed to have waived Tenant's right to terminate this Lease pursuant to this Section 2.02(d).]

(e) [Tenant shall have the right to enter the Premises prior to the Commencement Date for the purpose of installing data and telecommunication cabling and wiring; provided, that in all cases such access shall be permitted only to the extent that Landlord reasonably determines that such early access and installation activities will not delay Substantial Completion of Landlord's Work. Any person granted access on behalf of Tenant pursuant to this Section shall comply with all reasonable requirements that Landlord and Landlord's contractor may impose and shall strictly observe all rules and regulations promulgated by Landlord and/or Landlord's contractor relating to the job site. Any delay in the performance of Landlord's Work resulting from such access shall constitute Tenant Delay.]

(f) [Landlord's Work shall be deemed to be substantially complete ("Substantially Complete," and with correlative meaning, "Substantially Completed" and "Substantial Completion") on the earlier of (i) the date upon which Landlord's Work has been completed, other than (A) minor details or adjustments, (B) items that, in accordance with good construction practice, should be performed after completion of Tenant's initial Alterations and (C) any part of Landlord's Work that is not completed due to Tenant Delay; provided, that in each case Landlord shall nevertheless remain obligated to complete Landlord's Work and (ii) the date Tenant takes possession of the Premises for the performance of Alterations or for any other reason.]

(g) ["Tenant Delay" means any delay that Landlord may encounter in the performance of Landlord's obligations under this Lease by reason of any act or omission of any nature of Tenant, its agents or contractors, including, without limitation, delays due to changes in or additions to Landlord's Work requested by Tenant, delays by Tenant in submission of information or giving authorizations or approvals or delays due to the postponement of any Landlord's Work at the request of Tenant. Tenant shall pay to Landlord any costs or expenses incurred by Landlord by reason of any Tenant Delay.]

2.3 Landlord Concerns

With respect to the condition of the premises, the more common landlord posture is stated in Section 2.01(a) (set forth in the sample clause in Section 2.2, *supra*): the tenant takes "as is," with no landlord representations about anything. For larger and/or more sophisticated tenants, that opening bid will not be enough, and the landlord will be required to do more, including (as illustrated in the bracketed text of Section 2.01(a) set forth in Section 2.2, *supra*) effectively guaranteeing the condition of the building's systems and the legal compliance of the common areas.

With respect to further "Landlord's Work," the landlord will wish to insulate itself from the effect of any tenant-caused delays and/or force majeure delays that frustrate the estimated date of completion, and any agreed penalty imposed on Landlord for late completion should be adjusted on this account. As a result of events such as Superstorm Sandy and the COVID-19 pandemic, the definition and impact of force majeure on landlord delivery dates are gaining greater attention by legal practitioners. Landlords have recently sought to expand the force majeure definition, insofar as doing so benefits landlords, to include delays in the supply chain; government-imposed restrictions and construction shutdowns; closure of governmental agencies; and other delays and impacts attributable to superstorms, pandemics, endemics, and similar public health crises.

If the landlord grants the tenant a right to terminate the lease in connection with late delivery of the premises (see Section 2.02(d) set forth in the sample clause in Section 2.2, *supra*), the provision should include a deadline for the tenant's delivery of written notice to the landlord of the tenant's election to so terminate the lease.

2.4 Tenant Concerns

A stronger tenant will bargain for further definition to the phrase "as is," adding "broom clean" at a minimum and going on from there to cover other concerns: (1) the condition of the base building systems; (2) the need for refurbishment of windows and/or convectors; (3) the delivery of an ACP-5 or ACP-7 certificate with regard to asbestos; (4) the presence of common area facilities sufficient to meet local or federal fire or handicapped access laws, and the like. These concerns can either be addressed in the text of the Lease or included on the Exhibit describing Landlord's Work.

Beyond this basic space delivery work lies the universe of "Landlord's Work," which can be as simple as the addition of a demising wall or as complex as a complete buildout by the landlord's contractors. If the tenant will have an overlay of work beyond the "Landlord's Work," then care must be taken to fix a date by which the landlord should be substantially completed, so the tenant's contractors can have scheduled the start of the tenant's improvements. The tenant should also obligate Landlord to remedy latent defects in the Landlord's Work or, in the alternative, assign to the tenant the warranties applicable thereto. Section 2.02 entitled "Landlord's Work" (set forth in Section 2.2, *supra*) describes the result of such a negotiation, where both parties are installing improvements in sequence.

2.5 Standard Real Estate Board of New York Form

In the REBNY form, the "demised premises" are effectively defined in the Witnesseth section on the form's first page, although the later-used terms of "premises" or "demised premises" are not set down in such section. The form makes no explicit reference to an annexed exhibit containing a graphic description of the space demised, and in no place does this form provide a specific blank to be filled for a description of the number of square feet being rented. All of this is done by making these required references in the Witnesseth clause in the three blank lines provided, or by attaching a landlord rider touching on most or all of these points.

Language describing the condition of the premises and any required "Landlord's Work" may be found in the second and third sentences of REBNY Article 15, "Occupancy," and provide as follows:

> Tenant has inspected the demised premises and accepts them as is, subject to the riders annexed hereto with respect to Owner's work, if any. In any event, Owner makes no representation as to the condition of the demised premises, and Tenant agrees to accept the same subject to violations, whether or not of record.

2.6 Comments on Standard Real Estate Board of New York Clauses

If the owner/landlord has undertaken to do no work for the tenant, then from the owner's perspective REBNY Article 15 may stand unchanged in its stark simplicity, and the absence of a rider will prove in any subsequent dispute that no work was required. If the landlord has promised, and the tenant expects, such work (whether simply repainting and recarpeting, or something considerably more elaborate), then the language in the sample clause, set forth in Section 2.2, *supra*, may be adapted for purposes of a rider. Also, both parties will benefit from the presence of an exhibit or rider that shows the floor plan of the demised premises. Finally, a statement of the square footage might be added, and will necessarily be if the rider includes tax and/or operating cost escalation clauses based on the percentage of the building occupied by tenant.

2.7 Litigation Issues

The phrases "as is" and "deemed to be" must be read within the context of other relevant lease provisions, and the facts of each case, in order to assess whether a landlord may rely on these phrases in a claim concerning the size or condition of the premises.

The court, in *Wohl v. Owen*,[2] utilizing a definition found in *Black's Law Dictionary*, defined the phrase "deemed to be" to mean "treat as if." "Deemed to be" is often used by landlords to describe the area of the premises for the purpose of calculating Additional Rent based upon the tenant's portion of the entire building. In the *Wohl* case, the tenant believed that it was being overcharged on porter's wage escalation rent because the premises, "deemed to be" 660 square feet, was actually 414.22 square feet. The court concluded that "the use of the word deemed bars any conclusion that the landlord has made a representation."[3] The court did not rely solely upon the "deemed to be" phrase; even if the landlord had misrepresented the area during lease negotiations, the tenant had the ability to, and should have, verified the area by measurement prior to finalizing the lease. The court further concluded that "the tenant should have been alerted to the need for inquiry, if he was concerned about the matter, from the very lease he ultimately signed since it did not represent that there were 660 square feet but only *deemed* there to be such area."[4]

The merger clause in the *Wohl* lease was held inapplicable to the tenant's claim concerning area because it was limited to physical condition. In *S.R. Leon Co., Inc. v. The Towers*,[5] the merger clause bolstered the "deemed to be" defense, thus preventing the tenant from asserting a challenge to a landlord's statement concerning the usable square footage of the building where the premises was located. The merger clause negated any representations not only as to physical condition, but also as to ". . . any other matter or thing affecting or related to the premises, . . . Tenant has inspected the building and the demised premises . . . and agrees to take the same 'as is.'"[6] The inspection statement in the merger clause was particularly relied upon by the court, which also noted that the tenant waited eight years to assert its allegation of fraudulent inducement.

A commercial lease providing that a tenant takes possession of the premises "as is" negates any implied warranty of habitability.[7] If a condition requires extensive repairs in order to render premises safe for continued commercial use, and the lease repair clause does not impose upon a tenant the obligation to make structural repairs, the landlord is obligated neither to make such repairs nor to reimburse the tenant for making them, unless the lease contains an express covenant by the landlord to make such repairs.[8]

If the condition rendering the premises untenantable was known to the landlord at the inception of the lease, and the tenant abandoned possession as a result of the condition, constructive eviction may be alleged even in the absence of a landlord's express

2. 153 Misc. 2d 282, 580 N.Y.S.2d 854 (N.Y.C. Civ. Ct. Kings Cnty. 1992).
3. 580 N.Y.S.2d at 855.
4. *Id.* at 856–57.
5. 194 A.D.2d 600, 599 N.Y.S.2d 53 (2d Dep't 1993).
6. 599 N.Y.S.2d at 54.
7. Coulston v. Teliscope Prods., Ltd., 85 Misc. 2d 339, 378 N.Y.S.2d 553 (1st Dep't 1975).
8. Refrigeration for Sci., Inc. v. Deacon Realty Corp., 70 Misc. 2d 500, 334 N.Y.S.2d 418 (Sup. Ct. Nassau Cnty. 1972).

covenant to repair. A tenant may be relieved of its rental obligations because of a condition of the premises. To allege an eviction, the tenant must be deprived of the beneficial enjoyment or actual possession of the premises, as a result of the denial of some right under the lease, by reason of a wrongful act of the landlord.[9] If a tenant is actually evicted, or ousted from possession of part or all of the premises, the entire rent for the premises is suspended, even though the tenant may remain in possession of part of the premises. If the landlord substantially and materially deprived the tenant of beneficial use and enjoyment, and as a consequence, the tenant vacated all of the premises, the tenant is deemed to have been constructively evicted, and the rent is abated.

Constructive eviction can be asserted if the tenant abandons part of the demised premises.[10] In *Barash v. Pennsylvania Terminal Real Estate Corp.*,[11] the tenant complained that the building was not properly ventilated after hours. Constructive eviction could not, however, be asserted because the tenant remained in possession during regular business hours. Furthermore, since there were no landlord covenants concerning HVAC after business hours, it could not be argued that the landlord wrongfully deprived the tenant of a leasehold benefit.

Where the condition that a tenant may find inconvenient, even intolerable, such as excessive noise made by adjoining industrial tenants, is neither caused by the landlord nor results from a breach of a landlord's covenant, the condition cannot serve as the basis for a constructive eviction.[12]

A tenant is deprived of a substantial leasehold benefit when it is compelled to abandon part of the premises because of the landlord's failure to make repairs expressly required by the lease.[13] Such abandonment occurs, for example, when a restaurant is required to close on numerous occasions, without totally abandoning use of the premises, because of the landlord's failure to repair a leak around the grill area of a restaurant, thus preventing the preparation and service of food.[14]

An untenantable condition may be asserted as a defense to an action for the payment of rent, even if there is no actual or constructive eviction. In *West Broadway Glass Co. v. I.T.M. Bar Inc.*,[15] the landlord rented premises it knew was subject to water and sewer problems. Although the problems interfered with renovation work, the tenant continued with the renovation. The court determined that while the tenant was not entitled to a full rent abatement because it had retained possession, it was entitled to damages based upon diminution of rental value, and to dismissal of the nonpayment proceeding.

---

9. Barash v. Pa. Terminal Real Estate Corp., 26 N.Y.2d 77, 308 N.Y.S.2d 649 (1970).
10. Minjak Co. v. Diane Randolph, 140 A.D.2d 245, 528 N.Y.S.2d 554 (1st Dep't 1988).
11. *See Refrigeration for Sci., Inc.*, 70 Misc. 2d 500, 334 N.Y.S.2d 418.
12. Finkelstein v. Levinson, 74 Misc. 2d 105, 343 N.Y.S.2d 849 (N.Y.C. Civ. Ct. N.Y. Cnty. 1973).
13. Frame v. Horizons Wine & Cheese, Ltd., 95 A.D.2d 514, 467 N.Y.S.2d 630 (2d Dep't 1983).
14. Manhattan Mansions v. Moe's Pizza, 149 Misc. 2d 43, 561 N.Y.S.2d 331 (N.Y.C. Civ. Ct. N.Y. Cnty. 1990).
15. 245 A.D.2d 232, 666 N.Y.S.2d 629 (1st Dep't 1997).

In *Polak v. Bush Lumber Co.*,[16] it was determined that a landlord may be liable for tort damages resulting from the abandonment of a premises by a tenant, even in the absence of a covenant to repair. The tenant was forced to abandon the premises when part of the building facade fell. The court in *Polak* stated: "A landlord has a duty as an owner to use reasonable care in keeping in suitable condition such portions of the premises as are subject to his control."[17] An obligation imposed by law on a landlord, such as asbestos removal, will impose liability to reimburse a tenant for costs incurred for such removal during renovations conducted by the tenant, notwithstanding express repair obligations and compliance with law obligations imposed upon the tenant.[18]

If the landlord obligates itself to improve the condition of the premises and to construct the tenant's space, the landlord's obligations must be made specific enough to enforce. When a landlord agrees to construct premises for a tenant pursuant to plans to be approved by tenant, subsequent to the execution and delivery of the lease, the lease may fail as indefinite. The inclusion of preliminary plans, showing the intent of the parties as to the type of premises to be built, may be sufficiently detailed to result in a binding lease.[19] If the space is not completed in accordance with the plans, the measure of damages due the tenant is diminution in rental value, not the tenant's cost in completing the space as agreed to by the landlord.[20]

16. 170 A.D.2d 932, 566 N.Y.S.2d 757 (3d Dep't 1997).

17. 566 N.Y.S.2d at 759.

18. Marine Midland Bank v. 140 Broadway Co., 236 A.D.2d 232, 653 N.Y.S.2d 118 (1st Dep't 1997).

19. Dickenor Rest., Inc. v. Hotel Exec. on Madison Ave., Ltd., 13 A.D.2d 909, 215 N.Y.S.2d 580 (1st Dep't 1961).

20. Woodruff v. Castaldo, 113 A.D.2d 403, 496 N.Y.S.2d 875 (4th Dep't 1985).

CHAPTER 3

Term

3.1 General Purpose

The commencement date of the lease may be fixed or sliding. A fixed commencement date may be the date that the lease is executed and delivered, or a date certain that is later in time. A sliding commencement date usually is the earlier to occur of the date that the tenant takes possession of the space to perform work in preparation for its business occupancy, or the date that the space is available for the tenant's occupancy.

The lease should specify clearly when the various rights and obligations of the landlord and the tenant begin and end. Generally, not all of the rights and obligations of the parties commence on the date that the lease is signed or, for that matter, simultaneously on that or any other date. Rent and occupancy may be delayed, for example, if the space is not available for the tenant's use on the date that the lease is signed either because there is an existing tenant in the premises, or because the landlord must perform work in the premises to get it ready for the tenant's occupancy. The landlord will want the term to commence no later than the date upon which the tenant enters the space for any purpose so that the landlord can be protected by the appropriate lease provisions. When the tenant enters the premises to perform work or some other pre-occupancy function, the tenant generally will be required to meet some or all of its obligations under the lease, even though it has not opened the premises for business. At this point, at a minimum, the tenant should be obligated to carry appropriate insurance, indemnify the landlord for events occurring during the construction and/or move-in period, and, possibly, pay for its use of electricity. In addition, the rights and obligations of the parties in respect of maintenance, repairs, casualty, and compliance with law should commence no later than that time. Finally, the tenant may take possession of portions of the space as they become available or according to a predetermined schedule. In that case, the tenant's obligations may be phased in.

Once the demised premises are free of other occupancies and the work, if any, that the landlord is obligated to perform has been substantially completed, the tenant still may not be required to assume the full lease obligations if, for example, the landlord has agreed to a so-called "free rent" period. In that case, the obligation to pay rent will be delayed to a later rent commencement date, notwithstanding that many or all of the other obligations of the tenant under the lease may have commenced. The parties also must agree on whether the rent abatement applies only to fixed rent, or to fixed rent and to some or all of the additional rent provided for under the lease. If the premises are not available because of the presence of an existing tenant or work that the landlord must perform, the tenant is not likely to have any immediate obligations under the lease at the time that it is executed and delivered, other than perhaps to furnish plans and specifications to the landlord.

The expiration date of the lease will be a date certain but may not be known when the lease is signed. For example, if the expiration date is the date immediately preceding the fifth anniversary of the commencement date (or, more typically, the fifth anniversary of the last day of the month in which the commencement date occurs), and the commencement date depends on freeing the demised premises of a holdover tenant, the expiration date cannot be known until the commencement date is determined. In such circumstances, if the expiration date is fixed at the time the lease is executed (as is frequently the case), then, by definition, the duration of the term cannot be known when the lease is signed. The lease might also be extended pursuant to a renewal option or terminated earlier than the scheduled expiration date. An early termination can arise from the right of either party to terminate the lease pursuant to the casualty or condemnation provisions, any early termination option granted to the landlord or the tenant, or the right of the landlord to terminate the lease as a result of the tenant's default. For the purposes of administering the lease, it is probably easiest to have the expiration date fall on the last day of a month even if the commencement date is not the first day of a month, as shown in the sample clauses that follow.

If the commencement date is not a fixed date, it is advisable to require that upon a determination of the commencement date the parties will execute an agreement setting forth the commencement date and expiration date of the lease. Otherwise, there will be no agreed-upon record of when the commencement actually occurred and the expiration date is scheduled to occur.

3.2 Sample Clause

[Sample Clause A]

3.01 Term.

"Term" means the period commencing on the Commencement Date and ending, unless sooner terminated as herein provided, on the Expiration Date.

"Commencement Date" means [__________].

"Expiration Date" means [__________][, as the same may be extended pursuant to Article [___].

[Sample Clause B]

3.01 Term.

"Term" means the period commencing on the Commencement Date and ending, unless sooner terminated as herein provided, on the Expiration Date.

"Commencement Date" means the earlier to occur of (a) the date on which Landlord's Work is deemed to have been Substantially Completed in accordance with Exhibit E and (b) the date Tenant (or any person claiming by, through or under Tenant) occupies any portion of the Premises [for the conduct of business][the performance of Tenant's Initial Work].

"Expiration Date" means the last day of the calendar month in which the day preceding the [___] anniversary of the [Rent] Commencement Date occurs][, as the same may be extended pursuant to Article [___].

3.3 Landlord Concerns

The lease is binding when executed and delivered, but may be subject to a condition subsequent or a right of the landlord or tenant to cancel the lease if certain conditions are not met by some outside date. The landlord will vigorously seek to limit any such opportunity for the tenant to cancel the lease. The landlord will have invested time and incurred expense to obtain the tenant and negotiate the lease and will have taken the space off the market. If the tenant cancels the lease, the landlord will have to start the process again, losing additional time and incurring additional expense. Whether Sample Clause A or B (see Section 3.2, *supra*) is used depends on when the landlord can deliver vacant possession and whether the landlord is required by the lease to perform work in the space to prepare it for the tenant's initial occupancy. If a "sliding" (as distinguished from a fixed) Commencement Date or Rent Commencement Date is used, it is imperative that the Expiration Date is defined to be tied correctly to either the Commencement Date or the Rent Commencement Date per the terms of the business deal. In any event, the parties will have to deal with the issues of when their respective rights and obligations will arise under the lease. As noted in Section 3.1, *supra*, it is common for certain rights and obligations to arise prior to the commencement date and for others to arise later.

As noted in Section 2.3, *supra*, landlord and tenant practitioners are focusing more closely on the impacts of force majeure on their respective rights and obligations. Tenants generally bear the risk of force majeure events delaying their fit-out after landlords deliver their premises, and tenants' rent obligations commence regardless of those force majeure impacts. Tenants with significant negotiating leverage should at least seek to delay their obligation to commence paying rent to the extent their fit-out is delayed due to a specific, ongoing force majeure event if the lease is being negotiated during the pendency of such an event (for example, COVID-19 pandemic), and where landlords agree to such a concession the lease expiration date will likely extend in lock-step with the extension of the rent commencement date in order to avail landlords of a full term of rent.

3.4 Tenant Concerns

The tenant will want to make certain that it has no obligations under the lease until the latest possible date. Accordingly, the tenant has to be aware of the timing mechanisms in these clauses. If, as is usually the case, the tenant is not to take possession of the premises on the date that the lease is executed and delivered, the tenant will have to consider each of its obligations under the lease and determine which, if any, it is willing to perform prior to (1) the date that it takes possession of the premises for the purpose of performing work and (2) the date that it takes possession of the premises for the purpose of commencing its business operations. If portions of the premises are to be delivered to the tenant at differing times, it will be necessary to make the foregoing determinations with respect to each such portion of the premises.

If the occupancy date is not the date that the lease is executed and delivered, the tenant will have to think about the effect of delays, whether caused by the landlord or events beyond the landlord's control. From the tenant's perspective, the lease should set an outside date upon which the tenant could terminate the lease if the premises are not available for occupancy (see Section 2.02(d) set forth in the sample clause in Section 2.2, *supra*). Unfortunately, even a right to cause a termination of the lease prior to the commencement date may be a hollow remedy for a tenant that has to relocate on or before, as is usually the case, a fixed date. The tenant will attempt to gain additional remedies in the hope that these will "encourage" the landlord to deliver the premises on time. Remedies, other than the right to terminate the lease by reason of delays not caused by the tenant, include postponing the rent commencement date for a negotiated number of days for each day that the premises are not available for occupancy (see Section 2.02(c) set forth in the sample clause in Section 2.2, *supra*).

The landlord, of course, cannot allow a late delivery penalty to continue without limit, if at all. Also, the landlord should respond by asking for a right of its own to terminate the lease if, for reasons beyond the landlord's control, vacant possession cannot be obtained or the work cannot be completed on time. The landlord will try to limit any right of the tenant to impose a penalty on the landlord or to terminate the lease. The landlord will want one or more notices and an opportunity to cure any delay caused by its failure to timely perform its obligations under the lease.

3.5 Standard Real Estate Board of New York Clause

> Owner hereby leases to Tenant and Tenant hereby hires from Owner ______________ in the building known as ______________ in the Borough of ______________, City of New York, for the term of ______________ (or until such term shall sooner cease and expire as hereinafter provided) to commence on the ____ day of ______________ in the year ______, and to end on the ___ day of ______________ in the year ______, and both dates inclusive, at the annual rental rate of ______________. . .

3.6 Comments on the Standard Real Estate Board of New York Clause

This provision contemplates a fixed commencement date that may or may not be the same date as the date of execution and delivery of the lease and a fixed expiration date.

It fails to address many of the other issues discussed earlier, which would have to be covered in a rider.

3.7 Litigation Issues

The commencement date of a lease is more often determined by the occurrence of an event or condition than by the express statement of a specific date in the lease. The performance of such event may be by a third party, such as an existing tenant being required to vacate the demised premises; or by the landlord, who often covenants to "substantially complete" construction of the premises; or even by the tenant, who may be given a specified time to obtain a certificate of occupancy or zoning variance. A lease may be void if the term is indefinite or ambiguous;[1] but pegging a commencement date to the occurrence of a definite condition will not render the term indefinite.

The commencement date of the lease litigated in *67 Wall Street Co. v. Franklin National Bank*[2] was dependent on the prior tenant vacating the demised premises. No commencement date was actually set. The mechanism was a covenant by the landlord to "give notice to Tenant promptly after being advised by INCO [prior tenant] of the date on which it will actually vacate. . . ." If that event did not occur by August 31, 1970, either party could cancel the lease upon 60 days' notice. The prior tenant did not vacate by August 31, 1970; the tenant gave the requisite cancellation notice; and prior to the expiration of the 60-day period, the prior tenant vacated the premises.

The court held that the lease provided for a definitely ascertainable commencement. Interestingly, the court read an automatic recision into the cancellation provision if the agreed-upon contingency occurred prior to the expiration of the notice period. The better practice would have been to specifically incorporate a recision into the clause.

The lease term litigated in *510 Joint Venture v. Solcoor, Inc.*[3] was to commence on September 1, 1983, and end on August 31, 1988, or if the premises was not ready for occupancy on the commencement date, the lease would expire five years from the last day of the month in which the premises was substantially completed. At the commencement of the lease the landlord and tenant disputed when substantial completion occurred. The landlord gave tenant a notice fixing November 15, 1983, as the date of substantial completion and the tenant asserted that December 1, 1983, was the date.

The tenant decided not to exercise its renewal option and vacated the premises in the belief that its rental obligation ceased on August 31, 1988. The landlord sought to hold the tenant to a November 14, 1988, expiration date, and the court agreed. It was clear that the lease would commence on substantial completion and expire on the last day of the month five years thereafter. The fact that the parties may have disputed when substantial completion occurred did not render the occurrence of the event of

1. Genesee Conservation Found., Inc. v. Oatka Fish & Game Club, Inc., 63 A.D.2d 1115, 405 N.Y.S.2d 869 (4th Dep't 1978) (where the term was "for so long a period of time as the lessee remains an active club . . .").
2. 38 A.D.2d 460, 330 N.Y.S.2d 670 (1st Dep't 1972).
3. 177 A.D.2d 465, 575 N.Y.S.2d 897 (2d Dep't 1991).

substantial completion so indefinite that it could not be the determining condition of lease term commencement.

In the complex development lease discussed in *Omath Holding Co., Inc. v. the City of New York*,[4] the conditions for commencement were not asserted to be ambiguous. The lease for the marina complex was to commence on the earlier of one of the following: (1) the date on which the tenant substantially completed the project; (2) the date the tenant commenced business; or (3) 42 months after the tenant obtained rezoning of the premises. The term was defective because the lease contained no cancellation provision if the commencement conditions did not occur. The tenant could not achieve the rezoning and continued discussions with the city for 18 years as to how to develop the project. The tenant sought to enforce the lease when the city eventually gave notice to the tenant that it considered the lease null and void and was seeking to solicit new proposals.

The court held the lease void as an unreasonable restraint on alienation because the failure to include a cancellation provision resulted in an indefinite leasehold term. The court "drafted" in an implied "reasonable time period" for the tenant to rezone the premises and, as a matter of law, the expiration of 18 years was a reasonable period.

A lengthy delay in commencing the lease term does not always mean that a party may apply to a court to set a "reasonable" time for performance or termination. The facts in *RKO Century Warner Theatres, Inc. v. Morris Industrial Builders*[5] were similar to the *Omath* case in that nine years after the lease had been executed the tenant had yet to take occupancy, construct the premises as the lease required, or pay rent. The landlord and tenant bickered for that period of time over development and construction plans and unsuccessfully attempted to renegotiate the lease provisions. The landlord eventually declared the lease terminated as a result of the tenant's nonperformance and sought a judicial determination declaring the lease void as an unreasonable restraint on alienation.

Unlike the *Omath* decision, the court in this case found the lease to be valid. The landlord covenanted to provide a development plan, the tenant to provide construction plans and construct the theater; and the lease provided termination remedies if the covenants were breached. "In contrast [to *Omath*], the lease here sets forth the obligations of each party, and while the question of whether they have satisfied those obligations may need to be decided in court, there is no outside agency whose action or inaction can interfere with the parties' ability to carry out the terms of the contract."[6]

Stendig, Inc. v. Thom Rock Realty Co.[7] is another case where the term commencement was conditioned upon substantial completion. The lease contained an additional right of cancellation exercisable by either landlord or tenant if 250,000 square feet of leases in the building had not been signed. The tenant began to negotiate for space in

4. 149 A.D.2d 179, 545 N.Y.S.2d 557 (1st Dep't 1989).
5. 174 Misc. 2d 954, 667 N.Y.S.2d 217 (Sup. Ct. N.Y. Cnty. 1997).
6. 667 N.Y.S.2d at 219.
7. 163 A.D.2d 146, 558 N.Y.S.2d 917 (1st Dep't 1990).

another building, and alleged that it ended those negotiations based on representations made by the landlord's representative concerning modifications to the existing lease. After the tenant ceased negotiating for other space, the landlord terminated the existing lease based on the cancellation right. The court held that the landlord was estopped to rely on this provision, and waived the same. The estoppel argument is based on the principle that "the landlord, by conditioning the lease on the renting of 250,000 square feet of space, implicitly promised to use his good faith best efforts to bring about this result."[8]

General Obligations Law (GOL) section 5-905 regulates automatic renewal of lease term provisions that may be contained in a lease. The statute requires the landlord to notify the tenant of the automatic renewal provision not less than 15 days nor more than 30 days prior to the date by which a tenant must notify a landlord that it does not intend to renew a lease. This statute was construed in *Malone Associates v. Grand Union Co.*[9] Grand Union had assigned its lease, which by its terms provided for automatic renewal if the tenant held over after the expiration of the term. The assignee held over, and was held liable for the renewal term, notwithstanding the landlord's failure to provide notice pursuant to GOL section 5-905, as the result of its act of holding over. However, the assignor was discharged of any liability for rent during the renewal term because of the failure of the landlord to provide the required notice.

8. 558 N.Y.S.2d at 919.
9. 249 A.D.2d 830, 671 N.Y.S.2d 861 (3d Dep't 1998).

CHAPTER 4

Fixed Rent

4.1 General Purpose

The fixed rent clause is intended to set forth the amount and manner of the "fixed" or "base" rent required to be paid. The clause also sets forth the "Rent Commencement Date," that is, the date on which the fixed rent obligation accrues. This is typically a fixed period of time after the commencement date.

4.2 Sample Clause

4.01 Fixed Rent; Manner of Payment.

(a) Fixed Rent shall be payable by Tenant in advance on the Rent Commencement Date and on the first day of each calendar month thereafter; provided, that Tenant shall pay, upon the execution and delivery of this Lease by Tenant, [$__________] to be applied against the first full monthly installment of Fixed Rent following the Rent Commencement Date; and provided further, that if the Rent Commencement Date is not the first day of a month, then Fixed Rent for the month in which the Rent Commencement Date occurs shall be appropriately prorated.

"Rent Commencement Date" means the date occurring in the [___] month after the Commencement Date which is the same numerical date in the month as the Commencement Date (except that if no same numerical date shall exist in such [___] month, the Rent Commencement Date shall be the last day of such [___] month).

(b) Tenant shall pay all Rent as the same shall become due and payable under this Lease (i) in the case of Fixed Rent and recurring Additional Rent, by electronic transfer of immediately available funds as directed by Landlord and (ii) in the case of all other sums, either by electronic transfer as aforesaid or by check (subject to collection) drawn on a bank that clears through The Clearing House Payments Company L.L.C., in each case at the times provided herein without notice or demand (except as otherwise expressly provided in the Lease) and without setoff or counterclaim (except as otherwise expressly provided in the Lease or as required by Law). All Rent shall be paid in lawful money of the United States to Landlord at its office or such other place as Landlord may from time to time designate. If Tenant fails timely to pay any Rent, Tenant shall pay interest thereon from the date when such Rent became due to the date of Landlord's receipt thereof at the lesser of (A) 1½% per month and (B) the maximum rate permitted by law. Any Additional Rent for which no due date is specified in this Lease shall be due and payable on the 30th day after the date of invoice. All bills, invoices and statements rendered to Tenant with respect to this Lease shall be binding and conclusive on Tenant unless, within 60 days after receipt of same, Tenant notifies Landlord that it is disputing same.

4.3 Landlord Concerns

The landlord wants the first month's installment of fixed rent to be paid upon lease execution as additional short-term security for the tenant's obligations. If the free rent period is lengthy, and the landlord is performing a significant amount of work or providing a significant construction allowance, then the landlord will be incurring material costs specific to the tenant during a period when the tenant has no payment obligation. In addition, the landlord may have liability for brokerage commissions whether or not the tenant ever pays rent or occupies the premises.

The landlord wants the rents paid without notice (in the case of fixed rent and recurring escalation charges), and with only the notice otherwise prescribed in the lease for additional rent. The landlord also wants payments to be available in its account as soon as possible. Accordingly, the sample clause provides for the fixed rent and other recurring charges to be made by wire transfer and other payments to be issued by a bank, which enables the landlord's bank to use the shortest clearing time.

If any portion of the operating expenses attributable to services actually consumed by the tenant (e.g., electrical charges or cleaning) are payable by the tenant on a rent inclusion basis, the commencement of the applicable portion of the fixed rent payments should be adjusted to begin before the rent commencement date.

4.4 Tenant Concerns

The tenant does not want to pay the first month's rent in advance because doing so costs the tenant the use of such funds for the period up to the rent commencement date. Further, if the tenant terminates the lease before its fixed rent obligation commences, for example, because a non-disturbance agreement is not obtained or the landlord fails to timely perform its build-out, the tenant may have difficulty obtaining repayment.

The tenant will want to modify the provision that rent be paid without notice, demand, abatement, setoff, or counterclaim to state "except as otherwise expressly provided in this Lease" to reflect rights elsewhere granted the tenant.

4.5 Standard Real Estate Board of New York Clause

[At conclusion of Witnesseth clause on p. 11.] At the annual rate of ______ which Tenant agrees to pay in lawful money of the United States which shall be legal tender in payment of all debts and dues, public and private, at the time of payment, in equal monthly installments in advance on the first day of each month during said term, at the office of Owner or such other place as Owner may designate, without any set off or deduction whatsoever, except that Tenant shall pay the first _______ monthly installment(s) on the execution hereof (unless this lease be a renewal).

In the event that, at the commencement of the term of this lease, or thereafter, Tenant shall be in default in the payment of rent to Owner pursuant to the terms of another lease with Owner or with Owner's predecessor in interest, Owner may at Owner's option and without notice to Tenant add the amount of such arrears to any monthly installment of rent payable hereunder and the same shall be payable to Owner as additional rent.

4.6 Comments on Standard Real Estate Board of New York Clause

The board form includes what is in effect a cross-default clause, providing for the addition of overdue payments under another lease between the parties to the obligations under the lease at issue. The utility of this provision, as drafted, is questionable because it is unlikely that the exact same parties will be parties to another lease, other than in the building (in which event cross-defaulting the leases would be beneficial and appropriate). In addition, it is doubtful that a sophisticated tenant would accept this clause, which would limit its ability to default under another lease because it may put this lease at risk. The board form does not specify the manner of payment. Therefore, any landlord's lawyer utilizing the board form would want to set forth, in a rider, comparable provisions to the sample lease clause specifying wire transfers for base rent, and escalation rent and checks drawn on a New York Clearing House member bank for all other charges.

4.7 Litigation Issues

The standard form of lease contemplates the nature and liability associated with fixed rent and adequately protects a landlord's rights and remedies. When a practitioner drafts a lease without referring to a standard form, certain problems may arise. The drafter (1) may fail to designate that the rent shall be payable "in advance, on the first day of each month during the term," incorrectly assuming that the liability for rent accrues at the beginning of the rental period instead of at the end;[1] (2) may fail to provide that the rent is to be paid without offset or counterclaim, in order to avoid the consolidation of a summary eviction proceeding with a supreme court action for damages resulting

1. Smathers v. Standard Oil, 233 N.Y. 617 (1922).

from an alleged landlord breach; or (3) fail to provide for acceleration in case of default, preventing an action for damages until each subsequent rent installment is due.[2]

A situation requiring careful draftsmanship arises when the fixed rent does not commence on a specific date, but on a date determined by a future contingent event. In *Quik Snax at Herald Square, Inc. v. Herald Center Department Store, L.P.*,[3] payment of the fixed rent was contingent on the happening of a future event. Until the occurrence of the future event, the rent to be paid consisted of a percentage of the profits. The plaintiff-tenant's restaurant was located in a building within a "vertical" shopping mall intended to house 70 separate stores. The fixed rent was not payable "until 80% of the Units are leased and open for business in Herald Center." Although the project was not financially viable, the landlord eventually did lease more than 80 percent of the building's floor space to two department stores instead of 70 separate stores. The court ruled that the fixed rent was not payable. Having found that the landlord's drafting of the contingency was clear and unambiguous, the court was able to rule that the contingency that would require the tenant to pay fixed rent never occurred.

In *British American Development Corp. v. Fay's Drug Co., Inc.*,[4] the court found that the formula set forth in the lease for calculating the fixed rent was unambiguous and, as a consequence, as in the *Quik Snax* case, *supra*, resulted in the adoption of the tenant's assertions as to how the rent should be determined. The rent was to be calculated on "gross leasable area," measured from the outside face of the front and rear exterior walls and the midpoint of common walls on either side of the premises. The lease provided that the landlord would construct the premises pursuant to the tenant's plans. The plans called for a mezzanine area to be constructed for use as a lunchroom, bathroom, and office. Since there was no separate formula for measuring the gross leasable area of the mezzanine contained within the basic confines of the premises, the fixed rent determined by the formula was deemed to exclude any amount for the mezzanine.

The legal principle to be derived from both the *Quik Snax* and *British American* cases is that when a lease provision is clear and unambiguous, extraneous evidence, such as expert testimony of what "gross leasable area" might mean in the real estate industry, will not be admitted. Thus, in addition to drafting clear and unambiguous language, the landlord's attorney must anticipate contingencies, such as the failure of a project to be developed as planned, or a tenant using more floor area than anticipated.

Extrinsic evidence was permitted to establish the basic rental in *Grand Manor Health Related Facility v. Hamilton Equities, Inc.*[5] The rent was to be calculated on the "annual Medicaid reimbursement rate." This phrase was defined by neither statute nor lease. The court took into consideration the understanding of the lawyer who drafted the language of the provision and who negotiated for the landlord and tenant with the state. The result was the adoption of an interpretation most favorable to the tenant. In

2. Martin v. Glenzan Assoc., 75 A.D.2d 660, 426 N.Y.S.2d 347 (3d Dep't 1980).
3. 221 A.D.2d 154, 633 N.Y.S.2d 37 (1st Dep't 1995).
4. 178 A.D.2d 801, 577 N.Y.S.2d 528 (3d Dep't 1991).
5. 114 A.D.2d 776, 495 N.Y.S.2d 38 (1st Dep't 1985).

circumstances such as these, where a dollar amount is not specified in a lease, it is of utmost importance to incorporate a specific formula into a lease stating the manner in which the rent is to be calculated.

A payment made in lieu of rent may not be deemed to be a payment of rent as required by a lease. A payment made by a sublessee to a sublessor in order to obtain a cancellation of a sublease has been held not to be a prepayment of rent as to violate a covenant in a ground lease prohibiting the ground lessee from accepting a prepayment of rent for more than one month in advance.[6] In *Chusuk, Ltd. v. 461 Fifth Avenue Associates*,[7] the prohibition against accepting a prepayment of more than one month's rent was intended to preserve the sublease as security in the event of the ground lessee's default. Acceptance of a payment for cancellation has the same detrimental result: namely, the ground lessee receives compensation and the ground lessor loses rental income as security. However, the court will not "deem" a cancellation payment (made to obtain a right to surrender the premises) to be a rental payment, made in consideration of the right to occupy premises. The ground lessor should have specifically prohibited the ground lessee from canceling a sublease without consent.

The fixed rent provision should clearly state the due date, grace period, and termination notice periods. The landlord, through a course of conduct, may be considered to have waived due dates and time periods.[8] However, the acts of a landlord that may constitute a waiver of strict compliance of lease rent payments will not bind a subsequent purchaser who has no knowledge of the waiver and who has a right to enforce the clear requirements in a lease.[9] A successor landlord, who may have knowledge or be charged with knowledge of the prior landlord's waiver (such as an executor of the prior landlord's estate), can escape the effect of the waiver by entering into a new lease and faithfully enforcing its provisions.[10]

---

6. 154 Nassau St. Realty Co. v. Pinkerton's Nat'l Detective Agency, Inc., 17 A.D.2d 292, 233 N.Y.S.2d 747 (1st Dep't 1962).

7. 1997 WL 231173 (S.D.N.Y. 1997).

8. East 4th St. Garage, Inc. v. L.B. Mgmt. Co., 172 A.D.2d 292, 568 N.Y.S.2d 111 (1st Dep't 1991).

9. Tehan v. Thos. C. Peters Printing Co., Inc., 71 A.D.2d 101, 455 N.Y.S.2d 429 (4th Dep't 1979); Stoneybrook Realty, L.L.C. v. Cremkco, Inc., 176 Misc. 2d 589, 675 N.Y.S.2d 749 (Sup. Ct. App. Tm. 2d Dep't 1998).

10. Estate of Birnbaum v. Yankee Whaler, 75 A.D.2d 708, 427 N.Y.S.2d 129 (4th Dep't 1980).

CHAPTER 5

Additional Rent; Escalation

5.1 General Purpose

In the world of commercial leases, a stabilized rent, unvarying during the term of the lease, is now a matter of history. The modern lease virtually always includes "escalation clauses," which provide a means to "pass through" increases in a landlord's operating costs to its tenants, usually in proportion to each tenant's share of the premises on a square-footage basis. Tax escalations came first in time, and those applicable formulae remain relatively simple; when inflation became a persistent feature of our national economy, it became equally imperative for landlords to pass through increases in their other costs of operation, whether for labor or materials.

While operating escalation provisions show considerable variety, their purpose is to preserve the landlord's original profit margin—the purchasing power of the landlord's basic rent dollar—as calculated at term commencement. This is accomplished by causing the tenants to absorb, again proportionally, all increases in building operating costs running from the respective commencement dates of their leases after the passage of a "base year." These charges are always characterized as "additional rent" (additional, that is, to base or fixed rent), the nonpayment of which permits a landlord to employ all the remedies that it has for default in the payment of fixed rent. The landlord's aggregate rental income in its basic elements is thus sufficient to cover all costs of ownership: (1) debt service on the building is covered by the fixed rent; (2) real estate taxes for the base year are covered by the fixed rent and increases are covered by a specific escalation provision; (3) operating expenses for the base year are covered by the fixed rent and increases are covered by a similar escalation clause (actual cost increase or labor rate or price index rate); and (4) profit (25 percent to 50 percent, protected from erosion).

The Real Estate Board of New York (REBNY) commercial lease form does not, as printed, contain any provisions with respect to either real estate tax escalations or operating cost escalations; these are customarily the subject of one or more riders, which are virtually all building-specific. It is, of course, possible to treat even tax escalation as part of overall building costs escalation, and have only one provision for escalation costs, but often in a New York commercial lease there are two such articles (one for tax escalations, one for operating cost escalations), and a landlord using the REBNY form may have even more cost-specific riders (e.g., "public electric cost escalation," "steam escalation," "insurance cost escalation," as well as separate riders for tax escalation and operating cost escalation).

Furthermore, the operating cost escalation provisions have themselves varied in their formulae over time, and closely reflect the economic preoccupations of their respective eras. During the Great Depression, percentage rent arrangements were popular in order to keep the minimum rent as low as possible, and to allow the landlord to participate in gross sales in better times to come (a concept derived from oil and gas leases). After prosperity returned, for many years in New York, the "porter's wage clause"[1] held sway, creating an additional rent charge based on the increase of the regular hourly wage rate of porters as determined by the union contract of Local 32B and Local 32J of the Building Service Employees Union. A variation on the theme, in use nationally as well as locally, was and is to have a similar formula based on the Consumer Price Index, or CPI,[2] as periodically measured and published by the U.S. Department of Labor.

Both the porter's wage clause and the CPI attempted to measure the increase in a building's operating costs at a distance, assuming that the actual increase in such costs over time would be reflected, more or less accurately, by the increase in the index in question (and for a time, the "penny-for-penny" porter's wage clause seemed to do just that (see 5.05A(c))). The benefits to the landlord of an indexed increase were patent: no examination of books, no arguments over repairs versus capital improvements, no mere recoupment, and ease of administration. However, once owners discovered that the CPI "market basket of goods" (or, before that, the "penny-for-penny" increase in the union contract porter's wage) no longer seemed to reflect the inflationary rate of standard building costs (electricity and/or steam, cleaning, administrative overhead, etc.), the worth of these rigid equations in five-to-ten-year leases was limited at best. Thus, landlords have turned increasingly in the last several decades to operating cost escalation provisions that, in great detail, basically schedule all varieties of the building's operating costs to be shared by the occupants, and then invite the tenants to check the books if the landlord's annual increases seem suspect.

The sample clause set forth in Section 5.2, *infra*, consists of an omnibus "escalation" provision, which (in two sections) covers both tax escalations and operating cost escalations (the "proportionate share" elements of these two clauses are effectively the same, and this permits some drafting compression). The formula used in the operating cost section that is most frequently encountered today (instead of a CPI or porter's wage formula) is an enumeration of actual categories of operating costs (see Section 5.02 within Section 5.2, *infra*), followed by a list of excluded operating costs that tenants should not fairly be asked to bear (see Section 5.02(d) within Section 5.2, *infra*).

1. A sample of "porter's wage clause" is set forth in Section 5.5, *infra*.
2. Section 5.5, *infra*, also sets forth a sample form based on the CPI.

This omnibus clause is intended to be a relatively sophisticated set of provisions that might be used either as a rider to the REBNY form or as a stand-alone provision in a manuscripted lease.

In the chapter sections that follow, during the discussion of this lengthy provision from the perspectives of the landlord and tenant, additional concerns and draft clauses will be examined. No "sample" provision can possibly cover all the variations on the tax-and-operating-costs theme; the aim here is to provide the practitioner with a good sense of the range of issues raised by such an important set of clauses.

5.2 Sample Clause

5.01 Tax Payments.

(a) "Tax Year" means each period of 12 months, commencing on the first day of July of each such period, in which occurs any part of the Term, or such other period of 12 months occurring during the Term as hereafter may be adopted as the fiscal year for real estate tax purposes of the City of New York.

(b) "Base Tax Year" means the Tax Year commencing on July 1, [_____] and ending on June 30, [_____].

(c) "Base Tax Amount" means the Taxes for the Base Tax Year.

(d) "Taxes" means (i) the real estate taxes, vault taxes, assessments and special assessments levied, assessed or imposed upon or with respect to the Project by any federal, state, municipal or other government or governmental body or authority, including, without limitation, dues, levies or charges paid to any business improvement district or similar organization or to any entity on behalf of such an organization and (ii) all taxes assessed or imposed with respect to the rentals payable under this Lease other than general income and gross receipts taxes (note that taxes on rentals are based on the specific lease rent and not a percentage share of the building rent roll); *provided*, that any such tax shall exclude Commercial Rent or Occupancy Taxes imposed pursuant to Title 11, Chapter 7 of the New York City Administrative Code so long as such tax is required to be paid by tenants directly to the taxing authority. If at any time the method of taxation shall be altered so that in lieu of or as an addition to or as a substitute for, the whole or any part of such real estate taxes, assessments and special assessments now imposed on real estate, there shall be levied, assessed or imposed (x) a tax, assessment, levy, imposition, fee or charge wholly or partially as a capital levy or otherwise on the rents received therefrom, or (y) any other such substitute tax, assessment, levy, imposition, fee or charge, including without limitation, business improvement district and transportation taxes, fees and assessments, then all such taxes, assessments, levies, impositions, fees or charges or the part thereof so measured or based shall be included in "Taxes." If (A) Landlord or a Superior Lessor is exempt from the payment of taxes described in clauses (i) and (ii), but is required to make payments in lieu of Taxes, then there shall be included in Taxes the actual amount of such payments so required to be made and (B) a portion, but not all, of the Project is exempt from the payment of taxes described in clauses (i) and (ii) and no payments in lieu of Taxes are required to be paid by Landlord or any Superior Lessor in respect thereof, then there shall be included in "Taxes" the taxes described in clauses (i) and (ii) which would be so levied, assessed or imposed if such partial exemption did not exist and such taxes shall be deemed to have been paid by Landlord on the dates on which such taxes otherwise would have been payable in the absence of such exemption. Except as permitted in this Section 5.01(d), "Taxes" shall not include any income, franchise, capital stock, gains, inheritance, or transfer tax. Any assessments and special assessments included in Taxes which may be paid in installments without interest shall be deemed payable in the maximum number of installments permitted by law without incurring any penalties, and only such installment(s) as are payable within any Tax Year shall be included in Taxes for such Tax Year for the purposes of this Lease.

(e) "Tenant's Share" means [_____]% (calculated by dividing (i) [_____] by (ii) [_____], which Landlord and Tenant agree constitutes the rentable square foot area of the Building for purposes of computing Tenant's Share) [in the parenthetical the first blank (i) is the square footage of the Premises and the second blank (ii) is the square footage of the Building].

(f) If Taxes for any Tax Year, including the Tax Year in which the Commencement Date occurs, shall exceed the Base Tax Amount, Tenant shall pay to Landlord (each, a "Tax Payment") Tenant's Share of the amount by which Taxes for such Tax Year are greater than the Base Tax Amount. Landlord may furnish to Tenant, prior to the commencement of each Tax Year, a statement setting forth Landlord's reasonable estimate of the Tax Payment for such Tax Year. Tenant shall pay to Landlord on the first day of each month during such Tax Year, an amount equal to 1/12th of Landlord's estimate of the Tax Payment for such Tax Year. If Landlord shall not furnish any such estimate for a Tax Year or if Landlord shall furnish any such estimate for a Tax Year subsequent to the commencement thereof, then (i) until the first day of the month following the month in which such estimate is furnished to Tenant, Tenant shall pay to Landlord on the first day of each month an amount equal to the monthly sum payable by Tenant to Landlord under this Section 5.01(f) in respect of the last month of the preceding Tax Year; (ii) after such estimate is furnished to Tenant, Landlord shall notify Tenant whether the installments of the Tax Payment previously made for such Tax Year were greater or less than the installments of the Tax Payment to be made in accordance with such estimate, and (x) if there is a deficiency, Tenant shall pay the amount thereof within 30 days after demand therefor, or (y) if there is an overpayment, Landlord shall refund to Tenant the amount thereof; and (iii) on the first day of the month following the month in which such estimate is furnished to Tenant and monthly thereafter throughout such Tax Year, Tenant shall pay to Landlord an amount equal to 1/12th of the Tax Payment shown on such estimate. Landlord may, during each Tax Year, furnish to Tenant a revised statement of Landlord's estimate of the Tax Payment for such Tax Year, and in such case, the Tax Payment for such Tax Year shall be adjusted and paid or refunded as the case may be, substantially in the same manner as provided in the preceding sentence. After the end of each Tax Year Landlord shall furnish to Tenant a statement of Tenant's Tax Payment for such Tax Year (and shall endeavor to do so within 180 days after the end of each Tax Year). If such statement shall show that the sums paid by Tenant, if any, under this Section 5.01(f) exceeded the Tax Payment to be paid by Tenant for the applicable Tax Year, Landlord shall refund to Tenant the amount of such excess; and if such statement shall show that the sums so paid by Tenant were less than the Tax Payment to be paid by Tenant for such Tax Year, Tenant shall pay the amount of such deficiency within 30 days after demand therefor. If there shall be any increase in the Taxes for any Tax Year, whether during or after such Tax Year, or if there shall be any decrease in the Taxes for any Tax Year, the Tax Payment for such Tax Year shall be appropriately adjusted and paid or refunded, as the case may be, in accordance herewith. In no event, however, shall Taxes be reduced below the Base Tax Amount.

(g) If Landlord shall receive a refund of Taxes for any Tax Year in which Taxes exceeded the Base Tax Amount, Landlord shall pay to Tenant Tenant's Share of the net refund (after deducting from such refund the actual and reasonable costs and expenses of obtaining the same, including, without limitation, reasonable appraisal, accounting and legal fees); provided, that such payment to Tenant shall in no event exceed Tenant's Tax Payment paid for such Tax Year. If, with respect to any Tax Year after the Base Tax Year, Landlord shall incur any costs or expenses in an effort to reduce the Taxes for such Tax Year, and after final determination of such Taxes, Landlord has not recovered such costs and expenses by way of a deduction from a refund as set forth in the first sentence of this paragraph, then Tenant shall pay to Landlord, within 30 days after invoice, Tenant's proportionate share of the reasonable out-of-pocket costs and expenses so incurred.

(h) If the Taxes comprising the Base Tax Amount are reduced as a result of an appropriate proceeding or otherwise, the Taxes as so reduced shall for all purposes be deemed to be the Base Tax Amount and Landlord shall notify Tenant of the amount by which the Tax Payments previously made were less than the Tax Payments required to be made under this Section 5.01, and Tenant shall pay the deficiency within 30 days after demand therefor, which demand shall be accompanied by reasonable evidence of such reduction.

5.02 Operating Payments.

(a) "Base Operating Amount" means Operating Expenses for the Base Operating Year.

(b) "Base Operating Year" means calendar year [_____].

(c) "Landlord's Statement" means an instrument setting forth the Operating Payment payable by Tenant for a specified Operating Year.

(d) "Operating Expenses" means all expenses paid or incurred by or on behalf of Landlord in respect of the repair, replacement, maintenance, operation and security of the Project, including, without limitation, (i) salaries, wages, medical, surgical, insurance (including, without limitation, group life and disability insurance), union and general welfare benefits, pension payments, severance payments, sick day payments and other fringe benefits of employees of Landlord, Landlord's Affiliates and their respective contractors engaged in such repair, replacement, maintenance, operation and/or security; (ii) payroll taxes, worker's compensation, uniforms and related expenses (whether direct or indirect) for such employees; (iii) the cost of fuel, gas, steam, electricity, heat, ventilation, air-conditioning and chilled or condenser water, water, sewer and other utilities, together with any taxes and surcharges on, and fees paid in connection with the calculation and billing of, such utilities; (iv) the cost of painting and/or decorating all areas of the Project, excluding, however, any space contained therein that is demised to tenants; (v) the cost of casualty, liability, fidelity, rent and all other insurance regarding the Project; (vi) the cost of all supplies, tools, materials and equipment, whether by purchase or rental, used in the repair, replacement, maintenance, operation and/or security of the Project, and any sales and other taxes thereon; (vii) the fair market rental value of Landlord's Building office and any other premises in the Building utilized by the personnel of either Landlord, Landlord's Affiliates or Landlord's contractors not to exceed an aggregate of [_______] rentable square feet in the Project, in connection with the repair, replacement, maintenance, operation and/or security thereof, and all office expenses, such as telephone, utility, stationery and similar expenses incurred in connection therewith; (viii) the cost of cleaning, janitorial and security services, including, without limitation, glass cleaning, snow and ice removal and garbage and waste collection and disposal; (ix) the cost of all interior and exterior landscaping and all temporary exhibitions located at or within the Project; (x) the cost of all alterations, repairs, replacements and/or improvements made at any time following the Base Operating Year by or on behalf of Landlord, whether structural or non-structural, ordinary or extraordinary, foreseen or unforeseen, and whether or not required by this Lease, and all tools and equipment related thereto; provided, that if under GAAP, any of the costs referred to in this clause (x) are required to be capitalized, then such costs shall not be included in Operating Expenses unless they (I) are required by any Laws that first became effective (1) on or after the date of this Lease or (2) before the date of this Lease but with respect to which the obligation to comply first arises after the date of this Lease, (II) have the effect of reducing expenses that would otherwise be included in Operating

Expenses only to the extent of the reduction in Operating Expenses reasonably anticipated by Landlord, (III) constitute a replacement that in Landlord's reasonable judgment is prudent to make in lieu of repairs to the replaced item(s), so long as the same would be treated as such by comparable landlords in comparable buildings or (IV) are depreciable in accordance with generally accepted accounting principles consistently applied ("GAAP") over a period of not more than 10 years, in which event (except in the case of alterations, repairs, replacement, and/or improvements described in clause (III) of this clause (x), the cost of which shall be included in Operating Expenses in the Operating Year in which such costs are incurred) the cost thereof, together with interest thereon at either (A) if Landlord shall not finance such alterations, repairs, replacements, and/or improvements, the Interest Rate in effect on December 31 of the Operating Year in which such costs were incurred or (B) if Landlord shall finance such alterations, repairs, replacements, and/or improvements, the actual interest rate incurred by Landlord in connection with such financing, shall be amortized and included in Operating Expenses over the useful life of the item in question, as determined in accordance with GAAP; (xi) management fees not to exceed [__]% of the gross revenues from the Project; (xii) all reasonable costs and expenses of legal, bookkeeping, accounting and other professional services; (xiii) fees, dues and other contributions paid by or on behalf of Landlord to civic or other real estate organizations; (xiv) installation, operation and maintenance of holiday decorations; and (xv) all other fees, costs, charges and expenses properly allocable to the repair, replacement, maintenance, operation and/or security of the Project, in accordance with then prevailing customs and practices of the real estate industry in the Borough of Manhattan, City of New York. Notwithstanding the foregoing, "Operating Expenses" shall not include the following:

(A) depreciation and amortization (except with respect to the alterations, repairs, replacements, and/or improvements described in clauses (I), (II), (III) and (IV) of clause (x) of this Section 5.02(d));

(B) principal and interest payments and other costs incurred in connection with any financing or refinancing of the Project or any portion thereof (except as provided in clause (x) above);

(C) the cost of tenant improvements made for tenant(s) of the Building, including permit, license, and inspection fees related thereto;

(D) brokerage commissions and advertising expenses incurred in procuring tenants for the Building;

(E) cost of any work or service performed for any tenant of the Building (including Tenant), whether at the expense of Landlord or such tenant, to the extent that such work or service is in excess of the work or service that Landlord is required to furnish Tenant under this Lease at the expense of Landlord;

(F) [the cost of any electricity consumed in the Premises or in any other space in the Building demised or available for demise to tenants;] *[To be inserted if electricity is separately addressed]*

(G) Taxes;

(H) legal fees incurred in preparing or negotiating leases or lease amendments for tenants or in disputing, litigating or enforcing the terms of any lease;

(I) any cost to the extent Landlord is reimbursed therefor out of insurance proceeds or otherwise (other than by means of operating expense reimbursement provisions contained in the leases of other tenants);

(J) rent payable under any Superior Lease (other than amounts which constitute a reimbursement to the Superior Lessor for items which would have been included in Operating Expenses under this Lease if the same were paid directly by Landlord) and costs incurred with respect to the execution or modification of any Superior Lease (including, without limitation, fees for obtaining approvals from or otherwise dealing or negotiating with superior lessors or providing reports and information thereto or thereof and legal fees and disbursements in connection therewith);

(K) wages, salaries and benefits paid to employees of Landlord above the level of the immediate supervisor of the building manager;

(L) any costs of acquiring sculpture, paintings or other objects of fine art, but nothing contained herein shall be deemed to preclude Landlord from including as an Operating Expense the cost to clean, maintain, insure and secure any such works of art;

(M) the cost of any judgment, settlement or arbitration award resulting from any tort liability of Landlord, and all expenses incurred in connection therewith, or in connection with any such claims or disputes arising from Landlord's negligence or willful misconduct;

(N) all costs and expenses of abating or remediating any hazardous materials located in the Building that have been determined to be hazardous materials as of the date of this Lease (exclusive of any such costs with respect to hazardous materials used in compliance with all applicable Laws in the ordinary course of operating and maintaining the Project, which costs may be included in Operating Expenses);

(O) all amounts paid by Landlord to Affiliates of Landlord for services in the Project to the extent that the same exceeds the costs of such services rendered by unaffiliated third parties on a competitive basis in first class office buildings in *[insert market area]*;

(P) any compensation paid to clerks, attendants or other persons in commercial concessions operated by Landlord for profit;

(Q) to the extent any costs that are otherwise includable in Operating Expenses are incurred by or on behalf of Landlord and any Affiliate of Landlord with respect to both the Project and any other buildings owned by Landlord or its Affiliate(s), there shall be excluded from Operating Expenses the percentage thereof that is reasonably allocable to such other properties as reasonably determined by Landlord;

(R) the cost of correcting defects in any Building equipment or Building Systems or any other facilities located at the Project to the extent Landlord has an existing warranty that covers such costs;

(S) costs incurred with respect to a sale of all or any portion of the Project or any interest therein or in any person or entity of whatever tier owning an interest therein and the cost of maintaining, organizing or reorganizing the entity that is the landlord under this Lease;

(T) the costs of installing, operating and maintaining a specialty improvement, such as a cafeteria, lodging or private dining facility, or an athletic, luncheon or recreational club, unless Tenant is permitted to make use of any such facility without additional cost or on a basis consistent with other users;

(U) any interest, fine, penalty or other charge payable by Landlord by reason of the late payment of any Taxes or Operating Expenses, except to the extent the late payment was incurred with respect to a payment, part or all of which was the responsibility of Tenant hereunder and which Tenant did not make in a timely fashion or did not make at all; and

(V) general overhead costs of Landlord, as distinguished from the costs of the management, operation, repair and maintenance of the Project.

(e) "Operating Year" means each calendar year in which occurs any part of the Term.

(f) For each Operating Year, including the Operating Year in which the Commencement Date occurs, Tenant shall pay (each, an "Operating Payment") Tenant's Share of the amount, if any, by which Operating Expenses for such Operating Year exceed the Base Operating Amount.

(g) If during any relevant period (i) any rentable space in the Building above the ground floor shall be unoccupied, and/or (ii) the tenant or occupant of any space in the Building above the ground floor undertook to perform work or services therein in lieu of having Landlord perform the same and the cost thereof would have been included in Operating Expenses, then, in any such event, the Operating Expenses for such period shall be increased to reflect the Operating Expenses that would have been incurred if such space had been occupied or if Landlord had performed such work or services, as the case may be.

(h) Landlord may furnish to Tenant, prior to the commencement of each Operating Year, a statement setting forth Landlord's estimate of the Operating Payment for such Operating Year. Tenant shall pay to Landlord on the first day of each month during such Operating Year, an amount equal to 1/12th of Landlord's estimate of the Operating Payment for such Operating Year. If Landlord shall not furnish any such estimate for an Operating Year or if Landlord shall furnish any such estimate for an Operating Year subsequent to the commencement thereof, then (A) until the first day of the month following the month in which such estimate is furnished to Tenant, Tenant shall pay to Landlord on the first day of each month an amount equal to the monthly sum payable by Tenant to Landlord under this Section 5.02 in respect of the last month of the preceding Operating Year; (B) after such estimate is furnished to Tenant, Landlord shall notify Tenant whether the installments of the Operating Payment previously made for such Operating Year were greater or less than the installments of the Operating Payment to be made in accordance with such estimate, and (x) if there is a deficiency, Tenant shall pay the amount thereof within 30 days after demand therefor, or (y) if there is an overpayment, Landlord shall refund to Tenant the amount thereof; and (C) on the first day of the month following the month in which such estimate is furnished to Tenant and monthly thereafter throughout such Operating Year Tenant shall pay to Landlord an amount equal to 1/12th of the Operating Payment shown on such estimate. Landlord may, during each Operating Year, furnish to Tenant a revised statement of Landlord's estimate of the Operating Payment for such Operating Year, and in such case, the Operating Payment for such Operating Year shall be adjusted and paid or refunded as the case may be, substantially in the same manner as provided in the preceding sentence.

(i) Landlord shall furnish to Tenant a Landlord's Statement for each Operating Year (and shall endeavor to do so within 180 days after the end of each Operating Year). If Landlord's Statement shall show that the sums paid by Tenant, if any, under Section 5.02(h) exceeded the Operating Payment to be paid by Tenant for the applicable Operating Year, Landlord shall refund to Tenant the amount of such excess; and if the Landlord's Statement shall show that the sums so paid by Tenant were less than the Operating Payment to be paid by Tenant for such Operating Year, Tenant shall pay the amount of such deficiency within 30 days after demand therefor.

(j) (A) Tenant, upon notice given within 60 days after Tenant's receipt of a Landlord's Statement, may elect to have Tenant's designated (in such notice) certified public accountant (who may be an employee of Tenant but who may not, in any case, be retained by Tenant on a contingency fee basis or any other fee basis by which such accountant's compensation is based upon the amount refunded or credited by Landlord to Tenant as a result of such audit) examine such of Landlord's books and records (collectively, "Records") as are directly relevant to such Landlord's Statement, and Landlord shall promptly provide reasonable access to the Records upon reasonable prior notice. As a condition to Tenant's right to review the Records, Tenant shall pay all sums required to be paid in accordance with the Landlord's Statement in question. If Tenant shall not give such notice within such 60 day period, then such Landlord's Statement shall be conclusive and binding upon Tenant. Tenant and Tenant's employees, accountants and agents shall treat all Records as confidential, and, upon request by Landlord, shall confirm such confidentiality obligation in writing.

(B) Tenant, within 90 days after the date on which the Records are made available to Tenant, may send a notice ("Tenant's Statement") to Landlord that Tenant disagrees with the applicable Landlord's Statement, specifying in reasonable detail the basis for Tenant's disagreement and the amount of the Operating Payment Tenant claims is due. If Tenant fails timely to deliver a Tenant's Statement, then such Landlord's Statement shall be conclusive and binding on Tenant. Landlord and Tenant shall attempt to resolve such disagreement. If they are unable to do so, Tenant shall notify Landlord, within 90 days after the date on which the Records are made available to Tenant in connection with the disagreement in question, that such disagreement shall be determined by an Arbiter in accordance with this Section 5.02(j), and promptly thereafter Landlord and Tenant shall jointly designate a certified public accountant (the "Arbiter") whose determination made in accordance with this Section 5.02(j)(B) shall be binding upon the parties. If Tenant timely delivers a Tenant's Statement, the disagreement referenced therein is not resolved by the parties and Tenant fails to notify Landlord of Tenant's desire to have such disagreement determined by an Arbiter within the 90-day period set forth in the preceding sentence, then the Landlord's Statement to which such disagreement relates shall be conclusive and binding on Tenant. If the determination of the Arbiter shall substantially confirm the determination of Landlord, then Tenant shall pay the cost of the Arbiter. If the Arbiter shall substantially confirm the determination of Tenant, then Landlord shall pay the cost of the Arbiter. In all other events, the cost of the Arbiter shall be borne equally by Landlord and Tenant. The Arbiter shall be a member of an independent certified public accounting firm having at least 3 accounting professionals. If Landlord and Tenant shall be unable to agree upon the designation of the Arbiter within 15 days after receipt of notice from the other party requesting agreement as to the designation of the Arbiter, which notice shall contain the names and addresses of two or more certified public accountants meeting the requirements of this Section 5.02(j)(B) and who are acceptable to the party sending such notice, then either party shall have the right to request the American Arbitration Association (or any organization which is the successor thereto) (the "AAA") to designate as the Arbiter a certified public accountant meeting the requirements of this Section 5.02(j)(B) whose determination made in accordance with this Section 5.02(j)(B) shall be conclusive and binding upon the parties, and the cost of such certified public accountant shall be borne as provided above in the case of the Arbiter designated by Landlord and Tenant. Any determination made by an Arbiter shall not exceed the amount determined to be due in the first instance by Landlord's Statement, nor shall such determination be less than the amount claimed to be due by Tenant in Tenant's Statement, and any determination which does not comply with the foregoing shall be null and void and not binding on the parties. In rendering such determination such Arbiter shall not add to, subtract from or otherwise modify the provisions of this Lease, including the immediately preceding sentence. Pending the resolution of any contest pursuant to this Section 5.02(j)(B), and as a condition to Tenant's right to prosecute such contest, Tenant shall pay all sums required to be paid in accordance with the Landlord's Statement in question. If Tenant shall prevail in such contest, an appropriate refund shall be made by Landlord to Tenant. The term "substantially" as used in this Section 5.02(j)(B), shall mean a variance of [range of 3% to 10%] or more of the Operating Payment in question.

5.03 Tax and Operating Provisions.

(a) In any case provided in Section 5.01 or 5.03 in which Tenant is entitled to a refund, Landlord may, in lieu of making such refund, credit against future installments of Rent any amounts to which Tenant shall be entitled. Nothing in this Article 5 shall be construed so as to result in a decrease in the Fixed Rent. If this Lease shall expire before any such credit shall have been fully applied, then (provided Tenant is not in default under this Lease) Landlord shall refund to Tenant the unapplied balance of such credit.

(b) Landlord's failure to render or delay in rendering a Landlord's Statement with respect to any Operating Year or any component of the Operating Payment shall not prejudice Landlord's right to thereafter render a Landlord's Statement with respect to any such Operating Year or any such component[; provided, that such Landlord's Statement is delivered within 2 years after the end of the Operating Year in question], nor shall the rendering of a Landlord's Statement for any Operating Year prejudice Landlord's right to thereafter render a corrected Landlord's Statement for such Operating Year [within such 2-year period]. Landlord's failure to render or delay in rendering any statement with respect to any Tax Payment or installment thereof shall not prejudice Landlord's right to thereafter render such a statement [provided such statement is delivered within 2 years following the later of (i) the end of the Tax Year in question or (ii) the final determination of the Taxes for the Tax Year in question], nor shall the rendering of a statement for any Tax Payment or installment thereof prejudice Landlord's right to thereafter render a corrected statement therefor [within such 2-year period]. [If Landlord shall not render any statement (or corrected statement) within the relevant 2-year period, then Landlord shall be deemed to have waived any right to render such statement (or corrected statement).]

(c) Landlord and Tenant confirm that the computations under this Article 2 are intended to constitute a formula for agreed rental escalation and may or may not constitute an actual reimbursement to Landlord for Taxes and other costs and expenses incurred by Landlord with respect to the Project.

(d) Each Tax Payment in respect of a Tax Year, and each Operating Payment in respect of an Operating Year, which begins prior to the Commencement Date or ends after the expiration or earlier termination of this Lease, and any tax refund pursuant to Section 2.02(e), shall be prorated to correspond to that portion of such Tax Year or Operating Year occurring within the Term.

5.3 Landlord Concerns

The landlord's goals in this article are (1) to pass through every increase in costs of operation of the building incurred during the term; (2) to make those incremental collections from tenants on a current basis, even though final numbers may not be available until year-end accounting; and (3) where the increase in costs is not a function of a non-landlord-controlled index (Consumer Price Index [CPI] or porter's wage) already publicly available, but is instead a measurement of landlord's provable expenses, to keep business confidentiality to the extent possible, while allowing tenants some opportunity to examine the landlord's books and records to confirm its numbers.

The first goal will never be achieved. If the landlord is using a CPI or porter's wage formula, the rate of increase in those indices may not match the rate of actual increases in the landlord's real-world group of costs (which neither CPI nor the porter's wage formula was invented to measure). If, on the other hand, the landlord chooses to use a comprehensive listing of actual operating costs, tenants will argue for several exceptions, as detailed earlier in the sample clause (see Section 5.2, *supra*), on the grounds that many landlord expenses (such as legal fees for leasing activity or lease enforcement) are a cost of doing business, which should be built into the landlord's bargained-for base rent on the deal in question, and not passed on to all other tenants, who reap no benefits from that landlord expenditure. In a perfect world for landlords, of course, the operating expense definition would be: "The term 'Operating Expenses' shall mean any and all costs and expenses (except real estate taxes, treated elsewhere in this lease) paid or incurred by or on behalf of the landlord in connection with the operating, servicing, management, and maintenance of the building," but such is not usually the omnibus definition that survives negotiations.

A landlord should also be aware of its need for inclusion of a "gross-up" provision, so that if a less-than-full building is experiencing a depressed amount of actual operating costs (other than taxes), those costs are "grossed up"—sometimes simply by setting forth an automatic assumption of an appropriate "full building" occupancy rate of, say, 95 percent (see Section 5.02(g) set forth in the sample clause in Section 5.2, *supra*)—so that the amount a tenant pays of its proportionate share formula is increased to the level it would have achieved if the building were effectively fully leased.

Taxes, of course, are a matter of public record, and the individual tenant's share is easily computed, once the tenant accepts that its "proportionate share" of the building's square footage has been appropriately calculated. It should be noted, however, that in some leases (and not in the preceding sample clause), the tenant's proportionate share for tax payment escalations may be less than its proportionate share for operating escalation payments. This occurs when the office building has retail space operations, where those retail tenants are picking up their own real estate tax payments, thereby reducing both the square footage of the balance of the building that is shared by the office space tenants and each tenant's respective share of that balance.

The landlord's second goal is to make current collection of those rising incremental costs, which requires both reasonable (tenant-credible) projections of those costs and a periodic billing system, with a "true-up" at year's end to match receipts with actual costs. In the "true-up," as reported to the tenants, is the danger to the third goal, securing landlord's business confidentiality. The tenant's representatives must be given a reasonable opportunity to examine the books and records on which the landlord's bills are based, but landlord sensitivity to attacks from "tenant audit" consultants, who offer to discover landlord escalation overbillings in exchange for a percentage of the proven savings, has caused landlords to be cautious about who is permitted to make the record examinations and how wide-ranging they may be. The landlord will also want to reach closure quickly, setting a maximum period (90 days in the sample clause) within which the tenant must protest any figures that it disputes. The landlord should also make it clear that, despite the expiration of the lease term, for some period tenant remains liable for recalculated or otherwise adjusted tax and operating cost escalations.

On tax escalations, the landlord has fewer concerns but will want to emphasize that it has no duty to apply for reduction in its real estate taxes, even though tenants may benefit from such an application. When a tax certiorari proceeding in reduction of an assessment has been successful, the landlord will also have to pay its counsel out of the projected savings, so any reductions to be shared with tenants must in such a lease provision be described as net of those legal costs.

Also, if the building is in the suburbs, and subject to several taxing jurisdictions with differing fiscal years (e.g., village, town, school, county), the tax escalation provision must make clear what those jurisdictions are, what fiscal years they have established, and even in some instances whether tax payments are retrospective instead of prospective. Finally, if the taxes to be paid are on the "building," this word must be defined elsewhere in the lease as both "land and building" where the assessor provides separate assessments for each component, to avoid a tenant argument that it is liable for tax increases only on the improvements, and not the land. The sample clause addresses this concern by using the defined term "project," which is defined as the land and the building.

5.4 Tenant Concerns

Once the tenant has chosen to occupy a building that utilizes either a CPI operating expense clause or a porter's wage operating expense clause, its escalation rent will merely be a function of the chosen formula as applied to its initial fixed rent, and the result is the degree of inflation. These two varieties of escalation clause will naturally also embody the features of projection, monthly collection, and annual reconciliation, but will not involve any period for protest or examination of the landlord's books and records.

If, on the other hand, the building of the tenant's choice employs an escalation clause like the sample clause, based on actual operating expenses (see Section 5.02 set forth in the sample clause in Section 5.2, *supra*), the tenant will want to carve out expense categories (see clauses (A) through (V) of Section 5.02(d) set forth in the sample clause in Section 5.2, *supra*) that should not fairly be borne by the tenant, but rather by the landlord as a business expense, or by some other tenant that is more directly benefitting from the expenditure in question. An individual tenant's ability to negotiate such a list is often, as with other aspects of lease negotiation, a function of a tenant's economic heft, but the larger the tenant, the more important economically is the expanded list of exclusions, and the more achievable.

Generally, exclusions for which tenants may successfully negotiate include the following general categories: (1) executive salaries; (2) depreciation (many variables); (3) capital improvements (see Section 5.02(d) set forth in the sample clause in Section 5.2, *supra*, for certain capital improvements that are commonly includable in operating expenses); (4) mortgage and ground lease payments; (5) amounts reimbursed by tenants or specifically included in the rent of tenants (such as electricity); (6) above-building-standard work or services; (7) brokerage commissions and other general leasing expenses; (8) preparation of space for tenant occupancy; (9) expenses of enforcing leases; and (10) expenses arising out of the landlord's negligence. If the landlord is permitted to include cost-saving or labor-saving capital expenditures, then the charge to a tenant should not outrun the savings.

Tenants generally have the right to inspect the landlord's books. The tenant should seek a reasonably extensive period for its initial review and right to register protest. A landlord will conversely insist on both confidentiality and the professional independence of the tenant's accountants doing the examination. A landlord may also prohibit tenants from using accountants who charge on a "contingency" basis, which incentivizes the accountants to allege significant overcharges because their compensation is a function of tenant refunds.

On tax escalations, as noted earlier, a tenant in a building with retail tenancies should probably have its proportionate share for tax escalation reduced below the percentage obtaining for the same tenant for operating costs. Furthermore, in the definition of "taxes," tenant should seek specifically to exclude the categories of taxes listed Section 5.01(d) (see Section 5.2, *supra*). Similarly, selection of the actual base tax year is important, so that the fiscal year of "base" is mostly in the future, postdating the commencement date of the lease, to delay the increase in the tenant's required cumulative rental payments.

In new buildings, it is also important for a tenant or its broker to discover if the structure is benefitting from a tax abatement that could result in an abnormally low basis, meaning a sudden hike a few years into the term when the abatement expires; here, the tenant might negotiate for the taxes included in the base year and each subsequent tax year to be unaffected by such tax abatements, or at least bargain for being charged only a portion of that jump in the transition year or years so as to phase in the impact of the increase.

A building under construction or in transition (e.g., the subject lease will result in a significant increase in real estate taxes once the income attributable to the lease is reported) presents special problems. If there is no clearly defined figure for a known fiscal or calendar base year, or tenant anticipates materially higher escalations than would be expected in a stabilized building, then tenant could seek to negotiate (1) a fixed cost per square foot in lieu of escalations until the building is assessed or operated (as applicable) as a fully completed building and stabilized building, whereinafter the first stabilized year will be established as the "base year" and the fixed rent will be increased by the sum of the previous years' escalations, (2) escalations based on those seen in a "basket" of comparable buildings until the first stabilized year as described earlier, or (3) some other methodology to put the landlord and the tenant in the same position with respect to escalations as if the building was assessed or operated as a fully completed and stabilized building at lease signing.

Since the landlord is passing through all its real estate tax increases, it may be feared that such a landlord will not be vigilant to keep taxes down, and so the large tenant might press for the right to compel a tax assessment reduction proceeding. Most landlords will refuse, but the tenant might then negotiate for a situation where a critical mass of tenants—say, 40 percent in rentable area of the building (which might even be the amount of footage a single tenant occupies)—can compel a contest, upon agreement to pay legal expenses in excess of the reduction or refund achieved. Also, the tenant may wish to clarify that its obligation to share the costs of tax reduction proceedings can never exceed the tax savings achieved in same.

5.5 Alternative Sample Clauses

1. *"Porter's Wage" Clause*

Section 5.05(A): In addition to the fixed rent herein reserved (Sec. 1.01), Tenant agrees to pay to Landlord additional rental calculated as follows:

5.05(A)(a) "Wage Rate" shall mean one-half of the combined total of the minimum regular hourly wage rate plus all other sums required to be paid to or for the benefit of (i) porters, and (ii) female cleaners engaged in the general maintenance and operation of office buildings of the type and in the vicinity of the Building pursuant to a collective bargaining agreement between Realty Advisory Board on Labor Relations, Inc. (or any successor) and 32B-32J Service Employees International Union AFL-CIO (or any successor). The Wage Rate shall include but not be limited to sums paid for pensions, welfare funds, vacations, bonuses, social security, unemployment, disability benefits, health, life, accident and other types of insurance. If any such agreement is not entered into or such parties or their successors shall cease to bargain collectively, the Wage Rate shall be one-half the combined total of the minimum regular hourly wage rate and other sums as aforesaid payable to or for the benefit of porters and female cleaners engaged in the maintenance and operation of the Building and payable by either Landlord or the contractor furnishing such services, but not in excess of the minimum rate of wages and other sums above described for porters and female cleaners engaged in the general maintenance and operation of office buildings in the vicinity of and of the same type as the Building.

5.05(A)(b) "Base Wage Rate" shall mean the Wage Rate in effect on [__________].

5.05(A)(c) For purposes of this article the number of square feet of rentable area contained in the Demised Premises is hereby fixed at ___ square feet. If the Wage Rate shall be changed at any time during the term of this Lease and shall be greater than the Base Wage Rate, Tenant shall pay to Landlord as additional rent an annual sum equal to 1.50 [*or whatever multiple is agreed upon*] times the product obtained by multiplying (i) the number of cents (including any fraction of a cent) by which the Wage Rate exceeds the Base Wage Rate by (ii) the number of square feet of rentable area in the Demised Premises. Such amounts shall be payable in equal monthly installments commencing with the first monthly installment of fixed rent falling due after the effective date of such change in the Wage Rate and continuing thereafter until a new adjustment in the additional rental shall be established and thereupon become effective in accordance with the provisions of this Article 5, except that notwithstanding any change in the Wage Rate downwards the fixed minimum annual rental shall not be reduced [*or alternatively:* Provided, however, that if there be a change in Wage Rate downward, there shall be a corresponding reduction in the additional rental beginning with the first monthly installment of fixed rent falling due after the effective date of such downward revision and continuing thereafter until a new adjustment of additional rental shall be established and become effective, but in no circumstance shall the fixed rent be reduced below that stated in Sec. 1.02 hereof.] In the event any change in the Wage Rate shall be made retroactive, Tenant shall pay Landlord the amount of such retroactive adjustment within ten (10) days after the billing therefor.

Section 5.05(B). If any controversy shall arise as to correctness of the Wage Rate or Base Wage Rate, the difference shall be resolved by arbitration in accordance with the provisions governing arbitration, stated in Article __ hereof [or alternatively, beginning after "resolved by": *New York Simplified Procedure for Court Determination of Disputes (CPR. 3031 et seq.)*].

2. CPI or Cost of Living Adjustment Clause Section 5.05(C). The fixed annual rent reserved in this lease and payable hereunder shall be adjusted, as of the times and in the manner set forth in this Article:

5.05(C)(a) Definitions: For the purposes of this Article, the following definitions shall apply:

(1) The term "*Base Year*" shall mean the full calendar year during which the term of this lease commences.

(2) The term "*Price Index*" shall mean the "Consumer Price Index" published by the Bureau of Labor Statistics of the U.S. Department of Labor, All Items, [New York, N.Y.-Northeastern New Jersey] for urban wage earners and clerical workers, or a successor or substitute index appropriately adjusted.

(3) The term "*Price Index for the Base Year*" shall mean the average of the monthly All Items Price Indexes for each of the 12 months of the Base Year.

5.05(C)(b) Effective as of each January and July subsequent to the Base Year, but in no event sooner than six months after the commencement date of this lease, there shall be made a cost of living adjustment of the annual rental rate payable hereunder. The July adjustment shall be based on the percentage difference between the Price Index for the preceding month of June and the Price Index for the Base Year. The January adjustment shall be based on such percentage difference between the Price Index for the preceding month of December and the Price Index for the Base Year.

(1) In the event the Price Index for June in any calendar year during the term of this lease reflects an increase over the Price Index for the Base Year, then the fixed annual rent originally herein provided to be paid as of the July 1st following such month of June (unchanged by any adjustments under this Article) shall be multiplied by the percentage difference between the Price Index for June and the Price Index for the Base Year, and the resulting sum shall be added to such fixed annual rent, effective as of such July 1st. Said adjusted annual rent shall thereafter be payable hereunder, in equal monthly installments, until it is readjusted pursuant to the terms of this lease.

(2) In the event the Price Index for December in any calendar year during the term of this lease reflects an increase over the Price Index for the Base Year, then the fixed annual rent originally herein provided to be paid as of January 1st following such month of December (unchanged by any adjustments under this Article) shall be multiplied by the percentage difference between the Price Index for December and the Price Index for the Base Year, and the resulting sum shall be added to such fixed annual rent effective as of such January 1st. Such adjusted annual rent shall thereafter be payable hereunder, in equal monthly installments, until it is readjusted pursuant to the terms of this lease.

Illustration of the Parties' Intentions

The following illustrates the intentions of the parties hereto as to the computation of the aforementioned cost of living adjustment in the annual rent payable hereunder:

Assuming the said fixed annual rent is $10,000, that the Price Index for the Base Year was 102.0 and that the Price Index for the month of June in a calendar year following the Base Year was 105.0, then the percentage increase thus reflected, i.e., 2.941% (3.0/102.0), would be multiplied by $10,000, and the said fixed annual rent would be increased by $294.10 effective as of July 1st of said calendar year.

In the event that the Price Index ceases to use 1967=100 as the basis of calculation, or if a substantial change is made in the terms or number of items contained in the Price Index, then the Price Index shall be adjusted to the figure that would have been arrived at had the manner of computing the Price Index in effect at the date of this lease not been altered. In the event such Price Index (or a successor or substitute index) is not available, a reliable governmental or other non-partisan publican evaluating the information theretofore used in determining the Price Index shall be used.

No adjustments or recomputations, retroactive or otherwise, shall be made due to any revision which may later be made in the first published figure of the Price Index for any month.

5.05(C)(c) The statements of the cost of living adjustment to be furnished by Lessor as provided in subdivision (b) shall consist of data prepared for Landlord by a firm of certified public accountants (who may be the firm now or then currently employed by the Landlord for the audit of its accounts). The statements thus furnished to Tenant shall constitute a final determination as between Landlord and Tenant of the cost of living adjustment for the periods represented thereby, absent manifest computational error.

5.05(C)(d) In no event shall the fixed annual rent originally provided to be paid under this lease (exclusive of the adjustments under this Article) be reduced by virtue of this Article.

5.05(C)(e) Any delay or failure of Landlord, beyond July or January of any year, in computing or billing for the rent adjustments hereinabove provided, shall not constitute a waiver of or in any way impair the continuing obligation of Tenant to pay such rent adjustments hereunder.

5.05(C)(f) Notwithstanding any expiration or termination of this lease prior to the lease expiration date (except in the case of a cancellation by mutual agreement), Tenant's obligation to pay rent as adjusted under this Article shall continue and shall cover all periods up to the lease expiration date, and shall survive any expiration or termination of this lease.

5.6 Standard Real Estate Board of New York Clause

None.

5.7 Litigation Issues

There is no dearth of litigation concerning disputes over rent escalation provisions.[3] The amount of "additional rent" (see generally Section 5.1, *supra*) a tenant may have to pay as the result of an escalation clause may come as an unpleasant surprise,[4] even where substantial negotiation between counsel for both sides[5] has gone into preparing

3. *See* Treanor & Goldfaden, *Challenges to Rent Escalation Clauses in Commercial Leases*, Prob. & Prop. Mag. 6 (June 4, 1990).

4. George Backer Mgmt. v. Acme Quilting Co., 46 N.Y.2d 211, 413 N.Y.S.2d 135, 385 N.E.2d 1062 (1978).

5. 75 Henry St. Garage, Inc. v. Whitman Owner Corp., 79 A.D.2d 1001, 435 N.Y.S.2d 26 (2d Dep't 1981).

the lease. Although Real Property Law section 235-c[6] may afford some protection for a tenant attempting to avoid payment under an escalation clause, it must be established that the provision in question is more than merely a "burdensome bargain" and that it is "so onerous as to shock the conscience."[7] Additionally, it has been held that a sophisticated tenant who fails to keep its "eye" on the cumulative effect of compounding of rent under a porter's wage escalation provision will not be relieved of its obligations.[8]

In the case of *Wendel Foundation v. Moredall Realty Corp.*,[9] the Court of Appeals held that a tenant was not obligated to reimburse a tax-exempt landlord for taxes the landlord would never be required to pay. In *Wendel*, when the lease was first negotiated, the property was privately owned and the tenant was required to reimburse the landlord for taxes actually paid. When the property passed into the hands of a charitable institution (the plaintiff), an attempt by the tax-exempt entity to collect the taxes it would have had to pay were it not a charitable entity was denied by the court. The court stated: "There is no obligation on the tenant to pay as further rent a sum equal to taxes that might be imposed were the landlord not exempt from taxation. The obligation of the tenant was to pay if and when the landlords were required to pay and not otherwise."[10]

In *Fairfax Co. v. Whelan Drug Co., Inc.*,[11] the tax escalation clause provided for added rent based on tenant's stated percentage share of an increase in taxes or assessments. The assessment, in fact, was increased when the building was renovated and converted from commercial to residential (other than plaintiff's store) use. However, the landlord became entitled to substantial tax abatements because of the renovation, resulting in a tax payment decrease. The court prevented a windfall to the landlord, who sought to collect a tax escalation rent based on the new and higher assessment without taking into consideration the substantial tax abatement granted.

The *Fairfax* case has been followed where the tax obligation has been shifted to a third party, by a sale to a cooperative corporation and partial leaseback,[12] and to a ground sublessee.[13] In *1100 Avenue of the Americas Associates v. Bryant Imports,*

---

6. Real Property Law § 235-c. Unconscionable lease or clause:

1. If the court as a matter of law finds a lease or any clause of the lease to have been unconscionable at the time it was made the court may refuse to enforce the lease, or it may enforce the remainder of the lease without the unconscionable clause, or it may so limit the application of any unconscionable clause as to avoid any unconscionable result.

2. When it is claimed or appears to the court that a lease or any clause thereof may be unconscionable the parties shall be afforded a reasonable opportunity to present evidence as to its setting, purpose and effect to aid the court in making the determination.

7. *George Backer Mgmt.*, 46 N.Y.2d at 218, 413 N.Y.S.2d at 138.

8. CBS, Inc. v. P.A. Bldg. Co., 200 A.D.2d 257, 606 N.Y.S.2d 674 (1st Dep't 1994).

9. 282 N.Y. 239, 26 N.E.2d 241 (1940).

10. 282 N.Y. at 245.

11. 105 A.D.2d 647, 481 N.Y.S.2d 366 (1st Dep't 1984).

12. S.B.S. Assoc. v. Weissman-Heller, 190 A.D.2d 529, 593 N.Y.S.2d 28 (1st Dep't 1993).

13. 1100 Avenue of the Americas Assoc. v. Bryant Imports, Inc., 161 Misc. 2d 582, 616 N.Y.S.2d 848, *aff'd* 234 A.D.2d 101, 650 N.Y.S.2d 725 (1st Dep't 1996).

Inc.,[14] the additional rent clause required the tenant to pay 3 percent of the increase in taxes above the taxes payable during the base year. When the lease was entered into, the landlord paid the taxes and passed the increases on to the tenant. The landlord, a net lessee of the building, subsequently entered into a further net sublease of the entire building except for the ground floor stores. The ground floor sublease required the lessee to pay the real estate taxes for the entire building, notwithstanding that the ground lessor reserved to its benefit the store space and its rental income. Since the obligation to pay taxes was passed on to the ground floor sublessee, and was not in fact paid by the plaintiff, 1100 Avenue of the Americas Associates, the court held it could not collect the percentage increases under the escalation clause.

The dissent in *1100 Avenue of the Americas Associates* appears to have reached a better-reasoned conclusion, albeit the losing one. According to the dissent, the plaintiff landlord not only remained liable for the tax if not paid by the sublessee but may actually not have reaped a windfall. The ground sublessee's rent was otherwise reduced to account for the realty tax payments.

In the case of *Credit Exchange, Inc. v. 461 Eighth Avenue Associates*,[15] the court protected a tenant where increases in assessments resulted from improvements solely benefitting the landlord, notwithstanding the fact that no such limitation appeared in the tax escalation provision. The landlord in *Credit Exchange, Inc.* sought to recoup a tenant's percentage increase in an assessment resulting from the addition of two floors to the building where the tenant's premises was located.

Although the courts seem to come to the aid of tenants in order to prevent the unfair application of tax escalation clauses, attempts by tenants seeking to set aside these provisions on the ground of unfairness mostly fail. Although Real Property Law section 235-c[16] permits a challenge to a lease provision on the ground of unconscionability, and may be resorted to in attacking an escalation provision, most challenges are unsuccessful.[17]

In *J. Henry Schroder Bank & Trust Co. v. South Ferry Building Co.*,[18] it appeared to the tenant that the landlord was not deducting from operating expenses the amounts received from other tenants pursuant to porter's wage escalation clauses and, as a consequence, was not fairly calculating the operating expense escalation charges. Unlike the other tenants, whose leases employed the porter's wage formula escalation clauses (see Section 5.5, *supra*), the Schroder lease had an actual operating expense escalation provision (see Section 5.2, paragraph 5.01(I)(a) of the sample clause). The tenant even had the following provision to rely on: "Such expenses shall not include . . . any expenses referred to in subparagraph (a) of this Section 22.02 for which Landlord shall

---

14. *Id.*

15. Credit Exchange, Inc. v. 461 Eighth Ave. Assoc., 69 N.Y.2d 994, 517 N.Y.S.2d 903, 511 N.E.2d 47 (1987).

16. The text of Real Property Law § 235-c is set forth in note 6, *supra.*

17. *See, e.g.*, Adelphia Lamps & Shades, Inc. v. 41 Madison Ave. Co., 84 A.D.2d 501, 443 N.Y.S.2d 66 (1st Dep't 1981).

18. 99 A.D.2d 736, 472 N.Y.S.2d 382 (1st Dep't 1984).

have been reimbursed or is entitled to reimbursement." The court held that the additional rent paid by the other tenants pursuant to the porter's wage provisions was not intended to reimburse the landlord for wages actually paid, but was merely a provision used to calculate additional rent.

The Court of Appeals upheld enforcement of a porter's wage escalation provision in *George Backer Management v. Acme Quilting Co.*,[19] even though the landlord in fact paid its employees at a lower wage rate than that set forth in the escalation clause. In order to meet the statutory requirement of unconscionability, more than a burdensome bargain was necessary; the provision in question must shock the conscience. The court in *George Backer Management* found the provision had been the product of extensive negotiations and was not unconscionable.

The tenant in *City of Hope v. Fisk Building Associates*[20] had hopes of recovering damages resulting from paying additional rent pursuant to both a Consumer Price Index (see Section 5.5, *supra*) escalation and a cost of electric energy escalation. The tenant argued that the landlord was unjustly enriched because the CPI included the cost of electricity, and thus overlapped the additional rent paid under the electric energy escalation clause. The court rejected the argument, and instead held the tenant to its bargain.

The attempt to negotiate a "cap" to an escalation provision has resulted in litigation. The A&P's lease, interpreted by the court of appeals in *Bensons Plaza v. Great Atlantic & Pacific Tea Co., Inc.*,[21] contained the following cap added to the tax escalation clause: "provided, however, that in no event shall the rental fixed under this clause vary from the *rental under this lease* [emphasis added] by more than $1,006.50 per year." The italicized language in the previous quote was held by the court to mean the rent stipulated for the first year. As a consequence, the tenant could not be required to pay more than $1,006.50 in any one year over the amount of the first year's rental. The landlord should have more explicitly drafted the cap to support its position. The court stated: "If the landlord intended otherwise, it should have been made explicit."[22]

19. 46 N.Y.2d 211, 413 N.Y.S.2d 135, 385 N.E.2d 1062 (1978).

20. 63 A.D.2d 946, 406 N.Y.S.2d 472 (1st Dep't 1978).

21. 44 N.Y.2d 791, 406 N.Y.S.2d 33, 377 N.E.2d 477 (1978).

22. 44 N.Y.2d at 793, 406 N.Y.S.2d at 34. *See also* Wiener v. GaRo Die Cutting, Inc., 104 A.D.2d Dep't 331, 479 N.Y.S.2d 35 (1st Dep't 1984) (permitting extraneous proof to establish the applicability of a cap, added to an insurance additional rent clause, to other additional rent clauses) and Kenilworth Realty Trust v. Bankers Trust Co. 112 Misc. 2d 523, 447 N.Y.S.2d 210 (Sup. Ct. N.Y. Cnty. 1982) (landlord bound to 25-year course of conduct in interpreting cap).

CHAPTER 6

Use and Occupancy

6.1 General Purpose

The use clause sets forth, and thereby also limits, the permitted use of the premises. The broadest possible permitted use is for any lawful purpose. That assures the landlord that the tenant's use will conform to the certificate of occupancy covering the premises and all building, zoning, environmental, and other laws, codes, and regulations, and at the same time allow the tenant the broadest flexibility legally permissible. In an office building the landlord is likely to be more specific and, at least, state that the space may be used only as general and executive offices, for general office use or, if applicable, for retail use.

The tenant may well prefer to be able to use the premises for any lawful purpose, but that language is rarely conceded to an office tenant unless the tenant is under a long-term net lease. A somewhat more restrictive provision limits such office use to the operations of the tenant's specific type of business. Tenants object to such limitations because the tenant's business may change during the term of the lease and because such limitations will limit severely the tenant's ability to assign the lease or sublet the premises. The tenant may attempt to broaden the office use clause by adding "and any use incidental thereto, including, without limitation, the following incidental uses . . . ," some of which are suggested in Section 6.4, *infra*. The landlord may desire to restrict the use of the premises to the tenant's particular business or, in response to the tenant's concerns about a provision that is too restrictive, may limit the use of the premises without going so far as to specify the tenant's particular business. Under these circumstances the landlord may set forth a list of prohibited businesses, some of which are suggested in the sample clause (see Section 6.2, *infra*).

It is important to note that the use provision not only affects the latitude that the existing tenant will have in utilizing the premises, but will also affect the tenant's ability to assign the lease and sublet the demised premises. Any assignee or sublessee will have to conform its use to that of the lessee.

6.2 Sample Clause

6.01 Permitted Use.

The Premises shall be used and occupied by Tenant (and its permitted subtenants) solely for executive and general offices (the "Permitted Use") (including such ancillary uses in connection therewith as shall be reasonably required by Tenant in the operation of its business and are customarily permitted by landlords, and engaged in by tenants, in first class office buildings in *[insert market area]*); provided, that in no event shall the Premises be used for any of the following: (a) any retail use (including, without limitation, any financial industry use, and any restaurant, bar or other sale of food or beverage use), in each case open for business to the general public, (b) any manufacturing use, (c) an employment or travel agency, (d) a school or classroom, (e) medical or psychiatric offices, (f) conduct of an auction, (g) gambling activities, (h) conduct of obscene, pornographic or similar disreputable activities, (i) offices of an agency, department or bureau of the United States Government or any foreign government, any state or municipality within the United States or any foreign government, or any political subdivision of any of them, (j) offices of any charitable, religious, union or other not-for-profit organization, (k) offices of any tax exempt entity within the meaning of Section 168(h)(2) of the Internal Revenue Code of 1986, as amended, or any successor or substitute statute, or rule or regulation applicable thereto, (l) the operation of a business, the purpose of which is to provide to unrelated third parties for sublease or license a flexible workplace center consisting primarily of executive and general office suites and shared office workplaces or (m) the operation of a business, the primary business purpose of which is to provide space to third parties for the conduct of business meetings, conferences, co-working office suites and event spaces. The Premises shall not be used for any purpose that would tend to lower the first-class character of the Building, create unreasonable or excessive elevator or floor loads, impair or interfere with any of the Building operations or the proper and economic heating, ventilation, air-conditioning, cleaning or other servicing of the Building, constitute a public or private nuisance, interfere with, annoy or disturb any other tenant or Landlord, or impair the appearance of the Building.

6.3 Landlord Concerns

Landlords want to retain as much control as possible over the use made of their buildings. For that reason, a provision that limits the permitted use to the specific business of the tenant is most advantageous to the landlord. The landlord's consent will be required if the tenant wants to change its business, sublet the premises, or assign the lease to a subtenant or assignee operating a different business from the business of the tenant. The landlord's best interests also are served by refusing to make any representations about the condition of the premises or the building. From the landlord's perspective, the tenant should perform its own due diligence and satisfy itself on these issues. Further, if any permits, licenses, or amendments to the certificate of occupancy will be required because of the nature of the tenant's business or the alterations that the tenant makes to the premises, the landlord will want to place the cost and responsibility squarely on the tenant.

Regardless of the specific permitted use, the landlord will want it made clear that no other use will be permitted. For that reason, the phrase "and for no other purpose" commonly is added to the provision.

As an additional clarification, the landlord can specify certain prohibited uses. Banks, brokerage houses, travel agencies, schools, and auctions all attract large numbers of people into the building, increasing the security risks and taxing the building services, particularly the elevators. A restaurant facility poses all of these problems plus the added problems of venting, fire safety, vermin, and increased rubbish; the need to amend the certificate of occupancy to permit the facility if one does not already exist; and the requirement to restore the premises at the end of the term. Medical offices also may require additional plumbing and handicap facilities in the building. Governmental agencies, because of special immunities they may have and the difficulty in obtaining jurisdiction should legal proceedings become necessary, are undesirable as tenants. There are concerns, too, for the peaceable enjoyment by all tenants of their respective spaces and maintaining the quality and reputation of the building.

6.4 Tenant Concerns

The tenant will want to be able to use the premises for any lawful purpose. This kind of provision gives the tenant the most flexibility if its business changes, or if it wants to assign the lease or sublet the premises to another party. A second choice for the tenant would be general and executive offices and all uses incidental thereto. Among the incidental uses that a tenant will want to consider are the following: (1) kitchen and cafeteria; (2) dining room; (3) vending machines; (4) the use of photographic reproduction, offset, and data processing facilities for the use of the tenant and its employees; and (5) a travel agency, medical facility, or classrooms for the use of the employees of the tenant. A landlord seeking to prohibit many of these uses may agree to them if they are utilized only by the employees of the tenant and are not available to the public. Any facility that involves cooking or the preparation and service of food may well be limited in size by the landlord and subject to special venting, rubbish removal, and other requirements. At a minimum, a tenant concerned about its ability to assign the lease or sublet the premises will want to mitigate some of the specifically prohibited uses set forth in the sample clause. For example, a landlord should not object to the use of the premises for the general and executive offices of a bank or even of a restaurant. In addition, many tenants are concerned that language such as, "activities that would adversely affect the character or reputation of the Building . . ." is unduly vague and subjective.

It is the responsibility of the tenant to use the premises in compliance with applicable laws (see Chapter 10, *infra*), including, without limitation, obtaining necessary permits and approvals for the operation of the tenant's business and the performance of any alterations. Depending on the amount of due diligence that the tenant is prepared to undertake, the tenant will want to have the landlord represent that the tenant's permitted use of the premises will not violate any legal or insurance requirement. The tenant will also want to have the landlord agree not to amend the certificate of occupancy during the term so as to limit the scope of the permitted use of the premises as set forth in the lease. The tenant is not the owner of the building and will at least need the landlord's agreement to cooperate in obtaining any such permits and approvals, as necessary.

6.5 Standard Real Estate Board of New York Clause

Occupancy: 2

Tenant shall use and occupy the demised premises for *(insert description of tenant's use)* and for no other purpose.

6.6 Comments on the Standard Real Estate Board of New York Clause

The standard clause is limited in scope and would have to be augmented to cover the subjects discussed previously. The landlord and the tenant will each be concerned with incorporating more detailed language to express their respective concerns.

6.7 Litigation Issues

The use clause of a commercial lease may read as an innocuous grant of permission to use the premises for a particular purpose. The cases, however, reveal that if a tenant fails to anticipate the manner in which it may conduct its business during the term of the lease, the impact of a restrictive use clause may result in a lost opportunity to reasonably expand its revenues[1] or, perhaps, the forfeiture of a leasehold when the permitted use is no longer financially viable.[2]

There are three basic principles involved in analyzing a landlord/tenant dispute concerning the use restriction. *First*, the use clause of a lease will be strictly construed, and strictly limited to the precise terms of any restrictions set forth in the provision.[3] *Second*, the court will construe a lease in its entirety in order to ascertain the intent of

1. 72nd & Broadway Gourmet Rest., Inc. & Otto Gourmet, Ltd. v. Stahl Real Estate Co., 118 Misc. 2d 372, 460 N.Y.S.2d 408 (Sup. Ct. N.Y. Cnty. 1981) (prohibiting fast-food restaurant from installing video games).

2. *In re* Baime v. Martin's, 88 A.D.2d 595, 449 N.Y.S.2d 775 (2d Dep't 1982); 30-88 Steinway Street, Inc. v. H.C. Bohack Co., Inc., 65 Misc. 2d 1076, 319 N.Y.S.2d 679 (NYC Civ. Ct. Queens Cnty. 1971).

3. Kem Cleaners, Inc. v. Shaker Pine Inc., 217 A.D.2d 787, 629 N.Y.S.2d 492 (3d Dep't 1995).

the parties as to the use.[4] *Third*, a landlord has the right to control the use of the premises leased to a tenant.[5]

The application of these principles does not consistently result in a pro-tenant or pro-landlord decision, although recent cases may be tipping the scale in favor of the tenant.[6] *Qwakazi, Ltd. v. 107 West 86th Street Owners Corp.*[7] shows how a narrowly drawn use restriction can prevent a merchant from expanding its inventory and profits. The store lease use clause stated that "tenant shall use and occupy demised premises for sale of comic books, toys, posters, books solely." The landlord sought to call the tenant in default for selling and renting videotapes. The court that held the specifically drafted use restriction "is clear and unambiguous in its exclusion of plaintiff's right to sell video cassettes." Although generically, comic books, books, and videotapes are similar in entertainment value, the court held that "the sale and rental of video cassettes is not incidental to the sale of the items expressly permitted in the lease."[8]

A similar, narrowly drawn use clause restricting a tobacco shop to "sell pipes and tobacco and . . . items related to pipes and tobacco, such as ash trays, cigar lighters . . . and the right to sell cigarettes, cigars, boxed candy, pre-packaged glazed and dried fruit and specialty nuts and loose chocolates, and for no other purpose," prevented a tobacco, candy, and gift shop from selling lottery tickets.[9]

These cases can be contrasted with *Kem Cleaners, Inc. v. Shaker Pine Inc.*,[10] where a dry-cleaning establishment was not clearly prohibited from selling and renting videotapes. The use clause stated that tenant "shall use and occupy the Premises for no purpose other than a dry cleaning establishment or other retail use reasonably acceptable to" the landlord. This restriction was strictly construed against the landlord. By including the phrase "other retail use reasonably acceptable to" the landlord, the court held that there was no absolute and unambiguous restriction on use of the premises. The phrase "other retail use" was not narrow enough to limit the tenant to the sale of merchandise incidental to operation of a dry cleaners. The use of the "reasonably acceptable" standard was construed to limit the landlord to consider objective economic reasons for rejecting the tenant's new use.

The principle of examining the intent of the entire lease in construing a use restriction most often applies to restrictions that generically describe the type of use permitted at the demised premises. *Burber v. Jilamb Prime Meat, Inc.*[11] provides an excellent discourse on this principle. The use clause simply stated that the premises was to be

4. Burber v. Jilamb Prime Meat, Inc., 115 Misc. 2d 976, 455 N.Y.S.2d 44 (NYC Civ. Ct. N.Y. Cnty. 1982).

5. *In re Baime*, 88 A.D.2d 595, 449 N.Y.S.2d 775.

6. Astoria Bedding, Mr. Sleeper Bedding Ctr., Inc. v. Northside P'ship, 239 A.D.2d 775, 657 N.Y.S.2d 796 (3d Dep't 1997).

7. 123 A.D.2d 253, 506 N.Y.S.2d 162 (1st Dep't 1986).

8. 506 N.Y. S.2d at 163.

9. Smokes 'N' Sweets, Inc. v. West Lake Assoc., 227 A.D.2d 757, 642 N.Y.S.2d 358 (3d Dep't 1996).

10. 217 A.D.2d 787, 629 N.Y.S.2d 492 (3d Dep't 1995).

11. 115 Misc. 2d 976, 455 N.Y.S.2d 44 (NYC Civ. Ct. N.Y. Cnty. 1982).

used and occupied only for a butcher store. The tenant sold, in addition to meat, lard, margarine, eggs, milk, juice, soda, bread, frozen vegetables, spaghetti, grits, and other "grocery items," which happened to be items sold in the landlord's nearby grocery store. The court decided against the tenant after considering the (1) apparent intentions expressed in the lease; (2) when the lease was entered into; (3) the traditional concept of items sold in the type of use permitted; (4) current market customs and variations; (5) reasonableness of the restriction in view of the size of the store, percentage of objectionable items sold to total sales (or area devoted to the sale of the objectionable item); and (6) customer service. Although grocery items represented only 5 to 10 percent of gross sales, the court relied most heavily on the competition with neighborhood stores (probably the landlord's) in concluding that the use clause was violated.

Although *Burber* was decided against the tenant, it would appear that tenants fare better with generic use restriction clauses than with specific item restriction clauses. Generic use clauses are generally broad, and thus fall within the rule of construction that ambiguity and doubt are to be resolved against the drafter, which is usually the landlord. A store use clause permitting the premises "to be used and occupied only for a convenience food market" was deemed as not prohibiting sale of lottery tickets. The court considered the competitive marketplace and concluded that "when a convenience store is viewed in the light of modern stores of the same character in a commercial setting . . . the sale of lottery tickets is consistent with the use clause in the subject lease. . . ."[12]

A restrictive use clause may come into apparent conflict with other provisions of the lease such as subletting or alteration restrictions. The tenant in *Times Square Stores Corp., Inc. v. Bernice Realty Co., Inc.*[13] was permitted to use a building as its corporate headquarters and warehouse. The tenant was required to use the premises in conformity with the existing certificate of occupancy. In order to accommodate the number of employees required at the corporate headquarters, the certificate of occupancy had to be amended to permit expansion. The landlord sought to increase the rent provided for in the lease in consideration of approving an application to alter the certificate of occupancy, which the lease did not specifically require. The court held the refusal unreasonable, holding that "In executing the lease the defendant impliedly promised to refrain from unreasonably obstructing the plaintiff's expansion. . . . Because the plaintiff's use had not changed from the date the lease was executed, the defendant's refusal to execute the application was unreasonable."[14]

The balance of use restrictions against other lease provisions appears to have moved in the tenant's favor with the ruling in *Astoria Bedding, Mr. Sleeper Bedding Center, Inc. v. Northside Partnership.*[15] The use clause permitted use only for the purpose of conducting and operating a retail bedding, home furnishings, and accessory

---

12. Sky Four Realty Co. v. C.F.M. Enters, Inc., 128 A.D.2d 1011, 513 N.Y.S.2d 546 (3d Dep't 1987).
13. 141 A.D.2d 535, 529 N.Y.S.2d 148 (2d Dep't 1988).
14. 529 N.Y.S.2d at 150.
15. 239 A.D.2d 775, 657 N.Y.S.2d 796 (3d Dep't 1997).

business. The tenant also negotiated a sublet clause requiring that the landlord not unreasonably withhold consent to a proposed sublet. The tenant sought to sublease the premises to a packaging and mailing service. The court ignored the use restriction and held that the landlord could not merely consider use in rejecting the sublessee. It held that "Moreover, where a landlord affirmatively promises not to unreasonably withhold its consent, its refusal can only be based upon a consideration of objective factors, such as the financial responsibility of the subtenant, the subtenant's suitability for the particular building, the legality of the proposed use and the nature of the occupancy."[16] It would appear that *Astoria Bedding* contributes to the erosion of the traditional right of a lessor to specifically restrict the use of a demised premises.[17] Enforcement of a use restriction may be waived or estopped where the landlord knew a tenant expended substantial sums to alter the premises for the purpose of amending its use, and did not object to the alterations.[18]

16. 657 N.Y.S.2d at 797.
17. Lyon v. Bethlehem Eng'g Corp., 253 N.Y. 111, 170 N.E. 512 (1930).
18. Bethpage Theatre Co., Inc. v. Shekel, 133 A.D.2d 62, 518 N.Y.S.2d 408 (2d Dep't 1987).

CHAPTER 7

Alterations

7.1 General Purpose

As its title proclaims, this lease section is concerned with setting the ground rules for (1) changes to the premises made by or on behalf of the tenant; (2) whether they can be made; (3) the protections and costs to be incorporated into the approval and post-approval construction processes; (4) the possible tenant duty to remove these alterations and restore the premises at term's end; and (5) the declaration of the landlord's claim of title to all such changes. Virtually no lease forbids all alterations, and virtually no lease permits the occupant a free hand to make physical changes.

As more fully discussed later in the chapter, a landlord desires to ensure the safety of the process and the compatibility of the alterations with the future use and occupancy of the premises. A normal tenant, with a standard office operation and installation, requires some flexibility during the term to accommodate changing numbers of personnel, new office machines, and even new forms of business activity or requirement not reasonably anticipated at term commencement. The tenant is also concerned with preserving its right to remove trade fixtures without questions of title. The balancing of these interests is the goal of the alterations provisions.

7.2 Sample Clause

7.01 Alterations.

(a) Tenant shall make no improvements, changes or alterations in or to the Premises ("Alterations") without Landlord's prior approval. Notwithstanding the foregoing, Landlord's approval shall not be required for any non-Material Alteration that (A) is purely decorative in nature (such as wallpapering, painting or carpeting) or (B) does not require a building permit or other approval of any governmental authority (Alterations described in clause (A) or clause (B) are collectively called "Decorative Alterations"); *provided*, that Tenant shall give to Landlord not less than 5 Business Days prior notice of the performance of any Decorative Alterations. Landlord shall not unreasonably withhold or condition its approval to any Alteration requiring Landlord's consent that is not a Material Alteration. "Material Alteration" means an Alteration that (i) is not limited to the interior of the Premises or that affects the exterior (including the appearance) of the Building or any portion thereof, (ii) is structural or affects the strength of the Building or any portion thereof, (iii) adversely affects the usage or the proper functioning of any of the Building systems, (iv) has a cost greater than $[__________], (v) requires the consent of any Superior Mortgagee or Superior Lessor or (vi) requires a change to the Building's certificate of occupancy.

(b) Tenant, in connection with any Alteration, shall comply with any rules and regulations as may be from time to time established by Landlord. Tenant shall not proceed with any Alteration (other than Decorative Alterations) unless and until Landlord approves Tenant's plans and specifications therefor. Any review or approval by Landlord of plans and specifications with respect to any Alteration is solely for Landlord's benefit, and without any representation or warranty to Tenant with respect to the adequacy, correctness or efficiency thereof, its compliance with Laws or otherwise. If, within [___] days after Tenant's submission to Landlord of complete and coordinated plans and specifications with respect to any non-Material Alteration requiring Landlord's consent pursuant to Section 7.01(a) above, Landlord shall fail to notify Tenant of Landlord's approval or objection thereto (in the latter case, setting forth the reasons therefor), then Tenant may provide to Landlord a reminder notice which shall contain a legend in not less than 14 point font bold upper case letters as follows: "**THIS IS A TIME SENSITIVE REQUEST AND THE FAILURE OF LANDLORD TO RESPOND WITHIN 5 BUSINESS DAYS FOLLOWING RECEIPT OF THIS NOTICE SHALL RESULT IN LANDLORD'S DEEMED APPROVAL OF THE [specify Tenant's plans in question].**" If Landlord shall fail to respond within such 5 Business Day period, then Landlord shall be deemed to have given its consent to the applicable plans and specifications submitted by Tenant to Landlord; provided, that the proposed plans and specifications otherwise comply with the terms of this Section 7.01.

(c) Tenant shall pay to Landlord upon demand Landlord's reasonable costs and expenses (including, without limitation, the fees of any architect or engineer employed by Landlord or any Superior Lessor or Superior Mortgagee for such purpose) for reviewing plans and specifications and inspecting Alterations. In addition, Tenant shall pay to Landlord or its designee, upon demand, an administrative fee with respect to the performance of the Alterations and the scheduling of Building equipment, facilities and personnel in connection therewith, which fee shall be payable as follows: [___%] of the cost of Tenant's Alterations.

(d) Before proceeding with any Alteration that will cost more than [$__________] (exclusive of the costs of decorating work and items constituting Tenant's Property), as estimated by a reputable contractor designated by

Landlord, Tenant shall furnish to Landlord one of the following (as selected by Landlord): (i) a cash deposit, (ii) a performance bond and a labor and materials payment bond (issued by a corporate surety licensed to do business in New York reasonably satisfactory to Landlord) or (iii) an irrevocable, unconditional, negotiable letter of credit, issued by a bank and in a form satisfactory to Landlord; each to be equal to 125% of the cost of the Alteration, estimated as set forth above. Any such letter of credit shall be for one year and shall be renewed by Tenant each and every year until the Alteration in question is completed and shall be delivered to Landlord not less than 30 days prior to the expiration of the then current letter of credit, failing which Landlord may present the then current letter of credit for payment. Upon (A) the completion of the Alteration in accordance with the terms of this Section 7.01 and (B) the submission to Landlord of (x) proof evidencing the payment in full for said Alteration, (y) written unconditional lien waivers of mechanics' liens and other liens on the Project from all contractors performing said Alteration and (z) all other submissions as may be, from time to time required by Landlord, the security deposited with Landlord (or the balance of the proceeds thereof, if Landlord has drawn on the same) shall be returned to Tenant. Upon Tenant's failure properly to perform, complete and fully pay for any Alteration, as determined by Landlord, Landlord may, upon notice to Tenant, draw on the security deposited under this Section 7.01(d) to the extent Landlord deems necessary in connection with said Alteration, the restoration and/or protection of the Premises or the Project and the payment of any costs, damages or expenses resulting therefrom.

(e) Tenant shall obtain (and furnish copies to Landlord of) all necessary governmental permits and certificates for the commencement and prosecution of Alterations and for final approval thereof upon completion, and shall cause Alterations to be performed in compliance therewith, and in compliance with all Laws and with the plans and specifications approved by Landlord. Alterations shall be diligently performed in a good and workmanlike manner, using new materials and equipment at least equal in quality and class to the then standards for the Building established by Landlord. Alterations shall be performed by architects, engineers and contractors first approved by Landlord (which approval for non-Material Alterations shall not be unreasonably withheld or delayed); provided, that any Alterations in or to the systems of the Building shall be performed only by the contractor(s) designated by Landlord as long as such contractors charge commercially reasonable rates (Landlord shall, from time to time upon Tenant's request made prior to Tenant's commencement of each such Alteration, designate at least 3 contractors for each Building system except for the Class E system for which Landlord may designate one contractor and Landlord may elect to designate only one approved filing agent/expediter to be used in connection with all Alterations). The performance of any Alteration or any other work in the Project shall not be carried out in a manner that would violate Landlord's union contracts affecting the Project, or create any work stoppage, picketing, labor disruption, disharmony or dispute or any interference with the business of Landlord or any tenant or occupant of the Building. Tenant shall immediately stop the performance by any person of any work or service or any labor practice engaged in by Tenant if Landlord notifies Tenant that continuing same would violate Landlord's union contracts affecting the Project, or create any work stoppage, picketing, labor disruption, disharmony or dispute or any interference with the business of Landlord or any tenant or occupant of the Building, and Tenant shall not resume the performance of such work or service until such time as the same may be performed in a manner that shall not violate such union contracts or create such work stoppage, picketing, labor disruption, disharmony or dispute or interference.

(f) Throughout the performance of Alterations, Tenant shall carry, or cause its contractor, architect, or engineer to carry, workers' compensation insurance in statutory limits together with employer's liability insurance, "all risk" Builders Risk coverage, commercial general liability insurance, with coverage for ongoing and products-completed operations by endorsement, for any occurrence in or about the Project, automobile liability, and umbrella/excess liability insurance in like form and limits in accordance with the terms and conditions required of Tenant under Section 13.01 hereof, and such other insurance coverage and limits as Landlord may otherwise require, which may include, without limitation, reasonable amounts of professional liability insurance with respect to architects and engineers, as well as contractor's pollution liability with respect to contractors. Tenant shall also require any such contractor, architect, or engineer to satisfy the same additional coverage terms as required of Tenant under Section 13.01 with respect to naming Landlord and its managing agent, if any, and any Superior Lessor and Superior Mortgagee whose name and address have been furnished to Tenant each as an additional insured by way of endorsement ISO CG 20 37 together with CG 20 10 or their equivalent, which shall be primary and any other insurance that may be available to Landlord and any such additional insured will be excess and non-contributory, waiving all rights of recovery and subrogation, with insurers reasonably satisfactory to Landlord. Tenant shall furnish Landlord with evidence that such insurance is in effect at or before the commencement of Alterations and, on request, at reasonable intervals thereafter during the continuance of Alterations.

(g) Should any mechanics' or other liens be filed against any portion of the Project by reason of the acts or omissions of, or because of a claim against, Tenant or anyone claiming under or through Tenant, Tenant shall cause the same to be canceled or discharged of record by bond or otherwise within 20 days after notice from Landlord. If Tenant shall fail to cancel or discharge said lien or liens within said 20 day period, Landlord may cancel or discharge the same and, within 30 days after Tenant's receipt of Landlord's demand, Tenant shall reimburse Landlord for all costs incurred in canceling or discharging such liens, together with interest thereon at the Interest Rate from the date incurred by Landlord to the date of payment by Tenant, such reimbursement to be made within 10 days after receipt by Tenant of a written statement from Landlord as to the amount of such costs. Tenant shall indemnify and hold Landlord harmless from and against all costs (including, without limitation, attorneys' fees and disbursements and costs of suit), losses, liabilities or causes of action arising out of or relating to any Alteration, including, without limitation, any mechanics' or other liens asserted in connection with such Alteration.

(h) Tenant shall deliver to Landlord, within 30 days after the completion of an Alteration, "as-built" drawings thereof using the AutoCAD Computer Assisted Drafting and Design System, Version 12 or later, or such other system or medium as Landlord may accept. During the Term, Tenant shall keep records of Alterations [costing in excess of $____________] including plans and specifications, copies of contracts, invoices, evidence of payment and all other records customarily maintained in the real estate business relating to Alterations and the cost thereof and shall, within 30 days after demand by Landlord, furnish to Landlord copies of such records.

(i) All Alterations to and Fixtures installed by Tenant in the Premises shall be fully paid for by Tenant in cash and shall not be subject to conditional bills of sale, chattel mortgages, or other title retention agreements.

7.02 Landlord's and Tenant's Property.

(a) All fixtures, equipment, improvements and appurtenances attached to or built into the Premises, whether or not at the expense of Tenant (collectively, "<u>Fixtures</u>"), shall be and remain a part of the Premises and shall not be removed by Tenant. All Fixtures shall be the property of Tenant during the Term and, upon expiration or earlier termination of this Lease, shall become the property of Landlord.

(b) All movable partitions, business and trade fixtures, machinery and equipment, and all furniture, furnishings and other articles of movable personal property owned by Tenant and located in the Premises (collectively, "Tenant's Property") shall be and shall remain the property of Tenant and may be removed by Tenant at any time during the Term; *provided*, that if any Tenant's Property is removed, Tenant shall repair any damage to the Premises or to the Building resulting from the installation and/or removal thereof. Notwithstanding the foregoing, any equipment or other property identified in this Lease as having been paid for with any allowance or credit granted by Landlord to Tenant shall not be considered Tenant's Property and shall be and remain a part of the Premises, shall, upon the expiration or earlier termination of this Lease, be the property of Landlord and shall not be removed by Tenant.

(c) At or before the Expiration Date, or within 15 days after any earlier termination of this Lease, Tenant, at Tenant's expense, shall remove Tenant's Property from the Premises (except such items thereof as Landlord shall have expressly permitted to remain, which shall become the property of Landlord), and Tenant shall repair any damage to the Premises or the Building resulting from any installation and/or removal of Tenant's Property. Any items of Tenant's Property that remain in the Premises after the Expiration Date, or more than 15 days after an earlier termination of this Lease, may, at the option of Landlord, be deemed to have been abandoned, and may be retained by Landlord as Landlord's property or disposed of by Landlord, without accountability, in such manner as Landlord shall determine, at Tenant's expense.

(d) Landlord, by notice given to Tenant at any time prior to the Expiration Date or not later than 30 days after any earlier termination of this Lease, may require Tenant, notwithstanding Section 7.02(a), to remove all or any Fixtures that do not constitute a standard office installation (each, a "Specialty Alteration"), such as, by way of example only, kitchens, vaults, safes, raised flooring, slab cuts and stairwells. If Landlord shall give such notice, then Tenant, at Tenant's expense, prior to the Expiration Date, or, in the case of an earlier termination of this Lease, within 15 days after the giving of such notice by Landlord, shall remove the same from the Premises, shall repair and restore the Premises to the condition existing prior to installation thereof and shall repair any damage to the Premises or to the Building due to such removal. [Tenant may request, upon submitting to Landlord plans and specifications for any Alteration, that Landlord advise Tenant, together with Landlord's approval of the plans and specifications in question, whether or not any portion of such Alteration constitutes a Specialty Alteration that must be removed by Tenant at the end of the Term. If Tenant so requests and Landlord shall fail to so advise Tenant together with Landlord's approval of the plans and specifications in question, then Landlord shall be deemed to have advised Tenant that no portion of such Alteration constitutes a Specialty Alteration that must be removed by Tenant upon the expiration or earlier termination of this Lease.]

7.3 Landlord Concerns

The landlord has much to protect when permitting its asset to be modified by a tenant-proposed premises modification. There will be no attempt here to restate the paragraphs of the sample clause. Reference will be made here to its numbered provisions (all set forth in Section 7.2, *supra*) to illustrate the appropriate landlord precautions in reconciling the tenant's need for physical flexibility with a long list of legitimate ownership concerns.

The first thing to be guarded is the integrity and safety of the base building itself, since alterations can severely interfere with the proper functioning of the overall structure's mechanical systems (see sample clause 7.01(a) and—on using only landlord's contractors for work affecting special building systems—sample clause 7.01(e)). The second concern is ensuring the legality of the installation and conformance with all codes and permit conditions (sample clauses 7.01(d) and (e)), while leaving all liability for faulty design or installation with the tenant (sample clause 7.01(b)). A third landlord concern is what might be styled the installation's "regularity," that is, will the alteration to be approved be welcomed by the next commercial office tenant, or will it more likely have to be demolished and the original premises layout restored? A fourth potential problem is labor competence (a judgment call, but one inherent in the standard landlord demand for pre-approval of all tenant contractors, sample clause 7.01(e)). A fifth area of concern is labor harmony—will permitting the tenant's contractors in likely provoke a work stoppage because of the use of nonunion labor (sample clause 7.01(e)).

Also important to the landlord is securing coverage against mishap, not only in the traditional manner of requiring construction-specific standard policy coverages (sample clause 7.01(f)) but also in demanding indemnification from the tenant (sample clause 7.01(g)). The landlord is equally concerned with defending itself against liens for unpaid work (sample clause 7.01(g)), and recovering its out-of-pocket costs in the review of the tenant's plans, including the fees of any experts hired for that review (sample clause 7.01(c)).

Finally, the landlord is rightfully concerned with process: how the tenant is to make application for the right to alter, the level of sophistication of the plans and specifications that are submitted for review, and the definition of turnaround time for that review (sample clause 7.01(b)); the pre-approval of all contractors (sample clause 7.01(e)); the pre-work-commencement delivery of all governmental approvals and insurance certificates (sample clause 7.01(e)); the right to inspect work in progress (sample clause 7.01(c)); and the delivery of "as-builts" at the end of the day (sample clause 7.01(h)).

7.4 Tenant Concerns

The tenant also benefits from a clear statement of the alteration application process to avoid surprise and delay, and requires some protections not always volunteered by the building ownership. By way of a first example, some alterations are really a matter of indifference to the landlord if merely decorative in nature (see sample clause 7.01(a)), and the landlord should be asked to agree that decorative alterations do not need prior consent.

The tenant should be entitled to the exercise of reasonableness by the landlord regarding the approval of nonmaterial alterations; the reasons for disapproving initial submissions of plans and specifications; and in approving or disapproving contractors. That standard is built into the sample clause (see sample clause 7.01(a)), thus modifying the landlord's absolute discretion on these questions. If the tenant has contractors in mind prior to lease execution, these names may be pre-approved and incorporated into the lease form. By the same token, if the tenant contemplates what might otherwise be nonstandard alterations (a service kitchen or an interior stairway), it should secure the landlord's consent in advance, while the landlord is still disposed to bargain, and also obtain a clear agreement on whether such special installation may be left in place at term's end (or at least require a ruling as to removal policy when the alteration is approved, but before its installation—see sample clause 7.02(d) within the sample clause).

Furthermore, the tenant should insist on strict time periods of review of its plans and specifications, and bargain for a "default rule" that will result in the plans being "deemed to have been approved" if the landlord is not timely in its response (sample clause 7.01(b)).

Finally, while it is not a feature for the lease itself, the tenant should make sure that its architects and engineers have reviewed the draft provisions and know, before the lease is executed and delivered, what performance standards are to be imposed on their conduct, so that they can perform efficiently and economically within those expectations. (By the same token, in pre-execution due diligence, the insurance provision of the alterations clauses should be reviewed by the tenant's insurance advisor at the same time this advisor reviews the main insurance clauses, to make sure that tenant's insurer can indeed supply what is required, and that the coverages demanded by landlord are those obtaining in the current market.)

With respect to liens, the tenant should bargain for the right to bond them off, in order to buy time to fight contractors who have improperly liened the job, lest the landlord (seeking to avoid a default with its own lender) discharge the lien by payment and then bill the tenant.

Regarding end-of-term removal of installations, the tenant should have in place a clear definition of "Tenant's Property" which can be removed without the landlord claim of title (sample clause 7.02(b)). Removal of fixtures and other improvements affixed to the premises can be expensive and time-consuming. In fact, the obligation to do so may result in an inadvertent holding-over. The tenant certainly does not want to be responsible for removing anything installed in the premises by any former tenant or other occupant or, if it can help it, for anything installed by the landlord, whether for the benefit of the tenant or any prior tenant. In order to protect itself, the tenant should negotiate the right to remove only what it wants to remove from the premises on lease expiration and to leave all remaining improvements in the premises with no obligation to remove them and in some instances specifically enumerate the only type of "specialty alterations" that landlord could require removal of (sample clause 7.02(d)). As a compromise and included as a negotiated provision in the sample provision Section 7.01(d), the tenant should request that at the time the landlord approves any plans for tenant work (whether for initial or subsequent improvements), if requested by the tenant, the landlord must designate what property the tenant will be required to remove on lease expiration. Depending on the property so designated, the tenant may be able to revise its plans or the construction of the improvements in order to avoid its removal obligation or at least to make removal less costly and easier to accomplish. Even if this is not possible, the tenant will have enough advance notice to plan to remove all required property on or before the lease termination.

7.5 Standard Real Estate Board of New York Clause

The section on alterations, befitting its importance, is the third in this printed form. (The subheadings and paragraph breaks that follow have been added to make it easier to identify different aspects of the clause.)

> *Tenant Alterations. 3.* Tenant shall make no changes in or to the demised premises, of any nature without Owner's prior written consent. Subject to the prior written consent of Owner, and to the provisions of this article, Tenant, at Tenant's expense, may make alterations, installations, additions or improvements which are nonstructural and which do not affect utility services or plumbing and electrical lines, in or to the interior of the demised premises by using contractors or mechanics first approved in each instance by Owner.
>
> *[Permits and Insurance:]* Tenant shall, before making any alterations, additions, installations or improvements, at its expense, obtain all permits, approvals and certificates required by any governmental or quasi-governmental bodies and (upon completion) certificates of final approval thereof, and shall deliver promptly duplicates of all such permits, approvals and certificates to Owner, and Tenant agrees to carry, and will cause Tenant's contractors and sub-contractors to carry, such workman's compensation, commercial general liability, personal and property damage insurance as Owner may require.
>
> *[Discharge of Liens:]* If any mechanic's lien is filed against the demised premises, or the building of which the same forms a part, for work claimed to have been done for, or materials furnished to, Tenant, whether or not done pursuant to this article, the same shall be discharged by Tenant within thirty days thereafter, at Tenant's expense, by payment or filing the bond required by law.
>
> *[Alterations Landlord's Property Unless Ordered Removed:]* All fixtures and all paneling, partitions, railings and like installations, installed in the premises at any time, either by Tenant or by Owner on Tenant's behalf, shall, upon installation, become the property of Owner and shall remain, upon and be surrendered with the demised premises unless Owner, by notice to Tenant no later than twenty days prior to the date fixed as the termination of this lease, elects to relinquish Owner's rights thereto and to have them removed by Tenant, in which event same shall be removed from the demised premises by Tenant prior to the expiration of the lease, at Tenant's expense.
>
> *[Tenant's Property:]* Nothing in this article shall be construed to give Owner title to, or prevent Tenant's removal of, trade fixtures, moveable office furniture and equipment, but upon removal of same from the demised premises or upon removal of other installations as may be required by Owner, Tenant shall immediately, and at its expense, repair and restore the premises to the condition existing prior to installation and repair any damage to the demised premises or the building due to such removal. All property permitted

or required to be removed by Tenant at the end of the term remaining in the premises after Tenant's removal shall be deemed abandoned and may, at the election of Owner, either be retained as Owner's property or may be removed from the premises by Owner, at Tenant's expense.

7.6 Comments on Standard Real Estate Board of New York Form Clause

As the (added) subheadings make clear, when compared with the sample clause in Section 7.2, *supra*, the majority of the landlord's classic concerns are addressed by the REBNY form. However, the printed form does not describe any process for requesting the very consent that it requires. There is no description of plans and specifications, no stated periods for plan review, no pre-clearance of contractors, no disclaimer of liability for approving tenant's proposed work, no insurance of labor harmony, no stated rights of on-site inspection, no requirement of reimbursement for landlord expenses, no insistence on special landlord-approved contractors for building systems work, no indemnification of landlord and its lender by contractors, and no requirement of as-built plans to be delivered at job's end. All of these subjects, as exemplified and discussed in the sample clause (set forth in Section 7.2 of this chapter), would greatly benefit a landlord. The sample clause provisions can be profitably adopted as riders to the REBNY language for the landlord's benefit.

The tenant, as always, needs to expand this REBNY lease provision's coverage to secure some basic protections. The landlord should agree to review applications for alterations within a limited period, to be reasonable in its review, and (reasonably) to permit all nonstructural alterations that are customary in commercial offices. Decorative alterations (painting, wall coverings, carpeting) should be permitted without consent. A tenant should have a right to protest liens if they are first bonded off. The landlord should be asked to approve certain contractors in advance, if they are already identified.

Note, too, that, in this printed form, any alteration affecting the building mechanical systems is flatly forbidden, a prohibition that seems completely unacceptable in an increasingly "wired" world where the standard tenant's technology needs are increasing every day. Finally, if there are alterations that the tenant knows it will make but does not want to be forced to remove at term's end, the right to leave them in place should be bargained for prior to lease execution. Again, language for all these protections may be taken from the sample clause and inserted as riders to the printed form.

7.7 Litigation Issues

A landlord or tenant lawyer who is able to anticipate the needs of his or her client and thus draft provisions that contemplate factual contingencies beyond those addressed by standard form provisions will justify his or her fee. The alteration clause certainly is a provision requiring such attention.

In *Newport Associates v. Solow*,[1] the lease covered a building for a term of 99 years, if options to extend are taken into account. The alteration restriction provided that no structural alteration or change in excess of an estimated cost of $25,000 could be made without the prior approval of the landlord and that such approval would not be unreasonably withheld. The foregoing alteration restriction is garden variety; the facts of the case are not. The tenant constructed a 45-story office building, on a lot contiguous to the leased premises, that it owned in fee. The tenant was permitted, under applicable zoning regulations, to treat the leased and contiguous property as a single zoning lot, thus permitting the newly constructed building to conform to zoning floor area requirements. The plaintiff-landlord sought to prevent the use of the air rights over the leased premises from being effectively transferred to the tenant's fee property, in conformity with the zoning ordinance, as a violation of the alteration provision of the lease. The landlord of the leased premises asserted it was harmed because the completion of the tenant's new building meant that the landlord had no remaining air rights to transfer for consideration to other adjacent property.

The court of appeals held that the restriction did not prevent an alteration on property other than the leased premises, and that transfer of development rights was not restricted. Furthermore, the consolidation of zoning lots inured to the benefit of the long-term lessee under the applicable ordinance, and not to the reversionary owner. Had the landlord anticipated the value of its air rights in the draft of its lease, it could have restricted the tenant from using the rights, and required the tenant to transfer the same at landlord's direction.

Real Property Actions and Proceedings Law (RPAPL) section 803[2] was enacted to change the common-law rule that a tenant had no right to alter leased premises. The statute permits a tenant for a term of five or more years to alter leased premises if the proposed alteration is (1) prudent in view of existing neighborhood conditions; (2) would not reduce the market value for the reversionary owner; and (3) would not otherwise violate any other agreement regulating the conduct of the tenant or restricting the land. In *Two Guys from Harrison-N.Y., Inc. v. S.F.R. Realty Associates*,[3] the Court of Appeals, in construing this statute and a comprehensive alteration provision, prevented a tenant from structurally altering premises in connection with a sublease that would have otherwise permitted the alteration.

The tenant's store lease anticipated the possibility of having to cease operations and sublease to another, more viable tenant. The lease permitted subletting and subdividing of the premises. The lease also contained an alteration restriction provision permitting workmanlike, nonstructural alterations that would not weaken the structure and would comply with law. The provision also permitted the removal of any wall to afford entrance or connection with tenant's improvements on adjoining premises, provided the landlord could require the wall to be restored 90 days prior to the lease

1. 30 N.Y.2d 263, 332 N.Y.S.2d 617, 283 N.E.2d 600 (1972).
2. Real Property Law § 803.
3. 63 N.Y.2d 396, 482 N.Y.S.2d 465, 472 N.E.2d 315 (1984).

expiration. The sublessee requested certain structural alterations other than the specific structural removal of a wall as contemplated and permitted in the alteration clause. The tenant argued that since the alteration clause did not expressly prohibit other structural alterations, in view of RPAPL section 803, the alterations requested were not prohibited. Furthermore, argued the tenant, the right to subdivide the store impliedly included the right to make such alterations needed to complete the job. Noting that the lease was prepared by the tenant, the Court of Appeals disagreed with the tenant and held that the alteration clause comprehensively covered the issue, and "the specification of certain permitted activities in Paragraph 6 (a) should be read as implicitly prohibiting other alterations."[4] The proposed structural alterations were not necessary to effect the permitted subdivision, and thus were not permitted as "customarily and necessarily incidental thereto."[5] The comprehensive alteration clause, although not expressly prohibiting structural alterations, was deemed an agreement regulating and restricting the tenant's alteration rights, thus overriding the rights of a tenant to alter pursuant to RPAPL section 803.

Notwithstanding lease restrictions requiring landlord consent for structural or other alterations, courts have ruled that alterations performed without the required consent were impliedly permitted as being "necessarily incidental" to the permitted use. In *Harar Realty Corp. v. Michilin & Hill, Inc.*,[6] a tenant was held not to be in default for installing a stairway between floors, without obtaining consent, where the tenant was required to perform extensive renovations to make the two-floor offices habitable, and the hallway staircase, not within the leased premises, was in poor condition. The court reasoned that the lease could be forfeited only for alterations in violation of the lease that constituted waste; the necessary and removable stairway could not be deemed waste.[7]

All contracts, including leases, contain an implied covenant of fair dealing. Thus a landlord, who may wish to block an otherwise permitted alteration, cannot do so by failing to cooperate by refusing to take action not specifically required by a lease, such as applying to modify a certificate of occupancy to accommodate the permitted use as "corporate headquarters." Nor may a landlord refuse to execute an application for a building permit, where the lease clearly permitted structural alterations for a particular permitted sublease.[8] The court, in *Med Mac Realty Co. v. Lerner*,[9] held that a "landlord is under a duty to refrain from unreasonably obstructing the tenant's use of the premises."

4. 63 N.Y.2d at 404, 482 N.Y.S.2d at 468.
5. 63 N.Y.2d at 405, 482 N.Y.S.2d at 469.
6. 86 A.D.2d 182, 449 N.Y.S.2d 213 (2d Dep't 1982).
7. 86 A.D.2d at 185, 449 N.Y.S.2d at 215.
8. 154 A.D.2d 656, 547 N.Y.S.2d 65 (2d Dep't 1989).
9. 154 A.D.2d at 659, 547 N.Y.S.2d at 67.

CHAPTER 8

Repairs and Maintenance

8.1 General Purpose

The primary aim of the lease's provisions on repairs and maintenance is to fix the tenant's responsibility for preservation of the demised premises to the standard of their original delivery and/or construction, and for restoring them to that condition when damaged, for whatever reason, by the tenant or anyone connected with the tenant. The secondary aim is to fix on the tenant the responsibility for the cost of repair to any other portion of the building through which the tenant and its employees, contractors, and business visitors move, if that movement causes damage. The third intent is to reserve to the landlord the general maintenance responsibility for the structural and exterior portions of the building and building systems. The last major aim is to divide the responsibility for that work, with the tenant to perform all repairs within the demised premises, and the landlord to perform all work required elsewhere in the building, including all building systems.

8.2 Sample Clause

Section 8.01 Repairs and Maintenance.

(a) Tenant shall keep the Premises (including, without limitation, all Fixtures) in good condition and, upon expiration or earlier termination of the Term, shall surrender the same to Landlord in the same condition as when first occupied, reasonable wear and tear and damages from fire, other casualty or condemnation, excepted. Tenant's obligation shall include, without limitation, the obligation to repair all damage caused by Tenant, its agents, employees, invitees and licensees to the equipment and other installations in the Premises or anywhere in the Building, subject to the release and waiver of subrogation contained herein. Any maintenance, repair or replacement to the windows, the Building systems, the Building's structural components or any areas outside the Premises and that is Tenant's obligation to perform shall be performed by Landlord at Tenant's expense. Tenant shall not commit or allow to be committed any waste or damage to any portion of the Premises or the Project.

(b) Subject to the second sentence of Section 8.05(a), Landlord, at Landlord's expense (subject to reimbursement as Operating Expenses, but only if and to the extent such expenses are not excludable therefrom pursuant to the express provisions of Section 5.02 above), shall operate, maintain, repair and replace (if necessary) (i) all structural portions of the Building, such as, by way of example only, the roof, foundation, footings, exterior walls, load-bearing columns, ceiling and floor slabs, windows, window sills and sashes, (ii) all common and public service areas of the Building, including, without limitation, all elevators, and (iii) all Building systems serving the common and public service areas and the Premises, throughout the Term, and in such a manner as is consistent with the maintenance, operation and repair standards of [first-class office][comparable] buildings located in [__________]. Landlord's obligations under this Section 8.01(b) shall be subject to the provisions of Section 13.02.

(c) Except as expressly set forth in Articles 14 and 15 and Section 31.02(b), there shall be no allowance to Tenant for a diminution of rental value and no liability on the part of Landlord by reason of inconvenience, annoyance or injury to business arising from Landlord, Tenant or others making, or failing to make, any repairs, alterations, additions or improvements in or to any portion of the Building or the Premises or in or to any Building systems, fixtures or equipment therein, or in or to any appurtenances thereof.

(d) Landlord shall use commercially reasonable efforts to minimize interference with Tenant's use and occupancy of the Premises in making any repairs, alterations, additions or improvements; provided, however, that Landlord shall have no obligation to employ contractors or labor at so-called overtime or other premium pay rates or to incur any other overtime costs or expenses whatsoever.

8.3 Landlord Concerns

The building owner has three goals here: (1) to maintain control of the physical integrity and appearance of all areas outside of the premises defined as demised to tenant; (2) to confirm tenant's continuous financial responsibility for any damage to those premises or to the public areas of the building and the shared building systems; and (3) to compel tenant to repair its own premises.

The landlord is also concerned that the performance of these repairs, whether at the landlord's cost or the tenant's, provide no excuse for the tenant to reduce its rent, even though such work will necessarily have some effect on the use or peace of, or access to, the premises. Furthermore, the landlord does not want to spend more than is strictly necessary in performance of those repairs for which landlord is responsible, whether in public areas or leased areas, and so will resist any language that may imply a duty to perform such work in overtime conditions or nonbusiness hours. The landlord may also seek exculpation from liability for interruption of the tenant's business in the performance of repairs not only as may be required or permitted to be made under the language of the lease, but for any repairs "required by law" or even those that the landlord "deems appropriate in its reasonable discretion."

8.4 Tenant Concerns

The tenant, of course, is not in negotiating the lease so concerned with its own repair-and-maintenance responsibility, since that goes with the territory; rather, the tenant is concerned to limit and delimit the landlord's forays into the tenant's space.

Most landlords will not agree to use overtime labor to shorten the duration of any such in-space repair, but the tenant may legitimately require (1) that such be performed "with reasonable diligence and in a good and workmanlike manner"; (2) that they shall be performed upon reasonable prior notice to the tenant; (3) that in any event repairs be conducted so as to minimize interference with the tenant's business operations; and (4) that the landlord shall restore the premises (to the extent adversely affected by such repairs) as nearly as practicable to the condition of the premises prior to the making of such repairs, including the restoration of wall coverings and paneling, or the performance of touch-up painting.

Where possible, the landlord's own covenants to maintain the building, building systems, sidewalks, plazas, and public areas adjacent to the building at all times should be positively stated (or if stated, strengthened), to a first-class office building standard (if appropriate, that is, if the building is indeed considered a first-class office building), with the positive covenants to make all repairs and replacements necessary to keep the same in proper order and good repair, and to keep the same free of ice, snow, and debris.

8.5 Standard Real Estate Board of New York Clause

The REBNY parallel paragraph, Article 4, touches on many but not all of these concerns of the parties. The italicized, bracketed headings have been added for the purpose of emphasizing different aspects of the paragraph.

> *Maintenance and Repairs. 4.* Tenant shall, throughout the term of this lease, take good care of the demised premises and the fixtures and appurtenances therein. Tenant shall be responsible for all damage or injury to the demised premises or any other part of the building and the systems and equipment thereof, whether requiring structural or nonstructural repairs caused by or resulting from carelessness, omission, neglect or improper conduct of Tenant, Tenant's subtenants, agents, employees, invitees or licensees, or which arise out of any work, labor, service or equipment done for or supplied to, Tenant or any subtenant, or arising out of the installation, use or operation of the property or equipment of Tenant or any subtenant. Tenant shall also repair all damage to the building and the demised premises caused by the moving of Tenant's fixtures, furniture or equipment. Tenant shall promptly make, at

Tenant's expense, all repairs in and to the demised premises for which Tenant is responsible, using only the contractor for the trade or trades in question, selected from a list of at least two contractors per trade submitted by Owner. Any other repairs in or to the building or the facilities and systems thereof for which Tenant is responsible shall be performed by Owner at the Tenant's expense.

[Owner's Repairs] Owner shall maintain in good working order and repair the exterior and structural portions of the building, including the structural portions of the demised premises, and the public portions of the building interior and the building plumbing, electrical, heating and ventilating systems (to the extent such systems presently exist) serving the demised premises. Tenant agrees to give prompt notice of any defective condition in the premises for which Owner may be responsible hereunder.

[No Setoff] There shall be no allowance to Tenant for diminution of rental value and no liability on the part of Owner by reason of inconvenience, annoyance or injury to business arising from Owner or others making repairs, alterations, additions or improvements in or to any portion of the building or the demised premises or in and to the fixtures, appurtenances or equipment thereof. It is specifically agreed that Tenant shall not be entitled to any setoff or reduction of rent by reason of any failure of Owner to comply with the covenants of this or any other article of this Lease. Tenant agrees that Tenant's sole remedy at law in such instance will be by way of an action for damages for breach of contract. The provisions of this Article 4 shall not apply in the case of fire or other casualty which are dealt with in Article 9 hereof.

8.6 Comments on Standard Real Estate Board of New York Clause

The landlord's concerns are well covered by the REBNY article, and so any changes made are virtually all to do with further tenant protections of the kinds described in Section 8.4, *supra*. If the tenant has managed to work into Article 9 ("Destruction, Fire and Other Casualty") provisions wherein the landlord agrees to shorter time frames for lease cancellation than such article normally provides, the tenant might also argue in this Article 4 for protective language allowing the tenant to get some rent relief (if not the right to cancel the lease) if the landlord fails to make repairs, particularly to the building systems, which could amount to constructive eviction (where the elevator breakdown prohibits access, or HVAC failure makes working conditions unbearable); but these will be difficult to achieve for all but the largest tenants.

Tenants may argue with greater success to expand the number of contractors from which they may choose and require that the landlord give good-faith consideration to any suggested addition to such list. Furthermore, at the end of the laundry list of systems, "and elevators" should be added. This was omitted from both the 1984 and 1994 REBNY forms. Again, the tenant's obligation to notify the landlord of the need for repairs should be "after knowledge."

Finally, before the penultimate sentence, tenants should seek the following insertion:

> Except in the case of an emergency in which case no notice is required, all such non-emergency entries to the demised premises by Owner or its employees, contractors or agents for the purpose of making repairs, alterations, additions or improvements shall be performed upon reasonable prior notice to Tenant (which notice may be oral or written) and at such times and in such a manner as to reasonably minimize interference or disruption to Tenant's use, occupancy and quiet enjoyment of the demised premises.

8.7 Litigation Issues

There are virtually no implied obligations requiring a landlord to maintain a premises in good repair. There are, however, statutory obligations that go beyond a duty to perform ordinary repairs.[1] Since the tenant's common-law duty to "make tenantable repairs in order to avoid permissive waste of the leasehold"[2] is considered to be a tort liability, rather than contract liability arising out of the lease,[3] the drafting and negotiating of repair covenants becomes a matter of concern to both the landlord's and the tenant's lawyers. The cases in this area of litigation reveal that counsel must often attempt to overcome deficiencies created by negotiations that failed to properly protect one of the parties to the lease.

In *First Federal Savings and Loan Association of Rochester v. Minkoff*,[4] the court stated that "Net lease provisions are typically presumed to impose the responsibility for *all* expenses arising from the property, including the costs of repair of every nature, upon the tenant." However, in determining a repair obligation, the entire lease, not merely its characterization as "net," must be considered. The case of *First Federal v. Minkoff* demonstrates that conflicts may exist between a landlord and tenant pertaining to repair covenants in a "net, net, net" lease that were not clearly contemplated when the lease was drafted. The landlord constructed the tenant's leased building and covenanted to perform all repairs during the first year. The provision concerning repairs during the first year contained the statement that "all other repairs of a structural nature shall be the obligation of landlord."[5] Subsequent to the expiration of the first year of the lease

1. Wolf v. 2539 Realty Assoc., 161 A.D.2d 11, 560 N.Y.S. 2d 24 (1st Dep't 1990) (requiring landlord to abate asbestos condition); Bush Terminal Assoc. v. Federated Dep't Stores, Inc., 73 A.D.2d 943, 424 N.Y.S.2d 28 (2d Dep't 1980) (landlord's obligation to install sewer could not be imposed on tenant pursuant to compliance with law or repair covenants).

2. Watner v. P & C Food Mkts., Inc., 138 A.D.2d 959, 526 N.Y.S.2d 292 (4th Dep't 1988).

3. P.B.N. Assoc. v. Xerox Corp., 141 A.D.2d 807, 529 N.Y.S.2d 877 (2d Dep't 1988) (action for waste denied as barred by three-year statute of limitations, but permitted action, based on lease covenant, to continue).

4. First Fed. Sav. $ Loan Ass'n of Rochester v. Minkoff, 176 A.D.2d 1049, 575 N.Y.S.2d 197, 199 (3d Dep't 1991) (The case reached the appellate court on cross-appeals from a denial of motions for summary judgment. The lower court determination denying the motions for summary judgment was affirmed on the ground that the lease was ambiguous.).

5. 575 N.Y.S.2d at 197.

term, it was determined that approximately $190,000 in structural repairs were needed. The appellate court, affirming the lower court denial of motions for summary judgment, held that the lease was ambiguous and that it was appropriate to admit extrinsic evidence because the tenant's general covenants to perform all repairs in a "net" lease may have been intended to apply after the first year of the term. Additionally, the location of the landlord's covenant to perform structural repairs may have been intended to be limited to those required in the first year, since it was located in that clause. If the tenant had expected the landlord to continue to be liable for structural repairs after the expiration of one year, it should have negotiated for a distinctly numbered provision in the lease setting forth that obligation.

Generally, absent an express covenant by the landlord, a tenant would be responsible for structural repairs under a "net" lease in which the tenant agreed to pay all expenses in connection with maintenance of the demised premises.[6] A landlord's covenant to make structural repairs must be expressly stated, and will not be implied from a provision exempting the tenant from making structural repairs.[7] A provision permitting a landlord to enter upon the premises for the purpose of making repairs as may be necessary for the preservation and safety of the premises does not create such an obligation by implication.[8] Thus, when a tenant's lease failed to contain any repair covenant by the landlord, the tenant could not force the landlord to remedy a structural problem concerning the building's slab, even if the defect resulted in a notice of building violation, which the tenant was not required to cure.[9]

A properly drafted lease can shift a statutory repair obligation from the landlord to the tenant. The drafter of a lease should be particularly concerned when the use of the premises involves hazardous substances such as oil and gas. In this regard, two decisions concerning statutorily mandated gasoline cleanup may be compared.[10] In *101 Fleet Place Associates v. New York Telephone Co.*,[11] the landlord sought reimbursement from the tenant for a cleanup it performed in order to cure a violation issued to the tenant. The reimbursement was sought pursuant to a leasehold covenant requiring the tenant to keep and maintain the interior of the garage premises in a good state of preservation and repair. The lease also provided that "The landlord at his sole expense shall comply with all laws, orders and regulations . . . which shall impose any violation, order or duty upon landlord or tenant with respect to the demised premises or the use or

---

6. 1833 Assoc. v. Frying Carpets Co., Inc., 156 Misc. 2d 696, 594 N.Y.S.2d 121 (NYC Civ. Ct. N.Y. Cnty. 1992).

7. Refrigeration for Science, Inc. v. Deacon Realty Corp., 70 Misc. 2d 500, 334 N.Y.S.2d 418 (Sup. Ct. Nassau Cnty. 1972).

8. 334 N.Y.S.2d at 426.

9. *Id.* at 425, noting that a covenant to comply with laws does not generally require the tenant to perform a structural repair.

10. Star Nissan, Inc. v. Frishwasser, 253 A.D.2d 491, 677 N.Y.S.2d 145 (2d Dep't 1998) (holding for landlord); and 101 Fleet Place Assoc. v. New York Tel. Co., 197 A.D.2d 27, 609 N.Y.S.2d 896 (1st Dep't 1994) (holding for tenant).

11. 197 A.D.2d 27, 609 N.Y.S.2d 896.

occupation thereof."[12] Even though the tenant may have failed to maintain the gasoline tanks, the cleanup resulted from a violation of law. The tenant's repair covenant did not expressly require maintenance of the tanks so as to override the landlord's covenant to comply with legal requirements and orders.

In *Star Nissan, Inc. v. Frishwasser,*[13] however, even though state law imposed a similar cleanup obligation upon the property owner, the "net" lease provisions of the lease requiring the tenant to function "as though it were the sole owner . . . obligations of every kind . . . including the cost of interior and exterior repairs, both ordinary and extraordinary . . ." and further requiring the tenant to comply with all present and future laws, was held sufficient to shift the burden of the mandated cleanup to the tenant.[14]

A tenant's covenant to repair may impose an unfair monetary obligation. The tenant's covenant to maintain a pier in good and sufficient repair, and to surrender possession of the pier repaired, painted, and in good order and condition, imposed a liability of thousands of dollars upon the tenant to carry out such a repair, notwithstanding that the landlord intended to demolish the pier at the expiration of the lease and not actually perform the repairs.[15] A tenant leasing office space should have a similar concern when it is likely that the tenant's premises will be demolished to accommodate the succeeding tenant.

12. 609 N.Y.S.2d at 898.
13. 253 A.D.2d 491, 677 N.Y.S.2d 145.
14. *Star Nissan, Inc.*, 253 A.D.2d 491, 677 N.Y.S.2d 145.
15. City of New York v. Farrell Lines, Inc., 30 N.Y.2d 76, 330 N.Y.S.2d 358 (1972).

CHAPTER 9

Window Cleaning

9.1 General Purpose

New York State Labor Law section 202 provides:

> **Protection of the public and of persons engaged at window cleaning and cleaning of exterior surfaces of building**
>
> The owner, lessee, agent and manager of every public building and every contractor involved shall provide such safe means for the cleaning of the windows and of exterior surfaces of such building as may be required and approved by the board of standards and appeals.[1] The owner, lessee, agent, manager or superintendent of any such public building and every contractor involved shall not require, permit, suffer or allow any window or exterior surface of such building to be cleaned unless such means are provided to enable such work to be done in a safe manner for the prevention of accidents and for the protection of the public and of persons engaged in such work in conformity with the requirements of this chapter and the rules of the board of standards and appeals. A person engaged at cleaning windows or exterior surfaces of a public building shall use the safety devices provided for his protection. Every employer and contractor involved shall comply with this section and the rules of the board and shall require his employee, while engaged in cleaning any window or exterior surface of a public building, to use the equipment and safety devices required by this chapter and rules of the board of standards and appeals.
>
> The provisions of this section shall not apply to (1) multiple dwellings six stories or less in height located anywhere in this state; nor to (2) any building three stories or less in height in cities, towns or villages having a population of less than forty thousand; nor to (3) the windows or exterior surfaces of any building which may be exempted under any rule adopted by the board of standards and appeals.

1. Now Industrial Board of Appeals.

> The board of standards and appeals may grant variations pursuant to the provisions of section thirty of this chapter. All existing variations heretofore made by the board relating to the cleaning of windows are hereby validated and continued in full force and effect until amended or terminated by the board.
>
> The board of standards and appeals may make rules to effectuate the purposes of this section. Notwithstanding any other law or regulation, local or general, the provisions of this section and the rules issued thereunder shall be applicable exclusively throughout the state and the commissioner shall have exclusive authority to enforce this section and the rules issued thereunder.

The purpose of the lease provision relating to window cleaning is to make the tenant aware of Labor Law section 202 and to provide for the tenant's agreement not to violate its requirements. Additionally, this lease provision provides the landlord with a remedy in the event the tenant fails to comply with it by making such failure a default under the lease.

9.2 Sample Clause

> *9.01 Window Cleaning*
>
> Tenant shall not clean, nor require, permit, suffer or allow any window in the Premises to be cleaned from the outside in violation of § 202 of the Labor Law, or any other Legal Requirement, or of the rules of the Board of Standards and Appeals, or of any other board or body having or asserting jurisdiction.

9.3 Landlord Concerns

Landlords are concerned about any possible violation of Labor Law section 202 by any of their tenants because any such violation could be deemed to be a violation by the landlord.

9.4 Tenant Concerns

Tenants have no concern or interest in negotiating this provision, which essentially is redundant and superfluous, since its requirements fall under the general umbrella of lease provisions requiring compliance with laws generally.

9.5 Standard Real Estate Board of New York Clause

> *Window Cleaning: 5* Tenant will not clean, nor require, permit, suffer or allow any window in the demised premises to be cleaned, from the outside in violation of § 202 of the Labor Law or any other applicable law or of the rules of the Board of Standards and Appeals, or of any other Board or body having or asserting jurisdiction.

9.6 Comments on the Standard Real Estate Board of New York Clause

There is no substantial difference between the sample clause and the Standard Real Estate Board of New York clause. The Standard Real Estate Board of New York form as well as virtually every customized form contains such provisions.

9.7 Litigation Issues

Labor Law section 202 imposes upon the owner, lessee, agent, and manager of a public building an obligation to "provide safe means for the cleaning of the windows and exterior surfaces of such building . . . [and] shall not require, permit, suffer or allow any window or exterior surface of such building to be cleaned unless such means are provided to enable such work to be done in a safe manner. . . ." A tenant contemplated by this section is a lessee of all or substantially all of a building, so that the lessor is excluded from control of the windows and exterior.[2] If a lease does give the lessee total, exclusive control of an entire building during the term of a lease, the tenant and not the landlord may be liable to a window washer pursuant to the statute.[3] However, factual circumstances may result in liability imposed upon landlord and tenant.[4] The fact that the tenant may have hired the window cleaner will not relieve a landlord who is in control of the building from liability to an injured window cleaner, where it is apparent that the exterior of the windows are being cleaned by tenants.[5]

---

2. Durham v. Metro. Elec. Protective Ass'n, 18 N.Y.2d 433, 276 N.Y.S.2d 601, 223 N.E.2d 17 (1966); Schneier v. Owen Realty Co., 271 A.D. 983, 68 N.Y.S.2d 58 (2d Dep't 1957).

3. Homin v. Cleveland & Whitehill Co., 281 N.Y. 484, 24 N.E.2d 136 (1939) (holding that reserved right of entry to inspect or make repairs did not impose liability on landlord if building was wholly leased); Lowenhar v. Com. Outfitting Co., 260 A.D. 211, 21 N.Y.S.2d 112 (2d Dep't 1940).

4. France v. Abstract Title Div. of Title Guarantee Co., 50 A.D.2d 711, 374 N.Y.S.2d 886 (4th Dep't 1975).

5. Pollard v. Trivia Bldg. Corp., 291 N.Y. 19, 50 N.E.2d 287 (1943).

CHAPTER 10

Requirements of Law

10.1 General Purpose

The purpose of this lease section is to allocate responsibility for bearing the expenses generated by a legal requirement (and/or a fire insurance requirement). The general rule should be one of equitable application. The party whose conduct, use, or manner of use triggers the legal or insurance requirement to make physical changes to the premises or the larger building, in order to bring the premises or the building into legal or insurable compliance, is the party to bear the cost of alteration. This rule becomes harder to apply when a law of general application is passed, such as the *Americans with Disabilities Act of 1991* (ADA). Under such circumstances, neither the landlord nor the tenant has "done" anything, yet expensive changes are mandated by a new legal requirement. Another trap for the unwary is the legal requirement to remove asbestos, which is only triggered when the status quo is disturbed (and so tenants redoing their interiors find themselves bearing the cost of removing asbestos sprayed on years before by landlords). For coverage of all these situations, close attention must be paid to the language of this provision. Finally, with increased attention being paid to the storage and handling of hazardous materials, this article might provide a natural home for special provisions regarding these concerns.

10.2 Sample Clause

10.01 Compliance with Laws.

Tenant shall comply with all laws, ordinances, rules, orders and regulations (present, future, ordinary, extraordinary, foreseen or unforeseen) of any governmental, public or quasi-public authority and any other entity performing similar functions, at any time duly in force (collectively "Laws"), attributable to any work, installation, occupancy, use or manner of use by Tenant of the Premises or any part thereof. Nothing contained in this Section 10.01 shall require Tenant to (i) cure any violations of Laws existing prior to the

Commencement Date, or (ii) make any changes to the structural components of the Building unless the same are necessitated by reason of Tenant's performance of any Alterations, Tenant's particular manner of use of the Premises (as distinguished from office use generally) or the use by Tenant of the Premises for purposes other than normal and customary ordinary office purposes. Tenant shall procure and maintain all licenses and permits required for its business.

10.02 Compliance with Insurance Standards.

(a) Tenant shall not violate, or permit the violation of, any condition imposed by any insurance policy then issued in respect of the Project and shall not do, or permit anything to be done, or keep or permit anything to be kept in the Premises, that would subject Landlord, any Superior Lessor or any Superior Mortgagee to any liability or responsibility for personal injury or death or property damage, or that would increase any insurance rate in respect of the Project over the rate that would otherwise then be in effect or that would result in insurance companies of good standing refusing to insure the Project in amounts reasonably satisfactory to Landlord, or that would result in the cancellation of, or the assertion of any defense by the insurer in whole or in part to claims under, any policy of insurance in respect of the Project.

(b) If, by reason of any failure of Tenant to comply with this Lease, the premiums on Landlord's insurance on the Project shall be higher than they otherwise would be, Tenant shall reimburse Landlord, within 30 days after demand, for that part of such premiums attributable to such failure on the part of Tenant. A schedule or "make up" of rates for the Project or the Premises, as the case may be, issued by any body making rates for insurance for the Project or the Premises, as the case may be, shall be conclusive evidence of the facts therein stated and of the several items and charges in the insurance rate then applicable to the Project or the Premises, as the case may be.

10.3 Landlord Concerns

The landlord's aim here is to cause its tenants to bear every post-lease-execution cost of building alterations compelled, or otherwise caused, by a change in the law or the insurance regulatory system governing the building. To that end, such a clause must make clear the tenant's responsibility to bear such costs not only when the application arises out of the tenant's use (e.g., alterations) or "manner of use" (e.g., wood-burning fireplaces) of the affected premises, but also from the tenant's mere occupancy of the space in question at the time that the triggering law or insurance requirement comes into force (e.g., ADA, where tenants with full floors bear the cost of restroom conversion on their respective floors). Insurance requirements and legal requirements, as concepts, must be broadly defined to include all possible insurance regulatory boards and governmental authorities.

10.4 Tenant Concerns

The tenant's primary aim (not always achievable) is to avoid liability for the cost of compliance with legal or insurance requirements that do not arise out of its specific "use or manner of use" of its space, as long as it is utilizing the space for the purpose specified in the "use" clause of its lease (e.g., "general and executive offices"). If the tenant is liable for the cost of alterations compelled by legal or insurance requirement changes of general application, the tenant is improving the landlord's building for the next tenant using the space for the same purpose, without regard to the amount of the expense and when it falls during the first tenant's term. Consequently, when agreeing to be responsible for the expense of complying with legal and insurance requirements during its term, the tenant should bargain hard for exclusion of "the use of the Premises as permitted under Section X of this Lease." One partial solution, embodied in the REBNY clause set forth later, is to secure an exemption from any requirement to make structural repairs or alterations, unless required by the tenant's "manner of use."

In agreeing to be liable for all insurance requirements, the careful tenant will seek qualification that such insurance will be that customary in buildings of the type being occupied, and that noncompliance with such requirements has a measurable negative impact on the landlord (policy cancellation or premium increase). Also, if the tenant is on a partial floor, it is probable that the costs of compliance with legal requirements of common facilities, such as restrooms or life safety systems, would fall entirely on the landlord, since such common facilities are not defined as being within the premises. If, on the other hand, the landlord insists that the costs of legal compliance for the common facilities are to be borne by all multi-tenant floor occupiers, the tenant should secure language in its lease that limits its share to its pro rata proportion of the floor or building.

10.5 Standard Real Estate Board of New York Clause

> *Requirements of Law, Fire Insurance, Floor Loads: 6.* Prior to the commencement of the lease term, if Tenant is then in possession, and at all times thereafter, Tenant, at Tenant's sole cost and expense, shall promptly comply with all present and future laws, orders and regulations of all state, federal, municipal and local governments, departments, commissions and boards and any direction of any public officer pursuant to law, and all orders, rules and regulations of the New York Board of Fire Underwriters, Insurance Services Office, or any similar body which shall impose any violation, order or duty upon Owner or Tenant with respect to the demised premises, whether or not arising out of Tenant's use or manner of use thereof (including Tenant's permitted use) or, with respect to the building if arising out of Tenant's use or manner of use of the premises or the building (including the use permitted under the lease). Nothing herein shall require Tenant to make structural repairs or alterations unless

Tenant has, by its manner of use of the demised premises or method of operation therein, violated any such laws, ordinances, orders, rules, regulations or requirements with respect thereto.

[*Bonding for Contest*] Tenant may, after securing Owner to Owner's satisfaction against all damages, interest, penalties and expenses, including, but not limited to, reasonable attorney's fees, by cash deposit or by surety bond in an amount and in a company satisfactory to Owner, contest and appeal any such laws, ordinances, orders, rules, regulations or requirements provided same is done with all reasonable promptness and provided such appeal shall not subject Owner to prosecution for a criminal offense or constitute a default under any lease or mortgage under which Owner may be obligated, or cause the demised premises or any part thereof to be condemned or vacated.

[*No Insurance-Violating Acts*] Tenant shall not do or permit any act or thing to be done in or to the demised premises which is contrary to law, or which will invalidate or be in conflict with public liability, fire or other policies of insurance at any time carried by or for the benefit of Owner with respect to the demised premises or the building of which the demises premises form a part, or which shall or might subject Owner to any liability or responsibility to any person or for property damage. Tenant shall not keep anything in the demised premises except as now or hereafter permitted by the Fire Department, Board of Fire Underwriters, Fire Insurance Rating Organization or other authority having jurisdiction, and then only in such manner and such quantity as not to increase the rate for fire insurance applicable to the building, nor use the premises in a manner which will increase the insurance rate for the building or any property located therein over that in effect prior to the commencement of Tenant's occupancy.

[*Liability for Costs and Premiums*] Tenant shall pay all costs, expenses, fines, penalties, or damages, which may be imposed upon Owner by reason of Tenant's failure to comply with the provisions of this article, and if by reason of such failure the fire insurance rate shall, at the beginning of this lease or any time thereafter, be higher than it otherwise would be, then Tenant shall reimburse Owner, as additional rent hereunder, for that portion of all fire insurance premiums thereafter paid by Owner which shall have been charged because of such failure by Tenant. In any action or proceeding wherein Owner and Tenant are parties, a schedule or "make-up" of rate for the building or demised premises issued by the New York Fire Insurance Exchange or other body making fire insurance rates applicable to said premises shall be conclusive evidence of the facts therein stated and of the several items and charges in the fire insurance rates then applicable to said premises.

[*Floor Load*] Tenant shall not place a load upon any floor of the demised premises exceeding the floor load per square foot area which it was designed to carry and which is allowed by law. Owner reserves the right to prescribe the weight and position of all safes, business machines and mechanical equipment. Such installations shall be placed and maintained by Tenant, at Tenant's expense, in settings sufficient, in Owner's judgment, to absorb and prevent vibration, noise and annoyance.

10.6 Comments on Standard Real Estate Board of New York Clause

As is so often the case with the REBNY form, the owner/landlord has no particular need to modify this provision (unless the landlord wishes to add language about hazardous substances being subject to specific legal requirements, in which case language from the sample clause set forth in Section 10.2, *supra,* could be utilized).

The tenant, seeking the distinction between suffering liability for its "manner of permitted use," instead of merely "permitted use" itself being a foundation for liability, will seek to insert the first phrase before the second in the twelfth and thirteenth lines of the printed form, and in the printed form's tenth line, to strike "whether or not" and substitute "but only if," and to add the word "particular" before "use or manner of use thereof" in the printed form's eleventh line.

Also, the language about the owner being secured, in the face of the tenant mounting a legal contest of a legal requirement, to landlord's satisfaction should be modified to say to its "reasonable" satisfaction (in two places in the printed form), if the tenant's right to contest a *Requirements of* legal requirement is to be realizable with a highly nervous owner. See the second paragraph in Section 10.5, *supra*, bearing the following italicized heading: "[*Bonding for Contest*]."

In the sentence beginning on the twenty-first line from the bottom of this provision in the printed form, tenant might seek to insert: "In no event shall Tenant be deemed to have violated any provision of any insurance policy unless Tenant shall have first received notice of the substance of such provision."

10.7 Litigation Issues

The cases construing compliance with law provisions demonstrate the need for careful negotiation and draftsmanship by the landlord's and tenant's lawyers, especially when a change in use or construction is contemplated. The following cases exhibit the need for caution when negotiating this aspect of a lease.

In *Marcy v. Perlman,*[1] the use clause restricted the tenant's use to "*professional use—commodity consultant.*" The requirements of law clause required the tenant to conform to all laws, orders, and regulations. The premises was located in a building within a residential zone. The lease contained a negotiated provision stating that the tenant would not be required to expend any sums to comply with the requirements of law provision unless the use clause was violated. The tenant's use was held to be in

1. 92 A.D.2d 511, 459 N.Y.S.2d 279 (1st Dep't 1983).

violation of a zoning ordinance, and thus constituted a default under the lease. Notwithstanding the negotiated provision, the court held:

> This provision cannot be read as requiring defendant landlord to incur the requisite expenses. Since the use by the Tenant violates the zoning resolutions, the provision imposes the obligation on plaintiff to incur the requisite expense to seek an amendment to the certificate of occupancy and a zoning variance, or to cure the violation by conforming to the permitted use. The lease does not permit what the zoning resolution prohibits.[2]

The possibility that a variance needed may not be obtainable underscores the importance of (1) investigating the applicable zoning ordinances; (2) negotiating for a period of time to obtain the required variances; and (3) negotiating for a right to cancel.

Obtaining a landlord's representation or warranty concerning legality of use may not impose an obligation on the landlord to expend the sums necessary to allow a tenant to legally use the premises, but it will permit the tenant to cancel the lease. The courts, generally, have broadly construed such warranties to protect the tenants who negotiated for this protection. In *Benderson Development Co., Inc. v. Commenco Corp.*,[3] the landlord warranted "that the use by Lessee of the premises for the preparation, sale and consumption of food and beverages will be a permitted use under the zoning classification and local laws and ordinances applicable to the demised premises."[4] The tenant may have known that it could not obtain a building permit and legally build and use the premises until a public sewer was completed. As a result of the sewer not being completed until two years and nine months after the lease was signed, the court permitted the tenant to cancel the lease because the landlord breached the warranty.

In *Turmon v. Fantasia Auto, Inc.*,[5] the court permitted a tenant to cancel a lease when the landlord represented that the premises could be used for an auto body shop "pursuant to the Certificate of Occupancy." The building was constructed before certificates of occupancy were required. The previous use as an auto body shop was a prior legal nonconforming use. However, in order for the tenant to obtain a necessary permit from the state to legally operate an auto body shop, a certificate of occupancy proving that the building could be legally used for that purpose was required. Since no such certificate existed, the landlord was deemed to have breached the warranty, and the tenant was permitted to cancel the lease.

A landlord must also take considerable care in negotiating a compliance with law provision, since technical compliance may not achieve the use restriction desired by the landlord. In *LCB v. Butterfield House, Inc.*,[6] the cooperative corporation landlord sought to prohibit its tenant, a garage operator, from parking transient cars on a daily

2. 459 N.Y.S.2d at 292. *See also* Schlesinger v. Levine, 28 Misc. 2d 654, 212 N.Y.S.2d 904 (Sup. Ct. N.Y. Cnty. 1961).
3. 44 A.D.2d 889, 355 N.Y.S.2d 859 (4th Dep't 1974).
4. 355 N.Y.S.2d at 860.
5. 147 Misc. 2d 450, 556 N.Y.S.2d 195 (Dist. Ct. Nassau Cnty. 1990).
6. 142 Misc. 2d 995, 538 N.Y.S.2d 921 (Sup. Ct. N.Y. Cnty. 1989).

basis. Since the applicable zoning ordinances permitted parking of cars on a daily basis, the tenant's technical compliance with the ordinance resulted in a use of the premises found to be undesirable by the landlord. The landlord could have achieved the desired use limitation by strengthening the use clause restrictions.

Where an ordinance imposes an obligation upon a landlord, such as New York City Local Law 76 of 1985 (asbestos abatement), a standard provision requiring a tenant to repair or alter the premises in compliance with the law will not shift the burden of compliance to the tenant.[7] If a landlord expects a tenant to bear the expense of such compliance, a specific covenant to that effect should be incorporated into the lease. Unless clearly stated otherwise, a covenant requiring a tenant to comply with legal requirements affecting the premises mandates a tenant only to perform structural alterations or repairs when such repairs result from the character of a tenant's particular occupancy.

In *1165 Broadway Corp. v. Dayana of N.Y. Sportswear, Inc.*,[8] the petitioner-landlord commenced proceedings pursuant to Real Property Law section 231(1) and Real Property Actions & Proceedings Law section 715(1) against occupants of the premises who were engaged in the illegal manufacture and sale of counterfeit trademark apparel. The court, recognizing that these statutes were ordinarily employed to protect landlords and the surrounding neighborhoods against drug dealers and prostitutes, held that both statutes were sufficiently unambiguous to encompass "any illegal trade, manufacture or other business,"[9] and granted the petitions terminating the tenancies.

7. Marine Midland Bank v. 140 Broadway Co., 236 A.D.2d 232, 653 N.Y.S.2d 118 (1st Dep't 1997). *See also* Wolf v. 2539 Realty Assoc., 161 A.D.2d 11, 560 N.Y.S.2d 24 (1st Dep't 1990); and Bush Terminal Assoc. v. Federated Dep't Stores, Inc., 127 A.D.2d 574, 511 N.Y.S.2d 372 (2d Dep't 1980) (landlord unsuccessfully sought to compel warehouse tenant to install required sewer lines under standard requirements of law provision).

8. 166 Misc. 2d 939, 633 N.Y.S.2d 724, (N.Y.C. Civ. Ct. Bronx Cnty. 1995).

9. *See* Real Property Law § 231(1) and RPAPL § 715(1).

CHAPTER 11

Subordination and Attornment

11.1 General Purpose

In this aspect of the lease, the landlord wishes to fix its tenant's position within the hierarchy of interests in land. This is accomplished by (1) ensuring that the tenant's leasehold interest is subordinate,[1] and (2) by ensuring that all the covenants in a space lease are made anew to any succeeding landlord.

With respect to subordination, this book's text is not the proper place to fully explicate the theory of senior and subordinate interests in land, except to note the paramount principle that a mortgage is subordinate to existing recorded leases,[2] as well as to (1) existing unrecorded leases on the mortgaged property if the tenant is in open possession of the property, or (2) if the preexisting lease permits the landlord/borrower to mortgage the property. Foreclosure of such a mortgage yields a fee title still subject to the lease, as it would be to a prior mortgage. Apart from statutory provisions, in a foreclosure action, the holder of a leasehold affecting the mortgaged premises that is subordinate in lien to a mortgage being foreclosed is in the position of a junior lender, such that the tenant may pay the mortgage debt and be subrogated to the rights of the prior holder.

Subordination, however, gives the mortgage priority over the lease and assures the lender that the lease is and will remain in full force and effect as security for the loan, while leaving the lender the option (if, say, the rent is well below current market) to name the tenant thereunder in a foreclosure action and thereby terminate the lease. Landlords are keenly aware of the lending community's desire for such flexibility, and so routinely require their tenants to subordinate to present and future mortgages and ground leases. Only large-scale, strong-credit tenants will have the clout to demand in

1. The landlord wishes to ensure that the tenant's lease is subordinate, that is, lower or lesser, and therefore subject to extinguishment by a foreclosing lender or terminating ground lessee who is seeking to regain the mortgaged or ground leased premises free and clear of any space leasehold interests, even though they predate the mortgage or ground lease.

2. New York Real Property Law § 321(3).

return a "non-disturbance and attornment agreement" with the lender that will leave such tenants in place if the landlord is foreclosed out.

Note the interplay between a subordination provision and the covenant of quiet enjoyment (see Chapter 25, *infra*): where a lease with such a provision making the lease subordinate to any new mortgage does not contain an express covenant of quiet enjoyment, no covenant of quiet enjoyment will be implied as against any mortgage that existed at the time the lease was given. Conversely, where a lease expressly subordinate to all mortgages (present or future) on the premises contains an express covenant of quiet enjoyment, the lease is subordinate to the rights of the mortgagee, notwithstanding the presence of the covenant.

The source of the word "attornment" is the medieval Old French "attorn," to turn over. Thus, "attornment," in feudal law, was initially the turning over or transfer, by a lord, of the services and allegiance ("seignory") of his tenant to the new grantee. The concept of attornment eventually came to mean the act of a person, holding a leasehold interest, agreeing to become the tenant of a stranger who has acquired the fee interest or remainder or reversion in the land leased. At common law, then, the consent of the tenant was essential to a grant of the reversion. Furthermore, prior to the enactment of St. 32 Hen. VIII, c. 34 (1540), the assignee of the reversion could not maintain an action upon a covenant in the lease, even if the covenant ran with the land, unless the tenant attorned to the assignee and accepted him as landlord. The Henrician statute created, as between landlords and tenants and their respective assigns, an exception to the rule that one who is not a party to a covenant can neither sue nor be sued upon it.

Today, as noted in a New York Court of Appeals case to address the issue, *In re O'Donnell*:[3]

> Attornment in its primary sense, as it was understood at common law, is thus an idle ceremony. The transfer of the reversion, whether with the consent of the tenant or without it, is a transfer of the lease and of its rights and obligations.[4]

As set forth more succinctly in New York Real Property Law section 248: "An attornment to a grantee is not requisite to the validity of a conveyance of real property occupied by a tenant, or of the rents or profits thereof, or any other interest therein." Further, Henry VIII's legislation of 1540, made part of New York law through the adoption of the common law after the American Revolution, may now be found, more than 450 years later, embodied in Real Property Law section 223. Thus, new landlords are allowed to sue preexisting tenants (and tenant-assignees to sue preexisting landlords) on all covenants in leases that are "real"—that is "run with," or "touch and concern" the land (as the old English common law and later New York state cases have refined those concepts).

However, the act of attornment in still significant in a secondary sense. As the court in *O'Donnell* observed, it can also mean the acknowledgment by a tenant that it holds

3. 240 N.Y. 99, 147 N.E. 541 (1925).
4. 240 N.Y. at 105.

under a new landlord who claims by title paramount, and not by grant of the reversion or as privy to the reversioner. Since the act of attornment is deemed a new contract and a new demise (which may incorporate, expressly or by implication, the terms of the old demise, including the term of duration), payment of rent by a tenant, holding under an unexpired lease subject to a mortgage, following a subsequent foreclosure sale, results in a new lease on the old terms if the rent is accepted by the new landlord. However, if nothing more is shown in this situation than the payment of rent, and the acceptance thereof by the owner of a paramount title, the result (under *O'Donnell*) will be the creation of a tenancy at will or, at best, a tenancy from year to year.

Accordingly, where, after a foreclosure sale, a tenant formally attorns to the purchaser and thereby creates a new lease, which by implication incorporates the terms of the old lease, the tenant cannot avoid liability for the rent for the remainder of the term by subsequently abandoning possession of the premises. Furthermore, formal written attornment also forestalls any arguments by the tenant (which may be made in New York, through its continued reliance on post-Revolution English common-law cases) that certain original lease covenants were "personal" to the prior landlord and need not be fulfilled to the new owner if not "touching and concerning" the demised premises. (Finally, note that New York Real Property Law section 224 provides that the attornment of a tenant to a stranger is absolutely void, and does not in any way affect the possession of the landlord, unless such attornment is made with the consent of the landlord, or pursuant to or in consequence of a judgment, order, or decree of a court of competent jurisdiction, or to a purchaser at a foreclosure sale.)

11.2 Sample Clause

11.01 Subordination

(a) This Lease is subject and subordinate to each mortgage (a "Superior Mortgage") and each underlying lease (a "Superior Lease") that may now or hereafter affect all or any portion of the Project or any interest therein. The lessor under a Superior Lease is called a "Superior Lessor" and the mortgagee under a Superior Mortgage is called a "Superior Mortgagee." Tenant shall execute, acknowledge and deliver any instrument reasonably requested by Landlord, a Superior Lessor or Superior Mortgagee to evidence such subordination, but no such instrument shall be necessary to make such subordination effective. Tenant shall execute any reasonable amendment of this Lease requested by a Superior Mortgagee or a Superior Lessor; provided, that such amendment shall not result in any material increase in Tenant's obligations or liabilities under this Lease or material reduction in the rights, remedies or other benefits available to Tenant. In the event of the enforcement by a Superior Mortgagee of the remedies provided for by law or by such Superior Mortgage, or in the event of the termination or expiration of a Superior Lease, Tenant, upon request of such Superior Mortgagee, Superior Lessor or any person succeeding to the interest of such mortgagee or lessor (each, a "Successor Landlord"), shall automatically become the tenant of such Successor Landlord without change in the terms or provisions of this Lease (it being understood that Tenant shall, if requested, enter into a new lease on terms identical to those in this Lease); *provided*, that any Successor Landlord shall not be (i) liable for any act, omission or default of any prior landlord (including, without limitation, Landlord); (ii) liable for the return of any moneys paid to or on deposit with any prior landlord (including, without limitation, Landlord), except to the extent such moneys or deposits are delivered to such Successor Landlord; (iii) subject to any offset, claims or defense that Tenant might have against any prior landlord (including, without limitation, Landlord); (iv) bound by any Rent that Tenant might have paid for more than the current month to any prior landlord (including, without limitation, Landlord) unless actually received by such Successor Landlord; (v) bound by any covenant to perform or complete any construction in connection with the Project or the Premises or to pay any sums to Tenant in connection therewith; or (vi) bound by any waiver or forbearance under, or any amendment, modification, abridgment, cancellation or surrender of, this Lease made without the consent of such Successor Landlord. Upon request by such Successor Landlord, Tenant shall execute and deliver an instrument or instruments, reasonably requested by such Successor Landlord, confirming the attornment provided for herein, but no such instrument shall be necessary to make such attornment effective.

(b) Tenant shall give each Superior Mortgagee and each Superior Lessor a copy of any notice of default served upon Landlord, provided that Tenant has been notified of the address of such mortgagee or lessor. If Landlord fails to cure any default as to which Tenant is obligated to give notice pursuant to the preceding sentence within the time provided for in this Lease, then each such mortgagee or lessor shall have an additional 30 days after receipt of such notice within which to cure such default or if such default cannot be cured within that time, then such additional time as may be necessary if, within such 30 days, any such mortgagee or lessor has commenced and is diligently pursuing the remedies necessary to cure such default (including, without limitation, commencement of foreclosure proceedings or eviction proceedings, if necessary to effect such cure), in which event this Lease shall not be terminated and Tenant shall not exercise any other rights or remedies under this Lease or otherwise while such remedies are being so diligently pursued. Nothing herein shall be deemed to imply that Tenant has any right to terminate this Lease or any other right or remedy, except as may be otherwise expressly provided for in this Lease.

11.3 Landlord Concerns

As will be apparent from study of the sample clause set forth in Section 11.2, *supra*, in a sophisticated version of this provision, the landlord will be seeking much more than to secure the tenant's twin agreements to subordinate to present and future mortgages and ground leases, and to attorn to any purchaser at foreclosure or other successor landlord (such as a terminating ground lessor).

First, the landlord will find it useful, when seeking financing for its building, to have all the space leases contain clauses that clarify that, notwithstanding compelled attornment, the new landlord (lender or other foreclosure purchaser) will not be liable for certain acts or omissions of the original landlord. This list is the very list that appears in lenders' forms of subordination and non-disturbance, to give the same protections against a tenant that has successfully bargained not to be terminated in the event of foreclosure. A parallel protection of the lender/foreclosure purchaser is embodied in sample clause Section 11.01(a) (set forth in Section 11.2, *supra*), which provides that, upon the successor landlord's election, the tenant will automatically become the tenant of the successor landlord.

Second, this expanded set of provisions may require that the lender be permitted to cure any default by the landlord prior to the tenant terminating or exercising other remedies under the lease (see sample clause Section 11.01(b) set forth in Section 11.2, *supra*).

Finally, an aggressive landlord may insist, as a condition of the original lease, that the tenant agree to make future modifications at the behest of the landlord's lender, as long as the basic economic deal is not affected and the requested change is not otherwise materially adverse to the tenant's beneficial enjoyment of its leasehold (see sample clause Section 11.01(a), set forth in Section 11.2, *supra*).

11.4 Tenant Concerns

The tenant will often have no choice but to accept a subordination and attornment provision. However, if it is concerned with the protection of its leasehold investment, it must, as part of the original lease negotiations, insist on a non-disturbance and attornment agreement from the present mortgagee, and clarify that its subordination to future mortgagees is only on condition of receiving a similar non-disturbance. Unless the tenant is major in terms of the size of the building (one or more floors), this request will normally be strongly resisted by the landlord as an unacceptable infringement on its control of the building, in reducing the universe of lenders to whom it can turn in the future.

If the tenant's lease contains significant concessions to come from the landlord in the future, such as payment for the tenant's improvements, or rent abatement periods to come staggered through the term, it is in this provision that the tenant should make clear that it will not waive its claim for such items against future purchasers or lenders. This may involve the landlord and the tenant in a three-way negotiation with the current lender, but otherwise the tenant may be at significant risk that these deferred concessions will not be honored by a successor landlord.

The tenant may argue with equal force that if it loses the non-disturbance and/or future concession claims battles, any landlord request for advance agreement to future lease modifications at the behest of the selfsame lenders is similarly unacceptable, as it would impair the tenant's present contract.

11.5 Standard Real Estate Board of New York Clause

The REBNY form clause is extremely simple, and, presumably relying on New York Real Property Law sections 223 and 248, does not require attornment:

> *Subordination. 7.* This lease is subject and subordinate to all ground or underlying leases and to all mortgages which may now or hereafter affect such leases or the real property of which demised premises are a part and to all renewals, modifications, consolidations, replacements and extensions of any such underlying leases and mortgages. This clause shall be self-operative and no further instrument of subordination shall be required by any ground or underlying lessor or by any mortgagee, affecting any lease or the real property of which the demised premises are a part. In confirmation of such subordination, Tenant shall from time to time execute promptly any certificate that Owner may request.

11.6 Comments on Standard Real Estate Board of New York Clause

The REBNY provision is about as stripped-down as a subordination clause might be. As described at length earlier (see Section 11.3, Landlord Concerns), the landlord may have several more goals to achieve in seeking various tenant agreements that will enhance the landlord's abilities for future financing by dramatically increasing the number of tenant covenants, as in the sample clause. Alternatively for the tenant, unless its size is such as to make a non-disturbance agreement a bargaining possibility, or unless it wishes, in this clause, to make clear that certain rights to tenant improvement monies, or stretched-out rent abatements, must nevertheless be honored by present and future lenders, the REBNY provision might be left unamended.

11.7 Litigation Issues

A mortgagee may be a silent or even a nonexistent presence during lease negotiations, but if the mortgagee's rights are not considered, particularly when a tenant's interest and investment in the building are substantial, the exercise of those rights may be costly to the tenant in unanticipated ways. Investigation, negotiation, and imagination are needed to "avert a severe decree." Implementing the need to maintain a relationship with its lender, a landlord is often used as a surrogate negotiator for the tenant by agreeing to use "best" or "diligent" efforts to obtain a non-disturbance agreement in favor of a tenant. A tenant, however, may fare better by reserving the right to deal directly with the lender in order to negotiate non-disturbance protection.[5]

5. KVR v. Treasure Star, Inc., 58 N.Y.2d 793, 459 N.Y.S.2d 258, 445 N.E.2d 641 (1983).

The consequences of being subject, and subordinate, to a mortgage go beyond the possibility of foreclosure of a leasehold interest. A tenant contemplating a substantial leasehold transaction, whether a new lease or modifications of an existing lease, must take into consideration the rights of superior mortgagees. The tenant in *Resolution Trust Corp. v. 53 West 72nd Street Realty Associates*[6] entered into a "sandwich" lease with the fee owner and the five floors of residential tenants in the building. The tenant paid an annual rent of about $100,000 plus a share of the taxes and operating expenses; the residential rent roll was $300,000. The prior recorded mortgage contained a provision requiring the mortgagee's consent to a lease such as the tenant's lease, and also required an assignment of leases and rents as additional security for the loan. The landlord failed to obtain the consent of the mortgagee to the "sandwich" lease. The court held that the mortgagee's receiver could require the residential subtenants to attorn to and pay rent directly to the receiver, and not to the tenant. The court stated that ". . . the Lease, entered into without the mortgagee's permission, cannot prevent the Receiver from requiring the Sub-Tenants to attorn to himself, and his collection of their rent." The tenant, to no avail, argued that the receiver's rights should be limited to collection of the sandwich lease rent, and that it (the tenant) had the right to receive its bargained-for income from the residential subtenants. The tenant might have avoided the unfavorable outcome by examining the terms of the mortgage and insisting upon compliance with the mortgagee's consent requirements.

Even during the term of a lease, a tenant must continue to consider the rights of a superior mortgagee before taking significant actions pertaining to its leasehold. In *Dime Savings Bank of New York v. Montague Street Realty Associates*,[7] European American Bank (EAB), a nonparty tenant, entered into a lease with Montaco Realty Company in 1982. The lease was for a ten-year period running from June 1, 1983, to May 31, 1993. Prior to 1987, Montaco sold the property to the defendant. In April 1987, the defendant mortgaged the premises to the plaintiff bank. The mortgage, recorded in 1987, expressly prohibited the defendant from accepting prepayments of rent without the prior written consent of the plaintiff-mortgagee. The mortgage also provided that each new lease was subject and subordinate to the mortgage.

In 1992, EAB signed an amendment to the lease with the defendant extending the lease for a period of five years and providing for a prepayment of rent in the amount of $160,000 representing the rental for the period of June 1, 1993, to May 31, 1994. The amendment also incorporated the terms of the 1982 lease. The 1982 lease had a provision that stated that the lease was subject and subordinate to all mortgages that may "now or hereafter" encumber the property. EAB prepaid the rent in accordance with the agreement. The defendant subsequently defaulted on the mortgage, and, in January

6. 1991 WL 156260, S.D.N.Y., 1991; 1992 WL 183741, S.D.N.Y. 1992, No. Civ. 3299, but see Country Fin. Servs., Inc. v. Century 22 Props., Inc., 28 Misc. 3d 1232(A), 958 N.Y.S.2d 60, 2010 N.Y. Misc. LEXIS 4320 (Sup. Ct. Nassau Cnty. 2010) (distinguishing Resolution Trust Corp., where the rental rate was the result of a negotiated settlement. Thus, a receiver in a foreclosure action could not show that the rental agreement between owner and tenant was not bona fide.).

7. 90 N.Y.2d 539, 664 N.Y.S.2d 246, 686 N.E.2d 1340 (1997).

1993, the plaintiff commenced a foreclosure action. The court-appointed receiver served EAB with a notice to attorn for rents. EAB paid the rent to the receiver but refused to pay the $160,000 for the period of June 1, 1993, to May 31, 1994, because it had paid that amount to the defendant in accordance with the lease extension agreement. The receiver moved by order to show cause to compel EAB to attorn for rents due. The Supreme Court granted the motion and entered judgment against EAB directing it to pay the $160,000. The appellate division affirmed, and the court of appeals affirmed the appellate division.

EAB argued that the lease extension it entered into with the defendant was not a new lease but a continuation of the 1982 lease. As a consequence, asserted EAB, its tenancy predated the plaintiff's mortgage recorded in 1987 and it was not, therefore, bound by the provision in the Dime Savings Bank mortgage prohibiting prepayments of rent.

The court of appeals held that the lease extension represented a new agreement with a new landlord rather than a continuation of the old agreement.

> Although this new agreement incorporated terms of the Montaco lease, it also included several new provisions which were to take effect after the termination of that lease. The most significant provision, the prepayment of rent, was to be applied to the new lease term and not to the original lease term. Under these circumstances, we conclude that the lease extension was a new agreement rather than a continuation of the old agreement. Because the new contract postdated the Dime mortgage and because pledged collateral cannot be impaired by a postdated agreement . . . whatever right EAB had pursuant to that contract was subordinate to the terms of the mortgage.[8]

In *Fidelity Mutual Life Insurance Co. v. American Broadcasting Co., Inc.*,[9] the American Broadcasting Company canceled and surrendered its lease pursuant to a settlement agreement. The lease was subject to a prior collateral assignment of leases to the mortgagee. The lease contained a covenant not to abandon the premises, with a provision for continuing liability for rent if such abandonment occurred. Furthermore, in a subsequent assignment of rents in favor of the lender, the tenant agreed not to modify the lease. The mortgagee argued that since the lease was security for the mortgage, the tenant could not cancel the lease without the lender's consent, and should therefore be liable for a mortgage deficiency judgment. The judgment would have exceeded remaining rental for the balance of term of the surrendered lease. The appellate court noted that there were factual issues for a trial court's determination; however, failure to seek and obtain the lender's consent to the surrender may have resulted in continued liability of the tenant to the lender even though it surrendered possession of the premises.

8. 90 N.Y.2d at 543, 664 N.Y.S.2d at 248.

9. Fid. Mut. Life Ins. Co. v. Am. Broadcasting Co., Inc., 58 A.D.2d 780, 396 N.Y.S.2d 382 (1st Dep't 1977).

Dominion Financial Corp. v. 275 Washington Street Corp.[10] demonstrates the value of negotiating a subordination clause even when an existing lender is not required to deliver a non-disturbance agreement. The tenant was able to negotiate a limitation on automatic subordination to future mortgages. The superior mortgage would have to be either (1) an extension of the existing mortgage; (2) a mortgage to an institutional mortgagee, as defined; or (3) the mortgagee would have to provide non-disturbance protection. The new lender, a mortgage company, took an assignment of the existing superior mortgage in the amount of $56,000 and consolidated it with a new $216,750 mortgage. The court held that the tenant remained subordinate to the principal balance of the first mortgage despite the consolidation. However, since the new lender was not a defined institutional lender, the lease was superior to the new mortgage amount. The tenant was thus able to retain its tenancy by paying the $56,000 balance.

The practitioner should be aware of a mortgage subordination provision specifically set forth in the quiet enjoyment clause. A landlord, who took back a purchase money mortgage, has been permitted to terminate a lease subordinate to all mortgages, despite that landlord's covenant of quiet enjoyment, where that covenant was expressly subordinate to any and all mortgages.[11]

10. 64 Misc. 1044, 316 N.Y.S.2d 803 (Sup. Ct. Westchester Cnty. 1970).

11. 220 West 42d Assocs. v. Ronbet Newmark Co., 53 A.D.2d 829, 385 N.Y.S.2d 304 (1st Dep't 1976).

CHAPTER 12

Rules and Regulations

12.1 General Purpose

Most leases contain a provision requiring the tenant to comply with the rules and regulations established by the landlord for the building. Generally, these rules and regulations are promulgated by the landlord and set forth in a separate exhibit to the lease. The rules and regulations are intended to apply to all office tenants and to govern their conduct and that of their visitors in the building. Possibly because of their placement in an exhibit to the lease or because of their regulatory nature, they often are not a focus of the landlord/tenant negotiations. However, they do comprise enforceable lease provisions and should be given appropriate attention.

12.2 Sample Clause

> *12.01 Rules and Regulations.*
>
> Tenant shall comply with, and Tenant shall cause its licensees, employees, contractors, agents and invitees to comply with, the rules of the Building set forth in Exhibit C, as the same may be reasonably modified or supplemented by Landlord from time to time. Landlord shall not be obligated to enforce the rules of the Building against Tenant or any other tenant of the Building or any other party, and Landlord shall have no liability to Tenant by reason of the violation by any tenant or other party of the rules of the Building; *provided*, that Landlord shall not enforce the rules of the Building in a manner that discriminates against Tenant. If any rule of the Building shall conflict with any provision of this Lease, such provision of this Lease shall govern.

12.3 Landlord Concerns

The landlord has an obvious interest in maintaining order and cleanliness in the building. The landlord does not want any tenant to damage the building or infringe on the rights of other tenants in the building. The landlord also has an obligation to maintain a safe and secure environment for all persons in the building, including visitors, and will incur liability if he or she does not take reasonable steps to ensure the safety and security of tenants and others. The rules and regulations supply additional provisions to the lease that, for the most part, address these concerns, are enforceable by the landlord, and, in a relatively uniform format, can be attached to and made a part of every lease of space in the building.

12.4 Tenant Concerns

While recognizing the landlord's right to maintain a safe, clean, and secure environment for all tenants, the tenant has a right to enjoy the benefits of the negotiated provisions of the lease, which should not be superseded by the rules and regulations. In addition, the tenant should not be lulled into thinking that because the rules and regulations apply to all tenants, they are not negotiable (whether pursuant to edits to the rules and regulations exhibit or, more likely, negotiated provisions in the body of the lease). Finally, the tenant should not agree in advance to be governed by future rules and regulations unless they are reasonable and consistent with the provisions of the lease and do not add to the tenant's burdens or detract from its benefits in any meaningful way. The tenant should seek adequate advance notice in writing of all new or modified rules and regulations and a reasonable opportunity to dispute them. While a landlord is not likely to accept a provision requiring it to enforce all rules and regulations against other tenants, it should agree not to discriminate in the enforcement of the rules and regulations.

12.5 Standard Real Estate Board of New York Clause

> *Rules and Regulations: 33.* Tenant and Tenant's servants, employees, agents, visitors, and licensees shall observe faithfully, and comply strictly with, the Rules and Regulations and such other and further reasonable Rules and Regulations as Owner and Owner's agents may from time to time adopt. Notice of any additional rules or regulations shall be given in such manner as Owner may elect. In case Tenant disputes the reasonableness of any additional Rule or Regulation hereafter made or adopted by Owner or Owner's agents, the parties hereto agree to submit the question of the reasonableness of such Rule or Regulation for decision to the New York office of the American Arbitration Association, whose determination shall be final and conclusive upon the parties hereto. The right to dispute the reasonableness of any additional Rule or Regulation upon Tenant's part shall be deemed waived unless the same shall be asserted by service of a notice, in writing upon Owner within fifteen (15) days after the giving of notice thereof. Nothing in this lease contained shall be construed to impose upon Owner any duty or obligation to enforce the Rules and Regulations or terms, covenants or conditions in any other lease, as against any other tenant and Owner shall not be liable to Tenant for violation of the same by any other tenant, its servants, employees, agents, visitors or licensees.

RULES AND REGULATIONS ATTACHED TO AND MADE A PART OF THIS LEASE IN ACCORDANCE WITH ARTICLE 33.

1. The sidewalks, entrances, driveways, passages, courts, elevators, vestibules, stairways, corridors or halls shall not be obstructed or encumbered by any Tenant or used for any purpose other than for ingress or egress from the demised premises and for delivery of merchandise and equipment in a prompt and efficient manner using elevators and passageways designated for such delivery by Owner. There shall not be used in any space, or in the public hall of the building, either by any Tenant or by jobbers or others in the delivery or receipt of merchandise, any hand trucks, except those equipped with rubber tires and sideguards. If said premises are situated on the ground floor of the building, Tenant thereof shall further, at Tenant's expense, keep the sidewalk and curb in front of said premises clean and free from ice, snow, dirt and rubbish.
2. The water and wash closets and plumbing fixtures shall not be used for any purposes other than those for which they were designed or constructed and no sweepings, rubbish, rags, acids or other substances shall be deposited therein, and the expense of any breakage, stoppage, or damage resulting from the violation of this rule shall be borne by the Tenant who, or whose clerks, agents, employees or visitors, shall have caused it.
3. No carpet, rug or other article shall be hung or shaken out of any window of the building and no Tenant shall sweep or throw or permit to be swept or thrown from the demised premises any dirt or other substances into any of the corridors or halls, elevators, or out of the doors or windows or stairways of the building and Tenant shall not use, keep or permit to be used or kept any foul or noxious gas or substance in the demised premises, or permit or suffer the demised premises to be occupied or used in a manner offensive or objectionable to Owner or other occupants of the building by reason of noise, odors, and/or vibrations, or interfere in any way with other Tenants or those having business therein, nor shall any bicycles, vehicles, animals, fish, or birds be kept in or about the building. Smoking or carrying lighted cigars or cigarettes in the elevators of the building is prohibited.
4. No awnings or other projections shall be attached to the outside walls of the building without the prior written consent of Owner.
5. No sign, advertisement, notice or other lettering shall be exhibited, inscribed, painted or affixed by any Tenant on any part of the outside of the demised premises or the building or on the inside of the demised premise if the same is visible from the outside of the premises without the prior written consent of Owner, except that the name of

Tenant may appear on the entrance door of the premises. In the event of the violation of the foregoing by any Tenant, Owner may remove same without any liability, and may charge the expense incurred by such removal to Tenant or Tenants violating this rule. Interior signs on doors and directory tablet shall be inscribed, painted or affixed for each Tenant by Owner at the expense of such Tenant, and shall be of a size, color and style acceptable to Owner.

6. No Tenant shall mark, paint, drill into, or in any way deface any part of the demised premises or the building of which they form a part. No boring, cutting or stringing of wires shall be permitted, except with the prior written consent of Owner, and as Owner may direct. No Tenant shall lay linoleum, or other similar floor covering, so that the same shall come in direct contact with the floor of the demised premises, and, if linoleum or other similar floor covering is desired to be used an interlining of builder's deadening felt shall be first affixed to the floor, by a paste or other material, soluble in water, the use of cement or other similar adhesive material being expressly prohibited.
7. No additional locks or bolts of any kind shall be placed upon any of the doors or windows by any Tenant, nor shall any changes be made in existing locks or mechanism thereof. Each Tenant must, upon the termination of his Tenancy, restore to Owner all keys of stores, offices and toilet rooms either furnished to or otherwise procured by such Tenant, and in the event of the loss of any keys so furnished, such Tenant shall pay to Owner the cost thereof.
8. Freight, furniture, business equipment, merchandise and bulky matter of any description shall be delivered to and removed from the premises only on the freight elevators and through the service entrances and corridors, and only during hours and in a manner approved by Owner. Owner reserves the right to inspect all freight to be brought into the building and to exclude from the building all freight which violates any of these Rules and Regulations or the lease of which these Rules and Regulations are a part.
9. Canvassing, soliciting and peddling in the building is prohibited and each Tenant shall cooperate to prevent the same.
10. Owner reserves the right to exclude from the building all persons who do not present a pass to the building signed by Owner. Owner will furnish passes to persons for whom any Tenant requests same in writing. Each Tenant shall be responsible for all persons for whom he requests such pass and shall be liable to Owner for all acts of such persons. Tenant shall not have a claim against Owner by reason of Owner excluding from the building any person who does not present such pass.

11. Owner shall have the right to prohibit any advertising by any Tenant which in Owner's opinion tends to impair the reputation of the building, or its desirability as a building for offices, and upon written notice from Owner, Tenant shall refrain from or discontinue such advertising.
12. Tenant shall not bring or permit to be brought or kept in or on the demised premises any inflammable, combustible, explosive or hazardous fluid, material, chemical or substance, or cause or permit any odors of cooking or other processes, or any unusual or other objectionable odors to permeate in or emanate from the demised premises.
13. If the building contains central air conditioning and ventilation, Tenant agrees to keep all windows closed at all times and to abide by all rules and regulations issued by Owner with respect to such services. If Tenant requires air conditioning or ventilation after the usual hours, Tenant shall give notice in writing to the building superintendent prior to 3:00 p.m. in the case of services required on weekdays, and prior to 3:00 p.m. on the day prior in case of after-hours service required on weekends or on holidays. Tenant shall cooperate with Owner in obtaining maximum effectiveness of the cooling system by lowering and closing venetian blinds and/or drapes and curtains when the sun's rays fall directly on the windows of the demised premises.
14. Tenant shall not move any safe, heavy machinery, heavy equipment, bulky matter, or fixtures into or out of the building without Owner's prior written consent. If such safe, machinery, equipment, bulky matter or fixtures require special handling, all work in connection therewith shall comply with the Administrative Code of the City of New York and all other laws and regulations applicable thereto and shall be done during such hours as Owner may designate.
15. Refuse and Trash. *(1)* Compliance by Tenant. Tenant covenants and agrees, at its sole cost and expense, to comply with all present and future laws, orders, and regulations of all state, federal, municipal, and local governments, departments, commissions and boards regarding the collection, sorting, separation and recycling of waste products, garbage, refuse and trash. Tenant shall sort and separate such waste products, garbage, refuse and trash into such categories as provided by law. Each separately sorted category of waste products, garbage, refuse and trash shall be placed in separate receptacles reasonably approved by Owner. Such separate receptacles may, at Owner's option, be removed from the demised premises in accordance with a collection schedule prescribed by law. Tenant shall remove, or cause to be removed by a contractor acceptable to Owner, at Owner's sole discretion, such items as Owner may expressly designate. *(2)* Owner's Right in Event of Noncompliance. Owner has the option to refuse to collect

or accept from Tenant waste products, garbage, refuse or trash *(a)* that is not separated and sorted as required by law or *(b)* which consists of such items as Owner may expressly designate for Tenant's removal, and to require Tenant to arrange for such collection at Tenant's sole cost and expense, utilizing a contractor satisfactory to Owner. Tenant shall pay all costs, expenses, fines, penalties, or damages that may be imposed on Owner or Tenant by reason of Tenant's failure to comply with the provisions of this Building Rule 15, and, at Tenant's sole cost and expense, shall indemnify, defend and hold Owner harmless (including reasonable legal fees and expenses) from and against any actions, claims and suits arising from such noncompliance, utilizing counsel reasonably satisfactory to Owner.

12.6 Comments on the Standard Real Estate Board of New York Clause

The treatment in the standard Real Estate Board of New York clause of the landlord's rights to enforce, modify, and add to rules and regulations for the building and the substance of the rules and regulations themselves is similar to such treatment and to the rules and regulations in the sample clause (see Section 12.2, *supra*), albeit somewhat less extensive. Each lease form, including the standard Real Estate Board of New York form, has its own set of rules and regulations. Generally, they are similar. Each, however, has certain provisions that are absent from others and lack some that are present in others. The differences should reflect the concerns of the applicable landlord or the characteristics of the particular building or its operations. The essential point for the tenant is that they all count and, therefore, should all be considered.

12.7 Litigation Issues

Rules and regulations appended to lease agreements are provisions usually deemed "necessary for the reputation, safety, care or appearance of the building, or the preservation of good order therein, or the operation or maintenance of" a building.[1] They will be enforced as leasehold covenants and agreements, under the rule of construction that "[R]estrictive conditions in a lease are to be construed so as to carry out the intent of the parties as shown by the words used, considered in connection with the surrounding circumstances, and such intent must be ascertained from an examination of the whole lease and not from the particular clause alone."[2]

As building appearance and safety are often the reasonable goals of enforcing rules and regulations, they are often drafted as requiring a lessor's approval for certain

1. Eagle Spring Water Co., Inc. v. Webb & Knapp, Inc., 236 N.Y.S.2d 266, 281 (Sup. Ct. N.Y. Cnty. 1962).
2. 236 N.Y.S.2d at 281.

conduct. Such approval requirements will be looked at under the foregoing rule of construction, so that a rule requiring a landlord's approval of a tenant's suppliers did not require a tenant to use only suppliers identified by landlord.[3] Furthermore, the courts will restrict the remedy of enforcement of rules and regulations to those reasonably needed to enforce compliance. Where building rules required prior approval of store window signs, a court will not substitute its judgment for that of the landlord in imposing the rule, but it will limit the remedy to injunctive relief and not lease termination.[4]

3. 236 N.Y.S.2d 266.

4. Louis & Anne Abrons Found., Inc. v. 29 East 64th St. Corp., 78 A.D.2d 814, 433 N.Y.S.2d 132 (1st Dep't 1980).

CHAPTER 13

Insurance

13.1 General Purpose

Each party to a lease will have obligations imposed on it and risks allocated to it by the terms of the lease. It is in both the landlord's and tenant's interest that such obligations (e.g., rebuilding in the event of casualty-related damage) and risks (e.g., liability to third parties for damage or injury) be adequately covered by insurance. Whether drafting or commenting on a form of lease, counsel should be aware of the interaction between the insurance requirements and the indemnities and waivers set forth in the lease (in the case of liability insurance) and the restoration provisions of the lease (in the case of property losses), and should be careful to distinguish between claims made by third parties and claims made by either the landlord or tenant.

13.2 Sample Clause

13.01 Tenant's Insurance.

(a) Tenant, at Tenant's expense, shall maintain at all times during the Term:

(i) property insurance written on an ISO CP 10 30-Cause of Loss-Special Form, commonly referred to as the "all risk" policy form, or equivalent, including, without limitation, coverage against sprinkler leakage and other damage due to water, insuring all present and future Tenant's Property and Fixtures and any other personal property leased by or in the care, custody and control of Tenant and located in the Premises in an amount of not less than the full replacement cost thereof, with an agreed amount endorsement (waiving applicable co-insurance clause);

(ii) business interruption insurance covering any loss due to the occurrence of any of the hazards insured against by Tenant in Section 13.01(a)(i), in an amount sufficient to cover Tenant's monetary obligations under this Lease for a period of at least twelve months;

(iii) commercial general liability insurance written on an ISO CG 00 01 occurrence policy form or equivalent, including a Separation of Insureds clause and coverage for contractual liability, covering Tenant's contractual obligations under this Lease as an "insured contract," personal injury liability, host liquor liability, premises-operations and hazards thereto, as well as liability arising out of this Lease, in respect of the Premises and the conduct or operation of business therein, with Landlord and Landlord's managing agent, if any, and each Superior Lessor and Superior Mortgagee whose name and address shall have been furnished to Tenant, each as an additional insured (including for ongoing and products-completed operations coverage), which shall be primary, and any other insurance that may be available to Landlord and any such additional insured will be excess and non-contributory, in amounts of not less than [$__________] per occurrence and [$__________] general aggregate (applying per location) for bodily injury (including death) and property damage liability, [$__________] personal and advertising injury, and [$__________] products-completed operations (for which coverage shall be maintained continuously for a minimum period equal to three years after the completion of Tenant's operations under this Lease);

(iv) workers' compensation in statutory limits together with employer's liability insurance in amounts of not less than $1,000,000 each accident, $1,000,000 disease policy limit, and $1,000,000 disease each employee;

(v) business automobile liability insurance covering liability arising from any auto (including, owned, non-owned, and hired auto, provided that such non-owned and hired auto liability may be satisfied by endorsement to the commercial general liability policy) in an amount of not less than $1,000,000 combined single limit per accident for bodily injury and property damage, which names Landlord and Landlord's managing agent, if any, and each Superior Lessor and Superior Mortgagee whose name and address shall have been furnished to Tenant, each as an additional insured, which shall be primary, and any other insurance that may be available to Landlord and any such additional insured will be excess and non-contributory;

(vi) [liquor liability insurance, if Tenant sells or dispenses alcoholic beverages, in amounts of not less than $5,000,000 per occurrence and $5,000,000 annual aggregate, which names Landlord and Landlord's managing agent, if any, and each Superior Lessor and Superior Mortgagee whose name and address shall have been furnished to Tenant, each as an additional insured, which shall be primary, and any other insurance that may be available to Landlord and any such additional insured will be excess and non-contributory;]

(vii) umbrella/excess liability insurance on a follow form basis in amounts of not less than [$__________] per occurrence and [$__________] annual aggregate (applying per location) in excess of commercial general liability, employer's liability, and automobile liability, as well as liquor liability (if applicable) insurance policies, concurrent to, and not more restrictive than such underlying insurance policies, which names Landlord and Landlord's managing agent, if any, and each Superior Lessor and Superior Mortgagee whose name and address shall have been furnished to Tenant, each as an additional insured. Such umbrella/excess liability policy must be endorsed to provide that it is primary to, and non-contributory with, any other insurance on which Landlord and any such additional insured are an insured, whether such other insurance is primary, excess, self-insurance, or insurance on any other basis, which must cause the umbrella/excess coverage to be vertically exhausted, whereby such coverage is not subject to any "Other Insurance" provision under Tenant's umbrella/excess liability policy. The limits of liability may be satisfied by a combination of primary and excess liability insurance;

(viii) [boiler and machinery, if there is a boiler, supplemental air conditioning unit or pressure object or similar equipment in the Premises, with Landlord and Landlord's managing agent, if any, and each Superior Lessor and Superior Mortgagee whose name and address shall have been furnished to Tenant, as loss payees as their interests may appear, with limits of not less than the full replacement cost thereof, with an agreed amount endorsement; and]

(ix) when Alterations are in process, the insurance specified in Section 7.01(f) above.

(b) The limits of such insurance shall not limit the liability of Tenant. Tenant shall deliver to Landlord and any additional insureds, prior to the Commencement Date, certificates of insurance as evidence of such policies required herein, in form reasonably satisfactory to Landlord and issued by the insurance company or its authorized agent. Tenant shall provide copies of policies to Landlord upon request. Tenant shall procure and pay for renewals of such insurance from time to time before the expiration thereof, and Tenant shall deliver to Landlord and any additional insureds such renewal policy or a certificate thereof at least 30 days before the expiration of any existing policy. In no event will any acceptance of certificates of insurance by Landlord, or failure of Tenant to provide certificates of insurance as required hereunder, be construed as a waiver or limitation of Tenant's obligations to maintain insurance coverage pursuant to this Section 13.01. Tenant shall endorse all such liability policies to waive rights of subrogation against Landlord and Landlord's managing agent, if any, and each Superior Lessor and Superior Mortgagee whose name and address shall have been furnished to Tenant. All such policies shall be issued by companies of recognized responsibility licensed to do business in the State of New York State and rated by Best's Insurance Reports or any successor publication of comparable standing as [_____] or better or the then equivalent of such rating. In addition, all such policies shall not be canceled, allowed to lapse, or modified unless Landlord and any additional insured are given at least 30 days prior written notice of such cancellation, lapse, or modification, which shall be afforded by endorsement extending such notice of cancellation rights to Landlord and any additional insureds. The deductible or self-insured retention amount required under any insurance policy maintained by Tenant shall be the sole responsibility of Tenant and shall not exceed [$__________], unless otherwise approved by Landlord in writing. The proceeds of policies providing "all risk" property insurance of Tenant's Property and Fixtures shall be payable to Landlord, Tenant and each Superior Lessor and Superior Mortgagee as their interests may appear. Tenant shall cooperate with Landlord in connection with the collection of any insurance moneys that may be due in the event of loss and Tenant shall execute and deliver to Landlord such proofs of loss and other instruments which may be required to recover any such insurance moneys. Landlord may from time to time require that the amount of the insurance to be maintained by Tenant under this Section 13.01 be increased, so that the amount thereof adequately protects Landlord's interest.

13.02 Subrogation Waiver.

Landlord and Tenant shall each include in each of its insurance policies (insuring the Building in case of Landlord, and insuring Tenant's Property and Fixtures in the case of Tenant, against loss, damage or destruction by fire or other casualty) a waiver of the insurer's right of subrogation against the other party during the Term or, if such waiver should be unobtainable or unenforceable, (a) an express agreement that such policy shall not be invalidated if the assured waives the right of recovery against any party responsible for a casualty covered by the policy before the casualty or (b) any other form of permission for the release of the other party. Each party hereby releases the other party with respect to any claim (including a claim for negligence) that it might otherwise have against the other party for loss, damage or destruction with respect to its property occurring during the Term to the extent to which it is, or is required to be, insured under a policy or policies containing a waiver of subrogation or permission to release liability. Nothing contained in this Section 13.02 shall be deemed to relieve either party of any duty imposed elsewhere in this Lease to repair, restore or rebuild or to nullify any abatement of rents provided for elsewhere in this Lease.

13.3 Landlord Concerns

Nearly all space leases spell out the tenant's obligation to carry property insurance covering the property that a tenant will be obligated to restore following a casualty, and liability insurance benefitting the landlord and its related parties in the event liability is sought from such parties by reason of the tenant's acts or omissions.

Before landlord's counsel can draft the property insurance provisions of an office lease, it is first necessary to determine the extent of the parties' respective obligations to restore (or, if different, to pay for restoration) following the occurrence of a casualty. Each party will then be obligated to carry property insurance to cover that portion of the improvements in the building for which it has the economic responsibility to restore. In a typical space lease, the landlord will carry property insurance covering the core and shell, common systems, and mechanical and public areas of a building, while the tenant will carry insurance covering the improvements within the premises. If a tenant net leases an entire building, it may well be obligated to insure the entire building.

If the property is subject to a mortgage or if there is a ground lease in place, the loan documents or the ground lease will invariably impose insurance obligations on the landlord, and counsel should make sure that any requirements passed through to tenants will conform to such provisions.

Prudent counsel will always seek input from the client's insurance agent or risk manager in drafting insurance provisions. Insurance forms and coverages change over time, and a list of insurance coverages to be carried by a tenant that worked before may no longer be meaningful. For example, many older lease forms refer to policies of "comprehensive general liability insurance" and "fire insurance, with extended coverage," neither of which (if available at all) is desirable.

Obtaining mutual waivers of subrogation from the parties' insurers is of paramount importance to both landlords and tenants. Pursuant to the waiver, which is obtained only in connection with property insurance, the insurer waives its rights to step into the shoes of the insured and seek to recover any amount paid by the insurer on a claim from another party whose negligent actions may have led to the claim. The effect of this waiver, when combined with the parties' mutual releases relating to any such claims, is that the landlord and tenant will each look to their respective insurance to cover losses to their respective property, and will not seek to recover any such losses from the other or the other's insurer. Thus, if a building employee negligently starts a fire that destroys all of a tenant's brandnew build-out and furnishings, the waiver of subrogation (combined with the tenant's release) assures the landlord that the tenant will look only to its insurance company and will not make a claim against the landlord.

Many lease forms, including the REBNY form, talk about alternatives to a waiver of subrogation and a requirement that the party benefitting therefrom pay any cost incurred by the party obtaining the waiver. In practice, waivers of subrogation have for many years now been routinely provided by insurers without additional charge, and it is not uncommon for the parties to agree to unconditional requirements that the waivers be obtained.

Although, on its face, the waiver of subrogation obtained by the landlord would appear to violate New York General Obligations Law section 5-321, which voids as against public policy any provision in a lease that exempts a landlord from liability for its own negligence, the New York courts have enforced mutual agreements to obtain a waiver of subrogation on the theory that the parties are not exempting one another from liability, but merely agreeing to allocate the risk of that liability to a third-party insurer.

Because of GOL 5-321, however, many New York landlords are reluctant to permit tenants to self-insure or to carry large deductibles. In these cases, it can be argued that the tenant is exempting the landlord from liability for its negligence in violation of the statute, without shifting the liability risk to a third-party insurer. Many landlords avoid the risk by refusing to allow tenants to self-insure for property losses and limiting to relatively small amounts the deductibles under property insurance policies.

Landlords typically seek to preserve flexibility to require tenants to maintain greater levels of insurance or additional or different types of insurance if customs change during the course of the lease. Tenants will typically resist this provision and seek limits on the extent to which insurance requirements can be increased during the term of a lease.

13.4 Tenant Concerns

The tenant's first task in considering the insurance requirements imposed in a lease is to review the relevant provisions (which should include the indemnity provisions of the lease as well) with its insurance adviser or risk manager to confirm that the tenant's insurance program complies with the lease requirements (or can be modified without significant additional expense to so comply).

Most leases do not address the specifics of the insurance that the landlord will carry, and landlords are usually reluctant to include their own insurance requirements in a tenant lease. Because tenants typically pay for the landlord's insurance premiums by way of operating expense or similar charges (and will similarly pay the amount of any deductibles incurred by the landlord), it is not inappropriate for the tenant to know what it will be paying for. Tenants with significant leverage usually can and will push the landlord to include in the lease express insurance requirements parallel to those imposed on the tenant. In addition to the landlord's property and liability insurance, the tenant will want the landlord also to commit to carrying rent insurance, because it is the rent insurance policy that will effectively enable the landlord to grant the tenant a rent abatement in those instances for which an abatement has been bargained for (e.g., during the restoration period following a casualty).

In those instances where the landlord refuses to include its own insurance requirements, a fallback for the tenant may be to get the landlord to agree to a more general obligation to carry the kinds and amount of insurance that would be carried by a similarly situated prudent landlord. Where even this is not available, most tenants can count on the fact that the landlord's mortgagee (and/or, if applicable, ground or other superior lessor) will impose insurance requirements on the landlord.

The mutual waivers of subrogation and mutual releases relating to casualty damage are no less important to the tenant than they are to the landlord. If one of the tenant's employees negligently starts a fire that results in the entire building burning down, the waivers of subrogation and mutual releases assure the tenant that it will not have liability to the landlord for the restoration of the building, but that the landlord will look solely to its insurer (and the insurer will not seek recovery from the tenant) for such restoration. Indeed, the tenant should be willing to waive subrogation and extend a release to the other tenants of the building as well (provided they each do so in return in favor of the tenant) so that the tenant similarly need not be concerned about the restoration of the other tenants' premises.

13.5 Standard Real Estate Board of New York Clauses

Requirements of Law, Fire Insurance, Floor Loads:

> 6. . . . Tenant shall not do or permit any act or thing to be done in or to the demised premises which is contrary to law, or which will invalidate or be in conflict with public liability, fire or other policies of insurance at any time carried by or for the benefit of Owner with respect to the demised premises or the building of which the demised premises form a part, or which shall or might subject Owner to any liability or responsibility to any person or for property damage. Tenant shall not keep anything in the demised premises except as now or hereafter permitted by the Fire Department, Board of Fire Underwriters, Fire Insurance Rating Organization or other authority having jurisdiction, and then only in such manner and such quantity so as not to increase the rate for fire insurance applicable to the building, nor use the premises in a manner which will increase the insurance rate for the building or any property located therein over that in effect prior to the commencement of Tenant's occupancy. Tenant shall pay all costs, expenses, fines, penalties, or damages which may be imposed upon Owner by reason of Tenant's failure to comply with the provisions of this article and, if by reason of such failure the fire insurance rate shall, at the beginning of this lease or at any time thereafter, be higher than it otherwise would be, then Tenant shall reimburse Owner, as additional rent hereunder, for that portion of all fire insurance premiums thereafter paid by Owner which shall have been charged because of such failure by Tenant. In any action or proceeding wherein Owner and Tenant are parties, a schedule or "make-up" of rate for the building or demised premises issued by the New York Fire Insurance Exchange or other body making fire insurance rates applicable to said premises shall be conclusive evidence of the facts therein stated and of the several items and charges in the fire insurance rates then applicable to said premises.

Destruction, Fire and Other Casualty:

> 9. . . . Notwithstanding anything contained to the contrary in subdivisions (a) through (e) hereof, including Owner's obligation to restore under subparagraph (b) above, each party shall look first to any insurance in its favor before making any claim against the other party for recovery for loss or damage resulting from fire or other casualty, and to the extent that such insurance is in force and collectible and to the extent permitted by law, Owner and Tenant each hereby releases and waives all right of recovery with respect to subparagraphs (b),

(d), and (e) above, against the other or any one claiming through or under each of them by way of subrogation or otherwise. The release and waiver herein referred to shall be deemed to include any loss or damage to the demised premises and/or to any personal property, equipment, trade fixtures, goods and merchandise located therein. The foregoing release and waiver shall be in force only if both releasors' insurance policies contain a clause providing that such a release or waiver shall not invalidate the insurance. If, and to the extent, that such waiver can be obtained only by the payment of additional premiums, then the party benefiting from the waiver shall pay such premium within ten days after written demand or shall be deemed to have agreed that the party obtaining insurance coverage shall be free of any further obligation under the provisions hereof with respect to waiver of subrogation. Tenant acknowledges that Owner will not carry insurance on Tenant's furniture and/or furnishings or any fixtures or equipment, improvements, or appurtenances removable by Tenant and agrees that Owner will not be obligated to repair any damage thereto or replace the same. (f) Tenant hereby waives the provisions of section 227 of the Real Property Law and agrees that the provisions of this article shall govern and control in lieu thereof.

13.6 Comments on Standard Real Estate Board of New York Clauses

The biggest deficiency in the REBNY form from the landlord's perspective is the absence of any specific requirements as to the insurance that must be carried by a tenant. If the tenant elected not to carry any liability insurance, it would not be in violation of any provision of the lease. Even the mutual waiver is drafted to say that it applies only "to the extent that such insurance is in effect and collectible." If the tenant does not carry any casualty insurance, it would appear that the waiver does not apply, and the tenant could seek to recover its losses from the landlord and the landlord's insurer.

13.7 Litigation Issues

Cases concerning lease insurance provisions are usually litigated by and for the benefit of the insurance industry rather than the real estate industry. This does not mean that the lease drafter can ignore these rulings. Uninsured losses, enhancement of required tenant coverage, and impact on insurance rates must be considered.

New York General Obligations Law (GOL) section 5-321 provides that "every covenant . . . exempting the lessor from liability for damages for injuries to person or property caused by or resulting from the negligence of lessor, his agents, servants or employees, in the operation or maintenance of the demised premises or the real property containing the demised premises, shall be . . . void . . . and unenforceable." A landlord attempts to limit the impact of this statute, for example, by requiring a tenant to carry liability insurance naming the landlord as additional insured. If the tenant fails to comply with this covenant, it will be liable to the landlord for damages for personal injury or property damage resulting from the landlord's negligence.[1]

A landlord further attempts to limit GOL 5-321 by setting forth the mutual obligation of landlord and tenant to first look to their own insurance before asserting a claim against the other, and releasing each other from liability directly and by way of subrogation for such insured losses.

KAF-KAF, Inc. v. Rodless Decorations, Inc.,[2] demonstrates how the standard form Real Estate Board of New York waiver of subrogation and release provisions protect a landlord. The tenant's insurer paid the tenant for business interruption losses and property damage resulting from a fire and sued the landlord under its policy subrogation rights. The standard form waiver of subrogation provided a release for "all right of recovery," not merely for damage to the demised premises. Thus, claims for damage to personalty and business interruption were waived. Furthermore, the limitation required by GOL 5-321 for liability caused by the landlord's negligence set forth in the standard exculpation clause was deemed subject to the parties' agreement to look first to insurance. The landlord could be held liable only for uninsured losses.

This decision can be contrasted with the interpretation of a nonstandard form waiver of subrogation clause in *Periphery Loungewear, Inc. v. Kantron Roofing Corp.*,[3] which was held ineffective to bar a claim by a subtenant for losses due to business interruption. The lease required the tenant to cover "public liability and property damage" insurance. The waiver of subrogation clause released liability "to the extent that such polices shall not be invalidated" and was held to apply only to property damage and not business interruption losses. The landlord was relieved of liability, however, pursuant to a provision stating that there was "no liability . . . by reason of . . . injury to business. . . ." This exculpation was valid notwithstanding GOL 5-321, which was held to apply only to damage to property, not business losses.

The standard form waiver of subrogation provision was interpreted in *Interested Underwriters at Lloyds v. Ducor's Inc.*[4] as not protecting a landlord against an insurer's subrogation claim arising out of a fire that occurred in a building owned by the landlord adjacent to the demised premises. The court held that the waiver applied only to circumstances involving the landlord–tenant relationship.[5] The damage was deemed occurring outside the landlord–tenant relationship.

---

1. Turillo v. Helmsley, 251 A.D.2d 243, 674 N.Y.S.2d 669 (1st Dep't 1998). See 747 Third Ave. Corp. v. Killarney, 255 A.D.2d 375, 639 N.Y.S.2d 32 (1st Dep't 1996) (imposing liability on a tenant for damages resulting from its insurer's subrogation claim against landlord, where tenant breached covenant to obtain waiver of subrogation clause in insurance policy).

2. 90 N.Y.2d 654, 665 N.Y.S.2d 47, 687 N.E.2d 1330 (1997); *see also* General Accident Ins. Co. v. 80 Maiden Lane Assoc., 252 A.D.2d 391, 675 N.Y.S.2d 85 (1st Dep't 1998).

3. 190 A.D.2d 457, 599 N.Y.S.2d 554 (1st Dep't 1993).

4. 103 A.D.2d 76, 478 N.Y.S.2d 285 (1st Dep't 1984); *see also* H&M Hennes & Mauritz LP v. Skanska USA Bldg., Inc., 67 F. Supp. 2d 152 (2008) (holding that parties can extend the waiver of subrogation to parties beyond the landlord–tenant relationship through express languages. In this case, the waiver was extended to a contractor as a "landlord party.").

5. 478 N.Y.S.2d at 287.

A tenant's obligation to carry certain specified insurance is an essential complement to the waiver of subrogation, as the release from liability is only effective to the extent that insurance is in force and collectible.[6] If a lease requires a tenant to carry insurance against liability "occasioned by accident on or about the demised premises or any appurtenances thereto . . . ," naming the landlord as additional insured, the landlord is not covered for liability to a tenant's employee injured outside of the demised premises.[7]

Being named as an additional insured on a tenant's policies provides a different measure of protection from the waiver of subrogation clause. The waiver has been held to apply only to tort claims. Generally, an insurer cannot sue its insured for a covered loss. An insurer has been permitted to enforce by way of subrogation a landlord's contractual obligation to restore premises damaged by fire, despite the waiver of subrogation provision in the lease.[8] The claim could have been defended if the landlord were named as an additional insured on the tenant's policy. The drafter must take care in specifying the policies to which the landlord is to be named as additional insured. Being named as added insured on a liability policy will not prevent a subrogation claim by a property damage insurer; nor will it prevent a claim against a landlord additional insured for damage to a tenant's property in which the landlord has no interest.[9]

6. Empire Bias Binding Co., Inc. v. Andors Realty Corp., 210 A.D.2d 198, 619 N.Y.S.2d 745 (2d Dep't 1994).

7. Axelrod v. Maryland Cas. Co., Inc., 209 A.D.2d 336, 619 N.Y.S.2d 10 (1st Dep't 1994).

8. Viacom Int'l, Inc. v. Midtown Realty Co., 235 A.D.2d 332, 652 N.Y.S.2d 740 (1st Dep't 1997).

9. Commerce & Industry Ins. Co. v. Admon Realty, Inc., 168 A.D.2d 321, 562 N.Y.S.2 655 (1st Dep't 1990), *but see* H&M Hennes & Mauritz LP v. Skanska USA Bldg., Inc., 617 F. Supp. 2d 152 (2008) (distinguishing Commerce & Indus. Ins. Co. v. Admon Realty because that case was based on waiver of subrogation clause that explicitly required each party to obtain an insurance policy permitting the insured to waive the right of subrogation).

CHAPTER 14

Destruction (Fire or Other Cause)

14.1 General Purpose

The landlord's primary object in the damage-or-destruction provisions (after the fact of the casualty) is to keep control of the tenant long enough to permit rebuilding and re-occupancy, or alternatively, to be able to cancel all space leases and begin afresh. In the absence of such a provision in the lease, the tenant's rights, within New York state, are controlled by Real Property Law (RPL) section 227. This statute permits a tenant (if not negligently or criminally responsible with respect to the casualty in question) to quit or abandon the premises and thereby effectively terminate future obligations under its original lease. RPL section 227 reads in its entirety as follows:

> Where any building, which is leased or occupied, is destroyed or so injured by the elements, or any other cause as to be untenantable, and unfit for occupancy, and *no express agreement to the contrary has been made in writing*, the lessee or occupant may, if the destruction or injury occurred without his or her fault or neglect, quit and surrender possession of the leasehold premises, and of the land so leased or occupied; and he or she is not liable to pay to the lessor or owner, rent for the time subsequent to the surrender. Any rent paid in advance or which may have accrued by the terms of a lease or any other hiring shall be adjusted to the date of such surrender. [emphasis added]

Thus, the provision of a damage-or-destruction clause in a lease will provide the alternate disposition of rights, overcoming the innocent tenant's option to quit the premises, which is otherwise enshrined by RPL section 227.

Unsurprisingly, the landlord is also concerned with the interplay of liability and financial responsibility. Thus, standard versions of such lease articles also speak about insurance, mutual releases, and waivers of liability, even though such topics are also treated again, or more extensively, in the lease's insurance provisions. The tenant is invariably reminded that any personal property losses incurred in such a disaster, and the expenses involved in replacing its leasehold improvements, are to be covered by the tenant's insurance, as the landlord positively disclaims responsibility. The tenant and the landlord also have a community of interest in exchanging mutual releases and insurance waivers, prior to any casualty's occurrence, and this provision normally contains such clauses.

A tenant, however, particularly one of any business magnitude, will often not be content to wait and see if its landlord's promise to restore the damaged premises is fulfilled in a timely fashion, while it figuratively treads water in substitute space. Such a tenant must negotiate, in this clause, for a decrease of the expansive time periods that the landlord's lease draft will provide, while the building owner decides whether to do a partial restoration or, alternatively, to terminate all leases and clear the site. Small-space tenants will not often prevail in such a contest. A larger tenant, however, has both reason and the economic clout to insist that the landlord go beyond its bold promise to restore, and provide an independent architect's or contractor's estimate of the probable time to rebuild; or allow the tenant to terminate, if the restoration timetable is estimated to be, or in fact is, beyond the negotiated benchmark.

14.2 Sample Clause

14.01 Casualty.

(a) If the Building or the Premises shall be partially or totally damaged or destroyed by fire or other casualty (each, a "**Casualty**") and if this Lease is not terminated as provided below, then (i) Landlord shall repair and restore the Building and the Premises (excluding all Fixtures and Tenant's Property) with reasonable dispatch (but Landlord shall not be required to perform the same on an overtime or premium pay basis) after notice to Landlord of the Casualty and the collection of the insurance proceeds attributable to such Casualty and (ii) Tenant shall repair and restore in accordance with Section 7.01 all Fixtures and Tenant's Property with reasonable dispatch after the Casualty.

(b) If all or part of the Premises shall be rendered untenantable (including by reason of Tenant not having reasonable access to the Premises) by reason of a Casualty, the Fixed Rent and the Additional Rent under Articles 4 and 5 shall be abated in the proportion that the untenantable area of the Premises bears to the total area of the Premises, for the period from the date of the Casualty to the earlier of (i) the date the Premises is made tenantable (provided, that if the Premises would have been tenantable at an earlier date but for Tenant having failed diligently to prosecute repairs or restoration, then the Premises shall be deemed to have been made tenantable on such earlier date and the abatement shall cease) or (ii) the date Tenant or any subtenant reoccupies a portion of the Premises which had been untenantable for the ordinary conduct of business (in which case the Fixed Rent and the Additional Rent allocable to such reoccupied portion shall be payable by Tenant from the date of such occupancy). Landlord's determination of the date the Premises is tenantable shall be controlling unless Tenant disputes same by notice to Landlord within 10 days after such determination by Landlord, and pending resolution of such dispute, Tenant shall pay Rent in accordance with Landlord's determination. Nothing contained in this Section 14.01 shall relieve Tenant from any liability that may exist as a result of any Casualty.

(c) If by reason of a Casualty (i) the Building shall be totally damaged or destroyed, (ii) the Building shall be so damaged or destroyed (whether or not the Premises are damaged or destroyed) that Landlord's repair or restoration shall require more than 270 days or the expenditure of at least 20% of the full insurable value of the Building (which, for purposes of this Section 14.01(c), shall mean replacement cost less the cost of footings, foundations and other structures below the street and first floors of the Building) immediately prior to the Casualty or (iii) at least 30% of the Premises shall be damaged or destroyed (as estimated in any such case by a reputable contractor, architect or engineer designated by Landlord), then in any such case Landlord may terminate this Lease by notice given to Tenant within 180 days after the Casualty. If this Lease is so terminated, (A) the Term shall expire upon the date set forth in Landlord's notice and Tenant shall vacate the Premises and surrender the same to Landlord no later than the date set forth in the notice, (B) all Rent shall be prorated and paid as of such termination date and (C) Landlord shall be entitled to the proceeds of insurance policies held by Tenant providing coverage for Fixtures, but only to the extent of the unamortized value (amortized on a straight line basis from the Commencement Date or later date of installation or payment through the termination date) of any such Fixtures that were installed or paid for by Landlord, whether by contribution, offset or otherwise.

(d) [*negotiated provision*—Supplementing the foregoing provisions of this Section 14.01, within 60 days after Landlord has actual knowledge of any Casualty that results in more than 50% of the Premises being untenantable, Landlord shall deliver to Tenant an estimate prepared by a reputable contractor selected by Landlord setting forth such contractor's estimate as to the time reasonably required to repair such damage in order to make the Premises (or such portion thereof) no longer untenantable. If the period set forth in any such estimate exceeds eighteen months from the date of such Casualty, or if such Casualty occurred during the last year of the Term and there will be less than 120 days remaining in the Term after the period set forth in such estimate, Tenant may terminate this Lease by notice to Landlord given not later than 30 days following Tenant's receipt of such estimate (time of the essence). If Tenant shall exercise such election, the Term of this Lease shall terminate on the 30th day after notice of such election shall be given by Tenant, and Tenant shall vacate the Premises and surrender the same to Landlord in accordance with the terms of this Lease. Upon any such termination of this Lease, Tenant's liability for Fixed Rent and Additional Rent hereunder shall cease as of the date of such termination, and any prepaid portion of Rent for any period after such date shall promptly be refunded by Landlord to Tenant.]

(e) Landlord shall not be obligated to carry any insurance on any Tenant's Property or Fixtures and shall not be obligated to repair or replace Tenant's Property or Fixtures. Tenant shall look solely to Tenant's insurance for recovery of any damage to or loss of Tenant's Property or Fixtures. Tenant shall notify Landlord promptly of any Casualty in the Premises.

(f) This Section 14.01 shall be deemed an express agreement governing any damage or destruction of the Premises by fire or other casualty, and Section 227 of the New York Real Property Law providing for such a contingency in the absence of an express agreement, and any other law of like import now or hereafter in force, shall have no application.

14.3 Landlord Concerns

In dealing with a fire or other property-destroying casualty at its building (and New York leases tend not to identify other casualty types, since they may be imagined, and may well be outside either the landlord's or the tenant's control, such as utility explosions or terrorist attacks), the landlord has three aims: (1) to restore, if possible; (2) to demolish, if necessary; and (3) to control, as far as possible, the choice and timing of these decisions by limiting the tenant's participation in the process.

Thus, most such lease articles begin with a landlord covenant to restore and repair the damage to the premises and/or the building wherein the premises is located. However, most such lease articles will exclude —what the sample clause (see Section 14.2, *supra*) calls the "Tenant's Property" and "Fixtures." A less detailed clause than the sample clause in Section 14.2, *supra*, may speak only of restoration of the "demised premises," and both parties to the lease might benefit from the clarification, especially if the lease's insurance provisions already place on tenant the responsibility to insure tenant's space fit-out (as well as tenant's personal property).

The second necessary promise to be made by the landlord to the tenant in such a damage-or-destruction provision, beyond the promise to restore in all but the most extreme building wide-destruction scenarios, is that the tenant's rent will be abated. This, after all, is what has long been the automatic result under common law, and now New York state statutory law. However, the prudent landlord will seek to make this abatement proportionate on the quantum of the premises that have become "untenantable" due to the destruction, since most building casualties are fires, and fires (and/or attendant water damage) often do not devastate the entire premises.

The landlord is also naturally concerned with limiting the period of abatement as much as possible, with rent to recommence as soon as the restored premises are "substantially" repaired and access thereto is assured for the tenant's reentry. To further limit the effect of abatement, if the landlord has substitute space in which the tenant can set up temporary shop, the landlord might wish to provide for just such a contingency in advance.

Optimally, the landlord will seek to trade rent abatement for preservation of the original lease deal. Where, however, the damage is extensive or virtually total, or where the damage occurs so near the end of the term of the lease that restoration to that tenant's original plans makes little economic sense, the landlord will want the right to terminate. The tenant might find the landlord's interpretation of "substantial" destruction to be self-serving. Under these circumstances, an independent analysis from a contractor is often sought to estimate the time required to complete restoration. Of course, depending on the particular terms in the damage-or-destruction clause, the same contractor's estimate may support a tenant's, as well as the landlord's, right to terminate the lease.

Restoration clauses are in their nature forward-looking, but meanwhile the tenant presumably had a going concern and might prefer to relocate its business permanently. The landlord desires to forestall any claim that the tenant's business interruption, resulting from the fire or other casualty, even without reference to the amount or location of the damage, permits the tenant either to terminate the lease or to sue the landlord for damages. Furthermore, any landlord covenant to use due diligence in effecting the restoration will be qualified with specific language that overtime is not required.

A landlord disclaimer of any liability to replace the tenant's personal property will find a prominent place in such a set of clauses, and this may be coupled with a positive statement of the tenant's obligation to replace furniture and furnishings so destroyed.

Finally, since the entire damage-and-destruction clause is intended to restrict what would, in this major article's absence from the lease, be the tenant's right to terminate, the landlord will here demand a specific tenant acknowledgment that these alternative provisions are the very "express agreement" that Real Property Law section 227 requires for its own negation.

14.4 Tenant Concerns

Given real estate industry necessity, the overall shape of this provision is so favorable toward the landlord that most tenants will be unable to effect many changes. The tenant will first be concerned with decreasing the time frame within which the landlord may make decisions, so that at least the period of uncertainty is reduced, regarding potential lease termination in the event of a major restoration. The tenant would be well advised to seek further comfort with its insurer, by procuring business interruption insurance to cushion the blow of the costs of temporary relocation.

The tenant will also be concerned with clarifying, if possible, the standard of "untenantability," moving from or supplementing a sheer quantitative standard, in recognition of the fact that the localized destruction of certain areas of its premises—such as a communications center—may effectively put the tenant "out of business" even though the rest of the demised premises is relatively unscathed. Equal attention should be given to the definition of the abatement period. It is only fair for the tenant to have advance notice of the landlord-predicated date of "substantial" restoration if the abatement is to end on that date (rather than the five-day grace/move-in period contained in the REBNY clause set forth in Section 14.5, *infra*).

The tenant will want assurances that the landlord will not be able to terminate the tenant's lease unless leases for some large percentage of the building are also being terminated, and/or it would take a very long period of time (for example, more than 18 months) to restore the building. The tenant will also want a right to terminate the lease if the restoration work will take a long period of time to perform (for example, more than 18 months) based on estimates obtained by a general contractor selected by the landlord and the tenant, or in fact takes longer to complete than was estimated, or a significant casualty occurs near the end of the lease term.

Finally, if the landlord should seek to condition its restoration obligations on receiving adequate insurance proceeds, then the tenant should negotiate to require the landlord to keep the building insured for its full replacement value (exclusive of foundations and footings), and not permit the landlord to self-insure.

14.5 Standard Real Estate Board of New York Clause

The REBNY parallel paragraph, Article 9, touches on many but not all of these concerns of both the landlord ("Owner") and tenant in its letter-labeled clauses (the bracketed titles have been added):

> *Destruction, Fire and Other Casualty: 9*
>
> *(a) [Tenant Notice of Damage]* If the demised premises or any part thereof shall be damaged by fire or other casualty, Tenant shall give immediate notice thereof to Owner and this lease shall continue in full force and effect except as hereinafter set forth.
>
> *(b) [Partial Damage]* If the demised premises are partially damaged or rendered partially unusable by fire or other casualty, the damages thereto shall be repaired by and at the expense of Owner and the rent and other items of additional rent, until such repair shall be substantially completed, shall be apportioned from the day following the casualty according to the part of the demised premises which is usable.
>
> *(c) [Total Damage]* If the demised premises are totally damaged or rendered wholly unusable by fire or other casualty, then the rent and other items of additional rent as hereinafter expressly provided shall be proportionately paid up to the time of the casualty and thenceforth shall cease until the date when the premises shall have been repaired and restored by Owner (or if sooner reoccupied in part by the Tenant, then rent shall be apportioned as provided in subsection (b) above), subject to Owner's right to elect not to restore the same as hereinafter provided.
>
> *(d) [Owner Demolition and Termination]* If the demised premises are rendered wholly unusable or (whether or not the demised premises are damaged in whole or in part) if the building shall be so damaged that Owner shall decide to demolish it or to rebuild it, then, in any of such events, Owner may elect to terminate this lease by written notice to Tenant, given within 90 days after such

fire or casualty, or 30 days after adjustment of the insurance claim for such fire or casualty, whichever is sooner, specifying a date for the expiration of the lease, which date shall not be more than 60 days after the giving of such notice, and upon the date specified in such notice the term of this lease shall expire as fully and completely as if such date were the date set forth above for the termination of this lease and Tenant shall forthwith quit, surrender and vacate the premises without prejudice, however, to Landlord's rights and remedies against Tenant under the lease provisions in effect prior to such termination, and any rent owing shall be paid up to such date and any payments of rent made by Tenant which were on account of any period subsequent to such date shall be returned to Tenant. Unless Owner shall serve a termination notice as provided for herein, Owner shall make the repairs and restorations under the conditions of (b) and (c) hereof, with all reasonable expedition, subject to delays due to adjustment of insurance claims, labor troubles and causes beyond Owner's control. After any such casualty, Tenant shall cooperate with Owner's restoration by removing from the premises, as promptly as reasonably possible, all of Tenant's salvageable inventory and moveable equipment, furniture, and other property. Tenant's liability for rent shall resume five (5) days after written notice from Owner that the premises are substantially ready for Tenant's occupancy.

(e) [Insurance Recovery] Nothing contained hereinabove shall relieve Tenant from liability that may exist as a result of damage from fire or other casualty. Notwithstanding anything contained to the contrary in subdivisions (a) through (e) hereof, including Owner's obligation to restore under subparagraph (b) above, each party shall look first to any insurance in its favor before making any claim against the other party for recovery for loss or damage resulting from fire or other casualty, and to the extent that such insurance is in force and collectible and to the extent permitted by law, Owner and Tenant each hereby releases and waives all right of recovery with respect to subparagraphs (b), (d), and (e) above, against the other, or any one claiming through or under each of them by way of subrogation or otherwise. The release and waiver herein referred to shall be deemed to include any loss or damage to the demised premises and/or to any personal property, equipment, trade fixtures, goods and merchandise located therein. The foregoing release and waiver shall be in force only if both releasors' insurance policies contain a clause providing that such a release or waiver shall not invalidate the insurance. If, and to the extent, that such waiver can be obtained only by the payment of additional premiums, then the party benefiting from the waiver shall pay such premium within ten days after written demand or shall be deemed to have agreed that the party obtaining insurance coverage shall be free of any further obligation under the provisions hereof with respect to waiver of subrogation. Tenant acknowledges that Owner will not carry insurance on Tenant's furniture and/

or furnishings or any fixtures or equipment, improvements, or appurtenances removable by Tenant and agrees that Owner will not be obligated to repair any damage thereto or replace same.

(f) [Tenant Waiver] Tenant hereby waives the provisions of Section 227 of the Real Property Law and agrees that the provisions of this article shall govern and control in lieu thereof.

14.6 Comments on the Standard Real Estate Board of New York Clause

While the comparatively lengthy REBNY clause (Article 9) touches on most of the points just discussed, it is once again more deficient from the tenant's viewpoint than the landlord's (although it contains some points not found in the sample clause, such as the tenant covenant to remove its goods from the damaged premises).

To avoid future controversy, the landlord using this form may want to add language for the measuring of "substantial" damage, since the REBNY form really only contains two standards, namely "partial" damage, which the owner/landlord is required to restore, and "wholly unusable," with the right to terminate. The owner/landlord could benefit from a middle category, which is not total destruction but which nevertheless gives the owner/landlord the right *not* to restore and to terminate.

Tenants may want the same fine-tuning where major damage, while not total, requires so much restoration time that the tenant wants the right to exit. As noted earlier, the tenant will also want to seek a commitment that the landlord will restore the interior of the premises to the plans-and-specifications standard of the original lease. The REBNY language on this topic (requiring restoration of "the damages to" the "demised premises," which phrase is never actually defined in the form) is at best ambiguous, if not landlord favorable, in permitting merely a restoration of raw space only.

14.7 Litigation Issues

Real Property Law (RPL) section 227[1] was enacted to relieve a tenant of the harshness of the common-law rule that destruction of the premises did not relieve a tenant of its rental obligations. Since this statute was enacted, landlords have been perfecting lease provisions that expressly waive the benefits of section 227. The practitioner representing a tenant must be aware of this, and not fail to negotiate for the relief provided for in RPL section 227.

---

1. REAL PROPERTY LAW § 227 states:

Where any building, which is leased or occupied, is destroyed or so injured by the elements, or any other cause as to be untenantable, *and no express agreement to the contrary has been made in writing,* the lessee or occupant may, if the destruction or injury occurred without his or her fault or neglect, quit and surrender possession of the leasehold premises, and of the land so leased or occupied; and he or she is not liable to pay to the lessor or owner, rent for the time subsequent to the surrender. Any rent paid in advance or which may have accrued by the terms of a lease or any other hiring shall be adjusted to the date of such surrender [emphasis added].

The harshest result would be the inclusion of a clause that reinstates the common-law rule. In *Rodriguez v. Nachamie*,[2] the court upheld a provision in a lease requiring a tenant to carry fire and casualty damage insurance, naming the landlord as loss payee, on the building where the tenant's medical office was located. It was further provided that partial or total destruction by casualty would not result in a rent abatement. The lease stated that the tenant expressly waived the provision of any and all laws that provide otherwise. Having entered into the agreement without negotiating the provision, the tenant could not argue unconscionability.

Cases construing the standard REBNY fire and casualty damage clause reveal the problems faced by tenants whose premises have sustained serious casualty damage. In *Schwartz, Karlan & Gutstein v. 271 Venture*,[3] the plaintiff law firm desired to recommence its practice as soon as possible after a fire substantially damaged its offices. It sought a declaratory judgment permitting cancellation of its lease because the premises was unusable. The appellate division reversed the lower court's ruling in favor of the tenant. The appellate court stated that under the "standard" casualty damage provision:

> The tenant is not only not afforded a corresponding right to terminate, it expressly waives that option. . . . Thus, section 9 *[of the REBNY clause set forth in section 14.5, supra]* proscribes constructive eviction as a basis of terminating the lease. In the event of a fire rendering the premises unusable, tenant's sole remedy is a rent abatement during the restoration period.[4]

Self-help is another remedy denied the tenant pursuant to a standard form casualty damage clause. In *Mawardi v. Purple Potato, Ltd.*,[5] the tenant defendant wanted to resume business after the building where it leased its restaurant burned. The tenant commenced restoration at its own cost and expense. Not only was the landlord able to enjoin the tenant from completing the restoration, but its right to cancel the lease was enforced even though the entire building could be repaired for about $75,000 to $100,000. The REBNY clause permitted the landlord to cancel the lease if the premises were rendered wholly unusable, or if the building was so damaged that the owner decided to demolish or rebuild it. This cancellation right was deemed broader than a provision requiring total or substantial destruction, which would have permitted cancellation only if the cost of restoration exceeded half of the value of the building. As a consequence, the tenant was divested of a valuable business location even though the cost of restoration was relatively modest.

These cases underscore certain deficiencies, from a tenant's point of view, in the operation of the REBNY standard casualty damage clause: (1) only the landlord can cancel the lease; (2) the decision to restore is made in the landlord's discretion; and

2. 57 A.D.2d 920, 395 N.Y.S.2d 51 (2d Dep't 1977), *but see* Inchaustegui v. 666 5th Ave. P'ship, 268 A.D.2d 121, 706 N.Y.S.2d 396 (1st Dep't 2000).
3. 172 A.D.2d 226, 568 N.Y.S.2d 72 (1st Dep't 1991).
4. 568 N.Y.S.2d at 73 [bracketed language added].
5. 187 A.D.2d 569, 590 N.Y.S.2d 132 (2d Dep't 1992).

(3) the landlord has an extended time to decide to cancel the lease. The result is that the tenant's ability to resume operations is in the hands of the landlord.

In *Adams Drug Co., Inc. v. Knobel*,[6] the plaintiff negotiated a more favorable casualty damage clause in order to protect its significant investment and location. The landlord and tenant both had rights of cancellation in the event of casualty damage. The right had to be exercised within 30 days of the casualty event. In order for the landlord to terminate the lease, the damage had to affect more than 50 percent of the gross area of the building; restoration could not reasonably be completed within 120 days of the casualty; and the landlord had to decide not to rebuild the building. The Court of Appeals determined that this last condition, whether the landlord exercised good faith in deciding not to rebuild the premises, had to be determined at a new trial.

The obligation of a landlord to restore premises to the same condition as it was prior to casualty damage does not include tenant leasehold improvements—nor does it include an obligation to obtain a certificate of occupancy for the restoration, unless the landlord has covenanted in the fire and casualty or other provision to obtain the certificate.[7] If a building is sold after a fire but before restoration, the grantee can exercise a right to cancel a lease pursuant to a casualty damage clause.[8]

The usual fire and casualty damage clause provides for a rent abatement, but without a right of cancellation. The untenantable condition caused by casualty damage does not give the tenant a right to assert constructive eviction.[9] The tenant must promptly advise the landlord of casualty damage in order to benefit from the rent abatement; but absent a tenant's cancellation right, it must await a landlord's decision to restore or cancel. If the landlord, after notice, fails to either restore or cancel, a tenant may assert an eviction.

6. Adams Drug Co., Inc. v. Knobel, 64 N.Y.2d 768, 485 N.Y.S.2d 983, 475 N.E.2d 451(1986), *on remand, see* 129 A.D.2d 401, 513 N.Y.S.2d 674 (1st Dep't 1987).

7. Silver v. Moe's Pizza, 121 A.D.2d 376, 503 N.Y.S.2d 86 (2d Dep't 1986).

8. Jim, Jack & Joe Realty Corp. v. Rothenburg, 78 A.D.2d 634, 432 N.Y.S.2d 110 (2d Dep't 1980).

9. Milltown Park Inc. v. Am. Felt & Filter Co., 180 A.D.2d 235, 584 N.Y.S.2d 927 (3d Dep't 1992).

CHAPTER 15

Condemnation

15.1 General Purpose

Drafting and negotiating the condemnation provisions of a lease require consideration of the following elements: (1) how to define a condemnation; (2) under what circumstances the lease is to remain in effect or be terminated by either the landlord or the tenant, or both; (3) the restoration obligations of the landlord and the tenant; (4) the availability of the condemnation proceeds to pay for such restoration; (5) how the rent will be abated if the lease is not terminated; and (6) what claims the parties may make for the award. Furthermore, all of these considerations must be negotiated while being mindful of the interests of the landlord's lender—a party almost never at the negotiating table, but whose interest in, and influence over, the negotiation of the condemnation provisions of a lease is so overwhelming that it is not abated even if the property is free and clear at time of the lease negotiations (i.e., even if the lender does not exist at the time of the lease negotiation). Under such circumstances, the landlord must be protective of its ability to mortgage the property in the future.

The scope of the condemnation provisions of the lease should be broadened to include a sale or other transfer by reason of an agreement in lieu of condemnation between the landlord and any governmental or quasi-governmental entity authorized to exercise the power of eminent domain. Expanding the scope is necessary because a settlement may be reached in anticipation of a condemnation, the effect of which would be the same on the parties as if a condemnation had taken place. For the purposes of this chapter, a condemnation or a sale or other transfer by reason of an agreement in lieu thereof will be referred to as a "taking."

If there is a total, permanent taking or a partial, permanent taking that renders the premises incapable of being restored to an economically viable whole for the use intended by the lease, the parties should be relieved of their obligations to repair and restore the premises and the lease should be terminated as of the date of the taking. The parties may wish to set an objective standard for determining when, in the case of a partial-permanent taking, the premises no longer can be restored to an economically viable whole for the use intended by the lease. This may be accomplished by stipulating the portion (stated either as a percentage or as a square foot area) of the premises or the essential amenities, such as parking and access, that if taken would render the property incapable of being restored to an economically viable whole for the use intended by the lease.

In the case of a partial taking, if the premises can be restored, the parties still have to agree upon any rights to terminate the lease based on such factors as the time it would take to complete the repair and restoration work and the cost of such work.

In considering these issues, it will be necessary to take into account the rights of any existing or future lender to receive all or part of the award to reduce the landlord's indebtedness, perhaps leaving insufficient sums to pay for the cost of restoration or repair, or, on the other hand, any requirement in the mortgage or deed of trust to apply the award to the cost of the repair and restoration work. Unless the lease is superior to the mortgage (a very rare occurrence), the lender's right to receive the award will be paramount. The respective interests of the landlord and the tenant to the award are discussed in Sections 15.3 and 15.4, *infra*. In addition, it will be necessary to work within any other constraints imposed by the lender, such as an inability of the landlord and/or the tenant to effect an early termination of the lease without the consent of the lender.

If the lease is terminated, rent will be required to be paid up to the date of termination of the lease. In the case of a partial taking, an abatement of the rent based on the square footage that is taken may not reflect the true value of what is lost. An abatement of the rent based on the difference in the rental value of the premises before and after the taking is more appropriate, but also more difficult to ascertain. For example, if a parking area outside the premises is essential to the tenant's business, and it is only the parking area that is taken, the tenant would not be entitled to a rent abatement if the criteria for abatement depended solely on lost square footage within the premises.

If the taking is temporary, there should be no abatement of rent. The tenant, however, should receive the portion of the award attributable to the premises for the period of the taking that occurs during the term of the lease.

15.2 Sample Clause

15.01 Condemnation.

(a) If there shall be a total taking of the Building in condemnation proceedings or by any right of eminent domain, this Lease and the term and estate hereby granted shall terminate as of the date of taking of possession by the condemning authority and all Rent shall be prorated and paid as of such termination date. If there shall be a taking of any material (in Landlord's reasonable judgment) portion of the Land or the Building (whether or not the Premises are affected by such taking), then Landlord may terminate this Lease and the term and estate granted hereby by giving notice to Tenant within 60 days after the date of taking of possession by the condemning authority. If there shall be a taking of the Premises of such scope (but in no event less than 20% thereof) that the untaken part of the Premises would in Tenant's reasonable judgment be uneconomic to operate, then Tenant may terminate this Lease and the term and estate granted hereby by giving notice to Landlord within 60 days after the date of taking of possession by the condemning authority. If either Landlord or Tenant shall give a termination notice as aforesaid, then this Lease and the term and estate granted hereby shall terminate as of the date of such notice and all Rent shall be prorated and paid as of such termination date. In the event of a taking of the Premises that does not result in the termination of this Lease (i) the term and estate hereby granted with respect to the taken part of the Premises shall terminate as of the date of taking of possession by the condemning authority and all Rent shall be appropriately abated for the period from such date to the Expiration Date and (ii) Landlord shall with reasonable diligence restore the remaining portion of the Premises (exclusive of Tenant's Property) as nearly as practicable to its condition prior to such taking.

(b) In the event of any taking of all or a part of the Building, Landlord shall be entitled to receive the entire award in the condemnation proceeding, including, without limitation, any award made for the value of the estate vested by this Lease in Tenant or any value attributable to the unexpired portion of the Term, and Tenant hereby assigns to Landlord any and all right, title and interest of Tenant now or hereafter arising in or to any such award or any part thereof, and Tenant shall be entitled to receive no part of such award; provided, that nothing shall preclude Tenant from intervening in any such condemnation proceeding to claim or receive from the condemning authority any compensation to which Tenant may otherwise lawfully be entitled in such case in respect of Tenant's Property or moving expenses, provided the same do not include any value of the estate vested by this Lease in Tenant or of the unexpired portion of the Term and do not reduce the amount available to Landlord or materially delay the payment thereof.

(c) If all or any part of the Premises shall be taken for a limited period, Tenant shall be entitled, except as hereinafter set forth, to that portion of the award for such taking that represents compensation for the use and occupancy of the Premises, for the taking of Tenant's Property and for moving expenses, and Landlord shall be entitled to that portion that represents reimbursement for the cost of restoration of the Premises. This Lease shall remain unaffected by such taking and Tenant shall continue responsible for all of its obligations under this Lease to the extent such obligations are not affected by such taking and shall continue to pay in full all Rent when due. If the period of temporary use or occupancy shall extend beyond the Expiration Date, that part of the award that represents compensation for the use and occupancy of the Premises shall be apportioned between Landlord and Tenant as of the Expiration Date. Any award for temporary use and occupancy for a period beyond the date to which the Rent has been paid shall be paid to, held and applied by Landlord as a trust fund for payment of the Rent thereafter becoming due.

(d) In the event of any taking that does not result in termination of this Lease, (i) Landlord, whether or not any award shall be sufficient therefor, shall proceed with reasonable diligence to repair the remaining parts of the Building and the Premises (other than those parts of the Premises that constitute Tenant's Property) to substantially their former condition to the extent that the same may be feasible (subject to reasonable changes that Landlord deems desirable) and so as to constitute a complete and rentable Building and Premises and (ii) Tenant, whether or not any award shall be sufficient therefor, shall proceed with reasonable diligence to repair the remaining parts of the Premises that constitute Tenant's Property, to substantially their former condition to the extent that the same may be feasible.

15.3 Landlord Concerns

From the landlord's perspective, the lease should provide maximum flexibility, control, and cash flow; limit any right of the tenant to terminate the lease; and protect the landlord's interest in the condemnation award. The sample clause makes it clear that the lease will terminate only in the case of a total taking, if the landlord elects to terminate the lease in the case of a taking of a material portion of the land or building, or if the tenant elects to terminate the lease in the case of a taking of the premises (or requisite portion thereof) such that in the tenant's reasonable judgment the untaken part of the premises will be uneconomic to operate. The landlord is concerned that the tenant pay rent right up to the date of the taking. Accordingly, the date of termination of the lease is the date of the acquisition or vesting of title in the condemning authority. If the lease is not terminated, the rent is apportioned based on lost square footage, which is likely to be more easily determined than an apportionment based on lost rental value.

The common landlord concern that an award given to the tenant for the value of its leasehold interest will leave the landlord with an award only for the residual value of the property is eliminated by the sample clause, in which the tenant is prohibited from making any claim for the unexpired portion of the term of the lease or for its leasehold interest. The tenant is limited to making a claim for moving expenses and the value of its personal property, and, even then, only if an award made pursuant to any such claim will not in any way diminish the award given to the landlord.

If the taking is temporary, the tenant gets the award but must continue to pay rent. Accordingly, the landlord gets the benefit of its bargain with the tenant; the temporary taking does not affect the rental stream from the lease.

The landlord's paramount concern is the ability to finance the property and to reap the benefits of being a property owner. If the value of the leasehold has appreciated since the lease was negotiated, the landlord will want to benefit from that appreciation. The argument is similar to a landlord asking for the profits on an assignment of the lease or subletting of the premises. The landlord (and any lender) would not want that appreciation to go into the tenant's pockets.

15.4 Tenant Concerns

The tenant will want more control than the sample clause allows. If the lease is terminated, depending on the circumstances, the tenant may prefer to be released from its lease obligations at an earlier point in time when the certainty of a taking is determined, or to remain in the space in order to have time to arrange for another location. In the case of a partial taking, the tenant will not want to give the landlord absolute discretion to terminate the lease. The tenant will want assurances that all tenants will be treated the same and that the landlord will not be able to terminate the tenant's lease unless some large percentage of the building is taken, or it would take a very long period of time (more than 18 months) to restore the building.

On the other hand, the tenant will want a right to terminate the lease if the restoration work will take a long period of time to perform (more than 18 months) based on estimates obtained by a general contractor selected by the landlord and the tenant, or in fact takes longer to complete than was estimated. The tenant also will be concerned that the space remaining after a partial taking may not be adequate for the tenant's continued operation of its business in a commercially reasonable manner and will require the tenant to lease additional or substitute space elsewhere. In that case, too, the tenant will want a right to terminate the lease. The tenant may prefer to have an apportionment of rent based on the lost rental value of the demised premises rather than the diminution of square footage, as the sample clause provides. It may be that the portion of the space having some view, access, or other amenity is taken, leaving a less desirable space, in which case the tenant would be better off with an apportionment based on lost rental value. While the opposite may also occur, the tenant will generally prefer to take its chances with the lost rental value formulation because it is a more precise measure.

The tenant will argue that having negotiated its lease, it should not be subject to the condemnation provisions of any superior lease or mortgage that may deprive the tenant of the benefit of its bargain. If the superior instrument is negotiated after the lease, such a provision, in effect, will allow the landlord and the superior party to renegotiate the lease without the consent of the tenant. As a practical matter, the tenant's legitimate concerns frequently are subordinated to the landlord's need to be able to finance the property and a lender's need to control the disposition of the award in the event of a taking. As a consequence, the tenant is frequently inhibited from even commenting on the condemnation provisions of a lease, and the economic imperatives often result in no modifications being made for the tenant that does voice its concerns. A tenant with a strong bargaining position should be able, however, to protect its legitimate needs.

The tenant will also be concerned if the lease limits the amount that the landlord is required to spend on the restoration to the amount of the award. The tenant is interested in being made whole, and the amount of the award may not be sufficient to permit the landlord to rebuild to the same standard as the original construction.

The tenant must also be concerned about the portions of the lease governing a temporary taking. If the taking is for more than a de minimis period of time, the tenant will have to look elsewhere for temporary space, relocate, and then move back once the temporary taking is over. That involves two relocations, and the balance of the term of the lease remaining after the temporary taking may not be sufficient to justify the second move. Also, it will be difficult for the tenant to make adequate plans if it does not know the duration of the temporary taking up front. The tenant also will be obligated to perform the restoration work. This places very heavy burdens on the ability of the tenant to plan and to operate its business. The tenant would prefer to have a right to terminate the lease and relocate permanently if the circumstances make that option more commercially reasonable.

Finally, the tenant will want the amount of the award that is attributable to improvements it has made that cannot be removed from the realty, the amount by which the fair market rental value of the demised premises exceeds the amount of the rent payable under the lease (especially if the tenant is entitled to sublet and assignment profits under the terms of the lease), loss of goodwill for having to relocate its business, relocation costs, and moving expenses. As the sample clause provides, a landlord usually will permit the tenant to make a claim only for relocation costs and moving expenses, and then only if a separate award is made that does not diminish the landlord's award. The tenant will argue that, in addition, it wants the benefit of its bargain with the landlord and the right to that portion of the award that is attributable to the value of its leasehold interest. If the rent is below market, the tenant will want to get the benefit of the amount by which the value of the lease has appreciated. Although there is a logic to this argument, it will prevail only in extremely unusual circumstances in which the bargaining position of the tenant so outweighs that of the landlord that the landlord is willing to sacrifice the ability to mortgage the property in order to make the lease. It is an unusually bold tenant that even will ask for such a provision.

15.5 Standard Real Estate Board of New York Clause

> *Eminent Domain: 10* If the whole or any part of the demised premises shall be acquired or condemned by Eminent Domain for any public or quasi-public use or purpose, then, and in that event, the term of this lease shall cease and terminate from the date of title vesting in such proceeding, and Tenant shall have no claim for the value of any unexpired term of said lease, and assigns to Owner, Tenant's entire interest in any such award. Tenant shall have the right to make an independent claim to the condemning authority for the value of Tenant's moving expenses and personal property, trade fixtures and equipment, provided Tenant is entitled pursuant to the terms of the lease to remove such property, trade fixtures and equipment at the end of the term, and provided further such claim does not reduce Owner's award.

15.6 Comments on Standard Real Estate Board of New York Clause

This provision handles the issue of a taking by automatically terminating the lease without drawing any distinction between a total taking and a partial taking. Therefore, even in the event of a de minimis taking, the standard clause provides for a termination of the lease. The provision allows the tenant to make a claim for moving expenses, personal property, and moveable trade fixtures and equipment provided that the award made to the tenant does not reduce the landlord's award. The short shrift given to this provision may reflect a lack of concern in many urban areas that a taking will occur. There is no discussion at all of a temporary taking, and in the case of a partial taking there is no requirement to restore the premises under any set of circumstances. Further, the standard provision does not deal with an agreement in anticipation of a taking or with the rights or requirements of superior parties. These contingencies would have to be addressed in a rider to the lease.

15.7 Litigation Issues

A prospective office tenant may have little interest in negotiating a condemnation provision in a lease, especially if the landlord builds the tenant's space. However, a tenant of a free-standing building, or land on which one is to be constructed, particularly if located near a highway, can be severely affected by a condemnation clause drafted from a landlord's perspective.

Regardless of the amount expended by a tenant to improve its premises, or how much of the lease term remains at the time of a condemnation, "It is a fundamental principle that the Court of Claims has jurisdiction, and indeed an obligation, to make an award in compliance with the terms of an agreement between a landlord and a tenant and that in so doing it may exclude one of the parties from part or all of an award to which it might otherwise be entitled."[1] The Court of Claims of the state of New York determines the value of what has been taken. The lease, however, may determine what interests are to be divided and how the compensation will be divided upon a taking,[2] and may exclude a tenant from all or part of the award. A typical division of a condemnation award limits a tenant's claim to the value of its equipment and fixtures; thus, an award to a tenant for the value of its lease term, without considering a lease provision limiting a recovery to the value of fixtures and equipment, was improper.[3]

The parties may also agree to a division of an award on a monetary basis, but the court of claims will look beyond the condemnation clause in making its award. In

---

1. Castellano v. State of New York, 43 N.Y.2d 909, 403 N.Y.S.2d 724, 726, 374 N.E.2d 618 (1978).
2. Traendly v. State of New York, 51 A.D.2d 489, 382 N.Y.S.2d 365, 367 (3d Dep't 1976).
3. 382 N.Y.S.2d at 367.

Arlow v. Vinyl Masters, Inc.,[4] the landlord reserved in its lease the first $325,000 of an entire condemnation award, or of the aggregate of any separate award to landlord and tenant. Notwithstanding what appeared to be unambiguous language concerning the monetary division of a condemnation award, the landlord was not permitted to share in any portion of the tenant's award for trade fixtures. The condemnation clause divided an award for a taking of the "demised premises"; however, another provision of the lease defined the demised premises as including all improvements and fixtures, except for trade fixtures. Since trade fixtures were not part of the demised premises, the tenant retained its "absolute right to receive compensation for the appropriation of its trade fixtures if, under the terms of its lease . . . it has reserved its ownership and title to the fixtures."[5]

Of course, the "absolute" right can be waived by the provisions of a lease, and that waiver need not expressly refer to "trade" fixtures. *Interlake Service Station, Inc. v. State of New York*[6] is a good example of when and why a small-business tenant must be attentive to a condemnation clause. The tenant was a service station operator adjacent to a state highway. The state condemned the premises for an entrance/exit ramp. The possibility of a road widening or other highway improvement made condemnation of a free-standing building adjacent to a public highway more than a remote, hypothetical possibility. The tenant's claim for part of the condemnation award was entirely denied, and thus the tenant could not recoup the value of the trade fixtures it installed. The lease stated that "any alterations or additions to any buildings or permanent improvements . . . shall upon installation become the property of [Lessor] and Lessee shall have no right or interest therein. . . ." Improvements have been held to include trade fixtures, and the lease provided that ownership would pass to the landlord upon installation.

A tenant affixing specialized, removable fixtures to vacant land must consider the alteration clause in addition to the condemnation provision. *City of New York v. G & C Amusements*[7] involved the construction of amusement rides in violation of a lease of land to be used solely for parking, but the case would apply equally to permissible improvements. The tenant lost all claim to the value of the rides they installed, which were deemed trade fixtures, because the lease provided that all improvements would become property of the landlord upon annexation. Similarly, a tenant was denied a claim for the diner it improved on leased land not because of the condemnation clause but as a result of language in the surrender provision permitting the landlord to claim any property not removed by the tenant at the expiration of the term.[8] A sympathetic dissent articulated a better argument. The dissent reasoned that the lease terminated

4. 61 A.D.2d 994, 402 N.Y.S.2d 649 (2d Dep't 1978).

5. 402 N.Y.S.2d at 651.

6. 249 A.D.2d 275, 670 N.Y.S.2d 914, *leave to reargue denied*, 92 N.Y.2d 809, 680 N.Y.S.2d 54, 702 N.E.2d 839 (1998).

7. 55 N.Y. 2d 353, 449 N.Y.S.2d 671, 434 N.E.2d 1038, *re-argument denied*, 56 N.Y.2d 805, 452 N.Y.S.2d 1026, 434 N.E.2d 1038 (1982).

8. Conklin v. State of New York, 46 A.D.2d 936, 361 N.Y.S.2d 743 (3d Dep't 1974).

upon an appropriation, and thus the improvements belonged to the state and the tenant's claim for removable fixtures should have been granted.

Landlords do not want to diminish their award by a tenant's claim for the value of the unexpired portion of the lease, which can be expressly waived; such a claim may also be waived by providing for termination of the lease upon a vesting of title to the condemnor.[9]

9. Albany Cmty. Dev. Agency v. Abdelgader, 205 A.D.2d 905, 613 N.Y.S.2d 473 (3d Dep't 1994).

CHAPTER 16

Assignment and Subletting

16.1 General Purpose

For the tenant, this vital provision establishes its rights to modify the terms of its occupancy, with respect to the amount of rent expended or the length of term, or both, after the commencement of the term, through substitution of another occupant on pre-agreed terms for the landlord's consent to such substitution. For the landlord, assuming such flexibility to assign or sublet is to be given to a tenant, the goal is to ensure, for the term of the subject lease, that the substitute's creditworthiness, reputation, and conduct meet the original standards of the bargain.

The tenant, in other words, demands flexibility to accommodate the vicissitudes of the business cycle, whether bad times or good, which demand that space costs be decreased for survival, or that space secured be traded off for more room elsewhere while covering original costs in the first location. The landlord must respond to this demand but needs control of its own building, including not only the right to approve the substitute, but the opportunity to reclaim the space to accommodate the landlord's larger plans for the building and its tenant mix and disposition. The balancing of these interests makes the assignment and subletting clauses some of the longest, most complicated, and most negotiated of any provision in the lease form.

16.2 Sample Clause

16.01 Assignment; Etc.

(a) Subject to the further provisions of this Article 16, neither this Lease nor the term and estate hereby granted, nor any part hereof or thereof, shall be assigned, mortgaged, pledged, encumbered or otherwise transferred voluntarily, involuntarily, by operation of law or otherwise, and neither the Premises, nor any part thereof, shall be subleased, be licensed, be used or occupied by any person or entity other than Tenant or be encumbered in any manner by reason of any act or omission on the part of Tenant, and no rents or other sums receivable by Tenant under any sublease of all or any part of the Premises shall be assigned or otherwise encumbered, without the prior consent of Landlord.

The dissolution or direct or indirect transfer of control of Tenant (however accomplished including, by way of example, the addition of new partners or members or withdrawal of existing partners or members, or transfers of interests in distributions of profits or losses of Tenant, issuance of additional stock, redemption of stock, stock voting agreement, or change in classes of stock) shall be deemed an assignment of this Lease regardless of whether the transfer is made by one or more transactions, or whether one or more persons or entities hold the controlling interest prior to the transfer or afterwards, unless Tenant is a public company (*i.e.*, whose stock is publicly held and traded through a nationally recognized stock exchange). An agreement under which another person or entity becomes responsible for all or a portion of Tenant's obligations under this Lease shall be deemed an assignment of this Lease. No assignment or other transfer of this Lease and the term and estate hereby granted, and no subletting of all or any portion of the Premises shall relieve Tenant of its liability under this Lease or of the obligation to obtain Landlord's prior consent to any further assignment, other transfer or subletting. Any attempt to assign this Lease or sublet all or any portion of the Premises in violation of this Article 16 shall be null and void.

(b) Notwithstanding Section 16.01(a), without the consent of Landlord, this Lease may be assigned to (i) an entity created by merger, reorganization or recapitalization of or with Tenant or (ii) a purchaser of all or substantially all of Tenant's assets; *provided*, in the case of both clause (i) and clause (ii), that (A) Landlord shall have received prior notice of such assignment from Tenant, (B) the assignee assumes by written instrument satisfactory to Landlord all of Tenant's obligations under this Lease, (C) such assignment is for a valid business purpose and not to avoid any obligations under this Lease, and (D) the assignee is a reputable entity of good character and shall have, immediately after giving effect to such assignment, an aggregate tangible net worth (computed in accordance with GAAP) at least equal to the aggregate tangible net worth (as so computed) of Tenant immediately prior to such assignment or on the date of this Lease, whichever is greater.

(c) Notwithstanding Section 16.01(a), without the consent of Landlord, Tenant may assign this Lease or sublet all or any part of the Premises to an Affiliate of Tenant; *provided*, that (i) Landlord shall have received prior notice of such assignment or sublease from Tenant; and (ii) in the case of any such assignment, (A) the assignment is for a valid business purpose and not to avoid any obligations under this Lease, and (B) the assignee assumes by written instrument satisfactory to Landlord all of Tenant's obligations under this Lease. "Affiliate" means, as to any designated person or entity, any other person or entity that controls, is controlled by, or is under common control with, such designated person or entity. "Control" (and with correlative meaning, "controlled by" and "under common control with") means ownership or voting control, directly or indirectly, of 50% or more of the voting stock, partnership interests or other beneficial ownership interests of the entity in question.

[(d) Notwithstanding Section 16.01(a), Tenant may from time to time, subject to all of the provisions of this Lease and without the consent of Landlord, permit portions of the Premises to be used or occupied under so called "desk sharing" arrangements by a Desk Space User; *provided*, that (i) any such use or occupancy of desk or office space shall be without the installation of any separate entrance, (ii) at any time during the Term, the aggregate of the rentable square footage then used by Desk Space Users pursuant to this Section 16.01(d) shall not exceed [___%] of the rentable area of the Premises, (iii) each Desk Space User shall use the Premises in accordance with all of the provisions of this Lease, and only for the use expressly permitted pursuant to this Lease, (iv) in no event shall the use of any portion of the Premises by a Desk Space User create or be deemed to create any right, title or interest of such Desk Space User in any portion of the Premises or this Lease, (v) such "desk sharing" arrangement shall terminate automatically upon the termination of this Lease, (vi) such Desk Space User shall not have any signage outside of the Premises, (vii) each Desk Space User shall be engaged in a business or activity which is in keeping with standards of the Building and (viii) such desk sharing arrangement is for a valid business purpose and not to circumvent the provisions of this Article 16. Upon request of Landlord, Tenant shall notify Landlord of any Desk Space Users in the Premises, which notice shall include (A) a description of the nature and character of the business being conducted in the Premises by such Desk Space User and (B) the rentable square feet of the Premises occupied by such Desk Space User, together with a copy of the agreement, if any, relating to the use or occupancy of such portion of the Premises by such Desk Space User. "Desk Space User" means a bona fide client, service provider or other person or entity with which Tenant has a significant ongoing business relationship.]

16.02 Landlord's Right of First Offer.

(a) If Tenant desires to assign this Lease or sublet all or part of the Premises (other than in accordance with Sections 16.01(b) or (c), Tenant shall give to Landlord notice ("Tenant's Offer Notice") thereof, specifying (i) in the case of a proposed subletting, the location of the space to be sublet and the term of the subletting of such space, (ii) (A) in the case of a proposed assignment, Tenant's good faith offer of the consideration Tenant desires to receive or pay for such assignment or (B) in the case of a proposed subletting, Tenant's good faith offer of the fixed annual rent that Tenant desires to receive for such proposed subletting (assuming that a subtenant will pay for Taxes, Operating Expenses and electricity in the same manner, and utilizing the same base year or base amount, as Tenant pays for such amounts under this Lease) and (iii) the proposed assignment or sublease commencement date.

(b) Tenant's Offer Notice shall be deemed an offer from Tenant to Landlord whereby Landlord (or Landlord's designee) may, at Landlord's option, (i) sublease such space from Tenant (if the proposed transaction is a sublease of all or part of the Premises), (ii) have this Lease assigned to it or terminate this Lease (if the proposed transaction is an assignment or a sublease of all or substantially all of the Premises for all or substantially all of the remaining Term), or (iii) terminate this Lease with respect to the space covered by the proposed sublease (if the proposed transaction is a sublease of part of the Premises for all or substantially all of the remaining Term). Said option may be exercised by Landlord by notice to Tenant within 30 days after a Tenant's Offer Notice, together with all information required pursuant to Section 16.02(a), has been given by Tenant to Landlord.

(c) If Landlord exercises its option under Section 16.02(b)(ii) to terminate this Lease, then this Lease shall terminate on the proposed assignment or sublease commencement date specified in the applicable Tenant's Offer Notice and all Rent shall be paid and apportioned to such date.

(d) If Landlord exercises its option under Section 16.02(b)(ii) to have this Lease assigned to it (or its designee), then Tenant shall assign this Lease to Landlord (or Landlord's designee) by an assignment in form and substance reasonably satisfactory to Landlord, effective on the date that is the proposed assignment or sublease commencement date specified in the applicable Tenant's Offer Notice. Tenant shall not be entitled to consideration or payment from Landlord (or Landlord's designee) in connection with any such assignment. If the Tenant's Offer Notice provides that Tenant will pay any consideration or grant any concessions in connection with the proposed assignment or sublease, then Tenant shall pay such consideration and/or grant any such concessions to Landlord (or Landlord's designee) on the date Tenant assigns this Lease to Landlord (or Landlord's designee).

(e) If Landlord exercises its option under Section 16.02(b)(iii) to terminate this Lease with respect to the space covered by a proposed sublease, then (i) this Lease shall terminate with respect to such part of the Premises on the effective date of the proposed sublease; (ii) from and after such date the Rent shall be adjusted, based upon the proportion that the rentable area of the Premises remaining bears to the total rentable area of the Premises and (iii) Tenant shall pay to Landlord, within 30 days after demand, the costs incurred by Landlord in demising separately such part of the Premises and in complying with any Laws relating to such demise unless the applicable Tenant's Offer Notice states that the proposed subtenant shall be responsible for the cost of such demising work in which case Tenant shall not be obligated to make such payment to Landlord.

(f) If Landlord exercises its option under Section 16.02(b)(i) to sublet the space Tenant desires to sublet, such sublease to Landlord or its designee (as subtenant) shall be in form and substance reasonably satisfactory to Landlord at the lower of (i) the rental rate per rentable square foot of Fixed Rent and Additional Rent then payable pursuant to this Lease or (ii) the rental set forth in the applicable Tenant's Offer Notice with respect to such sublet space, and shall be for the term set forth in the applicable Tenant's Offer Notice, and:

(A) shall be subject to all of the terms and conditions of this Lease except such as are irrelevant or inapplicable, and except as otherwise expressly set forth to the contrary in this Section 16.02(f);

(B) shall be upon the same terms and conditions as those contained in the applicable Tenant's Offer Notice and otherwise on the terms and conditions of this Lease, except such as are irrelevant or inapplicable and except as otherwise expressly set forth to the contrary in this Section 16.02(f);

(C) shall permit the sublessee, without Tenant's consent, freely to assign such sublease or any interest therein or to sublet all or any part of the space covered by such sublease;

(D) shall provide that any assignee or further subtenant of Landlord or its designee may, at the election of Landlord, make alterations, decorations and installations in such space or any part thereof, any or all of which may be removed, in whole or in part, by such assignee or subtenant, at its option, prior to or upon the expiration or other termination of such sublease, provided that such assignee or subtenant, at its expense, shall repair any damage caused by such removal; and

(E) shall provide that (1) the parties to such sublease expressly negate any intention that any estate created under such sublease be merged with any other estate held by either of said parties, (2) any assignment or subletting by Landlord or its designee (as the subtenant) may be for any purpose or purposes that Landlord shall deem appropriate, and (3) except as set forth in clause (D) above, at the expiration of the term of such sublease, Tenant shall accept the space covered by such sublease in its then existing condition, subject to the obligations of the sublessee to make such repairs thereto as may be necessary to preserve such space in good order and condition (and Tenant shall have no obligation to remove or restore any Alterations made by Landlord or its designee).

(g) In the case of a proposed sublease, Tenant shall not sublet any space to a third party at a rental which is less (on a per rentable square foot basis) than 95% of the rental (on a per rentable square foot basis) specified in Tenant's Offer Notice with respect to such space, without complying once again with all of the provisions of this Section 16.02 and re-offering such space to Landlord at such lower rental. In the case of a proposed assignment, Tenant shall not assign this Lease to a third party where Tenant pays greater consideration or grants a greater concession to such third party for such assignment than 105% of the consideration offered to be paid or concession offered to be granted to

Landlord in Tenant's Offer Notice, or receives less consideration from such third party for such assignment than 95% of the consideration offered to be paid by Landlord in Tenant's Offer Notice, in each case without complying once again with all of the provisions of this Section 16.02 and re-offering to assign this Lease to Landlord and pay such consideration or grant such concession to Landlord.

16.03 Assignment and Subletting Procedures.

(a) If Tenant delivers to Landlord a Tenant's Offer Notice with respect to any proposed assignment of this Lease or subletting of all or part of the Premises and Landlord does not timely exercise any of its options under Section 5.02, and Tenant thereafter desires to assign this Lease or sublet the space specified in Tenant's Offer Notice, Tenant shall notify Landlord (a "Transfer Notice") of such desire, which notice shall be accompanied by (i) a copy of the proposed assignment or sublease and all related agreements, the effective date of which shall be at least 30 days after the giving of the Transfer Notice, (ii) a statement setting forth in reasonable detail the identity of the proposed assignee or subtenant, the nature of its business and its proposed use of the Premises, (iii) current financial information with respect to the proposed assignee or subtenant, including without limitation, its most recent financial statements and (iv) such other information as Landlord may reasonably request and Landlord's consent to the proposed assignment or sublease shall not be unreasonably withheld or delayed, provided that:

(i) Such Transfer Notice shall be delivered to Landlord within 90 days after the delivery to Landlord of the applicable Tenant's Offer Notice.

(ii) Tenant shall not be in default under this Lease beyond applicable notice and grace periods.

(iii) In Landlord's judgment the proposed assignee or subtenant will use the Premises in a manner that (A) is in keeping with the then standards of the Building, (B) is limited to the use expressly permitted under this Lease, and (C) will not violate any negative covenant as to use contained in any other Lease of space in the Building.

(iv) The proposed assignee or subtenant is, in Landlord's judgment, a reputable person or entity of good character and with sufficient financial worth considering the responsibility involved.

(v) [Provided that there is space in the Project that is comparable in size and location to the Premises (in the case of a proposed assignment) or the space covered by the proposed sublease, that is then available for leasing, or is expected to become available within the next 6 months, for the then balance of the term of this Lease (in the case of a proposed assignment) or for approximately the same term as the proposed sublease, n] [N]either the proposed assignee or sublessee, nor any Affiliate of such assignee or sublessee, is then an occupant of any part of the Building.

(vi) [Provided that there is space in the Project that is comparable in size and location to the Premises (in the case of a proposed assignment) or the space covered by the proposed sublease, that is then available for leasing, or is expected to become available within the next 6 months, for the then balance of the term of this Lease (in the case of a proposed assignment) or for approximately the same term as the proposed sublease, t][T]he proposed assignee or sublessee is not a person with whom Landlord is then negotiating or has within the prior 6 months negotiated to lease space in the Building.

(vii) The form of the proposed sublease shall be reasonably satisfactory to Landlord and shall comply with the applicable provisions of this Article 16.

(viii) There shall not be more than [___] subtenants [on any floor] of the Premises [or more than [__] subtenants of the Premises in the aggregate].

(ix) Tenant shall reimburse Landlord within 30 days after demand for any reasonable out of pocket costs incurred by Landlord in connection with said assignment or sublease, including, without limitation, the costs of making investigations as to the acceptability of the proposed assignee or subtenant, and legal costs incurred in connection with the granting of any requested consent.

(b) If Landlord consents to a proposed assignment or sublease and Tenant fails to execute and deliver the assignment or sublease to which Landlord consented within 45 days after the giving of such consent, then Tenant shall again comply with this Article 16 before assigning this Lease or subletting all or part of the Premises.

16.04 General Provisions.

(a) If this Lease is assigned, whether or not in violation of this Lease, Landlord may collect rent from the assignee. If the Premises or any part thereof are sublet or occupied by anybody other than Tenant, whether or not in violation of this Lease, Landlord may, after default by Tenant, and expiration of Tenant's time to cure such default, collect rent from the subtenant or occupant. In either event, Landlord may apply the net amount collected against Rent, but no such assignment, subletting, occupancy or collection shall be deemed a waiver of any of the provisions of Section 16.01(a), or the acceptance of the assignee, subtenant or occupant as tenant, or a release of Tenant from the performance of Tenant's obligations under this Lease.

(b) No assignment or transfer shall be effective until the assignee delivers to Landlord (i) evidence that the assignee, as Tenant hereunder, has complied with the requirements of Sections 13.01 and 13.02, [and] (ii) an agreement in form and substance satisfactory to Landlord whereby the assignee assumes Tenant's obligations under this Lease [and (iii) a ratification by Guarantor of the Guaranty].

(c) Notwithstanding any assignment or transfer, whether or not in violation of this Lease, and notwithstanding the acceptance of any Rent by Landlord from an assignee, transferee, or any other party, the original named Tenant and each successor Tenant shall remain fully liable for the payment of the Rent and the performance of all of Tenant's other obligations under this Lease. The joint and several liability of Tenant and any immediate or remote successor in interest of Tenant shall not be discharged, released or impaired in any respect by any agreement made by Landlord extending the time to perform, or otherwise modifying, any of the obligations of Tenant under this Lease, or by any waiver or failure of Landlord to enforce any of the obligations of Tenant under this Lease.

(d) Each subletting by Tenant shall be subject to the following:

(i) No subletting shall be for a term (including any renewal or extension options contained in the sublease) ending later than one day prior to the Expiration Date.

(ii) No sublease shall be valid, and no subtenant shall take possession of the Premises or any part thereof, until there has been delivered to Landlord, both (A) an executed counterpart of such sublease, and (B) a certificate of insurance evidencing that (x) Landlord is an additional insured under the insurance policies required to be maintained by occupants of the Premises pursuant to Section 13.01, and (y) there is in full force and effect, the insurance otherwise required by Section 13.01.

(iii) Each sublease shall provide that it is subject and subordinate to this Lease, and that in the event of termination, reentry or dispossess by Landlord under this Lease Landlord may, at its option, take over all of the right, title and interest of Tenant, as sublessor, under such sublease, and such subtenant shall, at Landlord's option, attorn to Landlord pursuant to the then executory provisions of such sublease, except that Landlord shall not be liable for, subject to or bound by any item of the type that a Successor Landlord is not so liable for, subject to or bound by in the case of an attornment by Tenant to a Successor Landlord under Section 11.01(a).

(e) Each sublease shall provide that the subtenant may not assign its rights thereunder or further sublet the space demised under the sublease, in whole or in part, without Landlord's consent and without complying with all of the terms and conditions of this Article 16, including, without limitation, Section 16.04, which for purposes of this Section 16.04(e) shall be deemed to be appropriately modified to take into account that the transaction in question is an assignment of the sublease or a further subletting of the space demised under the sublease, as the case may be.

(f) Tenant shall not publicly advertise the availability of the Premises or any portion thereof as sublet space or by way of an assignment of this Lease, without first obtaining Landlord's consent, which consent shall not be unreasonably withheld or delayed provided that Tenant shall in no event advertise the rental rate or any description thereof.

16.05 Assignment and Sublease Profits.

(a) If the aggregate of the amounts payable as fixed rent and as additional rent on account of Taxes, Operating Expenses and electricity by a subtenant under a sublease of any part of the Premises and the amount of any Other Sublease Consideration payable to Tenant by such subtenant, whether received in a lump-sum payment or otherwise shall be in excess of Tenant's Basic Cost therefor at that time then, promptly after the collection thereof, Tenant shall pay to Landlord in monthly installments as and when collected, as Additional Rent, 50% of such excess. Tenant shall deliver to Landlord within 60 days after the end of each calendar year and within 60 days after the expiration or earlier termination of this Lease a statement specifying each sublease in effect during such calendar year or partial calendar year, the rentable area demised thereby, the term thereof and a computation in reasonable detail showing the calculation of the amounts paid and payable by the subtenant to Tenant, and by Tenant to Landlord, with respect to such sublease for the period covered by such statement. "Tenant's Basic Cost" for sublet space at any time means the sum of (i) the portion of the Fixed Rent, Tax Payments and Operating Payments that is attributable to the sublet space, plus (ii) the amount payable by Tenant on account of electricity in respect of the sublet space, plus (iii) the amount of any costs reasonably incurred by Tenant in making changes in the layout and finish of the sublet space to prepare the sublet space for the subtenant's occupancy amortized on a straight-line basis over the term of the sublease, plus (iv) the amount of any reasonable brokerage commissions and reasonable legal fees paid by Tenant in connection with the sublease amortized on a straight-line basis over the term of the sublease. "Other Sublease Considerations" means all sums paid for the furnishing of services by Tenant and the sale or rental of Tenant's fixtures, leasehold improvements, equipment, furniture or other personal property less, in the case of the sale thereof, the then net unamortized or undepreciated cost thereof determined on the basis of Tenant's federal income tax returns.

(b) Upon any assignment of this Lease, Tenant shall pay to Landlord 50% of the Assignment Consideration received by Tenant for such assignment, after deducting therefrom customary and reasonable closing expenses. "Assignment Consideration" means an amount equal to all sums and other considerations paid to Tenant by the assignee for or by reason of such assignment (including, without limitation, sums paid for the furnishing of services by Tenant and the sale or rental of Tenant's fixtures, leasehold improvements, equipment, furniture, furnishings or other personal property, less, in the case of a sale thereof, the then net unamortized or undepreciated cost thereof determined on the basis of Tenant's federal income tax returns).

(c) The provisions of this Section 16.05 shall not apply to the transactions described in Sections 16.01(b), or (c) [or (d)].

16.3 Landlord Concerns

No landlord is compelled by law to consent to a tenant's request to permit assignment or subletting, and all such clauses begin with an absolute prohibition against such action. Only market forces, expressed through other building owners' attitudes on the question, can compel a landlord to consider this question. These market forces, however, do exist in New York's and other states' urban centers, and, as a result, it is a rare lease form that does not permit, subject to certain stated conditions, some form of subletting and/or assignment.

Having made its bargain with the tenant for a fixed period of years, the landlord is concerned that consent to an assignment or sublet will not leave the building owner in any lesser position, with respect to creditworthiness or character of the substituted occupant. Additionally, having erected the absolute prohibition against assignment or subletting without prior consent, the violation of which constitutes a default for which the lease may be terminated, the landlord will be determined to see that the balance of this article's provisions set forth in precise detail (1) those circumstances under which consent will be sought, with the provision of adequate information by the tenant, and (2) defensible reasons stated in advance for refusing the request, with no consequences to the landlord.

A primary consideration for the landlord is whether it wants the space back to use for its own business plan. If the tenant's primary goal is to cut its occupancy costs, and if tenant must in any event remain secondarily liable following any approved assignment or sublease, then the landlord's termination of that liability through exercise of "recapture" or "takeback" rights (see Section 16.02 set forth in the sample clause in Section 16.2, *supra*) is a solution that benefits both parties. Often these rights are conditioned on some (defined) "substantial" portion of the original space being on offer, so that the right is not triggered by the tenant's effort to sublease a small amount of space, perhaps for less than the balance of the term, but few tenants will have any reason to resist a building owner's insistence that it have such rights when such tenant is looking to reduce its space dramatically, or even effectively to leave the building. In a rising market, of course, where the tenant might look at its original space as a profit center if it could move to cheaper space while subletting at a premium, the recapture right means landlord has the power to allocate that gain to itself.

If there is to be no recapture option triggered within the defined period for its exercise, then the landlord will want to have established in advance (see Section 16.03 set forth in the sample clause in Section 16.2, *supra*) what conditions will be imposed on the exercise of its discretion. These conditions often find expression in standards that the proposed assignee or sublessee must meet before the application for consent will be considered (and which, if not met, are grounds for "reasonable" refusal). Some are clear tests, like proposed use (see Section 16.03(a)(iii) set forth in the sample clause in Section 16.2, *supra*), or candidates having no prior or current negotiations with landlord (see Section 16.03(a)(vi) set forth in the sample clause in Section 16.2, *supra*), or having too many occupants on a single floor (see Section 16.03(a)(viii) set forth in the sample clause in Section 16.2, *supra*). Other standards may be more nebulous, such as character and creditworthiness (see Section 16.03(a)(iv) set forth in the sample clause in Section 16.2, *supra*), where, like pornography, the building owner cannot precisely define it, but knows it when he sees it.

Besides the establishment of preconditions, which narrow the field for requests for consent that the landlord must seriously consider, the landlord will want to set forth the data required for the evaluation of those proposals that otherwise meet the precondition standards, which at a minimum will include a description of the sublessee or assignee, its business, and its finances (see Section 16.03(a) set forth in the sample clause in Section 16.2, *supra*). This information is customarily required to be submitted with a fully executed document of sublease, or instrument of assignment and assumption, so that the landlord is reacting to a "done deal," rather than a wish list. Some tenants, however, will resist going to the trouble and expense of concluding a sublease or an assignment (conditional on the landlord's consent) without some indication of the landlord's attitude, and may bargain for a form of "pre-clearance."

The landlord may find it useful, having set forth its recapture rights and approval procedure, to remind the tenant of the collateral consequences of a request for consent: (1) the tenant nonetheless remains financially liable post-assignment or post-sublease; (2) the first consent is not blanket and must be requested again for each new transaction; (3) any amendment of an approved sublease requires a new consent; and (4) the landlord's out-of-pockets for its lawyers to review the documents and other such costs are to be reimbursed.

Further rules of the process might also be usefully set forth: provisions to be contained in every sublease as to its term, subordination, and so on, and the requirement of formal assumption in the case of an assignment. Most landlords will prohibit any advertisement of proposed sublease rental rate.

Leases usually contain a provision allocating a portion of sublease or assignment "profits" back to the landlord from the tenant. This provision prevents a tenant from generating profit from a below-market lease without the landlord sharing in the benefit. Such a clause (see Section 16.05 set forth in the sample clause in Section 16.2, *supra*), in order to be workable, requires a fairly specific definition of the tenant's costs of subletting (or assignment) to be netted out.

Another basic landlord protection to be incorporated is to define any change in control of the business entity comprising the tenant (whether a corporation, partnership, or other business form such as a limited liability company) as an assignment (see Section 16.01(a) set forth in the sample clause in Section 16.2, *supra*). Under New York law, forbidding assignment of a lease, while failing to define assignment as a change in control, means that the lease in question can effectively be assigned by a transfer of shares, without violation of the no-assignment provisions, since such clauses are strictly construed (as constituting restraints against alienation), and very easy methods have been blessed by the courts for defeating them (see, e.g., *Rowe v. Great Atlantic & Pacific Tea Co.*[1] and *Brentsun Realty Corp. v. D'Urso Supermarkets, Inc.*[2]).

With respect to a tenant requesting "desk-sharing" rights that allow for certain third parties with whom the tenant has a business relationship (e.g., auditors, accountants, mail/porter service providers) to utilize a negotiated portion of the premises without the formality of entering into a sublease or obtaining the landlord's consent (see Section 16.01(d) set forth in the sample clause in Section 16.2, *supra*), landlords will want to include protections that prevent a tenant from using these rights to circumvent the assignment and subletting provisions entirely. For example, a desk-sharing provision will often cap the portion of the premises that may be occupied by desk space users, prohibit separately demising the desk-sharing space or the creation of a separate entrance for desk-space users, prohibit signage for the desk-space users, and prohibit the payment of rent by desk-space users.

16.4 Tenant Concerns

Generally speaking, the larger the space taken by a tenant, the more important it is to secure rights to future subletting and/or assignment, in the event of a business downturn or a need for expansion that may occur later in the term. Most landlords will accommodate such flexibility, as long as the primary tenant's liability is continued and the replacement tenant (whether assignee or subtenant) is of a financial strength and business character that is compatible with the tenant mix of the building. The tenant must realize, of course, that other rights it may have secured as part of the initial bargain, such as expansion or renewal rights, may be lost or severely curtailed upon an assignment of the lease, or after the subletting of a substantial portion of the original premises. Nevertheless, the ability to sublet and assign is certainly vital to have at the outset, despite the possibility of later forfeiture. However, a tenant with renewal or expansion rights should review the effect of a proposed sublease on the viability of those clauses before committing to the sublease, if the sublease is being entered into simply to lay off space temporarily, instead of as a winding-down of the tenant's tenure in the building.

A tenant is also concerned here to ensure that the issues of its internal business organization, or consolidation and/or disposition, do not become hampered by the landlord's rules against assignment without consent, and should therefore negotiate to secure agreement that normal internal stock transfers to officers, and even the sale or merger of the tenant in its entirety or an upstream change of control, do not run afoul of such provisions. Similarly, if the tenant is but one division of a larger company or a group of affiliated companies, the ability to transfer the lease as an asset to such an affiliate or successor company is also a right worth having, and such a transfer should not trouble the landlord if the net worth securing the lease is effectively the same after as before assignment, and the premises' use is not changed.

---

1. 46 N.Y.2d 62, 412 N.Y.S.2d 827, 385 N.E.2d 566 (1978).
2. 182 A.D.2d 604, 582 N.Y.S.2d 216 (2d Dep't 1992).

In addition, tenants will negotiate for "desk-sharing" rights that allow for certain third parties with whom the tenant has a business relationship (e.g., auditors, accountants, mail/porter service providers) to utilize a negotiated portion of the premises on a temporary or full-term basis without the formality of entering into a sublease or obtaining the landlord's consent (see Section 16.01(d) set forth in the sample clause in Section 16.2, *supra*).

As noted earlier, in the discussion in Section 16.3, Landlord Concerns, on the process of approval of sublessees, the tenant may want to argue for a "pre-clearance" procedure that will indicate whether, all other standards being met, the landlord will approve the subtenant with whom the tenant intends to negotiate. Even more important, the tenant should be sure that the "laundry list" of reasonableness standards (see Section 16.03(a) set forth in the sample clause in Section 16.2, *supra*) are plainly expressed, in order to avoid later controversy as each side proceeds in (presumed) good faith to identify approvable subtenants and/or assignees.

In bargaining for a "net profits" division that will direct some of the excess proceeds of a successful sublease or assignment into the tenant's coffers, the tenant should seek to have named specifically all costs likely to be incurred, instead of merely undifferentiated "expenses." For example, tenants may seek to enumerate brokerage commissions, legal fees, marketing and advertising costs, takeover expenses, and cash contributions. In addition, tenants with negotiating leverage may seek to include the unamortized cost of the tenant's initial fit-out as an expense and may seek to recoup all applicable expenses from the first payments of sublease rent (as opposed to amortizing the costs over the sublease term) in order to recoup those expenses before any sublease or assignment revenue is shared with the landlord.

16.5 Standard Real Estate Board of New York Clause

The clause to be found in the REBNY form is simple, direct, and composed entirely of landlord protections:

> *Assignment, Mortgage, etc.: 11.* Tenant, for itself, its heirs, distributees, executors, administrators, legal representatives, successors and assigns, expressly covenants that it shall not assign, mortgage or encumber this agreement, nor underlet, or suffer or permit the demised premises or any part thereof to be used by others, without the prior written consent of Owner in each instance. Transfer of the majority of the stock of a corporate Tenant or the majority partnership interest in any partnership or other legal entity which is Tenant shall be deemed an assignment. If this lease be assigned, or if the demised premises or any part thereof be underlet or occupied by anybody other than Tenant, Owner may, after default by Tenant, collect rent from the assignee, undertenant or occupant, and apply the net amount collected to the rent herein reserved, but no such assignment, underletting, occupancy or collection shall be deemed a waiver of this covenant, or the acceptance of the assignee, undertenant or occupant as tenant, or a release of Tenant from the further performance by Tenant

of covenants on the part of Tenant herein contained. The consent by Owner to an assignment or underletting shall not in any way be construed to relieve Tenant from obtaining the express consent in writing of Owner to any further assignment or underletting.

16.6 Comments on Standard Real Estate Board of New York Clause

Even the owner/landlord may wish to add some provisions to the standard form, such as recapture rights (Section 16.03), indemnification of owner/landlord (Subsection 16.06.4), a "net profits" provision (Section 16.07), and a prohibition on damages for refusing consent (Section 16.09). If the owner/landlord, in bargaining to secure the tenant, must agree to permit assignment and subletting, then the incorporation of clear standards (Section 16.05) and a procedure for requesting consent (Subsection 16.05.2) should also be added. A provision setting forth clear standards is a benefit to both parties.

The tenant, of course, has many more reasons to want a substantial expansion of these REBNY provisions, not only with regard to ensuring that the owner/landlord will not unreasonably withhold its consent to an assignment or sublease to a creditworthy candidate of good character, but also with regard to adding the standards for business flexibility discussed in Section 16.4, *supra*, entitled "Tenant Concerns" (in particular, the straitjacket in this Article 16's second sentence must be loosened to permit the transfer of the lease as part of a bona fide merger or sale of all the tenant's assets). Except in the isolated case of the smallest of tenants, who irrationally have no fear of business cycle disruptions occurring during their terms, it is hard to identify another provision of the REBNY form that requires the addition of more tenant protections, which are virtually standard in most manuscript lease forms (and are exemplified in detail in Section 16.4, *supra*, entitled "Tenant Concerns").

16.7 Litigation Issues

A fundamental provision contained in commercial leases, except those drafted by tenants of economic strength, is a restriction against assignment and subletting. These restrictions are strictly construed because they represent a restraint on alienation.[3] Although strictly construed, they are also strictly enforced. Thus a tenant must be certain to negotiate for the right to assign and sublet, even for the purpose of a transfer to a subsidiary entity.[4]

---

3. Rowe v. Great Atl. & Pac. Tea Co., Inc., 46 N.Y.2d 62, 412 N.Y.S.2d 827, 385 N.E.2d 566 (1978).

4. Guardia v. 250 West St. Corp., 205 A.D.2d 306, 613 N.Y.S.2d 10 (1st Dep't 1994) (upholding restriction against assignment without consent as applying to assignment to wholly owned subsidiary of tenant).

In *Rowe v. Great Atlantic & Pacific Tea Co., Inc.*,[5] the defendant, being a major chain store, was able to induce the landlord to enter into a lease with no restriction on assignment or subletting. No doubt the identity of the tenant was the most significant factor in granting the lease, and the financial viability of the tenant enhanced the value of the percentage rental provision. The court, in *Rowe*, would not imply a restriction against assignment where none was expressly stated. It did note that an implied covenant restricting an assignment could "be recognized only if it is clear that a reasonable landlord would not have entered into the lease without such an understanding."[6] A party attempting to prove such an implied restriction bears "a heavy burden."[7] The Court of Appeals, in *Rowe*, cited *Nassau Hotel Co. v. Barnett & Barse Corp.*[8] as an example of a situation where a restriction against assignment was implied. *Nassau Hotel Co.* involved the leasing of a hotel by the owner to two persons, one of whom was an experienced hotel manager. The lease gave them, among other rights, the exclusive possession of the hotel, and they agreed that they would operate it "at all times in a first-class business-like manner."[9] The tenants attempted to sublease the premises to a corporation and the owner sued to recover the premises. The attempt to sublet failed because a fundamental premise of the agreement with the owner was that *these two persons* would operate the hotel. Since the owner had agreed to accept a percentage of the receipts in place of rent, he had the right to depend on the fact that the hotel would be operated by the persons with whom he contracted. Permitting the sublease, under these circumstances, would have deprived the owner of a substantial element of his reasonable and legitimate contractual expectations. However, such a restriction will rarely be implied.

In strictly construing an assignment restriction, the courts will look at the form of the restricted transaction. A landlord may thus be unable to prevent a transaction to which it had reasonable business objections. In *Dennis' Natural Mini-Meals, Inc. v. 91 Fifth Avenue Corp.*,[10] a restriction requiring consent to an assignment did not prohibit an effective change in ownership of the tenant by the sale of the tenant's stock, notwithstanding the landlord's absolute right to withhold consent to an assignment of a lease to the ultimate purchaser of the tenant's stock. In *Brentsun Realty Corp. v. D'Urso Supermarkets, Inc.*,[11] it was held that a restriction against transferring 50 percent or more of the stock of a corporation did not restrict a corporate merger. Notwithstanding the reasonable objection to conducting business with a lease holdover, the court, in *29 W. 25th Street Parking Corp. v. Penn Post Parking, Inc.*,[12] held that a sale of a new

---

5. 46 N.Y.2d 62, 412 N.Y.S.2d 827, 385 N.E.2d 566 (1978).
6. 46 N.Y.2d at 70, 412 N.Y.S.2d at 831.
7. 46 N.Y.2d at 69, 412 N.Y.S.2d at 831.
8. 162 A.D. 381, 147 N.Y.S. 283, *aff'd* 212 N.Y. 568, 106 N.E. 1036 (1914).
9. 46 N.Y.2d at 71, 412 N.Y.S.2d at 832. The quote in *Rowe* is from the *Nassau Hotel Co.* case.
10. 172 A.D.2d 331, 568 N.Y.S.2d 740 (1st Dep't 1991).
11. 182 A.D.2d 604, 582 N.Y.S.2d 216 (2d Dep't 1992).
12. 105 A.D.2d 610, 481 N.Y.S.2d 345 (1st Dep't 1984). Reversed by 29 W. 25th St. Parking Corp. v. Penn Post Parking, Inc., 64 N.Y.2d 1085, 479 N.E.2d 250, 489 N.Y.S.2d 905 (N.Y. Ct. App.

lessee's stock to the existing holdover tenant was not prohibited by a restriction against assignment.

Leases have been drafted that restrict either an assignment or sublease, but not both. This may be due to inadvertence[13] or may be intentional, as in the case of *Nedick's Stores, Inc. v. T.S.N.Y. Realty Corp.*,[14] where a franchisor tenant was permitted to sublease to a franchisee but was restricted from assigning the lease. In *Nedick's*, the subtenant sold its business; the tenant "assigned" its lease with a right to a reassignment in the event of a default under the terms of the lease. The court held that the transaction was a true assignment because the right to reenter upon the "assignee's" default was not a true reversionary interest, which distinguishes a sublease from an assignment. The distinction must also be considered by a tenant in structuring a transaction, because in a true assignment the assignor is divested of privity of estate and has no further possessory interest, but remains liable for the contractual lease covenants, including the obligation to pay rent.[15]

By negotiating a covenant that a landlord will "not unreasonably" withhold its consent to an assignment or sublease, a tenant effectively turns an absolute restriction into a qualified right.[16] Having agreed not to unreasonably withhold consent, a "refusal can only be based upon a consideration of objective factors, such as the financial responsibility of the subtenant, the subtenant's suitability for the particular building, the legality of the proposed use and the nature of the occupancy."[17] A landlord could reasonably object to a sublease if its terms were contrary to the terms of the original lease, or gave greater or inconsistent rights to the subtenant. However, even if those terms were objectionable, a subsequently submitted document between tenant and subtenant, binding the subtenant to every provision of a prime lease, would render such an objection unreasonable.[18] A request for a consent that also requested an estoppel as to the tenant's lack of leasehold defaults could permit a reasonable withholding of the landlord's consent.[19] A landlord who agrees not to unreasonably withhold consent may expressly

---

1985) (The Appellate Division denied plaintiff tenant, 29 W. 25th St. Parking Corp., an extension of the lease term (as the lease requires in the case of the landlord being unable to give possession on the date specified). The only reason defendant landlord was unable to give possession to plaintiff tenant, 29 W. 25th St. was because plaintiff tenant, W. 25th St. Parking Corp., refused to surrender the premises at the end of the lease. The appellate division did not disturb the trial term ruling that the defendant landlord's refusal to consent was unreasonable.).

13. Krasner v. Transcon. Equities, Inc., 70 A.D.2d 312, 420 N.Y.S.2d 872 (1st Dep't 1979) (subtenant was permitted to effectively surrender premises to landlord in instrument deemed an assignment, where sublease only restricted further subletting).

14. 156 A.D.2d 123, 548 N.Y.S.2d 172 (1st Dep't 1989).

15. Howard Stores Corp. v. Robison Rayon Co., Inc., 64 Misc. 2d 913, 315 N.Y.S.2d 720 (Sup. Ct. App. Tm. 1st Dep't 1970).

16. Arlu Assoc., Inc. v. Rosner, 14 A.D.2d 272, 220 N.Y.S.2d 288 (1st Dep't 1961) (upholding right of the tenant to sue for damages if landlord unreasonably withholds consent).

17. Astoria Bedding, Mr. Sleeper Bedding Ctr. Inc. v. Northside P'ship, 239 A.D.2d 775, 657 N.Y.S.2d 796 (3d Dep't 1997).

18. Filmways, Inc. v. 477 Madison Ave., Inc., 36 A.D.2d 609, 318 N.Y.S.2d 506, *aff'd* 30 N.Y.2d 597, 331 N.Y.S.2d 31, 282 N.E.2d 119 (1972).

19. F.H.R. Auto Sales, Inc. v. Scutti, 144 A.D.2d 956, 534 N.Y.S.2d 266 (4th Dep't 1988).

state the conditions to be considered in evaluating its decision. Unless compliance with other lease provisions is expressly stated as such a condition, such other lease defaults cannot be considered.[20]

The landlord must carefully draft those conditions, as they will be strictly construed and may be interpreted as being permissive and not restrictive. In *International Chefs, Inc. v. Corporate Property Investors*,[21] one of the factors the landlord expressly stated that it would consider when deciding whether it would reasonably withhold consent to an assignment was "the nature of the business of the proposed assignee 'in relation to the tenant mix or balance in the shopping center.'"[22] The court in *International Chefs, Inc.* stated that a landlord did not have unfettered discretion to withhold consent to an assignment by a shopping center tenant to a proposed tenant that was not engaged in the same exact business as the tenant. The appellate court held that there was a triable issue of fact as to whether the defendant had unreasonably withheld consent and affirmed the lower court determination denying summary judgment.

20. 534 N.Y.S.2d at 267.
21. 240 A.D.2d 369, 658 N.Y.S.2d 108 (2d Dep't 1997).
22. 658 N.Y.S.2d at 109.

CHAPTER 17

Electricity

17.1 General Purpose

The purpose of the electricity provision, from the landlord's point of view, is to ensure that the building owner is getting back from all of the individual tenants what is being charged to the building owner by the utility for their individual uses, above and beyond the base building's consumption of electric power (and, for the same reason, base building energy cost escalation clauses are also being used more frequently). The tenant, on the other hand, is anxious to minimize the "profit center" aspect of power repurchase from its landlord—and, on a multi-tenant floor, paying a "proportionate share," may fear the fate of the member of the large restaurant party who orders cheaply but has to pay the bill of the arithmetically average diner. Tenants also want the flexibility to increase consumption in future, if need be.

Thus, the type of electricity clause as to measurement and payment provisions will vary among buildings and, often, among tenants of different sizes in the same building, where the smallest-space tenants may be too small (or vary their demising walls too often) for cost-effective submetering. This discussion of sample electricity provisions, then, to be comprehensive, must examine both the "rent inclusion" and submetering varieties of charging the tenant, although other components of electric power provision are common to both, and to the New York Real Estate Board form (which, in its very first sentence, invites the addition of a rider for "rates and conditions with respect to submetering or rent inclusion").

17.2 Sample Clause

[Metered Sample Provision]

17.01 Electric Charges.

(a) Tenant's demand for, and consumption of, electricity serving the Premises shall be determined by meter or meters installed (or, if existing, retrofitted) by Landlord at Tenant's expense. Tenant shall pay for such electric consumption from and after the Commencement Date within 15 days after rendition of bills therefor, which bills shall be rendered by or on behalf of Landlord separately for each meter.

(b) The amount payable by Tenant per "KW" and "KWH" for electricity consumed within the Premises shall be [_____%] of the amount (as adjusted from time to time, "Landlord's Rate") at which Landlord from time to time purchases each KW and KWH of electricity for the same period from the utility company and/or alternate providers (including, without limitation, all surcharges, taxes, fuel adjustments, market supply and market adjustment charges, taxes passed on to consumers by the public utility, and other sums payable in respect thereof), plus all surcharges, taxes and other sums payable in respect of Landlord's sale of electricity to Tenant.

(c) If the Commencement Date shall occur prior to the installation of meters in the Premises, then Tenant shall pay [$3.50] ([$1.50] during the period of Tenant's construction of Tenant's Initial Work to the Premises) per rentable square foot of space in the Premises per annum (the "Interim Electric Charge"), on account of Tenant's use of electricity in the Premises for the period commencing on the Commencement Date and ending on the date that the meters measuring Tenant's consumption of electricity in the Premises are installed and are operational. The Interim Electric Charge shall be paid by Tenant monthly within 10 days after submission of a bill therefor.

(d) At Landlord's option, Landlord shall furnish and install all replacement lighting, tubes, lamps, bulbs and ballasts required in the Premises, and Tenant shall pay to Landlord or its designated contractor upon demand Landlord's then established charges therefor.

[Rent Inclusion Sample Provision]

17.01 Electric Charges.

(a) For purposes of this Section 17.01:

(i) "Electric Rate" means at the time in question [_____%] of the public utility rate schedule (including all surcharges, taxes, fuel adjustments, taxes regularly passed on to consumers by the public utility, and other sums payable in respect thereof) for the supply of electricity to Landlord for the Building. Notwithstanding the foregoing, if the public utility rate schedule (with such inclusions) applicable to Landlord for the purchase of electricity for the Building shall be less than the public utility rate schedule applicable to Landlord if Landlord were to purchase electricity solely for the Premises, then the higher rate schedule shall be used in determining the Electric Rate.

(ii) "Base Electric Rate" means the Electric Rate in effect on the date of this Lease.

(iii) "Adjusted Electric Charge" means an amount, included as a component of Fixed Rent, equal to the sum of the Base Electric Charge plus all increases thereto pursuant to the provisions of this Section 17.01.

(b) Landlord shall furnish electricity to Tenant on a "rent inclusion" basis and there shall be no separate charge to Tenant for such electricity, such charge being included in Fixed Rent. The Base Electric Charge represents the amount initially included in the annual Fixed Rent set forth in Article 4 and such Base Electric Charge component of Fixed Rent shall not be subject to reduction, but may be subject to increase as hereinafter provided.

(c) At any time, and from time to time, after the Commencement Date, Landlord may survey the electrical fixtures, appliances and equipment in the Premises and Tenant's consumption of electricity therein to determine whether the then Adjusted Electric Charge included in Fixed Rent is less than the Adjusted Electric Charge computed as a result of said survey and to adjust the Adjusted Electric Charge component of Fixed Rent in accordance with such computation, which computation and adjustment shall be made as follows:

(i) In the case of the first such survey, if the product of (A) the Electric Rate in effect on the Commencement Date and (B) the electric consumption shown by the survey on a kilowatt and kilowatt hour basis shall exceed the Adjusted Electric Charge, then the Adjusted Electric Charge shall be increased by the amount of such excess, retroactive to the Commencement Date.

(ii) In the case of each subsequent survey, the computation shall be made by (A) dividing the Adjusted Electric Charge in effect immediately prior to such survey (the "Existing Adjusted Electric Charge") for which the computation is being made, by the number of kilowatt hours of electricity supplied to the Premises as determined by the last prior survey made by Landlord, thus arriving at an electrical consumption per kilowatt hour rate ("KWH Rate"), and (B) multiplying the number of kilowatt hours of consumption, as determined by the survey for which the computation is being made, by the KWH Rate. If such survey shall show that the Existing Adjusted Electric Charge is different from the Adjusted Electric Charge computed in accordance with such survey, then effective as of the earlier of the date of such survey or the earlier date(s), if any, on which changes in the connected power load or changes in electrical consumption occurred (as determined by Landlord), the Existing Adjusted Electric Charge included as a component of Fixed Rent shall be adjusted by an amount equal to the difference between the Existing Adjusted Electric Charge and the then Adjusted Electric Charge but in no event shall the Adjusted Electric Charge be reduced below the Base Electric Charge.

(d) If Tenant disagrees in good faith with any such computation or adjustment made by Landlord, Landlord, at Tenant's request, shall retain, at Tenant's expense, an independent electrical consultant reasonably satisfactory to Tenant who shall survey the demand for, and consumption of, electricity by Tenant, and the determination made by such electrical consultant shall be binding on

Landlord and Tenant (provided that in no event shall the Adjusted Electric Charge be less than the Base Electric Charge). Pending the determination of such consultant, Tenant shall pay Fixed Rent based on the Adjusted Electric Charge determined by Landlord, and upon such determination by the consultant, appropriate adjustment shall be made retroactive to the date of determination by the consultant.

(e) Surveys of Tenant's electrical consumption shall be based upon the use of electricity during Business Hours on Business Days, and on such other days and hours when electricity is used in the Premises; and if cleaning services are provided by Landlord, such survey shall include Landlord's normal cleaning hours for lighting within the Premises and for electrical equipment normally used for such cleaning.

(f) If at any time during the Term the Electric Rate shall exceed the Base Electric Rate or be decreased below the then applicable Electric Rate (as previously increased pursuant to this Section 17.01), then, effective as of the date of each such change in the Electric Rate, the Adjusted Electric Charge included in Fixed Rent shall be increased or decreased in proportion to such change in the Electric Rate (as determined by Landlord; but in no event shall the Adjusted Electric Charge be reduced below the Base Electric Charge).

(g) At Landlord's request, Tenant shall execute and deliver an agreement confirming any change in Fixed Rent under this Section 17.01, but any such change shall be effective even if such agreement is not executed and delivered.

(h) Anything in this Section 17.01 to the contrary notwithstanding, for the period occurring prior to the date Tenant first occupies the Premises for the conduct of business, Tenant shall pay for electricity consumed in the Premises at the rate of [$1.50] per rentable square foot per annum, payable within 10 days after being billed therefor by Landlord.

(i) At Landlord's option, Landlord shall furnish and install all replacement lighting, tubes, lamps, bulbs and ballasts required in the Premises, and Tenant shall pay to Landlord or its designated contractor upon demand Landlord's then established reasonable charges therefor.

17.3 Landlord Concerns

The landlord's choice of pricing mechanism—rent inclusion or submetering—will be responsive to each market (where occupants of larger spaces may well insist on submetering), the subject building's particular capacities (submeters have installation costs), and the size mix of tenancies (multi-tenant floors of small users with shorter terms invite application of the "proportionate share" and/or rent inclusion formulas). In either case, there will be landlord overhead to cover, even with submetering, and that may be met with either a fixed annual fee or a percentage (e.g., 103 percent to 110 percent) of the submetered electricity bill. Since electricity bills may be rendered separately from fixed rent and escalation rent invoices, it is important to set a maximum payment period, for default purposes, and to characterize these payments as "additional rent" in order to permit nonpayment penalties to be applied.

If the landlord begins with a rent inclusion system, or reserves a right to switch to one, it will need the right to survey the tenant's use from time to time in order to make sure the initially chosen price point (see Section 17.01(c), under the "Rent Inclusion" portion of the sample clause set forth in Section 17.2, *supra*) is correctly adjusted to protect the landlord. The tenant, in turn, will desire a right to contest the survey, but may resort to arbitration, if necessary, to settle the point. Opportunity to adjust, constantly and instantly, for the utility's own cost variables (time of day, fuel surcharge, etc.) should be reserved by the landlord, and any such consultant's survey should include the electrical power cost component of the periodic cleaning of the premises.

Given the vicissitudes in the power supply industry and the vagaries of the regulatory authorities, either of which may "change the rules" in the middle of a lease term and dramatically change the building owner's economics or flexibility, some landlords will want to give themselves the ability to change and choose between delivery systems. This flexibility permits such landlords to move from rent inclusion to submetering, or even direct tenant purchase from the utility, without incurring liability to the tenant.

Finally, most landlords will want to insist on the right to "relamp"—that is, provide all lighting supplies on a regular (and frequently profitable) basis.

17.4 Tenant Concerns

If the tenant otherwise likes the proposed space, it will probably not have any choice as to the landlord's method of charging for electricity. If the space is already (or is permitted to be) submetered, the tenant may feel relatively comfortable that its power costs are being adequately measured and appropriately priced (as long as the landlord's supervisory overhead charge is reasonable). If the only available charging method is rent inclusion, the tenant would be well advised to confirm that the per square foot electricity price figure being named is at least comparable to other buildings in the same business district.

More important for the tenant is the maximization of the basic capacity that the landlord undertakes in writing will be available (e.g., 6 watts per rentable square foot). Consultation with a professional engineer may be necessary to confirm that what the landlord can deliver is adequate for the tenant's immediate needs. For the larger or otherwise technology-intensive office user, the ability to increase the capacity as delivered to the tenant's space and/or disproportionately distribute the capacity across its footprint is also important and should be the subject of negotiation.

In any lease contemplating rent inclusion, the ability of the tenant to hire its own electrical consultant is vital, as is the ability to go to binding arbitration in the event the parties or the consultants fail to agree. In any lease allowing the landlord to discontinue power resale service to tenants, a tenant should bargain for an explicit delay in the cutoff date until such time as the direct contract with the private or public utility is secured. Additionally, in any lease where the landlord reserves the right to relamp, that is, to provide lighting supplies to the tenant on a regular basis, the tenant should seek some formal cost control on a comparable-building standard.

17.5 Standard Real Estate Board of New York Clause

> *Electric Current: 12.* Rates and conditions in respect to submetering or rent inclusion, as the case may be, to be added in RIDER attached hereto. Tenant covenants and agrees that at all times its use of electric current shall not exceed the capacity of existing *feeders* to the building or the risers or wiring installation and Tenant may not use any electrical equipment which, in Owner's opinion, reasonably exercised, will overload such installations or interfere with the use thereof by other tenants of the building. The change at any time of the character of electric service shall in no way make Owner liable or responsible to Tenant for any loss, damages or expenses which Tenant may sustain.

17.6 Comments on Standard Real Estate Board of New York Clause

As noted at the very beginning of this chapter, the REBNY form invites the addition of a rider to set the pricing mechanism. Otherwise, these few sentences merely establish that the tenant is not to exceed the system's capacity (without stating that capacity, or undertaking to deliver some "not less than" number of watts per square foot), and further that the owner/landlord is exculpated from any damage resulting from irregularity of supply (including, apparently, even in the event of owner's gross negligence). The prudent tenant will, at a minimum, wish to modify the REBNY form clause in at least those two respects, and may also wish to bargain for some future expansion of capacity, as set forth in the sample clause.

If the owner/landlord's form rider provides for rent inclusion rather than submetering, or for owner/landlord's ability to move to rent inclusion, the tenant will want all the protections discussed in Section 17.4, *supra* ("*Tenant Concerns*"), with regard to that pricing method, and with regard as well to the owner/landlord's possible ability to cut off service before a new direct contract is secured.

17.7 Litigation Issues

Many lawyers representing small office tenants have read language similar to that appearing in the lease construed in *Joffe v. Gramercy Park Bldg. Corp.*[1] without fully comprehending that a landlord could legally, on notice to the tenant, exercise its right to discontinue electric service, thereby causing considerable tenant expense to wire the premises. "The law is plain that a landlord is under no obligation to furnish any service

1. 121 N.Y.S.2d 521 (Sup. Ct. N.Y. Cnty. 1953).

in the absence of a covenant and that a covenant to do so will not be enlarged beyond the express terms of the lease . . . the lease governs completely as to the landlord's obligation to furnish services and the court has no authority to write into the lease an agreement to furnish services not provided for therein."[2] Therefore, when a lease clause merely states that "[I]f Landlord shall purchase or produce the necessary electric current, Tenant shall purchase from Landlord the current consumed . . . ,"[3] there is no express covenant to continue to provide electric service, and none will be implied. Additionally, if a landlord fails to include a provision in a lease requiring a tenant to pay for electricity, none will be implied; nor may the landlord obtain relief under New York Real Property Law section 235-c asserting that the inability to charge a tenant for its electric consumption was unconscionable.[4]

Tenants who pay for electric service on a "rent inclusion" basis are paying a form of rent and not for direct electric consumption. The landlord, in fact, may profit from the additional rent collected. That potential profit, if realized by the landlord, may not form the basis of a defense when billed to the tenant.[5] A tenant should seek the advice of a consultant when establishing the initial charge for the electricity, since that amount is not based on actual consumption.[6] Unless a provision states that the charge is based on the landlord's actual electric cost, the fact that the actual cost is less than the amount billed does not state a cause for relief.[7] The final determination of a rent inclusion amount will be in the hands of a consultant, and provisions deeming such determinations to be binding and final are enforced.[8]

---

2. *Id.* at 524.
3. *Id.* at 522–23.
4. Long Island Ophthalmologic Assoc. v. West Broadway Pro. Bldg., Inc., 88 A.D.2d 585, 449 N.Y.S.2d 793 (2d Dep't 1982).
5. Compton Advert., Inc. v. Madison-59th St. Corp., 91 Misc. 2d 607, 398 N.Y.S.2d 607, *aff'd* 63 A.D.2d 942, 407 N.Y.S.2d 436(1st Dep't 1978).
6. 398 N.Y.S.2d at 612.
7. Revlon Consumer Prods. Corp. v. Arnow, 238 A.D.2d 223, 657 N.Y.S.2d 9 (1st Dep't 1997) (construing a settlement agreement).
8. 99 Realty Co. v. Wall St. Transcript Corp., 165 Misc. 2d 454, 632 N.Y.S.2d 742 (1st Dep't 1995).

CHAPTER 18

Access to the Premises; Changes to the Building

18.1 General Purpose

Notwithstanding that a lease has been entered into, the landlord remains the owner of the leased premises and, accordingly, has an interest in controlling the premises that in many ways overrides the rights granted to the tenant.

A landlord often requires access to, and through, the premises leased to a tenant in order to perform its repair and maintenance obligations toward all tenants in the building, to common areas, and to the building's mechanical systems.

In addition, a landlord wants as much freedom as possible with respect to making alterations to the building, including the tenant's premises. In reserving to itself the right to rearrange and reconstruct the building's public areas, the landlord is simply reconfirming an incontrovertible power over its retained property, and the assertion of the power to control visitor access through such areas. Tenants, of course, are legitimately concerned with maintaining their ease of access during periods of renovation or alteration by the landlord. Tenants may also be dismayed or alarmed at the prospect of lobby reconstruction; but few have the power and/or influence to either demand or prevent it under their lease provisions. Less likely to be viewed as "public" areas are the exteriors of the tenant's windows, or any terraces or roof surfaces that lie beyond them; but the prudent landlord is equally rigorous here. New York was the first state to reject the common law's Law of Ancient Lights (in England a landowner had a right of action against the construction of a neighboring building that cut off his sunlight) on the grounds that "it cannot be applied in the growing cities and villages of this country, without working the most mischievous consequences."[1] The Real Estate Board form brutally reminds the tenant that the darkening of its windows, even if caused by owner/landlord's own acts, is not grounds for rent abatement or eviction. The tenant facing onto a terrace may similarly have its view obscured after lease commencement

1. Parker & Edgarton v. Foote, 19 Wend. 309 (1838).

by erection of a sign or—even more likely today—communications dishes and other such equipment. Also, the landlord commonly reserves the right to change the street address of the building, or the name by which it is commonly known, especially as the latter may be subsequently "sold" to a major tenant as an inducement to lease a large block of space.

Additionally, a landlord requires the right to show the premises to third parties (e.g., prospective tenants, purchasers, and current and prospective lenders). The primary purpose of the access provision is access. Unless this right is specifically stated in the lease, a landlord gives up its rights to the premises for the term of the lease, and may not enter the leased premises without the tenant's permission. The access provision ensures that (1) the landlord has the maximum flexibility in dealing with its property, and (2) the landlord's entry into the tenant's premises for the foregoing reasons will not give rise to a claim by the tenant that its right of quiet enjoyment (see Chapter 25) has been violated.

18.2 Sample Clause

18.01 Access to the Premises; Changes to the Building.

(a) Landlord reserves the right, at any time, to make changes in or to the Project as Landlord may deem necessary or desirable, and Landlord shall have no liability to Tenant therefor, provided any such change does not deprive Tenant of access to the Premises. Landlord may install and maintain pipes, fans, ducts, wires and conduits concealed behind the walls, floors or ceilings of the Premises[, provided that no such installation shall, except to a *de minimis* extent, reduce the size or adversely affect Tenant's use of the Premises]. In exercising its rights under this Section 18.01, Landlord shall endeavor to minimize any interference with Tenant's use of the Premises for the ordinary conduct of Tenant's business, but the foregoing shall not be construed as to require Landlord to perform any associated work on an overtime or premium pay basis. Tenant shall not have any easement or other right in or to the use of any door or any passage or any concourse or any plaza connecting the Building with any other building or to any public conveniences, and the use of such doors, passages, concourses, plazas and conveniences may, without notice to Tenant, be regulated or discontinued at any time by Landlord.

(b) Except for the space within the inside surfaces of all walls, hung ceilings, floors, windows and doors bounding the Premises, all of the Building, including, without limitation, exterior Building walls, core corridor walls and doors and any core corridor entrance, any terraces or roofs adjacent to the Premises, and any space in or adjacent to the Premises used for shafts, stacks, pipes, conduits, fan rooms, ducts, electric or other utilities, sinks or other Building facilities, and the use thereof, as well as access thereto through the

Premises, are reserved to Landlord and are not part of the Premises. Landlord reserves the right to name the Project or any portion thereof, and to change the name or address of the Project or any portion thereof, at any time and from time to time.

(c) Landlord shall have no liability to Tenant if at any time any windows of the Premises are either temporarily darkened or obstructed by reason of any repairs, improvements, construction, maintenance and/or cleaning in or about the Building (or permanently darkened or obstructed if required by Law), or covered by any translucent material for the purpose of energy conservation, or if any part of the Project, other than the Premises, is temporarily or permanently closed or inoperable.

[Alternate Provision: If at any time the windows of the Building are temporarily darkened, or the light, air or view therefrom is obstructed (i) on a temporary basis by reason of any repairs, improvements, maintenance or cleaning in or about the Building or on a permanent basis by reason of a requirement of Law (in which latter event, Tenant shall be entitled to an equitable reduction in base rent to compensate it for the loss of such light, air or view, which reduction shall be as agreed between Landlord and Tenant and, in the absence of agreement, shall be determined by arbitration in accordance with this Lease), or (ii) by reason of any structure that may be erected on lands in the vicinity of the Building, the same shall be without liability to the Landlord and without any reduction or diminution of Tenant's obligations under this Lease and shall not be deemed to constitute an eviction.]

(d) Landlord and persons authorized by Landlord shall have the right, upon prior notice to Tenant (except in an emergency), to enter the Premises (together with any necessary materials and/or equipment), at reasonable times, to inspect or perform such work as Landlord may reasonably deem necessary or to exhibit the Premises to prospective purchasers or, during the last [___] months of the Term, to prospective tenants provided, that, in all cases, Landlord endeavors to minimize interference with the ordinary conduct of business by Tenant in the Premises (without requiring Landlord to perform any work on an overtime or premium pay basis), and provided further, that Landlord and such authorized persons are accompanied by a designated representative of Tenant if Tenant shall have made such representative available. Landlord shall have no liability to Tenant by reason of any such entry. Landlord shall not be required to make any improvements or repairs of any kind or character to the Premises during the Term except as otherwise expressly provided in this Lease.

(e) The exercise of any right reserved to Landlord and such parties in this Article 18 shall be without abatement of rent, without entitling Tenant to claim an eviction and without liability of Landlord or such parties to Tenant.

18.3 Landlord Concerns

The provision gives the landlord maximum flexibility to make alterations to the building, building systems, and common areas, limited only to the extent that such alterations do not deprive the tenant of access to its space. Almost by definition, lobby improvements will be welcomed by all, though there is the potential that the access for certain tenants on certain elevator banks may be diminished in grandeur, if not efficiency; still, that is customarily the landlord's choice. Similarly, the landlord will wish to reserve the right to renumber or rename the building in the future, as a marketing exercise, since a major tenant may as a condition of occupancy desire that the building bear the tenant's name.

Similarly, the landlord should prepare itself against the necessity to darken windows either on a temporary or permanent basis. The "darkening" herein guarded against may result from temporary repairs or construction or result from modern fire laws, requiring windows to be secured by fireproof grates or meshes against flames jumping from a new building constructed nearby (as to the requirements of law, generally, see Chapter 10, *supra*).

Finally, the landlord will be concerned with having access to the tenant's premises so that it may use and manage its property as it wishes, including meeting its obligations in repairing and maintaining the building, the building systems, and the common areas. The provision makes it clear that the landlord is entitled to enter and use the tenant's premises for performing repairs, maintenance, or any alterations it chooses to make. The sample clause specifically identifies those areas of the landlord's property that are not included within the demised premises and reserves the use of, and access to, such areas to the landlord. If, in fact, the landlord agrees to let the tenant use any of the areas specifically excluded from the definition of the premises (e.g., the roof—see Chapter 52), it must be careful to strictly regulate the manner of the tenant's use and access so as not to invalidate any guaranties or warranties the landlord may have, and not to disrupt the proper functioning of building systems and equipment. The landlord also should require an indemnity from the tenant in order to protect it in the event of any such invalidation or disruption caused by the tenant or its agents.

Finally, in the context of a re-letting of the tenant's premises or a sale, financing, or refinancing of the building, it may be desirable or necessary to exhibit the tenant's premises to prospective tenants, prospective purchasers, and existing and prospective ground lessors and lenders. The sample provision permits access for these purposes as well.

18.4 Tenant Concerns

The tenant's concern with this provision in general is that it is overly broad. The tenant wants to limit the landlord's rights as much as possible, giving the landlord certain access rights, but only to the extent necessary for the landlord to comply with its legal obligations (i.e., to other tenants or in the context of compliance with laws).

A tenant is concerned that changes, improvements, or additions made by the landlord to the building could have the effect of impacting the tenant's path of access from the street, through the building and to the tenant's premises, or increasing operating expenses (and thereby increasing the tenant's operating expense escalation payments).

A tenant wants to know, with as much certainty as possible, that throughout the term of the lease it will enjoy all of the benefits bargained for when it entered the lease. Even a "reasonable" deprivation of access to its space, an "immaterial" reduction of the size of its space, or the presence of the landlord's contractor and equipment in its space for a "reasonable" amount of time, may not be acceptable to the tenant. Such being the case, the prudent tenant should endeavor to define what is not acceptable (e.g., reduction in size over percent or square feet; landlord's use of the premises for more than a specified number of days; any permanent loss of visibility of the premises or its signage [for a retail tenant]; loss of a particular means of ingress/egress, etc.).

With respect to sample clause 18.01(b) (see Section 18.2, *supra*), a tenant may want the right to make use of (1) the space above the hung ceiling of the premises (it may even want this space included in the definition of the premises being demised), (2) roof space (to the extent it desires to install antennas, satellite dishes, or other communications equipment) and the building core (in order to install and maintain conduits between the premises and such space), and (3) all common areas and facilities, streets, and sidewalks (on a nonexclusive basis).

Most tenants will be indifferent as to the building name and will rely on the landlord's self-interest not to change it whimsically, or to pick an embarrassing designation for the structure. However, a major tenant whose name recognition is important within its own industry will not want to find itself leasing space in an office tower newly renamed for a major competitor. Such a tenant should demand that this type of name change not occur during its own lease term.

The window closure issue is more sensitive, even if as statistically unlikely as a major lobby renovation during any given tenant term. In the alternate provision set forth in sample clause 18.01(c), *supra*, the tenant has managed to secure agreement for an equitable reduction of base rent if there is a permanent window darkening as a matter of law; but this, admittedly, is a highly unusual landlord concession.

Generally, the tenant wants the landlord to agree to use commercially reasonable efforts not to interfere with the conduct of the tenant's business while the landlord performs any work in or from the premises. Depending on the type of business being operated by the tenant, it may negotiate for no work to be performed during certain hours, days, or seasonal periods.

A tenant would also like to restrict any installations made by the landlord to the areas above the ceiling of the premises, below the floor of the premises, or within the walls of the premises. It would want the landlord to agree to use overtime labor in order to minimize the amount of time spent by the landlord, its agents, or contractors in the tenant's space. If the tenant's business is unreasonably interrupted, the tenant will want an abatement of rent until the landlord has completed its use of the tenant's premises and, if applicable, removed all equipment therefrom. A tenant also wants to make sure the landlord agrees to clean up the premises and restore it to the condition it was in prior to the landlord's entry; repair any damage caused to the premises arising out of any work performed by the landlord, its contractors, or other agents; and to indemnify the tenant against all claims and expenses arising from this work.

In order to protect its property, the tenant should require that the landlord may enter the premises only if accompanied by a representative of the tenant, except in an emergency situation, in which event the landlord should be obligated to use reasonable efforts to contact the tenant before entering. Again, depending on its business, the tenant may want to consider having secured areas in the premises to which access is not permitted except in the case of an emergency, and landlords may be amenable to agreeing subject to capping the amount of space that may be designated as "secure."

Finally, the tenant may try to limit the period during which the landlord may show the premises to prospective tenants (e.g., if a tenant has an unexpired renewal option, the tenant may seek to permit the landlord to show the premises to prospective tenants only after the tenant's right to exercise such renewal option lapses without the tenant having exercised it). It should not be necessary to place "For Rent" signs on the premises in a high-rise office building, and a tenant should request that this statement in the lease be deleted. Any ground- or street-level tenant also should object to this provision because of the potentially negative impact such a sign could have on the tenant's clients/customers.

18.5 Standard Real Estate Board of New York Clause

> *Access to Premises: 13* Owner or Owner's agents shall have the right (but shall not be obligated) to enter the demised premises in any emergency at any time, and, at other reasonable times, to examine the same and to make such repairs, replacements and improvements as Owner may deem necessary and reasonably desirable to the demised premises or to any other portion of the building or which Owner may elect to perform. Tenant shall permit Owner to use and maintain and replace pipes, ducts, and conduits in and through the demised premises and to erect new pipes, ducts, and conduits therein provided they are concealed within the walls, floor, or ceiling. Owner may, during the progress of any work in the demised premises, take all necessary materials and equipment into said premises without the same constituting an eviction, nor shall the Tenant be entitled to any abatement of rent while such work is in progress nor to any damages by reason of loss or interruption of business or otherwise. Throughout the term hereof Owner shall have the right to enter the demised premises at reasonable hours for the purpose of showing the same to prospective purchasers or mortgagees of the building, and during the last six months of the term, for the purpose of showing the same to prospective tenants. If Tenant is not present to open and permit an entry into the demised premises, Owner or Owner's agents may enter the same whenever such entry may be necessary or

permissible by master key or forcibly, and, provided reasonable care is exercised to safeguard Tenant's property, such entry shall not render Owner or its agents liable therefor, nor in any event shall the obligations of Tenant hereunder be affected. If during the last month of the term Tenant shall have removed all or substantially all of Tenant's Property therefrom, Owner may immediately enter, alter, renovate or redecorate the demised premises without limitation or abatement of rent, or incurring liability to Tenant for any compensation, and such act shall have no effect on this lease or Tenant's obligations hereunder.

18.6 Comments on the Standard Real Estate Board of New York Clause

The standard clause addresses the same general concerns as the sample provision. The sample provision, however, elaborates on the following issues: (1) the specific description of areas reserved to the owner/landlord; (2) the specific rights of the owner/landlord to make changes to building common areas and facilities (and the limitations on such rights), to expand the building, and to change ingress and egress; (3) the limitations on the rights of the owner/landlord to make changes in the tenant's premises and the owner/landlord's obligations to minimize interference with the tenant's business; (4) the rights of access of receivers, governmental authorities, ground lessors and lenders; and (5) the ability to place "For Rent" signs on the premises. In addition, the standard clause provides that the owner/landlord may exhibit the premises to prospective tenants only during the last six months of the lease term.

18.7 Litigation Issues

Without an express reservation in a lease for access to a tenant's premises, a landlord has no right to enter the premises,[2] except to comply with an order to cure a serious violation or other emergency.[3]

In *Cohen v. Trestina Dress Manufacturing Co.*,[4] a case involving a landlord's right to access, the court resorted to the rule of reading an entire lease in order to determine the intent of the parties. The lease had a standard right of access, but the tenant argued that other lease provisions should be construed to prohibit the landlord from entering the premises to cure a fire violation by removing a partition between it and another

---

2. Elkar Realty Corp. v. Mitsuye T. Kamada, 6 A.D.2d 155, 175 N.Y.S.2d 669 (1st Dep't 1958) (denying access to permit alteration required by other tenant to comply with law; see also Chapter 7, *supra*); Zwerin v. Geiss, 38 Misc. 2d 306, 237 N.Y.S.2d 280 (NYC Civ. Ct. N.Y. Cnty. 1963) (denying landlord duplicate tenant keys as lease had no right of access).

3. Cohen v. Trestina Dress Mfg. Co., Inc. 15 Misc. 2d 813, 180 N.Y.S.2d 899 (NYC Mun. Ct. 1958) (access sought to cure fire safety hazard). *See also* Klugherz v. Sutphin Food Shop, Inc., 90 Misc. 2d 63, 393 N.Y.S.2d 638 (NYC Civ. Ct. Queens Cnty. 1977) (clean up vacant premises as required by Multiple Dwelling Law), modified by Klugherz v. Sutphin Food Shop, Inc., 91 Misc. 2d 262, 397 N.Y.S.2d 869 (Sup. Ct. N.Y. Cnty. 1977).

4. 15 Misc. 2d 813, 180 N.Y.S.2d 899.

tenant. The partition denied fire exit access to the other tenant. The tenant argued that the premises would be changed by the alteration in that it would share the floor and no longer have a distinct premises. The tenant also asserted that since the landlord consented to the construction of the partition pursuant to the alteration provisions of the lease, the landlord could not remove the partition. The court relied on the tenant's standard compliance with law covenant to conclude that the intent of the lease was to allow access for the purpose of an alteration required to cure a violation.

This case can be contrasted to *Opatoshu v. Concord Properties, Inc.*,[5] a case involving residential tenants. The landlord sought access to certain apartments in order to affix a fire escape to the wall outside their apartments. The alteration was required in order for the landlord to add apartments to the building by subdividing other larger apartments. The lease had a standard access clause, permitting the landlord to "enter the premises . . . to make such alterations and improvements or additions as landlord may deem necessary or desirable, and landlord shall be allowed to take all material into and upon said premises that may be required therefor. . . ." Notwithstanding the broad right of access granted by the lease, the court looked to the covenant of quiet enjoyment in ruling that access for the desired alteration would be denied. The tenant's security and ventilation would be impaired by the alteration, which was intended to increase landlord's profits.

The right of access may also be used not merely to gain access but to counter the defenses, in summary eviction proceedings, of acceptance of surrender[6] or partial eviction.[7] The inclusion of the usual access provision in a lease would appear to be a necessity, but it is not without its problems. Tort lawyers have successfully argued that the inclusion of a right of access provision in a lease (even net leases where all repair and compliance with law provisions are contractually imposed upon the tenant) imposes a duty to effect repairs of conditions that are dangerous or constitute building violations. The right of access charges the landlord with constructive notice of defects in parts of the building where the landlord has access, and deems the landlord to have sufficient control over the premises to impose liability.[8] These cases underscore the need for a landlord, especially in a net lease situation, to carefully draft and monitor the tenant's liability insurance requirements.

The courts have restricted the liability of landlords based on constructive knowledge arising from a reserved right of access. When a lease clearly imposes maintenance obligations upon a tenant, "the general rule has been that, absent statutory duties, a landlord's reservation of the right to enter the leased premises to make repairs or

---

5. 38 Misc. 2d 544, 237 N.Y.S.2d 545 (Sup. Ct. N.Y. Cnty. 1963).

6. 91 Misc. 2d 262, 397 N.Y.S.2d 869 (where landlord entered vacated restaurant to remove vermin and odors; such entry was deemed not to affect an acceptance of a surrender).

7. Winston Churchill Owners Corp. v. Churchill Operating Corp., 193 A.D.2d 396, 597 N.Y.S.2d 62 (1st Dep't 1993) (where right to enter for repairs defeated defense partial eviction, even if time of entry was unreasonable).

8. Guzman v. Haven Plaza Hous. Dev. Fund Co., Inc., 69 N.Y.2d 559, 516 N.Y.S.2d 451, 509 N.E.2d 51 (1987).

correct improper conditions does not impose liability for a subsequently arising dangerous condition."[9] When all leases required tenants to "take good care of the demised premises, including bathroom and lavatory facilities," and a tenant sustained damage due to a leaking toilet in another tenant's premises, "the out-of-possession defendant-landlord is not responsible for plaintiff's losses notwithstanding the right to reenter under the lease."[10] Proof of actual or constructive knowledge of the condition would have to arise from more than mere inclusion of a right of access in the lease.

---

9. Manning v. New York Tel. Co., 157 A.D.2d 264, 555 N.Y.S.2d 720 (1st Dep't 1990) (distinguishing itself from *Guzman v. Haven Plaza*, because the injury arose from ordinary maintenance, which was a tenant obligation, and there was no statutory obligation on the landlord to remedy the slippery floor causing plaintiff's fall).

10. Sally Lu Fashions Corp. v. A-Chau Realty Corp., 191 A.D.2d 276, 595 N.Y.S.2d 23 (1st Dep't 1993).

CHAPTER 19

Certificate of Occupancy

19.1 General Purpose

In most jurisdictions, a certificate of occupancy issued by the local buildings department or similar municipal authority is generally a prerequisite to the occupancy of space. The certificate of occupancy may specify the use or uses for which occupancy is permitted (as is the case in New York City). If permitted uses are not set forth in the certificate of occupancy, then local zoning laws must be consulted to determine what uses are and are not permitted. In some jurisdictions, including in New York City, the certificate of occupancy also sets forth the maximum permitted floor loads for each floor of a building. Certificates of occupancy may be temporary or permanent; and it is common for temporary certificates to be issued for new construction and to be maintained by many New York City buildings pending completion of certain requirements of the municipality. Certificates of occupancy may be issued for entire buildings (as they are in New York City) or may be issued for individual spaces within a building.

19.2 Sample Clause

See the Standard Real Estate Board of New York clauses set forth in Section 19.5, *infra*. Most New York office leases do not include a separate section with respect to certificates of occupancy, but merely include references in other locations such as those in the board form.

19.3 Landlord Concerns

Most landlords will not and, indeed, should not make representations to tenants as to the uses that are permitted under applicable laws in a particular demised premises. Even if a lease permits the premises to be used solely for office purposes, and the governing certificate of occupancy states that "office" use is permitted in the premises, the meaning of "office" use under local zoning laws, and the question of what ancillary and incidental uses may or may not be encompassed therein is not always a straightforward question. As a result, landlords routinely maintain that the burden is on the tenant to determine that its intended use of the premises is permissible under law. Some lease forms go a step further and include a disclaimer that the statement of permitted uses in the lease does not constitute a representation that such uses are legally permissible. Such a disclaimer merely highlights the landlord's position that it is the tenant's burden, and not the landlord's, to determine permitted uses under law.

19.4 Tenant Concerns

The provisions of a certificate of occupancy are one more factor to be considered (together with the use clause of the lease—see Chapter 6, *supra*) in a tenant's determination of whether its intended use of any premises is permissible, and a review of the governing certificate of occupancy should always be a part of the tenant's due diligence before signing a lease. As set forth earlier, landlords will rarely accept the burden of ensuring that all of the tenant's desired uses will be permitted under law, and it is left to the tenant to ensure that its occupancy will not violate applicable laws.

A tenant must bear in mind that the meaning of terms under applicable zoning laws must be properly interpreted. For example, the fact that a certificate of occupancy states that "office" use is permitted in a certain space does not necessarily mean that one is permitted to operate a large-scale cafeteria; install an auditorium; provide banking, travel, or other services that may be considered retail; or conduct light manufacturing such as operating printing presses. In other words, the same issues that arise in negotiating a lease's use clause with respect to permitted incidental and ancillary uses in the demised premises must also be addressed in the context of what is permitted under law. If a tenant believes that any aspect of its intended use will in fact require a change to the governing certificate of occupancy, it should seek to have included in the lease an obligation on the part of the landlord to diligently prosecute such change.

A tenant may want the landlord to covenant that it will keep a certificate of occupancy in effect at all times, particularly where, at the inception of a lease, there is only a temporary certificate of occupancy that must be periodically renewed. The tenant can also seek to have the landlord covenant that the landlord will not take actions that will result in a certificate of occupancy being suspended, or the permitted uses of the premises being changed. Finally, while the landlord will rarely agree to representations as to what uses constitute permitted uses, most landlords will be willing to represent that a particular form constitutes the certificate of occupancy that exists on the date a lease is signed.

19.5 Standard Real Estate Board of New York Clause

> *Requirements of Law, Fire Insurance, Floor Loads: 6. …* Tenant shall not place a load upon any floor of the demised premises exceeding the floor load per square foot area which it was designed to carry and which is allowed by law.
>
> *Occupancy: 15.* Tenant will not at any time use or occupy the demised premises in violation of the certificate of occupancy issued for the building of which the demised premises are a part.

19.6 Comments on Standard Real Estate Board of New York Clause

As set forth earlier, the board form clauses adequately set forth the basic concerns of a landlord relevant to a certificate of occupancy. The tenant's concerns with respect to such clause are described in detail in Section 19.4, *supra*.

19.7 Litigation Issues

The absence of a certificate of occupancy does not render a lease void due to illegality;[1] nor does the mere lack of a certificate alone give a tenant a right to cancel a lease,[2] even when the landlord agreed to procure an amended certificate of occupancy and failed to do so;[3] nor does the issuance of a building violation because the permitted use in the lease violated the existing certificate of occupancy constitute a defense to payment of rent.[4]

The outcome in favor of the landlord in the nonpayment proceeding in *Phillips & Huyler Associates v. Flynn*[5] represents what a tenant should expect in a standard lease, without any warranties as to legality of use or compliance of the permitted use with the certificate of occupancy. The tenant leased an apartment for the permitted use as an office for psychotherapy. The certificate of occupancy, however, only permitted residential use. The tenant was not permitted to defend the nonpayment proceedings on the basis of the lack of a certificate of occupancy. The landlord had made no representation that the use complied with the certificate, and the tenant used the premises despite the violation.

When a tenant does obtain a representation that the permitted use complies with the certificate of occupancy, and as a result of the breach of that representation is unable to use the premises, there are grounds to cancel a lease.[6] Even without an affirmative representation, if, for reasons beyond the tenant's control, the tenant is unable to obtain a change in a certificate of occupancy permitting the manner of use contemplated by a lease, the lease may be voided.[7] When a tenant asserts that the lack of a certificate of occupancy should be the grounds for cancellation of a lease, the courts will look to see if the actual use of the premises is interfered with, and whether the proper certificate

1. Kosher Konvenience, Inc. v. Ferguson Realty Corp., 171 A.D.2d 650, 567 N.Y.S.2d 131 (2d Dep't 1991).

2. Jordache Enters., Inc. v. Gettinger Assocs., 176 A.D.2d 616, 575 N.Y.S.2d 58 (1st Dep't 1991); *but see* Jack Kelly Partners LLC v. Zegelstein, 140 A.D.3d 79, 82, 33 N.Y.S.3d 7, 8 (N.Y. App. Div. 2016) (noting that Jordache Enters. dealt with a scenario where the lack of a valid certificate could be readily cured, rather than a case where the certificate may not be remediable).

3. Cutler-Hammer, Inc. v. One Lincoln Assocs., Etc., 79 A.D.2d 512, 433 N.Y.S.2d 455 (1st Dep't 1980).

4. Abright v. Shapiro, 92 A.D.2d 452, 458 N.Y.S.2d 913 (1st Dep't 1983).

5. 164 Misc. 2d 347, 627 N.Y.S.2d 868 (Sup. Ct. App. Tm. 1st Dep't 1995).

6. Turmon v. Fantasia Auto, Inc., 147 Misc. 2d 450, 556 N.Y.S.2d 195 (Dist. Ct. Nassau Cnty. 1990) (the court permitted a tenant to cancel a lease when the landlord represented that the premises could be used for an auto body shop "pursuant to the Certificate of Occupancy").

7. Elkar Realty Corp. v. Mitsuye T. Kamada, 6 A.D.2d 155, 175 N.Y.S.2d 669 (1st Dep't 1958).

can easily be obtained.[8] A landlord may not have represented that the certificate of occupancy allows the use permitted by the lease, but it has a good faith obligation to assist the tenant in changing the certificate of occupancy if that permitted use would violate the limitations of the certificate.[9]

Roli-Blue, Inc. v. 69/70th Street Associates[10] is an interesting case showing that the inability to use the premises because of a certificate of occupancy violation, not caused by the tenant, can impose liability on a landlord despite the absence of breach of lease representations.

At the time a lease was signed, the certificate of occupancy permitted restaurant use. The tenant expended hundreds of thousands of dollars to improve the premises; the landlord also substantially renovated the building where the restaurant was located. The building department refused to grant a new certificate of occupancy to the landlord until it complied with building code regulations. Until the new certificate was issued, the tenant could not obtain an assembly permit required to operate a restaurant. As the tenant was not ousted from possession, it could not maintain an action against the landlord for breach of a covenant of quiet enjoyment. The landlord asserted that it had no liability to the tenant pursuant to the lease because no representation was made as to the certificate of occupancy, and the lease stated that "Landlord does not warrant that the Demised Premises may be used for the purposes mentioned in the Lease. In the event that the occupancy by Tenant is or becomes in violation of the rules and regulations of any City or State Department, Tenant shall commence curing such violations at Tenant's own cost and expense. . . ." The landlord further sought protection from the merger clause negating any representation as to the condition of the building.

Neither the absence of a warranty concerning the legality of the use pursuant to the certificate of the occupancy, nor either of the preceding stated provisions, could insulate the landlord from a suit for damages for breach of contract. The court held that

> While ordinarily, denial of a license precluding further use of the premises lawfully for the purpose for which the lease was intended does not relieve a lessee of an unconditional promise to pay rent, where the parties understood that a license had to be obtained before the premises could be so used . . . a landlord may not render the contemplated use unlawful by his own conduct. An obligation on the part of a landlord to maintain a building's certificate of occupancy will be implied if it may rightfully be assumed that the parties themselves would have imposed such an obligation had their attention been drawn to it, and their conduct inspired by principles of justice.[11]

---

8. Jordache Enters., Inc. v. Gettinger Assoc., 176 A.D.2d 616, 575 N.Y.S.2d 58 (1st Dep't 1991); Kosher Konvenience, Inc. v. Ferguson Realty Corp., 171 A.D.2d 650, 567 N.Y.S.2d 131(2d Dep't 1991); Cutler-Hammer, Inc. v. One Lincoln Assoc., Etc., 79 A.D.2d 512, 433 N.Y.S.2d 455 (1st Dep't 1980).

9. Time Square Stores Corp., Inc. v. Bernice Realty Co., Inc., 141 A.D.2d 536, 529 N.Y.S.2d 148 (2d Dep't 1988).

10. 119 A.D.2d 173, 506 N.Y.S.2d 159 (1st Dep't 1986).

11. 506 N.Y.S.2d at 161.

CHAPTER 20

Default (Conditional Limitation)

20.1 General Purpose

The provisions in a commercial space lease entitled "Default" or "Conditional Limitations" are the clauses that provide that the term of a lease must (or may, at landlord's option and notice) terminate and end, if an event defined in the lease occurs. Because of their length and complexity, these provisions are customarily separated from and followed by the provisions on "remedies" (see Chapter 21, *infra*), which spell out the choices that a landlord has to recoup its losses following the original tenant's termination upon the now-occurred and properly noticed condition of the "default" or "breach."

Discussion of some technical distinctions is in order here because "conditional limitations" and "conditions" are different legal classifications, despite their customary combination under the general heading of "default." Where the lease describes an event, the occurrence of which ends the term ("expires" or "terminates" or "is canceled" are all common and legally effective phrases), a "conditional limitation" has been created, and upon the happening of the event the lease automatically expires. A conditional limitation may be what has been styled as an "objective contingency," that is, an event that is not controlled by the landlord or the tenant, such as the involuntary bankruptcy of the tenant. Another type of conditional limitation may arise from the conduct of one of the parties, such as the sale of the premises by the landlord (followed by the occurrence of the event of receipt by tenant of the landlord's notice of sale, which receipt terminates the lease).

The last and most familiar form of conditional limitation, which is really the category of classic tenant "default," is the provision for the earlier expiration of the lease upon the occurrence of a specified contingency. Most frequently this contingency constitutes the lapse of time fixed in a notice given by a landlord upon the notice-identified breach of the lease by tenant. If the lease clearly provides that the term shall automatically expire upon the lapse of time fixed in a notice from the landlord, courts will rule this to be a conditional limitation, but the lack of such language may result in a finding that the provision is a "condition." In and of itself, the breach of a condition does not terminate the lease. It continues on unchanged unless and until the landlord, if it has the right to declare a forfeiture based on the breach of the condition, elects to exercise that right.

It may be argued that a "condition," coupled with a landlord right to declare forfeiture for the condition's breach, is effectively what happens, with the giving of the notice of forfeiture, with a "conditional limitation," and indeed a New York court has parsed the connective proposition in this manner:

> The breach is only an event antecedent to, and not the direct cause of, the expiration. The landlord is given the privilege in the original instrument to cancel it by notice, which practically substitutes a short period for the original term, and whether the occasion of this notice is the breach of the condition or a cause which does not reflect upon the tenant's conduct is quite immaterial. The lease expires by a mode of limitation which the landlord is granted the sole privilege to exercise.[1]

To avoid what this decision styled "subtle distinctions between conditions and limitations," it is better and safer landlord practice to employ the narrow and precise and case-law–tested language of conditional limitation.

What is therefore imperative, to protect a landlord, is that the occurrence of a stated event will end the lease, as if by its terms the lease had been originally limited to that time, even though the initiation of the determining event (the passage of time after the sending of a notice that need not necessarily be sent) is entirely optional with landlord. If the conditional limitation is properly stated, New York case law holds that a further provision granting the landlord the choice of either repossessing the property (reentry), or of reletting the premises as agent for tenant and holding tenant liable for any deficiency, does not negate the conditional limitation. (See Chapter 21, Remedies and Damages, *infra*.)

Note that, generally, a conditional limitation providing the landlord with a termination option is deemed to "run with the land" and thus benefits successors in interest to the original landlord. Conversely, the burden of a conditional limitation runs with the leasehold estate, allowing enforcement against an assignee. Nothing prevents the parties, however, from limiting a right to terminate the lease to such individually identified persons as they choose (e.g., a conditional limitation respecting the original tenant's continued possession of a particular license for its specialized business, the loss of which terminates the lease).

20.2 Sample Clause

Section 20.01 Default (Conditional Limitation).

This Lease and the term and estate hereby granted are subject to the limitation that:

---

1. Burnee Corp. v. Uneeda Pure Orange Drink Co., 132 Misc. 435, 443, 230 N.Y.S. 239, 251 (Sup. Ct. App. Tm. 1st Dep't 1928).

(a) if Tenant defaults in the payment of any Rent, and such default continues for 5 Business Days after Landlord gives to Tenant a notice specifying such default, or

(b) if Tenant defaults in the keeping, observance or performance of any covenant or agreement (other than a default of the character referred to in Sections 20.01(a), (c), (d), (e), (f), (g), or (h)), and if such default continues and is not cured within 30 days after Landlord gives to Tenant a notice specifying the same, or, in the case of a default that for causes beyond Tenant's reasonable control cannot with due diligence be cured within such period of 30 days, if Tenant shall not promptly after the receipt of such notice, (A) advise Landlord of Tenant's intention duly to institute all steps necessary to cure such default (B) institute and thereafter diligently prosecute to completion all steps necessary to cure the same and (C) actually cure the same within [90] days after Landlord gives to Tenant such initial notice specifying the same, or

(c) if there shall be any direct or indirect assignment (including, without limitation, any direct or indirect transfer of the interests in Tenant which is deemed to constitute an assignment hereunder), subletting or other transfer of this Lease or the term and estate granted hereby or of the right to occupy all or any portion of the Premises, whether voluntary, involuntary, by operation of law or otherwise, except as expressly permitted by Article 16, or

(d) if Tenant shall abandon the Premises (and the fact that any of Tenant's Property remains in the Premises shall not be evidence that Tenant has not abandoned the Premises), or

(e) if a default of the kind set forth in Section 20.01(a) or (b) shall occur and have been cured, and if a similar default shall occur more than once within the next 365 days, whether or not such similar defaults are cured within the applicable grace period, or

(f) if Tenant fails to deliver to Landlord any Letter of Credit within the time period required under this Lease, or

(g) (i) if Tenant shall (A) make a general assignment for the benefit of creditors, (B) admit in writing its inability to pay its debts as they become due, (C) file a voluntary petition in bankruptcy, (D) become insolvent, (E) file any petition or answer seeking for itself any reorganization, arrangement, composition, readjustment of debt, liquidation or dissolution or similar relief under any present or future statute, law or regulation of any jurisdiction, (F) petition or apply for any receiver, custodian or any trustee for any substantial part of its property, (G) take any formal action for the purpose of effecting any of the foregoing or looking to its liquidation or winding up, (H) die or (I) become incompetent, or

(ii) if an order for relief is entered under any bankruptcy or similar law or any other decree or order is entered by a court of competent jurisdiction (A) adjudicating Tenant bankrupt or insolvent, (B) approving as properly filed a petition seeking reorganization, arrangement, adjustment or composition of or in respect of Tenant, (C) appointing a receiver, liquidator, assignee, trustee, custodian, sequestrator (or other similar official) of Tenant or of any substantial part of its property, or (D) ordering the winding up or liquidation of the affairs of Tenant, and any such decree or order continues unstayed and in effect for a period of 90 days,

(h) (i) if the Guaranty shall for any reason cease to be in full force and effect, or

(ii) if (A) any representation or warranty made by Guarantor in the Guaranty shall at any time be false or misleading in any material respect, (B) Guarantor fails to comply with any covenant made by it in the Guaranty and such failure continues beyond any applicable notice and/or grace period, or (C) Guarantor attempts to revoke, disavow, contest, commence any action or, except as may be expressly permitted under the Guaranty, raise any defense against its obligations under the Guaranty, or

(iii) if Guarantor shall (A) cease to be actively involved in Tenant's business, (B) make a general assignment for the benefit of creditors, (C) admit in writing its inability to pay its debts as they become due, (D) file a voluntary petition in bankruptcy, (E) become insolvent, (F) file any petition or answer seeking for itself any reorganization, arrangement, composition, readjustment of debt, liquidation or dissolution or similar relief under any present or future statute, law or regulation of any jurisdiction, (G) petition or apply for any receiver, custodian or any trustee for any substantial part of its property, (H) take any formal action for the purpose of effecting any of the foregoing or looking to its liquidation or winding up, (I) die or (J) become incompetent, or

(iv) if an order for relief is entered under any bankruptcy or similar law or any other decree or order is entered by a court of competent jurisdiction (A) adjudicating Guarantor bankrupt or insolvent, (B) approving as properly filed a petition seeking reorganization, arrangement, adjustment or composition of or in respect of Guarantor, (C) appointing a receiver, liquidator, assignee, trustee, custodian, sequestrator (or other similar official) of Guarantor or of any substantial part of its property, or (D) ordering the winding up or liquidation of the affairs of Guarantor, and any such decree or order continues unstayed and in effect for a period of 90 days, then, in any of such cases, in addition to any other remedies available to Landlord at law or in equity, Landlord shall be entitled to give to Tenant a notice of intention to end the Term at the expiration of 3 days from the date of the giving of such notice, and, in the event such notice is given, this Lease and the term and estate hereby granted shall terminate upon the expiration of such 3 days with the same effect as if the last of such 3 days were the Expiration Date, but Tenant shall remain liable for damages as provided herein or pursuant to law.

20.3 Landlord Concerns

The task of a landlord's counsel is to clearly identify those circumstances that, when they occur, will permit the landlord to quickly reenter the premises in order to salvage the situation threatened by the original tenant's nonpayment, nonperformance, or (within the bankruptcy/insolvency categories) the imminent threat of future nonpayment. These are the three classic categories of default: nonpayment, nonperformance of a tenant covenant that does not involve payment (e.g., subletting without permission, or failure to provide proof of insurance coverage, or to renew insurance coverage), and a tenant's insolvency. The prudent landlord will also wish to protect himself against the tenant who is chronically late with the rent, or careless in adhering to other covenants of performance or behavior. Under these circumstances a "multiple breach" provision may be added to convert the succession of such breaches within a stated period into a conditional limitation.

Since "performance" breaches may not be as clear-cut as nonpayment breaches, and therefore not so easily cured by the tenant, the landlord must ensure that notice provisions of the lease (which customarily include notice of default, see Chapter 30, *infra*) are precise and strictly followed in the event of the need to give notice. A tenant will customarily request that the standard 30-day provision for cure of a performance default be extended in those cases where it is unreasonable to expect a cure to be effected within such a short period of time. Under these circumstances it is equally important, as a matter of practice for the landlord, to give a prompt notice once the default becomes known in order to start the tolling of the expanded time period.

In any event, if the tenant is to be granted more than 30 days to cure a breach in performance, the landlord should insist that tenant (1) advise landlord of tenant's intention duly to institute all steps necessary to cure such default, (2) institute and thereafter diligently prosecute to completion all steps necessary to cure the same, and (3) in any case cure the applicable default before a firm deadline beyond which not even that effort would prevent the expiration of the lease.

Also, the landlord should provide that any language affording the tenant an extended cure period will apply only to defaults outside those specifically identified in this article's (see Section 20.2, *supra*) numbered schedule, and not to the enumerated conditional limitations, which have much shorter or even no grace periods (by way of illustration, see the first parenthetical in Section 20.01(b) of the sample clause set forth in Section 20.2, *supra*).

Finally, the landlord must be prepared for the imposition of the automatic stay in a bankruptcy proceeding, or the resort by a tenant to a so-called *Yellowstone*[2] injunction proceeding brought to stop a termination.

20.4 Tenant Concerns

Termination may be an appropriate remedy for a tenant's default, but given the value of the leasehold interest at stake, the tenant's counsel is entitled to insist that the litany of default clauses be fair, and that unintentional minor omissions do not bring on doomsday.

With respect to rent defaults, tenants must be keenly aware that courts will allow forfeiture for late payment, since timely payment of rent is the primary covenant of their breed.[3] Nevertheless, there must be reasonable allowance for occasional lax procedures, human error, or the sometime failure of the postal or federal funds wiring system; thus, a grace period of five business days, with the rent due on the first of the month, is usually both requested and granted. However, a grace period without more is not wholly sufficient, if the tenant remains unaware that a payment duly made has not been received. Thus, the careful tenant will insist that the cure period commence from

2. The *Yellowstone* injunction derives its name from First Nat'l Stores v. Yellowstone Shopping Ctr., 21 N.Y.2d 630, 290 N.Y.S.2d 721, 237 N.E.2d 868 (1968). "The purpose of the Yellowstone injunction is to allow a tenant confronted by a threat of termination of the lease to obtain a stay tolling the running of the cure period so that, after a determination of the merits, the tenant may cure the defect and avoid a forfeiture of the leasehold." Empire State Bldg. Assocs. v. Trump Empire State Partners, 245 A.D.2d 225, 667 N.Y.S.2d 31, 34 (1st Dep't 1997); *see also* 159 MP Corp. v. Redbridge Bedford LLC, 33 N.Y.3d 353, 128 N.E.3d 128 (Ct. App. 2019) (upholding a waiver in a commercial lease of a tenant's right to bring a declaratory judgment action with respect to the provisions of said lease); NYRP § 235-h (superseding the 159 MP Corp. v. Redbridge Bedford LLC decision and disallowing such waivers). In 159 MP Corp. v. Redbridge Bedford LLC, a commercial landlord served its tenant with a notice to cure various defaults within 15 days, failing which the lease would terminate. The tenant commenced an action seeking a declaratory judgment that it was not in default and moved for a *Yellowstone* injunction to toll the cure period and prevent the landlord from terminating the lease or commencing summary proceedings. The trial court denied the tenant's motion for a *Yellowstone* injunction and dismissed the action based on a waiver in the lease of tenant's right to seek a declaratory judgment as to the terms of the lease. The trial court's decision was appealed, and upheld by both the Appellate Division and the Court of Appeals. As the Court of Appeals explained, clear and complete contracts should be enforced according to their terms, particularly in the context of real property transactions involving sophisticated, counseled parties. The Court of Appeals stated that only a limited set of public policy interests outweigh the public policy favoring freedom of contract, none of which were at issue in the case. In response to the Court of Appeal's decision in 159 MP Corp. v. Redbridge Bedford LLC, the legislature enacted NYRP § 235-h, which disallows the waiver or prohibition of a commercial tenant's right to bring a declaratory judgment action with respect to any provision, term, or condition of a commercial lease. Such waivers are deemed null and void as against public policy.

3. See Fifty States Mgmt. Corp. v. Pioneer Auto Parts, Inc., 46 N.Y.2d 573, 415 N.Y.S.2d 800, 389 N.E.2d 113 (1979) (reversing the Appellate Division determination that enforcing an acceleration clause due to nonpayment of rent would be an unconscionable forfeiture).

the date of the landlord's notice of nonpayment, and not merely from the date on which the lease defines payment as having been "due."

A lease contains numerous performance covenants other than merely the payment of rent and other sums, and the breach of any such nonmonetary covenants that are not themselves specifically enumerated defaults should not trigger an immediate default so long as the tenant commits to the landlord that the tenant will cure such breach and in fact exercises reasonable diligence in doing so. A tenant should seek to negotiate the longest possible time period to cure such breaches so as to avoid losing its leasehold estate as the result of a harmless "foot fault" or a breach that, by its nature, cannot reasonably be cured within a shorter time frame.

20.5 Standard Real Estate Board of New York Clause

The REBNY article, although loosely entitled "Default," correctly employs the standard language of conditional limitation (bracketed captions have been added):

> *Default*
>
> *17(1) [Defaults and Periods to Cure]* If Tenant defaults in fulfilling any of the covenants of this lease other than the covenants for the payment of rent or additional rent; or if the demised premises become vacant or deserted; or if any execution or attachment shall be issued against Tenant or any of Tenant's property whereupon the demised premises shall be taken or occupied by someone other than Tenant; or if this lease be rejected under § 365 of Title 11 of the U.S. Code (Bankruptcy Code); or if Tenant shall have failed, after five (5) days written notice, to redeposit with Owner any portion of the security deposit hereunder which Owner has applied to the payment of any rent and additional rent due and payable hereunder; or if Tenant shall be in default with respect to any other lease between Owner and Tenant; or if Tenant shall fail to move into or take possession of the premises within thirty (30) days after the commencement of the term of this lease, then, in any one or more of such events, upon Owner serving a written fifteen (15) days' notice upon Tenant specifying the nature of said default and upon the expiration of said fifteen (15) days, if Tenant shall have failed to comply with or remedy such default, or if the said default or omission complained of shall be of a nature that the same cannot be completely cured or remedied within said fifteen (15) day period, and if Tenant shall not have diligently commenced curing such default within such fifteen (15) day period, and shall not thereafter with reasonable diligence and in good faith proceed to remedy or cure such default, then Owner may serve a written five (5) days' notice of cancellation of this lease upon Tenant, and upon the expiration of said five (5) days this lease and the term thereunder shall end and expire as fully and completely as if the expiration of said five (5) day period were the day herein definitely fixed for the end and expiration of this lease and the term hereof and Tenant shall then quit and surrender the demised premises to Owner, but Tenant shall remain liable as hereinafter provided.

(2) [Re-entry, Dispossession, Waiver of Notices] If the notice provided for in (1) hereof shall have been given, and the term shall expire as aforesaid; or if tenant shall make default in the payment of the rent reserved herein or any item of additional rent herein mentioned or any part of either or in making any other payment herein required; then and in any of such events Owner may, without notice, reenter the demised premises either by force or otherwise, and dispossess Tenant by summary proceedings or otherwise, and the legal representative of Tenant or other occupant of demised premises and remove their effects and hold the premises as if this lease had not been made, and Tenant hereby waives the service of notice of intention to re-enter or to institute legal proceedings to that end. If Tenant shall make default hereunder prior to the date fixed as the commencement of any renewal or extension of this lease, Owner may cancel and terminate such renewal or extension agreement by written notice.

20.6 Comments on the Standard Real Estate Board of New York Clause

The REBNY provisions on default/conditional limitations leave little to be desired from the landlord's perspective, unless one would wish to add a requirement (noted in the sample clause set forth in Section 20.2, *supra*) that the tenant send a notice in a situation where the cure was foreseen to take longer than the 15-day cure period permitted by the clause.

Not surprisingly, with this landlord-sponsored form, the tenant has rather more improvements to seek. First, since a conditional limitation for the premises becoming "vacant or deserted" is a bit vague, a time period definition ("for more than three consecutive months") might be added. Also, the Bankruptcy Code reference is properly section 365 of Title 11, not section 235. Next, the conditional limitation on the move-in date, set in the form at 15 days, should perhaps be expanded to 30 days. In any event, it should be made to conform to other lease provisions that may make the occupancy/rent commencement date occur far beyond a mere 30 days after the formal "commencement" (execution) date of the lease. Expanding this period will have the happy result of simultaneously expanding the cure period for all other performance defaults, as contained in the very first clause of subsection (1) of REBNY article 17 (for the cure of which, see the sample clause discussion in Section 20.4, *supra*, suggesting that 20 to 30 days is more customary).

The tenant should argue that the five-day periods of limitation could be expanded to ten or even 15 days, thus providing the tenant with useful recovery time, without the owner/landlord suffering significant additional harm. Finally, in subparagraph (2), it is clearer and fairer to insert stated time periods on the rent defaults, such as five days after the mandated date of payment of "the rent reserved herein," and ten days for making "any other payment herein required" (since the tenant's treasurer will not have been able to put periodic procedures in place for more irregular or unusual types of lease payments, for overtime services, or what-have-you), and those payments should clearly be due within those time periods running from the delivery of invoices, by way of appropriate notice.

20.7 Litigation Issues

Equity may abhor a forfeiture, but such is the daily grist of landlord-tenant court. A tenant's attorney may attempt to cure an adjudicated rent default by resorting to Real Property Actions and Proceedings Law (RPAPL) section 751(1), which provides for a stay upon the payment of rent, or upon supplying an undertaking, to the court.[4] Notwithstanding the aforesaid abhorrence and statutory protection, the court will enforce the termination of a commercial lease for nonpayment of rent by conditional limitation;[5] and if nonpayment of rent is set forth among the events that trigger a conditional limitation, a tenant's attorney would serve his client well by carving the rent default out of the clause.[6]

If a lease is terminated by conditional limitation, the remedy is summary holdover proceedings, and the sole issue is whether the tenant is in possession beyond the expiration of the term. In *Perrotta v. Western Regional Off-Track Betting Corp.*,[7] the court stated that in order for a provision to constitute a conditional limitation,

> the tenancy must be ended automatically by lapse of time and not by election of the landlord to forfeit the lease for breach of a condition *[references omitted]*. If a clause in a lease provides that the lease cannot endure beyond the time when a contingency happens, it creates a conditional limitation upon the occurrence of which the lease automatically expires; a summary proceeding will lie to evict a tenant who remains thereafter *[references omitted]*.[8]

The court in *Perrotta* held that the following language did not constitute a conditional limitation:

> That the Tenants . . . shall not . . . make any alterations on the premises without the Landlord's consent in writing; . . . and *in the event of a breach the term*

4. *See generally* FINKELSTEIN & FERRARA, LANDLORD AND TENANT PRACTICE IN NEW YORK, ch. 14, "Nonpayment Proceedings" (1997).

5. B. Boman & Co., Inc. v. Pro. Data Mgmt., Inc., 218 A.D.2d 637, 631 N.Y.S.2d 19 (1st Dep't 1995) (applying conditional limitation in overlease to sublease since default provisions of master lease were incorporated in sublease by reference); Ranalli v. Burns, 157 A.D.2d 936, 550 N.Y.S.2d 192 (3d Dep't 1990). [NOTE: this case and the subsequent case law deal with the sufficiency of notice for a summary proceeding. *See* J.D. Realty Assocs. v. Jorrin, 166 Misc. 2d 17d, distinguishing itself from Ranalli because although the notice of default there did not include a dollar amount of rent, Ranalli involved a contractual notice provision and the court in Ranalli cited to the notice statute at issue in J.D. Assocs. by mistake, thus the sufficiency of the notice in Ranalli wasn't relevant to the sufficiency of notice in J.D. Assocs. Either way, it seems that the statement is not made untrue by J.D. Assocs.]

6. Lambert Houses Redevelopment Co. v. Adam & Peck Org., Inc., 169 Misc. 2d 667, 652 N.Y.S.2d 202 (Sup. Ct. App. Tm. 1st Dep't 1996).

7. 98 A.D.2d 1, 469 N.Y.S.2d 504, 505 (4th Dep't 1983); *see also* S. St. Seaport Ltd. P'ship v. Jade Sea Rest., Inc., 151 Misc. 2d 725, 573 N.Y.S.2d 568 (NYC Civ. Ct. N.Y. Cnty. 1991).

8. 469 N.Y.S.2d at 505.

herein shall immediately cease and determine at the option of the Landlord as if it were the expiration of the original term.[9]

The *Perrotta* court stated further that "Although the clause specifies that the term 'shall immediately cease' upon the happening of the contingency (i.e., making of alterations without the landlord's consent), this language does not become operative unless and until the landlord elects to exercise its option to give it effect."[10]

The court in *Perrotta* did find that another provision was a conditional limitation. In the event of a default, such as a default in payment of rent, ". . . the Landlord may, if the Landlord so elects, at any time thereafter terminate this lease and the term hereof, on giving Tenant five days' notice in writing . . . , and this lease and the term hereof shall expire and come to an end on the date fixed in such notice as if the said date were the date originally fixed in this lease for expiration hereof."[11] The landlord's election is to give a notice of termination; once the notice is given, the lease term automatically expires on the date set forth in the notice.

In *South Street Seaport Ltd. Partnership v. Jade Sea Restaurant, Inc.*,[12] the court found that a landlord's right to terminate the lease due to the tenant's gross sales falling below $2,000,000, and the tenant's failure to submit a required certification of sales, created a condition subsequent and not a conditional limitation. The pertinent provision stated that ". . . if Tenant's Gross Sales during the calendar year 1990 do not exceed $2,000,000 Landlord shall have the option to terminate the lease. . . ."[13] The "option" to terminate rendered the clause a condition subsequent, and thus the landlord had to resort to an action in ejectment and not summary proceedings.

Where a lease contains a conditional limitation, the tenant's attorney must advise a tenant that, in the event of receipt of a notice to cure, a *Yellowstone* injunction[14] should be immediately sought before the cure period expires. Absent tenant obtaining an injunction (or actual cure of the alleged default) prior to the date set forth in the notice for the lease termination, the lease will terminate by its terms and cannot be revived by a court.[15] As such, a tenant's attorney should negotiate for the longest cure period to provide the tenant with sufficient time to obtain a *Yellowstone* injunction.

A *Yellowstone* injunction maintains the status quo so that a commercial tenant, when confronted by a threat of termination of its lease, may protect its investment in the leasehold by obtaining a stay tolling the cure period so that upon an adverse

---

9. *Id.* at 506 (emphasis added).
10. *Id.*
11. *Id.* at 507.
12. 151 Misc. 2d 725, 573 N.Y.S.2d 568 (NYC Civ. Ct. N.Y. Cnty. 1991).
13. 573 N.Y.S.2d at 568.
14. First Nat'l Stores, Inc. v. Yellowstone Shopping Ctr., Inc., 21 N.Y.2d 630, 290 N.Y.S.2d 721, 237 N.E.2d 868 (1968) (holding that a tenant could not cure a default, thereby preventing lease from expiring pursuant to notice to cure, where the tenant did not obtain the temporary restraining order until after the cure period had expired).
15. *Id.*

determination on the merits the tenant may cure the default and avoid a forfeiture.[16] In order to obtain a *Yellowstone* injunction, a tenant must establish that (1) it holds a commercial lease; (2) it received from the landlord either a notice of default, a notice to cure, or a threat of termination of the lease; (3) it requested injunctive relief prior to the termination of the lease; and (4) it is prepared and maintains the ability to cure the alleged default by any means short of vacating the premises.[17] Thus, prompt application for the injunction is essential to preserve the leasehold and the right to cure if held in default.

In *Lexington Ave. & 42nd St. Corp. v. 380 Lexchamp Operating, Inc.*,[18] a *Yellowstone* injunction was issued in a case where the default was based on the nonpayment of rent. Citing the *Garland* criteria, the appellate division reversed a lower court decision denying the injunction. The landlord had billed the tenant for 30 years of unbilled electric charges totaling nearly $500,000. Numerous subsequent decisions have confirmed that a *Yellowstone* injunction is available even where the default in question is nonpayment of rent; however, in such cases, courts often require some assurance from the tenant that it can/will pay arrears as well as use and occupancy during the pendency of the litigation.[19]

The ability to "cure" an allegedly "incurable" default was considered in the appellate division's reversal of a denial of a *Yellowstone* injunction in *Empire State Building Associates v. Trump Empire State Partners.*[20] At issue in the appeal was one of a series of default notices sent by *Trump* in a continuing attempt to remove *Empire* from the premises. The notice involved implied claims that *Empire* falsely obtained variances as to its air conditioning and sprinkler systems. *Trump* argued that the false filing was an incurable default, because it would be exposed to immediate criminal liability due to the false filing; and that the default was based uon an act that could not be undone. The court disagreed, noting that the tenant could resubmit the correct information or alter

16. Graubard Mollen Horowitz Pomeranz & Shapiro v. 600 Third Ave. Assocs., 93 N.Y.2d 508, 514, 715 N.E.2d 117 (1999).

17. *Id.*; 225 E. 36th St. Garage Corp. v. 221 E. 36th Owners Corp., 211 A.D.2d 420, 421, 621 N.Y.S.2d 302 (1995).

18. 205 A.D.2d 421, 613 N.Y.S.2d 402 (1st Dep't 1994).

19. 93 N.Y.2d 508; Sokoloff Arts Found. Inc. v. Nur Ashki Jerrahi Cmty., 140 N.Y.S.3d 418, 419 (1st Dep't 2021) ("plaintiffs' significant rental arrears warrant the injunction to issue upon the condition that plaintiffs post an undertaking"); Physicians Planning Serv. Corp. v. 292 Estates, Inc., 451 N.Y.S.2d 425, 425–26 (1st Dep't 1982) (granting injunction "on condition that plaintiff tender to landlord all rent due and owing and that shall become due during the pendency of that action pursuant to the terms of the lease, without prejudice to landlord by the acceptance thereof"); P.J. Clarke's On the Hudson, LLC v. WFP Retail Co., L.P., 2014 N.Y. Misc. LEXIS 3163, at *4–5 (Sup. Ct. N.Y. Cnty. July 17, 2014) (finding that the only way that tenant could sufficiently establish its ability to cure payment default was by depositing arrears and monthly rent in escrow); Gap, Inc. v. 170 Broadway Retail Owner, LLC, No. 652732/2020, 2020 N.Y. Misc. LEXIS 9794, *1–2 (Sup. Ct. N.Y. Cnty. Oct. 30, 2020) (conditioning injunction on plaintiff filing an undertaking in the form of a bond with the Clerk of the County in the total amount of $5,500,000, comprised of the sum of $2,500,000 to secure payment of future use and occupancy and $3,000,000 to secure the payment of rent arrears allegedly owed).

20. 245 A.D.2d 225, 667 N.Y.S.2d 31 (1st Dep't 1997).

the premises to bring it into compliance. "While these cures cannot 'undo' the filing of purportedly inaccurate information, it is not necessary, in order to cure, that a tenant show that it is able to erase the past, as long as it can show that it is able to bring itself into compliance with the lease without vacating the premises."[21]

When drafting nonstandard provisions, the landlord's counsel must consider which covenants should be dependent and draft conditions that expressly trigger lease-terminating defaults. In *Friedman v. Fooderama Supermarkets, Inc.*,[22] the tenant entered into two leases requiring the construction of a supermarket and satellite store. The landlord was required, after a request, to reimburse the tenant for the cost of construction. The failure to reimburse was deemed a default by the landlord, permitting the tenant to cancel. The tenant did not complete the satellite store and canceled the leases because the lessor failed to make a reimbursement. The court held that there was no implied condition that the tenant construct both stores to receive reimbursement. If the landlord intended reimbursement to be tied to tenant's obligation to complete, it should have drafted a schedule of completion, tied reimbursement thereto, and clearly denominated failure to complete a default permitting termination and withholding of reimbursement.

21. 667 N.Y.S.2d at 35.

22. 50 A.D.2d 246, 377 N.Y.S.2d 45 (1st Dep't 1975) (interpreting Pennsylvania law, but noting that New York law was substantially the same).

CHAPTER 21

Remedies and Damages

21.1 General Purpose

Despite the best of intentions, a tenant may default in the performance of its obligations under its lease. The purpose of this chapter is to enumerate the remedies available to the landlord following a tenant's default. In general, these provisions tend to be very broad. The courts in New York have tended to be protective of tenants and, therefore, landlords want all possible remedies set forth in the lease so that if a court will not enforce any particular remedy, the landlord nevertheless will be entitled to the others.

21.2 Sample Clause

21.01 Re-entry by Landlord.

If Tenant defaults in the payment of any Rent and such default continues for 3 days, or if this Lease shall terminate as in Section 20.01[1] provided, Landlord or Landlord's agents and servants may immediately or at any time thereafter re-enter into or upon the Premises, or any part thereof, either by summary dispossess proceedings or by any suitable action or proceeding at law, without being liable to indictment, prosecution or damages therefor, and may repossess the same, and may remove any persons therefrom, to the end that Landlord may have, hold and enjoy the Premises. The words "re-enter" and "re-entering" as used in this Lease are not restricted to their technical legal meanings. Upon such termination or re-entry, Tenant shall pay to Landlord any Rent then due and owing (in addition to any damages payable under Section 21.02).

21.02 Damages.

If this Lease is terminated under Section 20.01, or if Landlord re-enters the Premises under Section 21.01, Tenant shall pay to Landlord as damages, at the election of Landlord, either:

1. See Chapter 20, Default (Conditional Limitation), *supra*.

(a) a sum that, at the time of such termination, represents the then value of the excess, if any, of (1) the aggregate of the Rent that, had this Lease not terminated, would have been payable hereunder by Tenant for the period commencing on the day following the date of such termination or re-entry to and including the Expiration Date over (2) the aggregate fair rental value of the Premises for the same period (for the purposes of this clause (a) the amount of Additional Rent that would have been payable by Tenant under the Lease shall, for each calendar year ending after such termination or re-entry, be deemed to be an amount equal to the amount of such Additional Rent payable by Tenant for the calendar year immediately preceding the calendar year in which such termination or re-entry shall occur), or

(b) sums equal to the Rent that would have been payable by Tenant through and including the Expiration Date had this Lease not terminated or had Landlord not re-entered the Premises, payable upon the due dates therefor specified in this Lease; provided, that if Landlord shall relet all or any part of the Premises for all or any part of the period commencing on the day following the date of such termination or re-entry to and including the Expiration Date, Landlord shall credit Tenant with the net rents received by Landlord from such reletting, such net rents to be determined by first deducting from the gross rents as and when received by Landlord from such reletting the expenses incurred or paid by Landlord in terminating this Lease and of re-entering the Premises and of securing possession thereof, as well as the expenses of reletting, including, without limitation, altering and preparing the Premises for new tenants, brokers' commissions, and all other expenses properly chargeable against the Premises and the rental therefrom in connection with such reletting, it being understood that any such reletting may be for a period equal to or shorter or longer than said period; provided, further, that (i) in no event shall Tenant be entitled to receive any excess of such net rents over the sums payable by Tenant to Landlord under this Lease, (ii) in no event shall Tenant be entitled, in any suit for the collection of damages pursuant to this Section 21.02(b), to a credit in respect of any net rents from a reletting except to the extent that such net rents are actually received by Landlord on account of any period that is the subject of such suit, (iii) if the Premises or any part thereof should be relet in combination with other space, then proper apportionment on a square foot rentable area basis shall be made of the rent received from such reletting and of the expenses of reletting, and (iv) Landlord shall have no obligation to so relet the Premises and Tenant hereby waives any right Tenant may have, at law or in equity, to require Landlord to so relet the Premises.

Suit or suits for the recovery of any damages payable hereunder by Tenant, or any installments thereof, may be brought by Landlord from time to time at its election, and nothing contained herein shall require Landlord to postpone suit until the date when the Term would have expired but for such termination or reentry.

21.03 Other Remedies.

Nothing contained in this Lease shall be construed as limiting or precluding the recovery by Landlord against Tenant of any sums or damages to which, in addition to the damages particularly provided above, Landlord may lawfully be entitled by reason of any default hereunder on the part of Tenant. Anything in this Lease to the contrary notwithstanding, during the continuation of any default by Tenant, Tenant shall not be entitled to exercise any rights or options, or to receive any funds or proceeds being held, under or pursuant to this Lease.

21.04 Right to Injunction.

In the event of a breach or threatened breach by Tenant of any of its obligations under this Lease, Landlord shall also have the right of injunction. The specified remedies to which Landlord may resort hereunder are cumulative and are not intended to be exclusive of any other remedies or means of redress to which Landlord may lawfully be entitled, and Landlord may invoke any remedy allowed at law or in equity as if specific remedies were not herein provided for.

21.05 Certain Waivers.

Tenant waives and surrenders all right and privilege that Tenant might have under or by reason of any present or future law to redeem the Premises or to have a continuance of this Lease after Tenant is dispossessed or ejected therefrom by process of law or under the terms of this Lease or after any termination of this Lease. Tenant also waives the provisions of any law relating to notice and/or delay in levy of execution in case of any eviction or dispossession for nonpayment of rent, and the provisions of any successor or other law of like import.

21.06 No Consequential Damages.

Notwithstanding anything in this Lease to the contrary, and except as set forth in Article 24, in no event shall Landlord or Tenant be liable for special, punitive, or consequential damages in matters arising under this Lease or otherwise with respect to the Premises or the Building.

21.3 Landlord Concerns

Under New York law, a distinction is made between a dispossess proceeding brought in connection with (1) a tenant's default in the payment of rent (in this case, because the lease has not ended, the default is curable by the tenant) or (2) a dispossess proceeding brought against a holdover tenant. A holdover situation may arise where the lease has ended either on its stated expiration date or sooner, following a casualty, a right of early termination granted to the landlord or the tenant, or after the expiration of a stated, usually brief, notice period following a default; and, because the lease has ended, there is no right to cure. The sample clause states that a default in the payment of rent provides the landlord with the grounds to terminate the lease before the stated expiration date following such a default.

The landlord wants to reserve all its options with respect to the enforcement of available remedies following a tenant's default, in part, at least, because the landlord's choice of remedies may be limited by the courts. Also, depending on the conditions of the rental market at the time, certain remedies may be more attractive than others and the landlord needs the ability to choose the most favorable. This provision permits the landlord to repossess the premises, make alterations to prepare the premises for a subsequent tenancy and re-let the premises, all without releasing the defaulting tenant, who remains liable for, in addition to all amounts due prior to termination of the lease by the landlord, the landlord's damages, calculated on the difference between the rent the tenant would have paid for the rest of the lease term and the rent actually collected by the landlord from a re-letting, if any (less expenses incurred by the landlord in connection with the re-letting). This amount is payable monthly by the tenant for the balance of what would have been the lease term. The landlord has the option, however, in lieu of collecting damages on a monthly basis as just described, of collecting liquidated damages in a lump sum, in this case calculated on the difference between the rent the tenant would have paid for the rest of the lease term and the fair market rental value of the premises for what would have been the rest of the lease term. Also, the sample clause gives the landlord the right to injunctive relief in case of a breach or threatened breach of the lease.

21.4 Tenant Concerns

The major concern of the tenant relating to the remedies clause is that the tenant could be faced with a draconian remedy (loss of its lease) in a situation where the default may have occurred as a result of a clerical error or technical oversight on the tenant's part, or failure to receive the five-day notice referred to, or another failure that the tenant easily could and would cure. A tenant should demand service of a second default notice from the landlord highlighting the possible consequences of failing to cure the default promptly and a reasonable opportunity, following such second notice, to cure the default before the landlord sends a third notice terminating the lease.

In addition, with respect to Section 21.01 of the sample clause (set forth in Section 21.2, *supra*), a tenant should negotiate (1) to require the landlord to limit its right of reentry to only those instances permitted pursuant to legal process (and not "by force or otherwise"), (2) to preserve any liability the landlord might have in connection with an improper reentry, and (3) to preserve its right to any notice to which the tenant might otherwise be entitled under law.

With respect to Section 21.02, a tenant would want the landlord to agree to use reasonable efforts to mitigate its damages by re-letting the premises. In some states, even if not specified in the lease, the landlord is required by law to mitigate. New York, however, is not one of those states, and a landlord views this suggestion as an inappropriate interference with its control of the premises and an invitation to litigate. From its perspective, the premises is the landlord's property and the tenant, generally after notice and an opportunity to cure, has defaulted, and the landlord does not want the courts to speculate whether the landlord should have re-let the premises (perhaps to a tenant that the landlord deemed to be unacceptable) or, if the landlord has in fact re-let the premises, whether it could have done so at a higher rental.

Generally, landlords are not amenable to heavy negotiation of remedies provisions; first, because they only come into play if the tenant is in default, and, second, because of the limitations placed on the enforcement of these provisions by the courts. The tenant would do better to consider carefully the various aspects of the default provisions themselves (e.g., the specific occurrences constituting a default, the requirements for notice, and the length of the cure periods) and would likely meet with more success in negotiating these provisions.

21.5 Standard Real Estate Board of New York Clause

The clause has been divided, and bracketed italicized introductory headings added, in order to enhance the readability and comprehension of the provision. The number "18" refers to the section within the actual Real Estate Board Form wherein this clause may be found.

> *Remedies of Owner and Waiver of Redemption: 18*
>
> *[Landlord's rights upon default, re-entry, or expiration of lease]* In case of any such default, re-entry, expiration and/or dispossess by summary proceedings or otherwise, *(a)* the rent shall become due thereupon and be paid up to the time of such reentry, dispossess and/or expiration, *(b)* Owner may re-let the premises or any part or parts thereof, either in the name of Owner or otherwise, for a term or terms, which may at Owner's option be less than or exceed the period which would otherwise have constituted the balance of the term of this lease and may grant concessions or free rent or charge a higher rental than that in this lease, and/or *(c)* Tenant or the legal representatives of Tenant shall also pay Owner as liquidated damages for the failure of Tenant to observe and perform said Tenant's covenants herein contained, any deficiency between the rent hereby reserved and/or covenanted to be paid and the net amount, if any, of the rents collected on account of the lease or leases of the demised premises for each month of the period which would otherwise have constituted the balance of the term of this lease. The failure of Owner to re-let the premises or any part or parts thereof shall not release or affect Tenant's liability for damages.
>
> *[Computation of liquidated damages]* In computing such liquidated damages there shall be added to the said deficiency such expenses as Owner may

incur in connection with re-letting, such as legal expenses, reasonable attorneys' fees, brokerage, advertising and for keeping the demised premises in good order or for preparing the same for re-letting. Any such liquidated damages shall be paid in monthly installments by Tenant on the rent day specified in this lease and any suit brought to collect the amount of the deficiency for any month shall not prejudice in any way the rights of Owner to collect the deficiency for any subsequent month by a similar proceeding.

[Rights and remedies upon re-rental by Landlord] Owner, in putting the demised premises in good order or preparing the same for re-rental may, at Owner's option, make such alterations, repairs, replacements, and/or decorations in the demised premises as Owner, in Owner's sole judgment, considers advisable and necessary for the purpose of re-letting the demised premises, and the making of such alterations, repairs, replacements and/or decorations shall not operate or be construed to release Tenant from liability hereunder as aforesaid. Owner shall in no event be liable in any way whatsoever for failure to re-let the demised premises, or in the event that the demised premises are re-let, for failure to collect the rent thereof under such re-letting, and in no event shall Tenant be entitled to receive any excess, if any, of such net rents collected over the sums payable by Tenant to Owner hereunder. In the event of a breach or threatened breach by Tenant of any of the covenants or provisions hereof, Owner shall have the right of injunction and the right to invoke any remedy allowed at law or in equity as if reentry, summary proceedings and other remedies were not herein provided for. Mention in this lease of any particular remedy shall not preclude Owner from any other remedy, in law or in equity.

[Waiver of redemption by Tenant] Tenant hereby expressly waives any and all rights of redemption granted by or under any present or future laws in the event of Tenant being evicted or dispossessed for any cause, or in the event of Owner obtaining possession of demised premises, by reason of the violation by Tenant of any of the covenants and conditions of this lease, or otherwise.

21.6 Comments on the Standard Real Estate Board of New York Clause

The standard clause addresses many of the same concerns as the sample clause. In addition, some of the provisions contained in the sample clause are, in fact, found in other sections of the Real Estate Board form. One major difference is that the standard clause does not give the landlord the option to collect accelerated liquidated damages (i.e., the remedy set forth in Section 21.04(e) of the sample clause set forth in Section 21.2, *supra*). Another difference is the absence in the standard clause of the various waivers by the tenant contained in sample clause Section 21.02. A third difference is the inclusion in the sample clause of Section 21.05 that gives the landlord the right to cure, at the expense of the tenant, any breach by the tenant of its obligations with respect to the condition and repair of the premises.

21.7 Litigation Issues

The space leased by the landlord is its stock and trade. Thus, if some problem is created by a tenant resulting in an interruption of the orderly administration of its properties, summary nonpayment and holdover proceedings to recover possession are the remedies of choice.[2] Cases supporting other landlord remedies, such as acceleration,[3] mitigation,[4] and liquidation of damages[5] hold the tenant to its bargain, despite the fact that forfeiture may result. On the other hand, cases supporting the tenant's defenses generally refuse to permit a forfeiture, notwithstanding the express language of the bargain reflected in the lease.

The New York Court of Appeals in *Fifty States Management Corp. v. Pioneer Auto Parks, Inc.*[6] upheld a provision in a commercial lease permitting acceleration of rent for the entire term upon a rental default, even though the lease did not provide for a notice to accelerate or a cure period. The tenant argued that the acceleration created a penalty that necessitated a forfeiture since a cure required payment of the rent for the full term.

The court upheld the acceleration provision, but the facts, not merely the drafting, were relevant to the decision. First, the tenant's arrogance irked the court, which noted that the tenant "blithely sat by and exacerbated the effects of its willful breach." Second, there was no fraud, unknowing assent, overreaching or unconscionable conduct on the part of the landlord or any indication that the acceleration clause "was anything but the result of intensive negotiations between commercial parties of equal bargaining strength."[7] Third, the rent reserved for the term was reasonably related to the damages sustained: it was a means of receiving the rentals actually payable as a condition for a defaulting tenant to remain in occupancy.[8]

The case does stand for the proposition that acceleration of rent, when a remedy for nonpayment, which is deemed to be the essential tenant covenant, will be enforced. However, it leaves the tenant with certain equitable defenses. Acceleration will not be enforced as the result of the breach of any lease covenant, and will be deemed an unenforceable penalty, (1) if the acceleration was buried in the boilerplate language of the lease; (2) the negotiating position of the tenant was not on par with the landlord; (3) there are other indicia of unconscionability; or (4) if the rent default was the result

---

2. A discussion of summary nonpayment and holdover proceedings is beyond the scope of this text. However, these procedures and related case law are thoroughly discussed in FINKELSTEIN & FERRARA, LANDLORD AND TENANT PRACTICE IN NEW YORK (West 1997).

3. Fifty States Mgmt. Corp. v. Pioneer Auto Parks, Inc., 46 N.Y.2d 573, 415 N.Y.S.2d 800, 389 N.E.2d 113 (1979).

4. Holy Properties Ltd., L.P. v. Kenneth Cole Prods., Inc., 87 N.Y.2d 130, 637 N.Y.S.2d 964, 661 N.E.2d 964 (1995).

5. Lexington Bldg. Co., L.P. v. S-Fer Int'l Corp., 225 A.D.2d 406, 640 N.Y.S.2d 1 (1st Dep't 1996).

6. *See* 46 N.Y.2d 573, 415 N.Y.S.2d 800, 389 N.E.2d 113 (1979).

7. 415 N.Y.S.2d at 804.

8. *Id.* at 802.

of "a good faith mistake, promptly cured by the party in default with no prejudice to the other creditor. . . ."[9]

Having accelerated the rent to an amount that the tenant cannot cure, a landlord can both legally and contractually hold the tenant to its bargain without making an effort to re-let, as landlord-tenant law does not impose the usual contract obligation to mitigate damages.[10] The landlord can refuse to make any attempt to re-let; accept a tenant's surrender and thereby release the tenant; or regain possession by summary proceedings and hold the tenant liable for contract damages, which must be mitigated. The Court of Appeals in *Holy Properties*, following the rule that a tenant must live up to the detriments of its bargain, held that a lease provision requiring a tenant to pay rent for the entire term subsequent to the lessor's recovering possession by summary proceedings is valid, and further continued the rule that a landlord has no contract obligation to mitigate damages if the landlord-tenant relationship is not terminated.

Courts will enforce the agreement of the parties as to liquidated damages where the liquidated amount bears a reasonable relation to the probable loss. Thus the court in *Lexington Building Co., L.P. v. S-Fer International Corp.*[11] upheld a provision that did not set forth a definite monetary amount, but required the holdover tenant to indemnify the landlord for any liability resulting from the delay in surrendering possession, including claims asserted by a succeeding tenant. As a consequence, the holdover's liability increased beyond the damages for its use and occupancy. This case may be contrasted to *Square Lex 48 Corp. v. Shelton Towers Associates*,[12] where the court refused to enforce a $6,000-a-day measure of liquidated damages in the event of a holdover. The test of whether a liquidated damage provision will be deemed an unenforceable penalty depends on whether the amount is grossly disproportionate to the probable loss, or if anticipated damages were readily ascertainable at the time the contract was entered into.[13] Where the same amount of "liquidated damages" is provided for the breach of every lease covenant, the court will find the damages to be an unenforceable penalty.[14]

A lease should provide for some liquidated damages reasonably related to the anticipated loss that may occur as a result of specified material breaches, such as holding over. In *437 Madison Avenue Associates v. A.T. Kearney, Inc.*,[15] the court refused

9. *Id.*

10. *See* Holy Properties Ltd., L.P. v. Kenneth Cole Prods., Inc., 87 N.Y.2d 130, 637 N.Y.S.2d 964, 661 N.E.2d 964 (1995); Sage Realty Corp. v. Kenbee Mgmt.-New York, Inc., 182 A.D.2d 489, 582 N.Y.S.2d 182 (1st Dep't 1992).

11. Lexington Bldg. Co., L.P. v. S-Fer Int'l Corp., 225 A.D.2d 406, 640 N.Y.S.2d 1 (1st Dep't 1996).

12. 98 Misc. 2d 1039, 415 N.Y.S.2d 325 (Sup. Ct. N.Y. Cnty. 1978).

13. Pyramid Centres & Co. Ltd. v. Kinney Shoe Corp., 244 A.D.2d 625, 663 N.Y.S.2d 711 (3d Dep't 1997) (refusing to enforce as a penalty a provision that if tenant cease store operations damages would be the average annual percentage rent or double the fixed rent provided for in the lease).

14. Vernitron Corp. v. CF 48 Assocs., 104 A.D.2d 409, 478 N.Y.S.2d 933 (2d Dep't 1984) (clause providing for a sum equal to one year's rent as liquidated damages for the breach of any lease covenant).

15. 127 Misc. 2d 37, 488 N.Y.S.2d 950 (Sup. Ct. App. Term 1st Dep't 1985).

to hold a tenant liable for consequential damages, the fair rental value of the premises where tenant held over, where the lease contained no liquidated damages provision.

Notwithstanding a clearly drafted, enforceable conditional limitation arising out of a definite tenant default, the courts will not always permit lease termination as a remedy. When insubstantial provisions are violated, or the violations themselves are deemed insubstantial, the landlord will be relegated to injunctive relief, and forfeiture will be avoided.[16]

The courts are particularly reluctant to permit landlords to terminate leases on the grounds of unconsented-to alterations. Notwithstanding that a lease clearly requires the landlord's prior consent for all alterations, a violation of this covenant is usually not deemed a default unless the court finds that the alteration constituted waste. Installation of trade fixtures and other alterations reasonably required to permit the tenant to conduct its business, and which are removable without damage upon lease expiration, will generally not be considered lease violations.[17]

The landlord may not be able to resort to a remedy clearly set forth in the lease, when an alternate remedy provided in the lease is more reasonable and less onerous on the tenant. In *SKD Enterprises, Inc. v. L & M. Offset, Inc.*,[18] the landlord sought to enforce the standard provision permitting it to perform any covenant, at the expense of the tenant, upon which the tenant defaulted. The lease clearly provided that the tenant had to comply with all laws, including the installation of a sprinkler system if so required. The landlord could terminate the lease in the event of a uncured default, or cure the default at tenant expense. The lease was for five years at a rental of about $3,000 per year. The sprinkler system, which tenant was legally required to install, was installed by the lessor at a cost of $24,500. The court held that the intent of the lease was to safeguard the landlord from incurring the cost of installing a sprinkler system. This intention, the court went on to hold, was best served by terminating the lease, rather than imposing upon the tenant a cost of multiple times the remaining rent that would be used to significantly improve the value of the building for the landlord, with no corresponding benefit to the tenant.

---

16. Rubinstein Bros. v. Ole of 34th St., Inc. 101 Misc. 2d 563, 421 N.Y.S.2d 534 (NYC Civ. Ct. N.Y. Cnty. 1979) (refusing to terminate lease where tenant may have violated use restriction by selling some items in violation thereof, relegating lessor to injunction); Madison 52d Corp. v. Ogust, 49 Misc. 2d 663, 268 N.Y.S.2d 126 (NYC Civ. Ct. N.Y. Cnty. 1966) (relegating landlord to injunctive relief in lieu of termination where tenant failed to obtain required consent with respect to a window sign).

17. Dennis' Nat. Mini-Meals, Inc. v. 91 Fifth Ave. Corp., 172 A.D.2d 331, 569 N.Y.S.2d 740 (1st Dep't 1991); Harar v. Michilin & Hill, Inc., 86 A.D.2d 183, 449 N.Y.S.2d 213 (1st Dep't 1982).

18. 65 Misc. 2d 612, 318 N.Y.S.2d 539 (NYC Civ. Ct. N.Y. Cnty. 1971).

CHAPTER 22

Landlord's Fees and Expenses; Self-Help

22.1 General Purpose

The primary purpose of a landlord's fees and expenses provision is to give the landlord the right to perform the obligations of a tenant that the tenant fails to perform, and to receive reimbursement for costs or expenses incurred therewith. The right to perform the tenant's obligation gives the landlord the ability to ensure that the covenant the landlord bargained for will in fact be complied with, albeit by the act of the landlord rather than the tenant. The right to receive reimbursement for any costs incurred by the landlord helps to ensure that the rent payable by the tenant pursuant to its lease will be net of any costs or expenses the landlord may incur in connection with the ownership, operation, and maintenance of the building, except, of course, for the general operating expenses of the building that are incurred in the ordinary course, and the debt service payable on the mortgage encumbering the building. For example, if, in connection with the performance of alterations by a tenant, the tenant damages an electric riser running through its premises that serves other portions of the building, the landlord should have the right to repair the riser if the tenant fails to do so and have the cost of repair paid by the tenant. Similarly, if the landlord incurs attorneys' fees in enforcing its rights against a tenant, or in defending itself against claims by third parties arising out of the tenant's acts, the landlord wants those attorneys' fees to be paid directly by the tenant. The obligation of the tenant to pay these fees and expenses, in addition to fixed rent and escalation charges, is essential to ensuring that the landlord receive a net fixed rent.

22.2 Sample Clause

Section 22.01 Right to Perform Tenant Covenants.

If Tenant fails to perform any of its obligations under this Lease, Landlord, any Superior Lessor or any Superior Mortgagee (each, a "**Curing Party**") may perform the same at the expense of Tenant (a) immediately and without notice (except that Landlord shall give notice to Tenant as soon as practicable) in the case of emergency or in case such failure materially or unreasonably interferes with the use of space by any other occupant in the Building or with the operation of the Building or is reasonably likely to result in a violation of any Law or in a cancellation of any insurance policy maintained by Landlord and (b) in any other case if such failure continues beyond any applicable grace period. If a Curing Party performs any of Tenant's obligations under this Lease, Tenant shall pay to Landlord the reasonable costs thereof, together with interest at the Interest Rate from the date incurred by the Curing Party until paid by Tenant, within 30 days after receipt by Tenant of a statement as to the amounts of such costs. If the Curing Party effects such cure by bonding any lien that Tenant is required to bond or otherwise discharge, Tenant shall obtain and substitute a bond for the Curing Party's bond and shall reimburse the Curing Party for the reasonable cost of the Curing Party's bond. "**Interest Rate**" means the lesser of (i) the base rate from time to time announced by Citibank, N.A. (or, if Citibank, N.A. shall not exist or shall cease to announce such rate, such other bank in New York, New York, as shall be designated by Landlord in a notice to Tenant) to be in effect at its principal office in New York, New York plus [__]% and (ii) the maximum rate permitted by law.

Section 22.02 Landlord's Fees and Expenses.

(a) If Landlord places the enforcement of this Lease or any part thereof, or the collection of any Rent due or to become due hereunder, or recovery of the possession of the Premises, in the hands of an attorney, or files suit upon the same, or in the event any bankruptcy, insolvency or other similar proceeding is commenced involving Tenant, Tenant shall, upon demand, reimburse Landlord for Landlord's attorneys' fees and disbursements and court costs.

(b) Subject to Section 22.02(a), the prevailing party in any action or proceeding between Tenant and Landlord shall be reimbursed by the losing party, within 30 days after demand, for its reasonable, out-of-pocket attorneys' fees and disbursements and court costs.

22.3 Landlord Concerns

In addition to the payment of rent, there are many tenant obligations under a lease, the performance of which requires the expenditure of money. Maintenance and repair, compliance with law, maintaining insurance and the lien-free completion of tenant alterations are a few. Although it is rare that a landlord will actually perform and pay for the cost of performing an obligation that is supposed to be performed by the tenant, there are circumstances under which the landlord may be left with no alternative. In those instances, the landlord should have the right to self-help and to collect any amounts from the tenant that the landlord expends in exercising such right.

From the landlord's perspective, the triggering event giving rise to the landlord's right to perform an obligation the tenant failed to perform should be broad and easily met. If the tenant defaults in *any* obligation, the landlord should have the right to perform such obligation immediately after the applicable notice to the tenant and expiration of the grace period, if any, in the lease for the cure of defaults, and without the requirement of notice in the case of an emergency.

Having been put in the position of spending money that should have been spent by the tenant, the landlord also does not want to be second-guessed about the amount expended. Language that qualifies the tenant's reimbursement obligation, such as the tenant will pay the "reasonable" or "competitive" cost incurred by the landlord, creates the opportunity for a hindsight reevaluation. If the landlord spends $20,000 to repair damage to the building HVAC system caused by a tenant performing its initial alterations, and provides proof of that expenditure, the landlord does not want to be faced with assertions by the tenant that the amount spent in repairs was unreasonable. In addition, to ensure that the landlord is made whole, it should also be provided that the tenant is obligated to pay interest, at a default rate, on the sums expended by the landlord from the date incurred until the date actually reimbursed.

In most contract disputes, the American rule provides that each party to the dispute is responsible for its own attorneys' fees, regardless of which party ultimately prevails in the dispute. This rule is inconsistent with the landlord's "net rent" concept since, even if it successfully sues a tenant and collects all of the unpaid rent and other sums due, it would have to use a portion of the rents to pay for the legal fees and disbursements incurred in the dispute. Thus, a lease should provide that if the landlord incurs attorneys' fees in any way arising out of the tenant's default under its lease, and the landlord prevails in the action, the tenant is obligated to reimburse the landlord for the reasonable fees and disbursements incurred.

With respect to all of the reimbursement obligations of the tenant to the landlord discussed in this chapter, the lease should expressly provide that the sums due from the tenant are "additional rent." Using this term of art gives the landlord the same rights and remedies under the lease for the nonpayment of these sums as for the nonpayment of the fixed rent. Instead of being limited to a contract action for collection, the landlord can then pursue a summary eviction proceeding and seek to terminate the lease. Finally, there should be a measured period of time within which the tenant must reimburse the landlord. After the expiration of this designated period (e.g., within ten days after demand), the tenant will be deemed to have failed to comply with the payment requirement and appropriate action may be taken.

22.4 Tenant Concerns

A significant tenant's primary concern with respect to self-help, fees, and expenses is achieving mutuality. Where a tenant has failed to perform an obligation under the lease, it is difficult for the tenant to argue that the landlord should not be entitled to perform that obligation, and that it should not be reimbursed for the cost of that performance. However, a tenant with a significant amount of leverage should ask for a similar right to seek reimbursement for expenses it incurs in performing the landlord's obligations that the landlord fails to perform. Landlords are likely to firmly resist granting such a right (and materially limit the right if granted) because, as a practical matter, it is much more likely that a tenant will actually spend money in this regard because of the need to continue business operations in the premises, and landlords are concerned about potential liability to other occupants, building employees, and vendors attributable to an action taken by a tenant that is typically reserved to landlords.

Of course, the tenant should be sure that the landlord is obligated to provide notice and an opportunity to cure before exercising self-help (except in the case of an emergency), and the tenant should be willing to provide the same before exercising any tenant self-help remedy. The tenant should also attempt to limit the expenses for which the landlord may seek reimbursement to reasonable out-of-pocket expenses paid to unaffiliated third parties, in order to minimize the opportunity for abuse.

In the case of legal fees and disbursements, the tenant should be sure to have the right to collect its legal fees and disbursements if it is the prevailing party in a dispute with the landlord; or if it incurs legal fees and disbursements in defending itself against claims by third parties arising out of a landlord's acts. Finally, if a tenant justifiably incurs expenses arising from the landlord's default, and the landlord does not properly reimburse the tenant, it may attempt to seek a right of offset against the fixed rent as a remedy for collection.

22.5 Standard Real Estate Board of New York Clause

> *Fees and Expenses: 19.* If Tenant shall default in the observance or performance of any term or covenant on Tenant's part to be observed or performed under or by virtue of any of the terms or provisions in any article of this lease, after notice if required and upon expiration of any applicable grace period if any (except in any emergency), then, unless otherwise provided elsewhere in this lease, Owner may immediately or at any time thereafter and without notice perform the obligation of Tenant thereunder. If Owner, in connection with the foregoing or in connection with any default by Tenant in the covenant to pay rent hereunder, makes any expenditures or incurs any obligations for the payment of money, including but not limited to reasonable attorneys' fees, in instituting, prosecuting or defending any action or proceeding, and prevails in any such action or proceeding, then Tenant will reimburse Owner for such sums so paid or obligations incurred with interest and costs. The foregoing expenses incurred by reason of Tenant's default shall be deemed to be additional rent hereunder and shall be paid by Tenant to Owner within ten (10) days of rendition of any bill or statement to Tenant therefore. If Tenant's lease term shall have expired at the time of making of such expenditures or incurring of such obligations, such sums shall be recoverable by Owner, as damages.

22.6 Comments on the Standard Real Estate Board of New York Clause

The Real Estate Board form, not unexpectedly, addresses most of the owner/landlord concerns, and virtually none of the tenant concerns, regarding self-help and owner/

landlord's fees and expenses. The triggering event is any default; there is no qualification regarding "reasonable" expenses; and sums are due with interest and are characterized as additional rent. A tenant has no similar rights or any stated ability to challenge the amount of expenses incurred by the landlord. Depending on its negotiating leverage, a tenant should endeavor to add a provision similar to Section 22.03 of the sample clause (set forth in Section 22.2, *supra*), giving the tenant mutual rights with respect to self-help and being reimbursed for costs arising from a landlord default.

22.7 Litigation Issues

Recovery of legal fees is of equal importance to the client as it is to the attorney drafting the lease, and the recovery of these fees is directly governed by the applicable lease provision.

The customary lease provisions permit recovery of legal fees in prosecuting a summary proceeding for nonpayment of rent, and deem such fees added rent, which may be the basis of such an action[1] or a holdover action to recover possession.[2] Real Property Law section 234, providing for an implied right of a tenant to recover legal fees if a lease provides for the landlord to recover such expense, does not apply to a commercial lease. Thus, the commercial tenant is relegated to having to negotiate for an express provision to recover attorney fees.[3]

In *Frank B. Hall & Co. v. Orient Overseas Associates*,[4] the landlord sought to recover attorneys' fees incurred in the defense of a declaratory judgment action commenced by the tenant asserting that the landlord used the wrong base year in calculating certain escalation charges. The tenant's action for declaratory judgment was eventually decided in accordance with landlord's interpretation of the lease. The tenant paid the added rent when billed, but was thereafter served a notice demanding additional rent based on the landlord's legal fees incurred in the declaratory judgment action. The landlord sued the tenant and was successful at the trial court level. On appeal, however, the appellate court reversed the trial court and denied the claim for legal fees. Three lease provisions were discussed by the appellate court. Of two of these provisions the court said that "when considered together . . . they cannot and do not serve as a contractual predicate for the recovery of attorneys' fees incurred in defense of a prior action for declaratory judgment. . . . These paragraphs would, however, operate as a basis for recovery of attorneys' fees in a situation, not present here, where the landlord has undertaken some action, either by summary proceeding or otherwise, to re-enter the demised premises or to dispossess the tenant." In order to activate these two provisions,

1. Clemons Mgmt. Corp. v. Quick Quality Copies, Inc., 164 Misc. 2d 144, 623 N.Y.S.2d 498 (NYC Civ. Ct. N.Y. Cnty. 1995).

2. Chatanow Assoc., Inc. v. 527 MDN Prop., Inc.,161 A.D.2d 258, 555 N.Y.S.2d 50 (1st Dep't 1990).

3. Taylor v. Eli Haddad Corp., 118 Misc. 2d 253, 460 N.Y.S.2d 886 (Sup. Ct. N.Y. Cnty. 1983) (commercial lease did not include tenant's right to legal fees, but if residential use was permitted, then implied right to legal fees under Real Property Law section 234 would apply).

4. 84 A.D. 2d 338, 446 N.Y.S.2d 59 (1st Dep't 1982).

the landlord had to engage in some prior affirmative action and "since the defense of a declaratory judgment action is not that type of action contemplated which will trigger these provisions, the claim for attorneys' fees [under these two paragraphs] is ill founded."[5] The third paragraph considered by the court provided that the landlord could only seek attorneys' fees incurred in connection with performing an obligation for the account of the tenant. The court observed that this provision required the tenant to owe an obligation to some third party that could be performed by the landlord. This provision did not permit the recovery of attorneys' fees under the circumstance of this case because, as "additional rent," the sum was owed to no one else other than the landlord.

The U.S. District Court was also asked by a tenant to render a declaratory judgment concerning rent escalation charges, in *Schechter v. Carter*,[6] but awarded the landlord legal fees for defending the action. The court distinguished the lease provisions from those in the *Hall* case. The legal fee provision stated that "If the Landlord shall necessarily incur or become liable for any reasonable legal fees or expenses to secure compliance by the Tenant . . . the Tenant shall pay said reasonable legal fees and expenses. . . ."[7] Since in defending the declaratory judgment action the landlord incurred legal fees to secure compliance, it could recover those legal defense costs. However, legal fees have been denied in connection with the successful defense by a landlord of a tenant's action to recover an alleged rent overcharge because the lease only provided for legal fees when a tenant default is asserted.[8]

In *Taylor v. Eli Haddad Corp.*[9] a tenant was relying on the protection of Real Property Law section 234 to seek attorney fees in its *Yellowstone* action to prevent eviction on the grounds that his residential use violated the lease use clause. The statute implies a right to legal fees resulting from the failure of the landlord to perform a lease covenant. The right did not apply where the tenant sought to invalidate a landlord's notice to cure, an act that does not constitute a landlord default. In another case it was held that a lease that provided that "Lessor shall reimburse Lessee for Lessee's reasonable expenses, if Lessee shall prevail in enforcing or performing such covenants, including reasonable attorneys' fees . . ." gave no right to reimbursement for attorneys' fees in connection with the successful prosecution of an action involving the establishment of the base rental and commencement date of a lease; there may have been a dispute, but there was no default by the landlord in the performance of any lease covenant.[10]

5. 446 N.Y.S.2d at 61.
6. 580 F. Supp. 1526 (S.D.N.Y. 1984).
7. 580 F. Supp. 1528.
8. Altieri v. Net Realty Holding Trust, 237 A.D.2d 551, 655 N.Y.S.2d 984 (2d Dep't 1997).
9. 118 Misc. 2d 253, 460 N.Y.S.2d 886 (Sup. Ct. N.Y. Cnty. 1983).
10. Grand Manor Health Related Facility v. Hamilton Equities, Inc., 147 A.D.2d 118, 541 N.Y.S.2d 425 (1st Dep't 1989).

CHAPTER 23

No Representation by Landlord

23.1 General Purpose

The aim of this provision is to negate a tenant's subsequent claim that the landlord misrepresented the premises. Such a misrepresentation, if tantamount to fraud in the inducement, would permit the tenant to rescind the lease. The implementation of this goal, if astutely defended by tenant's counsel, is more difficult. Obviously, in agreeing to take the space, the tenant is relying on certain facts being true, and now in the document to be signed is being asked to make a statement to the contrary—that tenant is relying on "no" representations of any kind regarding the space.

For the landlord's draftsman, then, there are two possible initial results in the first draft of the lease, namely, (1) a statement that there are no representations, with a savings clause ("except as herein expressly set forth"), or (2) a slightly more elaborate statement of no representations, followed by a laundry list of categories of information (meant to be all-inclusive) as to which the overarching statement applies. This compels tenant's counsel, in self-defense, to negotiate in other clauses of the lease for specific representations that can be preserved by this provision's savings clause.

Since the representations being denied have primarily to do with the condition, quality, or cost of the premises, this lease section often contains a second, concluding thought, that once the tenant occupies the premises, it is in effect estopped from protesting any subsequent disappointment, regardless of what the landlord, its broker, building engineer, or other agents may, or may not, have said to tenant.

23.2 Sample Clause

23.01 No Representations.

Tenant expressly acknowledges and agrees that Landlord has not made and is not making, and Tenant, in executing and delivering this Lease, is not relying upon, any warranties, representations, promises or statements, except to the extent that the same are expressly set forth in this Lease. All understandings and agreements heretofore had between the parties are merged in this

Lease and any other written agreement(s) made concurrently herewith, which alone fully and completely express the agreement of the parties and which are entered into after full investigation, Tenant is not relying upon any statement or representation not embodied in this Lease.

23.3 Landlord Concerns

While New York is among the states that have adopted a statute providing for an implied warranty of habitability in all residential leases, this covenant or warranty does not extend to leases of commercial property. Thus, the decisions of courts regarding residential property, which have held that an implied covenant of habitability has been violated by such conditions as the lack of heat, hot water, or elevator service; the presence of dirt or debris; or unpleasant odors, and that such violations if sufficiently severe can relieve the residential tenant of its rent obligation, are of no help to the commercial tenant. To combat these same conditions, a commercial tenant must plead constructive eviction and act on that argument by moving out.

This landlord's provision is inserted in the lease as a defense against a commercial lessee attempting to rescind the lease on some contract theory such as fraud in the inducement, mutual mistake, or misrepresentation. Thus the prudent landlord begins by requiring, as a condition of delivery of the lease, that the tenant expressly agree that it has not relied on any statement by the landlord, or anyone purporting to speak for the landlord, regarding the quality or adequacy of the premises or the building wherein the premises are located, or indeed about any other matter pertaining to the premises (especially the amount or rate of increase of escalation rents for taxes and operating costs).

23.4 Tenant Concerns

For a tenant that is asked to sign off on such a provision (and virtually all commercial tenants are required to do so), the protective response must be threefold:

First: Before signing the lease, the tenant should make whatever physical inspections it deems necessary, taking into consideration all material concerns, for example, from the condition of the electrical, the elevators, HVAC, and other building systems. The tenant should insist that the landlord repair (at landlord's own cost and expense) or contribute for anything needed to bring the premises up to operable and customary market standard. Thus, this clause should contain a carve-out for the landlord's work or tenant improvements to be performed prior to the tenant moving into the premises.

Second: The tenant, in other provisions of the lease, must find or otherwise establish standards for, among other things, service delivery, thresholds from minimum KW per rentable square foot in available electrical power to the business hours and numbers of passenger and freight elevators. This is necessary in order to establish those "representations" behind which the landlord must stand even if the lease cannot be rescinded, or the rent withheld or setoff, because of these inadequacies.

Third: The tenant should press the landlord to exclude from its "no representations" hard line those things that the normal levels of inspection by the tenant's architect and engineer cannot or might not reveal, such as latent defects in the building or hazardous materials within the premises hidden behind the walls or above the plenum and other items that the landlord is representing in the lease itself.

23.5 Standard Real Estate Board of New York Clause

The REBNY clause is starkly simple, although it contains some additions (separately captioned here), namely, the "merger" clause and the "amendments only in writing" clause, which usually constitute separate sections in longer, more sophisticated leases.

> *No Representations by Owner. 21.* Neither Owner [Landlord] nor Owner's agent have made any representations or promises with respect to the physical condition of the building, the land upon which it is erected or the demised premises, the rents, the leases, expenses of operation or any other matter or thing affecting or related to the premises except as herein expressly set forth and no rights, easements or licenses are acquired by Tenant by implication or otherwise except as expressly set forth in the provisions of this lease. Tenant has inspected the building and the demised premises and is thoroughly acquainted with their condition and agrees to take the same "as is" and acknowledges that the taking of possession of the demised premises by Tenant shall be conclusive evidence that the said premises and the building of which the same form a part were in good and satisfactory condition at the time such possession was so taken, except as to latent defects. *["Merger clause":]* All understandings and agreements heretofore made between the parties hereto are merged in this contract, which alone fully and completely expresses the agreement between Owner and Tenant and *["Amendments only in writing clause":]* any executory agreement hereafter made shall be ineffective to change, modify, discharge or effect an abandonment of it in whole or in part, unless such executory agreement is in writing and signed by the party against whom enforcement of the change, modification, discharge or abandonment is sought.

23.6 Comments on Standard Real Estate Board of New York Form Clause

As is usually the case, the need to seek modifications of this clause falls mainly to the prospective tenant. The standard sweeping scope of the REBNY "no landlord reps" clause is already qualified by an exception for latent defects, but the tenant may also insist on an exception for asbestos or other hidden hazardous materials. This is particularly true if the tenant intends to make alterations, either immediately or at some subsequent time, that require expensive encapsulation or removal of these hazardous materials; see "requirements of law" (REBNY Article 6 set forth in Chapter 10) and performing "tenant alterations" at tenant's sole expense (REBNY Article 3 set forth in Chapter 7).

The other recommended tenant change in the REBNY clause is the insertion in the second sentence, before Tenant's agreement to take the premises "as is," of the phrase "except as otherwise provided herein," so as to exclude from the tenant's acquiescence any lease-imposed owner/landlord obligations to perform improvements or repairs.

23.7 Litigation Issues

Of course, the landlord and his renting agent, despite the "no representations" recital in a lease merger clause, do in fact make representations concerning the building, its services, and condition. The purpose of such merger clauses is to limit all rights and obligations to the four corners of the lease document. *Lemkin v. Gulde*[1] is an interesting case showing how certain types of representations, not expressly incorporated in a lease, may become enforceable rights. The plaintiff leased space for his medical practice in a medical center to be constructed. Newspaper advertisements stated, in an appealing manner, that the center "will occupy 5 acres of ground with approximately 2 acres in front of the building set aside as a tastefully landscaped and shrubbed botanic setting forming a park-like atmosphere. . . ." Signs on the premises repeated this description of the premises, as did the landlord's leasing representatives. In fact, the two-acre park was dedicated to the village and the park was established. The landlord's successor planned to fill the "park-like atmosphere" with two apartment buildings and brought an action to invalidate the park dedication, asserting that it resulted from improper zoning by private contract. The tenant urged that the premises included an interest in the park, and that removal would violate the covenant of quiet enjoyment, even though the lease only demised "Suite No. 2A" in a building located on a plot bounded by four named streets. There was no mention of the park, or any appurtenant rights therein. The court held that the lease included an implied easement of necessity for enjoyment of the park, which was deemed necessary to the full enjoyment of the leased premises. Further, the right to the park was deemed to be an easement by representation and estoppel. The court noted that "Plaintiff testified . . . that setting was materially persuasive on him in moving from his former location in a highly commercial area; it requires no stretch of imagination to infer that the lease as made would not have been concluded had it been clear that the building would be located on a dead end street off the main thoroughfare behind two apartment buildings and their 94 car parking lot." Because of the recording of the declaration of trust establishing the park, the landlord's successor was bound by inquiry knowledge to all of the rights that the tenants had in the park, and was enjoined from attempting to void it. The case contains no discussion of a merger clause defense, which would have probably failed because the park dedication made it a vested appurtenant right.

In *New York Fruit Auction Corp. v. City of New York*[2] the parol evidence rule, in the absence of an express merger clause, helped a landlord defend a similar claim (as in

1. 25 Misc. 2d 144, 205 N.Y.S.2d 658 (Sup. Ct. Nassau Cnty. 1960).
2. 81 A.D.2d 159, 439 N.Y.S.2d 648 (1st Dep't 1981).

Lemkin, supra) that the premises was part of an overall development plan. The tenant asserted that it opted to stay in New York, and entered into a lease for its executive offices and auction facility, based on the city's representation that it intended to develop the blighted Hunt's Point area into a modern food-processing and distribution center. The plan was never fully implemented, and the tenant sought to void or reform the lease on the grounds of fraud and misrepresentation. The lease incorporated a reference to the plan in a provision where the tenant acknowledged that the premises was part of the food-processing and distribution center "being developed," and which required the tenant's improvements to be in conformity with the plan specifications and subject to approval of the project designer. However, there was no provision expressly conditioning the tenant's performance under the lease on the implementation of the plan. Even without a merger clause, such a condition was considered "of such controlling importance" that it should have been an integral part of the lease. The parol evidence rule barred proof that the plan was incorporated as such a condition.

An effective merger clause leaves the tenant with a claim of fraud or mutual mistake, and the burden to prove that a representation should have been incorporated in a lease.[3] Tenants seldom prevail on these grounds. Courts regularly conclude that a tenant's "attempt to reform this agreement made between sophisticated parties, after arm's length negotiation, is not supported by adequate evidence of mutual mistake."[4] Furthermore, even a fraud claim can be prevented by a specific merger clause in which the tenant acknowledged that no representations were made or relied upon and the tenant, in fact, made its own inspection and investigation.[5] Cases where merger clauses, combined with other disclaimers, have protected landlords from claims of fraud include instances where (1) a tenant asserted that the electric service was inadequate for its use;[6] (2) a tenant challenged the area of the premises used for escalation purposes;[7] or (3) a tenant claimed the landlord represented that a basement could be used for manufacturing purposes.[8]

---

3. Barash v. Pa. Terminal Real Estate Corp., 26 N.Y.2d 77, 308 N.Y.S.2d 649, 256 N.E.2d 707 (1970) (holding that tenants allegations that landlord made fraudulent representations about after-hours ventilation in an office building must have been accompanied by an allegation of unilateral mistake on tenant's part for a successful claim for reformation).

4. Sioris v. 25 West 43d St. Co., 223 A.D.2d 475, 637 N.Y.S.2d 78 (1st Dep't 1996).

5. Dannan Realty Corp. v. Harris, 5 N.Y.2d 317, 184 N.Y.S.2d 599, 157 N.E.2d 597 (1959) (holding that a merger clause stating the parties may not rely on any representations not embodied in the contract disallows a party from making claims of fraud based on an oral representation).

6. Lewis Frimel Co., Inc. v. U.S. Trust Co. of New York, 42 A.D.2d 516, 344 N.Y.S.2d 212 (1st Dep't 1973).

7. S.R. Leon Co., Inc. v. The Towers, 194 A.D.2d 600, 599 N.Y.S.2d 53 (2d Dep't 1993). Even though the general merger clause alone was not sufficient to bar a claim of fraud in *Wohl v. Owen*, 153 Misc. 2d 282, 580 N.Y.S.2d 854 (NYC Civ. Ct. Kings Cnty. 1992), use of the phrase "deemed to be" negated a representation and put the burden of inspection on tenant.

8. Zazu, Inc. v. Giora Manor, 148 A.D.2d 400, 539 N.Y.S.2d 348 (1st Dep't 1989) (upholding the lease, the court relied on a merger clause, a use clause requiring tenant to conform to certificate of occupancy, and a specific disclaimer as to fitness for intended use).

CHAPTER 24

End of Term; Surrender of Premises

24.1 General Purpose

When the term of a lease has ended, whether upon the scheduled expiration date or an earlier termination date following the tenant's default or other accelerating event, the principal concerns of the parties relate to (1) the timeliness of the surrender of the premises, and (2) the condition in which the premises are to be left.

The purpose of end-of-term provisions is to ensure that the tenant will vacate the premises at the time specified in the lease (which may be of particular importance to the landlord if it has re-let the premises in reliance on the original tenant vacating by a certain date) and to minimize the costs to the landlord of having to prepare the premises for a subsequent tenancy.

24.2 Sample Clause

24.01 Surrender of Premises.

On the Expiration Date or upon any earlier termination of this Lease, or upon any reentry by Landlord upon the Premises, Tenant shall quit and surrender the Premises to Landlord "broom-clean" and in good order, condition and repair, except for ordinary wear and tear and such damage or destruction as Landlord is required to repair or restore under this Lease, vacant and free and clear of all lettings, occupancies, liens and encumbrances caused or created by Tenant or any person claiming through or under Tenant, and Tenant shall remove all of the Tenant's Property therefrom except as otherwise expressly provided in this Lease. Tenant shall not be required to remove any Alteration, except for Specialty Alterations which must be removed at the end of the Term in accordance with this Lease or otherwise expressly required to be removed pursuant to this Lease. With respect to surrender of the Premises prior to the Expiration Date or a surrender that is not pursuant to Tenant's right to terminate this Lease as provided in this Lease, no act or thing done by Landlord or its agents shall be deemed an acceptance of such surrender, and no agreement to accept such surrender shall be valid unless in writing and signed by Landlord.

24.02 Tenant Waivers.

Notwithstanding anything to the contrary contained in this Lease, the acceptance of any rent paid by Tenant pursuant to Section 24.03 below shall not preclude Landlord from commencing and prosecuting a holdover or summary eviction proceeding, and the preceding sentence shall be deemed to be an "agreement expressly providing otherwise" within the meaning of Section 223-c of the Real Property Law of the State of New York.

24.03 Damages.

If Tenant holds over without the consent of Landlord after expiration or termination of this Lease, the parties agree that it is difficult, if not impossible, to ascertain the lost rent that the Landlord will suffer as a result of Tenant's holdover. As a result, Landlord and Tenant have mutually agreed to the following liquidated damages as a reasonable pre-estimate of the probable amount of damages for lost rent and not as a penalty: Tenant shall (a) pay as holdover rental for each month of the holdover tenancy an amount equal to the Applicable Percentage of the greater of (i) the fair market rental value of the Premises for such month (as reasonably determined by Landlord) or (ii) the Rent which Tenant was obligated to pay for the month immediately preceding the end of the Term; and (b) [if such holdover continues for more than [30] days,] be liable to Landlord for and indemnify Landlord harmless against (i) any payment or rent concession which Landlord may be required to make to any tenant obtained by Landlord for all or any part of the Premises (a "New Tenant") by reason of the late delivery of space to the New Tenant as a result of Tenant's holding over or in order to induce such New Tenant not to terminate its lease by reason of the holding over by Tenant, (ii) the loss of the benefit of the bargain if any New Tenant shall terminate its lease by reason of the holding over by Tenant and (iii) any claim for damages by any New Tenant. No holding over by Tenant after the Term shall operate to extend the Term, and the acceptance of any rent paid by Tenant pursuant to this Section shall not preclude Landlord from commencing and prosecuting a holdover or summary eviction proceeding. "Applicable Percentage" shall mean [(A) 150% for the first 30 days of such holdover, and (B) 200% thereafter.]

24.04 Survival of Article 24.

Tenant's obligations under this Article 24 shall survive the termination of this Lease.

24.3 Landlord Concerns

A landlord needs to know with as much certainty as possible that once a lease has terminated, the tenant will move out. This is necessary so that arrangements may be made to re-let the premises with as small a gap as possible between tenancies. Accordingly, as an incentive to a tenant vacating in a timely manner, most leases provide that at the landlord's option a holdover tenant will be deemed to be a month-to-month tenant (which under New York law may be dispossessed by the landlord at the end of any month on not less than 30 days' notice); and provide for a holdover rent equal to a multiple of the fixed and additional rent payable under the lease immediately prior to termination or the fair market value of the demised premises, whichever is greater; provided, that a court will likely not enforce what it considers to be a penalty and may so construe a provision for triple rent. Therefore, many leases provide only for double rent in a holdover situation. Note, however, that the burden is on the tenant challenging the holdover rent amount to provide that it is unequitable or unreasonable, and a court will analyze whether the amount is a reasonable prediction of damages or is grossly disproportionate to the harm actually suffered by the landlord. As an added incentive for the tenant to vacate on time, many leases provide that the tenant is liable for any losses suffered by the landlord by reason of the tenant's holding over, which losses may be substantial if the landlord has re-let the premises. The landlord may be forced to make monetary concessions or payments to the succeeding tenant, or may lose the succeeding tenant and be faced with a substantial loss of income if it becomes necessary to start the process to re-let all over again.

Additionally, the landlord requires the tenant to waive its rights to utilize the stay provisions of section 223-c of the Real Property Law of the State of New York to prevent the tenant from obtaining a stay of enforcement of the landlord's judgment of dispossession.

A landlord is also concerned that the premises are in reasonably good condition upon the tenant's vacation in order that the landlord will have less to do to prepare the premises for the next tenant. In addition to requiring the tenant to deliver vacant possession of the premises to the landlord, the landlord wants to require the tenant to remove all of its personal property and nonstandard office installations from the premises. Such tenant obligations are more particularly addressed in Section 7.3 and Section 42.3.

24.4 Tenant Concerns

Assume that a lease terminates according to its terms and the tenant intends to vacate at the time required and, in fact, has entered into a lease for other premises. Now assume that the new space is not ready to be delivered to the tenant (whether due to delays in the landlord's work, a holdover tenant, or otherwise). The tenant may have little choice but to hold over in its current space, and therefore is concerned about the amount of the holdover rent, and should endeavor to negotiate a lower multiple. A tenant may be even more concerned about the potential for open-ended liability if the lease provides that the tenant is also responsible for the landlord's losses as a result of the tenant's holding over. Depending on the deal the landlord has made with the new tenant (i.e., it may be at a much higher rent than the original tenant is paying, depending on the conditions of the rental market), or the circumstances that may require the new tenant to occupy the premises by a certain date, the tenant's exposure could be very substantial. At a minimum, a tenant should seek to negotiate for such losses to be limited to the landlord's "actual" (as opposed to consequential) damages and to commence only after the tenant is holding over in the premises for an extended period (for example, at least 30 days).

In the event the tenant contemplates renewing its lease, it should request that the lease provide that if at its expiration the landlord and the tenant are engaged in good faith renewal negotiations, the rental due during the holdover period will continue at the rate in effect immediately prior to termination. The landlord's usual response to this request is that even a brief or one-time discussion with a tenant relating to the possibility of lease renewal might serve as a basis for defending a holdover by the tenant. If, upon renewal negotiations, the parties intend for the tenant to hold over without an increase in rent, they can so provide at that time. Accordingly, the landlord should not alter the lease but should consider such a request by the tenant only in the context of actual renewal negotiations.

With respect to the tenant's waiver of the stay provisions of section 223-c of the Real Property Law of the State of New York, the tenant may have valid grounds on which to dispute the landlord's judgment of dispossession, and by waiving this right available to the tenant by law, the tenant effectively loses its ability to contest the judgment.

24.5 Standard Real Estate Board of New York Clause

> *End of Term:* 22. Upon the expiration or other termination of the term of this lease, Tenant shall quit and surrender to Owner the demised premises, broom clean, in good order and condition, ordinary wear and damages which Tenant is not required to repair as provided elsewhere in this lease excepted, and Tenant shall remove all its property. Tenant's obligation to observe or perform this covenant shall survive the expiration or other termination of this lease. If the last day of the term of this lease or any renewal thereof falls on Sunday, this lease shall expire at noon on the preceding Saturday unless it be a legal holiday in which case it shall expire at noon on the preceding business day.
>
> All fixtures and all paneling, partitions, railings and like installations, installed in the premises at any time, either by Tenant or by Owner on Tenant's behalf, shall, upon installation, become the property of Owner and shall remain upon and be surrendered with the demised premises unless Owner, by notice to Tenant no later than twenty days prior to the date fixed as the termination of this lease, elects to relinquish Owner's right thereto and to have them removed by Tenant, in which event the same shall be removed from the premises by Tenant prior to the expiration of the lease, at Tenant's expense. Nothing in this Article shall be construed to give Owner title to or to prevent Tenant's removal of trade fixtures, moveable office furniture and equipment, but upon removal of any such from the premises or upon removal of other installations as may be required by Owner, Tenant shall immediately and at its expense, repair and restore the premises to the condition existing prior to installation and repair any damage to the demised premises or the building due to such removal. All property permitted or required to be removed by Tenant at the end of the term remaining in the premises after Tenant's removal shall be deemed abandoned

and may, at the election of Owner, either be retained as Owner's property or may be removed from the premises by Owner, at Tenant's expense.

24.6 Comments on Standard Real Estate Board of New York Clause

While the standard clause is similar to the sample clause with respect to requirements that the tenant remove its property and repair any damage, it does not provide for holdover rent, liability for the landlord's consequential damages, or the tenant's waiver of CPLR 2201.

24.7 Litigation Issues

A landlord has two separate concerns about surrender of premises: (1) damages resulting from loss of rent from a successor lessee; and (2) costs that may be incurred in repairing the premises. As to the first concern, there is no implied right to consequential damages, even though obviously foreseeable; as to the second concern, the courts may award damages greater than the actual loss sustained by the lessor due to tenant's surrender of the premises in a damaged condition. Notwithstanding that consequential damages may be foreseen, the damages recoverable by the landlord are generally limited to the legal cost of eviction, plus the value of tenant's use and occupancy. In *1009 Second Avenue Associates v. New York City Off-Track Betting Corp.*,[1] an off-track betting (OTB) parlor did not vacate the premises at the lease expiration because its new premises were still under construction. The landlord notified the tenant in writing that it needed the premises immediately in order to construct premises for a new tenant whose lease was to commence in about six months, the time required for construction. The holdover tenant was advised that the failure to vacate could result in the loss of the successor tenant who would be paying $500,000 in annual rent. The trial court refused to dismiss the landlord's claim, holding that "even if consequential damages are not foreseeable at the time of the contract, they are recoverable if foreseeable at the time of the holdover."[2] In reversing the lower court, the appellate division reaffirmed that "settled law" imposes no liability on a tenant for consequential damages resulting from its holding over; and that the prevailing law when the lease was entered should continue to apply because "parties who engage in transactions based on prevailing law must be able to rely on the stability of such precedents."[3] The court held that the terms of the lease refuted the assertion that the tenant should have expected to pay consequential damages for holding over. An express provision imposed liability for consequential damages if the tenant held over after notice that the building was to be demolished. The inclusion of this provision "operates to preclude such damages under circumstances that are not expressly stated. . . . Second, the inclusion of a provision for consequential

1. 248 A.D.2d 106, 669 N.Y.S.2d 540 (1st Dep't 1998).
2. 669 N.Y.S.2d at 542.
3. *Id.*

damages reflects their 'unusual and extraordinary' nature. . . ." so that an express provision imposing such liability in case of holding over after the term expired should have been in the lease.[4]

A provision requiring a tenant to surrender the premises broom clean, in good order and condition, ordinary wear and tear excepted, has been interpreted to mean that the tenant is required to repair and restore actual damage, deterioration, or waste. This covenant is not an obligation to restore the premises, and thus unless there is an express provision to restore the premises to its condition prior to commencement of the lease, none will be implied. Thus, in *Civic Realty Co. v. New York Telephone Co.*,[5] where the landlord consented to a structural alteration converting the existing men's and women's bathrooms into a single, larger women's bathroom, the tenant was not required to restore two separate bathrooms at the end of the term.

Typically, several lease provisions govern obligations on surrender of the premises. There is an obligation to surrender the premises broom clean, in good order and condition, reasonable wear and tear excepted. The tenant may also be required to remove its trade fixtures, on notice from the landlord, and upon removal the tenant is obligated to repair and restore the premises to the condition prior to installation, and to repair damage due to removal. The tenant usually covenants, in a separate provision, to take good care of the premises and make nonstructural repairs. The application of these provisions led to the conclusion in *Akron Meats, Inc. v. 1418 Kitchens, Inc.*[6] that the tenant defaulted in its lease obligations. The tenant left large holes in the floor when removing trade fixtures and otherwise left the premises in a state of disrepair. The trial court held that the tenant had not breached its obligations on surrender and removal of the fixtures because the premises was initially delivered to tenant in deteriorated condition. The lower court decision was reversed, as the lease obligated the tenant to "leave the premises in good repair" and "to repair the damage caused by such removal. . . ." The appellate court held that

> the express obligation imposed by a lease to leave premises in good condition has long been interpreted to require the tenant not only to keep the premises in as good a condition as when it enters, but to put, keep and leave the premises in a good state of repair. . . . Here, notwithstanding the age of the building, it was demonstrated, without question, that plaintiff did not leave the premises in good repair. Although plaintiff may have left the premises in no worse condition than when it first took occupancy, it clearly failed to fulfill the specific obligation . . . to leave the premises in "good order and condition."[7]

4. *See also* 437 Madison Ave. Assoc. v. A.T. Kearney, Inc., 127 Misc. 2d 37, 488 N.Y.S.2d 950 (Sup. Ct. App. Tm. 1st Dep't 1985) and Chapter 21, Remedies and Damages, *supra*.
5. 16 Misc. 2d 660, 190 N.Y.S.2d 3 (Sup. Ct. N.Y. Cnty. 1959).
6. 160 A.D. 2d 242, 553 N.Y.S.2d 355 (1st Dep't 1990).
7. 553 N.Y.S.2d at 357.

The measure of damages in *Akron Meats* was not the cost of repair, but the loss of an alteration reimbursement payment, due on cancellation by the landlord provided the tenant was not in default. Since the failure to restore was deemed a default, a condition precedent to the payment was not met and payment was properly withheld, regardless of the actual cost of repair.[8]

8. *See also* Chapter 8, Repairs and Maintenance, *supra*, and City of New York v. Farrell Lines, 30 N.Y.2d 76, 330 N.Y.S.2d 358, 281 N.E.2d 162 (1972) (holding tenant liable for cost of repairs even though lessor was to demolish premises).

CHAPTER 25

Quiet Enjoyment

25.1 General Purpose

A covenant of quiet enjoyment is an agreement on the landlord's part that, for the period of the lease term, the tenant shall not be disturbed in its enjoyment of the occupancy of the premises by any wrongful act of landlord, its successors in interest, or by the enforcement of any title superior to that of landlord. Such covenant also constitutes a warranty that the landlord has title or power to grant a valid lease. Thus, this landlord's covenant is for the benefit of the tenant. It is not, as a surprising number of tenants seem to think, in reading the customary language of boilerplate leases, including the REBNY form quoted next, intended to assure literal "peace and quiet" to the occupant of the premises. Rather its purpose is to guarantee that the tenant's possession will not be disturbed by another real estate interest-holder among the sets of interests that make up the bundle of rights in the property in question. The landlord will, in such a clause, make exculpatory reference to other identified interests that may, under certain circumstances, claim a right to evict the tenant. An example of such an interest would be the holder of a prior or later mortgage or ground lease to which the tenant has agreed to make its interest subordinate (see Chapter 11, Subordination and Attornment, *supra*). Except for those situations, and as long as the tenant is not in default under other terms of the lease, it has the right to "quietly enjoy" its tenure in the premises without needing to defend any legal action seeking ouster.

25.2 Sample Clause

25.01 Quiet Enjoyment.

Tenant shall and may peaceably and quietly have, hold and enjoy the Premises, subject to the other terms of this Lease and to Superior Leases and Superior Mortgages, provided that Tenant pays the Fixed Rent and Additional Rent to be paid by Tenant and performs all of Tenant's covenants and agreements contained in this Lease.

25.3 Landlord Concerns

There is no legitimate reason for a landlord to refuse to include such a standard provision. Such a covenant means that the landlord, at the time, has a title to the premises that enables him to give to the tenant a legal right of entry and enjoyment during the defined term. By the same token, the landlord is also entitled to add the standard qualifiers that relieve the building owner from the consequences of the covenant, namely, (1) that the tenant perform all its payment and other lease obligations in a timely manner and (2) that the tenant may still lose its space lease in a foreclosure by a mortgagee to whose mortgage the lease is subordinated, or be terminated upon the termination of a ground or underlying lease to which the tenant's space lease is subordinated, in each case by agreement in the lease.

25.4 Tenant Concerns

A covenant for quiet enjoyment under New York state law is implied in every lease, whether created by parol (oral contract) or in writing (although a lease may apparently legally stipulate that such lease may not be construed to that effect). Still, the prudent tenant will insist both upon the inclusion of such a clause and, in its reference to the covenant not being binding if the tenant is in default, will also require the tenant to propose language indicating that default here is measured by the passage of the cure period after notice as required by the lease.

25.5 Standard Real Estate Board of New York Clause

The REBNY clause, article 23, is straightforward:

> *Quiet Enjoyment: 23.* Owner covenants and agrees with Tenant that upon Tenant paying the rent and additional rent and observing and performing all the terms, covenants and conditions, on Tenant's part to be observed and performed, Tenant may peaceably and quietly enjoy the premises hereby demised, subject, nevertheless, to the terms and conditions of this lease including, but not limited to Article 31 hereof and to the ground leases, underlying leases and mortgages hereinbefore mentioned.

25.6 Comments on Standard Real Estate Board of New York Clause

The reference in the REBNY form to Article 31 apparently refers to the definition of "owner" (landlord), making clear that the transfer of the land and building frees the owner/landlord of any covenants in the lease, including the covenant of quiet enjoyment. Appropriate changes from the tenant's perspective would be the additions described earlier with respect to the sample clause (see discussion in Section 25.4, Tenant Concerns, *supra*) making the performance of the tenant's obligations "after periods of notice and opportunity to cure," and making the owner/landlord's covenant itself one that explicitly "runs with the land."

25.7 Litigation Issues

The covenant of quiet enjoyment is virtually the only obligation implied in a commercial lease.[1] The covenant is an assurance that the landlord has the legal title and right to grant the lease, and that the tenant may have exclusive use of the premises for any legal purpose.[2]

Leases, ordinarily, expressly provide for a covenant of quiet enjoyment. The leading case interpreting contractual quiet enjoyment covenants is *Dave Herstein Co. v. Columbia Pictures Corp.*[3] In this case a tenant that had ceased payment of rent sought damages from the landlord alleging a breach of the covenant of quiet enjoyment. The landlord's alterations on part of the premises used as a storeroom, and the removal of a toilet, were argued to constitute a partial actual eviction. The court set forth the essential elements constituting a breach of this covenant. The landlord must create a nuisance or perform an act that precludes the tenant from the beneficial enjoyment of the property, resulting in the abandonment of the premises by the tenant. The key element is ouster, or forced abandonment of the premises, except actual ouster will not be required when the tenant attorns to a successor by foreclosure. The express language in the lease conditioned landlord's covenant on payment of the rent by the tenant when due. Since the tenant had ceased payment of rent prior to the act allegedly constituting the breach by landlord, the tenant was barred from maintaining its action. The court held "that unless there is an eviction, actual or constructive, there is no breach of the covenant of quiet enjoyment; and further, that to maintain an action on the covenant, plaintiff must have performed all covenants which are conditions precedent to his right to insist upon the covenant. . . ."[4]

In order to prevail on a claim, either affirmatively for damages or defensively in a non-payment proceeding, the tenant must establish that the condition complained of was caused by the landlord. Thus, if a tenant is constructively evicted due to a leak in the building where the premises is located, and the landlord had no knowledge of the condition causing the leak, a claim for breach could not be sustained. Once the landlord was on notice of the condition, such knowledge, and failure to remedy the condition, constituted a breach of the covenant of quiet enjoyment.[5] Excessive noise

---

1. Fifth Ave. Bldg. v. Kernochan, 221 N.Y. 370, 117 N.E. 579, *rearg. denied* 222 N.Y. 525, 118 N.E. 1057 (1917). *See also* LANDLORD AND TENANT PRACTICE IN NEW YORK, FINKELSTEIN & FERRARA, sections 10.41, 10.62 (West 1997).
2. Forsee Corp. v. Pergament Enters. of S.I., 198 A.D.2d 397, 604 N.Y.S.2d 123 (2d Dep't 1993).
3. 4 N.Y.2d 117, 172 N.Y.S.2d 808, 149 N.E.2d 328 (1958).
4. 172 N.Y.S.2d at 811; *see also* 220 West 42d Assoc. v. The Ronbet Newmark Co., 53 A.D.2d 829, 385 N.Y.S.2d 304 (1st Dep't 1976) (covenant was expressly subordinate to all mortgages, thus insulating the landlord from liability when it later cutoff the lease when acting as mortgagee under a purchase money mortgage).
5. Finkelstein v. Levinson, 74 Misc. 2d 105, 343 N.Y.S.2d 849 (NYC Civ. Ct. N.Y. Cnty. 1973).

may constitute a breach; however, a tenant who rented space in a noisy manufacturing area could not assert a breach of the covenant of quiet enjoyment by the landlord where other tenants caused the noise. The breach could not be asserted even though the noise interfered with tenant's use of the premises as offices and conference rooms, and would require the tenant to incur costly alterations to muffle the noise.[6] The act resulting in the breach may be a failure to provide services such as heat, even when there is no express requirement to provide heat, if the covenant of quiet enjoyment can be implied.[7]

Another element essential to the assertion of a breach of the covenant is that there must be an actual or constructive eviction. Thus where a restaurant was required to cease operations because of a lack of water, resulting from a clogged pipe outside of the premises, but on other property owned by the landlord, the tenant stated a case for a breach of the covenant of quiet enjoyment.[8] However, a tenant's failure to vacate the premises precludes constructive eviction and prevents reliance upon the covenant.[9]

6. Lanin v. Thurcon Props., Ltd., 197 A.D.2d 423, 602 N.Y.S.2d 388 (1st Dep't 1993).
7. Adams v. Green, 114 Misc. 2d 633, 452 N.Y.S.2d 143 (NYC Civ. Ct. Kings Cnty. 1982).
8. Hidden Ponds of Ontario, Inc. v. Hresent, 209 A.D.2d 1025, 622 N.Y.S.2d 168 (4th Dep't 1994).
9. 343 N.Y.S.2d at 854.

CHAPTER 26

No Waiver

26.1 General Purpose

Landlords and tenants may not always act quickly in response to, and indeed may not always quickly become aware of, the other party's breach of its lease obligation. In addition, either party may even knowingly waive a breach but, due to a change in circumstances, may not want to waive a subsequent breach. Furthermore, a landlord wants to be able to deposit all rent checks and have access to the funds as soon as possible without such deposit or use of funds constituting a waiver of an existing breach by the tenant/payor. Finally, a landlord does not want to inadvertently have a tenant released from its liability under its lease. The purpose of the no waiver provisions is to address these concerns.

26.2 Sample Clause

26.01 No Waivers.

Failure by either party to declare any default immediately upon its occurrence or delay in taking any action in connection with such default shall not waive such default but such party shall have the right to declare any such default at any time thereafter. Any amounts paid by Tenant to Landlord may be applied by Landlord, in Landlord's discretion, to any items then owing by Tenant to Landlord under this Lease. Receipt by Landlord of a partial payment shall not be deemed to be an accord and satisfaction (notwithstanding any endorsement or statement on any check or any letter accompanying any check or payment) nor shall such receipt constitute a waiver by Landlord of Tenant's obligation to make full payment. No act or thing done by Landlord or its agents shall be deemed an acceptance of a surrender of the Premises, and no agreement to accept such surrender shall be valid unless in writing and signed by Landlord.

26.3 Landlord Concerns

A landlord wants to ensure that neither anything done by the landlord nor by any of the landlord's agents will constitute the landlord's agreement to a surrender of the premises (and a concomitant release of the tenant from its liability under the lease) prior to lease expiration. This provision is especially important to a landlord whose offices are not located in the building where the premises are located or in a building having numerous employees of the landlord on-site, such as concierges, security personnel, elevator personnel, porters, and maintenance staff. A landlord wants to know that no tenant will be released from its lease obligations unless the landlord has agreed to it in writing.

A landlord also is concerned that neither a delay in responding to the tenant's breach nor a failure to respond at all will be construed as a waiver of the landlord's rights under the lease when a response to that breach or a subsequent similar or dissimilar breach is eventually forthcoming. Also, while a landlord may overlook a nonmaterial breach, it wants to preserve its rights with respect to any such subsequent breach, because at some point repeated nonmaterial breaches can become material. In addition, circumstances may change, and a landlord wants the flexibility to enforce its rights under the lease with respect to what was once overlooked. To ensure that neither the landlord's failure to act nor an oral statement made or allegedly made by an employee or agent of the landlord will be deemed to be a waiver of any lease provision, the sample clause provides that any waiver must be in writing and signed by the landlord.

A landlord is concerned with cash flow, and therefore wants to be able to deposit and utilize all rental payments as soon as possible. If a tenant disputes an amount owed to the landlord, or believes that the landlord is not fulfilling its obligations under the lease and consequently pays to the landlord less than the required rental, the landlord wants to be able to use the payment received without such act constituting an admission that the tenant is correct. The lease provision preserves the landlord's rights to recover the full amount of the required payment.

26.4 Tenant Concerns

While a tenant might like the ability to be relieved of its lease obligations by handing over its keys to the landlord, it cannot reasonably expect that the landlord will be amenable to negotiating this provision. The same can be said for the balance of this article and, accordingly, substantial changes are rarely requested (and even more rarely given). However, as drafted, a tenant will typically receive reciprocal provisions providing that neither the tenant's failure to address a breach by the landlord of its obligations under the lease nor the payment of rent by the tenant when it is aware of a breach by the landlord will be deemed to be a waiver of the tenant's rights. Also, it is reasonable for a tenant to request that the payment of the full amount of rent billed by the landlord will not be deemed to be a waiver of the tenant's right to dispute the amount actually owed.

26.5 Standard Real Estate Board of New York Clause

No Waiver: 25. The failure of Owner to seek redress for violation of, or to insist upon the strict performance of any covenant or condition of this lease or of any of the Rules or Regulations, set forth or hereafter adopted by Owner, shall not prevent a subsequent act which would have originally constituted a violation from having all the force and effect of an original violation. The receipt by Owner of rent and/or additional rent with knowledge of the breach of any covenant of this lease shall not be deemed a waiver of such breach and no provision of this lease shall be deemed to have been waived by Owner unless such waiver be in writing signed by Owner. No payment by Tenant or receipt by Owner of a lesser amount than the monthly rent herein stipulated shall be deemed to be other than on account of the earliest stipulated rent, nor shall any endorsement or statement of any check or any letter accompanying any check or payment as rent be deemed an accord and satisfaction, and Owner may accept such check or payment without prejudice to Owner's right to recover the balance of such rent or pursue any other remedy in this lease provided. No act or thing done by Owner or Owner's agents during the term hereby demised shall be deemed an acceptance of a surrender of said premises, and no agreement to accept such surrender shall be valid unless in writing signed by Owner.

No employee of Owner or Owner's agent shall have any power to accept the keys of said premises prior to the termination of the lease and the delivery of keys to any such agent or employee shall not operate as a termination of the lease or a surrender of the premises.

26.6 Comments on Standard Real Estate Board of New York Clause

The standard clause addresses all of the concerns addressed by the sample clause.

26.7 Litigation Issues

"A waiver is the voluntary abandonment or relinquishment of a known right. It is essentially a matter of intent which must be proved."[1] More than merely a matter of intent, it is a matter of conduct; the more egregious the conduct, the more it approaches an estoppel, the less a "no waiver" clause will protect the landlord.

The New York Court of Appeals has heard several cases on the narrow issue of whether acceptance of rent during a period of default constitutes a waiver of the default.[2] Acceptance of rent is an act not easily resisted on the part of the landlord, and it is also a definite act that can clearly be drafted into a non-waiver clause.[3]

---

1. Jefpaul Garage Corp. v. Presbyterian Hosp. in City of New York, 61 N.Y.2d 442, 474 N.Y.S.2d 458, 462 N.E.2d 1176 (1984).

2. *Id.*; TSS-Seedman's, Inc. v. Elota Realty Co., 72 N.Y.2d 1024, 534 N.Y.S.2d 925, 531 N.E.2d 646 (1988); Atkin's Waste Materials, Inc. v. May, 34 N.Y.2d 422, 358 N.Y.S.2d 129, 314 N.E.2d 871 (1974).

3. *See* P&D Cards & Gifts, Inc. v. Matejka, 150 A.D.2d 660, 541 N.Y.S.2d 533 (2d Dep't 1989) (holding that acceptance of rent for 40 months without demanding required security deposit was waiver, where non-waiver clause did not refer to acceptance of rent).

In *Atkin's Waste Materials, Inc. v. May*,[4] the tenant conducted a scrap business on land leased from the city of Rochester, and some burning of scrap metal on the premises may have violated lease terms. The landlord sought to reject an exercise of an option to renew the lease four months after notice by tenant exercising the renewal, stating that the tenant failed to fully perform every lease term. The landlord had accepted rent for the months following the renewal notice, and for years without noticing the tenant for the alleged defaults. The court held that "When rent is accepted with knowledge of particular conduct which is claimed to be a default, the acceptance of such rent constitutes a waiver by the landlord of the default. . . . The acceptance of rent is in effect an election by the landlord to continue the relationship of landlord and tenant."[5] Although it seems that the court is setting down black letter law, factors other than mere acceptance of rent were considered in determining that a waiver occurred. The tenant in fact served the city lessor in disposing of scrap, and thus the landlord accepted performance not only as lessor but in fulfillment of tenant's other contractual obligations. Therefore, the tenant's conduct was also considered in substantial compliance. Furthermore, the landlord gave the tenant a vague notice of default without appropriate opportunity to cure.

In *Jefpaul Garage Corp. v. Presbyterian Hospital in City of New York*,[6] the Court of Appeals supported the landlord wherein rental defaults constituted the grounds for rejecting the exercise of a lease renewal. Unlike *Atkin's*, the lease in *Jefpaul* contained a non-waiver clause that specifically stated that "The receipt by Landlord of rent with knowledge of the breach of any covenant shall not be deemed a waiver of such breach. . . ."[7] The court stated that the provision of lease was ". . . clear and unambiguous. The parties having mutually assented to its terms, the clause should be enforced to preclude a finding of waiver of the conditions precedent to renewal."[8]

The court in *Jefpaul* made other distinctions between the two cases. In *Jefpaul* the landlord promptly rejected the exercise of the renewal option, on the grounds of particular and repeated defaults in payment of rent; in *Atkin's* the landlord waited four months to reject the renewal. Thus the waiver in *Atkin's* was of the condition that the lease not be in default when the renewal was exercised. Furthermore, the landlord in *Jefpaul* accepted rent, but noticed the tenant for rental defaults during the term, whereas the city in *Atkin's* never formally asserted a default for the alleged tenant conduct.

Gimbel Holding Co. v. Hirschman[9] points out how the failure to comply with a condition constitutes conduct that prevents reliance on the non-waiver clause. Similar to the one in *Jefpaul*, the non-waiver clause specifically provided that receipt of rent with knowledge of a breach shall not be a waiver. The landlord's predecessor did not bill rent escalations because it had problems providing services to the tenants and, in fact, eventually went bankrupt. The successor purchaser from the bankruptcy trustee

4. 34 N.Y.2d 422, 358 N.Y.S.2d 129, 314 N.E.2d 871 (1974).
5. 34 N.Y.2d at 427, 358 N.Y.S.2d at 132.
6. 61 N.Y.2d 442, 474 N.Y.S.2d 458, 462 N.E.2d 1176 (1984).
7. 61 N.Y.2d at 446, 474 N.Y.S.2d 460.
8. *Id.*
9. 1997 WL 724562 (S.D.N.Y.) *[This case was not reported in the Federal Supplement.]*.

sought to bill the tenant for added rent since the lease inception, but was barred from doing so notwithstanding the non-waiver clause. The additional rent provisions called for providing a statement and billing the rent on an annual basis. This was deemed a condition to collection of the added rent; and because of the failure to provide the timely notice required by the lease, the court held that the non-waiver clause did not prevent a determination that the landlord's (Gimbel Holding Co.) conduct constituted a waiver of its claim to rent overages.[10]

In *TSS-Seedman's, Inc. v. Elota Realty Co.*,[11] the Court of Appeals found that acceptance of rent waived termination of a lease due to a nonpayment default, notwithstanding the non-waiver clauses in the lease. The lease contained a conditional limitation providing for termination in the event of default upon five days' notice; it did not provide a right to effect a cure even during the five-day period. The rent payment was accepted prior to issuing the termination notice as provided for in the lease. The essential act constituting termination of the lease, that is, giving the notice of termination, never occurred prior to the payment of rent. However, non-waiver clauses have protected landlords who accept rent after the serving of a termination notice pursuant to lease provisions.[12]

When conduct other than acceptance of rent is alleged to constitute a waiver, courts consider the egregiousness of the conduct in order to determine whether a landlord should be estopped from relying on a non-waiver clause. In *Taylor v. Eli Haddad Corp.*,[13] the landlord asserted that the tenant's joint residential and commercial use of the premises constituted a violation of the use clause permitting the premises to be used only as a photographic studio. The tenant alleged that the landlord knew at the inception of the lease that the tenant intended to reside in the premises and nevertheless entered into the lease. The court held that the tenant could assert a defense that "Despite the no waiver clause in the lease, defendant's alleged instigation and participation in the offending condition from the inception of the lease is so pervasive and active that it may be estopped from relying on the no waiver clause."[14]

Conduct may be so willful that it may constitute an actual agreement to waive. In *Compton Advertising, Inc. v. Madison-59th Street Corp.*,[15] a tenant unsuccessfully challenged an electric additional rent provision. However, during negotiations prior to the litigation, the landlord's agent advised the tenant that electric increases would not be passed on; and "increases were not revealed or passed on during this period merely in order to avoid irritating the tenant during negotiations respecting escalation charges for other services. . . ."[16] The court held that the landlord waived the right to collect the electric increases not billed, as "It smacks of fraud to withhold secretly the claim for

10. 1997 WL 724562, *4 (S.D.N.Y.).

11. 72 N.Y.2d 1024, 534 N.Y.S.2d 925, 531 N.E.2d 646 (1988).

12. Kallen v. Kasin, 226 A.D.2d 505, 641 N.Y.S.2d 76 (2d Dep't 1996); Castaldo v. Harrington, 212 A.D.2d 1004, 633 N.Y.S.2d 94 (4th Dep't 1995).

13. 118 Misc. 2d 253, 460 N.Y.S.2d 886 (Sup. Ct. N.Y. Cnty. 1983).

14. 460 N.Y.S.2d at 890.

15. 91 Misc. 2d 768, 398 N.Y.S.2d 607 (Sup. Ct. N.Y. Cnty. 1977).

16. 398 N.Y.S.2d at 612–13.

such increases, to be asserted later, in order to procure an advantageous resolution of the escalation dispute. . . ."[17]

The longer the period of time the landlord's conduct of accepting rent or having knowledge of an alleged default persists, the more likely a waiver will be found.[18] However, despite the length of time such conduct persisted, a successor landlord without actual knowledge of a waiver of performance of a lease covenant would not be charged constructive knowledge of the prior landlord's conduct. The new landlord has a right to expect performance pursuant to the terms of the lease.[19]

17. *Id.* at 613.

18. Sea Cliff Delicatessen, Inc. v. Skrepek, 199 A.D.2d 510, 605 N.Y.S.2d 389 (2d Dep't 1993) (five years acceptance of rent from alleged unconsented to assignee); East 4th St. Garage, Inc. v. L.B. Mgmt. Co., 172 A.D.2d 292, 568 N.Y.S.2d 111 (1st Dep't 1991) (long-standing practice of accepting late rent payment); El-Kam Realty Co. v. Epstein, 148 Misc. 2d 835, 568 N.Y.S.2d 259 (Sup. Ct. App. Tm. 1st Dep't 1990) (lessor knew of alleged illegal commercial use for five years).

19. Tehan v. Thos. C. Peters Printing Co., Inc., 71 A.D. 2d 101, 421 N.Y.S.2d 465 (4th Dep't 1979); Stoneybrook Realty, L.L.C. v. Cremktco Inc., 176 Misc. 2d 589, 675 N.Y.S.2d 749 (2d Dep't 1998) (possession does create constructive knowledge of a waiver).

CHAPTER 27

Waiver of Trial by Jury

27.1 General Purpose

Although most landlord-tenant relationships will run their term without serious disagreement between the parties, others will not be so amicable. Either or both parties to a lease may, on one or more occasions during the course of the lease term, resort to the courts for the resolution of their disputes.

When a jury, rather than a judge, is the fact finder at a trial, the trial most likely will take longer to complete, and the cost and expense to the litigants, particularly attorneys' fees, will increase. The parties' agreement to waive trial by jury streamlines the expensive and time-consuming dispute resolution process. In addition, many people believe that it will lessen the risk of a biased or otherwise surprising result.

27.2 Sample Clause

> *Article 27 Waiver of Trial by Jury.*
>
> Landlord and Tenant hereby waive trial by jury in any action, proceeding or counterclaim brought by either against the other on any matter whatsoever arising out of or in any way connected with this Lease, the relationship of Landlord and Tenant, Tenant's use or occupancy of the Premises, including, without limitation, any claim of injury or damage, and any emergency and other statutory remedy with respect thereto.

27.3 Landlord Concerns

When faced with a tenant that has failed to pay its rent or to perform some other obligation under its lease, a landlord desires a swift resolution of its dispute with the tenant and the prompt payment of the past due sums or prompt performance of the other defaulted obligations. The landlord does not want to engage in the expensive and time-consuming effort of empaneling a jury and allowing it to hear and determine the issues being litigated.

The vast majority of landlords are dependent on the timely receipt of rental income in order to pay debt service on the mortgage encumbering their property. A mortgagee will not permit its borrower, the landlord, to default in making timely mortgage payments simply because a tenant is in default in the payment of rent. Thus, landlords require the timely payment of rent in order to avoid defaulting on their mortgage, thereby avoiding the expense of defending against foreclosure and perhaps even losing their property. Therefore, landlords view the possibility of a jury trial in any matter affecting their relationship with their tenants, especially, but not exclusively, in matters effecting the timely payment of rent, as a very real threat to their ownership of their property and, thus, to their very survival. Their concern is real and legitimate.

Juries are comprised of "natural persons," and there are many more natural persons who are tenants than landlords. A jury pool selected more or less at random from the citizenry of a particular county is likely to be populated by a majority of persons who are tenants and will tend to be sympathetic with the position of a tenant at trial. Therefore, it is no surprise that landlords believe that they stand a better chance of receiving an unbiased result when a judge rather than a jury sits as the finder of fact.

When a landlord is the defendant in an action or proceeding brought by its tenant, the landlord may not desire the swift resolution of the action and, accordingly, may want the ability to have the case heard before a jury. A landlord with this concern could, if its interest in a protracted process outweighs its concern about the possible bias of a jury populated largely by tenants, draft the waiver to provide that only the tenant waives its right to a jury trial. It is unlikely, however, that a tenant's attorney would agree to such a waiver if it were not reciprocal.

27.4 Tenant Concerns

Tenants, too, are benefitted by prompt and economical conflict resolution processes. But, as noted earlier, jury pools tend to be more heavily populated by tenants than by landlords, and their sympathies might sway them toward more pro-tenant decisions.

Also, delays in the trial process can be extremely costly to a tenant. When a landlord fails to provide a service required to be performed by it under the lease and necessary for the tenant to operate its business at the demised premises, generally the tenant must resort to legal action to enforce its right to receive such service (unless the lease affords the tenant a self-help remedy or the landlord's breach is so severe as to constitute a constructive eviction). Whether or not the tenant is capable of operating its business at the demised premises absent such service, it is likely that the lease requires the tenant to continue to pay rent, without abatement or setoff, at all times during the term, including throughout the entire period of time that the landlord fails to provide such necessary services. A resolution in court may be the tenant's only practical means of enforcing its rights under the lease and/or recovering damages resulting from the landlord's breach. A tenant may suffer great harm if the court proceedings are not expeditiously concluded.

Therefore, tenants rarely have a legitimate basis for objecting strenuously to waiver of trial by jury provisions, and it is very rare that such provisions are stricken or even modified in any material way.

27.5 Standard Real Estate Board of New York Clause

> *Waiver of Trial by Jury: 26.* It is mutually agreed by and between Owner and Tenant that the respective parties hereto shall and they hereby do waive trial by jury in any action, proceeding or counterclaim brought by either of the parties hereto against the other (except for personal injury or property damage) on any matters whatsoever arising out of or in any way connected with this lease, the relationship of Owner and Tenant, Tenant's use of or occupancy of said premises, and any emergency statutory or any other statutory remedy. It is further mutually agreed that in the event Owner commences any proceeding or action for possession including a summary proceeding for possession of the premises, Tenant will not interpose any counterclaim of whatever nature or description in any such proceeding including a counterclaim under Article 4 except for statutory mandatory counterclaims.

27.6 Comments on Standard Real Estate Board of New York Clause

The standard Real Estate Board of New York clause differs from the sample clause in two material respects.

First, the standard Real Estate Board clause excludes actions for personal injury or property damage from the mutual waiver of trial by jury. It is possible that a court under certain circumstances might be unwilling to enforce a waiver of trial by jury by a tenant in the case of a personal injury action and, rather than risk the possibility that the entire article be declared unenforceable, the standard real estate board clause has anticipated such possibility and carved it out of the scope of the waiver. The introductory phrase of the sample clause, limiting the waiver *in its entirety* to the extent the parties may lawfully waive their rights to trial by jury, obviates not only the concern of unenforceability in the case of personal injury actions but in other unforeseen and unforeseeable cases as well.

Second, the standard real estate board clause includes an agreement by the tenant, absent in the sample clause, that the tenant will not interpose any counterclaims in the event the landlord brings an action to terminate the tenant's right of possession. While such a waiver is entirely appropriate and, in fact, for the reasons stated in Section 27.3, *supra*, necessary for the landlord's economic survival, it is absent from the sample provision simply because it is included, in broader form, in another provision of the sample lease. (See Chapter 43, sample clause Section 43.03.)

27.7 Litigation Issues

Section 259-c of the Real Property Law states that a clause in a lease that provides for the waiver of a jury trial in any action, proceeding, or counterclaim, for personal injury or property damage action, is void. Such a waiver is fully enforceable in a summary proceeding action for rent[1] and a holdover summary proceeding, even though the lease containing the waiver has expired.[2] When combined with a waiver of counterclaims, the waiver will permit a summary proceeding for possession to proceed without the delay in conducting a jury trial.[3] Although a commercial lease may contain a provision waiving the right to a trial by jury of any action arising out of that lease, it has been held that such a waiver does not apply to causes of action alleging an inducement to enter into a lease by fraudulent misrepresentations.[4]

Disagreement exists among the judicial departments as to whether a particular action or counterclaim constitutes damage to property and thus subject to a trial by jury. *81 Franklin Co. v. Ginaccini*[5] has an excellent summary of the case law and interpretations. The tenant was sued for nonpayment of rent, lost that proceeding, but sued the landlord for damages due to lost revenue arising from a partial eviction. The court held that the lost revenue constituted damage to the tenant's business and was therefore deemed to be property damage. The court followed First Department precedent in holding that damage to property, whether caused tortiously or caused by breach of lease, that is, contractually, was covered by R.P.L. section 259-c, and thus the jury waiver could not apply.[6]

The Southern District of New York in *Herman Miller, Inc. v. Thom Rock Realty Co., L.P.*[7] sided with the Second and Fourth Departments in ruling "That [R.P.L. § 259-c] provision is not applicable to an action to recover damages arising out of breach of the contractual provision of the lease because the words 'personal injury or property damage' traditionally refer to 'tort actions arising out of a liability imposed by law for negligence, or even a willful tort, but not out of contract.'"[8] The court upheld the waiver, by stating that the lost profits claimed by the tenant did not constitute physical property damage. The claim arose out of an alleged misrepresentation that the premises would be in a building used exclusively for furniture showrooms. Subsequent to the execution

1. Fay's Drug Co. v. P & C Prop. Coop., Inc., 51 A.D.2d 887, 380 N.Y.S.2d 398 (4th Dep't 1976).
2. Arol Dev. Corp. v. Goodie Brand Packing Corp., 83 Misc. 2d 477, 372 N.Y.S.2d 324 (NYC Civ. Ct. Bronx Cnty. 1975) (noting that terms of lease which expired are deemed to continue for holdover, absent a new agreement).
3. West Seventy-Ninth St. Assoc. v. Lemi, Inc., 141 Misc. 2d 830, 535 N.Y.S.2d 325 (NYC Civ. Ct. N.Y. Cnty. 1988) (severing counterclaim for damages for breach of covenant of quiet enjoyment, thus giving effect to jury trial waiver).
4. Ferry v. Poughkeepsie Galleria Co., 197 A.D.2d 913, 602 N.Y.S.2d 267 (4th Dep't 1993).
5. 149 Misc. 2d 124, 563 N.Y.S.2d 977 (NYC Civ. Ct. N.Y. Cnty. 1990).
6. The court notes that the Appellate Division, Second Department holds that R.P.L. § 259-c applies only to tort actions; the Fourth Department agrees with the Second Department, *see* Fay's Drug Co. v. P&C Property Cooperative, Inc., 51 A.D.2d 887, 380 N.Y.S.2d 398 (4th Dep't 1976).
7. 819 F. Supp. 307 (S.D.N.Y. 1993) (enforcing a jury waiver claim R.P.L. § 259-c as to a breach of the lease that led to lost profits and additional costs, which the court deemed a contractual loss).
8. 819 F. Supp. 308.

of the lease, other tenant uses were permitted. The tenant claimed lost profits because the building was no longer perceived by buyers as a significant showroom space and, as a consequence, attracted fewer visitors.[9] The court stated: "Merely characterizing the damage as lost profits does not convert an action for breach of a lease into a property damage or personal injury claim exempted from the waiver by [R.P.L.] § 259-c."[10]

The First Department has denied jury trials, upholding lease jury waivers, in cases where tenants allege damage to their business. In *Phoenix Garden Restaurant, Inc. v. Chu,*[11] the court denied a jury trial in action arising out of a claim that tenant's business was damaged because the landlord imprudently undertook a building renovation project. The tenant combined its action for damages with claims in equity for injunctive relief and to be relieved of certain debt and guarantee obligations. The nature of the pleadings meant a jury trial had to be waived. Similarly, in *Paralegal Institute, Inc. v. Big Sol Mfg. Co., Inc.*,[12] the tenant claimed damage to its business due to faulty window repairs. In addition to a claim for damages, the tenant sought to rescind the lease. The court held that both the jury waiver clause and the combining of requests for legal and equitable relief barred a jury trial.

9. *Id.* at 310.
10. *Id.* at 309.
11. 234 A.D.2d 233, 651 N.Y.S.2d 510 (1st Dep't 1996).
12. 190 A.D.2d 595, 593 N.Y.S.2d 797 (1st Dep't 1993).

CHAPTER 28

Inability to Perform; Force Majeure

28.1 General Purpose

This provision quite simply exculpates a landlord and tenant from any consequences of the failure to fulfill the building owner's obligations because of circumstances beyond its control (other than the payment of money). Because the exculpatory impact is of vital importance to the landlord and tenant, there has historically been little variation within this provision of a lease. However, recently landlords and tenants have focused more closely on the "force majeure" definition and the consequences of force majeure due to the impacts that Superstorm Sandy and the COVID-19 pandemic had (and the impacts that similar future events may have) on properties and business operations. The definition and consequences of force majeure are also relevant in the discussion of delivery of the premises, commencement of rent, and the consequences of service interruptions (see Section 2.02, *supra*, and Section 30.2, *infra*). A tenant may seek, and even receive, relief under other provisions of the lease where the landlord actually withdraws or denies some service, or access, for so long that the passage of time will trigger a rent abatement, release, or even a tenant right to terminate, but that situation is not normally covered in this provision (except by generic cross-reference).

28.2 Sample Clause

Article 28 Inability to Perform (Force Majeure).

Landlord or Tenant shall have no liability in connection with either party's inability to fulfill or delay in fulfilling any of its obligations under this Lease expressly or impliedly to be performed by Landlord or Tenant, as the case may be, (including, without limitation, Landlord's or Tenant's inability to make or delay in making any repairs, additions, alterations, improvements or decorations, or Landlord's or Tenant's inability to supply or delay in supplying any equipment or fixtures), if Landlord's or Tenant's inability or delay is due to or arises by reason of strikes, labor troubles or disruptions, disruption in the supply chain, or by accident, or by any cause whatsoever beyond Landlord's or Tenant's reasonable control, including, without limitation, Laws, other governmental actions, shortages or unavailability of labor, fuel, steam, water, electricity or materials, delays caused by other tenants or other occupants of the Building, acts of God, enemy or terrorist action, civil commotion, [*language recommended due to COVID-19 pandemic:* actual or threatened health emergency (including, without limitation, epidemic, pandemic, famine, disease, plague, quarantine, and other health risk)], fire or other casualty ("Force Majeure"). Notwithstanding anything to the contrary contained in the foregoing, any party's failure timely to fulfill an obligation required to be fulfilled by such party under this Lease shall not be excused or deemed to be an event of Force Majeure if (i) said obligation is an obligation to pay money, or (ii) said failure shall be attributable to such party's lack of funds.

28.3 Landlord Concerns

A landlord does not wish to give a tenant any excuse to claim constructive eviction and remove itself from the premises on such grounds while claiming termination of the lease. The failure to deliver any vital service to the tenants—elevator, power and light, rubbish removal—might have that consequence, without such a provision, even if the reason for the service failure was a labor strike, or public utility breakdown, or other circumstance beyond the landlord's reasonable control. The sample clause (see Section 28.2, *supra*) purports to cover the gamut of such risks of modern urban life, by redefining such a crisis situation as one in which the *status quo ante* of the lease relationship stays fixed until the crisis has passed. If the force majeure provision mutually benefits both parties, then landlords should be insistent on including the last sentence from the sample clause, which does not permit tenant to withhold the payment of monies due to a force majeure event.

28.4 Tenant Concerns

The first draft of a force majeure provision usually speaks to the landlord alone being prevented from performing its obligations, without reference to the tenant. However, there are periods during the term of the standard lease, such as fulfillment of a tenant's obligation to repair or restore, or even to move out at term's end, that can be seriously affected by a strike in one of the trades or by the movers. If this provision is altered to give the tenant the same protection afforded to the landlord, then the tenant is empowered to argue that its damage restoration or move-out date obligations should be extended for the practical duration of the strike (or other force majeure events) that prevented good faith performance. Thus, though the occasions for its use may be far fewer, the tenant may equally benefit from such protection. More recently, many tenants (particularly retail tenants) have unsuccessfully argued for a suspension of their rent obligations due to the COVID-19 pandemic. For example, in *1140 Broadway LLC v. Bold Food, LLC*,[1] an office tenant unsuccessfully argued that the doctrines of impos-

1. 1140 Broadway LLC v. Bold Food, LLC, 2020 NY Slip Op. 34017(U) (Sup. Ct. 2020).

sibility and frustration of purpose should excuse the tenant's nonpayment of rent. The tenant blamed their failure to pay rent in part on the fact that many of their own clients had suspended services or operation due to COVID-19-related public health directives. Similarly, in 53 E. 75th St. Cop. v. Christian Louboutin L.L.C.,[2] a retail tenant argued that the COVID-19 pandemic evoked the doctrines of impossibility and frustration of purpose because, inter alia, their business model was based on highly visible retail space and heavy foot traffic while COVID-19 kept potential buyers at home. The court granted summary judgment for the plaintiff and noted that the "frustrated purpose must be so completely the basis of the contract that, as both parties understood, without it, the transaction would have made little sense." Tenants should not expect landlords to agree to a lease provision excusing the payment of rent due to any force majeure event, and it is extremely unlikely in the absence of such a provision that the courts would grant such rent relief.

28.5 Standard Real Estate Board of New York Clause

The REBNY provision, Article 27, is along the same lines as the sample clause, but limits its coverage solely to the owner/landlord:

> *Inability to Perform:* 27. This Lease and the obligation of Tenant to pay rent hereunder and to perform all of the other covenants and agreements hereunder on part of Tenant to be performed shall in no way be affected, impaired or excused because Owner is unable to fulfill any of its obligations under this lease or to supply or is delayed in supplying any service expressly or impliedly to be supplied or is unable to make, or is delayed in making any repair, additions, alterations or decorations or is unable to supply or is delayed in supplying any equipment, fixtures, or other materials if Owner is prevented or delayed from so doing by reason of strike or labor troubles or any cause whatsoever including, but not limited to, government preemption or restrictions or by reason of any rule, order or regulation of any department or subdivision thereof of any government agency or by reason of the conditions which have been or are affected, either directly or indirectly, by war or other emergency.

28.6 Comments on Standard Real Estate Board of New York Clause

An owner/landlord has no need for further protection in this provision; the tenant, however, should seek some changes. First, following the words "any cause whatsoever," the phrase "beyond Owner's reasonable control" should be added. A second addition, to cross-reference back to other lease provisions that may give the tenant the right to a rent abatement or even lease termination after the passage of a certain period of

2. 53 E. 75th St. Cop. v. Christian Louboutin L.L.C., 2020 NY Slip Op. 34063(U) (Sup. Ct. 2020).

time, should be inserted at the head: "Except as elsewhere explicitly set forth in this Lease, . . ."

A third amendment, which the owner/landlord should not in logic resist, would be to add at the very end of the text, "but excluding Owner's financial condition" (note that the sample clause similarly excludes "obligations to pay money"). Finally, while the grammatical construction of the REBNY's one-sentence provision makes it difficult to insert a modification to give the tenant reciprocal protection, the following language might be sought:

> The foregoing events are here and elsewhere in this Lease described as force majeure events. Tenant shall have no liability whatsoever to Owner on account of the inability of Tenant to timely fulfill any of Tenant's obligations under this Lease (except for obligations to pay money) by reason of any force majeure events. If this Lease specifies a time period for performance of an obligation of Tenant (except for payment obligations), that time period shall be extended by the reason of any delay in Tenant's performance caused by any *force majeure* events.

The addition of this last sentence may be made to serve a further purpose. If it is further expanded to include the owner/landlord (i.e., made to track the last sentence of the sample clause in Section 28.2, *supra*), it will explicitly limit the period of the owner/landlord's excuse for nonperformance in a manner presently missing from the REBNY provision (although such language's absence should not prevent the tenant's counsel from arguing that the concept is inherent in the clause).

28.7 Litigation Issues

A force majeure clause does not always protect a landlord or tenant from the consequences of their inability to perform a leasehold covenant due to a cause beyond their control. The landlord in *Pyramid Investors Co. v. Medina-Maple, Inc.*[3] prepared a store lease containing a force majeure clause stating that:

> The period of time during which either party is prevented or delayed in the performance of the making of any improvement or repairs or fulfilling any obligation . . . due to unavoidable delays caused by . . . strikes or labor troubles . . . or other causes beyond such party's reasonable control, shall be added to such party's time for performance thereof. . . .

A rider to the commencement clause provided that if the premises were not ready for the occupancy by March 16, 1971, the lease would terminate. At the time the lease was executed there was a construction strike and the premises were completed by March 24, 1971. Examining the lease, the court noted that the force majeure clause specifically dealt with "improvements or repairs" and not specifically with "construction." The court examined the fire and casualty damage clause and the repair clause,

3. 72 Misc. 2d 893, 339 N.Y.S.2d 612 (Sup. Ct. Onondaga Cnty. 1973).

and found that both provisions contained obligations to effect certain repairs, by either the landlord and/or the tenant, within a specified time period. However, the court noted that "The very detailed language of this lease, which is silent as to any obligations on the part of the landlord to deliver possession . . . leads the Court to believe that the intent of the parties was that [the force majeure clause] would come into effect only after occupancy had been taken and not prior thereto."[4] It was the clear intention of the parties that if the premises were not ready by March 16, 1971, the lease would be terminated. As a consequence the court held that the tenant was not obligated to take possession after that date.

In *Kel Kim Corp. v. Central Markets, Inc.*,[5] the plaintiff-tenant operated a roller rink. Its lease contained a covenant to carry liability insurance from a solvent insurer in limits of not less than $500,000 for any individual and the aggregate of $1,000,000 for any single accident. The tenant's liability insurance was canceled because of the financial condition of the insurer. The tenant, thereafter, was unable to obtain coverage in the aggregate amount required by the lease.

Kel Kim Corporation was served with a notice of default providing that it vacate the premises within 30 days unless it cures the default. Kel Kim (and its individual guarantors under the lease) commenced an action to declare its rights under the lease, the defendant moved for summary judgment, and plaintiffs cross-moved for similar relief. Plaintiffs alleged that it should be excused under the force majeure clause for its inability to obtain the required coverage because a "nationwide insurance crises" made the coverage unavailable in the marketplace. The force majeure clause, in part, read:

> If either party to this Lease shall be . . . prevented from the performance of any obligation through no fault of their own by reason of labor disputes, inability to procure materials, failure of utility services, restrictive governmental laws, riots, insurrection, war, adverse weather, Acts of God, or other similar causes beyond the control of such party, the performance of such obligation shall be excused for the period of the delay.[6]

The landlord sought to enjoin the tenant from using the premises as a skating rink until the insurance was obtained. The use clause was broad, permitting any legal purpose. The court held that the doctrine of impossibility of performance could not be relied on to excuse the inability to procure insurance. Reliance on the doctrine "hinges

4. 339 N.Y.S.2d at 616.
5. Kel Kim Corp. v. Cent. Mkts., Inc., 131 A.D.2d 947, 516 N.Y.S.2d 806 (3d Dep't 1987). [**NOTE:** the Shepards report states that this case has been overturned by statute. That is not accurate, strictly speaking. The case cited in the Shepards report and the relevant statute in that case deal with domestic violence survivors. In that case, a woman experiencing domestic violence was evicted from her apartment based on the noise resulting from the attacks against her. She invoked a statute meant to protect victims of abuse from discrimination. If not for that statute, which was enacted in 2016, the only relevant considerations about eviction based on the noise would have been Kel Kim Corp., but in light of the domestic abuse statute, the tenant was protected from discrimination and not evicted despite the loud noise coming from her apartment.]
6. 516 N.Y.S.2d at 808.

upon a showing that performance of a condition is rendered impossible by an unanticipated event that could not be foreseen or guarded against in the contract." The tenant should have anticipated, in view of the use as a skating rink, that insurance might not be available at some period during the 20-year lease term and drafted some protection into the lease. Furthermore, the impossibility was deemed personal to the tenant, who could have legally used the premises for another use for which insurance may have been available. The court further refused to permit the tenant to use the force majeure clause as a defense, construing it under the principal of *ejusdem generis*: "words constituting general language of excuse are not to be given the most expansive meaning possible, but are held to apply only to . . . the same general kind or class as those specifically mentioned."[7]

The court concluded that:

> [T]he *force majeure* clause here contemplates irresistible forces which make consummation of any material obligation of the lease impossible. While compliance with the insurance aspect of the lease agreement is a material element of the lease, it is the lawful use and occupancy of the demised premises which is its centerpiece, and plaintiffs have not shown that they have been prevented from using the premises by reason of a frustrating circumstance not of their own making, for it is they who have chosen to use the premises for an enterprise for which they cannot obtain the necessary insurance; one simply cannot rely on his own act, or failure to act, as a *force majeure*.[8]

7. *Id.* at 809.
8. *Id.*

CHAPTER 29

Bills and Notices

29.1 General Purpose

Throughout the term of a lease (and sometimes even after its expiration), the parties will want or need to communicate with one another. Communications may relate to such mundane matters as a request by a tenant to add a new employee's name to a building lobby directory board, or to more significant or time-sensitive matters, such as a request for an estoppel certificate or a notice of a default in the timely payment of rent. In various circumstances, landlords and tenants need to be able to communicate their wants and needs efficiently, effectively, and with certainty. A lease must provide one or more approved methods by which communications may be given by one party to the other and should provide that communications given in any other manner will not be deemed to be effective notice under the lease. A notice clause also should provide the name and/or title of a particular person to receive notices.

29.2 Sample Clause

Article 29 Bills and Notices.

All notices, demands, consents, approvals, advices, waivers or other communications which may or are required to be given by either party to the other under this Lease (each, "Notice") shall be in writing and shall be delivered by (a) personal delivery, (b) the United States Postal Service mail, certified or registered, postage prepaid, return receipt requested or (c) a nationally recognized overnight courier, in the case of each Notice to Landlord at *[address of Landlord]* to the attention of *[Name of Individual]*, with a copy to (i) *[insert any other party to be copied]* and (ii) *[name and address of Landlord's attorneys]*, Attention: *[name of contact person at Landlord's attorneys' firm]*, Esq. and in the case of each Notice to Tenant at *[address of Tenant]* to the attention of *[Name of Individual]* with a copy to (i) *[insert any other party to be copied]* and (ii) *[name and address of Tenant's attorneys]*, Attention: *[name of contact person at Tenant's attorneys' firm]*, Esq. or to such other place as the party to be notified may from time to time designate by at least 5 days' notice to the notifying party. [Notwithstanding anything contained herein to the contrary, either party may give Notices to the other by email, in the case of each Notice to Landlord at *[email address of Landlord]*, with a copy to *[email address of Landlord's attorney]* and in the case of each Notice to Tenant at *[email address of Tenant]*, with a copy to *[email address of Tenant's attorney]*, provided that such Notice is also given pursuant to the methods set forth in clauses (a), (b) or (c) above within one (1) Business Day after such Notice is given by email.] Notices from Landlord may be given by Landlord's managing agent, if any, or by Landlord's attorney. The attorneys for Tenant may send notices on behalf of Tenant. Each Notice shall be deemed to have been given on the date such Notice is actually received as evidenced by a written receipt therefor, and in the event of failure to deliver by reason of changed address of which no Notice was given or refusal to accept delivery, as of the date of such failure.

29.3 Landlord Concerns

The most important purpose of a notice provision in a lease is to provide certainty, that is, to provide the parties with a method of giving a notice that the sender knows will be effective for all purposes even if the addressee does not receive it because, for example, the addressee has relocated and cannot be found. This is much more important to landlords than to tenants for two reasons: first, it is much less likely that a landlord will move and be difficult or impossible to locate since, after all, the landlord owns the property and derives income from it; and second, when a landlord sends an important notice to a tenant (such as a default notice), it will need to establish (especially in a court proceeding) that the notice was "given" (i.e., that it is effective). It will be much easier for the landlord to prove that it gave a notice in accordance with the terms of the lease than to prove that the tenant actually received it. Thus, the primary purpose of a well-drafted notice provision is to negate any need to deal with the issue of whether the addressee received it. Proof that the notice was properly sent should suffice for all purposes.

A secondary purpose of a notice provision in a lease is to limit the types of notices (by method of transmission) that will be effective, thereby limiting the notices that must be dealt with and/or responded to as substantive notices under the lease. Thus, landlords want to know that substantive notices received from tenants are given the attention they merit. For example, a landlord would be imprudent to permit a tenant to drop off a substantive notice with the lobby attendant at the building rather than requiring such notices to be delivered in an appropriate manner to the administrative or counsel's office at the landlord's main offices. Letters sent by certified mail, as well as packages delivered by overnight courier or other personal delivery services, each of which require the recipient's signature upon delivery, are likely to receive prompt attention by the addressee and are less likely to be lost in transit or neglected following receipt. Each of those methods should satisfy a landlord that the tenant's notice will receive the prompt attention at the landlord's office it is likely to require. In order to further ensure that notices from tenants are not lost in the shuffle of a busy landlord's day, a landlord may require a tenant to send a duplicate of any notice to the landlord's attorneys. The attorneys' copies of notices should also be sent by certified mail or overnight courier or other personal delivery service, requiring a signed receipt evidencing delivery.

The sample clause provides that delivery of notices is deemed to occur when it in fact is completed, as evidenced by the signed receipt, or when delivery is refused, which will be noted by the courier or messenger service. Since overnight and personal delivery services generally deliver within specific time frames and since the fact of delivery usually can be ascertained by means of a telephone call or electronic confirmation (supported by a documented receipt) from the delivery service, these methods also provide for certainty and have the added advantage, in most situations, of greater speed of delivery.

Landlords need the ability to change the address to which notices are to be delivered, and the sample clause sets forth the method by which a party may change the addresses to which notices must be given by the other party. A landlord also may want the ability to require a tenant to deliver copies of notices to additional addresses, such as to the landlord's attorneys (if not required in the lease as originally drafted) or as may be required by a mortgagee of the building. The notice clause should provide the landlord with the ability to require tenants to send notices to additional addresses upon the landlord's request.

Since certified mail cannot be sent to addresses outside the United States, to allow for the possibility of addressees outside the United States, both the sample clause and the Real Estate Board of New York clause provide that the alternative delivery method of registered mail may be used. This method would not normally be used within the United States since it is more costly and burdensome than certified mail. Similarly, neither overnight courier nor messenger service should be the exclusive method for giving notices since neither can be made to a post office box address.

29.4 Tenant Concerns

A tenant's primary concern is that it not be bound by the content of a notice it has not received and has not had an opportunity to act upon. If a notice is sent by ordinary mail, delivery (or the failure thereof) cannot be proven with certainty. If a notice is left at the tenant's premises, perhaps with a receptionist, or merely slipped under the door in the evening, it could easily be lost or mis-delivered within the tenant's organization. Further, although a tenant may occupy space within a particular building, that space may not be the office from which the tenant operates its business or administers its leases. Accordingly, a tenant should insist that bills and notices be sent to it at its proper administrative office address. Notwithstanding the burden that might be placed on a landlord, a tenant might prefer even routine notices and rent bills to be sent by a method assuring delivery to a particular person within the tenant's organization. This requirement would guard against the failure to respond to such bills and notices, and would ensure the necessary response within the time frames required by the lease, thereby avoiding a potential default by the tenant. A tenant might, for example, provide in its lease that bills be sent to its main office marked for the attention of the director of lease administration, and that notices of default be marked for the attention of its president or director of facilities with a duplicate sent to its general or outside counsel.

For the same reasons as apply to landlords, most tenants prefer that duplicate copies of any notice be sent to the tenant's attorney. The attorney's copy of notices should also be sent by certified mail or overnight courier or other personal delivery service. If a landlord is resistant to the burden of copying a tenant's attorney on *all* notices, the tenant might request that, minimally, the tenant's attorney receive duplicate copies of default notices.

If the tenant is unable to use its premises because the heat has failed on a cold winter day, the tenant will want the service to be restored immediately and will, in all likelihood, telephone or visit the landlord's management office in the building to present its demands. However, the landlord does not want to be deemed in default of its lease obligations if the porter on duty fails to communicate the tenant's concern to the appropriate supervisor. Accordingly, a landlord would be unwise to permit formal notice to be deemed given by a tenant upon mere oral notification. A tenant might be able to negotiate the right to give emergency notices by electronic mail. However, in order to better protect both the sender and the recipient of such electronic mail provision should state that the electronic mail notice must be confirmed electronically and immediately followed by duplicate notice sent by one of the more traditional methods.

Finally, tenants frequently concern themselves with the length of various grace periods provided for in the lease during which they must cure a default, but fail to analyze the related, and very important, issue of when notices are deemed effective. This, of course, can be a harmful omission.

29.5 Standard Real Estate Board of New York Clause

> *Bills And Notices: 28.* Except as otherwise in this lease provided, any notice, statement, demand or other communication required or permitted to be given, rendered or made by either party to the other, pursuant to this lease or pursuant to any applicable law or requirement of public authority, shall be in writing (whether or not so stated elsewhere in this lease) and shall be deemed to have been properly given, rendered or made, if sent by registered or certified mail (express mail, if available), return receipt requested, or by courier guaranteeing overnight delivery and furnishing a receipt in evidence thereof, addressed to the other party at the address hereinabove set forth (except that after the date specified as the commencement of the term of this lease, Tenant's address, unless Tenant shall give notice to the contrary, shall be the building), and shall be deemed to have been given, rendered or made (a) on the date delivered, if delivered to Tenant personally, (b) on the date delivered, if

delivered by overnight courier or (c) on the date which is two (2) days after being mailed. Either party may, by notice as aforesaid, designate a different address or addresses for notices, statements, demand or other communications intended for it. Notices given by Owner's managing agent shall be deemed a valid notice if addressed and sent in accordance with the provisions of this Article. At Owner's option, notices and bills to Tenant may be sent by hand delivery.

29.6 Comments on Standard Real Estate Board of New York Clause

The Real Estate Board of New York clause permits landlords to leave bills and notices at the premises, without the requirement for a signed receipt. The clause does not provide that notices be given to the attention of a particular person or officer or that copies of notices be sent to the parties' respective attorneys, which, as noted earlier, would be beneficial to both parties. Although the clause provides for certified mail as a permissible method, it does not require a return receipt, which is the basic evidence that will be received by the party sending a certified mail notice that the notice has, in fact, been delivered. It also does not require a receipt for hand deliveries and makes no mention of the very commonly used method of overnight courier. Finally, the clause rather harshly and unrealistically provides that notices sent by certified mail are deemed delivered when mailed.

29.7 Litigation Issues

Compliance with the notice provisions of a lease is important because the required notice is generally construed as a condition precedent to enforcement of the particular provision. Attempts to collect additional rent, especially after a substantial delay, are often successfully defended because the landlord has failed to give notice deemed to be a condition precedent to the tenant's obligation to pay. In *Winfield Capital Corp. v. Mahopac Auto Glass, Inc.*,[1] the landlord was obligated to provide a copy of the annual tax bill and to give the tenant notice of the tax escalation amounts by February 1st of each lease year. The court held that the notice requirement established a condition precedent to the tenant's obligation to pay the additional rent. Even the non-waiver clause, which the dissent urged should excuse the landlord's delay in billing the amounts due, was ignored by the majority in granting summary judgment to the tenant and denying the landlord's claim.[2]

---

1. 208 A.D.2d 715, 617 N.Y.S.2d 499 (2d Dep't 1994); *see also* Woodlaurel, Inc. v. Wittman, 199 A.D.2d 497, 606 N.Y.S.2d 39 (2d Dep't 1993).

2. *See also* Gimbel Holding Co., v. Hirschman, 1997 WL 724562 (S.D.N.Y.) (denying reliance on non-waiver clause where escalation rent was not billed in accordance with lease). *[This case was not reported in the Federal Supplement.]*

The case can be contrasted to *Goldstein v. City of New York*,[3] where the landlord sought to collect 11 years of escalation charges, totaling more than $625,000, arising in connection with a lease by New York City of premises for a day-care center. The lease required the landlord to provide the tenant with an estimate of operating costs 60 days prior to each lease year. The court held that the requirement was not a condition precedent, and if it was intended to be, the lease could have expressly stated that failure to provide the annual cost estimate would constitute a waiver of the added rent. It appears that this decision rests on precedent involving similar municipal leases and contracts. Failure to comply with a similar provision in a lease involving private parties would constitute failure to comply with a condition precedent to collection.[4]

Where a purchase option clause required a tenant to be in compliance with all the terms of a lease as a condition to exercising the option, the courts have held that the landlord must have previously given the tenant a notice of a default, as may be required by the lease, in order to deny the effective exercise of the option.[5] This "notice provision is a condition precedent to the landlord's ability to use a default as a reason to deny the . . . rights under the lease, including the . . . option to purchase."[6]

A notice requirement may also be a condition precedent to the exercise of a tenant's rights. When a casualty damage provision required a tenant to give prompt notice of a fire, and the notice provision required that notices be sent by certified mail, failure to give the notice barred the tenant from obtaining the benefits of the rent abatement portions of the casualty clause, notwithstanding the tenant's allegations that the landlord was aware of the fire and that the premises were unusable.[7]

The requirement, in an operating expense escalation clause, that the tenant give notice of a dispute with respect to an operating expense statement, within 30 days of its receipt, has been held to be a condition precedent to challenging the escalation charges, notwithstanding the landlord's discussions with the tenant concerning these charges subsequent to the expiration of the 30-day period.[8]

Failure to comply strictly with notice requirements concerning a tenant's default will provide the defaulting tenant with a defense. A conditional limitation requires that a notice be given to establish the condition, expiration of a time period, that will result in a lease termination. "It is the passage of time—the period of time specified in the

3. 159 A.D.2d 313, 552 N.Y.S.2d 594 (1st Dep't 1990), *but see* Mount Sinai Hosp. v. 1998 Alexander Karen Annuity Tr., 110 A.D.3d 288, 970 N.Y.S.2d 533 (App. Div. 1st Dep't 2013) (distinguishing Goldstein because Goldstein dealt with a lease to the City of New York as opposed to an ordinary commercial lease).

4. See Weisblatt v. Schwimmer, 249 A.D.2d 297, 670 N.Y.S.2d 891 (2d Dep't 1998) (where lease required landlord to provide tax bill or estimated bill and statement of operating costs prior to beginning of each calendar year, the failure to provide such figures precluded collection of added rent).

5. Cinema Dev. Corp. v. Two Thirty Eight Realty Corp., 149 A.D.2d 648, 540 N.Y.S.2d 305 (2d Dep't 1989).

6. 540 N.Y.S.2d at 306.

7. Milltown Park Inc. v. Am. Felt & Filter Co., 180 A.D.2d 235, 584 N.Y.S.2d 927 (3d Dep't 1992).

8. Silverstein Props., Inc. v. Paine, Webber, Jackson & Curtis, Inc., 104 A.D. 2d 769, 480 N.Y.S.2d 724 (1st Dep't 1984).

termination notice—that the lease automatically comes to an end; without service of a notice specifying the date of expiration of the lease there can be no termination and the lease remains in effect."[9]

Similarly, where a landlord seeks an acceleration of rent due to an alleged default, notice of acceleration must be given strictly in accordance with the notice provisions of a lease. Thus, notice by personal service or by certified or registered mail, which is deemed "sufficient" in a standard lease clause, has been held to be mandatory in order to enforce acceleration. The court in *Bijan Designer for Men, Inc. v. St. Regis Sheraton Corp.*[10] denied the acceleration, holding that "whether or not other unspecified methods of notice may be sufficient, I hold that where such a drastic result as acceleration of the full term's rent is sought, the type of notice provided for by mutual agreement must be adhered to." This ruling can be compared to a landlord's successful attempt to maintain nonpayment summary proceedings upon an oral demand, where the lease had essentially the same notice provision.[11] The court held that the notice provision applied to notices given under the lease and that the oral rent demand was permitted under Real Property Actions and Proceedings Law (RPAPL) section 711. The notice provision did not expressly provide for notice of a rent demand in a manner other than permitted by the statute.

The contents of a notice to cure, which may result in a lease termination, must also be carefully considered by a landlord. In *Filmtrucks, Inc. v. Express Industries & Terminal Corp.*[12] the landlord's attorney wrote a letter to the tenant advising it of certain alleged defaults, and stated that "unless the above is rectified . . . we would appreciate your immediately vacating the space and not require any action on our part." The court held this to be an ineffective notice to cure because it did not specifically refer to the cure provision in the lease, and to the 60-day cure period set forth therein. Nor did it advise the tenant that the lease would immediately terminate if the defaults were not cured in the 60-day period. Furthermore, since the lease did not provide for notices to be given by the landlord's attorney, the notice had to be signed by the owner to be effective.

---

9. TSS-Seedman's, Inc. v. Elota Realty Co., 72 N.Y.2d 1024, 534 N.Y.S.2d 925, 956, 531 N.E.2d 646 (1988) (lease did not make rent default curable after notice of termination, but no notice was given prior to cure, thus subsequent notice could not terminate lease).

10. 142 Misc. 2d 175, 536 N.Y.S.2d 951, 956 (Sup. Ct. N.Y. Cnty. 1989).

11. Four Star Holding Co. v. Alex Fur, Inc., 153 Misc. 2d 447, 590 N.Y.S.2d 667 (Sup. Ct. App. Tm. 1st Dep't 1992).

12. 127 A.D.2d 509, 511 N.Y.S.2d 862 (1st Dep't 1987).

CHAPTER 30

Services and Interruption of Services (HVAC, Elevator, Water, Cleaning)

30.1 General Purpose

The "Services" provision in an office lease is intended to establish the standards for delivery of various necessities or amenities associated with the use and enjoyment of the demised premises. Typically, these include heating, ventilating, and air conditioning (thus, HVAC), passenger and freight elevator access, hot and cold water, cleaning (often the subject of a separate lease exhibit), and sometimes electricity (which is often the subject, as in the Real Estate Board of New York printed form, of an entirely separate provision, and thus will be treated elsewhere in this book [Chapter 17, *supra*]).

More than in other standard office lease sections, the contents of these provisions are a function of the size and quality (class) of the office building in question. The landlord is prepared to offer a standard, rent-inclusive package of services, with defined (and effectively capped) quantities, but often indicates that other services (such as overtime HVAC, excessive cleaning, or freight elevator service) are, with sufficient notice, available on a per-use basis. The tenant, for its part, wants to establish minimum levels for such services, to minimize its extra-service costs (through sharing with neighboring tenants, where possible, or seeking a discount for or free allotment of freight elevator use in connection with its initial move-in to the premises), and to minimize the impact of service interruptions, perhaps with a rent abatement if landlord services are not provided for an extended period of time with the ultimate threat of lease cancellation.

30.2 Sample Clause

Section 30.01 Landlord Services.

From and after the date that Tenant first occupies the Premises for the conduct of Tenant's business, Landlord shall furnish the Premises with the following services (collectively, "Landlord Services") at no additional charge (other than by inclusion in Operating Expenses), except as otherwise expressly provided in this Lease:

(a) heat, ventilation and air-conditioning to the Premises from [8:00 a.m. to 6:00 p.m.] on each Business Day; if Tenant shall require heat, ventilation or air conditioning services at any other times, Landlord shall furnish such service (i) in the case of a Business Day, upon receiving notice from Tenant by noon of such Business Day and (ii) in the case of a day other than a Business Day, upon receiving notice from Tenant by noon of the immediately preceding Business Day, and Tenant shall pay to Landlord within 30 days after demand Landlord's then established charges therefor which, as of the date of this Lease are $[*insert per hour charge for overtime HVAC*] per hour, plus applicable sales tax; *provided*, that there shall be a minimum charge of 4 hours for any period of additional service that neither immediately precedes nor immediately follows the standard hours first set forth above in this Section 30.01(a), it being agreed that no such minimum shall otherwise apply;

(b) (i) passenger elevator service to each floor of the Premises at all times during Business Hours on Business Days, with at least one passenger elevator subject to call at all other times and (ii) freight elevator and loading dock service to the Premises on a first come-first served basis (i.e., no advance scheduling) on Business Days from [8:00 a.m. to 6:00 p.m.], and on a reserved basis at all other times upon the payment of Landlord's then established charges therefor which, as of the date of this Lease are $[*insert per hour charge for overtime freight elevator service*] per hour, plus applicable sales tax; *provided*, that there shall be a minimum charge of 4 hours for any period of additional service that neither immediately precedes nor immediately follows the standard hours first set forth above in this Section 30.01(b)(ii), it being agreed that no such minimum shall otherwise apply; Tenant's use of all elevators shall be on a non-exclusive basis; [notwithstanding the foregoing, there shall be no charge to Tenant for the first *[insert amount of free freight elevators hours]* hours of overtime freight elevator usage by Tenant in connection with Tenant's initial move-in to the Premises];

(c) reasonable quantities of hot and cold water to the floor(s) on which the Premises are located for core lavatory, pantry and cleaning purposes only; if Tenant requires water for any other purpose, Landlord shall furnish cold water at the Building core riser through a capped outlet located on the floor on which the Premises is located (within the core of the Building), and the cost of heating such water, as well as the cost of piping and supplying such water to the Premises, shall be paid by Tenant; Landlord may install and maintain, at Tenant's expense, meters to measure Tenant's consumption of water for such other purposes in which event Tenant shall reimburse Landlord for the quantities of water shown on such meters, at Landlord's actual cost therefor (including costs for sewer rents and taxes) plus [3–10]% within 30 days after demand;

(d) electric energy on a submetered basis through presently installed electric facilities for power and lighting and other electrical fixtures, appliances and equipment at a level of not less than *[insert minimum amount of electricity to be provided to the premises]* (exclusive of electricity for the Building HVAC system) ("Available Electric Capacity"); in no event shall Tenant's consumption of electricity exceed the capacity of existing feeders to the Building or the risers or wiring serving the Premises, nor shall Tenant be entitled to any unallocated power available in the Building [unless, in Landlord's reasonable judgment (taking into account the then existing and future needs of other then existing and future tenants, and other needs of the Building), the same is available and necessary for Tenant's use, and if Landlord shall provide any such additional power, Tenant shall pay Landlord within 30 days following demand the Building's then established connection charge for each additional amp of power or portion thereof provided to the Premises and the cost of installing additional risers, meters, switches and related equipment necessary to provide such additional power];

(e) cleaning services on Business Days in accordance with Exhibit *[exhibit with cleaning specifications to be attached]* attached hereto. Tenant shall pay to Landlord within 30 days after receipt of a reasonably detailed demand the costs incurred by Landlord for (i) extra cleaning work in the Premises required because of (A) carelessness, misuse or neglect on the part of Tenant, its subtenants or their respective employees or visitors, (B) interior glass partitions or an unusual quantity of interior glass surfaces, (C) non-standard materials or finishes installed in the Premises, and (ii) removal from the Premises and the Building of any refuse of Tenant in excess of that ordinarily accumulated in business office occupancy, including, without limitation, kitchen and pantry refuse, or, if expressly requested by Tenant in writing, at times other than Landlord's standard cleaning times. Notwithstanding the foregoing, Landlord shall not be required to clean any portions of the Premises used for preparation, serving or consumption of food or beverages, training rooms, trading floors, data processing or reproducing operations, private lavatories or toilets or other special purposes requiring greater or more difficult cleaning work than office areas and Tenant shall retain Landlord's cleaning contractor at Tenant's expense to perform such cleaning and any other cleaning services in excess of those provided for in Exhibit *[exhibit with cleaning specifications to be attached]* [and Landlord shall cause such contractor to charge Tenant for such extra cleaning services at rates reasonably competitive with those charged by reputable third-party contractors performing such work in comparable buildings]. Landlord's cleaning contractor shall have access to the Premises after [6:00 p.m. and before 8:00 a.m.] and shall have the right to use, without charge therefor, all light, power and water in the Premises reasonably required to clean the Premises;

(f) subject to Force Majeure and applicable law, access to and use of the Premises 24 hours per day, 7 days per week;

[if Landlord supplies condenser water to Tenant to support Tenant's supplemental cooling needs: up to [insert amount of tonnage to be provided to tenant] tons of condenser water for Tenant's supplemental HVAC system from the common cooling tower unit serving the Building 24 hours a day, 7 days a week. Tenant shall perform all necessary work and install all required equipment to permit Tenant to tap into Landlord's condenser water riser on the floor on which the Premises is located. Tenant shall pay to Landlord a fee of *$[insert tap in fee]* per tap and shall pay for Tenant's usage of condenser water an amount equal to *$[insert per annum per ton charge]* per connected ton per annum, which amount shall be adjusted on each anniversary of the Commencement Date to equal the product of (i) such amount multiplied by (ii) the percentage of increase, if any, in the Consumer Price Index for the month prior to the month in which the applicable anniversary occurs over the Consumer Price Index for the month prior to the month in which the Commencement Date occurs, which amount shall be payable within 10 days after rendition of a bill therefor. "Consumer Price Index" means the Consumer Price Index for All Urban Consumers published by the Bureau of Labor Statistics of the United States Department of Labor, New York, New York–Northeastern New Jersey Area (1982–84=100), or any successor index thereto, appropriately adjusted; *provided*, that if there shall be no successor index, a substitute index shall be reasonably selected by Landlord. If, on the first anniversary of the Commencement Date, Tenant's connected load of condenser water is less than *[insert amount of tonnage to be provided to tenant]* tons, then Landlord shall have no further obligation to reserve for Tenant's use any condenser water in excess of Tenant's then connected load]; and

(g) Subject to Force Majeure, security in the Building 24 hours per day, 7 days per week, of a type consistent in all material respects with the standards of comparable buildings; *provided*, that, Landlord shall have no liability to Tenant (or anyone claiming through or under Tenant) for loss to Tenant (or such other person) or their agents, contractors, employees, invitees or licensees, arising out of theft, burglary or damage or injury to persons or property caused by persons gaining access to the Building or other causes.

Section 30.02 General Services Provision.

(a) Landlord may stop or interrupt any Landlord Service, electricity, or other service and may stop or interrupt the use of any Building facilities and systems at such times as may be necessary and for as long as may reasonably be required by reason of Force Majeure, accidents, strikes, or the making of repairs, alterations or improvements, or inability to secure a proper supply of fuel, gas, steam, water, electricity, labor or supplies, or by reason of any other cause beyond the reasonable control of Landlord. Landlord may modify the delivery and scope of any Building services if required by reason of any Laws. Landlord shall have no liability to Tenant by reason of any stoppage, interruption or modification of any Landlord Service, electricity or other service or the use of any Building facilities and systems for any reason. Landlord shall use reasonable diligence (which shall not include incurring overtime charges) to make such repairs as may be required to machinery or equipment within Landlord's control to provide restoration of any Landlord Service and, where the cessation or interruption of such Landlord Service has occurred due to circumstances or conditions beyond Landlord's control, to cause the same to be restored by diligent application or request to the provider.

(b) Notwithstanding the foregoing, if without the fault or neglect of Tenant or any person claiming through or under Tenant, any Substantial Portion of the Premises is rendered Untenantable for a period of *[__—the length of interruption will depend on the negotiating leverage of the tenant]* consecutive Business Days after Tenant shall have notified Landlord of such Untenantability, by reason of any stoppage or interruption of any Landlord Service to be provided by Landlord to the Premises, but excluding by reason of a Casualty to the Building or any Force Majeure, and provided Tenant is not then in default under this Lease beyond any applicable notice or cure period, then for the period commencing on the 8th Business Day after Tenant's giving notice to Landlord that such Substantial Portion of the Premises is so Untenantable, until such Landlord Service is restored or such Substantial Portion of the Premises is no longer Untenantable, Fixed Rent, Tenant's Operating Payments and Tenant's Tax Payments shall be appropriately abated with respect only to such Substantial Portion. "Untenantable" means that Tenant shall be unable to access the Premises or Tenant shall be unable to use, and, in either case, shall not be using, the Premises or the applicable portion thereof for the conduct of business.

"Substantial Portion" shall mean any portion of the Premises consisting of [_____________*—the amount of rsf defined as a Substantial Portion will depend on the size and negotiating leverage of the tenant]* or more contiguous rentable square feet.

(c) Without limiting any of Landlord's other rights and remedies, if Tenant shall be in default under this Lease after the giving of notice to Tenant and the expiration of any applicable grace or cure period, Landlord shall not be obligated to furnish to the Premises any service outside of Business Hours on Business Days, unless Tenant pays for same in advance, and Landlord shall have no liability to Tenant by reason of any failure to provide, or discontinuance of, any such service outside of Business Hours on Business Days.

(d) "Business Hours" means [8:00 a.m. to 6:00 p.m.] "Business Days" means all days except (a) Saturdays, (b) Sundays and (c) Holidays. "Holidays" means New Year's Day, Martin Luther King Day, President's Day, Memorial Day, Independence Day, Labor Day, Thanksgiving, the day following Thanksgiving, Christmas and any other days which are either (i) observed by both the federal and the state governments as legal holidays or (ii) designated as a holiday by the 32B-32J Service Employees International Union AFL-CIO contract.

30.3 Landlord Concerns

The landlord, in addition to being a building owner, is a service vendor within the building. This role has cost, control, and safety/access implications with respect to the provision of those services.

First, the landlord has "priced" the space, not only within the context of the raw market value of similarly appointed commercial spaces but also with an eye toward the group of basic building services that all tenants, seeking space within a particular class of building, will expect to be available during normal business hours (i.e., passenger and freight elevators, cleaning, HVAC, and water). Additionally, the prospective tenant will expect no extra charges for the delivery of these basic services. Most tenants will, after a base year, be paying the landlord escalation rent, based on some formula (see Chapter 5, Additional Rent; Escalation, *supra*) that is intended to pass through to the individual tenant its proportionate share of the annual increase in the cost of those inclusive, nonpersonal/nonspecial order services. The majority, if not all, of those services, however (with the notable exception of electricity, which is submetered or proportionately billed), are "sold" on a "rent-inclusive" basis.

To properly determine its initial per square foot price point, the landlord must (1) clearly define the number, type, and volume of these services and (2) secure the tenant's agreement that services beyond those defined, if available, would be forthcoming only on an order-first, user-charge basis (which additional cost is often left undefined over the lease term except as "Landlord's standard charge").

The landlord's second concern is control. Building systems, for efficient operation, must be run from a centralized place in a balanced and safe manner. Thus, tenants may not, for example, be permitted to make individual adjustments in the HVAC system, without the landlord's knowledge, oversight, and ultimate veto. Additionally, the delivery of those services that require the devotion of building staff, such as freight elevators and overtime HVAC service, must be scheduled in advance and perhaps even rationed in times of heavy use (e.g., the initial tenant buildouts in a new building during lease-up); union personnel may also need to be used and are subject to the limitations of the union contract as to designated skills and hours.

Third, while the tenant has the right of use and occupancy of its own premises, the landlord has an entire building to operate, maintain, and repair. Thus, the landlord requires access to every tenant's premises from time to time in order to repair or alter building systems. Additionally, the landlord has the unfettered right to occasionally shut down those systems in the event of emergency, or as part of the building's regular maintenance program. Thus, the landlord must secure the right of service stoppage, while avoiding the risk of incurring a damage claim from a tenant during the resulting interruption of that tenant's business.

A final concern of the landlord is the determination of when, if at all, the landlord is willing to agree to a rent abatement or cancellation of the lease due to the continued suspension or interruption of some vital building service. Many landlords, confronted with a sufficiently strong tenant, will negotiate a rent abatement, but it is extremely rare for a landlord to make any concession regarding the cancellation of the lease. During negotiations, the parties will discuss how long a service interruption must persist, and how much of the premises must be affected, before a rent abatement will apply. The landlord will also want to exclude service interruptions by reasons originating outside of the landlord's control (i.e., a force majeure event). Landlords will argue that while they have fixed costs of operation regardless of any force majeure event, tenants are required to carry business interruption insurance to cover the possibility of such events and therefore should take the risk of liability. The landlord will usually win this argument unless a tenant has substantial leverage and is particularly sophisticated.

30.4 Tenant Concerns

The tenant should first satisfy itself that all the basic services are indeed included in the landlord's promise of general service delivery, and that their cost is included in the fixed rent (subject to any escalation for increase in such costs, as additional rent). Some of those services, such as HVAC, will have system-delivery specifications (perhaps to be examined by the tenant's engineer or architect) and qualifications on intensity of the tenant usage.

Beyond these standard constraints, however, the tenant has some negotiating room with the landlord. The right to after-hours services, particularly HVAC, should be clearly established if any need is anticipated (with a statement of per-hour charges for the current year). The tenant may also bargain for parity or cost-sharing with other tenants in the same building service bank, to spread the impact of such overtime charges. If the tenant is operating a supplemental HVAC system, the opportunity to buy some minimum volume of condenser water from the landlord will be important. Also, it is very typical for a landlord to absorb the cost of security obligations for the building. One security concern is access to and from the building and the premises. Tenants might provide their employees with key cards to access the premises, and landlords might provide key cards for access to the building and any common areas or amenities. The tenant should request, and it is common for the landlord to agree with larger tenants, that the landlord synchronize the key cards for the premises with the system for entry to the building so that the tenant's employees need only a single card.

Since the lease form may be otherwise silent, this article is perhaps also the best place to insert a guaranteed tenant right of access to the premises by at least one passenger elevator, 24 hours a day, all the year round. The tenant doing a major buildout might demand a waiver or discount on freight elevator costs during the period of its initial move-in (see Section 30.01(b)(ii). As the tenant is obliged (even if the lease does not so state) to pay for the electricity needed to run the landlord's cleaners' machines and after-hours lighting, securing a promise that the lights will be turned off upon completion of cleaning is useful.

Every landlord will insist on the right to service stoppage, but the prudent tenant will insist, in return, upon reciprocity in the form of formal advance notification (except in emergencies), and due diligence regarding the completion of the landlord's work, thus allowing the most prompt resumption of the interrupted service. The tenant would also be well advised to seek from the landlord a pledge of a good faith effort to minimize the tenant's business interruption and, perhaps, a promise to chase the outside power and/or water utility for correction of a service disruption beyond landlord's control.

Finally, as to the tenant-business-killers of condemnation, fire, or other casualty, the tenant should argue for the inclusion of language (e.g., see Section 30.02(b)) that provides for a rent abatement in the event of a prolonged service interruption. Tenants will be less likely to succeed in negotiating for rent abatement due to events originating outside of the building or force majeure, which rarely excuse a tenant's obligation to pay rent. The right to cancel is hardly ever granted, since the normal building service interruption not involving major reconstruction of the building or of the demised premises can often be ended within 30 days or less.

30.5 Standard Real Estate Board of New York Clause

The REBNY provision, Article 29 (here spaced and subtitled for easier review), touches on most of the major themes enlarged upon in the sample clause set forth in Section 30.2, *supra*.

> *Services Provided by Owners: 29.* As long as Tenant is not in default under any of the covenants of this lease beyond the applicable grace period provided in this lease for the curing of such defaults, Owner shall provide:

(*a*) *[Elevator]* necessary elevator facilities on business days from 8 a.m. to 6 p.m. and have one elevator subject to call at all other times;

(*b*) *[Heat]* heat to the demised premises when as required by law, on business days from 8 a.m. to 6 p.m.;

(*c*) [Water] water for ordinary lavatory purposes, but if Tenant uses or consumes water for any other purposes or in unusual quantities (of which fact Owner shall be the sole judge), Owner may install a water meter at Tenant's expense which Tenant shall thereafter maintain at Tenant's expense in good working order and repair to register such water consumption and Tenant shall pay for water consumed as shown on said meter as additional rent as and when bills are rendered;

(*d*) *[Cleaning]* Cleaning service for the demised premises on business days at Owner's expense, provided that the same are kept in order by Tenant. If, however, said premises are to be kept clean by Tenant, it shall be done at Tenant's sole expense, in a manner reasonably satisfactory to Owner and no one other than persons approved by Owner shall be permitted to enter said premises or the building of which they are a part for such purpose. Tenant shall pay Owner the cost of removal of any of Tenant's refuse and rubbish from the building;

(*e*) *[HVAC]* If the demised premises are serviced by Owner's air conditioning/ cooling and ventilating system, air conditioning/cooling will be furnished to tenant from May 15th through September 30th on business days (Mondays through Fridays, holidays excepted) from 8:00 a.m. to 6:00 p.m., and ventilation will be furnished on business days during the aforesaid hours except when air conditioning/cooling is being furnished as aforesaid. If tenant requires air conditioning/ cooling or ventilation for more extended hours or on Saturdays, Sundays or on holidays, as defined under Owner's contract with the applicable Operating Engineers contract, Owner will furnish the same at Tenant's expense. RIDER to be added in respect to rates and conditions for such additional service;

(*f*) *[Owner's Reservation of Service Interruption]* Owner reserves the right to stop services of the heating, elevators, plumbing, air-conditioning, electric, power systems or cleaning or other services, if any, when necessary by reason of accident or for repairs, alterations, replacements or improvements necessary or desirable in the judgment of Owner for as long as may be reasonably required by reason thereof. If the building of which the demised premises are a part supplies manually operated elevator service, Owner at any time may substitute automatic control elevator service and proceed diligently with alterations necessary therefore without in any way affecting this lease or the obligation of tenant hereunder.

30.6 Comments on Standard Real Estate Board of New York Clause

The REBNY version of the standard lease article pertaining to the provision of services (Article 29) covers the four types of basic services and concludes with the owner/landlord's reservation of the right to interrupt services. Unsurprisingly, the REBNY article contains no language providing for an abatement of rent as a result of a prolonged service interruption. Further, from the tenant's perspective, this clause could benefit from the other modifications and additions discussed in Section 30.4, Tenant Concerns, *supra*.

More importantly, a tenant will seek to delete the provision's opening words, making the delivery of services dependent on the tenant's not being "in default." Very few types of tenant default (or applicable municipal health laws allow) would justify the owner/landlord's cutting off a tenant's heat and hot water. This language, left unaltered, would permit such action. At the very least, the phrase "beyond applicable periods of notice and opportunity to cure" should be added. Furthermore, the REBNY printed form is often supplemented by a typewritten rider that modifies this printed provision. Care should be taken to avoid contradiction or inconsistency between the two separate provisions on the same subject.

Although the REBNY provision is more favorable to the owner/landlord, it may, nonetheless, be improved with the addition of new paragraphs modeled on those appearing in the sample clause set forth in Section 30.2, *supra*. The new paragraphs to be added would (1) provide terms and conditions of freight elevator service; (2) list above-standard, extra-charge cleaning services; (3) condition the delivery of HVAC temperatures on tenant employee density maintenance; (4) establish an overtime building service request system; (5) provide special standards for tenant's maintenance of any planned pantry; (6) create a class of owner/landlord-authorized service vendors for food, office maintenance, and so on; (7) add the services sales tax provision; and (8) negate any owner/landlord obligation to provide further or other services except as specified.

30.7 Litigation Issues

The prudent attorney, representing a tenant, must ensure that the express covenants contained in the lease provide for such services as heat,[1] air conditioning, water, electricity, elevator service, and parking. Additionally, the tenant's attorney would be well advised not to assume that, absent an express covenant, the landlord will provide adequate services for a client's special needs.

---

1. However, *see* Adams v. Green, 114 Misc. 2d 633, 452 N.Y.S.2d 143 (NYC Civ. Ct. Kings Cnty. 1982) (obligation to provide heat and hot water for commercial tenant was implied where there was no express covenant to provide those services, but building was heated from a central plant within the landlord's exclusive control).

In *Barash v. Pennsylvania Terminal Real Estate Corp.*,[2] an attorney rented office space in a new, glass-enclosed, air-conditioned building with sealed windows. He alleged that the rental agent confirmed that the building would be ventilated 24 hours a day, seven days a week, so that the attorney could comfortably put in the long hours required by his law practice. The final lease specifically stated that the building would be air conditioned from June to September on business days, from 9 a.m. to 6 p.m., and that the landlord would "at other times during business days and similar hours, ventilate the demised premises." In other words, after-hours ventilation was not provided for in the lease. The court noted that the absence of 24 hours a day ventilation did not constitute an actual eviction, but rather was only a constructive eviction requiring the tenant to abandon the premises before being relieved of the obligation to pay rent.

A lease, apparently, may require a tenant to obtain all services directly from public utilities. Such a requirement, however, does not relieve the landlord from the obligation to assist the tenant in obtaining those services. In *Lincoln Plaza Tenants Corp. v. MDS Properties Development Corp.*,[3] the lease clearly stated that "Tenant shall, at its own cost, make arrangements with the governmental and public utility companies serving the building for the direct supply to Tenant of water, electricity, gas, heat, steam, air conditioning and any other utilities to be used by Tenant in the conduct of its business at the demised premises." The lease also provided that the landlord install a switch at the electrical distribution box serving the premises and permit the tenant to hook up to the existing utility lines, pipes, risers, and feeders to the demised premises. The landlord rejected the tenant's various plans to hook up its utilities to the landlord's existing lines, pipes, risers, and feeders. The clear obligation on part of the tenant to pay for obtaining all of its required utilities was held as not clearly exculpating the landlord from cooperating with the tenant in effecting the installation. Although the lease may have clearly provided "that" the tenant obtain utilities directly from the suppliers, it did not clearly provide "how" that could be accomplished without the landlord's cooperation. *Lincoln Plaza* demonstrates the need for a cooperative effort between landlord and tenant to permit the tenant to fulfill its obligations under the lease.

Where a lease requires the landlord to provide services, the failure to perform that essential covenant can result in a partial eviction, suspending the obligation to pay rent,[4] or it may result in a judgment for monetary damages stemming from the deprivation of the services.[5] In *Union City Union Suit Co., Ltd. v. Miller*,[6] the tenant had leased loft manufacturing space in a building subsequently converted to residential use. During the course of renovation the premises was deprived of heat for extended periods, resulting in frozen and burst pipes, as well as an interruption and eventual termination of freight elevator service. The lack of heat required the tenant to purchase heat transfers used to

2. 26 N.Y.2d 77, 308 N.Y.S.2d 649, 256 N.E.2d 707 (1970).
3. 169 A.D.2d 509, 564 N.Y.S.2d 729 (1st Dep't 1991).
4. Johnson v. Cabrera, 246 A.D.2d 578, 668 N.Y.S.2d 45 (2d Dep't 1998); Union City Union Suit Co., Ltd. v. Miller, 162 A.D.2d 101, 556 N.Y.S.2d 864 (1st Dep't 1990).
5. 162 A.D.2d 101, 556 N.Y.S.2d 864.
6. *Id.*

print the T-shirts made by the tenant, at a cost of $350,000, instead of manufacturing the transfers at a cost of $35,000. The lease contained a clause exculpating the landlord from a rent reduction or liability by reason of inconvenience, annoyance, or injury to the tenant's business by reason of the landlord making alterations or improvements.

The court in *Union City* held that the exculpation clause could not be relied on as a defense to landlord's failure to provide heat and elevator service. Further, another lease clause required that alterations be made at such times so as not to unreasonably interfere with the tenant's use of the premises. The court concluded that "it is evident that plaintiff did not agree in the lease to countenance the extended and unreasonable interruption of essential services, predictably resulting in harm to its business, without remedy."[7] The court awarded full damages to the tenant for its monetary loss due to its inability to manufacture its own heat transfers, and entirely suspended the obligation to pay rent based on the actual partial eviction resulting from the loss of freight elevator service.

If a landlord fails to make repairs required under the lease, such as fixing a frozen pipe, the failure to provide heat and hot water resulting from the failure to repair can result in a constructive eviction and a suspension of the obligation to pay rent.[8] However, where a building renovation resulted in the reduction in elevator service, but no denial of access during the period of renovation, there is no liability to the tenant for a partial actual eviction.[9]

---

7. *Id.* at 866.

8. Johnson v. Cabrera, 246 A.D.2d 78, 668 N.Y.S.2d 45 (2d Dep't 1998). *See also* 246 A.D.2d 578, 668 N.Y.S.2d 45; 162 A.D.2d 101, 556 N.Y.S.2d 864.

9. Graubard Mollen Horowitz Pomeranz & Shapiro v. 600 Third Ave. Assoc., 240 A.D.2d 161, 658 N.Y.S.2d 272 (1st Dep't 1997).

CHAPTER 31

Vault Space

31.1 General Purpose

This provision is not found in the vast majority of manuscript office leases. Generally, the owner of the fee of a highway has the right to use the subsurface thereof if material interference with the enjoyment of the public easement is avoided. A "vault" is an area underneath the sidewalk, or otherwise all or partly outside the property line of the building being leased, which might be accessed through the first floor tenant's or basement tenant's space, and possibly used for storage by these or other tenants. For the standard office tenant, however, situated above the building's lobby level, the availability of a subsurface vault or utility is not an issue. If anything, the standard manuscript lease will precisely define the location of the premises (see Chapter 2, *supra*), and then perhaps go on to grant the tenant a right to use, on a nonexclusive basis, "common areas" such as sidewalks, driveways, entrances, passages, corridors, lobbies—but here, too, vaults would not be mentioned (even if existing at the building's perimeter), since these are not normally used in common.

However, if there are no other proper storage areas within the building, in the basement or elsewhere, a tenant might seek, and a landlord might agree to grant a revocable license to use the vault space of a building. Consequently and historically, the Real Estate Board of New York lease form has long contained a vault clause. Use of a vault will, however, trigger (possibly uncollected, long-dormant) annual vault charges or taxes (see Administrative Code of the City of New York Title 11, Chapter 27, for the effective rates), and so a landlord will want to ensure that the responsibility for the payment of such taxes falls solely on the user/occupier tenant. Furthermore, such space in the public ways, by virtue of its location, is subject to invasion or recapture by municipal authorities or (even more likely) public utilities. For this reason, the landlord's permission to use a vault is virtually always couched in the form of a revocable license, the loss of which would not subject the landlord to any liability. Additionally, the tenant, upon the loss of its vault license, would not receive any reduction of rent or license fee beyond that allocable to the use of the vault.

31.2 Sample Clause

See the standard REBNY clause set forth in Section 31.5, *infra*.

31.3 Landlord Concerns

As indicated in Section 31.1, *supra*, a landlord will want to grant the use of any vault space only on the basis of a revocable license, since its own claim of use to the vault or vaults in question may be interrupted through recapture by utilities or by a municipal department (most likely, in New York City, the Bureau of Operations of the Department of Transportation). The landlord will also want to insist on the tenant bearing any vault charges occasioned by active use of the space. Finally, if the vault area is to be enlarged or altered for a tenant's needs, the normal panoply of municipal building licenses and permits will be required (New York City Administrative Code 19-117), and the cost thereof clearly made the tenant's responsibility.

31.4 Tenant Concerns

A tenant requiring the use of a building's vault must realize its occupancy of the vault is insecure. Statistically, however, the risk of revocation of a vault license, probably, is only slightly higher than that of condemnation of the building itself. Thus, if the space is useful, and a satisfactory agreement is reached with the landlord without the need for significant alteration expense, the tenant has a fair chance of enjoying the use of valuable adjoining space for the full length of its term. Tenant's counsel would be well advised to determine the status of the vault charges of the space, so that an agreement to assume that expense does not engender a later controversy over unbilled vault charges predating the tenant's occupancy.

31.5 Standard Real Estate Board of New York Clause

The REBNY vault provisions are found in Article 14.

> *Vault, Vault Space, Area: 14.* No Vaults, vault space or area, whether or not enclosed or covered, not within the property line of the building is leased hereunder, anything contained in or indicated on any sketch, blue print or plan, or anything contained elsewhere in this lease to the contrary notwithstanding. Owner makes no representation as to the location of the property line of the building. All vaults and vault space and all such areas not within the property line of the building, which Tenant may be permitted to use or occupy, is to be used and/or occupied under a revocable license, and if diminished or required by any federal, state or municipal authority or public utility, Owner shall not be subject to any liability nor shall Tenant be entitled to any compensation or diminution or abatement of rent, nor shall such revocation, diminution or requisition be deemed constructive or actual eviction. Any tax, fee or charge of municipal authorities for such vault or area shall be paid by Tenant.

31.6 Comments on Standard Real Estate Board of New York Clause

For the reasons just set forth, the owner/landlord has no particular need to modify this provision. A tenant, however, if compelled to agree to pay the vault charges as part of its additional rent, will want to remove any ambiguity inherent in the last sentence of the REBNY form, and thus avoid any potential liability for unpaid, preterm vault charges, by adding the words "allocable to the term of this Lease, through the last date of Tenant's use and occupancy thereof in the event of revocation of Tenant's license prior to the expiration date hereof."

31.7 Litigation Issues

Street vaults were essential appurtenances in the days when coal and wood were used as fuel and had to be physically stored near the premises. Thus, even though no specific right to use a vault may have been set forth in a commercial lease, the improvement of the vault and fitting it for use as a coal and wood bin was sufficient to establish an appurtenant right to use the vault.

This does not mean that a tenant's attorney need not be concerned about street vaults, particularly if the tenant is leasing a ground-floor store with basement storage. First, there is an issue of liability for personal injury. More than once workmen have been injured because of jackhammers, or other work on the surface, resulting in a collapse of the sidewalk without realizing a vault was located below the work area.[1] The fact that a vault area was specifically not included in a lease relieved a tenant from liability for injuries caused by such an accident, even though the tenant used the vault.[2] Unless such use is contemplated by the tenant, it would seem to be the better practice that a tenant's attorney make certain that the lease not include the right to use vault space.

The tenant should be concerned with the vault tax charged by New York City. Based on the size of the vault, the tax can be costly. If a lease includes the vault area and imposes liability on the tenant for payment of the tax, the tenant's counsel must determine the amount of tax being charged and whether the tenant actually intends to use the vault. Unless the vault is sealed in the manner required by the Administrative Code, mere nonuse will not end the obligation to pay the tax.[3] It should be noted,

---

1. Times Square Improvement Co. Inc. v. Fleischmann's Vienna Model Bakery, Inc., 173 App. Div. 633, 160 N.Y.S. 346 (1st Dep't 1916).

2. Pouso v. City of New York, 177 A.D.2d 560, 575 N.Y.S.2d 928 (2d Dep't 1991); *see also* Curran v. Newport Assoc., Inc., 57 A.D.2d 882, 394 N.Y.S.2d 272 (2d Dep't 1977) (tenant could be liable to injured worker when elevator crashed into street vault, if it had control of vault area; evidence of who paid vault tax was relevant to whether tenant had possession and control).

3. 71 Fifth Ave. Co. v. City of New York Dep't of Finance, 73 N.Y.2d 861, 537 N.Y.S.2d 126, 534 N.E.2d 43 (1989).

however, that on and after June 1, 1998, "no annual vault charge or additional charge shall be imposed."[4]

Although the use of street vaults for storage of coal is obsolete, the vault may be used for storage in connection with conduct of tenant's business. Since the vaults, located in the bed of the street, may be subject to use of the municipality or a utility, it would be best to specifically provide for a relative value of this space in the event its use is lost. Without such provision, the loss of the vault space may not constitute a partial actual eviction.[5]

---

4. N.Y.C. ADMIN. CODE § 11-2702 was amended pursuant to L.L. 47/1997 § 1, effective June 23, 1997. Subdivision (a) paragraph (D) was added and provides as follows:

> "Notwithstanding any provision of law to the contrary, no annual vault charge or additional charge shall be imposed pursuant to this chapter on or after June first, nineteen hundred ninety-eight."

5. Syndicate Bldg. Corp. v. Quiros, 116 N.Y.S.2d 15, *aff'd* 281 A.D. 866, 120 N.Y.S.2d 239 (1st Dep't 1953).

CHAPTER 32

Security Deposit

32.1 General Purpose

The "security" sought by this provision is the landlord's; the "deposit" is the tenant's, made against future nonpayment of rent, additional rent, or of landlord expenditures in the tenant's name. The basic nature of a security deposit is to enable the landlord to attain the status of a protected creditor should the tenant breach the lease, but the tenant is not entitled to the deposit's return until his obligations to the landlord are satisfied, generally at term's end.

The amount of the deposit is beyond the scope of this chapter since that number, generally a multiple of several months' rent, is set by the market at the time the lease is signed, and is also affected (for better or for worse) by the particular tenant's creditworthiness. Once the amount is decided, its characterization as a "security deposit" creates certain statutory protections for the tenant, and imposes corollary obligations for the landlord. Monies that are styled or treated as "pre-paid rent" do not have the same protection, from a tenant's perspective, although under applicable case law, money paid over to the landlord may be a security deposit with trust status, even if the lease does not so state; alternatively, a court may sometimes refuse to be bound by labels that the parties have applied to lease payments.

Sometimes a security deposit is in the form a letter of credit that is provided by tenant's bank in the name of a tenant to a landlord as the beneficiary of the letter of credit. As such, the letter of credit will be delivered to the landlord simultaneously with execution of the lease and the landlord will hold same until the expiration of the lease, subject to the landlord's right to draw on such letter of credit in the event of a tenant default. The letter of credit should be evergreen (i.e., automatically renews) each year until the lease expires, plus an additional period of term beyond the lease expiration so that the landlord has security for tenant's obligations that survive the lease expiration (for example, any repair or restoration obligations).

If the security deposit is in the form of cash, then under the common law, the landlord-tenant relationship with respect to security deposits was that of debtor-creditor, but this has been abolished by statute. Now, New York General Obligations Law

(GOL) section 7-103 provides that all sums, with interest accrued thereon, deposited or advanced as security in connection with the use or rental of real property (residential and commercial, although the statute does not specifically say so) remain the property of the (tenant) depositor, and are to be held in trust and not commingled with funds of the landlord.

Pursuant to GOL section 7-103(2), security money deposited with the landlord into a "banking organization" must be one doing business within the state, and the tenant-depositor is required to be given the name and address of the bank, as well as a confirmation of the amount of the deposit. If the deposit is made into an interest-bearing account (or more than one account, even with the same tenant's monies, as permitted by Banking Law Section 237(4)), the principal and interest remain the property of the tenant-depositor (subject to application by landlord in accordance with the terms of the lease); however, under GOL section 7-103(2), the landlord is "entitled to receive, as administration expenses, a sum equivalent to one per cent per annum upon the security money, in lieu of all other administrative and custodial expenses." This interest is to be paid annually or, at the option of the depositor (the tenant, not the landlord), returned together with the principal upon termination of the tenancy.

Note that a tenant is not entitled to the payment of interest on a security deposit, unless, pursuant to GOL section 7-103(2), the lease is in a building containing six or more dwelling units. There is no exception in the statute for mixed commercial and residential buildings, and the applicability of the statute is conditioned on the nature of the building (i.e., whether or not the building has six or more dwelling units) and not dependent on whither the lease is commercial or residential. Notwithstanding the foregoing, an express agreement, however, to pay such interest would permit a tenant to sue for "legal interest" on its security if the monies are not deposited in an interest bearing account. If interest is mandated in a commercial lease security deposit provision, but a rate is not specified, the landlord is obligated to pay the legal statutory interest rate.

A cash security deposit, to be held in accordance with such laws or any permissible commercial variation agreed upon by the parties to the lease, is not the only form of security. Tenants and landlords sometimes rely on parents or other guarantors, or give and take liens of various kinds on tenant property (although Real Property Law section 231(4) voids a lease provision that purports to pledge as security "personal property exempt by law from levy and sale by virtue of an execution").

If the property is sold or otherwise conveyed, the landlord, pursuant to GOL section 7105(1), is required to turn over such security deposits to the new property owner or assignee within five days of the sale or conveyance of the real property. It is worth noting that pursuant to GOL section 7-105(3), "any failure to comply with this section is a misdemeanor."

To conclude this brief review of the case and statutory law respecting security deposits before looking at the sample clauses to be negotiated by the parties within this framework, it should also be noted that, on the tenant side, a breach of the obligation to make a security deposit (e.g., by depositing a bad check in the first place), or to keep it constant or "topped up" after legitimate landlord application of part or all of the deposit, will permit the landlord to declare a breach, terminate, and commence a holdover proceeding.

Alternatively, any mingling of security deposit funds with a landlord's personal funds is a conversion, which entitles the tenant to immediate recovery of the deposit intact, because a landlord who converts deposited funds forfeits his right to security (although he can segregate after tenant's renewed demand therefor and escape this penalty, if no damage has been suffered by tenant).

Also, absent any contrary provision, the renewal of a lease will operate as a renewal of the security deposit provision, and the tenant must maintain the security deposit for the renewal term (although he may bargain in advance for a reduced deposit in event of such renewal and in the absence of any default preventing exercise of the renewal option). Not surprisingly, the security deposit provision in the sophisticated commercial space lease reflects many if not all of these themes.

Only upon the original expiration date of a lease, when all of the landlord's damages can be confirmed, may a tenant claim the return of a deposit; however, if the parties to a lease agree the security deposit may "burn off" (i.e., be reduced) by an agreed upon amount at an agreed upon time during the lease term so long as tenant is not then in default.

32.2 Sample Clause

Article 32 Security Deposit.

(a) Simultaneously with Tenant's execution of this Lease, Tenant shall deliver to Landlord, as security for the performance of Tenant's obligations under this Lease, an unconditional, irrevocable letter of credit in the amount of [__________] in the form annexed hereto as Exhibit *[insert form of LOC]* and issued by a bank satisfactory to Landlord (the "Letter of Credit"). The Letter of Credit shall provide that it is assignable by Landlord without charge and shall either (i) expire on the date which is 60 days after the expiration or earlier termination of this Lease (the "LC Date") or (ii) be automatically self-renewing until the LC Date. If any Letter of Credit is not renewed at least 60 days prior to the expiration thereof or if Tenant holds over in the Premises without the consent of Landlord after the expiration or termination of this Lease, Landlord may draw upon the Letter of Credit and hold the proceeds thereof as security for the performance of Tenant's obligations under this Lease. Landlord may draw on the Letter of Credit (or the proceeds thereof) to remedy defaults by Tenant (beyond any applicable periods of notice and grace provided under this Lease) in the payment or performance of any of Tenant's obligations under this Lease, which default continues beyond the expiration of any applicable notice or grace period (except that no notice of default shall be required, and no grace period shall be applicable, if Landlord is prevented or prohibited from delivering notice of default under applicable bankruptcy, insolvency or other laws). If Landlord shall have so drawn upon the Letter of Credit (or the proceeds thereof), Tenant shall within 7 days after demand deposit with Landlord a sum equal to the amount so drawn by Landlord.

(b) Provided Tenant is not in default under this Lease beyond any applicable notice and cure period and Tenant has surrendered the Premises to Landlord in accordance with all of the terms and conditions of this Lease, on or before the LC Date: (i) Landlord shall return to Tenant the Letter of Credit (or the proceeds thereof) then held by Landlord or (ii) if Landlord shall have drawn upon such Letter of Credit (or the proceeds thereof) to remedy defaults by Tenant in the payment or performance of any of Tenant's obligations under this Lease after the expiration of any applicable notice and cure period, Landlord shall return to Tenant that portion, if any, of the proceeds of the Letter of Credit remaining in Landlord's possession.

[INCLUDE IF BURN-OFF CONCEPT IS CONTEMPLATED] Provided that on the Reduction Date (i) Tenant is not then in default under this Lease beyond any applicable notice and grace periods, (ii) Tenant shall occupy the entire Premises and (iii) Landlord has not theretofore drawn on the Letter of Credit by reason of any default on the part of Tenant, Tenant shall be entitled to a reduction in the amount of the Letter of Credit of [________________] (the "Reduction Amount") on the [___] anniversary of the Rent Commencement Date (the "Reduction Date"). In no event shall the Letter of Credit be reduced to less than [________________]. Tenant shall deliver to Landlord an amendment to the Letter of Credit (the form and substance of such amendment to be reasonably satisfactory to Landlord), reducing the amount of the Letter of Credit by the Reduction Amount, and Landlord shall execute the amendment and such other documents as are reasonably necessary to reduce the amount of the Letter of Credit in accordance with the terms hereof.

32.3 Landlord Concerns

Few tenants can legitimately resist the market demand requiring the payment of a security deposit. Thus, the landlord is concerned with avoiding the possibility of doing more than the law already requires, and with ensuring that the security deposit is available for all defaulted money obligations of the tenant, not just for the nonpayment of rent.).

The landlord has every right to insist that a letter of credit be exactly akin to a "cash equivalent," readily available upon landlord's own conclusion that a default has occurred, and transferrable to a successor landlord without cost to either assignor or assignee (attendant fees are the tenant's problem, always). It is also vital that the letter of credit, normally issued on an annual basis, be automatically renewable throughout the term, and that the landlord be able (within its unexpired term) to convert it to cash if a substitute letter of credit is not timely supplied.

If the security deposit is in the form of cash, then the landlord will want to limit its obligation to achieve or maintain any specific interest rate by generic reference to the rate achievable "from time to time" on such security accounts, and to openly state its right to the statutory 1% administrative fee in view of the possibility that the tenant may not be aware of this statutory entitlement.

In addition, if the security deposit is a cash security deposit, the standard provision that the tenant will not encumber the security deposit (which is also the final sentence of the REBNY form provision; see Sections 32.5 and 32.6, *infra*) is recognition that the deposit is legally the tenant's and could, conceivably, be pledged as security to someone else. If a tenant pledges the security deposit to someone else, the landlord's possession of the deposit, as well as its contractual and statutory rights to its application upon default, will normally block any attack by the tenant's creditor on such monies. The addition of a provision in the lease not to encumber the security deposit is a useful device for a subsequent assertion of actual notice to the tenant, and of constructive notice to the tenant's creditors, that any blanket pledge of personal property in connection with this tenant's other financial relations should not be deemed to include this security deposit with the landlord.

32.4 Tenant Concerns

If the security deposit is in the form of cash and as noted in the commentary to the REBNY provision (see Section 32.6, *infra*), unless the tenant bargains for the deposit of its security at interest, the landlord has no duty to make such a deposit. Virtually all landlords agree to deposit the security at interest when requested. Beyond the basic obligation, a tenant would also want a covenant that the interest be paid out annually (the landlord cannot legitimately refuse this request under the statute). Some landlords seek to add language that they shall not be required to credit any security with interest for any period during which the landlord does not receive interest on that money. Since, however, any delay in making the deposit would be the landlord's, and the choice of banking institution is up to landlord, there is no good reason for a tenant to grant this free pass.

For a tenant planning to avail itself of the letter of credit, it is imperative to confirm that the terms of the LC demanded by the landlord, either within this provision's text or in an attached exhibit, are terms that the tenant's customary bank, or some other bank, can meet. Just as with the lease's insurance provisions, the tenant must consult with the issuer before the lease is signed, not after. The tenant should also seek language that funds withdrawn under the LC will be deemed to be held under the terms originally established for the cash security deposit, including deposit at interest and annual interest payouts.

As for permitting the release from liability of the old landlord upon transfer of the security deposit or LC to a successor landlord, the prudent tenant should insist that the liability release be contingent upon notification of the identity of the new landlord (which would usually occur, if only as a function of the changeover of the address for payment of rent and notices), and of new notice of the location of the bank where the security deposit is held (which might stay put, but more likely will be transferred to the new landlord's bank).

32.5 Standard Real Estate Board of New York Clause

In the REBNY form, the relevant law is faithfully and economically restated [subparagraph captions and breaks have been added]:

> *Security. 34.* [*Deposit and Application*] Tenant has deposited with Owner the sum of $__________ as security for the faithful performance and observance by Tenant of the terms, provisions and conditions of this lease; it is agreed that in the event Tenant defaults in respect of any of the terms, provisions and conditions of this lease, including, but not limited to, the payment of rent and additional rent, Owner may use, apply or retain the whole or any part of the security so deposited to the extent required for the payment of any rent and additional rent or any other sum as to which Tenant is in default or for any sum which Owner may expend or may be required to expend by reason of Tenant's default in respect of any of the terms, covenants and conditions of this lease, including but not limited to, any damages or deficiency in the re-letting of the premises, whether such damages or deficiency accrued before or after summary proceedings or other re-entry by Owner. In the case of every such use, application or retention, Tenant shall, within five (5) days after demand, pay to Owner the sum so used, applied or retained which shall be added to the security deposit so that the same shall be replenished to its former amount.
>
> *[Deposit Return]* In the event that Tenant shall fully and faithfully comply with all of the terms, provisions, covenants and conditions of this lease, the security shall be returned to Tenant after the date fixed as the end of the Lease and after delivery of entire possession of the demised premises to Owner.
>
> *[Deposit Assignability and Landlord Release]* In the event of a sale of the land and building or leasing of the building, of which the demised premises form a part, Owner shall have the right to transfer the security to the vendee or lessee and Owner shall thereupon be released by Tenant from all liability for the return of such security; and Tenant agrees to look to the new Owner solely for the return of said security, and it is agreed that the provisions hereof shall apply to every transfer or assignment made of the security to a new Owner.
>
> *[No Encumbrance]* Tenant further covenants that it will not assign or encumber or attempt to assign or encumber the monies deposited herein as security and that neither Owner nor its successors or assigns shall be bound by any such assignment, encumbrance, attempted assignment or attempted encumbrance.

32.6 Comments on Standard Real Estate Board of New York Clause

The owner/landlord has no particular need to modify this provision (unless it wishes to add language, found in the sample clause set forth in Section 32.2, *supra*, that the tenant must restore the deposit to its original amount if any part thereof is applied for default during the term, and in the event the security is deposited at interest, that owner/landlord is entitled to a 1% administrative fee). However, the owner/landlord will be met with several demands from the tenant that the REBNY provision be modified.

First, the tenant will require language to be added compelling the deposit to be held in a single, interest-bearing account (even for a large security deposit), at not less than the market rate for the period or periods in question during the term. Second, unless the tenant is content to have all its interest at the end of its term, demand should be made for the payout of interest on an annual basis (allowing the owner/landlord its 1% administrative fee). Third, the tenant may wish to trigger the landlord's obligation to notify the tenant of the identity of the bank of deposit, by simply naming it in the lease. Although no statute requires this notification to be made in the lease, side letters or notices, often filed separately, are sometimes lost; thus, a reference within the lease is helpful to later administrators of the lease.

Also, if the tenant has a longer-term lease or one with renewal options, here is the place to incorporate provisions for reducing the amount of the security deposit in the later stages of the term, as a reward for good behavior. If a letter of credit is actually cheaper for a creditworthy tenant to maintain than to have a cash deposit so encumbered, the alternative proffer of an LC should be added to this provision to resemble the same alternative in Section 32.3, Letter of Credit Security, of the sample clause set forth in Section 32.2.

32.7 Litigation Issues

General Obligations Law (GOL) section 7-103, unlike most sections of the Real Property Law governing the landlord-tenant relationship, provides that any contractual provision that waives the protections of the section is void.[1] Advance rent payments, in addition to security deposits, remain the property of the depositor until applied when due or returned. Such funds must be held in trust for the depositor until so applied, and are not to be commingled with the landlord's funds.

LeRoy v. Sayers[2] demonstrates the consequences of a landlord's failure to comply with the requirements of the General Obligations Law. The tenant rented a summer home, and as is typical under such arrangements, was required to pay a large installment of the rent for the entire summer in advance, together with a security deposit.

1. GOL § 7-103(3) provides: "Any provision of such a contract or agreement whereby a person who so deposits or advances money waives any provision of this section is absolutely void."

2. 217 A.D.2d 63, 635 N.Y.S.2d 217 (1st Dep't 1995).

The landlord cashed the checks but failed to open separate accounts for the advance payment and security deposit. Prior to commencement of the lease term the house was substantially damaged by fire. The tenant sought to repudiate the lease and, in fact, did not take occupancy. The issue of whether the house was so damaged by fire that the landlord could not satisfy his lease obligations presented an issue of fact barring summary judgment. However, regardless of whether the tenant repudiated the lease, the failure of the landlord to comply with General Obligations Law section 7-103 meant that the "tenant has an immediate right to the funds in the event of a commingling. . . . Nor is the tenant's non-compliance with the lease terms a defense to a landlord's breach of his duty in this regard."[3] The landlord offered the argument that he was entitled to the advance rent payment and the security deposit because they represented liquidated damages. The court denied this argument and held that the liquidated damages clause represented a penalty and was unenforceable.

In *Glass v. Janbach Properties, Inc.*,[4] the landlord was pitted against the assignee for the benefit of the tenant's creditors in a claim as to who had the right to the tenant's security deposit. A security deposit account was properly set up, and as the tenant was in default, the landlord was permitted to apply the security deposit pursuant to the terms of the lease.

Central Savings Bank v. Fashoda, Inc.[5] instructs us that a successor in interest to real property is not liable to a tenant for a security deposit that was never returned to the tenant nor transferred to the successor in interest.

425 Fifth Avenue Realty Associates v. Yeshiva University[6] involved a security deposit in the form of a letter of credit. The lease provided that the deposit may be utilized upon a default by the tenant, and the landlord, in addition to terminating the lease, could draw down sums to make up for a deficiency in rent payments.

A creditworthy tenant may seek to post a letter of credit in lieu of cash as a security deposit, thus giving the tenant continued use of its cash. In negotiating the language in the security deposit provision, the tenant should realize that a landlord may, under certain circumstances, have a greater ability to access the funds evidenced by the Letter of Credit than a cash deposit. If the landlord asserts a default, the tenant may obtain a *Yellowstone* injunction and litigate the propriety of the notice of default. If the landlord were to withdraw a cash security deposit and then lose the trial on the merits of the alleged default, the lessor would have violated GOL section 7-103. However, where the security deposit provision calls for posting of a letter of credit and permits the landlord to draw on the letter upon presentation of a sight draft, or affidavit, asserting that the tenant has defaulted, the tenant cannot prevent the bank from honoring the letter of

3. 635 N.Y.S.2d at 221.
4. 73 A.D.2d 106, 425 N.Y.S.2d 343 (2d Dep't 1980).
5. 94 A.D.2d 927, 463 N.Y.S.2d 335 (3d Dep't 1983).
6. 228 A.D.2d 178, 643 N.Y.S.2d 542 (1st Dep't 1996).

credit, by *Yellowstone* or other preliminary injunction.[7] The court, in *Chiat/Day Inc. v. Kalimian*, held that

> It is a fundamental principle that the letter of credit is completely independent of the contract between the customer and the beneficiary. . . . The tenant herein is not a party to the letter of credit contract between the bank and the landlord. Thus, as the purchaser of the letter of credit, the tenant is not a party to the letter of credit transaction and cannot enjoin the bank from paying, or the beneficiary from demanding, the funds pursuant to the letter of credit.[8]

Unless the tenant succeeds in negotiating a notice provision, and a right to enjoin access to the letter of credit pending a contest of an alleged default, "the only way . . . to succeed on an action to defeat payment on that letter of credit is to demonstrate fraud in the transaction or presentment of the letter. . . . Fraud in the transaction is limited to instances of active intentional fraud."[9]

---

7. Chiat/Day, Inc. v. Kalimian, 105 A.D.2d 94, 483 N.Y.S.2d 235 (1st Dep't 1984); *see also* Titleserv, Inc. v. Zenobio, 210 A.D.2d 311, 619 N.Y.S.2d 765 (2d Dep't 1994).

8. 483 N.Y.S.2d at 239.

9. 410 Sixth Ave. Foods, Inc. v. 410 Sixth Ave., Inc., 197 A.D.2d 435, 602 N.Y.S.2d 835, 836 (1st Dep't 1993), citing 105 A.D.2d 94, 483 N.Y.S.2d 235.

CHAPTER 33

Captions

33.1 General Purpose

Leases are divided into articles and sections. The articles and sections customarily are numbered in order to permit the draftsperson to make cross-references within the document and to assist the reader in locating provisions efficiently. To further facilitate both functions, each article or section is headed with a title identifying its subject matter. It would be a mistake, however, to permit the title of an article or section, sometimes chosen more out of custom or habit than as a result of a careful analysis of the article or section that it purports to describe, to change or even influence the interpretation of the content or intent of the article or section, which, of course, usually is negotiated and drafted with great care. Accordingly, although titles are useful guides for the reader, a lease should include a provision to the effect that the captions themselves are not to be used in the interpretation of the document.

33.2 Sample Clause

Article 33 Captions.

The table of contents, captions, headings and titles in this Lease are solely for convenience of reference and shall not affect its interpretation.

33.3 Landlord Concerns

Captions usually are included in the first draft of a lease document prepared by the landlord or its attorneys, and generally reflect the subject matter of the articles or sections that they head. As the document is negotiated and revised, however, the content of particular articles or sections may change. Each time a provision is revised during the lease negotiation process, the heading should be revisited to confirm that it continues to reflect the evolving subject matter that follows it. Unfortunately, that task frequently is neglected. Landlords do not want those who may be required to interpret the lease to discount or misinterpret particular revisions because of an inappropriate heading or the inclusion of a particular substantive issue in an article or section, the title of which does not relate to the subject matter in question.

33.4 Tenant Concerns

In this rare instance, the interests of the tenant are perfectly aligned with those of the landlord. Neither party wants the lease to be ambiguous or prone to misinterpretation.

33.5 Standard Real Estate Board of New York Clause

> *Captions: 30.* The Captions are inserted only as a matter of convenience and for reference and in no way define, limit or describe the scope of this lease nor the intent of any provisions thereof.

33.6 Comments on Standard Real Estate Board of New York Clause

The standard Real Estate Board of New York clause is not materially different from the sample clause.

CHAPTER 34

Parties Bound; Successors and Assigns

34.1 General Purpose

The primary aim of the "successors and assigns" provision of a commercial space lease is to bind the entity or person succeeding the original landlord or tenant to the covenants and agreements made by the original party. In other words, its purpose is to ensure, to the degree permitted by the law of contracts, that there is no argument about a partial or otherwise incomplete assumption of all the promises of the initial contracting party. A lease article with such a caption may carry other conditions (as does the Real Estate Board of New York provision discussed in Sections 34.5 and 34.6, *infra*, with its stated limitation of landlord's liability to its estate in the real property subject to the lease). The primary purpose, however, is to preserve the original contract terms, so that the assignee of the lease and/or the purchaser of the landlord's reversion are certain of the terms of the tenancy to which successor interests must adhere.

Such a clause is not surplusage. The concept of "personal" or "collateral" covenants in leases, which do not "run with the land" and thus do not bind the assignees of the personal covenantor, is alive and well in New York state. At common law, one who is not a party to a covenant may neither sue nor be sued directly upon it. The parties to the covenants in a lease are the original tenant and the original landlord. If either conveys his estate, his grantee can neither sue nor be sued as a party to the covenant in the lease unless such covenants pass as an incident of the estate conveyed. This feature of English common law became critical when this "privity of estate" was interrupted in 1540, the date Henry VIII broke with the Catholic Church and caused the lands of many monasteries to be forfeited to the Crown. These forfeited properties were subsequently granted to others. Many of these estates were under lease, but as a consequence of the forfeiture it was impossible to argue that the leases had been "assigned" in the customary way.

Consequently, the grantees of the Crown received lands subject to leases, the covenants of which could not be enforced against the lessees because they (the grantees) were not parties to those leases. The necessary remedy was effected by St. (1540) 32 Hen. VIII, c. 34, which provided, in substance, that the grantees of the king and the heirs, executors, successors, and assigns of the lessors should have the same remedies against the lessees, their executors, administrators, and assigns as the lessors would have had, and conversely that the lessees, their executors, administrators, and assigns should have the same remedies against the grantees of the king and the lessors, their heirs, successors, and assigns as the lessees would have had. Thus, this Henrician statute (which applied to leases only, not deeds) created, as between landlords and tenants and their respective assigns, an exception to the rule that one who is not a party to a covenant can neither sue nor be sued upon it.

The Henrician statute was adopted by the state legislature of New York after the American Revolution and may now be found in New York Real Property Law (RPL) section 223.[1] However, New York courts also made their own adoption of the "English rule" against the enforcement of the burden of affirmative (also styled "positive") covenants, either at law or in equity, against successors in interest,[2] with the result that some covenants (to pay rent by the tenant, or to repair or restore in case of casualty on landlord's part) are deemed by law to "run with the land." Other covenants may not run with the land if found to be "personal" in nature. Consequently, the inclusion of an explicit "successors and assigns" clause in a lease confirms for each party to an assignment that all of the predecessor's covenants (landlord or tenant) are going to be honored after the assignment. This provision eliminates the allegation that they may be personal and thus unenforceable.

34.2 Sample Clause

Section 34.01 Successors and Assigns.

This Lease shall be binding upon and inure to the benefit of Landlord, its successors and assigns, and shall be binding upon and inure to the benefit of Tenant, its successors, and to the extent that an assignment may be approved by Landlord, is deemed approved or does not require the approval of Landlord, Tenant's assigns.

Section 34.02 Limitation of Landlord's Personal Liability.

Tenant shall look solely to Landlord's interest in the Project (including (a) all rent or other consideration received by Landlord in respect of its estate in the Project and (b) net proceeds of a sale), for the recovery of any judgment against Landlord, and no other property or assets of Landlord or Landlord's partners, officers, directors, shareholders or principals, direct or indirect, disclosed or undisclosed, shall be subject to levy, execution or other enforcement procedure for the satisfaction of Tenant's remedies under or with respect to this Lease.

---

1. *See* discussion in Commonwealth Mortg. Co. v. De Waltoff, 135 App. Div. 33, 119 N.Y. Supp. 781 (1st Dep't 1909).
2. *See, e.g.*, Miller v. Clary, 210 NY 127, 103 NE 1114 (1913).

34.3 Landlord Concerns

The landlord, elsewhere in the lease (see Chapter 16, Assignment and Subletting), may have permitted the assignment of the tenant's estate in the lease, often subject to certain conditions. Even if the lease is silent, there may, in the real world, be a succession by operation of law, as in a merger or acquisition. Assuming that the landlord must consent, or chooses to consent, to a successor-in-interest being the new tenant under the original lease, the prudent landlord would want to ensure that all of the co-tenants remain bound to such successor by contract, by operation of law, or both. Hence this provision fairly warns the assignee or successor-by-operation-of-law that its assumption of the tenant's role with respect to this lease brings with it not only all the rights but also all the obligations of the original signatory tenant.

The landlord is also concerned with warning an "unpermitted" or "unapproved" assignee, whose assumption of the tenant's position is otherwise forbidden by the lease's terms in the Assignment and Subletting article (see Chapter 16, *supra*) that such assignee has gained no rights against the landlord by virtue of the purported assignment. The language in the sample clause 34.01, set forth in Section 34.2, *supra*, emphasizes this point.

Sample clause 34.02, set forth in Section 34.2, *supra*, and the second sentence in the REBNY clause set forth in Section 34.5, *infra*, deal with yet another concern of the landlord, namely, the limitation on its liability to the value of the bricks and mortar and underlying land housing the leased premises. For a tenant, who procures the insurance usually required by another provision of the lease (see Chapter 13, *supra*), this is not really a significant limitation on its recovery rights, and most tenants accept this limitation without controversy.

34.4 Tenant Concerns

While the successor and assigns provision of the lease is of primary concern to the landlord, the tenant that finds itself with a new landlord is equally anxious to know that all of the prior covenants of landlord-supplied service levels and prices, as well as bargained-for agreements on rental rates and renewal options, will remain in place. The contract law language of sample clause 34.01, set forth in Section 34.2, *supra*, is couched in, and works in, a mutually beneficial manner, and the tenant should indeed ask for such language if it is not already present.

As for the landlord limitation on liability set forth in sample clause 34.02, set forth in Section 34.2, *supra*, the concept is quite customary in sophisticated leases (which means that a tenant officer may not be fairly criticized for agreeing to its inclusion), and it is difficult to conceive of a fact situation where a tenant's damages would exceed the value of the building of which it occupies a part, as long as the tenant has procured the usual insurance coverages. Tenants may seek recourse against the landlord's interest in insurance proceeds and condemnation awards relating to the estate of landlord and the land.

34.5 Standard Real Estate Board of New York Clause

The REBNY clause is a restatement of the first and third provisions of the sample clause set forth in Section 34.2, *supra*:

> *Successors and Assigns: 36.* The covenants, conditions and agreements contained in this lease shall bind and inure to the benefit of Owner and Tenant and their respective heirs, distributees, executors, administrators, successors, and except as otherwise provided in this lease, their assigns. Tenant shall look only to Owner's estate and interest in the land and building, for the satisfaction of Tenant's remedies for the collection of a judgment (or other judicial process) against Owner in the event of any default by Owner hereunder, and no other property or assets of such Owner (or any partner, member, officer or director thereof, disclosed or undisclosed) shall be subject to levy, execution or other enforcement procedures for the satisfaction of Tenant's remedies under or with respect to this lease, the relationship of Owner and Tenant hereunder, or Tenant's use and occupancy of the demised premises.

34.6 Comments on Standard Real Estate Board of New York Clause

The owner/landlord has no need to tinker with this language. By the same token, unless the tenant is that unusual entity that can persuade the owner/landlord, as the price of the deal, to strike the second sentence above, there is nothing here that the tenant really needs or can change.

34.7 Litigation Issues

Boilerplate lease provisions purporting to bind the landlord's and tenant's successors and assigns will not impose liability upon a successor for an agreement it does not expressly assume and that does not constitute an interest in the realty or a covenant running with the land. However, the presence of such a clause may result in finding an assumption, and its absence or negation may result in the loss of successor liability if the covenant sought to be enforced is held not to be a covenant running with the land.

In *Bank of New York, Albany v. Hirschfeld*,[3] the inclusion of a successor provision, together with the conveyance made "subject to a lease," of which the grantee has constructive notice, has been held by the New York Court of Appeals to constitute the assumption of a leasehold obligation. The landlord leased the premises to a bank and covenanted in the lease that it would provide ten parking spaces to the tenant in a garage under construction in an adjacent building. The landlord subsequently conveyed the bank building to the mortgagee in lieu of foreclosure, *subject to* the bank lease, a memorandum of which had been recorded. The successors provision stated that "in

3. 37 N.Y. 2d 501, 374 N.Y.S.2d 100, 336 N.E.2d 710 (1975).

the event of any sale . . . it shall be deemed and construed without further agreement between the parties or their successors in interest . . . that the purchaser . . . of the building has assumed and agreed to carry out any and all covenants and obligations of the landlord hereunder." The court held that the grantee, on notice of the lease provisions due to the recording of the memorandum, could be liable in damages for the refusal of the owner of the adjacent garage to provide the required spaces. The court stated that "it is true that, in the absence of an affirmative assumption, a grantee is not liable on any covenants or agreements by which the grantor may have bound himself, unless, or course, the covenant runs with the land. . . . Here, however, [the purchaser] by taking title 'subject to' the existing bank lease, without taking exception to the terms . . . affirmatively assumed the contractual liability of the original landlord to carry out the terms of the lease."[4]

Bank of New York, Albany does not stand for the proposition that all covenants in a lease, including the covenant to provide parking, are covenants running with the land and thus binding on a successor. The case imposed the assumption of a contractual obligation on a grantee where title was taken "subject to" a lease, with actual or constructive notice of its terms, containing an explicit successors clause as set forth above. This theory has bound successors to recognize a predecessor's waiver as an assumed obligation. "It is clearly the law of this State that a successor-in-interest to real property takes the premises subject to the conditions as to the tenancy, including any waiver of rights, that his predecessor in title has established if the successor-in-interest has notice of the existence of the leasehold and the waiver."[5]

A successor landlord who does not expressly assume the obligations under a license agreement will not be bound to its predecessor's obligations. In *Todd v. Krolick*,[6] the laundry agreement was the usual agreement to provide and maintain washers and driers in the laundry room of an apartment complex. It was for a term of ten years, and was binding upon successors and assigns. The landlord that entered into the agreement eventually deeded the property to its lender in lieu of foreclosure who further transferred the property. The landlord was permitted to repudiate the agreement, which it did not expressly assume, because it was "in the nature of a license rather than a lease or an easement. . . . The agreement did not give exclusive possession and control of any definite space. . . . Accordingly, defendants are not bound by the terms of the contract merely because they had knowledge of the agreement and may have accepted the benefits thereunder."[7]

A successor landlord does not have to perform the terms of an agreement that does not constitute a covenant running with the land. The usual successors and assigns provision in a lease will not impose liability on a purchaser of a building to pay a

---

4. 374 N.Y.S.2d at 103.

5. Tehan v. Thos. C. Peters Printing Co., Inc., 71 A.D.2d 101, 421 N.Y.S.2d 465, 468 (4th Dep't 1979) (successor was not bound to a waiver of rent payment provisions because the tenant's possession was not constructive notice of the waiver).

6. 96 A.D. 2d 695, 466 N.Y.S.2d 788 (3d Dep't 1983).

7. 466 N.Y.S.2d at 790.

broker's commission for a lease renewal, even though the renewal term may occur after the successor purchased the premises, if the purchaser did not assume the brokerage commission agreement.[8] Nor will it obligate a successor landlord who did not receive a security deposit to return the funds to a tenant.[9] For a discussion of security deposits, see Chapter 32, *supra*.

Furthermore, specific language in a lease may be construed to limit the effect of a boilerplate successors and assigns clause. The garage operator tenant in *Square Lex 48 Corp. v. Shelton Towers Associates*[10] negotiated a restriction preventing the landlord from leasing the parking garage to another operator after termination of the plaintiff-tenant's garage lease. This restriction was conditioned upon the landlord or any of its affiliates or subsidiaries owning the property. Thus, an unrelated successor landlord was not bound by the restriction. The specific negotiated language negated any implication that the restriction was a covenant running with the land.

8. Longley-Jones Assocs., Inc. v. Ircon Realty Co., 115 A.D.2d 272, 496 N.Y.S.2d 155 (4th Dep't 1985).

9. Central Savings Bank v. Fashoda, 94 A.D.2d 927, 463 N.Y.S.2d 335 (3d Dep't 1983).

10. 98 Misc. 2d 1039, 415 N.Y.S.2d 325 (Sup. Ct. N.Y. Cnty. 1978).

CHAPTER 35

Brokerage

35.1 General Purpose

In New York, a broker's claim for a commission must be based on an agreement (except for those rare claims based on a tortious interference with a broker's right to earn a commission). In addition, the General Obligations Law section 5-701 (Statute of Frauds) specifically excludes such agreements from the requirement of a writing. Subsection 5-701(a)(10) provides, in part, that the requirement of a writing subscribed by the party to be charged "shall not apply to a contract to pay compensation to an auctioneer, an attorney at law, or a duly licensed real estate broker or real estate salesman." Indeed, the agreement not only need not be in writing but may be, and frequently is, inferred.

In all but the rarest of circumstances, if a commission is to be paid with respect to a lease, it is to be paid only by the landlord. This is true whether the broker is the landlord's broker or the tenant's broker. Under New York law, a tenant may be liable for a commission only (1) if it entered into a contract with a broker in which it agreed to pay a commission or (b) if it tortiously interfered with a broker's ability to earn a commission (such as an improper dismissal for the purpose of preventing the broker from collecting its commission).

To establish a valid claim for a commission based on an agreement, a broker need only to prove that it was "employed" and the procuring cause of the lease. It is almost impossible for a landlord to refute a broker's assertion that it was "employed." This is so because a broker is "employed" by a landlord if the broker (1) attends an open house, (2) receives a flyer, (3) is made aware of the availability of the space through a listing arrangement or otherwise through the landlord's listing or exclusive broker, or (4) observes or learns about a sign or an advertisement placed by or on behalf of the landlord in which it is stated that brokers are protected.

Therefore, a landlord, who may have "employed" more brokers than it is aware of, will be liable to one or more of them depending not on its own actions but rather the actions of the tenant. In order to have a valid claim for a commission, a broker must establish that it was the procuring cause of the lease. In other words, were it not for the broker's contact with the tenant, the lease would not have been made. Thus, a broker may have a valid claim for a commission without the landlord being aware of the broker's involvement in the transaction; but the broker cannot have a valid claim for a commission without having actually dealt with the tenant. That is why landlords need brokerage provisions in their leases.

35.2 Sample Clause

Article 35 Brokerage

Each party represents to the other that such party has dealt with no broker other than the Brokers in connection with this Lease or the Building. Landlord shall indemnify Tenant from and against all loss, cost, liability and expense (including, without limitation, reasonable attorneys' fees and disbursements) arising out of any claim for a commission or other compensation by any broker (including the Brokers) who alleges that it has dealt with Landlord in connection with this Lease or the Building. Tenant shall indemnify and hold Landlord harmless from and against all loss, cost, liability and expense (including, without limitation, reasonable attorneys' fees and disbursements) arising out of any claim for a commission or other compensation by any broker other than the Brokers who alleges that it has dealt with Tenant in connection with this Lease or the Building. Landlord shall enter into a separate agreement with the Brokers which provides that, if this Lease is executed and delivered by both Landlord and Tenant, Landlord shall pay to the Brokers a commission to be agreed upon between Landlord and the Brokers, subject to, and in accordance with, the terms and conditions of such agreement.

35.3 Landlord Concerns

For the reasons just stated, a landlord is required to know of every broker with whom the tenant has dealt and the manner and extent of the connection with lease or the premises. It is the tenant's activities that will lead to claims, and, in all likelihood, those claims will be made exclusively against the landlord. Since a tenant's activities can create an exposure for its landlord without any awareness or meaningful participation by the landlord, the landlord is entitled to be indemnified by the tenant in the event the tenant's representation regarding its brokerage activities is not completely accurate. In addition, a reciprocal representation and indemnification from the landlord to tenant as drafted in the preceding sample clause is typically included; however, it arguably is inappropriate for a landlord to make such a representation and give such an indemnification for two reasons—first, the landlord, knowingly or otherwise, probably has "employed" just about every broker in town and, second, absent tortious interference or a written contract to the contrary, the tenant will not be liable for a commission.

35.4 Tenant Concerns

Organizationally, large tenants are concerned about making representations about brokers in such broad terms (i.e., beyond naming the procuring broker) because of the administrative difficulties and inherent uncertainties of policing all contacts that may have been made by any of its employees and agents. This, however, is a burden not reasonably imposed upon a landlord and tenant, and therefore need exists to establish a method for policing these activities. The issue of indemnifying against claims made by a broker (other than the brokers specifically named in the lease) alleging to have dealt with a tenant, as distinguished from a claim based on having, in fact, dealt with such tenant (i.e., getting past this issue at trial), raises the issue of who should bear the cost of the defense of a claim before it is established that the tenant's representation may, in fact, be a misrepresentation, and who should bear the cost of a claim that ultimately fails. Tenants will maintain that these claims are a cost of the landlord's business, not the tenant's, and as such, should be borne by the landlord.

Also, notwithstanding the preceding discussion regarding the reasons for a landlord not to give a tenant a reciprocal indemnity (including the fact that a tenant should not need one), many tenants, fearing that they will be named in an action brought by a broker against their landlord and thus have some exposure to at least the cost of defense, ask for and receive a reciprocal representation and indemnity from their landlord.

35.5 Standard Real Estate Board of New York Clause

None.

35.6 Comments on Standard Real Estate Board of New York Clause

In light of the almost universal practice of including some brokerage provision in a lease, and the preponderance of brokers in the Real Estate Board of New York, it is surprising that there is no brokerage provision in the Real Estate Board of New York form. In practice, the Real Estate Board of New York form almost always is used with a rider, and presumably any such rider will include a brokerage provision.

35.7 Litigation Issues

A review of the law of brokerage commissions arising out of leasing transactions is beyond the scope of this book. Both landlord and tenant must realize that they may each be liable to a broker for a leasing commission,[1] or damages resulting from the loss thereof,[2] and thus both should take steps to protect themselves from that liability.

A landlord is not protected from an "unwarranted" payment of a broker's leasing commission solely by obtaining a representation from a tenant identifying the broker together with an indemnification against claims by other brokers. The landlord must

1. Gronich & Co., Inc. v. 649 Broadway Equities Co., 169 A.D.2d 600, 565 N.Y.S.2d 18 (1st Dep't 1991).

2. Williams Real Estate Co. Inc. v. Viking Penguin, Inc., 228 A.D.2d 233, 644 N.Y.S.2d 19 (1st Dep't 1996); Curtis Properties Corp. v. Greif Cos., 212 A.D.2d 259, 628 N.Y.S.2d 638 (1st Dep't 1995).

enter into a commission agreement with the broker to whom a commission is being paid, not only to obtain similar representations but to determine the conditions to earning and payment of commissions. Thus, unless a commission agreement executed by the broker conditions payment upon some standard of financial viability of the tenant, such as taking possession and payment of rent over some period of time, the default by a tenant shortly after the commencement of a lease will not relieve a landlord from its obligation to pay a commission in connection with an executed and delivered lease.[3] The landlord must be aware "that absent an agreement to the contrary, a real estate broker earns his commission when he produces a party who is ready, willing and able to purchase or lease on the terms set by the lessor . . . the subsequent default by the tenant shortly after the lease was entered into does not affect the broker's right to recover a commission."[4]

Furthermore, there is no implied condition in an agreement to pay a commission in installments, nor that the payment of each future installment requires the continuation of the lease in good standing. It is possible that more than one broker may claim a commission pertaining to a single lease. Such multiple claims underscore the need for representations from the broker that it is the "sole" procuring cause of a lease or other indemnification from the broker to whom payment is made.[5] Even though a broker must establish that it was the procuring cause of a lease to earn a commission, suits are often filed by brokers who had shown premises to prospective tenants who subsequently negotiate leases through the services of other brokers.[6] Even if there is no liability to the claiming broker, there is a defense cost more appropriately borne by the tenant who may have utilized a broker's services.[7]

A properly drafted agreement will limit a broker's ability to claim it earned a commission for an "aborted" lease transaction. In *Holzer v. Robbins*,[8] the broker responded to an ad placed by the hopeful lessor to lease a commercial building. He presented a tenant, negotiated terms, and awaited a draft lease that the landlord thereafter refused to present. The broker subsequently presented the same party as a prospective buyer, and the sale was closed. Without a commission agreement "to the contrary," the leasing commission was deemed earned when the broker produced a tenant ready, willing,

---

3. Kaplon-Belo Assoc., Inc. v. Farrelly, 221 A.D.2d 321, 633 N.Y.S.2d 522 (2d Dep't 1995); Sauerhoff-Kessler Realty Corp. v. Roma Shopping Plaza, Inc., 201 A.D.2d 477, 607 N.Y.S.2d 404 (2d Dep't 1994).

4. Kaplon-Belo Assoc,, Inc. v. Farrelly, 633 N.Y.S.2d at 523.

5. *See* J. Grotto & Assoc., Inc. v. Lax, 174 A.D.2d 394, 572 N.Y.S.2d 293 (1st Dep't 1991).

6. *See* Thomas P. Reilly & Co., Inc. v. Rockefeller Ctr. Mgmt. Corp., 223 A.D.2d 477, 637 N.Y.S.2d 371(1st Dep't 1996); Kalmon-Dolgin Affiliates, Inc. v. Bush Terminal Assoc., 164 A.D.2d 790, 559 N.Y.S.2d 327 (1st Dep't 1990); Aegis Property Services Corp. v. Hotel Empire Corp., 106 A.D.2d 66, 484 N.Y.S.2d 555 (1st Dep't 1985).

7. Kenneth D. Laub & Co. v. 101 Park Ave. Assoc., 101 A.D.2d 744, 475 N.Y.S.2d 64 (1st Dep't 1984) (tenant indemnified landlord from claim of broker who obtained rental quotes from landlord for purpose of negotiating lease for tenant in its prior building, who did not participate in negotiations for space in landlord's building where tenant eventually located).

8. 141 A.D.2d 505, 520 N.Y.S.2d 130 (2d Dep't 1988).

and able to lease on the lessor's terms.[9] The court held that the broker could earn both the leasing commission for the aborted lease and the duly earned sales commission. A commission agreement, executed by the broker upon commencement of negotiations, stating that no commission is earned unless a lease is executed and delivered by and between landlord and tenant would be "an agreement to the contrary" that would have protected the lessor from this dual liability.

A tenant may become liable to a broker for payment of a commission by entering into a "brokerage" agreement retaining a broker to negotiate on its behalf. Such agreements typically state that the broker will only seek its compensation from the lessor. Nevertheless, the tenant can become liable to the broker if the tenant negotiates the lease without using the broker, thereby preventing the broker from becoming the procuring cause of a lease. In *Curtis Properties Corp. v. The Greif Companies*,[10] the court held that the tenant could be liable to the broker even though the broker agreed to look solely to the landlord for its commission, and the landlord refused to negotiate with or pay brokers. The court found that under those circumstances, the tenant could not proceed to negotiate the lease without the broker's assistance and not compensate the broker. It held that "The termination of plaintiff's [broker's] right to represent defendants obviates the condition precedent to plaintiff's compensation, preventing it from being the procuring cause of the transaction . . . and offends the principle that a part to a contract may not frustrate its performance by bringing about the failure of a condition precedent. . . . In this event, the law permits recovery on the theory of implied contract."[11]

The tenant need not enter into a written brokerage agreement to incur obligations to negotiate a lease through the services of a particular broker. There can be an oral brokerage agreement to "cover" or "protect" a broker with respect to premises introduced to the prospective tenant by the broker. By proceeding to negotiate on one of those properties without using the broker, the tenant prevents the broker from becoming the procuring cause of a lease.[12]

Lessor and lessee must realize that the law has long protected the broker, who, having brought the parties together, is often "frozen" out of the deal by the parties, preventing the broker from being the eventual procuring cause of the lease. In *Gronich & Co., Inc. v. 649 Broadway Equities Co.*,[13] the court found both landlord and tenant liable for the broker's commission, even though during the course of negotiating both landlord and tenant refused to agree to pay the broker's commission; and the landlord agreed to indemnify the tenant against any commission claim by the broker. The broker advised the tenant of the availability of the space and was authorized to negotiate

9. 520 N.Y.S.2d at 131.

10. Curtis Properties Corp. v. The Greif Cos., 212 A.D.2d 259, 628 N.Y. S.2d 628 (1st Dep't 1995).

11. 628 N.Y.S.2d at 632.

12. Williams Real Estate Co., Inc. v. Viking Penguin, Inc., 228 A.D.2d 233 644 N.Y.S.2d 19 (1st Dep't 1996).

13. 169 A.D.2d 600, 565 N.Y.S.2d 18 (1st Dep't 1991).

on its behalf. The landlord advised the broker that it would not pay a commission; the tenant refused to pay unless the amount of the commission was reimbursed as a rental off-set. Regardless of the indemnity in the lease protecting the lessee from commission claim, the court found both parties liable: "It cannot be assumed that a broker works gratuitously and the lessor and lessee are held to such knowledge when they accept the result of the broker's services."[14]

14. 565 N.Y.S. 2d at 20.

CHAPTER 36

Indemnity Exculpation

36.1 General Purpose

Lease articles entitled "Exculpation and Indemnification" or, alternatively, "Non-Liability and Indemnification" are, more than most other provisions in a sophisticated lease, pro-landlord. In other words, the "exculpation" or "non-liability" segments of these provisions relate exclusively to the landlord, and the "indemnification" portion tends to be limited to the tenant indemnifying and holding the landlord harmless, not the other way round (provided, that larger tenants will receive an indemnification from landlord as noted in the sample clause that follows).

The economic motive of a landlord for this posture is clear. The building owner is counting on a rental stream, less foreseeable and predictable expenses of operation, and not on suffering contingent liabilities for a tenant's negligence or willful misconduct during the lease term with active occupancy of the premises. In such circumstances, the tenant is reduced simply to making sure that, in agreeing to these terms, it is not indemnifying the landlord against landlord's own negligence (which is illegal in New York state). The tenant's primary practical response to the landlord demand for indemnification is the acquisition of sufficient personal property and liability insurance coverage, with special additional coverage at the time of performing any alterations, in each case naming the landlord as an additional insured.

36.2 Sample Clause

Section 36.01 Non-Liability.

Neither Landlord, any Superior Lessor or any Superior Mortgagee, nor any partner, director, officer, shareholder, principal, agent, servant or employee of Landlord, any Superior Lessor or any Superior Mortgagee (whether disclosed or undisclosed), shall be liable to Tenant for (i) any loss, injury or damage to Tenant or to any other person, or to its or their property, irrespective of the cause of such injury, damage or loss, nor shall the aforesaid parties be liable for any loss of or damage to property of Tenant or of others entrusted to employees of Landlord; *provided*, that, except to the extent of the release of liability and waiver of subrogation provided in Section 7.03 hereof, the foregoing shall not be deemed to relieve Landlord of any liability to the extent resulting from the negligence or willful acts or omissions of Landlord, its agents, contractors, servants or employees, or as a result of the breach by Landlord of its obligations hereunder, or (ii) any loss, injury or damage described in clause (i) above caused by other tenants or persons in, upon or about the Building, or caused by operations in construction of any private, public or quasi-public work.

Section 36.02 Tenant Indemnification

Tenant shall indemnify and hold harmless Landlord, all Superior Lessors and all Superior Mortgagees and each of their respective partners, members, directors, officers, shareholders, principals, agents and employees (each, an "Indemnified Party"), from and against any and all claims arising from or in connection with (i) the conduct or management of the Premises or of any business therein, or any work or thing done, or any condition created, in or about the Premises, (ii) any act, omission or negligence of Tenant or any person claiming through or under Tenant or any of their respective partners, directors, officers, agents, employees or contractors, (iii) any accident, injury or damage occurring in, at or upon the Premises (or outside the Premises if arising from or in connection with Tenant's installations in, or use of, areas outside the Premises), (iv) any default by Tenant in the performance of Tenant's obligations under this Lease and (v) any brokerage commission or similar compensation claimed to be due by reason of any proposed subletting or assignment by Tenant); together with all costs, expenses and liabilities reasonably incurred by an Indemnified Party in connection with each such claim or action or proceeding brought thereon, including, without limitation, all reasonable attorneys' fees and disbursements; *provided*, that the foregoing indemnity shall not apply to the extent such claim results from the negligence (other than negligence to which the release of liability and waiver of subrogation provided in Section [____] applies) or willful misconduct or omission of the Indemnified Party or any of their respective agents, contractors, servants, or employees. If any action or proceeding is brought against any Indemnified Party by reason of any such claim, Tenant, upon notice from such Indemnified Party shall resist and defend such action or proceeding (by counsel reasonably satisfactory to such Indemnified Party and counsel selected by Tenant's insurance company to resist and defend such action or proceeding is, absent a conflict, hereby deemed to be satisfactory to such Indemnified Party).

Section 36.03 Landlord Indemnification [ONLY TO BE INCLUDED IN LARGE LEASES UPON TENANT REQUEST

Landlord shall indemnify and hold harmless Tenant and Tenant's partners, members, directors, officers, shareholders, principals, agents and employees (each, a "Tenant Indemnified Party"), from and against any and all claims arising from or in connection with (i) any act, omission or negligence of Landlord or any person claiming through or under Landlord or any of their respective partners, directors, officers, agents, employees or contractors, (ii) any accident, injury or damage occurring in, at or upon the public and common areas of the Project, and (iii) any default by Landlord in the performance of Landlord's obligations under this Lease; together with all costs, expenses and liabilities reasonably incurred by a Tenant Indemnified Party in connection with each such claim or action or proceeding brought thereon, including, without limitation, all reasonable attorneys' fees and disbursements; provided, that the foregoing indemnity shall not apply to the extent such claim results from the negligence (other than negligence to which the release of liability and waiver of subrogation provided in Section [___] applies) or willful misconduct or omission of the Tenant Indemnified Party or any of their respective agents, contractors, servants, or employees. If any action or proceeding is brought against any Tenant Indemnified Party by reason of any such claim, Landlord, upon notice from such Tenant Indemnified Party shall resist and defend such action or proceeding (by counsel reasonably satisfactory to such Tenant Indemnified Party, and counsel selected by Landlord's insurance company to resist and defend such action or proceeding is, absent a conflict, hereby deemed to be satisfactory to such Tenant Indemnified Party).]

36.3 Landlord Concerns

Any prudent landlord, at a minimum, should be insured against the standard kinds of property damage, equipment explosions, and malfunctions. The prudent landlord will also compel its tenant (in one or more other lease provisions) to procure insurance protecting both the tenant and the landlord. In seeking to avoid financial responsibility for losses or claims that may arise from misadventures that are somehow not covered (or may be inadequately covered) by such policies, the prudent landlord will often require tenants both (1) to waive, or accept a disclaimer of, liability for such accidents, and (2) to indemnify the landlord (and its extended business family and lenders) against all the consequences of a mishap resulting from the activities of the tenant, its employees, business visitors, and contractors.

Some nonliability provisions are quite specific and favorable to the landlord. Such provisions provide for exculpation from the tenant against "claims resulting from: (a) any equipment or appurtenances becoming out of repair; (b) injury done or occasioned by weather conditions; (c) any defect in or failure of plumbing, heating or air conditioning equipment, gas, water, and steam pipes, stairs, railings, or walks; (d) broken glass; (e) the backing up of any sewer pipe or down spout; (f) the bursting, leaking, or running of any tank, tub, washstand, water closet, waste pipe, drain, or any other pipe or tank in, upon or about the building or the premises; (g) the escape of steam or hot water; (h) water, snow or ice being upon or *coming* through the roof or any skylight, trapdoor, stair, doorway, window, walk, or any other place upon or near the Building or the Premises or otherwise; and/or (i) the falling of any fixture, plaster, tile, or stucco." Such laundry lists, however, may provide the tenant with the argument that since the catastrophe in question was not specifically listed, it was not waived. Note, whether the language is couched in general terms or set forth in conjunction with a list of potential mishaps, care should be exercised to make sure that the tenant's recognition of the landlord's exculpation from liability extends beyond the perimeter of the tenant's premises to situations occurring anywhere within the building or on the property generally.

In such a provision the landlord may also seek to preempt further objections from a tenant by demanding from the tenant a waiver of landlord liability for "any indirect, consequential, or punitive damages, including loss of profits," and also for any claim of loss for any landlord or mortgagee "failure or refusal to grant its consent or approval with respect to any matter as to which any of them are entitled to give their consent or approval" pursuant to the lease (a question that arises most often in consents to a tenant's sublease or assignment requests).

Beyond the exculpation sought by a landlord through a tenant waiver of claims, protection in the form of indemnification will usually be sought against unlooked-for consequences of a tenant's occupancy. The tenant may lay off the financial impact of most such occurrence through insurance coverage, but the required indemnity is necessarily broader than any such policy protection, and thus provides a secondary layer of financial security to the landlord.

36.4 Tenant Concerns

A tenant is not well placed to resist the landlord's demands for exculpation and indemnity, except to make sure that the disclaimer of liability excludes the landlord's own negligence or willful misconduct (which demand a landlord can hardly refuse if the tenant thinks to ask for it).

Rather, the tenant should take other action that will reduce its potential liability such as (1) having appropriate insurance coverage, and (2), if possible, insisting that the landlord also have appropriate insurance coverage on the building and grounds, to be periodically exhibited to the tenant (which tenant request for proof, if the landlord is not seeking to self-insure, should be agreed to by the landlord in the lease document).

The tenant may also want to specifically note (as already provided in the Real Estate Board of New York clause, see Sections 36.5 and 36.6, *infra*) that its indemnity is limited to matters to which the landlord is not reimbursed by insurance (since the landlord, to avoid making a claim that could have an effect on future premiums, might choose to ignore its own insurance coverage, under a waiver of subrogation, and proceed directly on its indemnification).

36.5 Standard Real Estate Board of New York Clause

The REBNY form contains one paragraph, Article 8, entitled "Property Loss, Damage, Reimbursement, Indemnity," which appears following the paragraph entitled "Maintenance and Repairs" and is shown below. The range of provisions covered by the sample clause set forth in Section 36.2, *supra*, are scattered throughout the complete REBNY document:

Maintenance and Repairs: 4. . . . Tenant shall be responsible for all damage or injury to the demised premises or any other part of the building and the systems and equipment thereof, whether requiring structural or nonstructural repairs caused by or resulting from carelessness, omission, neglect or improper conduct of Tenant, Tenant's subtenants, agents, employees, invitees or licensees, or which arise out of any work, labor, service or equipment done for or supplied to Tenant or any subtenant or arising out of the installation, use or operation of the property or equipment of Tenant or any subtenant. . . . There shall be no allowance to Tenant for diminution of rental value and no liability on the part of Owner by reason of any inconvenience, annoyance or injury to business arising from Owner or others making repairs, alterations, additions or improvements in or to any portion of the building or the demised premises or in and to the fixtures, appurtenances or equipment thereof. It is specifically agreed that Tenant shall not be entitled to any setoff or reduction of rent by reason of any failure of Owner to comply with the covenants of this or any other article of this Lease. Tenant agrees that Tenant's sole remedy at law in such instance will be by way of an action for damages for breach of contract. The provisions of this Article 4 shall not apply in the case of fire or other casualty which are dealt with in Article 9 hereof.

Property Loss, Damage, Reimbursement, Indemnity: 8. Owner or its agents shall not be liable for any damage to property of Tenant or of others entrusted to employees of the building, nor the loss of or damage to any property of Tenant by theft or otherwise, nor for any injury or damage to persons or property resulting from any cause of whatsoever nature, unless caused by or due to the negligence of Owner, its agents, servants or employees. Owner or its agents will not be liable for any such damage caused by other tenants or persons in, upon or about said building or caused by operations in construction of any private, public or quasi public work.

If at any time any windows of the demised premises are temporarily closed, darkened or bricked up (or permanently closed, darkened or bricked up, if required by law) for any reason whatsoever including, but not limited to Owner's own acts, Owner shall not be liable for any damage Tenant may sustain thereby and Tenant shall not be entitled to any compensation therefore nor abatement or diminution of rent nor shall the same release Tenant from its obligations hereunder nor constitute an eviction.

Tenant shall indemnify and save harmless Owner against and from all liabilities, obligations, damages, penalties, claims, costs and expenses for which Owner shall not be reimbursed by insurance, including reasonable attorneys' fees, paid, suffered or incurred as a result of any breach by Tenant, Tenant's agents, contractors, employees, invitees or licensees. Tenant's liability under this lease extends to the acts and omission of any sub-tenant, and any agent, contractor, employee, invitee or licensee of any sub-tenant, in case any action or proceeding is brought against Owner by reason of such claim. Tenant, upon written notice from Owner, will, at Tenant's expense, resist or defend such action or proceeding by counsel approved by owner in writing, such approval not to be unreasonably withheld.

Building Alterations and Management: 20. . . . There shall be no allowance to Tenant for diminution of rental value and no liability on the part of owner by reason of inconvenience, annoyance or injury to business arising from Owner or other tenants making any repairs in the building or any such alterations, additions and improvements. Furthermore, Tenant shall not have any claim against Owner by reason of Owner's imposition of such controls of the manner of access to the building by Tenant's social or business visitors as the Owner may deem necessary for the security of the building and its occupants.

Inability to Perform: 27. This Lease and the obligation of Tenant to pay rent hereunder and perform all of the other covenants and agreements hereunder on part of Tenant to be performed shall in no way be affected, impaired or excused because Owner is unable to fulfill any of its obligations under this lease or to supply or is delayed in supplying any service expressly or impliedly to be supplied or is unable to make, or is delayed in making any repair, additions, alterations or decorations or is unable to supply, or is delayed in supplying, any equipment or fixtures if Owner is prevented or delayed from doing so by reason of strike or labor troubles or any cause whatsoever, including, but not limited to, government preemption in connection with a National Emergency or by reason of any rule, order or regulation of any department or subdivision thereof or of any government agency or by reason of the conditions of supply and demand which have been or are affected by war or other emergency.

Definitions: 31. . . . The term "Owner" means a landlord or lessor, and as used in this lease means only the owner, or the mortgagee in possession, for the time being of the land and building (or the owner of a lease of the building or of the land and building) of which the demised premises form a part, so that in the event of any sale or sales or conveyance, assignment or transfer of said land and building or of said lease, or in the event of a lease of said building, or of the land and building, the said Owner shall be and hereby is entirely free and relieved of all covenants and obligations of Owner hereunder, and it shall be deemed and construed without further agreement between the parties or their successors in interest, or between the parties and the purchaser, at any such sale, or the said lessee of the building, or of the land and building, that the purchaser, grantee, assignee or transferee of the building or the lessee of the building has assumed and agreed to carry out any and all covenants and obligations of Owner hereunder. . . .

36.6 Comments on Standard Real Estate Board of New York Clause

The sample clause (see Section 36.2, *supra*), with the word "exculpation" in its title, and REBNY Article 8 (see Section 36.5, *supra*) speaking of "nonliability" are designed, largely without qualification, to free the landlord from liability to a tenant. These provisions reach that goal by way of a unilateral declaration of such status, although the REBNY form will automatically include the carve-out for owner/landlord's own negligence, and the tenant should insist upon the addition of the phrase "and willful misconduct," and perhaps upon repetition of the entire phrase following the last sentence of Article 8's first paragraph. Also, while the REBNY language would not seem to prohibit the tenant from seeking injunctive relief against landlord for any owner/landlord activity (or omission to act) that might lead to damage to persons or property, the cautious tenant might seek to clarify this right by express owner/landlord acknowledgment in modification of this paragraph.

Article 8's reference to windows being bricked over without having effect on the rent or otherwise imposing landlord liability often surprises potential tenants from out of town, but is perhaps a practical landlord necessity in a city of frequently replaced low-rises for skyscrapers (and this particular provision has led to the dark joke that, indeed, the rent should be *increased* if the windows are blocked, since security has been automatically improved).

The indemnification provision in the REBNY form may also be fairer to the tenant than the sample provision, in that owner/landlord's indemnification protection is explicitly limited to matters not covered by insurance, which is not always the case in manuscripted articles like the preceding sample provision. However, both the sample clause (see Section 36.2, *supra*) and REBNY indemnification provisions (see Section 36.5, *supra*) are extraordinarily broad, and the average tenant is usually unable to limit them much in negotiation, except as noted herein.

Since the exercise of the owner/landlord's rights of maintenance and repair may interfere with tenant's ordinary business operations, the tenant might seek a positive owner/landlord covenant to minimize such interference with the tenant's business operations, even though no rent set-off or constructive eviction claim is allowed for such interruptions. See Chapter 8 entitled "Repairs and Maintenance" and Chapter 18 entitled "Access to the Premises," *supra*.

Unlike Article 8, which specifically excluded the owner/landlord's own negligence from its scope in connection with damage to property or persons at the building, REBNY Article 27 (see Section 36.5, *supra*) on landlord's inability to perform services should, from the tenant's side, have added a similar, explicit exclusion for such negligence or owner/landlord's willful misconduct.

The definition of "owner" (landlord) found in Article 31 (see Section 36.5, *supra*) has the same effect as the language in the sample clause (see Section 36.2, *supra*) in terminating the transferor owner/landlord's liability; however, as a result of its ambiguous phrasing, Article 31 is somewhat more generous to the tenant who claims unperformed obligations by the transferor. Notwithstanding this apparent generosity, the prudent tenant should seek to limit the transferor's release by adding an exception for "claims relating to Owner's breach of any provision in this Lease arising prior to the date of such conveyance or sale, which breach has been asserted in a written notice to Owner given prior to such conveyance or sale pursuant to the terms of this Lease." The inclusion of such language in a rider to the printed form will put the potential purchaser, performing due diligence lease review but not otherwise requiring delivery of tenant estoppels as a condition of closing, on notice that taking a deed might bring with it liability for unperformed covenants of the original owner/landlord.

36.7 Litigation Issues

In *Hogeland v. Sibley, Lindsay & Curr Co.*,[1] a customer of the tenant department store was injured when she tripped over a snow-covered planter located on the sidewalk outside the premises. While the sidewalk was not part of the leased premises, it and the planter were constructed by the landlord's contractor pursuant to plans drawn by the tenant's architects. The trial court found both the landlord and tenant jointly liable to plaintiff and allocated responsibility between the two defendants at 60 percent for the landlord and 40 percent for the tenant. The landlord sought indemnification for its proportionate share of damages from the tenant under a clause requiring the tenant to indemnify the landlord for any claim "arising from . . . negligence of tenant . . . in or about the Tenant's demised premises or . . . occurring outside the demised premises but within the Shopping Center." Another section of the lease provided that "nothing in this lease shall be construed to relieve the Landlord from responsibility to the Tenant for any loss or damage caused the Tenant wholly or in part by the negligent acts or omissions of the Landlord." This provision went on to state that ". . . the Landlord shall not be responsible for . . . loss or damage which is recovered or recoverable by the Tenant from insurance."

Ultimately, the court of appeals held that the landlord was entitled to indemnification. In reaching its conclusion, the court, inter alia, stated that General Obligations Law (GOL) section 5-321[2] did not prevent the landlord from being indemnified. The

1. 42 N.Y.2d 153, 397 N.Y.S.2d 602, 366 N.E.2d 264 (1977).
2. GOL § 5-321 provides in part:

> "Every covenant . . . in connection with . . . any lease of real property exempting the lessor from liability for damages from injuries to person or property caused by or resulting from the negligence of the lessor, in the operation or maintenance of the demised premises . . . shall be deemed to be void as against public policy and wholly unenforceable." (L. 1963, ch. 576, § 1, eff. Sept. 27, 1964).

See also A To Z Applique Die Cutting, Inc. v. 319 McKibbin St. Corp., 232 A.D.2d 512, 649 N.Y.S.2d 26 (2d Dep't 1996) (lease provisions purporting to hold landlord harmless were held unenforceable); Automatic Findings, Inc. v. Allied Outdoor Advertising, Inc., 214 A.D.2d 482, 625 N.Y.S.2d 220 (1st Dep't 1995) (lease provisions that shielded defendant/landlord from liability for losses, including lost profits, by requiring plaintiff/tenant to procure insurance did not violate GOL § 5-321); Fay's Drug Co., Inc. v. British Am. Dev. Corp., 140 A.D.2d 810, 528 N.Y.S.2d 201 (3d Dep't 1988) (lease provided that the landlord and the tenant would each be responsible for its own share of liability in a slip-and-fall action; landlord's personal injury insurer was required to defend the tenant because the landlord agreed to be responsible for common areas and the injury occurred in a common area); Reeves v. Welch, 127 A.D.2d 1000, 512 N.Y.S.2d 749 (4th Dep't 1987) (tenant entitled to contractual indemnification from the landlord where the parties' intent was clear from the agreement); Graphic Arts Supply, Inc. v. Raynor, 91 A.D.2d 827, 458 N.Y.S.2d 115 (4th Dep't 1982) (lease provision requiring tenant to maintain insurance against loss for damages caused by fire, theft, water, or other cause and to hold landlord harmless therefrom was void under GOL § 5-321

landlord was not exempting itself from liability to the injured party for its own negligence. "Rather, the parties are allocating the risk of liability to third parties between themselves, essentially through the employment of insurance."[3] GOL section 5-321, applicable in situations involving fraud and overreaching conduct on the part of a landlord, did not apply in *Hogeland*, "where the landlord contracted for no direct exculpation from negligence towards his indemnitor, where insurance was provided as a form of continued responsibility and where the parties were so equal in their relative bargaining positions."[4]

as purporting to exempt landlord from liability for its own negligence); Taylor v. City of New York, 150 Misc. 2d 528, 576 N.Y.S.2d 974 (Sup. Ct. App. Tm. 2d Dep't 1991) (indemnification clause in which the city agreed to hold the landlord harmless for injuries resulting from the city's negligence in connection with the occupancy of the premises did not extend to the landlord's acts of negligence and therefore the landlord was not entitled to indemnification).

3. 42 N.Y.2d at 161, 397 N.Y.S.2d at 607.

4. *Id.*

CHAPTER 37

Shoring

37.1 General Purpose

Construction is an inevitable part of life, at least in highly developed, densely populated urban areas. Sometimes construction, particularly excavation or other substructure work, undertaken at one site may pose a risk of causing damage to a building on a neighboring site or to the site itself. In such instances, it generally is prudent to allow the party undertaking such construction activity to have access to the neighboring site, in advance of performing the work, in order to enable such party to protect the neighboring site against possible damage. On occasion, owners and/or tenants of the property at risk are reluctant to grant access to their property for the purpose of taking such protective measures. This reluctance, most often, stems from a fear of inconvenience and business disruption rather than a concern as to how the work next door is done.

In 1968, the New York state legislature, in an effort to provide a mechanism to deal with conflicts between adjoining property owners arising out of a need for access to adjoining property in order to perform work on one's own property (a somewhat broader arena than just excavating and shoring), passed Real Property Actions and Proceedings Law (RPAPL) section 881, which provides:

> When an owner or lessee seeks to make improvements or repairs to real property so situated that such improvements or repairs cannot be made by the owner or lessee without entering the premises of an adjoining owner or his lessee, and permission so to enter has been refused, the owner or lessee seeking to make such improvements or repairs may commence a special proceeding for a license so to enter pursuant to article four of the civil practice law and rules. The petition and affidavits, if any, shall state the facts making such entry necessary and the date or dates on which entry is sought. Such license shall be granted by the court in an appropriate case upon such terms as justice requires. The licensee shall be liable to the adjoining owner or his lessee for actual damages occurring as a result of the entry.

The purposes of shoring provisions are (1) to afford landlords the benefits of RPAPL section 881 as against their own tenants in the event the landlord is performing excavation or other substructure work on its own property and to do so without the need to seek a court-imposed license; (2) to insulate landlords from liability to their tenants resulting from such work (whether performed by the landlord or by an adjoining owner); (3) to protect landlords in such instances from any claim by their tenants for abatement of rent or constructive eviction; (4) to assure landlords the opportunity to secure their property without any claim by their tenants of improper access or interference; and (5) to give landlords the exclusive right to negotiate the terms and conditions of any access license with an adjoining owner, or to litigate such adjoining owner's claim of entitlement, in each case without including their tenants in the process.

37.2 Sample Clause

Article 32 Shoring.

If an excavation shall be made upon land adjacent to or under the Building, or shall be authorized to be made, then, subject to any applicable provisions of Article 18 hereof, Tenant shall afford to the person causing or authorized to cause such excavation, license to enter the Premises for the purpose of performing such work as said person shall deem necessary or desirable to preserve and protect the Building from injury or damage to support the same by proper foundations, without any claim for damages or liability against Landlord and without reducing or otherwise affecting Tenant's obligations under this Lease. Such license to enter and such work shall be without liability of Landlord to Tenant and Tenant shall not have, and hereby waives, any right to or claim for damages, abatement of rent and constructive eviction as a result of such license to enter and such work.

37.3 Landlord Concerns

Landlords must have the ability, without threat of interference by their tenants, to protect or to allow others to protect their property from damage resulting from excavation or other substructure work, whether performed by the landlord or by an adjoining owner. In addition, landlords want to be insulated from claims of liability by their tenants, whether in respect of damaged property or loss of business, resulting from such work. Similarly, landlords want to be insulated from claims of rent abatement or constructive eviction. Finally, if an adjoining owner seeks access to the property for the purpose of protecting the property against possible damage from excavation or other substructure work on the adjoining property, landlords want to be able to negotiate the conditions of such access (e.g., timing, payment, insurance, indemnity, security, restoration and approval of plans, specifications, contractors and engineers) without the involvement of their tenants, whose interests may not be consistent with those of the landlord.

37.4 Tenant Concerns

From a tenant's perspective, the work contemplated by this section may be more intrusive, and have a greater impact, on the tenant than on the landlord. A tenant, therefore, should be very concerned about the negotiation of the terms and conditions of an access license, and should insist upon having a voice (perhaps on a not-to-be-unreasonably-withheld or delayed basis) in the process. Additionally, the tenant may decide that it is in its best interests to litigate an adjoining owner's entitlement to such a license. Certainly, a tenant should have some right of approval regarding the plans and specifications for, as well as the timing of, such work. In addition, such work may damage the tenant in terms of lost business (perhaps even forcing a temporary closing) or may cause damage to its property, and it therefore should not waive (and if possible, should even provide affirmatively for the possibility of) a reduction or abatement of rent or, if appropriate, a constructive eviction. A tenant should seek to be indemnified by its landlord from the effects of such work.

While a tenant's position with respect to these concerns may be stronger when the work is being done by its landlord on its own property, even when the work is being done on adjoining land without benefit to its landlord, a tenant reasonably can argue that the effects of such work are more easily dealt with by its landlord and that the tenant should be insulated from them under its landlord's covenant of quiet enjoyment.

37.5 Standard Real Estate Board of New York Clause

> *Adjacent Excavation-Shoring: 32.* If an excavation shall be made upon land adjacent to the demised premises, or shall be authorized to be made, Tenant shall afford to the person causing or authorized to cause such excavation, license to enter upon the demised premises for the purpose of doing such work as said person shall deem necessary to preserve the wall or the building of which demised premises form a part from injury or damage and to support the same by proper foundations, without any claim for damages or indemnity against Owner, or diminution or abatement of rent.

37.6 Comments on Standard Real Estate Board of New York Clause

The Real Estate Board of New York clause is not materially different from the sample clause, except that it does not include the possibility of work done by a landlord on its own property (which may or may not be covered adequately by the "access to premises" clause) and does not contain a waiver of a claim of constructive eviction.

CHAPTER 38

Commercial Rent Control

38.1 General Purpose

Various attempts have been made over the years, particularly in New York City, to impose controls over the amount of increased rent that a landlord can charge a tenant to lease, or to renew a lease, of commercial space. This movement was particularly active in the late 1980s as rents soared in the hot real estate market. Unlike rent control for residential renters, none of these efforts has ever been successful. The lease clause found in many New York City leases is an effort to preserve for the landlord, to the extent permitted by law, the rent for which the landlord bargained, even if the landlord is prohibited by law from collecting the full amount thereof.

38.2 Sample Clause

> *38.01.* If at any time during the Term, the Rent is not fully collectible by reason of any applicable laws, Tenant shall take such other steps as Landlord may request, and as may be legally permissible, to permit Landlord to collect the maximum rents which may during the continuance of such restriction be legally permissible (but not in excess of the Rent reserved under this Lease). Upon the termination of such restriction during the Term, Tenant shall pay to Landlord, in addition to the Rent for the period following such termination, if legally permissible, the portion of Rent which would have been paid pursuant to this Lease but for such legal restriction, less the Rent paid by Tenant to Landlord while such restriction was in effect, together with interest thereon at the Prime Rate.

38.3 Landlord Concerns

Suffice it to say that efforts to impose commercial rent control have not endeared politicians to landlords. The sample clause, set forth in Section 38.2, *supra*, attempts to give the landlord maximum flexibility to restructure the rent if the full amount, as stated in the lease, cannot be collected. For example, if a law were to limit or prohibit a particular type of rent or rent increase, it may be possible to bypass these limitations by categorizing the prohibited amount as something else. If all else fails, the clause would allow the landlord to retroactively collect any amounts that were previously uncollectible if and when the restrictions are subsequently rescinded.

38.4 Tenant Concerns

Arguably, a tenant should not find the rent control clause particularly troubling in that its effect is merely to obligate the tenant to pay the rent that it committed to pay at the outset. In addition, the tenant should find solace in the fact that the likelihood that commercial rent control will ever be imposed is fairly remote. Even if such controls were imposed, it is particularly unlikely that rentals set forth in existing leases would be affected. Thus, while the preference may be to strike the clause from a proposed lease, the tenant does not face much risk by leaving it in. If the clause remains in the lease, the tenant may wish to provide that any past due amounts that accrue while the rent controls are in effect may be paid out over a period of two or three years, rather than be faced with a large lump sum payment at one time. In addition, the tenant may wish to limit the obligation to pay amounts that were previously uncollectible to situations where the rent restriction is terminated during the term of the lease.

38.5 Standard Real Estate Board of New York Clause

None.

38.6 Comments on Standard Real Estate Board of New York Clause

None.

CHAPTER 39

Renewal Option

39.1 General Purpose

The mutual landlord/tenant initial choice of term length may be influenced by any number of factors: (1) the tenant's projected growth over that term for the size of office leased, and (2) the landlord's desire to retain flexibility in the building's stacking plan for this or other tenants. The tenant may wish to remain in the building, if the space has not been outgrown or become functionally obsolete by term's end, in order to avoid the cost and disruption of a move. The landlord is also interested in tenant stability and with the possibility of retaining a tenant with a demonstrated ability to pay the rent. Retention of a reliable tenant can eliminate the need for new tenant improvement expenditures, higher brokerage fees, and a major abatement period, resulting in major savings by the landlord. Both parties are, as well, keenly interested in the market rent to be paid during any renewal term: the tenant, not to exceed the market rent for comparable space while still garnering the benefits of staying put, and the landlord, not to be below the market for its own space although saving some outlay while accommodating the tenant who otherwise wishes to remain. Finally, both parties need sufficient time before the end of the stated initial term to make alternative plans: the tenant, to locate and have new space built-out before its current lease's expiration date (when the holdover penalty may be multiples of the stated rent and the tenant may be at risk of eviction), and the landlord, to find a new tenant and sign a lease within a time frame that similarly permits a build-out during that new tenant's free rent period while its old lease runs down. The resolution of these goals, some conflicting and some parallel, shapes the provisions of the standard renewal clause.

39.2 Sample Clause

39.01 Renewal Right.

(a) Provided that on the date Tenant exercises the Renewal Option and on the date of commencement of the Renewal Term, (i) this Lease shall not have been terminated, (ii) Tenant shall not be in default beyond any applicable notice and cure periods under this Lease and (iii) Tenant shall occupy [the entire Premises] [at least __% of the Premises], Tenant shall have the option (the "Renewal Option") to extend the term of this Lease for an additional _________ year period (the "Renewal Term"), to commence at the expiration of the initial Term.

(b) The Renewal Option shall be exercised with respect to [the entire Premises only][the entire Premises or a Renewal Portion of the Premises] and shall be exercisable by Tenant giving notice to Landlord (the "Renewal Notice") at least [18] months before the last day of the initial Term. Time is of the essence with respect to the giving of the Renewal Notice.

(c) ["Renewal Portion" means __________________________.]

39.02 Renewal Rent and Other Terms.

(a) The Renewal Term shall be upon all of the terms and conditions set forth in this Lease, except that (i) the Fixed Rent shall be as determined pursuant to the further provisions of this Section 39.02; (ii) Tenant shall accept the Premises in its "as is" condition at the commencement of the Renewal Term, and Landlord shall not be required to perform any work, to pay any amount or to render any services to make the Premises ready for Tenant's use and occupancy or to provide any abatement of Fixed Rent or Additional Rent, in each case with respect to the Renewal Term; (iii) Tenant shall have no option to renew this Lease beyond the expiration of the Renewal Term; and (iv) the Base Tax Amount shall be the Taxes for the Tax Year ending during the first 12 months of the Renewal Term and the Base Operating Year shall be the Operating Year ending during the first 12 months of the Renewal Term.

(b) The annual Fixed Rent for the Premises for the Renewal Term shall be [Fair Market Rent] [the greater of (i) the Fair Market Rent or (ii) an amount (the "Annual Rent") equal to the aggregate of (A) the Fixed Rent payable by Tenant for the 12 month period ending on the last day of the initial Term, (B) the Tax Payment payable with respect to the Tax Year ending immediately before the commencement of the Renewal Term and (C) the Operating Payment payable with respect to the Operating Year ending immediately before the commencement of the Renewal Term (the greater of Fair Market Rent and Annual Rent is called the "Rental Value").] "Fair Market Rent" means the fixed annual rent that a willing lessee would pay and a willing lessor would accept for the Premises during the Renewal Term, each party acting prudently and under no compulsion to lease, and taking into account all relevant factors including the Base Tax Amount and the Base Operating Year.

(c) If Tenant timely exercises the Renewal Option, Landlord shall notify Tenant (the "Rent Notice") at least 120 days before the last day of the initial Term of Landlord's determination of the Fair Market Rent ("Landlord's Initial Determination"). Tenant shall notify Landlord ("Tenant's Notice"), within 20 days after Tenant's receipt of the Rent Notice, whether Tenant accepts or disputes Landlord's Initial Determination, and if Tenant disputes Landlord's Initial Determination, Tenant's Notice shall set forth Tenant's determination of the Fair Market Rent ("Tenant's Initial Determination"). If Tenant fails to give Tenant's Notice within such 20 day period, or if Tenant gives Tenant's Notice within such 20 day period but fails to set forth therein Tenant's Initial Determination, then Tenant shall be deemed to have accepted Landlord's Initial Determination.

(d) (i) If Tenant timely disputes Landlord's Initial Determination and Landlord and Tenant fail to agree as to the Fair Market Rent within 20 days after the giving of Tenant's Notice, then the Fair Market Rent shall be determined by arbitration in the City of New York, as set forth in this Section 39.02(d). Tenant shall initiate the arbitration process by giving notice to that effect to Landlord within 20 days after the giving of Tenant's Notice, which notice shall include the name and address of Tenant's designated arbitrator. If Tenant fails to give such notice within such 20-day period, then Tenant shall be deemed to have accepted Landlord's Initial Determination. Within 30 days after the designation of Tenant's arbitrator, Landlord shall give notice to Tenant of the name and address of Landlord's designated arbitrator. If Landlord shall fail timely to appoint an arbitrator, then Tenant may request the AAA to appoint an arbitrator on Landlord's behalf. Such two arbitrators shall have 30 days to appoint a third arbitrator who shall be impartial. If such arbitrators fail to do so, then either Landlord or Tenant may request the AAA to appoint an arbitrator who shall be impartial within 30 days after such request and both parties shall be bound by any appointment so made within such 30 day period. If no such third arbitrator shall have been appointed within such 30 day period, either Landlord or Tenant may apply to the Supreme Court, New York County to make such appointment. The third arbitrator only shall subscribe and swear to an oath fairly and impartially to determine such dispute.

(ii) Within 7 days after the appointment of the third arbitrator, the three arbitrators will meet (the "Initial Meeting") and set a hearing date for the arbitration. The hearing shall not exceed two days and shall be scheduled to be held within 60 days after the meeting of the three arbitrators. At the Initial Meeting, Landlord and Tenant may each submit a revised Fair Market Rent determination (each, a "Final Determination"); *provided*, that Landlord's Final Determination may not be greater than Landlord's Initial Determination, and Tenant's Final Determination may not be lower than Tenant's Initial Determination. If either party shall fail so to submit a Final Determination, then Landlord's Initial Determination or Tenant's Initial Determination, as applicable, shall constitute such party's Final Determination.

(iii) There shall be no discovery in the arbitration. However, on reasonable notice to the other party, Tenant may inspect any portion of the Building relevant to its claims, and Landlord may inspect any portion of the space occupied by Tenant on the floors in issue. Thirty days prior to the scheduled hearing, the parties shall exchange opening written expert reports and opening written pre-hearing statements. Opening written pre-hearing statements shall not exceed 20 pages in length. Two weeks prior to the hearing, the parties may exchange rebuttal written expert reports and rebuttal written pre-hearing statements. Rebuttal written pre-hearing statements shall not exceed 10 pages in length. Ten days prior to the hearing, the parties shall exchange written witness lists, including a brief statement as to the subject matter to be covered in the witnesses' testimony. One week prior to the hearing, the parties shall exchange all documents which they intend to offer at the hearing. Other than rebuttal witnesses, only the witnesses listed on the witness lists shall be allowed to testify at the hearings. Closing arguments shall be heard immediately following conclusion of all testimony. The proceedings shall be recorded by stenographic means. Each party may present live witnesses and offer exhibits, and all witnesses shall be subject to cross-examination. The arbitrators shall conduct the two day hearing so as to provide each party with sufficient time to present its case, both on direct and on rebuttal, and permit each party appropriate time for cross examination; *provided*, that the arbitrators shall not extend the hearing beyond two days. Each party may, during its direct case, present evidence in support of its position and in opposition to the position of the opposing party.

(iv) The third arbitrator shall make a determination of the Fair Market Rent by selecting either the amount set forth in Landlord's Final Determination or the amount set forth in Tenant's Final Determination, whichever the third arbitrator determines is closest to Fair Market Rent for the Premises. The third arbitrator may not select any other amount as the Fair Market Rent. The fees and expenses of any arbitration pursuant to this Section 39.02(d) shall be borne by the parties equally, but each party shall bear the expense of its own arbitrator, attorneys and experts and the additional expenses of presenting its own proof. The arbitrators shall not have the power to add to, modify or change any of the provisions of this Lease. Each arbitrator shall be a licensed real estate broker having at least 10 years of experience in leasing of first class office buildings in Manhattan. After a determination has been made of the Fair Market Rent, the parties shall execute and deliver an instrument setting forth the Fair Market Rent, but the failure to so execute and deliver any such instrument shall not affect the determination of Fair Market Rent.

(e) If Tenant disputes Landlord's Initial Determination and if the final determination of Fair Market Rent shall not be made on or before the first day of the Renewal Term, then, pending such final determination, Tenant shall pay, as Fixed Rent for the Renewal Term, an amount equal to Landlord's Final Determination. If, based upon the final determination of the Fair Market Rent, the Fixed Rent payments made by Tenant for such portion of the Renewal Term were greater than the Fair Market Rent payable for the Renewal Term, Landlord shall credit the amount of such excess against future installments of Fixed Rent and/or Additional Rent payable by Tenant.

39.3 Landlord Concerns

If a landlord is prepared to grant a renewal option, enough time must remain to re-let the premises if the tenant does not exercise its renewal option. The length of that period is a function of the size of the subject premises; the smaller the space (and perhaps the need to do no extensive alterations for the next standard-use tenant), the shorter the time frame. If there is to be no renewal, the tenant must locate new space, negotiate a new lease, and build that new space in time for its move on or before the expiration date of the previous lease.

Landlord's other primary concern is price—the base or fixed rent (as discussed further in Chapter 50 (Fair Market Valuation on Renewals or Options), *infra*). If the initial term is five years or less, the landlord may be willing to "guesstimate" the likely market rent in that short-term future and agree upon a fixed number for the renewal term rent. If, however, the initial term is longer than five years, most landlords will seek some indexing mechanism—typically a fair market rent-setting mechanism (as set forth in Section 39.02, entitled "Sample Clause," *supra*) that will achieve the free market's fixed-rent level, which would hypothetically be equivalent to an offer from a new tenant. Thus, if a "fair market rent" standard is set, both parties are interested in defining the "fair market rent" to consider all relevant factors and, to the extent applicable, any particular factors the parties would specifically like to be included in the determination. In so doing, the parties are able to not only specify any known factors at the time that the lease is entered into but also to reserve the inclusion of factors that may not be apparent at such time. If arbitration or another determination method for the final rent number is in place, the lease should provide for some interim rental rate (usually landlord's determination of the fair market rent), if the determination process should be likely to overlap the renewal term commencement date.

The landlord will want to make explicit that (whether or not these were features of the initial term) the renewal term does not provide a rent abatement period, further tenant improvement contribution, or any other performance of work by the landlord. The existence of any future tenant renewal rights should also be explicitly negated. The question of the renewal term's base years (for operating and real estate tax escalation purposes) should be separately and particularly addressed, and either indicated to be the original base years, or to be new base years established (customarily, but not necessarily) in the calendar and tax year of the renewal term's commencement.

Finally, the landlord will legitimately want the tenant to be in good standing (no uncured defaults) both at the time of giving its renewal notice, and at the commencement of the renewal term. The landlord will also want tenant to renew substantially for its own use, not for an opportunity to make sublease profits, and so landlord will require protective provisions to that end (see sample clause set forth in Section 39.2, *supra*).

While, as a matter of law, the expiration or earlier termination of a lease would cause any renewal right contained within the lease to be extinguished, the landlord might insist on additional lease language clarifying that termination of the lease terminates any renewal option and, in the case of a lease with multiple renewal rights, that the tenant's failure to exercise one in a series has the effect of terminating the rest of that series.

39.4 Tenant Concerns

If the tenant wishes one or more renewal options, it will desire some mechanism to ensure a level playing field for the determination of the fixed rent. If that mechanism is "fair market," then the tenant's interest in that market's defining characteristics for the purposes of its lease renewal is a keen one, and if there are foreseeable features of a standard landlord offer to rent (such as a substantial contribution to the tenant's build-out) that the renewing tenant will not need, then the tenant may seek to clarify that the consideration of "all relevant factors" expressly contains an adjustment in the tenant's favor for the (missing) concession. Similarly, the tenant may also bargain for some percentage discount (e.g., 5 percent), even off the fair market, in consideration for saving the landlord the "down time" between the tenants that would otherwise be a landlord risk with a real, if indeterminate, cost.

The tenant cannot argue that its right to renew should remain regardless of its default status, but may wish to resist any requirement that the tenant not be in default as of the commencement of the term (as distinguished from such condition applying only as of the tenant's exercise of its renewal option), since at that point the tenant will have already foregone the opportunity, and time necessary, to locate, negotiate a lease for, and build-out alternative space. In any case, the tenant may seek to qualify the condition that it not be in default by specifying that all applicable notice and cure periods under the lease shall have elapsed.

The tenant may also wish to resist any conditional restriction on the amount of space it is actually occupying at the time of renewal on the grounds that if it has successfully bargained for the right to sublease some portion of its space (whether or not at a profit), it could choose to do so for a short term, and thus should be permitted nevertheless to renew the main lease to allow recapture of the subleased space in the renewal term when the tenant's occupancy needs have expanded once more.

If a tenant leases more than one floor, it may seek the ability to shrink its footprint after the initial term by exercising its renewal option with respect to less than the entirety of the premises. Landlords will likely be more sympathetic to tenants that lease a significant amount of space in a building for a longer initial term; however, landlords will require that any block of floors comprising the tenant's initial premises be renewed on a contiguous basis starting at the top floor or at the bottom floor of the stack, so that the landlord is not left with noncontiguous floors to market and re-let once the tenant returns the non-renewed floors to the landlord.

Assuming that the tenant, when moving to new space, will need a substantial time to build out, tenant will have reason to agree with the landlord's wanting to set a renewal exercise date upwards of a year prior to the expiration date. If the tenant is in a smaller (e.g., standard office suite) space, then it may wish to shorten the pre-expiration date exercise period in order to better gauge (by being nearer to it in time) the free market rent number for comparable space in other buildings.

While the tenant may be compelled to concede by signing the landlord's lease providing that termination of the tenant's lease also ends its renewal options, the tenant should conversely insist that any assignment of the lease permitted by its terms specifically includes the assignment of the tenant's renewal option(s).

Finally, and especially if the base rent number is fixed in advance for the renewal, the tenant wanting a renewal option may try (if the renewal rent is a fixed number, or is set at 100 percent of a fair market determination) to bargain for pre-agreed concessions during the renewal term, such as a small rent abatement of a few months, or minor work by the landlord, such as a repainting of the premises.

39.5 Standard Real Estate Board of New York Clause

None.

39.6 Comments on Standard Real Estate Board of New York Clause

None.

39.7 Litigation Issues

An option to renew is always a benefit to the tenant, if the renewal rental is better than the market at the time of the exercise of the option. It is in the best interests of the landlord to attempt to set aside deals negotiated years earlier during different market conditions. The court of appeals has addressed renewal option issues on numerous occasions: (1) whether a tenant's exercise of a renewal option could be defeated due to the existence of lease defaults;[1] (2) lessor's waiver of alleged tenant defaults that could have defeated the exercise of renewal options;[2] (3) excusing tenant's late exercise of its renewal option;[3] and (4) whether the terms of a renewal option are too vague to enforce.[4]

In *Jefpaul Garage Corp. v. Presbyterian Hospital*, the court notes that "the general rule is that if a tenant's right to renew is conditional . . . it cannot be exercised validly

1. Waldbaum, Inc. v. Fifth Ave. of Long Island Realty Assoc., 85 N.Y.2d 600, 627 N.Y.S.2d 298, 650 N.E.2d 1299 (1995).

2. Jefpaul Garage Corp. v. Presbyterian Hos., 61 N.Y.2d 442, 474 N.Y.S.2d 458, 462 N.E.2d 1176 (1984); Atkins Waste Materials v. May, 34 N.Y.2d 422, 358 N.Y.S.2d 129, 314 N.E.2d 871 (1974). *See* Chapter 26, "No Waiver," *supra*.

3. J.N.A. Realty Corp. v. Cross Bay Chelsea, Inc., 42 N.Y.2d 392, 397 N.Y. S. 2d 958, 366 N.E.2d 1313 (1977); Sy Jack Realty Corp. v. Pergament Syosset Corp., 27 N.Y.2d 449, 318 N.Y.S.2d 720, 267 N.E.2d 462 (1971).

4. 166 Mamaroneck Ave. Corp. v. 151 East Post Rd. Corp., 78 N.Y.2d 88, 571 N.Y.S.2d 686, 572 N.E.2d 104 (1991); Joseph Martin, Jr., Delicatessen, Inc. v. Schumarcher, 52 N.Y.2d 105, 436 N.Y.S.2d 247, 417 N.E.2d 541(1981).

unless the tenant is in full compliance with the conditions."[5] Although courts have excused a tenant's lack of full compliance under equitable principles, the tenant must usually demonstrate expenditure of substantial sums in contemplation of the valid exercise of the option. The court in *J.N.A. Realty Corp. v. Cross Bay Chelsea, Inc.* noted that "the reason is that the option itself does not create any interest in the property, and no rights accrue until the condition precedent has been met by giving notice within the time specified. Thus equity will not intervene because the loss of the option does not ordinarily result in the forfeiture of any vested right."[6]

The court has applied its power of equity to permit tenants who have not "fully complied" with the requirements of renewal options to exercise their renewal options, provided they have not caused prejudice and are diligently seeking to cure the non-compliance. In *Waldbaum, Inc. v. Fifth Avenue of Long Island Realty Associates*,[7] the renewal option contained the typical proviso that the lease could not be renewed "if, at the time of the exercise of the option or the commencement date of the option term, Tenant shall be in default under this lease."[8] The option had to be exercised one year prior to the expiration of the lease. The landlord served a notice on the tenant to cure a default of a covenant to operate the demised premises as a first class facility. The default provision permitted the landlord to terminate the lease if a default was not cured within 30 days of written notice of the breach. However, for defaults not curable within 30 days, the tenant could avoid termination by commencing and diligently continuing its efforts to cure the default. A referee in a *Yellowstone* hearing granted a six-month cure period, and a determination that the time to exercise the lease renewal option would be extended to 30 days after cure period. The tenant expended some $3.5 million to upgrade its facility during that period. The court held that the tenant did effect a timely cure. However, it also held that the referee had no authority in a *Yellowstone* proceeding to extend the time for the tenant to exercise its renewal option. The landlord argued that the tenant was thus in default at the time it was required to exercise the renewal option, and that the exercise of the option was not valid. The court determined that although the tenant may have breached a lease covenant, this breach could be distinguished from a default. It stated, "By definition, an event of default does not occur under the lease until the tenant has failed to effect a cure of the nonperformance of the obligation within the appropriate cure period after notice."[9] So long as the tenant was diligently pursuing the cure, as permitted by the lease default provision, there was no lease default. The court in *Waldbaum* also held that it would be inequitable for the tenant to forfeit its renewal right after having spent $3.5 million to improve the premises with full knowledge and consent of the landlord. The landlord was not prejudiced by the alleged late exercise of the option, as it took no steps to its detriment in the belief that the tenant would not renew.

5. 474 N.Y.S.2d at 461.
6. 397 N.Y.S.2d at 960.
7. 85 N.Y.2d 600, 627 N.Y.S.2d 298, 650 N.E.2d 1299 (1995).
8. 85 N.Y.2d at 603, 627 N.Y.S.2d at 299.
9. 85 N.Y.2d 606, 627 N.Y.S.2d at 301.

When the tenant's noncompliance with the renewal provision is the failure to provide a timely notice, the three-point test applied to determine if the delay will be excused is (1) has the tenant expended substantial sums to improve the premises, (2) has the landlord been prejudiced by the delay, and (3) was the delay the result of an honest or excusable mistake.[10] This test has been applied to excuse tenants who have delayed from a few days in exercising a renewal option[11] to as much as two months[12] and six and a half months.[13]

The application of this test has also resulted in the denial of the attempted renewal. Without proof of expending substantial funds, which were in contemplation of the renewal term, sending a notice one day before a lease expired, when the lease required nine months' notice, was held to be insufficient to renew the lease.[14] A two-and-a-half-month negligent delay was not excused when the tenant failed to establish that its initial leasehold improvements, the cost of which could be amortized over the initial lease term, were in contemplation of the renewal, and that the fixtures were removable and usable in another premises.[15] The court also noted that the delay was not excusable on grounds such as the lessor misleading the tenant as to the need to provide a timely notice.

The exercise of a purported renewal option could be set aside because the terms of the option are too vague to be enforced. A renewal option "at annual rentals to be agreed upon" is thus not enforceable.[16] In holding that the language constituted a mere unenforceable agreement to agree, the court, in *Joseph Martin, Jr. Delicatessen, Inc.*, stated: "This is not to say that the requirement for definiteness in the case before us now could only have been met by explicit expression of the rent to be paid. . . . It certainly would have sufficed, for instance, if a methodology for determining the rent was to be found within the four corners of the lease, for a rent so arrived at would have been the end product of agreement between the parties themselves. Nor would the agreement have failed for indefiniteness because it invited recourse to an objective extrinsic even, condition or standard on which the amount was made to depend."[17] An option based on a rent to be agreed upon will not be enforced even if the tenant expended substantial sums to improve the demised premises with a new building.[18]

---

10. J.N.A. Realty Corp. v. Cross Bay Chelsea, Inc., 42 N.Y.2d 392, 397 N.Y. S. 2d 958, 961–62, 366 N.E.2d 1313 (1977).

11. Godnig v. Belmont Realty Co., Inc., 124 A.D.2d 701, 508 N.Y.S.2d 213 (2d Dep't 1986).

12. Am. Power Industries, Ltd. v. Rebel Realty Corp., 145 A.D.2d 454, 535 N.Y.S.2d 99 (2d Dep't 1988).

13. Souslian Wholesale Beer & Soda, Inc. v. 380-4 Union Avenue Realty Corp., 166 A.D.2d 435, 560 N.Y.S.2d 491 (2d Dep't 1990).

14. 95 East Main St. Serv. Station, Inc. v. H & D All Type Auto Repair, Inc., 162 A.D.2d 440, 556 N.Y.S.2d 385 (2d Dep't 1980).

15. Soho Dev. Corp. v. Dean & DeLuca Inc., 131 A.D.2d 385, 517 N.Y.S.2d 498 (1st Dep't 1987).

16. Joseph Martin, Jr., Delicatessen, Inc. v. Schumarcher, 52 N.Y.2d 105, 436 N.Y.S.2d 247, 417 N.E.2d 541 (1981).

17. 52 N.Y.2d at 110, 436 N.Y.S.2d at 249–50.

18. Mulcahy v. Rhode Island Hos. Tr. Nat'l Bank, 83 A.D.2d 846, 441 N.Y.S.2d 752, (2d Dep't 1981).

In *166 Mamaroneck Avenue Corp. v. 151 East Post Road Corp.*,[19] the court held that a lease that provided for a renewal term rental to be agreed upon, subject to arbitration in the event landlord and tenant could not agree, did meet the test of certainty and was thus enforceable. Even though the lease did not set forth a manner for determining the rent, the parties to the lease "selected a process for the calculation of rent for the renewal term. They clearly intended to be bound by the arbitrator's determination. Arbitration, while a process and not a methodology per se, implicates the participation and decision making of a neutral third party. We conclude that by providing for this eventuality and agreeing to be bound by the result, the parties 'invited recourse to an objective extrinsic event, condition or standard' on which the amount was made to depend . . . and the renewal term is consequently definite and enforceable."[20]

A sublessee must be aware when negotiating a renewal option in its sublease that unless the sublessor has an option to renew the prime lease and agrees to exercise the option if the subtenant so requests, the sublessor is not obligated to do so.[21]

One of the detriments in granting an option to renew to a tenant is the restriction on the landlord from marketing the space until the tenant has exercised its option. The landlord in *Cobalt Blue Corp. v. 184 West 10th Street Corp.*[22] attempted to deal with this problem by drafting a requirement that if after the tenant exercised its renewal option the landlord received a bona fide offer to rent the premises for the period of the renewal term, at an increased rental, the existing tenant would lose its right to renew unless, within 30 days' after notice, it agreed to the superior offer. The landlord may have believed that by requiring the tenant to give at least 12 months' prior notice of its renewal, plus building in an "obligation to match a better offer" it clearly protected itself from losing the benefit of market increases in rent. The tenant had two five-year renewal options and it exercised both 12 months prior to the expiration of the initial lease term. The landlord obtained a bona fide offer at triple the rent for a ten-year initial and ten-year renewal term, and demanded that the tenant match this offer.

It took two trips to the appellate division, the last decided in December 1996, for a lease renewal term that was to commence on September 1, 1991, for the landlord to prevail and be permitted to proceed with its holdover proceeding. The appellate division first found that the lease provisions were ambiguous and that questions of fact were raised as to whether the alleged bona fide third-party offer varied so much from the terms of the tenant's lease that it did not fit within the lease term that the offer be at a "rental in excess of the rental provided to be paid by the Tenant . . . but otherwise on the same terms and conditions as are contained in this lease." Among the variances besides base rent were the rent escalation provisions, and the ten-year base plus ten-year renewal term, as opposed to the two five-year renewals provided for in the tenant's lease. The appellate division, on its second consideration, deemed both variances de

19. 78 N.Y.2d 88, 571 N.Y.S.2d 686, 572 N.E.2d 104 (1991).

20. 78 N.Y.2d at 92, 571 N.Y. S.2d at 688.

21. Tiger Crane Martial Arts Inc. v. Franchise Stores Realty Corp., 235 A.D.2d 994, 652 N.Y.S.2d 674 (3d Dep't 1997).

22. 227 A.D.2d 50, 650 N.Y.S.2d 720 (1st Dep't 1996).

minimis. The increase in rent that could be considered could include increases in additional rent. As a result of tenant's attempt to exercise both its renewal options at once, for a single ten-year renewal term, the court would not hear its complaint that the initial term of the bona fide offer was for ten rather than five years. The landlord's position may have finally been sustained, but it cannot be said, in view of all the litigation, that the lease provisions achieved the landlord's goal of renting the premises at its market value when the existing lease expired.

CHAPTER 40

Bankruptcy

40.1 General Purpose

Several provisions, customarily included in leases, attempt to provide a landlord with certain protections against a tenant's bankruptcy. Some of these provisions, however, are not enforceable under the current federal Bankruptcy Code. Statutory references to the bankruptcy law may be found in Title 11 of the United States Code Annotated (U.S.C.A.). Even where the Bankruptcy Code does not expressly prohibit enforcement of a particular provision, enforceability remains in doubt because of the bankruptcy court's broad equitable powers to act in the best interests of the bankrupt's estate.

The most common of these bankruptcy clauses, often referred to as an "ipso facto" clause, states that the landlord has the right to automatically terminate or modify a lease upon the tenant's bankruptcy, insolvency, or upon the appointment of, or loss of assets to, a custodian. Under the former federal Bankruptcy Act, which was in effect prior to 1978, such clauses were not expressly prohibited, and it may be for this reason that most lease forms continue to include such a provision.

Current federal bankruptcy law, however, in an effort to protect the debtor's rights to potentially valuable leaseholds, expressly provides that ipso facto clauses are not enforceable. Pursuant to section 365(e) of the federal Bankruptcy Code [11 U.S.C.A. § 365(e)], an unexpired lease may not be modified or terminated after the commencement of a bankruptcy case (1) solely on the basis of a provision that is conditioned on the insolvency or financial condition of the debtor, (2) the commencement of a bankruptcy case, or (3) the appointment of or taking possession of assets by a bankruptcy trustee, or by another custodian before the filing of a bankruptcy petition. Section 365(e)(2) sets forth certain narrow exceptions to the rule invalidating ipso facto clauses, but these do not typically apply to leases. In addition, under section 365(b)(2), a clause providing for a tenant's default on the ground of bankruptcy, financial difficulty, or the appointment of, or taking possession of assets by a trustee or other custodian, is not recognized as causing a default by the tenant; nor does it trigger any obligation to cure, or to provide adequate assurance of future performance prior to assumption of the lease by the tenant. Such adequate assurance will be required, however, if there are other non-bankruptcy defaults on the part of the tenant at the time of assumption, or if the tenant desires to assign its interest under the lease under section 365(f) of the Bankruptcy Code, notwithstanding prohibitions thereon in the lease.

Another provision often included in a lease may attempt to limit assignment of the lease in a bankruptcy and may seek to give the landlord a right of first refusal to acquire the lease on the same terms as a third-party assignee. Section 365(f) of the federal Bankruptcy Code states, with certain narrow exceptions, that if a debtor assumes an unexpired lease and provides adequate assurance of future performance, the debtor may assign the lease notwithstanding any provision in the lease or applicable law that prohibits, restricts, or conditions the assignment of the lease. As a consequence, a provision giving the landlord the right to terminate or modify the lease upon such assignment is not enforceable. Thus, a lease cannot restrict the tenant's ability to assign the lease in a bankruptcy proceeding. And, while a right of first refusal in favor of the landlord would, on its face, appear not to violate section 365(f), a court may not enforce that right if it determines that the right of first refusal might dissuade potential assignees from bidding to acquire the lease.

Similarly, courts have struck down lease provisions that would give the landlord a share of profits from an assignment made during the course of a bankruptcy. Such clauses have been stricken even when the profit-sharing provisions of the lease apply generally and are not triggered by the bankruptcy, and even when the sharing provision might otherwise be considered fair and reasonable (a landlord's share of as little as one-third of the profit has been held unenforceable). The view of the bankruptcy courts has been that the mere existence of a profit-sharing provision, regardless of its independent merit, limits the tenant's ability to realize the value of its lease in a bankruptcy and will be held unenforceable.

It should be noted that section 365(f), while permitting the assumption and assignment of a lease by a debtor, notwithstanding restrictions on transfer contained in the lease, does not permit the debtor to assume the lease and to sublease the premises in violation of the terms of the lease. Courts that have decided this issue have interpreted section 365 to require that a lease be assumed or rejected in its entirety, whereas to permit a sublease would be a change in the terms of the lease.

Another provision often included in leases attempts to define "adequate assurance," which, under section 365(f) of the Bankruptcy Code, must be provided to the landlord before a lease may be assigned under that section. The Bankruptcy Code does not define "adequate assurance," and courts have held that it must be determined on a case-by-case basis. There is no certainty that a bankruptcy judge will recognize the requirements of adequate assurance specified in the lease. Indeed, setting forth a definition of adequate assurance in a lease could limit the landlord by making it impossible to ask for more, or different, assurance than specified in the lease, even where warranted by the particular situation.

Sample clauses of the types just discussed are set forth in the next section.

40.2 Sample Clause

40.01 Insolvency of Tenant or Tenant's Guarantor. This Lease and the term and estate hereby granted are subject to the limitation that whenever Tenant, or any guarantor of Tenant's obligations under this Lease, shall make an assignment for the benefit of creditors, or shall file a voluntary petition under any bankruptcy or insolvency law, or an involuntary petition alleging an act of bankruptcy or insolvency shall be filed against Tenant or such guarantor under any bankruptcy or insolvency law, or whenever a petition shall be filed by or against Tenant or such guarantor under the reorganization provisions of the United States Bankruptcy Code or under the provisions of any law of like import, or whenever a petition shall be filed by Tenant, or such guarantor, under the arrangement provisions of the United States Bankruptcy Code or under the provisions of any law of like import, or whenever a permanent receiver of Tenant, or such guarantor, or of or for the property of Tenant, or such guarantor, shall be appointed, then Landlord (a) if such event occurs without the acquiescence of Tenant, or such guarantor, as the case may be, at any time after the event continues for 60 days, or (b) in any other case at any time after the occurrence of any such event, may give Tenant a notice of intention to end the term of this Lease at the expiration of 5 days from the giving of such notice of intention, and upon the expiration of said 5-day period this Lease and the term and estate hereby granted, whether or not the term shall theretofore have commenced, shall terminate with the same effect as if that day were the expiration date of this Lease, but Tenant shall remain liable for damages as provided in Article __.

40.02 Assignment of Lease; Requirement of Adequate Assurance.

(a) If pursuant to the Bankruptcy Code Tenant is permitted to assign this Lease in disregard of the restrictions contained in Article 16 (or if this Lease shall be assumed by a trustee), the trustee or assignee shall cure any default under this Lease and shall provide adequate assurance of future performance by the trustee or assignee including (i) the source of payment of rent and performance of other obligations under this Lease, for which adequate assurance shall mean the deposit of cash security with Landlord in an amount equal to the sum of one year's Fixed Rent then reserved hereunder plus an amount equal to all Additional Rent payable under Article 5 for the calendar year preceding the year in which such assignment is intended to become effective, which deposit shall be held by Landlord, without interest, for the balance of the term as security for the full and faithful performance of all of Tenant's obligations under this Lease, and that any such assignee of this Lease shall have a net worth exclusive of good will, computed in accordance with generally accepted accounting principles, equal to at least 10 times the aggregate of the annual Fixed Rent reserved hereunder plus all Additional Rent for the preceding calendar year as aforesaid and (ii) that the use of the Premises shall in no way diminish the reputation of the Building as a first-class office building or impose any additional burden upon the Building or increase the services to be provided by Landlord.

(b) If Tenant's trustee, Tenant or Tenant as debtor-in-possession assumes this Lease and proposes to assign the same (pursuant to Title 11 U.S.C. § 365, as the same may be amended) to any person or entity who shall have made a bona fide offer to accept an assignment of this Lease on terms acceptable to the trustee, Tenant or Tenant as debtor-in-possession, then notice of such proposed assignment, setting forth (i) the name and address of such person, (ii) all of the terms and conditions of such offer, and (iii) the adequate assurance to be provided to Landlord to assure such person's future performance under this Lease, including, without limitation, the assurances referred to in Title 11 U.S.C. § 365(b)(3) (as the same may be amended), shall be given to Landlord by the trustee, Tenant or Tenant as debtor-in-possession no later than 20 days after receipt by the trustee, Tenant or Tenant as debtor-in-possession of such offer, but in any event no later than 10 days prior to the date that the trustee, Tenant or Tenant as debtor-in-possession shall make application to a court of competent jurisdiction for authority and approval to enter into such assignment and assumption, and Landlord shall thereupon have the prior right and option, to be exercised by notice to the trustee, Tenant or Tenant as debtor-in-possession, given at any time prior to the effective date of such proposed assignment, to accept an assignment of this Lease upon the same terms and conditions and for the same consideration, if any, as the bona fide offer made by such person, less any brokerage commissions which may be payable out of the consideration to be paid by such person for the assignment of this Lease.

40.3 Landlord Concerns

As discussed in Section 40.1 (General Purpose), *supra*, the enforceability of the provisions described in Section 40.2 (Sample Clause), *supra*, at best, are questionable. Accordingly, we question whether any of them should be included in a modern office lease. While there would appear to be no downside to including a right of first refusal clause in favor of a landlord, its enforceability is not ensured.

Filing a federal bankruptcy case is not the only evidence of a tenant's financial difficulty. An argument might be made in favor of retaining ipso facto clauses where a tenant's financial problems manifest themselves in other forms, for example, seeking protection under state insolvency laws, so that the landlord, under such circumstances, would have the right to terminate the lease. Although state law insolvency remedies are sought less frequently than federal bankruptcy protections, there are certain entities, such as banks and insurance companies that are not eligible for federal bankruptcy protection and there are various reasons why the tenant might prefer state remedies to a bankruptcy filing. In addition, there is always the possibility that federal bankruptcy law will again change and permit enforcement of ipso facto bankruptcy termination clauses.

Lease provisions that create a tenant's default in the event of the bankruptcy or insolvency of a guarantor of the tenant do not violate the federal Bankruptcy Code and should be included in a lease whenever there is a guaranty of a tenant's obligations under the lease. It should be noted that where the guarantor is in bankruptcy but the tenant is not, the landlord should consider the possibility that calling such a default may force the tenant into bankruptcy.

40.4 Tenant Concerns

When faced with ipso facto bankruptcy termination clauses (see Section 40.1, *supra*) or other bankruptcy-triggered provisions that the tenant believes are not enforceable, two choices are presented. The tenant may attempt to have the provisions eliminated from the lease, or it can opt to ignore the provisions. The first course of action would be preferable. If, however, it cannot be accomplished due to the realities of the parties' relative bargaining strength, the latter course is acceptable. In any event, tenant should not spend a significant amount of time negotiating to improve these provisions. The tenant may, however, wish to make clear that any rights granted to the landlord under these provisions may be exercised, if at all, only during the pendency of the bankruptcy or insolvency event.

Clauses that create a default or other rights against a tenant upon the bankruptcy or insolvency of a guarantor of tenant may be guarded against by negotiating for the right to provide landlord with alternative security, in the form of a different guarantor, a security deposit, or some other acceptable form of security.

40.5 Standard Real Estate Board of New York Clause

> *Bankruptcy: 16.* (a) Anything elsewhere in this lease to the contrary notwithstanding, this lease may be canceled by Owner by the sending of a written notice to Tenant within a reasonable time after the happening of any one or more of the following events: (1) the commencement of a case in bankruptcy or under the laws of any state naming Tenant (or a guarantor of any of Tenant's obligations under this lease) as the debtor; or (2) the making by Tenant (or a guarantor of any of Tenant's obligations under this lease) of an assignment or any other arrangement for the benefit of creditors under any state statute. Neither Tenant nor any person claiming through or under Tenant, or by reason of any statute or order of court, shall thereafter be entitled to possession of the premises demised but shall forthwith quit and surrender the premises. If this lease shall be assigned in accordance with its terms, the provisions of this Article 16 shall be applicable only to the party then owing Tenant's interest in this lease.
>
> (b) It is stipulated and agreed that in the event of the termination of this lease pursuant to (a) hereof, Owner shall forthwith, notwithstanding any other provisions of this lease to the contrary, be entitled to recover from Tenant as and for liquidated damages an amount equal to the difference between the rent

reserved hereunder for the unexpired portion of the term demised and the fair and reasonable rental value of the demised premises for the same period. In the computation of such damages the difference between any installment of rent becoming due hereunder after the date of termination and the fair and reasonable rental value of the demised premises for the period for which such installment was payable shall be discounted to the date of termination at the rate of four percent (4%) per annum. If such premises or any part thereof be re-let by the Owner for the unexpired term of said lease, or any part thereof, before presentation of proof of such liquidated damages to any court, commission or tribunal, the amount of rent reserved upon such re-letting shall be deemed to be the fair and reasonable rental value for the part or the whole of the premises so re-let during the term of the re-letting. Nothing herein contained shall limit or prejudice the right of the Owner to prove for and obtain as liquidated damages by reason of such termination, an amount equal to the maximum allowed by any statute or rule of law in effect at the time when, and governing the proceedings in which, such damages are to be proved, whether or not such amount be greater, equal to, or less than the amount of the differences referred to above.

40.6 Comments on Standard Real Estate Board of New York Clause

Section 40.1 (General Purpose), *supra*, describes the various reasons why the REBNY form clause is not enforceable under federal law. If the board form is being relied on to cover actions under state law, it should be noted that it contains significant gaps. For example, while an assignment for the benefit of creditors is covered, the appointment of a receiver is not. Note, too, that the second paragraph set forth in Section 40.5 (Standard Real Estate Board of New York Clause), *supra*, providing for a measure of damages (which is in itself somewhat contradictory in that it purports to set forth a "stipulated and agreed" measure of "liquidated damages" but then goes on to say that owner/landlord is nevertheless entitled to any other measure of damages allowed under law) would, at least in a market that has been stable or risen since the lease was entered into, result in less damages than those to which the owner/landlord would be entitled under the federal Bankruptcy Code in the absence of such a clause. For example, if fair market rent is higher than the rent set forth in the lease, there would be no damage to the owner/landlord under the measure set forth in the form. In the absence of such provision, however, the owner/landlord could seek to recover the unpaid rent for the balance of the term, subject, however, to the limitation on damages in section 502(b)(6) of the federal Bankruptcy Code.

40.7 Litigation Issues

The truism ordinarily governing commercial leasing law in New York—that the rights of the parties are determined by the terms of the lease agreement—is, for the most part, untrue when a tenant comes under the protective aegis of a bankruptcy court. The best business judgment of a bankruptcy trustee or debtor will supersede a written lease document.[1] For a thorough review of the application of the Bankruptcy Code to the landlord and tenant relationship, see Finkelstein and Ferrara, *Landlord and Tenant Practice in New York*.[2]

There are certain fundamental bankruptcy concepts that must be confronted by a landlord when a tenant is in financial trouble or becomes a bankruptcy debtor. The landlord, dealing with a tenant in financial difficulty, must be concerned with avoiding a preferential[3] and/or fraudulent transfer.[4] Upon the filing of a bankruptcy petition, the landlord will be confronted with the following consequences of the filing: (1) an automatic stay;[5] (2) the law concerning assumption, rejection, or assignment of unexpired leases;[6] (3) the invalidation or refusal to enforce certain lease provisions, such as ipso facto bankruptcy termination clauses;[7] (4) restrictions on assignment of subletting;[8] and (5) the concept of "adequate assurance" of performance, as opposed to actual cure of defaults in lease provisions for leases being assumed[9] or assigned.[10]

Transactions with a tenant in financial difficulty that are voidable preferences or fraudulent transfers, consummated prior to the commencement of a bankruptcy case, may be set aside by a bankruptcy trustee after the petition is filed. The use of a security deposit within 90 days prior to the filing of a bankruptcy petition may, if the tenant was insolvent at the time, be deemed to be a preferential payment. The bankruptcy trustee, pursuant to section 547 of the Bankruptcy Code,[11] may recover the deposit. Furthermore, the acceptance of a surrender of a lease from an insolvent tenant may be set aside as a fraudulent transfer under section 548 of the Bankruptcy Code, if the surrender is obtained without payment to the tenant of an amount equal to the market value of the unexpired term. The landlord who relets the premises after accepting a surrender, which is subsequently set aside as a fraudulent transfer, may be required, under section 550 of the Bankruptcy Code,[12] to pay the increased rental it receives attributable to the balance of the lease term to the bankruptcy trustee.

If the landlord can complete legal proceedings to terminate a lease prior to the filing of a bankruptcy petition, the lease will not be deemed to be within the bankrupt's

---

1. *In re* Balco Equities Ltd., 323 B.R. 85 (Bankr. S.D.N.Y. 2005); *In re* Sok Jun Kong, 162 B.R. 86 (Bankr. E.D.N.Y. 1993); *In re* Child World, Inc., 142 B.R. 87 (Bankr. S.D.N.Y. 1990).
2. Finkelstein & Ferrara, Landlord and Tenant Practice in New York ch. 20 (2020–21).
3. 11 U.S.C.A. § 547.
4. *Id.* § 548.
5. *Id.* § 362 (a).
6. *Id.* § 365.
7. *Id.* § 365(e).
8. *Id.* § 365(f).
9. *Id.* § 365 (b)(1)(A).
10. *Id.* § 365(f)(2)(B).
11. Finkelstein & Ferrara, *supra* note 2, at § 20:289.
12. *In re* Brooklyn Overall Co., Inc., 57 B.R. 999, 1004 (Bankr. E.D.N.Y. 1986) (lease surrender could not be avoided under 11 U.S.C.A. § 549 because premises were re-let, but landlord had to pay increased rent for balance of debtor's term to trustee under 11 U.S.C.A. § 550).

estate and will be beyond the trustee's reach. In the case of termination of a lease by summary proceedings, the issuance of a warrant of eviction annuls the landlord-tenant relationship.[13] If the landlord, prior to the filing of a bankruptcy petition, obtains a judgment of possession and the issuance of a warrant of eviction, the premises will be freed from the bankrupt's estate,[14] even if the warrant is unexecuted.[15]

If, however, a warrant of eviction has not been issued, filing of a bankruptcy petition will invoke the section 362 automatic stay, which will not only prevent completion of legal proceedings but prevent the serving of a notice of termination[16] or from using a security deposit.[17] In order to enforce its state court remedies for default or access the security deposit, the landlord must obtain relief, under section 362(d), from the automatic stay. In deciding whether to grant such relief, the bankruptcy court will consider more than the default that would entitle the lessor to terminate the lease under applicable state law. Pursuant to section 362(d) of the Bankruptcy Code, relief from the stay may not be granted if the debtor has "equity" in the property or the property is necessary for the debtor's reorganization. Thus the hope for increased rent from a solvent tenant, which impels the landlord to evict an insolvent tenant, is the same reason that may move the trustee to oppose a motion for relief from the stay. The debtor's estate may have value if assigned for a market rent, and the realization of these funds would benefit the debtor and its creditors.

The impact of the automatic stay is so powerful that parties seeking to enforce rights against non-bankrupt parties are barred from taking steps adverse to the bankrupt. A landlord is prohibited from serving a notice terminating a prime lease, where the sublessee has filed for bankruptcy protection.[18] The Second Circuit, in *In re 48th*

---

13. Real Property Actions and Proceedings Law (RPAPL) § 749(3).

14. *In re* Éclair Bakery, Ltd., 255 B.R. 121, 133 (Bankr. S.D.N.Y. 2000) ("Under the law of New York, the issuance of a warrant of eviction cancels the lease between the parties and annuls the relationship of landlord and tenant."). *See also* Nadine Props., Inc. v. Henry Bergmann & Co., Inc., 583 N.Y.S.2d 114, 117 (N.Y. Civ. Cnty. Ct. 1991) (where the property owner was able to execute the eviction warrant against the debtor since the debtor had no legal interest in the premises at the time the bankruptcy since the warrant was executed the day before the bankruptcy petition was filed); *In re* Lady Liberty Tavern Corp., 94 B.R. 812 (Bankr. S.D.N.Y. 1988) (where judgment of possession and issuance of warrant obtained by default judgment, but noting that lease was properly terminated by exercise of conditional limitation prior to filing of petition).

15. *In re* Darwin, 22 B.R. 259, 262 (Bankr. E.D.N.Y. 1982) ("Under the laws of the state of New York it is not the execution of the warrant, but the issuance of a warrant for the removal of a tenant that 'cancels the agreement under which the person removed held the premises and annuls the relationship of landlord and tenant.'") *But see* Super Nova 330 LLC v. Gazes, 693 F.3d 138, 142 (2d Cir. 2012) ("Under New York law, therefore, while the issuance of a warrant of eviction cancels any existing lease and seemingly terminates the landlord-tenant relationship, the *tenant, in fact, retains a residual interest in the lease until the execution of the warrant.* Prior to such execution, the state court may vacate the warrant of eviction for good cause and thereby reinstate the lease.") (emphasis added).

16. *In re* Éclair Bakery, Ltd., 255 B.R. 121, 133 (Bankr. S.D.N.Y. 2000); *see also* Finkelstein & Ferrara, *supra* note 2, at § 20:298.

17. Finkelstein & Ferrara, *supra* note 2, at § 20:291.

18. *In re* Hartley, 458 B.R. 145 (Bankr. S.D.N.Y. 2011); *In re* Adelphia Commc'ns. Corp., 345 B.R. 69 (Bankr. S.D.N.Y. 2006); *In re* 48th St. Steakhouse, Inc., 835 F.2d 427 (2d Cir. 1987).

Street Steakhouse, Inc., noted that "if action taken against the non-bankrupt party would inevitably have an adverse impact on property of the bankrupt estate, then such action should be barred by the automatic stay."[19]

Section 365 of the Bankruptcy Code provides for a 60-day period, unless extended, for the trustee or debtor to assume or reject a lease. In reaching a decision whether to reject or assume a lease, the bankruptcy court is not primarily concerned with the landlord's state law right to evict a defaulting tenant. The court is concerned with whether, in the debtor's business judgment, assumption of the lease is advantageous to the debtor and its creditors.[20] The landlord, under section 365(b)(1), is entitled to adequate assurance of a prompt cure, prompt compensation for actual pecuniary loss, and adequate assurance of future performance. A prompt cure "depends on the facts and circumstances of each case,"[21] and may not necessarily occur prior to the expiration of the lease cure period. Adequate assurance of future performance is not a guaranty, but "rather, the test is whether there is a likelihood that the rent and other lease-related obligations will be met."[22] Thus, "courts will look for 'evidence of profitability' in the form of: (1) demonstrated reductions in operating costs, payroll, and inventory, coupled with an increase in sales; (2) a plan earmarking money exclusively for the landlord; or (3) the ability and willingness of the debtor or its assignee to fund the cure payments."[23]

In re Lafayette Radio Electronics Corp.[24] represents an excellent example of the analysis employed by a bankruptcy court in deciding whether a lease is to be assumed by the bankrupt, notwithstanding the landlord's objections. The court's overriding concern in reaching a decision whether the lease should be assumed for the purpose of obtaining sublease income is whether "the proposed sublease is in the best interests of the debtor and its creditors[.]"[25] The bankrupt electronics store sought to sublease its store premises to a discount women's clothing store as part of a sublease program in order to achieve a positive cash flow from the value of its various leaseholds. Achieving a certain income stream was important because it was a condition to a proposed merger. In approving the sublease, the court considered the importance of the merger to the reorganization of the debtor. The court also ruled that the landlord was provided with the necessary adequate assurance by considering (1) the income from the overall sublease program; (2) the proposed merger; (3) the fact that the proposed subtenant was part of a successful retail chain and had posted a security deposit and a promissory note

---

19. *48th Street*, 835 F.2d at 431. *See also In re* Comcoach Corp., 698 F.2d 571 (2d Cir. 1983) (denying relief from automatic stay to foreclosing fee mortgagee to cut off bankrupt tenant's lease which was expressly subordinate to the mortgage).

20. *In re* Lee Rd. Partners, 155 B.R. 55 (Bankr. E.D.N.Y. 1993); *In re* Child World, Inc., 142 B.R. 87 (Bankr. S.D.N.Y. 1990).

21. Finkelstein & Ferrara, *supra* note 2, at § 20:121 citing *In re* Embers 86th Street, Inc., 184 B.R. 892 (Bankr. S.D.N.Y. 1995) (debtor's proposal to cure rent default over 29-month period was not sufficiently "prompt" for purposes of assuming the lease).

22. Finkelstein & Ferrara, *supra* note 2, at § 20:82 (referencing *In re* Westview 74th Street Drug Corp., 59 B.R. 747 (Bankr. S.D.N.Y. 1986)).

23. *Id.* (referencing *In re* Embers 86th Street, Inc., 184 B.R. 892 (Bankr. S.D.N.Y. 1995)).

24. *In re* Lafayette Radio Electronics Corp., 9 B.R. 993 (Bankr. E.D.N.Y. 1981).

25. *Id.* at 1004.

from its principals. The court was not unmindful of specific lease provisions that may have prevented the sublease had the language in the lease been more restrictive. Had the debtor sought to assign the lease, the subtenant may not have provided adequate assurance that the lease's specific financial covenants would be met. Furthermore, the court analyzed, on a factual basis, each of the specific conditions to the subletting set forth in the lease. The court found, on a factual basis, that the use clause and manner of use provisions would not be violated by the subtenant's occupancy of the premises.

Section 365(f) of the Bankruptcy Code would overcome an objection by a landlord to a debtor's assignment of a lease, notwithstanding the existence of direct or implied restrictions or prohibitions against assignment. Under these circumstances, reliance on lease restrictions would not prevent an assignment. The landlord would be entitled to adequate assurance of future performance, which may take the form of an added security deposit, personal guarantees, or an analysis of the assignee's net worth. Thus, if the assignment is needed to further a reorganization or liquidation plan of the debtor, the court will permit it even if the assignee's use does not comply with the lease's express use restriction.[26]

Shopping center landlords are provided with a greater measure of protection with respect to a court's analysis of what constitutes "adequate assurance" under section 365(b)(3) of the Bankruptcy Code. When approving an application for the assumption or assignment of a shopping center lease, the court must consider whether the financial condition of the assignee is similar to the debtor's; that the percentage rent will not diminish by reason of the assignment; that the assignment or assumption is subject to all lease provisions; and that the tenant mix will not be disrupted. Thus a use restriction, which may be ignored in considering an assignment of a retail store lease in an office building, may prevent the assignment of a shopping center lease.[27]

---

26. *In re* U.L. Radio Corp., 19 B.R. 537 (Bankr. S.D.N.Y. 1982).
27. *In re* TSW Stores of Nanuet, Inc., 34 B.R. 299 (Bankr. S.D.N.Y. 1983).

CHAPTER 41

Estoppel Certificates

41.1 General Purpose

Throughout the term of a lease, landlords and tenants from time to time engage in transactions with third parties who may have a particular interest in the status of the lease. Most commonly, when the landlord intends to sell the real property subject to the lease, the prospective purchaser will want to confirm the terms of the lease and assure itself that the parties to the lease are not in default of their respective obligations. A prospective lender providing a loan to the landlord has similar concerns. Conversely, a tenant may be selling all of its assets and liabilities to another company, including its interest in the lease, and the purchaser will want certainty as to the leasehold obligations being assumed. An estoppel certificate is designed to provide this certainty.

Rather than merely relying on a representation from the party with whom the purchaser or lender is contracting, the estoppel certificate precludes the certifying party from alleging or denying facts that are inconsistent with the facts contained in the estoppel certificate. This enables the third party to rely uon the information and, should it succeed to the interest of the landlord or tenant, such third party may utilize the certificate to enforce or defend its rights against the certifying party. The provisions of a lease should obligate the landlord and tenant to deliver estoppel certificates, in a timely manner, that contain the information typically required by third parties with whom they may transact business during the term of the lease.

41.2 Sample Clause

Article 41

(a) Within 10 Business Days following request from Landlord, any Superior Mortgagee or any Superior Lessor, Tenant shall deliver to Landlord a statement executed and acknowledged by Tenant, in form reasonably satisfactory to Landlord, (i) stating the Commencement Date, the Rent Commencement Date and the Expiration Date, and that this Lease is then in full force and effect and has not been modified (or if modified, setting forth all modifications),

(ii) setting forth the date to which Fixed Rent and any Additional Rent have been paid, together with the amount of monthly Fixed Rent, Tax Payment and Operating Payment then payable, (iii) stating whether or not, to the best of Tenant's knowledge, Landlord is in default under this Lease, and, if Tenant asserts that Landlord is in default, setting forth the specific nature of any such defaults, (iv) stating whether Landlord has failed to complete any work required to be performed by Landlord under this Lease, (v) stating whether there are any sums payable to Tenant by Landlord under this Lease, (vi) stating the amount of the security deposit, if any, under this Lease, (vii) stating whether there are any subleases affecting the Premises, (viii) stating the address of Tenant to which all notices and communications under this Lease shall be sent, and (ix) responding to any other matters reasonably requested by Landlord, such Superior Mortgagee or such Superior Lessor. Tenant acknowledges that any statement delivered pursuant to this Section 41.01(a) may be relied upon by any purchaser or owner of the Real Property or the Building, or all or any portion of Landlord's interest in the Real Property or the Building or under any Superior Lease, or by any Superior Mortgagee or assignee thereof, or by any Superior Lessor or assignee thereof.

(b) Within 10 Business Days following request from Tenant (but in no event more than once in any twelve month period), Landlord shall deliver to Tenant a statement executed and acknowledged by Landlord, in form reasonably satisfactory to Tenant, (i) stating the Commencement Date, the Rent Commencement Date and the Expiration Date, and that this Lease is then in full force and effect and has not been modified (or if modified, setting forth all modifications), (ii) setting forth the date to which Fixed Rent and any Additional Rent have been paid, together with the amount of monthly Fixed Rent, Tax Payment and Operating Payment then payable and (iii) stating whether or not, to Landlord's knowledge, Tenant is in default under this Lease, and, if Landlord asserts that Tenant is in default, setting forth in reasonable specificity the nature of any such defaults. Any such statement may be relied upon by Tenant or any permitted assignee or sublessee or lender to Tenant.

41.3 Landlord Concerns

Three principal concerns occupy the landlord regarding the estoppel certificate provision of a lease. First, and of paramount importance, is the content of the certificate the tenant is required to deliver. An effective estoppel certificate should contain certifications about the terms and provisions of the lease, as well as the state of performance of the respective parties' obligations under the lease. The information addressed in this latter type of certification, which cannot be discerned from a mere reading of the lease, is of critical importance to the third parties who will be relying on the certificate. Information about the lease itself should include a specific description of the lease and all amendments or, preferably, an attachment of a true, correct, and complete copy of the lease. Other informational items regarding the lease itself may be the amount of square footage demised by the lease, a statement of the fixed rent that is payable, the current rate for the payment of overage or escalation rents such as tax and operating pass-throughs or common area maintenance charges, base years (or amounts) and the applicable tenant's percentage for these additional rent payments, the amount of any security deposit, the commencement and expiration dates of the lease, and the number and duration of renewal options.

The most common certifications regarding the state of the lease relate to whether the lease is in full force and effect and whether or not either party is in default of any of its obligations under the lease (and, if so, a specific description of each default). With regard to defaults, it is important that the tenant be obligated to specify not only its own defaults but, more importantly, its view of whether or not the landlord is in default. From the perspective of the third party who will be relying on the tenant's certificate, it is the landlord's actions that could trigger a set-off against the payment of rent or possible termination of the lease. If a tenant certifies that there are no landlord defaults, the third party may rely on there being no prior failure on the part of the landlord to perform its obligations under the lease which could inure to the detriment of the third party. Often, tenants will attempt to qualify this portion of the certificate with language such as "to the best of tenant's knowledge," or "tenant has not actual knowledge of any default." Of course, landlords should endeavor to require tenants to deliver certificates without these qualifications.

Other types of "outside of the lease" information may (1) include the date to which rents have been paid (and that no other rent has been paid more than one month in advance); (2) whether or not the tenant has accepted possession of the premises; (3) whether or not the landlord has completed and/or paid for all work that it was obligated to complete in order to ready the premises for the tenant's occupancy; (4) whether the tenant has any claim or defense against the landlord or has the right to assert any offset or credit against the payment of rent; and (5) whether the tenant has subleased any portion of the premises.

The second principal area of concern for the landlord is to ensure that the tenant is obligated to address the estoppel certificate directly to the third party who will be relying on its contents. Most prospective purchasers and lenders want to be able to directly enforce their rights against the certifying party and will not accept an estoppel certificate that is addressed to the landlord. Thus, the lease provision should require the tenant to deliver the certificate to the landlord or to any party specified by the landlord.

The third major area of concern to the landlord is the period of time given to the tenant to complete and return the certificate. Many sale and finance transactions happen very quickly or not at all; and the inability of a landlord to obtain the timely return of an estoppel certificate could jeopardize the transaction. It is difficult to establish an effective remedy for the failure of a tenant to execute and deliver a certificate in a timely manner, since most landlords, being in the position of needing the certificate, will not wish to send a notice of default or notice of termination of the lease to the tenant. One option is to include a provision in the lease that states that a tenant's failure to deliver an estoppel certificate will be deemed to be a certification by that tenant that there are no defaults under the lease. However, such a provision is of limited value since it is unlikely the third party will rely on such a deemed certification, and because this only addresses one of the many items that should be included in an estoppel.

41.4 Tenant Concerns

From the tenant's point of view, an estoppel provision should give it the right to request and receive the certificate from the landlord. In many landlord-friendly leases, including the Real Estate Board of New York form (set forth in Section 41.5, *infra*), a landlord is the only party who can request estoppel certificates. However, there are many instances in which a tenant's need for an estoppel certificate from the landlord is just as critical as the landlord's need for an estoppel certificate from the tenant. In addition to the sale of a business scenario described in Section 41.1 ("General Purpose"), *supra*, the tenant may wish to sublet all or a portion of its premises. In such a case the subtenant will justifiably require the delivery of a landlord estoppel certificate. In ground leases or other situations where the tenant may mortgage its leasehold interest, the tenant's lender will insist on a landlord estoppel certificate as a condition to making the leasehold mortgage. The purchaser of a ground lease position will similarly require an estoppel certificate from the ground lessor.

The contents of a landlord estoppel certificate should be similar to the contents of a tenant estoppel certificate in most respects, except for some of the more detailed "outside the lease" information. In this regard, rather than addressing whether the landlord has performed all required work and other items (which are more of a concern to a party that may succeed to a landlord's interest in the lease), the estoppel provision should require a certification from the landlord that it has not commenced any action or given or received any notice for the purpose of terminating the lease.

From the defensive perspective, the tenant should attempt to minimize its exposure by limiting the type of information set forth in the certificate, and by limiting the parties to whom the tenant is required to deliver the certificate at the request of the landlord. Ideally, the tenant should only be required to certify to three basic items: a description of the lease, a statement that it is in full force and effect, and that, to the tenant's actual knowledge, no event of default has occurred nor is continuing. A tenant should also try to limit its obligation to deliver an estoppel certificate only to an entity that is either purchasing, or making a loan secured by, the landlord's interest in the lease. In addition, the tenant should be sure it has sufficient time to complete and return the certificate so that it can conduct appropriate due diligence with its facilities and/or on-site personnel to verify that the information contained in the certificate is correct, and that any problems are adequately set forth in the certificate. Finally, tenants may wish to limit the frequency with which a landlord may request an estoppel certificate, as confirming or filling in the facts in an estoppel certificate usually requires the tenant to devote legal, accounting and possibly other resources that the tenant would prefer to be devoted to its underlying business. Therefore, it is typical and standard for tenants to request that landlords only be permitted to request an estoppel certificate once or twice in any 12-calendar-month period.

41.5 Standard Real Estate Board of New York Clause

> *Estoppel Certificate: 35.* Tenant, at any time, and from time to time, upon at least 10 days' prior notice by Owner, shall execute, acknowledge and deliver to Owner, and/or any other person, firm or corporation specified by Owner, a statement certifying that this Lease is unmodified and in full force and effect (or, if there have been modifications, that the same is in full force and effect as modified and stating the modifications), stating the dates to which the rent and additional rent have been paid, and stating whether or not there exists any default by Owner under this Lease, and, if so, specifying each such default and such other information as shall be required of Tenant.

41.6 Comments on Standard Real Estate Board of New York Clause

The standard Real Estate Board of New York clause is the classic example of a pro-landlord estoppel provision. There is no tenant right to request owner/landlord estoppel certificates; there is no "to the best of tenant's knowledge" qualification; there is no limit on the entities to which a tenant may be required to deliver an estoppel certificate; and there is no limitation on the frequency with which the owner/landlord may request estoppel certificates.

From the owner/landlord's perspective, the Real Estate Board provision does not require the tenant to state the more specific information outlined in Section 41.3 ("Landlord Concerns"), *supra*. In the sample clause set forth in Section 41.2, *supra*, in addition to the enumerated certifications, each party is required to state such other information as is reasonably requested and readily accessible. This is an alternative means of requiring the more specific information without containing a lengthy list of items in the lease provision itself. Another alternative way of addressing this issue is to attach a form of an owner/landlord and a tenant estoppel certificate to the lease. However, this still does not protect against the unexpected requirements of third parties who may have their own unique estoppel certificate requirements. Thus, the general language in the sample clause is recommended.

41.7 Litigation Issues

A party acquiring an interest in realty should inquire into the rights of the tenants in possession. These rights include defenses to the performance of lease covenants, and their rights to enforce performance of the landlord's obligations.[1] The customary way of

---

1. *See* Cutaia, Inc. v. Buyer's Bazaar, Inc. 224 A.D.2d 952, 637 N.Y.S.2d 857 (4th Dep't 1996) (tenant asserts prior landlord did not fulfill repair obligation); Won's Cards, Inc. v. Samsondale/

making the necessary inquiry is to obtain estoppel certificates from the tenants. Since there is no statutory obligation for a tenant to provide an estoppel to a buyer or lender, a lease provision obligating the tenant to provide an estoppel certificate is necessary.

The principles of waiver and promissory estoppel are pertinent to the analysis of cases involving estoppel certificates. In the case of *In Re Caldor, Inc.-NY,*[2] a tenant in Chapter 11 under the bankruptcy law was held not to have waived its right to recover overpayments of rent by having executed an estoppel certificate when an assignee acquired the shopping center, wherein the tenant was located, from the landlord. Nor did the doctrine of promissory estoppel prevent the tenant in Chapter 11 from recovering the rental overpayments. The opinion noted that tenant-debtor had stated in the certificate that to the best of its knowledge no lease default existed as to it or the landlord and that the debtor did not clearly and unambiguously represent that there were no defaults under the lease.

In the case of *Won's Cards, Inc. v. Samsondale/Haverstraw Equities, Ltd.,*[3] the tenant's lease contained a restriction prohibiting the landlord from renting to another tenant selling greeting cards and gifts. The landlord then leased to a drug store, permitting it to sell "items normally found in a super retail drug store." This, of course, included greeting cards. In connection with the sale of the shopping center, the tenant provided an estoppel certificate stating that the landlord is not in default under the lease and that it knew of no event that would constitute a default by the landlord under the lease. Within months after the sale, the tenant asserted that the drug store's sale of greeting cards violated the lease restriction.

The execution of the estoppel was held not to be an automatic waiver of its right to seek damages due to the violation of the use restriction continuing after the sale, and the court reversed grant of summary judgment to the successor landlord based on the estoppel certificate. The certificate would have to be evaluated together with all of the tenant's conduct to determine if the tenant waived the protection of its lease provisions. The execution of the estoppel certificate did not by itself "directly, unmistakably or unequivocally establish plaintiff's intentional relinquishment of the known right." The purchaser's conduct would also have to be considered in order to establish that it relied on the representations in the estoppel certificate to its detriment, and that it derived no knowledge of the facts constituting the lessor's alleged default from its exercise of due diligence.

A landlord may also request its tenants to execute estoppel certificates for the benefit of a prospective lender. The landlord does not have the right to rely on a certificate given to a lender to defend against a tenant's claim arising out of its leasehold

Haverstraw Equities, Ltd., 165 A.D.2d 157, 566 N.Y.S.2d 412 (3d Dep't 1991) (tenant claims prior landlord breached exclusive use restriction). [Criticized by: HRC Guam Co. v. Bayview II, L.L.C., 2017 Guam 25, 2017 Guam LEXIS 17, 2017 WL 6629217. The court in HRC Guam discussed the Won's Cards approach to estoppel certificates, but ends up following the California approach.].

2. 217 B.R. 121 (Bankr. S.D.N.Y. 1998).

3. 165 A.D.2d 157, 566 N.Y.S.2d 412 (3d Dep't 1991).

obligations.[4] However, tenants must be careful in executing such lender's forms, since they often contain provisions that impose obligations in favor of the lender that are not required by the underlying lease, such as subordination to the new financing.

The recitation in an estoppel agreement given to a lender that the certificate is an inducement for the lender to make a loan is sufficient consideration to support the agreements set forth in the certificate as a binding contract. In *General Electric Capital Corp. v. Domino's Pizza, Inc.*,[5] the defendant entered into a lease agreement with a landlord. After the lease was signed, the landlord refinanced the mortgage on the premises and executed a mortgage agreement and an assignment agreement to plaintiff containing a number of leases. One of the leases assigned was that of the defendant, Domino's Pizza, Inc. The defendant executed an estoppel certificate containing a number of provisions, one of which was the sole issue that occupied the court in this action. The relevant language of the estoppel certificate stated that the "Tenant *understands* [emphasis added] that under the provisions of the assignment, the lease cannot be terminated (either directly or by the exercise of any option which could lead to termination) . . . without the prior written consent of GECC [the plaintiff]."[6] The defendant terminated the lease without permission of the plaintiff. The issue presented was whether the defendant, pursuant to the terms of the estoppel certificate, was obligated to obtain written consent from the plaintiff prior to terminating the lease. The plaintiff contended that the certificate obligated the defendant to seek its written permission. The defendant asserted that the language of the estoppel certificate meant only that it "*understands*" that the lease cannot be terminated without the prior consent of the plaintiff, not that it was obligated to obtain that consent. The court held that the estoppel certificate constituted a contract between tenant and lender, and not merely an acknowledgment by the tenant of its landlord's obligations to the lender. As a consequence, the defendant was obligated under the terms of the certificate to obtain the plaintiff's written consent in order to terminate the lease. The court stated: "[i]nterpreting the document in its entirety, the only interpretation which is consistent with the remainder of the Estoppel Certificate, is one where 'understands' means 'agrees.'"[7]

4. *See* NHS Nat'l Health Serv., Inc. v. Kaufman, 250 A.D.2d 528, 673 N.Y.S.2d 129 (1st Dep't 1998) and Padell Nadell Fine Weinberger & Co. v. Midtown Realty Co., 245 A.D.2d 188, 665 N.Y.S.2d 891 (1st Dep't 1997) (dealing with tenants seeking refund of rental overcharges).

5. Gen. Elec. Cap. Corp. v. Domino's Pizza, 1994 WL 256776, Case 93 Civ. 5070 (S.D.N.Y. 1994) [case not reported in the Federal Supplement].

6. *Id.* at *1.

7. *Id.* at *4.

CHAPTER 42

Tenant Improvement Allowance

42.1 General Purpose

The tenant improvement allowance (along with rent, additional rent, "free-rent," landlord's work, length of term, and creditworthiness of the tenant or its guarantor) is one of the several basic, market-driven, financial terms of a lease. Because money is the ultimate fungible commodity, the amount of a tenant allowance can be increased or decreased in balance with a corresponding decrease or increase in another basic financial term (most obviously, landlord's work) without impacting the net present value of the effective rent as of the date of the lease or the commencement date of the term. Market practices prevalent at the time of the negotiation of the lease, and the respective cash flow and requirements of the landlord and tenant, will mitigate strongly against any material shifting of these factors, notwithstanding the ability to do so without impacting the bottom line.

The purpose of the tenant improvement allowance is to provide a fund for the tenant at the outset of the term to help defray some of the costs of the tenant's initial build-out. The allowance is usually calculated on a per-square-foot basis and is recovered by the landlord, through rent, over the term of the lease. Except in the rare instance when the tenant has an extraordinarily positive net worth (in which case the tenant improvement allowance is nothing more than a purely economic term of the lease), the landlord has an interest in seeing that the allowance is properly spent by the tenant, and the tenant has an interest in making certain that the tenant allowance will be available when necessary to meet its expenses. Each party should perform due diligence to be sure that the other party has the financial ability to perform its obligations under all sections of the lease, particularly those provisions regarding the tenant improvement allowance and the tenant's initial build-out.

42.2 Sample Clause

42.01 Work Allowance.

(a) Landlord shall reimburse Tenant for the cost of Initial Tenant Work in an amount (the "Work Allowance") equal to the lesser of (i) *[(insert amount)]* and (ii) the actual cost of Initial Tenant Work, upon the following terms and conditions:

[If payable in installments, insert alternative clauses (A) and (B)]

(A) Reimbursement shall be made to Tenant after all Initial Tenant Work has been completed as determined by Landlord;

(B) Tenant shall have supplied to Landlord: (1) a certificate signed by Tenant's architect and an officer of Tenant certifying that all Initial Tenant Work has been satisfactorily completed in accordance with the plans and specifications therefor approved by Landlord, (2) paid invoices evidencing the cost of all Initial Tenant Work, (3) a general release from all contractors, subcontractors and materialmen performing Initial Tenant Work and (4) all Building Department sign-offs and inspection certificates and any permits required to be issued by the Building Department or any other governmental entities having jurisdiction thereover; and

(C) Tenant is not then in default under this Lease.

(b) "Initial Tenant Work" means the installation of fixtures, improvements and appurtenances attached to or built into the Premises to prepare the Premises for Tenant's initial use and occupancy, and shall not include movable partitions, business and trade fixtures, machinery, equipment, furniture, furnishings and other articles of personal property.

(c) The right to receive reimbursement for the cost of Initial Tenant Work as set forth in this Section 42.01 shall be for the exclusive benefit of Tenant, it being the express intent of the parties hereto that in no event shall such right be conferred upon or for the benefit of any third party, including, without limitation, any contractor, subcontractor, materialman, laborer, architect, engineer, attorney or any other person, firm or entity. Without in any way limiting the provisions of Section *[insert indemnity provision reference]*, Tenant shall indemnify and hold harmless each Indemnified Party from and against any and all liability, damages, claims, costs or expenses arising out of or relating to Landlord's payment of any installment of the Work Allowance directly to Tenant's general contractor or construction manager, together with all costs, expenses and liabilities incurred in or in connection with each such claim or action or proceeding brought thereon, including, without limitation, all reasonable attorneys' fees and expenses.

(d) Notwithstanding anything to the contrary contained in this Section 42.01, in no event shall more than $________ of the Work Allowance be made available to Tenant for Tenant's soft costs of construction (including, without limitation, filing and permit fees and expenses, architecture, engineering and other consulting fees and expenses and moving expenses).

(e) If any portion of the Work Allowance remains after the 1st anniversary of the Commencement Date, such remaining portion (i.e., any portion of the

Work Allowance for which Tenant has not timely and properly submitted a request for disbursement as set forth in this Section 42.01 on or before the first anniversary of the Commencement Date) shall be retained by and belong to Landlord.

[(A) The Work Allowance shall be payable to Tenant (or to Tenant's general contractor or construction manager, as directed by Tenant) in installments as Initial Tenant Work progresses, but in no event more frequently than monthly. Installments of the Work Allowance shall be payable by Landlord within 30 days following Tenant's satisfaction of each of the conditions required for disbursement set forth in this Section 42.01(a).

(B) Prior to the payment of any installment, Tenant shall deliver to Landlord a request for disbursement which shall be accompanied by (1) paid invoices (or invoices if Tenant shall be directing Landlord to pay Tenant's general contractor or construction manager) for the Initial Tenant Work performed or incurred since the last disbursement of the Work Allowance, (2) a certificate signed by Tenant's architect and an officer of Tenant certifying that the Initial Tenant Work and services represented by the aforesaid invoices have been satisfactorily completed in accordance with the plans and specifications therefor approved by Landlord and have not been the subject of a prior disbursement of the Work Allowance, and (3) lien waivers by architects, contractors, subcontractors and all materialmen for all such work and services. Each installment payment of the Work Allowance shall be limited to an amount equal to the amount requested by Tenant pursuant to clause (1) above, multiplied by a fraction, the numerator of which is the amount of the Work Allowance, and the denominator of which is the total contract price (or, if there is no specified or fixed contract price for the Initial Tenant Work, then a reasonable estimate thereof in the opinion of Tenant's architect, construction manager or general contractor) for the performance of all of the Initial Tenant Work shown on all plans and specifications approved by Landlord. In addition, Landlord shall be permitted to retain from each disbursement an amount equal to 10% of the amount requested to be disbursed by Tenant. The aggregate amount of the retainages shall be paid by Landlord to Tenant upon the completion of all Initial Tenant Work and upon receipt from Tenant of (A) a certificate signed by Tenant's architect and an officer of Tenant certifying that all of the Initial Tenant Work has been satisfactorily completed in accordance with the plans and specifications therefor approved by Landlord, (B) all Building Department sign-offs and inspection certificates and any permits required to be issued by the Building Department or any other governmental entities having jurisdiction thereover, and (C) a general

release from all contractors and subcontractors performing the Initial Tenant Work releasing Landlord and Tenant from all liability for any of the Initial Tenant Work.]

[OFFSET RIGHT FOR FAILURE TO PAY ALLOWANCE:

If Landlord fails to pay to Tenant any amount of the Work Allowance on or before the date on which the same is due and payable to Tenant under this Section 42.01, and provided that such failure continues for 30 days after Tenant notifies Landlord of such failure (which notice shall state that Tenant intends to set off such amount against the next installment of Rent unless Landlord pays such amount to Tenant within such 30 day period), then Tenant may set off such amount (together with interest thereon at the Interest Rate from the date payable by Landlord until credited) against the next installments of Rent coming due under this Lease; provided, that if within 30 days after Tenant's notice to Landlord of such failure, Landlord notifies Tenant that Landlord disputes its obligation to pay such unpaid amount of the Work Allowance (which notice shall specify the basis for Landlord's dispute in reasonable detail and the portion of such installment of the Work Allowance to which such dispute relates), then Tenant shall not have the right to offset the portion of such installment of the Work Allowance so disputed, or interest thereon.]

42.3 Landlord Concerns

The foregoing provision illustrates the landlord's interests in controlling the payment of the tenant allowance. The landlord wants to be sure that its monies are going into the improvements and not into the tenant's pocket, and that the work is proceeding in accordance with the approved plans and specifications and that the building remains free of liens. This provision permits a capped amount of the tenant allowance to be applied only to certain specified soft costs, such as consultant fees, but not toward furniture, trade fixtures, and signage that may be removed from the premises by the tenant. Other than the specified soft costs, all of the tenant allowance must go into permanent leasehold improvements that will enhance the value of the space. Furthermore, section (e) of the sample clause is drafted so that if the tenant fails to use the tenant allowance by a date certain, then the tenant will lose the right to use the tenant allowance.

In addition, there are many conditions precedent to the landlord's payment of the tenant allowance. There is no payment if the tenant is in default. The tenant and the tenant's architect must certify that the work is being performed in accordance with the approved plans and specifications and that it is within the budget. If landlord pays tenant the allowance in installments, then 10 percent of the allowance will be retained until the end of the job. The tenant is required to complete the work whether or not the allowance is sufficient. Lien waivers are required with each draw request from all contractors, subcontractors, and materialmen for work previously performed and materials previously supplied. All of these provisions are designed to protect the landlord's interests.

Depending on which sample clause is used will dictate whether the tenant allowance will be paid along with rather than after tenant's own contribution. Very often a landlord will require the tenant's contributions to be made prior to the landlord's contributions in order to make certain that the tenant has an equity interest in the project, which is how the initial sample clause is drafted.

42.4 Tenant Concerns

The landlord's concern with controlling the payment of the tenant allowance must be balanced with the tenant's need to have the funds promised it as an inducement to enter into the lease. An advantage to the tenant found within the sample clause is that a certain percentage of the tenant allowance may be used for soft costs and, if the alternative clauses are used, the landlord's dollars will be advanced as the work progresses. Of course, from the tenant's point of view, a more favorable provision would have no restriction on the use of the tenant allowance, and would provide that the tenant allowance will be fully funded before the tenant makes any investment in the demised premises. The ability of a tenant to achieve these advantages will depend on its creditworthiness, the overall economics of the transaction, and, of course, the forces of the marketplace.

The provision permitting the landlord to withhold payment if the tenant is in default should be stricken by the tenant. The tenant should argue that the landlord has all appropriate remedies for tenant defaults, including lease termination, and that withholding the allowance should not be an additional remedy. At minimum, the landlord should agree that it will not withhold payments unless a default has occurred and is continuing beyond all applicable notice and cure periods, and the tenant should negotiate for the reinstatement of its entitlement to payments if the tenant ultimately cures the default in question.

The tenant, with the assistance of its representative or construction consultant, should make every effort to minimize the prerequisites (including materials to be delivered to the landlord) to the funding of the periodic draws. The tenant may also want to negotiate to increase the amount of the allowance allocable to permitted soft costs, and to decrease or eliminate the retainage.

The sample clause requires that the tenant provide lien waivers from all contractors, subcontractors and materialmen at the time of each draw request. If the first draw request is to cover the deposit given to the general contractor in advance of work being performed or materials supplied to the job, lien waivers will not be available in connection with the first draw request. The tenant should also argue that until the end of the job a lien waiver from the general contractor should suffice to protect the landlord's interests and simplify the draw request procedure for the tenant. Of course, lien waivers are not effective unless given against payment and, therefore, any obligation to deliver lien waivers should be limited to payments made from the prior requisition rather than payments to be made from the current requisition. The tenant should also attempt to exclude from the lease the provision permitting the landlord to be reimbursed for reviewing plans and inspecting the work for tenant's initial occupancy.

Since the amount of the tenant allowance is an important fundamental economic term of the lease, the tenant should make every effort to ensure receipt of the full tenant allowance even if the amount of the tenant allowance is greater than the cost of the work to be performed by the tenant in the premises or the tenant allowance will not be fully drawn by a specified outside date. If the tenant has a concern in this regard (i.e., if the tenant has determined that it may spend less than the full amount of the tenant allowance in preparing the space for its occupancy, or may not fully draw the tenant allowance by a specified outside date), the tenant should negotiate for the excess portion of the tenant allowance to be applied toward rent or any undrawn tenant allowance to be applied toward rent after the specified outside date.

In the event the landlord fails to fund the tenant allowance, the tenant will have no effective remedy other than a plenary action against the landlord, which will be both expensive and time-consuming. Thus, the tenant should negotiate for an offset right against rent in the event the landlord fails to pay the tenant allowance to the tenant when due, a sample provision for which is included earlier in the chapter.

42.5 Standard Real Estate Board of New York Clause

The REBNY form does not cover the subject of tenant improvement allowances.

42.6 Comments on Standard Real Estate Board of New York Clause

None.

CHAPTER 43

Miscellaneous; Interpretation

43.1 General Purpose

The general purpose of a closing lease article or section entitled "Miscellaneous" is to function as a catch-all for those terms and conditions that are often dismissed as "boilerplate" and do not readily fit in elsewhere.[1] It should be noted that several of these provisions are scattered throughout the Real Estate Board of New York form under captions that give no warning of their presence. However, even the REBNY form does not contain many standard provisions of this nature, which its users probably believe are buried somewhere in the fine print. To mitigate this problem, several of the paragraphs set forth in the sample clause (see Section 43.2, *infra*) may be incorporated into a rider for the REBNY form and improve its certainty for both parties.

Most of the provisions enumerated under "Miscellaneous" may fairly be characterized as terms of interpretation and procedure, and their various purposes are patent from the captions in the text; as such, they are found—or should be—in almost all leases. Under this provision's title, too, the landlord and the tenant will seek specific protections or rights that occur to the parties at the end of negotiations and find their way into the lease's badly titled last major article. In instances where the tenant is taking large amounts of space, a provision such as signage may be more heavily negotiated and addressed in its own dedicated lease section (as opposed to being relegated to the subclause of the "Miscellaneous" section).

43.2 Sample Clause

43.01 Severability. If any term or provision of this Lease, or the application thereof to any person or circumstances shall to any extent be invalid or

1. The following are included in the definition and interpretation of terms and procedures set forth in the sample clause found in Section 43.2, *infra*. The numbers in brackets are to the paragraphs of the sample clause: *[43.01]* Severability; *[43.02]* Certain Definitions; *[43.03]* Counterclaims; *[43.04]* Survival; *[43.05]* Certain Remedies; *[43.06]* No Offer; *[43.07]* Amendments; *[43.08]* Merger; *[43.09]* Applicable Law; *[43.10]* No Development Rights; *[43.11]* Condominium; *[43.12]* Embargoed Person; *[43.13]* Counterparts; *[43.14]* Signage.

unenforceable, the remainder of this Lease, or the application of such provision to persons or circumstances other than those as to which it is invalid or unenforceable, shall not be affected, and each provision of this Lease shall be valid and shall be enforceable to the extent permitted by law.

43.02 Certain Definitions.

(a) "Landlord" means only the owner, at the time in question, of the Building or that portion of the Building of which the Premises are a part, or of a lease of the Building or that portion of the Building of which the Premises are a part, so that in the event of any transfer or transfers of title to the Building or of Landlord's interest in a lease of the Building or such portion of the Building, the transferor shall be and hereby is relieved and freed of all obligations of Landlord under this Lease accruing after such transfer, and it shall be deemed, without further agreement, that such transferee has assumed all obligations and liabilities of Landlord during the period it is the holder of Landlord's interest under this Lease.

(b) "Landlord shall have no liability to Tenant" or words of similar import mean that Tenant is not entitled to terminate this Lease, or to claim actual or constructive eviction, partial, or total, or to receive any abatement or diminution of Rent, or to be relieved in any manner of any of its other obligations under this Lease, or to be compensated for loss or injury suffered or to enforce any other right or kind of liability whatsoever against Landlord under or with respect to this Lease or with respect to Tenant's use or occupancy of the Premises, except as otherwise may be expressly provided in this Lease.

43.03 Counterclaims.

If Landlord commences any summary proceeding or action for nonpayment of Rent or to recover possession of the Premises, Tenant shall not interpose any counterclaim of any nature or description in any such proceeding or action, unless Tenant's failure to interpose such counterclaim in such proceeding or action would result in the waiver of Tenant's right to bring such claim in a separate proceeding under applicable law.

43.04 Survival.

All obligations and liabilities of Landlord or Tenant to the other that accrued before the expiration or other termination of this Lease and all such obligations and liabilities that by their nature or under the circumstances can only be, or by the provisions of this Lease may be, performed after such expiration or other termination, shall survive the expiration or other termination of this Lease. Without limiting the generality of the foregoing, the rights and obligations of the parties with respect to any indemnity under this Lease, and with respect to Tax Payments, Operating Payments and any other amounts payable under this Lease, shall survive the expiration or other termination of this Lease, subject to any specific limitation of liability expressly contained herein.

43.05 Certain Remedies.

If Tenant requests Landlord's consent and Landlord fails or refuses to give such consent, Tenant shall not be entitled to any damages for any withholding by Landlord of its consent, it being intended that Tenant's sole remedy shall be an action for specific performance or injunction, and that such remedy shall be available only in those cases where this Lease provides that Landlord shall not unreasonably withhold its consent. No dispute relating to this Lease or the relationship of Landlord and Tenant under this Lease shall be resolved by arbitration unless this Lease expressly provides for such dispute to be resolved by arbitration.

43.06 No Offer.

The submission by Landlord of this Lease in draft form shall be solely for Tenant's consideration and not for acceptance and execution. Such submission shall have no binding force or effect and shall confer no rights nor impose any obligations, including brokerage obligations, on either party unless and until both Landlord and Tenant shall have executed a lease and duplicate originals thereof shall have been delivered to the respective parties.

43.07 Amendments.

This Lease may not be altered, changed or amended, except by an instrument in writing signed by the party to be charged.

43.08 Merger.

Tenant acknowledges that Landlord has not made and is not making, and Tenant, in executing and delivering this Lease, is not relying upon, any warranties, representations, promises or statements, except to the extent that the same are expressly set forth in this Lease. This Lease embodies the entire understanding between the parties with respect to the subject matter hereof, and all prior agreements, understanding and statements, oral or written, with respect thereto are merged in this Lease. The deletion of any printed, typed or other portion of this Lease shall not evidence the parties' intention to contradict such deleted portion. Such deleted portion shall be deemed not to have been inserted into this Lease.

43.09 Applicable Law.

This Lease shall be governed by, and construed in accordance with, the laws of the State of New York, without giving effect to any principles of conflicts of laws.

43.10 No Development Rights.

Tenant acknowledges that it has no rights to any development rights, air rights or comparable rights appurtenant to the Project, and consents, without further consideration, to any utilization of such rights by Landlord. Tenant shall promptly execute and deliver any instruments that may be requested by Landlord, including instruments merging zoning lots, evidencing such acknowledgment and consent. The provisions of this Section 43.10 shall be construed as an express waiver by Tenant of any interest Tenant may have as a "party in interest" (as such term is defined in Section 12-10 Zoning Lot of the Zoning Resolution of the City of New York) in the Project.

43.11 Condominium.

This Lease and all rights of Tenant hereunder are and shall be subject and subordinate in all respects to any condominium declaration and any other documents (collectively, the "Declaration") that are or shall be recorded in order to convert the Land and the improvements erected thereon to a condominium form of ownership in accordance with the provisions of Article 9-B of the Real Property Law, or any successor thereto, provided the Declaration does not, except to a de minimis extent, (a) increase Tenant's monetary obligations under this Lease, (b) increase Tenant's non-monetary obligations under this Lease, or (c) decrease Tenant's rights under this Lease. If any such Declaration is to be recorded, Tenant, upon the request of Landlord, shall enter into an amendment of this Lease confirming such subordination and modifying the Lease in such respects as shall be necessary to conform to such condominiumization, including, without limitation, appropriate adjustment to Tenant's Share and appropriate reductions in the Operating Expenses for the Base Operating Year and the Base Tax Amount; provided, that, such amendment shall not, except to a de minimis extent, (a) increase Tenant's monetary obligations under this Lease, (b) increase Tenant's non-monetary obligations under this Lease, or (c) decrease Tenant's rights under this Lease.

43.12 Embargoed Person.

Tenant represents that as of the date of this Lease, and Tenant covenants that throughout the term of this Lease: (a) Tenant is not, and shall not be, an Embargoed Person, (b) none of the funds or other assets of Tenant are or shall constitute property of, or are or shall be beneficially owned, directly or indirectly, by any Embargoed Person; (c) no Embargoed Person shall have any interest of any nature whatsoever in Tenant, with the result that the investment in Tenant (whether directly or indirectly) is or would be blocked or prohibited by law or that this Lease and performance of the obligations hereunder are or would be blocked or in violation of law and (d) none of the funds of Tenant are, or shall be derived from, any activity with the result that the investment in Tenant (whether directly or indirectly) is or would be blocked or in violation of law or that this Lease and performance of the obligations hereunder are or would be in violation of law. "Embargoed Person" means a person, entity or government (i) identified on the Specially Designated Nationals and Blocked Persons List maintained by the United States Treasury Department Office of Foreign Assets Control and/or any similar list maintained pursuant to any authorizing statute, executive order or regulation and/or (ii) subject to trade restrictions under United States law, including, without limitation, the International Emergency Economic Powers Act, 50 U.S.C. § 1701 et seq., The Trading with the Enemy Act, 50 U.S.C. App. 1 et seq., and any Executive Orders or regulations promulgated under any such laws, with the result that the investment in Tenant (whether directly or indirectly), is or would be prohibited by law or this Lease is or would be in violation of law and/or (iii) subject to blocking, sanction or reporting under the USA Patriot Act, as amended; Executive Order 13224, as amended; Title 31, Parts 595, 596 and 597 of the U.S. Code of Federal Regulations, as they exist from time to time; and any other law or Executive Order or regulation through which the U.S. Department of the Treasury has or may come to have sanction authority. If any representation made by Tenant pursuant to this Section 8.19 shall become untrue Tenant shall within 10 days give written notice thereof to Landlord, which notice shall set forth in reasonable detail the reason(s) why such representation has become untrue and shall be accompanied by any relevant notices from, or correspondence with, the applicable governmental agency or agencies.

43.13 Counterparts.

This Lease may be executed in counterparts each of which shall be an original and all of which counterparts taken together shall constitute one and the same agreement.

43.14 Signage.

Tenant may, at Tenant's expense, install (i) Building standard identification signage in the common corridor of the [insert floor of the Building on which the Premises is located] floor and (ii) Tenant identification signage on the entry doors to the Premises (such signage under clauses (i) and (ii) shall mean "Tenant's Signage"); *provided*, that Tenant's Signage shall be subject to Landlord's approval (including, without limitation, as to size, color and materials), and Tenant, at Tenant's expense, shall be responsible for supplying, installing, maintaining, repairing and replacing Tenant's Signage. On the Expiration Date or earlier termination of this Lease, Tenant shall (i) promptly remove all Tenant's Signage, and (ii) promptly repair in a good and workmanlike manner, in conformity with applicable Laws and all applicable provisions of this Lease, all damage to the Building caused by such removal. Tenant shall also be provided with a reasonable amount (but no more than its proportionate share) of entries in the Building directory, if any, at no cost to Tenant.

43.3 Landlord Concerns

The concern of the landlord common to most of these provisions is that the tenant have as few defenses as possible to an enforcement action under the lease. The provisions on Severability *[43.01]*, Amendments *[43.07]*, and Merger *[43.08]* are intended to defeat any defense attempting to introduce parol evidence, or in general denial of the plain terms of the document. The provisions on Applicable Law *[43.09]* require the application of New York state law without regard to conflicts of law principles. The provisions relating to Certain Definitions *[43.02]*, Counterclaims *[43.03]*, Survival *[43.04]*, and Embargoed Person *[43.12]* are intended to reduce arguments relating to interpretation and enforcement. The Condominium *[43.11]* provision is intended to enable the landlord to subject the building to a condominium form of ownership (which the landlord may desire to do to facilitate a sale, financing or other structured transaction for only a portion of the building, without the need to obtain the tenant's consent to do so.

The provision dealing with the No Offer *[43.06]* is geared toward providing the landlord with control over the lease creation process and eliminating any claim that there is a landlord-tenant relationship, or indeed a lease, prior to (1) the execution by both parties and (2) delivery of the instrument to both parties. As a practical matter, this leaves the landlord in control until the last minute, since the tenant is customarily required to sign the lease counterparts and deliver them with its security deposit and first month's rent checks to the landlord, without having "closed the deal" with the landlord's simultaneous signature.

The defensive side of this posture is shown in the detailed provision regarding Certain Remedies *[43.05]*, where the landlord has undertaken, in advance, to grant certain permissions under a rule of reason—such approval "not to be unreasonably withheld or delayed." Landlords remain fearful of damage actions in which tenants challenge what the landlord deems to be an exercise of the building owner's reasonable business judgment, and so the price of a tenant's demanding that a consent or approval will not be unreasonably withheld or delayed is to be forced to agree, in exchange, that compelling the landlord's consent by process of law will result only in securing such court-ordered consent, and not damages as well, as these have been waived in advance. One area in which this is of particular concern is assignment and subletting. Since the landlord is not compelled, except by the competitive standards of the market, to even consider the tenant's request to assign or sublet, and usually begins from the posture of absolute prohibition, it is not unreasonable for the building owner to demand that, in consideration for the concession of agreeing "not to unreasonably withhold consent," it be subject only to reversal of its decision by a court applying the standards of approval required by the lease form, and no more.

While court decisions have clearly established that space tenants have no proprietary rights outside the physical dimensions of their leased premises, some owners prefer to emphasize that in a provision such as No Development Rights *[43.10]* that the powers of disposition over such rights are exclusively within the domain of the landlord, and require the tenant to confirm in writing if required by the landlord.

Finally, the "Miscellaneous" lease article may be home to certain housekeeping details not found elsewhere in the standard lease form. If the landlord wishes to exercise more effective control over a tenant's contractors and suppliers within its building, the landlord may do so briefly in this article or in the articles dealing with alterations or building rules and regulations, which may be useful in ensuring labor harmony, as well as controlling traffic within the building. If the tenant proposes to install its own security system, then the ground rules for compatibility (with the overall building system) and accessibility (for the landlord) may be established here or in the articles dealing with landlord services or alterations. And finally, if not in a lease addendum on building rules and regulations, or addressed in a separate provision of the lease, the nature of the tenant's signage *[43.14]* on the premises door, corridor, and/or elevator landing should be stated in this article.

43.4 Tenant Concerns

A tenant will not have much to negotiate with regard to the majority of these Miscellaneous/Interpretation provisions. Being largely "contract" clauses, they arguably could benefit the tenant as much as the landlord in any future dispute. A tenant may try to assert mutuality to certain applicable provisions, such as with respect to Embargoed Person *[43.12]*.

Since the vast majority of first-draft leases say nothing about the tenant's rights to directory listings and signage, the tenant has a strong interest in a clear statement of those rights—and in getting them explicitly extended to its co-occupant affiliates, as well as to its sublessees and assignees. Similarly, if a separate security system is envisioned or contemplated, the tenant should bargain here (or in the alterations or landlord services article) for the landlord's pre-approval.

Additionally, the language of the No Offer *[43.06]* provision to the effect that neither the landlord nor the tenant is bound until executed leases are exchanged and delivered, is also mutually beneficial, and any tenant that fears that a landlord may delay the return of a fully executed lease because of possible higher-rent opportunities elsewhere can protect itself by insisting on an all-party, in-person lease signing, as opposed to the tenant's making its own first move by mail.

The tenant will also be concerned with the exculpation provision in the Certain Remedies *[43.05]* provision limiting the tenant to the right to, in effect, reverse the withholding of the consent, but protecting the landlord from any claim for damages. The tenant would like its landlord to be responsible for the consequences of its wrongdoing, if for no other reason than to discourage such wrongdoing. Landlords, however, have become very resistant to this position. A not uncommon compromise provides that the landlord will be liable only if it is found in arbitration (or, sometimes, only in a separate litigation) to have acted in bad faith in withholding its consent or approval.

43.5 Standard Real Estate Board of New York Clause

The vast majority of the items in the sample clause are not to be found in the REBNY form. The remainder are buried in provisions with captions that give little or no clue to their presence. The REBNY analogues to the sample clause's Merger *[43.08]* and Amendments *[43.07]* provisions may both be found in the last sentence of REBNY Article 21:

> All understandings and agreements heretofore made between the parties hereto are merged in this contract, which alone fully and completely expresses the

agreement between Owner and Tenant and any executory agreement hereafter made shall be ineffective to change, modify, discharge or effect an abandonment in whole or in part, unless such executory agreement is in writing and signed by the party against whom enforcement of the change, modification, discharge or abandonment is sought.

Also, the REBNY form in its Article 18's penultimate sentence does reflect the central thrust of the sample clause on Remedies Cumulative: "Mention in this lease of any particular remedy, shall not preclude Owner from any other remedy, in law or in equity"—but it is not mutual, as provided in the Sample Clause 43.05 for the tenant's protection. Similarly, REBNY Article 25, "No Waiver" (for text, see Chapter 26, Section 26.5), protects the owner/landlord from the charge of waiver, but not the tenant (which, again, the sample clause provides).

43.6 Comments on Standard Real Estate Board of New York Clause

Even for the benefit of the landlord, the REBNY form contains no provisions pertaining to (as set forth and labeled in the sample clause) Governing Law, Invalidity, Presumptions, Independent Covenants, Number and Gender, Exhibits, No Partnership, Submission of Lease, Authorized Signatories, Consent to Jurisdiction, Counterparts, Additional Instruments and Actions, Consents and Approvals, Confidentiality, No Rights of Other Tenants, Bankruptcy Code Rent, 360-Day Year, Tenant Financials for Landlord Financing, Designated Suppliers, and Managing Agent—all of which are certainly helpful to the landlord, and in many cases to the tenant as well, and so may be usefully added in a rider to the standard printed form.

The tenant, meanwhile, will wish to have inserted some language of mutuality in the sentences just quoted from REBNY Articles 18 and 25 on cumulative remedies and waivers, respectively; there is no good reason why such provisions should be one-sided. Finally, the tenant should seek in this article clear expression of its rights to directory listings, signage, and a separate security system, if not treated elsewhere in the lease.

CHAPTER 44

Relocation

44.1 General Purpose

One of the great challenges for any owner (and its leasing agent) in leasing space in an office building is properly managing its stacking plan so that it can coordinate renewal and expansion options granted to tenants and so that it can assemble blocks of contiguous space for future leasing. In leasing relatively small office spaces (i.e., anything less than a full floor), this becomes even more challenging as the owner is faced with the somewhat conflicting interests of both wanting to increase occupancy and wanting to preserve flexibility for its own needs and those of other tenants. Moreover, this is a problem faced not only by owners of largely vacant buildings as they progress through the initial leasing process but also by owners of well-leased buildings as space turns over.

Owners often seek to mitigate such problems by including a so-called relocation clause in the leases of such small tenants (owners generally understand that larger tenants are unlikely to agree to a relocation clause). Such a clause permits the owner to relocate the tenant to other available space in its building upon certain advance notice and subject to certain conditions (which can vary widely as described later). In negotiating a relocation clause, the landlord's interest in preserving as much flexibility as possible in relocating the tenant runs counter to the tenant's interest in limiting the landlord's ability to do so. As a result, numerous issues are raised by such clauses.

44.2 Sample Clause

Section 44.01 Relocation of Premises.

(a) Landlord, at any time, may elect by notice to Tenant to substitute for the Premises other office space in the Building (the "Substitute Premises") designated by Landlord, provided that the Substitute Premises contains substantially the same usable square foot area as the Premises and has a configuration substantially similar to the Premises. Landlord's notice shall be accompanied by a plan of the Substitute Premises, and such notice or the plan shall set forth the usable square foot area of the Substitute Premises. Tenant shall vacate and surrender the Premises and shall occupy the Substitute Premises promptly (and, in any event, not later than 15 days) after Landlord has substantially completed the work to be performed by Landlord in the Substitute Premises pursuant to Section 44.1(b). Tenant shall pay the same Fixed Rent and Additional Rent under Article 4 with respect to the Substitute Premises as were payable with respect to the Premises, without regard to the usable square foot area of the Substitute Premises.

(b) Landlord shall have no liability to Tenant by reason of any such relocation, including, without limitation, as a result of any inconvenience or interference with Tenant's business, but Landlord shall, at Landlord's expense, do the following: (i) furnish and install in the Substitute Premises fixtures, equipment, improvements and appurtenances substantially in kind and quality to those contained in the Premises at the time such notice of substitution is given by Landlord, (ii) provide to Tenant personnel to perform under Tenant's direction the moving of Tenant's Property from the Premises to the Substitute Premises, (iii) promptly reimburse Tenant for Tenant's actual and reasonable out-of-pocket costs incurred by Tenant in connection with the relocation of any telephone or other communications equipment from the Premises to the Substitute Premises, and (iv) promptly reimburse Tenant for any other actual and reasonable out-of-pocket costs incurred by Tenant in connection with Tenant's move from the Premises to the Substitute Premises provided such costs are approved by Landlord in advance, which approval shall not be unreasonably withheld. Tenant shall cooperate with Landlord so as to facilitate the prompt completion by Landlord of its obligations under this Section 44.1 and the prompt surrender by Tenant of the Premises. Without limiting the generality of the preceding sentence, Tenant shall (A) provide to Landlord promptly any approvals or instructions, and any plans and specifications or any other information reasonably requested by Landlord, and (B) promptly perform in the Substitute Premises any work to be performed therein by Tenant to prepare the same for Tenant's occupancy.

(c) From and after the date that Tenant shall actually vacate and surrender the Premises to Landlord, this Lease (i) shall no longer apply to the Premises, except with respect to obligations that accrued on or prior to such surrender date, and (ii) shall apply to the Substitute Premises as if the Substitute Premises had been the space originally demised under this Lease.

44.3 Landlord Concerns

The form of the landlord's relocation clause illustrates a straightforward desire to build into the lease the unconditional right to relocate the tenant at the lowest possible cost and as quickly as possible. Landlords are typically reluctant to remove such clauses from small leases because to do so can result in two harsh results: first, the landlord may not have any empty floors to lease to a large tenant and could lose a deal if the smaller tenant is unwilling to voluntarily move; and second, the smaller tenant, knowing that the landlord needs its space, may try to extract financial concessions and thus capitalize on its lease's "hold-up" value. As far as the landlord's interests are concerned, generally speaking, the less said in the relocation clause the better. A sophisticated landlord will try to limit the clause to addressing (1) the advance notice required to be delivered to the tenant and to the other mechanics of relocation (and the remedies possessed by the landlord if the tenant fails to move as required) and (2) the costs to be borne by landlord. Even the most demanding of landlords could not realistically hope to relocate a tenant without having to at least pay for moving expenses. Aside from moving expenses, there are other costs of relocation (some obvious and others less so as illustrated in Section 44.2, *infra*, entitled "Sample Clause") that the landlord will try to avoid paying. In terms of advance notice, the landlord will want to minimize the notice it must give since it will need to relocate the existing tenant and prepare the space for a new tenant's occupancy, all within a time frame that will be acceptable to the new tenant.

44.4 Tenant Concerns

A tenant's initial reaction to a relocation clause is to strike it. This is motivated by the belief that in signing a lease it is bargaining for the right to occupy certain specified space for the stated term (as opposed to the right to occupy a specified square footage in a building, the location of which may be changed from time to time). If the tenant—most likely very small tenants—cannot obtain a lease without a relocation clause, there are numerous issues it will be concerned with, which are addressed in the sample clause and discussed next.

These issues may be addressed as follows:

Issue (1): How often may the landlord exercise the relocation right?

Approach: If a tenant is willing to agree to a relocation provision, it should insist that the landlord only be permitted to exercise the relocation right once during the tenant's term. Even if a landlord is bearing all costs of the relocation, the disruption to the tenant's business can be great. It is not to be expected that a tenant suffer through such disruptions more than once during its initial term. Landlords usually recognize that it is not reasonable to require more than one relocation during the initial term, although they often will desire the ability to exercise such right again during a renewal term.

Issue (2): What is "equivalent," "comparable," or a "similarly configured" space in the building?

Approach: The space to which a tenant may be relocated is often described in the lease as having to be "comparable," "equivalent," or "similarly configured" to the original premises. But, the question remains, comparable, equivalent, or similarly configured in terms of what? The landlord will want the ability to move the tenant to any space that is comparable in terms of square footage without regard to its other characteristics. The tenant, however, will want to preserve (as closely as possible) all of the characteristics of the space it originally chose to lease. As a result, the tenant will be concerned with the following types of characteristics, among others: size, layout, view, floor location, and utility for the tenant's purposes, as opposed to relying on the general phrase "similarly configured." The more qualifications set forth in the lease regarding the standard for the relocation space, the fewer options the landlord will have for relocating the tenant (and the greater likelihood of claims by the tenant that the relocation space is not similarly configured to the original premises). In addition, incorporating these qualifications makes it more likely that the space eventually selected will satisfy the tenant's desires.

Issue (3): How much advance notice will be given?

Approach: With regard to advance notice, a tenant generally would like as much advance notice as possible so that it has time to prepare for the move and minimize disruption to its business. Ultimately, the advance notice granted to tenants may vary greatly from deal to deal and will likely depend on the size of the tenant being relocated.

Issue (4): Are there certain periods during which the landlord should not have the right to relocate the tenant?

Approach: In order to restrict the landlord from arbitrarily moving a tenant (which, in reality, a landlord has little incentive to do), and to ensure that it will have a minimum period of undisturbed occupancy, a tenant will want to establish certain restrictions on the landlord's exercise of the relocation right. For example, tenants often request and receive a "lockout" period during which the landlord cannot exercise the relocation right (which may be at the beginning of a tenant's term so it is not forced to move early in its tenancy, a period prior to the expiration date so that the tenant is not forced to move near the end of its term, or during an especially active time during the tenant's business cycle (e.g., "tax season" for an accounting tenant)). In addition, a tenant will want to condition the landlord's exercise of the relocation right on the landlord having a signed lease (or other binding agreement) covering the tenant's space and other contiguous space of a certain square footage so as to create a threshold for leases that permit the landlord to exercise its relocation right. For example, a tenant would not want the landlord to be able to relocate it if it found another comparably sized tenant merely because that tenant was willing to pay more rent for the space.

Issue (5): What costs will be paid by the landlord?

Approach: Tenant will want to make sure that all costs of relocation are paid for by the landlord so that the tenant is not out-of-pocket if the landlord exercises its relocation option. Often a lease will only cover reimbursement for the tenant's cost of moving its furniture, equipment, and other personal property. However, there are numerous other expenses that should be addressed: costs incurred with respect to the installation of telephone and computer equipment, construction of the relocation premises in a condition comparable to original premises (as set forth in Section 44.2, entitled "Sample Clause," *supra*), removal of any hazardous materials, ordering new stationery and other office supplies to reflect the tenant's new suite number, and legal fees and other consultants' expenses incurred with respect to the relocation.

Issue (6): What effect does relocation have on tenant's monetary obligations?

Approach: If the relocation premises are smaller than the original premises, the tenant will want to ensure that its fixed rent and percentage share of escalations are decreased proportionately. Moreover, the tenant will have to make certain that the relocation premises are not too much smaller or they may no longer satisfy the tenant's space requirements. If the relocation premises are larger than the original premises, most sophisticated tenants will insist that its fixed rent and percentage share not be increased, since the tenant's monetary obligations should not be increased by virtue of the landlord exercising its relocation option. As set forth in Section 44.2, entitled "Sample Clause," *supra*, these concerns are addressed from the outset by providing that the size of the relocation premises will not deviate substantially from the original premises, and that the tenant will pay the same fixed rent and additional rent as were payable with respect to the original premises, without regard to the usable square foot area of the relocation premises.

Issue (7): Should tenant have the right to terminate the lease rather than being forced to relocate?

Approach: A tenant will often seek the right to terminate its lease without penalty rather than being forced to relocate. However, this termination right is typically not given unless the relocation right is exercised within a short period prior to the expiration date of the tenant's lease. Frankly, such a termination right does not avoid the primary problem posed to tenants by relocation clauses (i.e., disruption to the tenant's business and the inconveniences of having to move). If a termination right existed and was exercised, the tenant would still have to move, only this time it would be at its own expense and, more inconveniently, to a new building. Nevertheless, such a termination right has a more practical benefit: since the landlord would face the possibility of losing the existing tenant by its exercise of a termination right, the landlord may be more circumspect about exercising its relocation option.

44.5 Standard Real Estate Board of New York Clause

None.

44.6 Comments on Standard Real Estate Board of New York Clause

None.

CHAPTER 45

Partnership Tenant Liability

45.1 General Purpose

When a corporation executes and delivers a lease as a tenant, the signature of the officer binds the entity to the lease (assuming due authorization or apparent authority). The corporate entity itself becomes liable under the lease, and the landlord may look only to the entity and its assets for the satisfaction of the tenant's obligations and liabilities. Neither subsequent changes in the respective ownership interest of any or all shareholders, nor the election of new officers or directors, alters the binding nature of the corporation's liability under the lease. Landlords therefore need not concern themselves with such changes as they may relate to the issue of the binding nature of the tenant's lease obligations (as distinguished from whether changes in the ownership or control of a corporate tenant may affect the creditworthiness of the tenant or the character or quality of the operations of the tenant's business at the premises).

When a partnership executes and delivers a lease, the lease becomes the binding obligation of the partnership entity and of each of its general partners. Limited partners, however, in a limited partnership generally are liable only to the extent of their interests in the entity. Changes in the ownership of general partnership interests effect changes both in control of the entity and in liability under the partnership's obligations; both landlord and general partners in partnership tenants need to protect themselves from the attendant risks and exposures.

45.2 Sample Clause

> *45.01 Partnership Tenant.* If Tenant is a partnership the following shall apply: (a) the liability of each of the parties comprising Tenant shall be joint and several, (b) each of the parties comprising Tenant hereby consents to, and agrees to be bound by, any written instrument which may hereafter be executed, changing, modifying or discharging this Lease, in whole or in part, or surrendering all or any part of the Premises to Landlord or renewing or extending this Lease and by any notices, demands, requests or other communications which

may hereafter be given, by Tenant or by any of the parties comprising Tenant, (c) any bills, statements, notices, demands, requests or other communications given or rendered to Tenant or to any of the parties comprising Tenant shall be deemed given or rendered to Tenant and to all such parties and shall be binding upon Tenant and all such parties, (d) if Tenant shall admit new Partners, all of such new Partners shall, by their admission to Tenant, be deemed to have assumed performance of all of the terms, covenants and conditions of this Lease on Tenant's part to be observed and performed, (e) Tenant shall give prompt notice to Landlord of the admission of any Partner or Partners, and upon demand of Landlord, shall cause each such Partner to execute and deliver to Landlord an agreement in form satisfactory to Landlord, wherein each such new Partner shall assume performance of all of the terms, covenants and conditions of this Lease on Tenant's part to be observed and performed (but neither Landlord's failure to request any such agreement nor the failure of any such new Partner to execute or deliver any such agreement to Landlord shall vitiate the provisions of this Section 45.01, and (f) on each anniversary of the Commencement Date, Tenant shall deliver to Landlord a list of all Partners together with their current residential addresses.

45.3 Landlord Concerns

A prudent landlord should know, at all times, the type of organization pursuant to which its tenant carries out its business. If the tenant is a partnership, the landlord should know which persons are the general partners. If a claim is made or an action is instituted by the landlord under the lease, the landlord may look to the assets of the partnership tenant and to the assets of each general partner of the partnership tenant for the satisfaction of any claim or judgment and, accordingly, should at all times know the identities of all such parties. The sample clause requires the tenant, periodically and on demand, to certify to the landlord the identities and addresses of all general partners in the partnership tenant, and to keep such information updated from time to time throughout the lease term. Current knowledge of the makeup of the partnership tenant affords the landlord the option of requiring any new partners to execute an agreement specifically assuming the tenant's lease obligations. If a general partner of a partnership tenant is involved in a bankruptcy proceeding, such partner's interest in the partnership (and, accordingly, its interest as tenant under the lease) may be affected, possibly causing a dissolution of the partnership tenant, drawing the landlord into a bankruptcy action and impairing the landlord's ability to collect rent and enforce its other rights under the lease.

Although a partnership agreement may allocate each partner's liabilities in accordance with their respective percentage ownership interests in the partnership, or according to some other formulae, the landlord wants to be able to look to the assets of each, or all, of the general partners for the full satisfaction of all claims and judgments under the lease. In subdivision 45.01(a) of the sample clause (see Section 45.2, *supra*), the tenant agrees that the liability under the lease of all partners will be joint and several.

Since any general partner of a partnership normally has the power and authority to enter into obligations that are binding upon the partnership, a landlord should be able to assure itself that if it deals with any one partner, no other partner will object or claim that the other partner did not have the right or power to bind the partnership. In the sample clause, the tenant agrees that any general partner has the authority, vis-à-vis the landlord, to enter into a binding agreement modifying the lease. Further, since any partner has a right to modify the lease, any partner can change the address to which notices intended for tenant are given under the lease agreement. Accordingly, the sample clause provides that any notice given by or to any general partner is deemed binding upon the partnership and all of its general partners.

45.4 Tenant Concerns

Although the general partners of a partnership tenant may be concerned with the unlimited nature of their liability under the lease, a landlord generally will be reluctant to afford protection against that concern. A release by a landlord of the individual liability of the general partners in a partnership would limit the landlord's ability to enforce the lease against the assets of the partnership itself and, unless those assets were significant enough and stable enough to give the landlord comfort as to the tenant's ability to operate its business as well as to satisfy all of its leasehold obligations over the entire term of the lease, the landlord would probably want to look further for financial comfort and security. On the other hand, the general partners may argue that while they choose to form a partnership rather than a corporation solely for tax reasons or other reasons personal to them and unrelated to the leasing of the space, the partnership tenant should be treated as a corporation for purposes of the lease and thus the general partners should enjoy the same exculpation from personal liability that they would enjoy if they were shareholders in a corporate tenant. The answer, of course, is dependent upon the nature and extent of the tenant's obligations under the lease, the net worth of the partnership tenant and of its various general partners, and, ultimately, the relative negotiating strength of the landlord and the tenant. It is possible, given all of the foregoing circumstances, that had the general partners formed a corporation and sought, as such, to lease the demised premises, the landlord would have required the same individuals who are the general partners of the partnership tenant to have fully guaranteed the corporate tenant's obligations under the lease, thus ending up essentially in the same place.

A partnership tenant might negotiate a non-recourse provision for the general partners, and provide, in exchange, a substantial cash or cash-equivalent security deposit or the personal guaranties of one or more (but perhaps fewer than all) of its general partners. These guaranties may be limited in terms of the scope of the tenant's obligations being guarantied or in the amount of total liability for which the guarantors are at risk. Alternatively, the partnership tenant might offer the landlord a "good-guy" guarantee of one or more of the general partners.

A landlord might agree that no modification of the lease will be binding upon the partnership tenant unless it is signed by a particular named general partner or partners.

A partnership tenant should be aware, however, that such an agreement might limit the tenant's ability to add and remove partners, transfer partnership interests, and change the internal management and structure of its partnership affairs. Accordingly, the general partner of a partnership tenant who is concerned that one of his or her co-partners might bind the partnership to a lease modification that is unacceptable to the partnership as a whole must generally address such a concern outside the scope of the lease.

The general partners of a partnership tenant have a legitimate concern about their ongoing liability for obligations under the lease that first accrue after they have left the partnership and given up all ongoing interest in it. A landlord may be sympathetic to this concern if the partner has left for legitimate business reasons having nothing to do with the avoidance of liability under the lease (such as a partner in a law firm partnership tenant retiring from the practice of law), provided that the remaining partnership meets certain minimum criteria relating to its financial condition and the number of remaining partners. The issue of individual partner liability in the context of large law firm and accounting firm leases is a highly contested one. There are a myriad of solutions, each of which is a function of the size and stability of the firm and of the respective negotiating positions of the parties which, in turn, are a function of the marketplace.

At a minimum, a departing general partner in a partnership tenant should demand that he or she not remain liable for any increased obligations of the partnership tenant that result from a modification of the lease (such as an increase in the size of the demised premises or the length of the lease term) made after the departure of such partner from the partnership tenant. A landlord should be able to make some level of accommodation in this regard.

45.5 Standard Real Estate Board of New York Clause

None.

45.6 Comments on Standard Real Estate Board of New York Clause

None.

45.7 Litigation Issues

Each general partner is liable for the debts of the partnership incurred in furtherance of partnership business.[1] Thus each partner is liable for the entire rental, not merely to the extent of the partner's proportionate interest in the partnership.[2] Every partner is not personally liable for all debts of the partnership "whenever" incurred. New York

1. PARTNERSHIP LAW § 26(a)(2). No partners in a limited liability partnership have personal liability unless a majority of the partners so agree in writing, subsections 2(b) and (d).

2. Lexington Ave. & 42nd St. Corp. v. Pepper, 221 A.D.2d 273, 634 N.Y.S.2d 87 (1st Dep't 1995).

Partnership Law section 28 states that "a person admitted as a partner into an existing partnership is liable for all the obligations of the partnership arising before his admission as though he had been a partner when such obligations were incurred, except that his liability shall be satisfied only out of partnership property." Absent an express assumption, a newly admitted partner cannot be held personally liable for existing lease obligations. Even a lease clause providing that "each person hereafter admitted as a general partner of Tenant during the term hereof shall be deemed to have assumed, jointly and severally, all of the obligations of Tenant under this lease" will not bind such a subsequently admitted partner absent an express assumption.[3]

In *600 Partners Co. v. Berger*,[4] it was determined that if a partner withdraws from the partnership prior to the partnership incurring liability, the partner who withdrew may not be held personally liable for that liability. In *600 Partners Co.* the lease specifically released a withdrawn partner from any liability incurred by the partnership after the partner's retirement, provided at least eight remaining partners remained liable under a personal guaranty. The partner who retired prior to the lease default was deemed released notwithstanding the fact that eight partners did not remain liable under the guarantee, since the rent default had not occurred at the time of the partner's withdrawal.

In *Barbro Realty Co. v. Newburger*,[5] the court held that the obligation to pay rent did not constitute a preexisting debt within the meaning of Partnership Law section 28. "The lease may have been executed prior to the entry of the defendants into the partnership, but the rent as a debt arose only when it became due *[cited cases omitted]*, and accordingly the defendants, who were partners at the time of the default, may be held personally liable therefor."[6]

---

3. C.E. Hooper, Inc. v. Perlberg, Monness, Williams & Sidel, 72 A.D.2d 687, 421 N.Y.S.2d 353 (1st Dep't 1979). [Facts distinguished by County of Oswego Indus. Dev. Agency v. Fulton Cogeneration Assocs., LP., 2007 U.S. Dist. LEXIS 19169, 2007 WL 838975].

4. 600 Partners Co. v. Berger, 245 A.D.2d 140, 666 N.Y.S.2d 158 (1st Dep't 1997); 59th & Park Assocs. v. Inselbuch, 68 A.D.2d 838, 414 N.Y.S.2d 537 (1st Dep't 1979) (refusing to bind withdrawn partner to surrender agreement entered into after withdrawal).

5. 53 A.D.2d 34, 385 N.Y.S.2d 68 (1st Dep't 1976).

6. 385 N.Y.S.2d at 70.

CHAPTER 46

Sovereign Immunity

46.1 General Purpose

Concern about a tenant's assertion of "sovereign immunity"—the legal doctrine that provides for absolute immunity both from eviction proceedings and from execution upon its assets—does not often arise in space lease negotiations, since the vast majority of tenants are private commercial entities without recourse to such a defense. However, a landlord should consider the implications of the foreign sovereign immunity doctrine in direct negotiations with tenants that are foreign governments, as well as in connection with assignment provisions in markets where foreign governments rent spaces.

Pursuant to the Foreign Sovereign Immunities Act of 1976 (FSIA, 28 U.S.C.A. §§ 1602, *et seq.*), a foreign state is not immune from the jurisdiction of the courts of the United States where, among other things, (1) the foreign state has waived its immunity, or (2) where the action is based upon a commercial activity carried on in the United States by the foreign state. Cases in New York have confirmed that leasing constitutes a commercial activity.[1]

Note, however, that without a waiver of inviolability, forcible eviction of a mission from private premises will be denied, even if a damages award for back rent is upheld.[2]

Furthermore, even under the FSIA, judicial action is expensive and time-consuming. Only two means for effective service of process on foreign states and their agencies are permitted under 28 U.S.C.A. section 1608, namely, either (a) "special arrangement for service between the plaintiff and the foreign state or political subdivision," or (b) in accordance with an applicable international convention on service of judicial documents (which means the Hague Convention on Service Abroad of Judicial and Extrajudicial Documents of 1965 (20 U.S.T. 361, T.I.A.S. No. 6638, U.N.T.S. 163)). If a landlord

---

1. Ford Motor Co. v. Russian Fed'n, No. 09 CIV. 1646 (JGK), 2010 WL 2010867, at *3 (S.D.N.Y. May 18, 2010); Kern v. Oesterreichische Elektrizitaetswirtschaft Ag, 178 F. Supp. 2d 367, 376 (S.D.N.Y. 2001).

2. *See* Mendik Realty Co., Inc. v. Permanent Mission of Libya, 767 Third Ave. Assoc. v. Permanent Mission of Republic of Zaire to the United Nations, 988 F.2d 295 (2d Cir. 1993). (notice provision in REBNY form did not constitute a "special arrangement").

wants to enter into a "special arrangement for service" pursuant to FSIA, it should not rely on boilerplate provisions regarding service in a lease.

With respect to assignments of leases, a landlord whose use provision states simply "general and executive offices" is implicitly allowing such use by a governmental agency to which the premises may be assigned or sublet, unless either the use clause lists government agencies as an occupancy type that is forbidden, or the assignment-and-subletting clause prohibits such agencies as either assignees or sublessees. A landlord can solve this issue in one of two ways. The most common response is an outright prohibition, in either the "Use" provision (see Chapter 6, *supra*, sample clause Section 6.01) or the "Assignment and Subletting" provision, which forbids sovereign immune entities from taking up occupancy (or which provides the landlord the right to reject a proposed assignment or sublease if the assignee or sublessee would use the premises in a manner not permitted under the lease (see Chapter 16, *supra*, sample clause Section 16.03(a)(iii)). In those markets where such governmental tenants are present and desired as customers, however, a more sophisticated set of provisions is recommended, with especial attention to (1) waiver of sovereign immunity, (2) consent to jurisdiction, and (3) some "special arrangement for service."

46.2 Sample Clause

Sample clauses of the types just discussed are set forth in Chapters 6 and 16 (within sample clause 6.01 and 16.03, respectively).

46.3 Landlord Concerns

The landlord is concerned with being able to move in court against a defaulting tenant, both for a judgment of eviction and also to enforce any resulting judgment lien against the tenant's property. A tenant (or assignee or subtenant of the original, non-sovereign tenant) claiming sovereign immunity can frustrate both these purposes. Consequently, the prudent landlord will make clear in its use clause that a governmental entity may not come in under the umbrella description of "general and executive offices" as a permitted form of occupancy, and in its assignment and subletting provisions that it may withhold consent to a proposed assignment or subletting to a sovereign immune entity.

If, however, such an entity's rental offer is too attractive to pass up, the landlord will want to bolster its own ability to effect eviction and enforce a money judgment by having the tenant formally waive its immunity (which, if properly drafted, it can do without endangering its claim of immunity for true political acts), and consent to the jurisdiction of local state and federal courts, and explicitly agree to a "special arrangement for service." Arguments of insufficiency of process and insufficiency of service of process, coming on top of the defense of lack of jurisdiction based on sovereign immunity, have often been devastating to the landlord's case.[3]

---

3. *See, e.g.*, 40 D 6262 Realty Corp. v. United Arab Emirates Gov't, 447 F. Supp. 710 (S.D.N.Y. 1978); Gray v. Permanent Mission of the People's Republic of the Congo in the United Nations, 443

46.4 Tenant Concerns

The average commercial tenant will have no claim to sovereign immunity and is already subject to the jurisdictional processes of the state in which the leased premises are located, and thus will have no concern with such provisions, except to be made to understand that a landlord will not automatically or readily consent, in an assignment or sublet situation, to a domestic or foreign state entity or department stepping into such tenant's place.

A tenant that does have sovereign immunity, however, whether the department or agency of a state of the United States, or a foreign embassy or consulate, or government-owned trading agency or bank, may be reluctant to grant any waiver, even in what is clearly a commercial context, and even though an explicit waiver is permitted under the FSIA (28 U.S.C.A. section 1605(a)(1). A waiver is also permitted under the Vienna Convention on Diplomatic Relations [Article 32, 23 U.S.T. 3227, at 3241]). In that case, the only alternative the tenant has to refusing to waive sovereign immunity is to agree to a considerably higher security deposit, in order to give the landlord some comfort that, in a rent dispute prolonged by a dispute over the applicable rules of sovereign immunity, the extra months of litigation will be covered by extra months of prepaid security.

46.5 Standard Real Estate Board of New York Clause

The landlord using the REBNY form without more is self-armored against the sovereign immunity problem, if the original tenant is not a sovereign immune entity, because the Assignment section (Article 11) forbids assignment or subletting without "the prior written consent of Owner in each instance." If, however, such landlord employs a rider that modifies this provision by setting forth standards to be met by a potential lease assignee or sublessee as to which owner/landlord will not unreasonably withhold its consent, then care should be taken to list the sovereign immune classification exception to the general rule.

As for the sovereign immune tenant signing the REBNY printed form (or being assigned such a lease or subleasing thereunder), without such an amendment in its text or by attached rider, the result is a lease without a "special arrangement" for service of process, which provides the tenant with ample opportunities to deploy the defenses of insufficiency of process and lack of effective jurisdiction described above in Section 46.3 (Landlord Concerns).

46.6 Comments on Standard Real Estate Board of New York Clause

As noted in Section 46.5, *supra*, the owner/landlord may wish to add to Article 11 that "In no event shall Owner permit an assignment or sublease to an entity or person

F. Supp. 710 (S.D.N.Y. 1978), and the *Mendik* case cited in note 2.

entitled, directly or indirectly, to diplomatic or sovereign immunity." An owner/landlord wishing to effect a REBNY form lease with just such an entity will need to employ a long-form rider provision like the second alternative set forth under Article 16 (Assignment and Subletting) in Section 46.2 (Sample Clause), *supra.* Since sovereign immunity is not really divisible, the governmental tenant will, if it wants the space, be required to agree to all the provisions of that sample clause—waiver, consent to jurisdiction, and specific ("special") arrangement for service of process—because its future landlord will demand all those protections.

46.7 Litigation Issues

The Foreign Immunities Act of 1976 (28 U.S.C.A. § 1602) governs actions against foreign governments. Section 1605 sets forth the exceptions to jurisdictional immunity of a foreign state that would make it viable for a landlord to rent commercial space to a foreign government or agency, and expect the remedy of eviction and collection of delinquent rent to be enforced.

Section 1605 provides for three exemptions from immunity that would protect a landlord: (1) under section 1605(a)(1), the tenant may waive immunity, expressly or impliedly; (2) if an action against a foreign government is based upon commercial activity, under section 1605(a)(2); and (3) under section 1605(a)(4) if the action concerns rights to "immovable property situated in the United States."[4] In dealing with a foreign government, or agency, or entity a landlord is well advised to include in a lease provisions reciting the facts establishing the foregoing exemptions.

Nevertheless, a landlord who leases property for use as consulate or mission will not be able to exercise the remedy of recovery of possession by eviction.[5] The Foreign Sovereign Immunities Act is inapplicable to United Nations missions, which are not subject to eviction or attachment pursuant to the Vienna Convention on Diplomatic Relations of 1961. The Foreign Sovereign Immunities Act was enacted subject to all treaties and international agreements, and the Vienna Convention provides that a mission is inviolable.[6] The landlord who rents to a consulate or mission can recover a judgment for monetary damages arising out of delinquency in rent payments; however, because of U.S. participation in the Vienna Convention, the landlord may not pursue eviction proceedings against a mission.[7] The prudent landlord, under these circumstances, would be well advised to secure a large security deposit when negotiating the lease in order to protect itself against the delinquency of a foreign mission. The Foreign

4. *See* Joseph v. Office of Consulate General of Nigeria, 830 F.2d 1018 (9th Cir. 1987) for a discussion of each exemption. [Tei Yan Sun v. Taiwan, 201 F.3d 1105 "questions" Joseph v. Office of Consulate. The "question" is in regard to statutory interpretation, not the exemptions laid out earlier.]

5. 767 Third Ave. Assoc. v. Permanent Mission of the Republic of Zaire, 988 F.2d 295, *cert. denied* 510 U.S. 819, 114 S. Ct. 74, 126 L. Ed. 2d 42 (1993); S & S Machinery Co. v. Masinexportimport, 802 F. Supp. 1109 (S.D.N.Y. 1992); 2 Tudor City Place Assoc. v. Libyan Arab Republic Mission, 121 Misc. 2d 945, 470 N.Y.S.2d 301 (N.Y.C. Civ. Ct. N.Y. Cnty. 1983).

6. *767 Third Ave. Assoc.*, 988 F.2d at 298.

7. *Id.* at 303.

Sovereign Immunities Act itself prohibits execution of a judgment establishing rights in property where the property is used for the purpose of maintaining a diplomatic or consular mission.[8]

Section 1608 provides for the method of service of process upon a foreign government, which expressly includes a "special arrangement for service" between the parties. A carefully drafted provision should be included in a lease to avoid the otherwise complex service requirements set forth in the act.[9] Thus service of a summons and complaint by certified mail, if provided for in a lease, can constitute sufficient service.[10] However, any such provision for special arrangement must be carefully drafted and the provisions thereof strictly followed. Thus where a lease provided for consent to personal jurisdiction in the *state* courts of New Jersey and further provided that service of process by certified mail was deemed personal service in "any such action," service by certified mail was not sufficient for an action commenced in federal district court.[11]

8. 2 Tudor City Place Assoc., 470 N.Y.S.2d at 305.

9. *Id.* at 302, 306.

10. Marlowe v. Argentine Naval Comm'n, 604 F. Supp. 703 (D.D.C. 1985). [Overruled in part by Lovati v. Bolivarian Republic of Venez., 2020 U.S. Dist. LEXIS 211458. "However, since *Marlowe*, the DC Circuit has rejected *Marlowe's* substantial compliance approach in favor of the strict adherence standard." Does not impact the statement above.]

11. Copelco Capital, Inc. v. General Consul of Bolivia, 940 F. Supp. 93 (S.D.N.Y. 1996).

CHAPTER 47

Memorandum of Lease

47.1 General Purpose

The purpose of a memorandum of lease, from the tenant's perspective, is to put the world on record notice of the tenant's space leasehold interest within the building. A lease for a term exceeding three years may be recorded in the local county clerk's office under New York Real Property Law (RPL) section 291. RPL section 291-c permits the recording with like effect of a memorandum of a lease, (1) if executed and acknowledged by all lease parties, and (2) if it contains, at a minimum, the following information: (a) the names of landlord and tenant; (b) their addresses as set forth in the lease; (c) the date of execution of the lease; (d) a description of the premises as described in the lease; (e) the term of the lease with the commencement and expiration dates, and if there is a right of extension or renewal, the maximum period to which (or number of times) it may be so extended or renewed, and the dates on which such rights (if any) are exercisable.

The purpose of the memorandum of lease clause in the standard landlord form, however, is normally to forbid such recording. The rationale behind this prohibition is that recording the lease could blemish the title to the property at the time of a sale. This is particularly true if the tenant has defaulted, or otherwise departed, without joining landlord in a duly executed-and-acknowledged cancellation of memorandum of lease. Since a memorandum of lease requires the signature and acknowledgment of both the landlord and the tenant, the landlord need say nothing in its form lease in order to prevent the recording. The tenant is prohibited simply by the absence of the landlord's signature and acknowledgment on any proposed memorandum. Thus, the lease may be completely silent on this point—as is the Real Estate Board of New York form itself. The prudent landlord, in order to remove any possibility of recording, may wish to be explicit on this point.

47.2 Sample Clause

Section 47.01

This Lease shall not be recorded [*include if Tenant permitted to enter into MOL*; however, at either party's request, Landlord and Tenant shall promptly execute, acknowledge and deliver a memorandum with respect to this Lease in a form attached hereto as Exhibit [__] (as well as a memorandum of any amendments to this Lease) sufficient for recording and Landlord or Tenant, as the case may be, may record the memorandum at such recording parties cost and expense. Within 10 days after the end of the Term, Tenant shall enter into such documentation as is reasonably required by Landlord to remove the memorandum of record.]

47.3 Landlord Concerns

The landlord desires to keep the record title to its commercial or retail building as free of encumbrances as possible. While a space lease with a term exceeding three years is a recordable encumbrance in New York, the normal office building owner avoids the issue by (1) not acknowledging the lease (so it is not recordable in its full form), and/or (2) forbidding any memorandum from being recorded within the lease's text, and/or (3) if the lease is silent, and the tenant presses the point, by refusing to sign and acknowledge any memorandum that a tenant might offer for signature and recording.

If this firm stand does not prevail—and it usually does—the landlord must be sure to procure a tenant covenant, of the type found in second part of the sample clause set forth in Section 47.2 (Sample Clause), *supra*, to cooperate with the landlord in removing the memorandum of record. As noted in the introduction to this chapter, many leases are silent on the point. A landlord, in order to remove all doubt, would be better advised to include a prohibition by incorporating the language found only in the first part of the sample clause in Section 47.2, *supra*.

47.4 Tenant Concerns

Where a tenant, under a written lease, is in active possession and use of its leased space, the risk that a bona fide purchaser for value will buy the building and, claiming ignorance, repudiate or otherwise challenge the tenancy is effectively nonexistent. A tenant with a lease of less than three years (which cannot be recorded) does not take up occupancy in such fear in New York state, and neither do tenants with longer terms.

It may be, as a matter of home office policy or general paranoia, that a tenant will insist on the ability to record such a memorandum, and a landlord, desirous of securing that tenant, may be compelled to agree to complete the deal. Larger and more sophisticated tenants whose leases include options to expand within the building will be more inclined to insist on the recording of a memorandum that references such expansion rights, putting other would-be tenants on notice that the premises they intend to lease may be encumbered and unavailable. The tenant, as the price of the landlord's concession, must expect to be asked to deliver a termination instrument to be held in escrow by the landlord's attorney. No landlord will run the risk of a tenant default or departure without being able, acting alone, to purge the public record of the tenant's memorandum of lease.

47.5 Standard Real Estate Board of New York Clause

As noted earlier, the REBNY form contains no language either forbidding or permitting a memorandum of lease, so the tenant is free to bargain for the right to record a memorandum as set forth in the option provision described in the sample clause, but the landlord is more likely to add a prohibition to the printed form and carry the point. See Section 47.2 (Sample Clause), *supra*, for both of these forms.

47.6 Comments on Standard Real Estate Board of New York Clause

None, for the reason stated in Section 47.5, *supra*.

47.7 Litigation Issues

A lease or memorandum need not be recorded for the lease to be valid. There is sufficient case law arising out of the tenant's possession of the premises to protect a tenant against subsequent buyers or lenders. "The rule that emerged is that mere possession is constructive notice of any and all rights the possessor can establish."[1]

While it may not be necessary to record a lease in order for it to be valid, the tenant who records the initial lease or memorandum *must*, in order to protect itself, record any subsequent modifications to that lease. Under these circumstances, pursuant to RPL section 291-cc, an unrecorded modification is void as against a subsequent good faith purchaser for value and *possession by the tenant is not deemed notice thereof.*

A tenant may wish to protect itself by recording the lease where it will not take possession of the leased space for an extended period of time, especially in circumstances where the premises are yet to be built. In *Jamaica Savings Bank v. Bregstein*[2] the tenant did obtain a recordable memorandum, but did not record the memo until after a subsequent construction loan was recorded. The memorandum was prior in time to the construction loan. The lease was by its terms subordinate to all bona fide mortgages thereafter placed on the premises on the condition that any mortgagee or purchaser at foreclosure agreed not to deprive the lessee of the use of the property. The mortgage did not provide this protection. The appellate court held that summary judgment was precluded because an issue of material fact existed as to whether the mortgagee was a purchaser in good faith so as to make a prior unrecorded lease void as against a recorded mortgage.

The recording of a memorandum provides a subsequent purchaser with notice of each of the covenants of the lease. Thus a grantee of a building, which is "subject to a lease," a memorandum of which was duly recorded, and which contained a covenant to provide certain parking spaces, and a covenant binding a successor to perform each

1. Tehan v. Thos. C. Peters Printing Co., Inc., 71 A.D.2d 101, 421 N.Y.S.2d 465 (4th Dep't 1979).
2. 49 A.D. 2d 617, 370 N.Y.S.2d 666 (2d Dep't 1975).

lease covenant, was bound to perform the covenant even though it did not assume the lease contractual covenants in writing.[3]

Not only must a memorandum be timely recorded, that is, prior to a conveyance protected by the recorded act, it must be properly indexed within the chain of title. Thus, if the lessor has conveyed the property prior to the recording of the memorandum, the recording of the memorandum after the conveyance will take the memo out of the chain of title and render it ineffective.[4] This would mean that the memo must not only be timely recorded, but recorded against all of the premises intended to be encumbered by the lease or the covenants therein. If easements or restrictive rights are to be asserted against premises adjacent to the leased premises, the memorandum must be recorded within the chain of title for this adjacent property to bind grantees thereof. A tenant should also require the recording of a memorandum if it intends to subject its leasehold to mortgage financing. Unless the lease memorandum is recorded, a mortgage recorded encumbering the lease will not be in the chain of title, and thus will not have the benefit of the recording act.

3. Bank of New York v. Hirschfeld, 37 N.Y.2d 501, 374 N.Y.S.2d 100, 336 N.E.2d 710 (1975).
4. Fekishazy v. Thomson, 204 A.D.2d 959, 612 N.Y.S.2d 276 (3d Dep't 1994).

CHAPTER 48

Arbitration of Disputes

48.1 General Purpose

A vast majority of landlords, tenants, and their respective attorneys believe that arbitration is an effective mechanism for resolving disputes without resort to litigation, which is generally believed to be a lengthier and more costly process. Three caveats must be considered, however, with regard to that perception. First, arbitration is not necessarily less expensive or less time consuming. Some participants come away from an arbitration saying, "never again" because they find it no less, and perhaps even more, expensive and time-consuming than litigation. Second, even assuming arbitration to be a less costly and a more efficient dispute resolution process, some landlords and even an occasional tenant believe that, given the respective strengths of the parties, the nature of the matter in dispute and the effect of a costly, drawn out process for resolving it, it may work to their advantage to require that all disputes either be resolved by negotiated settlement or, failing that, litigation. Third, many people believe that arbitrations tend to result in a compromised resolution rather than a "winner take all" determination. Nevertheless, after weighing the pros and cons of arbitration, most landlords include (and most tenants willingly accept) arbitration provisions in their leases, albeit not one that can be resorted to for all disputes. For example, it would be a rare, if not unique, landlord that would subject a nonpayment dispute to arbitration.

Generally speaking, arbitration does have certain qualities relative to litigation. Most often it is a faster, less costly process. It also allows the parties to exercise some control by setting boundaries and establishing rules. The expedited rules of arbitration set a relatively fast timetable for the resolution of disputes and can be particularly useful, for example, in determining whether the landlord has been reasonable in withholding its consent to a proposed assignment, subletting or alteration. With that in mind, an alternative (or additional) arbitration provision is included [set forth in Section 48.2, *infra*, and entitled "B. Expedited Arbitration Procedure (Consents and Approvals")] for use exclusively in the determination of disputes regarding the reasonableness of the withholding of consents or approvals by the landlord. It is important for the arbitration provisions to specify the qualifications of the arbitrator or arbitrators and to provide that the determination of the arbitrator or arbitrators will be binding on the parties and enforceable in a court of competent jurisdiction. In that way, the prevailing party can be assured of getting a judgment if the losing party does not follow the determination of the arbitrator or arbitrators. If the parties do not choose an expedited procedure, the arbitration rules set down by the parties usually require the arbitrators to hold hearings allowing the parties to present evidence that may include the presentation of witnesses and experts.

48.2 Sample Clause

The sample provisions provided below deal with the arbitration of nonmonetary issues.

A. Standard Arbitration Procedure of Nonmonetary Disputes

Article 48 Arbitration of Non-monetary Disputes

48.01 Either party may request arbitration of any matter in dispute which, pursuant to the terms of this Lease, expressly allows such dispute to be resolved by arbitration. The party desiring such arbitration shall give notice to the other party. If the parties shall not have agreed on a choice of an arbitrator within 15 days after the service of such notice, then each party shall, within 10 days thereafter, appoint an arbitrator and advise the other party of the arbitrator so appointed. A third arbitrator shall, within 10 days following the appointment of the 2 arbitrators, be appointed by the 2 arbitrators so appointed or by JAMS, if the 2 arbitrators are unable, within such 10 day period, to agree on the third arbitrator. If either party fails to appoint an arbitrator (the "Failing Party"), the other party shall provide an additional notice to the Failing Party requiring the Failing Party's appointment of an arbitrator within 5 Business Days after the Failing Party's receipt thereof. If the Failing Party fails to notify the other party of the appointment of its arbitrator within such 5-Business Day period, the appointment of the second arbitrator shall be made by JAMS in the same manner as hereinabove provided for the appointment of a third arbitrator in a case where the two arbitrators appointed hereunder are unable to agree upon such appointment. The 3 arbitrators shall render a resolution of said dispute or make the determination in question. In the absence, failure, refusal or inability of JAMS to act within 20 days, then either party, on behalf of both, may apply to a Justice of the Supreme Court of New York, [________] County, for the appointment of the third arbitrator, and the other party shall not raise any question as to the court's full power and jurisdiction to entertain the application and make the appointment. In the event of the absence, failure, refusal or inability of an arbitrator to act, a successor shall be appointed within 10 days as hereinbefore provided. Any arbitrator acting under this Article 48 in connection with any matter shall be experienced in the issue with which the arbitration is concerned and shall have been actively engaged in such field for a period of at least 10 years before the date of his appointment as arbitrator hereunder.

48.02 All arbitrators chosen or appointed pursuant to this Article 48 shall (x) be sworn fairly and impartially to perform their respective duties as such arbitrator, (y) not be an employee or past employee of Landlord or Tenant or of any other person, partnership, corporation or other form of business or legal association or entity that controls, is controlled by or is under common control with Landlord or Tenant and (z) in the case of the third arbitrator, has not represented or been retained for any reason whatsoever by Landlord or Tenant or any other person, partnership, corporation or other form of business or legal association or entity that controls, is controlled by or is under common control with Landlord or Tenant within the 5-year period prior to such arbitration. Within 60 days after the appointment of such arbitrators, such arbitrators shall determine the matter which is the subject of the arbitration and shall issue a written opinion. The decision of the arbitrators shall be conclusively binding upon the parties, and judgment upon the decision may be entered in any court having jurisdiction. Landlord and Tenant shall each pay the fees and expenses of the arbitrator selected by (or on behalf of) it. The losing party shall reimburse the prevailing party for the reasonable attorneys' fees and disbursements incurred by the prevailing party in connection with such arbitration, and the losing party shall pay for the fees and expenses of the arbitrator appointed by JAMS and the cost of the arbitration.

48.03 Landlord and Tenant shall sign all documents and to do all other things necessary to submit any such matter to arbitration and hereby waive any and all rights they or either of them may at any time have to revoke their agreement hereunder to submit to arbitration and to abide by the decision rendered thereunder. For such period, if any, that this agreement to arbitrate is not legally binding or the arbitrator's award is not legally enforceable, the provisions requiring arbitration shall be deemed deleted, and matters to be determined by arbitration shall be subject to litigation.

48.04 Any dispute which is required by this Lease to be resolved by expedited arbitration shall be submitted to final and binding arbitration in New York, New York, administered by JAMS in accordance with JAMS Optional Expedited Arbitration Procedures (pursuant to Rules 16.1(a) and 16.2 of JAMS Comprehensive Arbitration Rules & Procedures). In cases where the parties utilize such expedited arbitration, (a) if the arbitrator shall find that a party acted unreasonably in withholding or delaying a consent or approval, such consent or approval shall be deemed granted (but the arbitrators shall not have the right to award damages) and (b) the losing party in such arbitration shall pay the arbitration costs charged by JAMS and/or the arbitrator(s), together with the reasonable attorneys' fees and disbursements incurred by the prevailing party in connection with such arbitration. Any decision rendered by JAMS arbitrator shall be final, conclusive, and binding.

48.05 The arbitrators shall, in rendering any decision pursuant to this Article 48, answer only the specific question or questions presented to them. In answering such question or questions (and rendering their decision), the arbitrators shall be bound by the provisions of this Lease, and shall not add to, subtract from or otherwise modify such provisions.

48.06 Judgment may be had on the decision and award of the arbitrators rendered pursuant to the provisions of this Article 48 and may be enforced in accordance with the laws of the State of New York.

48.07 The provisions of this Article 48 shall not be applicable to any arbitration expressly contemplated to be conducted pursuant to arbitration provisions set forth in *[insert monetary provisions that deal with determining fair market rent]*

B. Expedited Arbitration Procedure (Consents and Approvals)

48.01 If Tenant requests Landlord's consent and Landlord fails or refuses to give such consent, Tenant shall not be entitled to any damages for any withholding by Landlord of its consent, it being intended that Tenant's sole remedy shall be an action for specific performance or injunction, and that such remedy shall be available only in those cases where this Lease provides that Landlord shall not unreasonably withhold its consent.

48.02 No dispute relating to this Lease or the relationship of Landlord and Tenant under this Lease shall be resolved by arbitration unless this Lease expressly provides for such dispute to be resolved by arbitration. Tenant shall have the right to submit a dispute relating to the reasonableness of the denial of a consent by Landlord under this Lease, where, pursuant to such provisions, Landlord's consent was not to be unreasonably withheld, to final and binding arbitration in New York, New York, administered by JAMS in accordance in accordance with JAMS Streamlined Arbitration Rules and Procedures in effect at that time (or, if JAMS is no longer in existence, then administered by National Arbitration and Mediation ("NAM"), in accordance with NAM's Comprehensive Dispute Resolution Rules and Procedures; and if NAM is no longer in existence, then administered by the American Arbitration Association under the Expedited Procedures of its Commercial Arbitration Rules in effect at that time; and if none of the preceding remains in existence, by the expedited arbitration procedures of any succeeding or substantially similar dispute resolution organization). A single arbitrator will be selected pursuant to such rules and procedures (the "JAMS Arbitrator"). The parties agree that: (A) the speedy resolution of any disputes or claims between them pursuant to this arbitration clause is a mutual and material inducement to enter into this Lease; (B) the unsuccessful parties in such arbitration shall pay to the successful parties all costs and expenses reasonably incurred by the successful parties, including reasonable attorney's fees and disbursements, and will pay any fees and disbursements due to JAMS and the JAMS Arbitrator and, to the extent the "successful" parties cannot be clearly identified, each party will bear its own costs and expenses and the parties will pay their equal share of any fees and disbursements due to JAMS and the JAMS Arbitrator and (C) this arbitration clause and all awards hereunder are to be enforced in the New York Supreme Court, New York County. The JAMS Arbitrator will be bound by the provisions of this Lease and will not have the power to add to, subtract from or otherwise modify such provisions, and will have the authority to, and may, order specific performance to remedy any breach of the terms of this Lease. The JAMS Arbitrator will consider only the specific issues submitted to him/her for resolution, and will be directed to make a determination as to the "successful" party or a specific determination that there is no prevailing party.

48.03 Landlord and Tenant agree to sign all documents and to do all other things necessary to submit any such matter to arbitration and further agree to, and hereby do, waive any and all rights they or either of them may at any time have to revoke their agreement hereunder to submit to arbitration and to abide by the decision rendered thereunder. For such period, if any, as this agreement to arbitrate is not legally binding or the arbitrator's award is not legally enforceable, the provisions requiring arbitration shall be deemed deleted and matters to be determined by arbitration shall be subject to litigation

48.3 Landlord Concerns

Arbitration generally is less advantageous to a landlord than a tenant because a lack of an effective remedy most often will prove to be more of a burden to the tenant than to the landlord. Nonetheless, landlords generally prefer to include arbitration provisions in their leases because efficiency should be beneficial for everyone.

It is very important for landlords to limit the application of arbitration provisions. For example, in no event should a landlord subject a nonpayment dispute or other default matter to arbitration and thereby give up the availability of a summary proceeding. Such a pervasive arbitration provision could render the landlord's property unfinanceable. To be safe, arbitration provisions should not be provisions of general application, but rather should be limited in their application to those specific lease provisions that the landlord has considered and determined to be subject to arbitration.

48.4 Tenant Concerns

Generally speaking, neither the determination to include or exclude arbitration in or from a lease, nor the specific considerations of an arbitration provision, if included, should be a matter of serious contention between a landlord and a tenant. Both the overall concept and the mechanics of a given provision are relatively neutral. Nevertheless, to the extent arbitration is more often favored by one party than the other, it is the tenant that finds arbitration attractive. Arbitration generally is more important to tenants because, as stated earlier, it is perceived to be (and most often is) a more efficient method of dispute resolution (thereby saving time and money) in comparison to litigation. The relative brevity and inexpensiveness of arbitration generally favors tenants who may be left without an effective remedy if they are limited to litigation as a sole method of resolving disputes with their landlords because litigation may be too costly and/or lengthy to serve as an effective remedy.

Expedited arbitration can be especially valuable to tenants. Without it, for example, a prospective subtenant or assignee, in all likelihood, will have found alternative space by the time the tenant is able to reverse its landlord's unreasonable withholding of consent to the proposed sublease or assignment.

48.5 Standard Real Estate Board of New York Clause

The REBNY form does not provide for arbitration.

48.6 Comments on Standard Real Estate Board of New York Clause

None.

48.7 Litigation Issues

In *Mendelsohn v. A & D Catering Corp.*,[1] the court stated that the policy of the state of New York "favors and encourages arbitration as a means of conserving the time and resources of the courts and the contracting parties." However, a party cannot be compelled to arbitrate "unless the agreement to arbitrate expressly and unequivocally encompasses the subject matter of the particular dispute."[2]

The lease for catering premises in *Mendelsohn* contained a broad arbitration clause that provided: "Except for the payment of rent any controversy regarding the interpretation of any provision of this lease which shall arise between the Lessor and Lessee regarding the rights, duties or liabilities hereunder shall be settled by a Board of Arbitrators." The landlord sold their catering business to the lessee, who was required to use the landlord's corporation, which had a liquor license that permitted the lessee to serve alcoholic beverages until such time as it obtained its own license. The lessee did not obtain the requisite license, and the lessor eventually refused to renew its company's liquor license. The tenant withheld rent, which resulted in the lessor's commencement of summary nonpayment proceeding, and an injunction action by the tenant to compel the lessor to renew the liquor license. The actions were discontinued and the dispute submitted to arbitration. Thereafter the landlord sought to terminate the lease and proceed with a summary dispossess action on the grounds that the tenant served liquor without a license. The landlord sought to stay the arbitration on the grounds that the arbitration clause was not broad enough to cover the liquor license dispute; that such a violation of the state liquor licensing laws should not be subject to arbitration as

1. Mendelsohn v. A&D Catering Corp., 100 A.D.2d 209, 473 N.Y.S.2d 481 (2d Dep't 1984). [Youshah v. Staudinger, 159 Misc. 2d 350 cites *Mendelsohn* as support that courts will not enforce illegal contract provisions.].

2. 100 William Co. v. Aetna Ins. Co., 163 A.D.2d 170, 558 N.Y.S.2d 34 (1st Dep't 1990) (held that arbitration clause required if manner of computation of rent adjustment clause was in dispute did not prevent court action concerning meaning of formula used in rent adjustment provision); *In re* We're Assoc. Co., 163 A.D. 2d 393, 557 N.Y.S.2d 930 (2d Dep't 1990); 140 Broadway Co. v. Dewey, Ballantine, Bushby, Palmer & Wood, 96 A.D.2d 482, 465 N.Y.S.2d 193 (1st Dep't 1983) (court held that arbitration clause provided for arbitration of amount of renewal rent, not date when rental value would be determined); *In re* Baime, 88 A.D.2d 595, 449 N.Y.S.2d 775 (2d Dep't 1982).

a matter of public policy; and that the tenant waived the right to compel arbitration because it commenced a legal action for a mandatory injunction.

The court held the provision broad enough to encompass the dispute concerning whether, and how long, the tenant may have sold liquor without a license. Furthermore, the court held that the arbitrator's determination concerning a possible criminal violation did not violate the state's public policy. The court noted that "this is a private controversy between the parties, involving the construction of their lease. . . . Arbitration would neither interfere with nor interdict the State's enforcement of the Alcoholic Beverage Control Law. Nor would arbitration impinge on the State's authority to impose the statutorily prescribed penalties if respondent were found to have violated the law."[3] The prior injunction action did not waive the right to arbitrate the dispute, but was deemed undertaken for protective relief to preserve the status quo.

The department store lease in the case of *In re Baime*[4] contained an agreement requiring arbitration of disputes arising from the execution of the terms of the lease. The tenant sought to stay a notice to cure a default in the leasehold obligations to continuously operate a first class department store on the premises. The store had become unprofitable and the tenant sought the landlord's approval to alter the premises for office rental, which the landlord refused. The tenant sought to arbitrate the dispute concerning the requested alteration of the premises and use. The court affirmed the stay of arbitration as the lease clearly required use of the premises as a department store. The arbitrator cannot rewrite the terms of a lease and is not "completely unfettered" by the terms of the lease in reaching its determination.

A party cannot compel arbitration of issues not expressly, directly, and unequivocally subject to the agreement to arbitrate. Thus, where a lease of a building constructed for the tenant by the landlord contained a construction warranty requiring the landlord to remedy any construction defects, and further requiring any disputes under the warranty to be resolved by arbitration, the tenant's claims for diminution of rental value as the result of alleged defective construction was not subject to mandatory arbitration.[5]

The breadth of an arbitration clause can result in compulsion to arbitrate rent payment issues, where the provision requires arbitration "of every dispute arising under this Lease other than non-payment of rent."[6] The issue of the date commencing the tenant's obligation to pay fixed rent was held not to be a dispute concerning nonpayment of rent.

3. 473 N.Y.S.2d at 486.

4. 88 A.D. 2d 595, 449 N.Y.S.2d 775 (2d Dep't 1982).

5. *In re* We're Associates Co., 163 A.D. 2d 393, 557 N.Y.S.2d 930 (2d Dep't 1990). *See also* 120 Wall St. Co. v. Cont'l Ins. Co., 1994 WL 107885 [not otherwise reported] (Sup. Ct., N.Y. Cnty. 1994) (where casualty damage clause provided for arbitration, claim to terminate lease due to asbestos contamination was not deemed to be within concept of casualty damage).

6. Cathedral Park Bldg. Assoc. v. Damon & Morey, 176 A.D.2d 1203, 576 N.Y.S.2d 972 (4th Dep't 1991).

CHAPTER 49

Roof Rights and Communication Equipment

49.1 General Purpose

With the advancement of telecommunications technology has come an ever increasing demand by tenants for the installation of "satellite dishes" or other rooftop equipment in order to transmit or receive signals. Previously, landlords were limited in the number of tenants who could be granted roof rights by the linear measurements of the rooftop (after taking into account the other sections of the roof that were needed for other purposes). Since the development of multitiered structures on which antennae can be erected at various elevations, the amount of rooftop equipment that can be accommodated has been dramatically increased. As roof rights have become viewed less as a benefit available only to major tenants and more as a right that is available even to smaller tenants, more attention has been focused on roof rights clauses.

49.2 Sample Clause

Article 49 Roof Rights.

Section 49.01

(a) Subject to the requirements of this Section 49, Tenant may install, maintain and operate, at Tenant's expense, one communications antenna (the "Antenna") on the roof of the Building and run a cable therefrom into the Premises through conduit space provided by Landlord in such locations as Landlord may designate. The size of the Antenna, and the location thereof on the roof of the Building, shall be subject to Landlord's reasonable approval. [If, on the first anniversary of the Commencement Date, Tenant has not installed an Antenna (or submitted plans to install an Antenna pursuant to Section 7.01), then this Section 49.01 shall be void and of no further force or effect.]

(b) Tenant acknowledges that (i) Tenant's use of the roof of the Building is a non-exclusive use and Landlord may permit any person or entity to use any other portion of the roof of the Building for any use, (ii) the installation of the Antenna constitutes a Material Alteration, (iii) if Landlord's structural engineer recommends structural reinforcement of the roof of the Building in connection with the installation of the Antenna, Tenant shall, prior to installation of the Antenna, perform such reinforcement at Tenant's expense in accordance with plans and specifications approved by Landlord, (iv) without limiting the other conditions set forth in this Section 49, such installation (including, without limitation, any structural reinforcements performed in connection therewith) shall be performed in compliance with all of the provisions of Section 7.01 and the other provisions of this Lease applicable to Alterations, (v) Tenant, at Tenant's expense, shall comply with all Laws and procure and maintain all necessary permits and approvals required therefor (Tenant hereby acknowledging that Landlord is making no representations as to the permissibility of any Antenna on the roof of the Building by any governmental authority having jurisdiction thereof), (vi) Tenant shall promptly repair any damage (whether structural or non-structural) caused to the roof or any other portion of the Building or its fixtures, equipment and appurtenances by reason of the installation, maintenance or operation of the Antenna (or, at Landlord's election, Landlord shall perform such repairs and Tenant shall reimburse Landlord for the reasonable costs thereof within 10 days after rendition of a bill therefor), (vii) the installation, operation and maintenance of the Antenna shall not interfere with the operation and maintenance of any installations existing on the date Tenant installs the Antenna, (viii) if Tenant's installation, operation or maintenance of the Antenna shall interfere with Landlord's rights (including, without limitation, Landlord's right to use the remainder of the roof of the Building for any purposes) or other present or future tenants in the Building, Tenant shall cooperate with Landlord or such other tenants in eliminating such interference; *provided*, that in cases where the interference affects installations existing on the date Tenant installs the Antenna the cost of remedying such interference shall be borne by Tenant and (ix) Tenant shall pay any additional or increased insurance premiums incurred by Landlord, and shall obtain and pay for any additional insurance coverage for the benefit of Landlord in such amount and of such type as Landlord may reasonably require in connection with the Antenna.

(c) If the installation, maintenance or operation of the Antenna shall revoke, negate or in any manner impair or limit any roof warranty or guaranty for the Building, then Tenant shall reimburse Landlord for any loss or damage sustained or costs or expenses incurred by Landlord as a result thereof. Tenant shall remove the Antenna upon the expiration or earlier termination of the Term and repair any damage to the roof of the Building caused by the installation or removal of the Antenna, all at Tenant's expense (or, at Landlord's election, Landlord shall perform such repairs and Tenant shall reimburse Landlord for the reasonable costs thereof within 10 days after rendition of a bill therefor). Landlord shall have no obligation to repair or maintain the Antenna, nor shall Landlord be liable for any damage to the Antenna.

(d) For the purpose of installing, operating or maintaining the Antenna, Tenant shall have access to the roof of the Building at reasonable times upon reasonable notice to Landlord, and Landlord shall have the right to require, as a condition to such access, that Tenant (or Tenant's employee, contractor or other representative) at all times be accompanied by a representative of Landlord who Landlord shall make available upon reasonable notice, and Tenant shall pay Landlord's reasonable out-of-pocket expenses incurred in making such representative available.

(e) Landlord shall have the right to relocate the Antenna, at Landlord's expense (or at Tenant's expense if the relocation shall be required due to the application of any Laws, the request of Tenant, or interference with rooftop equipment that was installed prior to the installation of the Antenna), to any other location on the roof of the Building, such right to be exercisable by Landlord giving Tenant 10 days prior notice thereof (except in the case of emergency in which case Landlord shall give such notice as is reasonably practicable). Tenant shall pay any amounts due to Landlord in connection with the relocation of the Antenna within 10 days after rendition of a bill therefor.

(f) The Antenna shall be connected to Tenant's submeters measuring Tenant's use of electricity in the Premises and Tenant shall pay all electricity costs in connection with the use of the Antenna in accordance with Section 17.02.

(g) The rights granted in this Section 49 are given in connection with, and as part of the rights created under this Lease, and are not separately transferable or assignable. Tenant shall not resell in any form the use of the Antenna, including, without limitation, the granting of any licensing or other rights.

49.3 Landlord Concerns

The landlord's concerns regarding the installation of rooftop equipment are similar in many respects to its concerns regarding alterations generally. These concerns are (1) that installation of the rooftop equipment be performed in compliance with laws; (2) that the tenant obtain all necessary permits for the installation and maintenance of the equipment; (3) that the tenant pay for any increased insurance premiums incurred by landlord arising from the installations; (4) that the tenant be responsible for the maintenance of the rooftop equipment; and (5) that the tenant remove the rooftop equipment at the end of the term and repair any damages caused by the installation. A landlord will, of course, want the right to review and approve all plans and specifications regarding the installation of rooftop equipment. In addition, issues unique to this type of installation are also raised. For instance, some landlords (particularly in low-rise office buildings) will require that (1) tenants install screening around the equipment so that it is not visible from the ground or from other buildings or (2) equipment will be installed below the parapet of the building. In addition, if deemed necessary by the landlord's structural engineer, the landlord will add structural reinforcement to the portions of the roof occupied by the rooftop equipment, and require the tenant to reimburse it for these additions. Moreover, the landlord will want the tenant to reimburse it for any losses suffered if the building's roof warranty is revoked or otherwise adversely affected by the erection and/or maintenance of rooftop equipment.

The landlord will want to specify both the location on the roof where the equipment will be installed and the location of the conduit shafts from the tenant's premises to the rooftop equipment. Additionally, the landlord will disclaim any responsibility for the tenant's ability to utilize the rooftop equipment for its intended purpose at such location. The tenant should have its consultant verify that it will have sufficient sight lines to transmit and receive signals to and from the designated location.

In this way the landlord can assemble and coordinate a "stacking plan" for its roof space much in the same way it does so with its office space. Landlords will generally want the ability to relocate the tenant's equipment to another location on the roof either to accommodate other tenants, or to permit the landlord to perform repairs to the areas of the roof on which the tenant's equipment stands. In addition, landlords will want to make sure that the installation of rooftop equipment does not interfere with or diminish the usefulness of other rooftop equipment that exists on the building prior to a tenant's installation.

While the tenant's concerns regarding relocation of rooftop equipment are not as extensive as those regarding relocation of office space, the tenant would want the landlord to pay all the costs of relocation, and will want to make sure the relocation is performed at a time, and in a manner, so as to minimize interference with the operation of the tenant's business. In addition, the tenant will want to ensure that the new location provides it with comparable ability to transmit and receive signals as its original location. A landlord would want the tenant to bear the costs of relocation when required in order to comply with legal requirements or insurance requirements; otherwise the landlord will generally pay these relocation costs.

Whether or not a tenant will be charged a base fee to use the rooftop space varies from building to building. It would be very unusual for a tenant to pay any escalation charges based on the square footage of its rooftop space. It is the norm, however, for the tenant to be billed for the electricity that is consumed by its rooftop equipment (either by connection to the tenant's meters, estimation by the landlord, or otherwise).

49.4 Tenant Concerns

As a threshold matter, a tenant will want to ensure that it will have roof rights throughout the term of its lease. Often, landlords will require a tenant to exercise its right to install rooftop equipment within a stated period following lease commencement (e.g., one year) or else such right would be waived. In this way, the landlord would not be required to reserve roof space indefinitely for a tenant. The tenant should also make sure that the lease provides it with the right to run conduits from its office space to the rooftop equipment. Since the landlord will have an approval right over the plans and specifications regarding the installation of the rooftop equipment, the tenant would be wise to have such plans and specifications prepared and pre-approved in the lease.

Since transmission and reception capabilities may vary depending on the rooftop location (and considering that, as mentioned earlier, landlords will generally not make any representations regarding the tenant's ability to use its equipment), the tenant will be concerned with the proximity of other equipment that could interfere with the functioning of its own equipment. As a consequence, the tenant will want to require the landlord not to grant roof rights to other tenants within a stated radius of its equipment, or in any other location that would interfere with the tenant's use of its equipment. Once installed, the tenant would not want to pay relocation costs under any circumstances (including relocation required by laws or insurance requirements). A negotiated compromise on this issue might be that the tenant bear these costs if the relocation is required by a law enacted after the installation of its equipment. If the tenant's consumption of electricity is not metered (but is estimated by the landlord), the tenant should request the right to contest the estimate and to have any dispute resolved by a survey performed by an independent electrical consultant.

While often overlooked, sophisticated tenants will ensure that the roof rights are transferable to the tenant's assignees and subtenants. If such rights are made personal to the named tenant, then the marketability of the space could be diminished dramatically.

Finally, the prudent tenant will also want to ensure that the lease specifically states that rooftop equipment is deemed to be the tenant's personal property or moveable trade fixtures (and not fixtures or installations) so that no question arises when the tenant wishes to remove the rooftop equipment at the end of the lease.

49.5 Standard Real Estate Board of New York Clause

None.

49.6 Comments on Standard Real Estate Board of New York Clause

None.

49.7 Litigation Issues

A party seeking to obtain rights to maintain rooftop equipment, such as a sign or an antennae, must be concerned with the nature of the right created by the operative document. A lease or easement will bind the realty; however, if deemed a license, the obligation to recognize the right of use of the roof is personal to the grantor and may be disavowed by a nonassuming successor.[1] Generally, notwithstanding the use of words such as "lease" or "let" or denomination of the grantor as "landlord," an agreement to maintain a rooftop sign will not be converted to a lease.[2] The test of whether the right

1. *See* Section 1.7, generally, in Chapter 1, "Demise," *supra*.

2. Bridge Hardware Co., Inc. v. Disosway & Fisher, Inc., 199 Misc. 359, 101 N.Y.S.2d 863 (Sup. Ct. N.Y. Cnty. 1950); *see also* Section 1.7, generally, in Chapter 1, *supra*.

will be recognized as a leasehold interest in the land, binding on successor owners, is the existence of an intent to deliver exclusive possession and control of a specifically defined premises to the grantee.[3]

A lease of an entire building impliedly includes use of the roof, even though not expressly permitted by the lease document.[4] In *Frequency Electronics, Inc. v. We're Associates Comp.*,[5] the tenant was required to obtain the landlord's prior written consent to make structural alterations. Without consent, the tenant undertook the installation of an exhaust and air conditioning system, including the location of blowers on the roof. The court held that the alteration, specifically including the roof installation, did not violate the lease provisions. The alterations were necessary to permit tenant to carry on its permitted use of the premises and could be removed at the end of the term without serious injury to the realty.

3. Pocher v. Hall, 50 Misc. 639, 98 N.Y.S. 754 (Sup. Ct. App. Tm. N.Y. Cnty. 1906).
4. Mammy's, Inc. & Pappy's, Inc. v. All Continent Corp., 106 N.Y.S.2d 635 (Sup. Ct. N.Y. Cnty. 1951).
5. 120 A.D. 2d 489, 501 N.Y.S.2d 693 (2d Dep't 1986).

CHAPTER 50

Fair Market Valuation on Renewals or Options

50.1 General Purpose

Leases are relatively long-term contracts, and if the term is long enough, fixed rent pricing at the outset may work an eventual market injustice on either of the parties, as the real estate industry goes through its cycle. In order to smooth out those bumps, landlords and tenants in recent years have agreed to what England's commercial property industry calls a "fair market rent review." This is a process that allows the tenant to elect to extend its tenancy at a price, initially suggested by the landlord to be "market" and, if challenged by tenant, submitted to adjustment by what is in effect binding arbitration. This adjustment to "fixed" or "base" rent, since it is an attempt to replicate what the tenant might find elsewhere in truly comparable space, is often accompanied by a re-setting of the base years for operating and real estate tax escalations.

For the landlord, there are substantial savings in the process, with no real "down time" during which the premises sit empty waiting for a new tenant; a reduced cost for brokerage (since computed as an extension, rather than a new lease) and no cost at all for tenant build-out contribution (which would be demanded by a new tenant). For the tenant, the disruption and costs of moving are avoided, as its familiar space is "marked to market" in terms of price, to the prevailing rate in the commercial space universe as at the date of renewal, taking into account all relevant factors.

50.2 Sample Clause

[Part of Renewal or Extension Term Article]

Section 50.01

(a) The Renewal Term shall be upon all of the terms and conditions set forth in this Lease, except that (i) the Fixed Rent shall be as determined pursuant to the further provisions of this Section 50.01; (ii) Tenant shall accept the Premises in its "as is" condition at the commencement of the Renewal Term, and Landlord shall not be required to perform any work, to pay any amount or to render any services to make the Premises ready for Tenant's use and occupancy or to provide any abatement of Fixed Rent or Additional Rent, in each case with respect to the Renewal Term; (iii) Tenant shall have no option to renew this Lease beyond the expiration of the Renewal Term; and (iv) the Base Tax Amount shall be the Taxes for the Tax Year ending during the first 12 months of the Renewal Term and the Base Operating Year shall be the Operating Year ending during the first 12 months of the Renewal Term.

(b) The annual Fixed Rent for the Premises for the Renewal Term shall be [Fair Market Rent] [the greater of (i) the Fair Market Rent or (ii) an amount (the "Annual Rent") equal to the aggregate of (A) the Fixed Rent payable by Tenant for the 12 month period ending on the last day of the initial Term, (B) the Tax Payment payable with respect to the Tax Year ending immediately before the commencement of the Renewal Term and (C) the Operating Payment payable with respect to the Operating Year ending immediately before the commencement of the Renewal Term (the greater of Fair Market Rent and Annual Rent is called the "Rental Value").] "Fair Market Rent" means the fixed annual rent that a willing lessee would pay and a willing lessor would accept for the Premises during the Renewal Term, each party acting prudently and under no compulsion to lease, and taking into account all relevant factors including the Base Tax Amount and the Base Operating Year.

(c) If Tenant timely exercises the Renewal Option, Landlord shall notify Tenant (the "Rent Notice") at least 120 days before the last day of the initial Term of Landlord's determination of the Fair Market Rent ("Landlord's Initial Determination"). Tenant shall notify Landlord ("Tenant's Notice"), within 20 days after Tenant's receipt of the Rent Notice, whether Tenant accepts or disputes Landlord's Initial Determination, and if Tenant disputes Landlord's Initial Determination, Tenant's Notice shall set forth Tenant's determination of the Fair Market Rent ("Tenant's Initial Determination"). If Tenant fails to give Tenant's Notice within such 20 day period, or if Tenant gives Tenant's Notice within such 20 day period but fails to set forth therein Tenant's Initial Determination, then Tenant shall be deemed to have accepted Landlord's Initial Determination.

(d) (i) If Tenant timely disputes Landlord's Initial Determination and Landlord and Tenant fail to agree as to the Fair Market Rent within 20 days after the giving of Tenant's Notice, then the Fair Market Rent shall be determined by arbitration in the City of New York, as set forth in this Section 50.01(d). Tenant shall initiate the arbitration process by giving notice to that effect to Landlord within 20 days after the giving of Tenant's Notice, which notice shall include the name and address of Tenant's designated arbitrator. If Tenant fails to give such notice within such 20 day period, then Tenant shall be deemed to have accepted Landlord's Initial Determination. Within 30 days after the designation of Tenant's arbitrator, Landlord shall give notice to Tenant of the name and address of Landlord's designated arbitrator. If Landlord shall fail timely to appoint an arbitrator, then Tenant may request the American Arbitration Association ("AAA") to appoint an arbitrator on Landlord's behalf. Such two arbitrators shall have 30 days to appoint a third arbitrator who shall be impartial. If such arbitrators fail to do so, then either Landlord or Tenant may request the AAA to appoint an arbitrator who shall be impartial within 30 days after such request and both parties shall be bound by any appointment so made within such 30 day period. If no such third arbitrator shall have been appointed within such 30 day period, either Landlord or Tenant may apply to the Supreme Court, New York County to make such appointment. The third arbitrator only shall subscribe and swear to an oath fairly and impartially to determine such dispute.

(ii) Within 7 days after the appointment of the third arbitrator, the three arbitrators will meet (the "Initial Meeting") and set a hearing date for the arbitration. The hearing shall not exceed two days and shall be scheduled to be held within 60 days after the meeting of the three arbitrators. At the Initial Meeting, Landlord and Tenant may each submit a revised Fair Market Rent determination (each, a "Final Determination"); provided, that Landlord's Final Determination may not be greater than Landlord's Initial Determination, and Tenant's Final Determination may not be lower than Tenant's Initial Determination. If either party shall fail so to submit a Final Determination, then Landlord's Initial Determination or Tenant's Initial Determination, as applicable, shall constitute such party's Final Determination.

(iii) There shall be no discovery in the arbitration. However, on reasonable notice to the other party, Tenant may inspect any portion of the Building relevant to its claims, and Landlord may inspect any portion of the space occupied by Tenant on the floors in issue. Thirty days prior to the scheduled hearing, the parties shall exchange opening written expert reports and opening written pre-hearing statements. Opening written pre-hearing statements shall not exceed 20 pages in length. Two weeks prior to the hearing, the parties may exchange rebuttal written expert reports and rebuttal written pre-hearing statements. Rebuttal written pre-hearing statements shall not exceed 10 pages in length. Ten days prior to the hearing, the parties shall exchange written witness lists, including a brief statement as to the subject matter to be covered in the witnesses' testimony. One week prior to the hearing, the parties shall exchange all documents which they intend to offer at the hearing. Other than rebuttal witnesses, only the witnesses listed on the witness lists shall be allowed to testify at the hearings. Closing arguments shall be heard immediately following conclusion of all testimony. The proceedings shall be recorded by stenographic means. Each party may present live witnesses and offer exhibits, and all witnesses shall be subject to cross-examination. The arbitrators shall conduct the two day hearing so as to provide each party with sufficient time to present its case, both on direct and on rebuttal, and permit each party appropriate time for cross examination; provided, that the arbitrators shall not extend the hearing beyond two days. Each party may, during its direct case, present evidence in support of its position and in opposition to the position of the opposing party.

(iv) The third arbitrator shall make a determination of the Fair Market Rent by selecting either the amount set forth in Landlord's Final Determination or the amount set forth in Tenant's Final Determination, whichever the third arbitrator determines is closest to Fair Market Rent for the Premises. The third arbitrator may not select any other amount as the Fair Market Rent. The fees and expenses of any arbitration pursuant to this Section 50.01(d) shall be borne by the parties equally, but each party shall bear the expense of its own arbitrator, attorneys and experts and the additional expenses of presenting its own proof. The arbitrators shall not have the power to add to, modify or change any of the provisions of this Lease. Each arbitrator shall be a licensed real estate broker having at least 10 years of experience in leasing of first class office buildings in Manhattan. After a determination has been made of the Fair Market Rent, the parties shall execute and deliver an instrument setting forth the Fair Market Rent, but the failure to so execute and deliver any such instrument shall not affect the determination of Fair Market Rent.

(e) If Tenant disputes Landlord's Initial Determination and if the final determination of Fair Market Rent shall not be made on or before the first day of the Renewal Term, then, pending such final determination, Tenant shall pay, as Fixed Rent for the Renewal Term, an amount equal to Landlord's Final Determination. If, based upon the final determination of the Fair Market Rent, the Fixed Rent payments made by Tenant for such portion of the Renewal Term were greater than the Fair Market Rent payable for the Renewal Term, Landlord shall credit the amount of such excess against future installments of Fixed Rent and/or Additional Rent payable by Tenant.

50.3 Landlord Concerns

If the landlord is prepared to make such a deal with a tenant, instead of guessing at a number a decade or more ahead, then the elements of a "fair" appraisal are relatively straightforward, and are recited earlier in the chapter. Additional considerations may be important, however. First, the landlord will have to decide whether the estimated or arbitrated fair market rent for the renewal term will be permitted to be less than the then-escalated rent at the end of the original or any stated previous renewal term. If this is to be allowed, then the bracketed language in the first sentence of Sample Clause 50.01(b) should be deleted. Alternatively, the landlord may want to put a floor on the new number, to be "in no event *less* than the aggregate of the Base Rent and Additional Rent payable in the month preceding the commencement of the Renewal Term." In such a case, if the tenant believes that the true fair market number is less than such aggregate figure, it will, well before the beginning of the renewal term, open further negotiations or choose to move. With respect to arbitrated fair market rent, the landlord should select an arbitration method in advance. In the sample clause, the parties agree to use "baseball" arbitration (aptly named after the arbitration method used by Major League Baseball to determine a player's salary when the team and player cannot reach agreement), whereby each party choses an arbitrator to present their fair market determination. Then, a third arbitrator must select either party's determination based on whichever such third arbitrator finds is closest to its determination of fair market value, and the third arbitrator cannot establish any other rental figure other than one of the two figures presented to it. Additionally, if arbitration does not conclude before the initial term expires, the landlord will want to stipulate that the tenant should pay rent at the landlord's fair market rent determination until the arbitration is complete so that the landlord is not short-changed pending the arbitration outcome.

The landlord may also wish to define further the concept of "comparable buildings," even identifying by address those nearby office buildings that the landlord deems (and to which the tenant must agree) are of the same class and amenity quality, though more modern practice is to direct the arbitrator to consider "all relevant factors."

Finally, as detailed in the sample clause (see Section 50.2, *supra*), the landlord is concerned to have a prompt and orderly process, where the lack of timely attention or cooperation by the tenant will not forestall a conclusion, or interrupt the rent stream.

50.4 Tenant Concerns

As observed earlier, a fair market rent review on a truly level playing field must effectively address all relevant factors. Perhaps the cardinal clause from the tenant's perspective is explicit language that the new number be calculated (depressed) to reflect what the landlord is not giving the tenant upon renewal (free rent, build-out allowance, etc.), which the landlord might otherwise be providing to another prospective tenant in the market at the commencement of the renewal term (and be increasing his market rental figure to amortize such costs over the projected term). Furthermore, the tenant will seek to direct the arbitrators to factor in this consideration when calculating the fair market rental number, though as noted earlier, modern-day practitioners tend to direct arbitrators to consider "all relevant factors" without specifying which ones apply and which ones do not.

The other important point from the tenant's perspective is to have the base years for escalation recalibrated to the year of renewal commencement. A new "fair market fixed rent," coupled with continuing historical base years for escalation, will not actually result in a fair market total number.

Finally, the aggressive tenant will want the fair market number to be specifically permitted to be less than the then-escalated rent, but the landlord will not invariably agree. It is more common for a landlord to concede a percentage discount off the finally agreed or arbitrated fair market rent number, as consideration for larger tenants staying on and removing uncertainty for landlord's rental future.

50.5 Standard Real Estate Board of New York Clause

The REBNY form simply does not address the question of fair market rent review, and so the entire set of provisions would need to be added by a rider if the parties had previously agreed to the concept.

50.6 Comments on Standard Real Estate Board of New York Clause

None. See Section 50.5, *supra.*

50.7 Litigation Issues

The court of appeals, in *Joseph Martin, Jr., Delicatessen, Inc. v. Schumacher,*[1] has ruled that a provision in a renewal option setting the renewal rent at an amount "to be agreed upon" was too uncertain to be enforceable. In *166 Mamaroneck Avenue Corp. v. 151 East Post Road Corp.,*[2] the state's highest court held that a renewal option in a lease providing for arbitration if the parties could not agree upon a rental for the renewal period was definite and enforceable notwithstanding that the option did not spell out the manner in which the rent was to calculated. The option provision, however, did establish a process for calculation and reflected the intention of the parties to be bound by the determination of an arbitrator. Although using the standard of "fair market value" for a renewal rent is not unenforceable for indefiniteness,[3] the use of that standard does not ensure that the issue of determining the renewal rent payable will not be litigated to the Court of Appeals.[4]

Having adopted a standard of fair market value for a renewal rental, the parties usually provide that, absent an agreement on the actual renewal rent, upon the exercise of the option, the determination should be made by an individual, such as an appraiser, who is an expert in determining value. In *Vitale v. Friedman,*[5] the defendant sought to vacate an appraisal and the appointment of a new neutral appraiser. Recognizing that "appraisers have broad discretion as to their methods and sources of information," the court held, since the defendants failed to demonstrate that the method of and factors considered by the appraiser fell outside the parameters of the appraisal as defined in the lease, "their disagreement with respect to the factors and various methods employed does not provide a basis for judicial review."[6] Absent proof of fraud, bias, or bad faith, the dissatisfied party will be unable to set aside what the parties agreed would be

1. 52 N.Y.2d 105, 436 N.Y.S.2d 247, 417 N.E.2d 541 (1981), *see also* Chapter 39, *supra*, entitled "Renewal Option."
2. 78 N.Y.2d 88, 571 N.Y.S.2d 686, 575 N.E.2d 104 (1991).
3. Northrup v. Hushard, 129 A.D.2d 1005, 514 N.Y.S.2d 304 (4th Dep't 1987).
4. Rice v. Ritz Assoc., 58 N.Y.2d 923, 460 N.Y.S.2d 510, 447 N.E.2d 58 (1983). *See also* N.Y. Overnight Partners, L.P. v. Gordon, 88 N.Y.2d 716, 649 N.Y.S.2d 928, 673 N.E.2d 123 (1996).
5. 245 A.D. 2d 14, 666 N.Y.S. 2d 403, Sup. Ct., A.D. 1st Dep't, 1997.
6. 666 N.Y.S.2d at 403.

binding and final determination of value by an appraisers;[7] nor can that party sue the appraiser for damages on the grounds that the appraiser's conclusion was incorrect.[8]

The appraiser must, however, arrive at a determination in accordance with the procedures set forth in the lease.[9] Thus the parties had better carefully consider those standards and procedures. In *Rice v. Ritz Assocs.*, a 1922 lease of vacant land was developed and contained long-term renewal options; the renewal rent was to be determined by a "fit and impartial person . . . considering [the premises] as a vacant piece or parcel of land as its full and fair worth at private sale free from encumbrances." In 1926 a building was completed on the site. The court stated that, in 1978, "it is to be noted at the outset that this standard eliminates virtually all the indicia of value of a piece of land usually considered in arriving at such a valuation . . . it is remembered that appraisers faced with the contract's unusual standard of evaluation can do little more than make an educated guess at what a naked piece of land at a certain location is worth."[10]

The court of appeals confronted a similar valuation provision in *New York Overnight Partner, L.P. v. Gordon.*[11] The renewal rental for the ground lease, where the Ritz Carlton Hotel in Manhattan stands, was to be the "appraised value of the land." The lease defined the land without the buildings and improvements thereon. This language was deemed to require the appraisers to take into account the best, most advantageous use of the land, as if vacant and unimproved, subject to existing zoning restrictions and contractual limitations. The zoning regulations at the time of the renewal would prohibit construction of the hotel, which was a prior, nonconforming use. The lessor argued that the land should be valued as permitting the use of the existing hotel, as the lease itself did not require that existing zoning and contractual restrictions be considered. Additionally, the lessor asserted that the "highest and best use" of the land was the maintenance of the existing hotel. The court rejected this argument as "nothing more than an attempt to enjoin appraisal of the land as raw and unimproved,"[12] as the "highest and best use" of the land was not the standard set forth in the lease.

A renewal clause requiring the rent to be determined by valuing the land as vacant and unimproved, free from all encumbrances and restrictions, requires consideration of the existing zoning, which dictates the use to which the land can be put. Zoning, as such, is not deemed a restriction, which is intended to mean a deed or private restriction on use.[13] Consideration free from existing structures means consideration free from the

---

7. 58 N.Y.2d 923, 460 N.Y.S.2d 510, 447 N.E.2d 58.

8. Perlbinder v. Jakubovitz, 239 A.D.2d 294, 658 N.Y.S.2d 267 (1st Dep't 1997).

9. Rice v. Ritz Assoc., 88 A.D.2d 513,450 N.Y.S.2d 7, *aff'd* 58 N.Y.2d 923, 460 N.Y.S.2d 510, 447 N.E.2d 58 (1983).

10. *Id.*, 450 N.Y.S.2d at 8.

11. 88 N.Y. 2d 716, 649 N.Y.S.2d 928, 673 N.E.2d 123 (1996).

12. 649 N.Y.S.2d at 930.

13. 201-203 Lexington Ave. Corp. v. 205/215 Lexington Ltd. P'ship, 224 A.D. 2d 183, 637 N.Y.S.2d 125 (1st Dep't 1996).

existing lease permitting such structure, even though that lease may be at below a current market rate, actually depressing the value.[14]

Fair market valuation for renewal terms is used in office leases. An office lease provided that the fair annual rental value would be determined by arbitration if the parties failed to reach an agreement. However, the renewal provision did not specify the date upon which the fair market value was to be determined, the date the option was exercised, or the date the renewal term was to commence. The option was exercised some two years prior to the commencement of the renewal term. The court held that it, and not the arbitrators, had the right to rule that the value would be determined as of the commencement date of the renewal term, and not the date of exercise of the option.[15] The arbitration clause only permitted the arbitrators to consider fair rental value, but the lease was silent as to the date that the value was to be determined. Since the agreement to arbitrate did not expressly and unequivocally encompass this issue, it had to be settled in court. The court noted that if arbitration was demanded prior to the renewal commencement date, "the arbitrators would certainly not have had to await the start of the new lease term but would have been warranted in proceeding to ascertain the anticipated fair rental value on the date the lease was to commence."[16] Notwithstanding the court's view of the scope of the arbitrators' authority, it is doubtful that the arbitrators could have anticipated the rapid inflation in commercial rental values which occurred in the early 1980s when the case was decided.

14. Olympia & York 2 Broadway Co. v. Produce Exch. Realty Tr., 93 A.D.2d 465, 462 N.Y.S.2d 456 (1st Dep't 1983).

15. 140 Broadway Co. v. Dewey, Ballantine, Bushby, Palmer & Wood, 96 A.D.2d 482, 465 N.Y.S.2d 193 (1st Dep't 1983).

16. 465 N.Y.S.2d at 195.

CHAPTER 51

Termination Option

51.1 General Purpose

The general purpose of the tenant's termination option is to provide the tenant with the flexibility to terminate the lease in the event of unforeseen circumstances that render continued use of the space economically unfeasible or otherwise undesirable. The tenant may have outgrown the space, downsized, or relocated its business. The termination option gives the tenant the certainty of knowing it can relieve itself of its lease obligations for a fixed dollar amount. From the landlord's perspective, the only reason for granting a tenant the right to terminate the lease prior to the agreed upon expiration date is to induce it to consummate the transaction. As with any option, the benefits only run one way—in favor of the option holder.

51.2 Sample Clause

51.01 Tenant shall have the one-time right (the "Termination Option") to terminate this Lease effective on the [_____] anniversary of the Rent Commencement Date (the "Termination Date"). Tenant may exercise the Termination Option on or before the date that is [____] months prior to the Termination Date (time being of the essence) only (a) by delivering to Landlord irrevocable notice of such exercise (the "Termination Notice") and (b) by delivering to Landlord the Termination Payment concurrently with the Termination Notice. If Tenant shall fail to timely to exercise the Termination Option, or shall fail to pay the Termination Payment together with the giving of the Termination Notice, Tenant shall conclusively be deemed to have waived Tenant's right to exercise the Termination Option and Tenant shall have no further rights under this Article.

51.02 "Termination Payment" means $[___________] [the sum of (i) the unamortized costs of any improvements to the Premises or otherwise made by Landlord for Tenant, (ii) the unamortized amount of the Work Allowance, (iii) the unamortized amount of brokerage commissions or fees, (iv) the unamortized legal costs incurred by Landlord attributable to the negotiation of this Lease and any documents related thereto, and (v) an amount equal to the Annual Rent for one-half of the Lease Year during which Tenant has terminated this Lease].

51.03 Anything in this Lease to the contrary notwithstanding, the provisions of this Article 51 granting to Tenant the Termination Option shall be null and void and of no force or effect if (i) *[insert tenant name]* is no longer the Tenant under this Lease or (ii) Tenant shall be in default under this Lease.

51.3 Landlord Concerns

Prior to granting a termination option to a tenant, several points must be considered, one of which is the effect of such a clause on the landlord's ability to finance the lease. Many lenders resist financing leases that grant a tenant the right to terminate. This resistance stems from the fear that upon the early termination of the lease the landlord will lose its rent stream, at least for a short period of time, thus impairing the security of the lender's loan. In addition to addressing the concerns raised by lenders, the landlord must determine the compensation to be paid by the tenant in the event the right to terminate is exercised prior to the stated expiration date. The amount of the early termination payment, and the date on which it is to be paid, must be negotiated by the landlord and the tenant at the time the option is granted. Factors that the landlord typically wants to include in the calculation of the early termination payment are (1) the unamortized costs of the tenant's improvements or tenant work allowance paid for by the landlord; (2) the unamortized amount of any brokerage fees or commissions; (3) a sum of money (usually a number of months' rent) to compensate the landlord for the down period during which attempts to re-let the premises are made; (4) any lease concessions, such as a free rent period or take-over lease costs, incurred by the landlord in leasing the premises to the tenant; and (5) legal fees and other consultants' fees incurred by the landlord in leasing the premises to the tenant (including those incurred during the negotiation of the lease and any other related documents). The landlord will want the early termination payment to be made at the same time that the tenant gives notice that it is exercising its option to terminate the lease. Payment at the time the option is exercised, rather than on the effective date of termination, helps ensure that the landlord will receive the early termination payment.

The landlord will want the tenant to provide it with a meaningful period between the date of the tenant's termination notice and the early termination date. The purpose of this notice period is to provide the landlord with sufficient time in which to re-let the space while still collecting rent from the tenant terminating its lease. Further, the landlord should require that upon termination of the lease, the tenant surrender the premises in the same condition as if the lease had expired on the original stated expiration date. Notwithstanding the tenant's surrender of the premises and termination of the lease, the landlord will want to obligate the tenant to pay all rent and other sums due under the lease, and to perform all of its obligations under the lease accruing prior to the early termination date.

The landlord will also want to limit the termination option to the tenant with whom it entered into the transaction (not its successors); although the landlord will usually permit the option to benefit permitted assignees under the lease (e.g., successors by merger or consolidation and controlled affiliates to whom the lease is assigned). Inasmuch as the termination option is a benefit to the tenant, the landlord should allow the exercise of this option only if the tenant is in good standing under the lease, that is, not in default.

51.4 Tenant Concerns

A right to terminate the lease prior to the stated expiration date is of considerable importance and is highly desirable by most tenants, especially in light of ever-changing economic conditions. Although assignment and subletting rights may be granted in the tenant's lease, a termination option is a more valuable tool to a tenant whose space needs have changed. If a tenant assigns or sublets, in most circumstances it will remain liable under the lease and, as such, will be relying on the credit of its assignee or subtenant. In addition, it is possible that despite the right to assign the lease or sublet the space, a tenant may, as a practical matter, be unable to do so, or may only be able to exercise the right at an unacceptable cost.

A tenant must negotiate the right to terminate its lease in order to be prepared for unforeseen circumstances that make it impractical for the tenant to continue to occupy and pay rent on the leased space. Such unforeseen events may include the tenant's inability to operate its business with sufficient profit to support the rented space, or the failure to properly project the amount of space resulting in more space than is required for tenant's needs. Additionally, the tenant may wish to quantify its costs if it ceases to operate its business. Anticipating the possibility of early termination of the lease at the negotiation stage, the tenant should attempt to fix the early termination payment at this stage so that it knows just what the costs will be to terminate the lease. Further, the tenant will want to give the landlord as little notice of termination as possible in order to preserve its flexibility in the event of a change in circumstances that would permit the tenant to continue to occupy the space.

51.5 Standard Real Estate Board of New York Clause

None.

51.6 Comments on Standard Real Estate Board of New York Clause

None.

51.7 Litigation Issues

Landlords often negotiate for early termination in the event of an intention to demolish the building where the leased premises is located. In *Jack LaLanne Biltmore Health*

Spa, Inc. v. Builtland Partners,[1] the lease had just such a provision. The 21-year lease could be canceled if the landlord entered into a bona fide arrangement to demolish the building. The building was the Biltmore Hotel and the tenant's space was located in the cellar and subcellar. The building was to be converted into an office building. In order to effect the renovation, the building was stripped down to its steel skeleton and two structural slabs, and other areas required to be preserved as landmarks. The court held that even though the building's steel shell remained, "for all practical purposes the Biltmore was demolished," as the exterior masonry, internal walls, floors, ceilings, elevators, fixtures, electrical and plumbing conduits were removed. A "common sense meaning of 'demolish' is not confined to razing the building."[2]

Lease provisions have been drafted that permit cancellation even if less than the entire building is to be demolished. In *North Shore Mart v. F.W. Woolworth Co.*,[3] the lease provided for the right to cancel if 50 percent of the ground floor area of the shopping center where the tenant's store is located was demolished. A clause of this nature should not go unchallenged by a tenant. Cancellation would not only mean terminating the lease of a store that might be able to operate during the renovation, but would also prevent the tenant from benefitting from the improvement of the shopping center.

A tenant should also negotiate a formula of compensation, based on the unamortized cost of its improvements, in the event the landlord exercises a demolition right of cancellation. However, care must be taken not only to obtain such a right but to carefully negotiate the language. In *Akron Meats, Inc. v. 1428 Kitchens, Inc.*,[4] the tenant was to be paid the unamortized portion of $100,000, provided the tenant was not then in default of the terms and conditions of the lease, and provided the tenant surrendered the premises broom clean, in good order and condition, except for ordinary wear and tear. The tenant in fact caused certain damage, which it did not repair when it removed its trade fixtures. The court held that the tenant failed to comply with the lease provisions and was therefore not entitled to the early cancellation payment. Note that the court did not consider the actual cost to repair the damage, but forfeited the entire payment. Also, the ultimate fate of the vacated premises is not clear from the opinion. It is interesting to speculate that if the building, in fact, was to be demolished or so substantially altered (such as in the *Jack LaLanne* case, *supra*), what would have been the damage to the landlord?

Tenants may also negotiate a right to cancel conditioned on future events making use of the premises less profitable, such as if the landlord is leasing space to a competing retail tenant;[5] the lessor fails to complete a "conversion" of a warehouse building

---

1. 99 A.D.2d 705, 471 N.Y.S.2d 854 (1st Dep't 1984).
2. 471 N.Y.S.2d at 855.
3. 124 A.D.2d 574, 507 N.Y.S.2d 718 (2d Dep't 1986) (denying summary judgment on the issue of whether the alteration plan in fact resulted in such degree of demolition).
4. 160 A.D.2d 242, 553 N.Y.S.2d 355 (1st Dep't 1990) (the lease provided for the right to cancel "on six months notice, in the event of the demolition, sale, or long term net lease of the building." 553 N.Y.S.2d at 355).
5. Binghamton Plaza, Inc. v. Fashion Bug #2470 of Binghamton Inc., 242 A.D.2d 822, 661 N.Y.S.2d 683 (3d Dep't 1997).

to office use;[6] or the tenant is unable to take occupancy because of the failure of an existing tenant to vacate the premises.[7] The parties may believe the conditions permitting cancellation are understood at the time of lease execution, but in fact they have failed to define the conditions sufficiently to avoid a trial. In *Pouch Terminal, Inc. v. Hapag-Lloyd (America), Inc.*,[8] the tenant could cancel the lease if the landlord had not "converted" 75 percent of the rentable space to non-warehouse commercial and office use. The warehouse use had in fact been discontinued, and a temporary certificate of occupancy permitting office use was obtained, but the space was neither rented to nor occupied by an office tenant when the lease was canceled. The court could not conclude as a matter of law that the "conversion" had or had not occurred.

A landlord or tenant exercising a cancellation right should carefully and strictly comply with the notice requirements. In *Siegel v. Kentucky Fried Chicken of Long Island, Inc.*,[9] the court held that a default notice signed by an attorney, other than the landlord or attorney named in the lease, was insufficient and could be ignored by the tenant. However, in *Prime Realty Holdings Co. v. Alpine Group, Inc.*,[10] the court found that it was clear from the record "that the defendant's attorney was authorized to act as its agent in matters concerning the leased premises."

---

6. Pouch Terminal, Inc. v. Hapag-Lloyd (America), Inc., 172 A.D.2d 735, 569 N.Y.S.2d 122 (2d Dep't 1991).

7. 67 Wall St. Co. v. Franklin Nat'l Bank, 37 N.Y.2d 245, 371 N.Y.S.2d 915, 333 N.E.2d 184 (1975).

8. Pouch Terminal, Inc. v. Hapag-Lloyd (America), Inc., 172 A.D.2d 735, 569 N.Y.S.2d 122 (2d Dep't 1991).

9. 67 N.Y.2d 792, 501 N.Y.S.2d 317, 492 N.E.2d 390 (1986).

10. 225 A.D.2d 533, 638 N.Y.S.2d 746 (2d Dep't 1996) (noting that cancellation fee also accompanied the notice establishing attorney's authority and compliance with lease requirements).

CHAPTER 52

Expansion Option

52.1 General Purpose

An expansion option will be included in leases at the request of a tenant where future expansion is contemplated, but not definitively determined, by a tenant at the time of lease execution. This concept provides tenant preferential rights to lease certain agreed upon space(s) in a building.

Throughout a portion of the lease term, which will be agreed upon and set forth in the lease, tenant will have the option to lease certain additional space in the building (the "expansion space"). The expansion space is typically a specific floor(s) or portion(s) thereof of identified in the lease, but occasionally may be to be determined space that is typically (1) adjacent space on the same floor as the then current tenant premises, (2) full floors that are directly above or below the then-current tenant premises, and/or (3) in the same elevator banks as the then-current tenant premises, and, in either case, such space will always be agreed upon and set forth in the lease prior to execution. Occasionally, tenant will have the option to take all or a certain agreed upon portion of such space.

The lease terms with respect to the expansion space will be the same as the then-current space for such tenant except for modifications to the economic obligations (i.e., base and additional rental obligations). There are two different approaches in determining the base rent for the expansion space. The rental amount will either (1) be based on the fair market rental value for the space, which such fair market rental value will be determined on relevant market factors (i.e., tenant allowance, free rent, landlord work, etc.), or (2) the greater of (a) said fair market rental value for the space and (b) the per rentable square foot rental that is in effect for the rest of tenant's premises immediately prior to the date the expansion space becomes part of the premises.

Occasionally, most often in new construction leases where there will be a significant period of time between signing the lease and the commencement of the lease term, a tenant may also request a pre-commencement expansion option, which works similarly to the expansion option just described, except that (1) a tenant usually must exercise this option prior to the occurrence of the commencement date, and (2) the rental amount will usually be the same as the rental amount for the rest of the premises initially lease by tenant. This option provides the tenant some extra flexibility, as it may be difficult to determine space needs so far in advance of when the lease term starts.

Even without an expansion option provision, it will be typical for a landlord to go to a tenant leasing space on a floor with a vacancy and inquire about such tenant's interest in leasing the vacant space.

52.2 Sample Clause

52.01 Expansion Option. (a) Provided that on the date Tenant exercises the Expansion Option and on the ES Inclusion Date (i) this Lease shall not have been terminated, (ii) Tenant shall not be in default under this Lease and (iii) Tenant shall occupy the entire Premises, Tenant shall have the option (the "Expansion Option") to lease the space on the ___ floor of the Building substantially as shown hatched on the floor plan annexed as Exhibit (the "Expansion Space"). Landlord and Tenant confirm that the Expansion Space is conclusively deemed to contain _____ rentable square feet. The Expansion Option shall be exercisable by Tenant giving Landlord notice thereof (the "Expansion Notice") on or before ______ (time being of the essence). If Tenant timely gives the Expansion Notice, then on the ES Inclusion Date, the Expansion Space shall become part of the Premises, upon all of the terms and conditions set forth in this Lease, except that:

(i) Fixed Rent shall be increased by [the ES Fair Market Rent] [the greater of (A) the ES Fair Market Rent and (B) an amount (the "ES Minimum Rent") equal to the product of (x) the annual Fixed Rent on a per rentable square foot basis applicable to the remainder of the Premises immediately prior to the ES Inclusion Date, and (y) ___________ **[THE RENTABLE SQUARE FOOTAGE OF THE EXPANSION SPACE]** (the greater of the amounts under clauses (A) and (B) is called the "ES Rental Value")];

(ii) Tenant's Share shall be increased by ___%;

[(iii) Electric inclusion - increase in charge per square foot]; and

(iv) Landlord shall not be required to perform Landlord's Work or any other work, to pay the Work Allowance or any other amount, or to render any services to make the Building or the Expansion Space ready for Tenant's use or occupancy or to provide any abatement of Fixed Rent or Additional Rent, and Tenant shall accept the Expansion Space in its "as is" condition on the ES Inclusion Date.

(b) The "ES Inclusion Date" shall be __________ (the "Anticipated ES Inclusion Date"); *provided,* that if on the Anticipated ES Inclusion Date there is a holdover tenancy in all or any part of the Expansion Space, then the ES Inclusion Date shall be the date that Landlord delivers vacant possession of the Expansion Space to Tenant. Landlord shall use reasonable efforts to deliver possession of the Expansion Space to Tenant on or before the Anticipated ES Inclusion Date, including, to the extent advisable in Landlord's business judgment, the institution and prosecution of holdover or other appropriate proceedings against any occupant of the Expansion Space. If Landlord is unable to deliver possession of the Expansion Space to Tenant for any reason on or before the Anticipated ES Inclusion Date, Landlord shall have no liability to Tenant therefor and this Lease shall not in any way be impaired. This Section 1.0__(b) constitutes "an express provision to the contrary" within the meaning of said Section 223(a) of the RPL and any other law of like import now or hereafter in effect.

(c) "ES Fair Market Rent" means the fixed annual rent that a willing lessee would pay and a willing lessor would accept for the Expansion Space, each party acting prudently and under no compulsion to lease, and taking into account all relevant factors. If Tenant timely exercises the Expansion Option, then on a date (the "ES Exchange Date") mutually agreed by Landlord and Tenant that is not more than 120 days nor less than 90 days before the Anticipated ES Inclusion Date (and in the absence of such agreement, then on the 90th day before the Anticipated ES Inclusion Date), Landlord and Tenant shall meet and simultaneously exchange notices setting forth their respective determinations of ES Fair Market Rent (each, an "Initial ES Determination"). [In no event shall Tenant's Initial ES Determination be less than the ES Minimum Rent.] After the ES Exchange Date, Landlord and Tenant shall negotiate in good faith to agree on the ES Fair Market Rent. If Landlord and Tenant fail to agree as to the ES Fair Market Rent within 30 days after the Exchange Date, then the ES Fair Market Rent shall be determined **[in the same manner as disputes regarding Fair Market Rent pursuant to Section 9.02(d); *provided*, that all references in Section 9.02(d) to "Fair Market Rent" shall be deemed to refer to "ES Fair Market Rent," all reference in Section 9.02(d) to "Initial Determination" shall be deemed to refer to "Initial ES Determination" and all references in Section 9.02(d) to the "Exchange Date" shall be deemed to refer to the "ES Exchange Date"] [IF NO FAIR MARKET RENEWAL, ADD ARBITRATION MECHANICS]**.

(d) If the final determination of the ES Fair Market Rent shall not be made on or before the ES Inclusion Date, then, pending such final determination, Tenant shall pay, as Fixed Rent for the Expansion Space, an amount equal to Landlord's ES Determination. If, based upon the final determination of ES Fair Market Rent, the Fixed Rent payments made by Tenant for the Expansion Space were greater than the ES [Fair Market Rent] [Rental Value], Landlord shall credit the amount of such excess against future installments of Fixed Rent and/or Additional Rent payable by Tenant.

(e) Anything in this Lease to the contrary notwithstanding, if the Expansion Space becomes vacant or, in Landlord's reasonable judgment, is likely to become vacant, before the Anticipated ES Inclusion Date, Landlord may notify Tenant of the date of anticipated availability thereof (which shall thereafter be deemed to be the Anticipated ES Inclusion Date for proposes of this

Section 1.0__) and, upon the giving of such notice to Tenant, Tenant shall have the right, to be exercised by notice to Landlord given within 20 days (time being of the essence) after receipt of Landlord's notice, to elect to lease the Expansion Space. If Tenant elects to lease the Expansion Space within such 20-day period, the Expansion Space shall become part of the Premises on the ES Inclusion Date upon the terms and conditions set forth in this Section 1.0__. If Tenant elects not to lease the Expansion Space or fails to deliver Tenant's notice of election within such 20 day period, Tenant shall be deemed to have irrevocably waived its right to lease the Expansion Space, and the Expansion Option shall be null and void and of no further force or effect.

(f) Promptly after the occurrence of the ES Inclusion Date, Landlord and Tenant shall confirm the occurrence thereof and the inclusion of the Expansion Space in the Premises by executing an instrument reasonably satisfactory to Landlord and Tenant; *provided*, that failure by Landlord or Tenant to execute such instrument shall not affect the inclusion of the Expansion Space in the Premises in accordance with this Section 1.0__.

[(g) Anything in this Lease to the contrary notwithstanding, the provisions of this Section 1.0__ granting to Tenant the Expansion Option shall be null and void and of no force or effect if (i) [INSERT NAME OF ORIGINALLY NAMED TENANT] __________ is no longer the Tenant under this Lease, (ii) __________ at any time fails to occupy at least __________ rentable square feet in the Premises or (iii) __________ shall at any time be in default under this Lease beyond any applicable period of grace.]

52.3 Landlord Concerns

As with any expansion rights that a tenant may have set forth in a lease, a landlord is ultimately concerned with having full autonomy to lease and control their investments, while not being burdened by having to wait for a tenant to decide if it wants to lease a space prior to going to the open market. Consequently, a landlord will want to minimize the circumstances in which a tenant will have the right to lease such space. To accomplish this goal, a landlord will, among other things, (1) limit the time frame during the term of a lease that tenant may elect to lease the space (i.e., any time during the term until a specified outside date or only within a particular time span specified in the lease), (2) limit the space that tenant has the option to lease, (3) make such expansion rights personal to the tenant initially named under the lease, and/or (4) require a tenant to satisfy a certain occupancy threshold in order to exercise such rights.

A landlord will establish the terms (other than rental obligations) at the execution of the lease for the expansion space so there is no dispute as to when tenant's right to lease the expansion space applies and when it expires. A landlord will most likely want the base rent to be the greater of the fair market value and the per rentable square foot rental that is then in effect for the rest of tenant's premises; however, it is more common that the rental of the expansion space will be at fair market value.

52.4 Tenant Concerns

A tenant will focus on making sure there are few limitations on the circumstances in which a tenant may elect to lease the expansion space. This includes, among other things, (1) extending the outside date for exercising tenant's option or expanding the time frame during which tenant may elect to lease the expansion space, (2) minimizing the amount of prior notice tenant must give in order to exercise its option to lease the space, (3) the right not being personal to the tenant initially named under the lease, and/or (4) reducing the occupancy threshold.

A tenant will also try to incentivize landlord to ensure that, if tenant elects to lease the expansion space, it will be delivered to tenant by a certain date by, among other things, having landlord agree that if the expansion space is not delivered by a specified outside date (1) landlord will pay to tenant all or a portion of any holdover rent (to the extent in excess of base rent that would be payable by tenant) received by landlord from a tenant who is holding over in the expansion space and delaying its delivery to tenant; (2) landlord will exercise any legal remedies available to it against a tenant who is holding over in the expansion space and delaying its delivery to tenant, or permit tenant to exercise such remedies in landlord's name; and/or (3) tenant will have the option to cancel tenant's election to lease the expansion space.

The expansion option is a right, not an obligation, so there is no downside for a tenant to include same in a lease. If a tenant needs to expand and the conditions for the expansion option are not satisfied, or tenant has already elected to lease the expansion space and now needs additional space, then a tenant must go to the landlord outside of the confines of the expansion option provision and the lease in order to expand their footprint in the building.

Even if a tenant does not intend to exercise the expansion option, a tenant may use such right to leverage other asks of a landlord, since a tenant could hold up a landlord from leasing the space to others until the tenant waives its rights to the space.

52.5 Standard Real Estate Board of New York Clause

None.

52.6 Comments on Standard Real Estate Board of New York Clause

None.

52.7 Litigation Issues

Litigations involving expansion options highlight the importance of avoiding ambiguities in such provisions. In each of the following cases, the court found that the provision was ambiguous, leading to further (potentially costly) litigation.

In *Goldsmith v. Ellenberg*,[1] the court considered an option in a lease that the restaurant tenant could exercise by "commenc[ing] renovation . . . for the purpose of extending the [dining area], from the now existing building line thereof to the property line." The plaintiff argued that the restaurant was required to extend the dining area "*all the way* to the property line" in order to exercise the option, while the restaurant contended that *any* extension into the designated space was a valid exercise. The court found that the extension option was ambiguous, and ordered further proceedings.

In *Isogon Corp. v. Fours on Seventh LLC*,[2] the bankruptcy court (applying New York law) found that the expansion option was ambiguous in two respects, and that a hearing was necessary to interpret the provision. *First*, the court found that the lease's definition of the expansion space in a hybrid ROFO/option provision—"at least one-half (1/2) of a full floor"—was ambiguous.[3] While the building was generally divided into north and south "halves," the north "half" was in fact only 48.05 percent of the floor space. *Second*, the court found that condition triggering the option—"should any vacant space become available"—was ambiguous because the lease provision failed to account for holdover tenants or otherwise define "vacant."

Additionally, several cases in New York have addressed the impact of the parties' course of conduct on an expansion option.

In *Kenyon & Kenyon v. Logany, LLC*,[4] the First Department affirmed the lower court's finding that the tenant had effectively exercised its option, despite never providing written notice as required by the lease and despite the presence of a non-waiver clause in the lease.[5] As the court explained, the defendant landlord's "failure to insist on such [written] notice for nearly 10 months . . . while acting as if it had accepted the oral exercise of the option . . . constituted a waiver of any right to insist on written notice."

In *Padded Accessories*,[6] the tenant, who leased two-thirds of a building, exercised its option to obtain the balance of the premises in accordance with the terms of the lease, by sending notice via registered letter. Subsequently, the tenant failed to occupy, demand possession of, or offer any rent for, the expansion space for at least 19 months from the date the tenant claimed to have exercised the option. Only after the landlord demanded that the tenant cease using outdoor common space for storage did the tenant seek to enforce its rights under the option. The court found that "having failed to exercise its right to possession over so long a period and having failed over the same period to perform its obligation to tender the rent specified in the option . . . the plaintiff may not now have specific performance" of the expansion option.

---

1. Goldsmith v. Ellenberg, 2011 N.Y. Misc. LEXIS 7164 (Sup. Ct. N.Y. Cnty. 2011).
2. Isogon Corp. v. Fours on Seventh LLC, 2000 Bankr. LEXIS 1648 (S.D.N.Y. 2002).
3. *See* Chapter 53 for more information on right of first offer (ROFO) provisions.
4. Kenyon & Kenyon v. Logany, LLC, 33 A.D.3d 538, 823 N.Y.S.2d 72 (1st Dep't 2006).
5. The *Logany* court followed *Dice v. Inwood Hills Condo.*, 237 A.D.2d 403, 655 N.Y.S.2d 562 (1st Dep't 1997) ("[T]he existence of a nonwaiver clause does not in itself preclude waiver of a contract clause.").
6. Padded Accessories Corp. v. Five Herriot St. Corp., 16 Misc. 2d 1060, 184 N.Y.S.2d 244 (Sup. Ct. Westchester Cnty. 1959).

Finally, in *2350 Fifth Ave. LLC v. 2350 Fifth Ave. Corp.*,[7] the court relied on "the course of conduct of the parties" to determine the tenant's rights with respect to permissible alterations to the expansion space. Prior to exercising the expansion option, plaintiff tenant had made substantial renovations to the original space without seeking consent, and without any objection, from the defendant landlord, despite restrictions on tenant's alteration rights in the lease. The court found that because "plaintiff performed alterations [to the original space] that could properly be deemed structural . . . without seeking or obtaining the [landlord's] consent," the landlord could not object to "similar alterations" to the expansion space.

7. 2350 Fifth Ave. LLC v. 2350 Fifth Ave. Corp., 22 Misc. 3d 1120(A), 880 N.Y.S.2d 876 (Sup. Ct. N.Y. Cnty. 2009).

CHAPTER 53

Right of First Offer

53.1 General Purpose

A "right of first offer" (ROFO) may be negotiated into leases by tenants that desire the option, but not the requirement, to expand their premises in the future by requiring the landlord to first offer space that is or will become available for leasing to the tenant before that landlord can lease it to a different user. Landlords generally resist ROFOs because they encumber the landlord's ability to freely fill building vacancies while affording the landlord no certainty that the tenant possessing the ROFO will actually exercise it. Therefore, landlords typically grant ROFOs only to large tenants or those with negotiating leverage.

There are generally two different approaches to determining the rent for space that is subject to a tenant's ROFO: either (1) the landlord will unilaterally set forth a proposed rent in its notice to the tenant that the ROFO space is becoming available, or (2) the lease will provide that the ROFO space rent will be based on the fair market rental value for the ROFO space. In the latter case, the fair market rental value is typically determined by arbitration should the landlord and the tenant fail to mutually agree on terms.

53.2 Sample Clause

53.01 Offer Space Option.

(a) As used herein:

"Available" means, as to any space, that such space is vacant and free of any present or future possessory right now or hereafter existing in favor of any third party; provided, that any space that is vacant on the date of this Lease shall not be deemed Available unless and until such space is first leased to another tenant and then again becomes Available. Anything to the contrary contained herein notwithstanding, Tenant's right of first offer pursuant to this Section 1. is subordinate to (x) any right of offer, right of first refusal, expansion right or similar right or option in favor of any third party existing as of the date of this Lease and (y) Landlord's right to renew or extend the term of any lease to another tenant, whether or not pursuant to an option or right set forth in such other tenant's lease.

"Offer Period" means the period commencing on the Commencement Date to and including the date that is 3 years prior to the Expiration Date.

"Offer Space" means [the space on the ___ floor of the Building substantially as shown hatched on the floor plan annexed as Exhibit. Landlord and Tenant confirm that the Offer Space is conclusively deemed to contain ___ rentable square feet] [any Available space on the ___ floor of the Building].

(b) Provided (i) this Lease shall not have been terminated, (ii) Tenant shall not be in default under this Lease, and (iii) Tenant shall occupy the entire Premises, if at any time during the Offer Period the Offer Space either becomes, or Landlord reasonably anticipates that within the next 12 months (but not later than the last day of the Offer Period) the Offer Space will become, Available, Landlord shall give to Tenant notice (an "Offer Notice") thereof, specifying (A) the fixed annual rental ("Offer Rental") which Landlord is then considering for the lease of the Offer Space, (B) the date or estimated date that the Offer Space has or shall become Available and (C) such other matters as Landlord may deem appropriate for such Offer Notice **[IF APPLICABLE, SPECIFY RENTABLE SQUARE FOOTAGE]. [OR USE THE FOLLOWING IF FMV RENT IS PREFERRED]**

Provided (i) this Lease shall not have been terminated, (ii) Tenant shall not be in default under this Lease, and (iii) Tenant shall occupy the entire Premises, if at any time during the Offer Period the Offer Space either becomes, or Landlord reasonably anticipates that within the next 12 months (but not later than the last day of the Offer Period) the Offer Space will become, Available, Landlord shall give to Tenant notice (an "Offer Notice") thereof, specifying (A) Landlord's determination of the Fair Offer Rent for such Offer Space, (B) the date or estimated date that the Offer Space has or shall become Available and (C) such other matters as Landlord may deem appropriate for such Offer Notice ***[IF APPLICABLE, SPECIFY RENTABLE SQUARE FOOTAGE].*** *"Fair Offer Rent" means the fixed annual rent that a willing lessee would pay and a willing lessor would accept for the Offer Space, each party acting prudently and under no compulsion to lease, and taking into account all relevant factors.*

(c) Provided that on the date that Tenant exercises the Offer Space Option and on the Offer Space Inclusion Date (i) this Lease shall not have been terminated, (ii) Tenant shall not be in default under this Lease, and (iii) Tenant shall occupy the entire Premises, Tenant shall have the option (the "Offer Space Option"), exercisable by notice (an "Acceptance Notice") given to Landlord on or before the date that is 30 days after the giving of the Offer Notice (time being of the essence) to include the Offer Space in the Premises. **[ADD IF USING FMV:** *Tenant shall notify Landlord in the Acceptance Notice whether Tenant accepts or disputes Landlord's determination of the Fair Offer Rent,* *and if Tenant disputes Landlord's determination of the Fair Offer Rent, the Acceptance Notice shall set forth Tenant's determination thereof. If Tenant fails timely to object to Landlord's determination in the Acceptance Notice and to set forth Tenant's determination, then Tenant shall be deemed to have accepted Landlord's determination.]*

(d) If Tenant timely delivers the Acceptance Notice, then, on the date on which Landlord delivers vacant possession of the Offer Space to Tenant (the "Offer Space Inclusion Date"), the Offer Space shall become part of the Premises, upon all of the terms and conditions set forth in this Lease, except (i) Fixed Rent shall be increased by the Offer Rental [or Fair Offer Rental], (ii) Tenant's Tax Share shall be increased by ___% and Tenant's Operating Share shall be increased by ___%, (iii) **[ELECTRICITY—INCREASE IN CHARGE PER SQUARE FOOT]**, (iv) Landlord shall not be required to perform Landlord's Work or any other work, to pay Landlord's Contribution or any other amount, or to render any services to make the Building or the Offer Space ready for Tenant's use or occupancy or to provide any abatement of Fixed Rent or Additional Rent, and Tenant shall accept the Offer Space in its "as is" condition on the Offer Space Inclusion Date and (v) as may be otherwise set forth in the Offer Notice.

[ADD IF USING FMV: *If in the Acceptance Notice Tenant disputes Landlord's determination of Fair Offer Rent, and Landlord and Tenant fail to agree as to the amount thereof within 20 days after the giving of the Acceptance Notice, then the dispute shall be resolved by arbitration* ***[in the same manner as disputes regarding Fair Market Rent pursuant to Section [reference the FMV renewal section] provided, that all references in said Section [___] to "Fair Market Rent" shall be deemed to refer to "Fair Offer Rent."] [If no fair market renewal, add arbitration mechanics].*** *If the dispute shall not have been resolved on or before the Offer Space Inclusion Date, then pending such resolution, Tenant shall pay as annual fixed rent for the Offer Space the Fair Offer Rent as determined by Landlord. Within 20 days after the final determination of Fair Offer Rent, an adjustment, if any, required to correct the amounts previously paid on account thereof shall be made by the appropriate party.]*

(e) If Landlord is unable to deliver possession of the Offer Space to Tenant for any reason on or before the date on which Landlord anticipates that the Offer Space shall be Available as set forth in the Offer Notice, the Offer Space Inclusion Date shall be the date on which Landlord is able to so deliver possession and Landlord shall have no liability to Tenant therefor and this Lease shall not in any way be impaired. This Section 1. (e) constitutes "an express provision to the contrary" within the meaning of Section 223(a) of the New York Real Property Law and any other law of like import now or hereafter in effect.

(f) If Tenant fails timely to give an Acceptance Notice, then (i) Landlord may enter into one or more leases of the Offer Space with third parties on such terms and conditions as Landlord shall determine, the Offer Space Option shall be null and void and of no further force and effect and Landlord shall have no further obligation to offer the Offer Space to Tenant, and (ii) Tenant shall, upon demand by Landlord, execute an instrument confirming Tenant's waiver of, and extinguishing, the Offer Space Option, but the failure by Tenant to execute any such instrument shall not affect the provisions of clause (i) above.

(g) Promptly after the occurrence of the Offer Space Inclusion Date, Landlord and Tenant shall confirm the occurrence thereof and the inclusion of the Offer Space in the Premises by executing an instrument reasonably satisfactory to Landlord and Tenant; provided, that failure by Landlord or Tenant to execute such instrument shall not affect the inclusion of the Offer Space in the Premises in accordance with this Section 1.

[(h) Anything in this Lease to the contrary notwithstanding, the provisions of this Section 1. granting to Tenant the Offer Space Option shall be null and void and of no force or effect if (i) __________ is no longer the Tenant under this Lease, (ii) __________ at any time fails to occupy at least __________ rentable square feet in the Premises or (iii) __________ shall at any time be in default under this Lease beyond any applicable period of grace.]

53.3 Landlord Concerns

As with any expansion rights that a tenant may have set forth in a lease, a landlord is ultimately concerned with having full autonomy to lease and control their investments, while not being burdened with the obligation to offer space to a specific tenant or tenants prior to marketing the space on the open market. Consequently, a landlord will want to minimize the circumstances in which they must first offer such space to a tenant prior to marketing the space to other tenants. To accomplish this goal, a landlord will, among other things, seek to (1) limit the time frame during the term of a lease that landlord must offer the space to the tenant (e.g., only up to a certain amount of time prior to the expiration of the lease term, which condition enables the landlord to freely enter into a longer term and more lucrative lease for the applicable space), (2) limit the portion(s) of the building that must be offered to a tenant, (3) make the ROFO personal to the named tenant under the lease, (4) require a tenant to satisfy a certain occupancy threshold in order to exercise such rights (e.g., the tenant must occupy at least 75 percent of its leased premises in order to avail itself of the ROFO), (5) limit the amount of times a landlord is required to offer such space to tenant (e.g., either (x) only once during the agreed upon period and/or (y) only after a space that is vacant as of the date of the lease is first leased to another tenant), (6) subordinate such tenants' rights to any other ROFO or expansion rights for other tenants in the building that the landlord has previously granted or thereafter may wish to grant, and/or (7) subordinate such tenants' rights to landlord's ability to negotiate an extension of any then-existing lease for the

ROFO space. A landlord will establish the terms (other than rental obligations) at the execution of the lease for the offer space so there is no dispute when the space must be offered to a tenant.

53.4 Tenant Concerns

A tenant will focus on making sure there are few limitations on the circumstances that landlord must offer the ROFO space to tenant and that the tenant's ROFO is superior to the rights of other existing and future tenants of the building. This includes, among other things, (1) requiring a landlord to offer the space without any limitation on the number of instances the space must be offered or the time frame during the term the space must be offered, (2) the right not being personal to the tenant named under the lease, and/or (3) reducing the occupancy test threshold.

The ROFO is a right, and not an obligation, so there is no downside for a tenant to seek to include a ROFO in a lease.

A tenant can simply elect not to exercise its ROFO, in which case the landlord will be free to lease that space to any other party. However, if the terms of the ROFO contemplate the landlord proposing the rental amount to the tenant, then in order to "keep the landlord honest" and afford the tenant the intended benefit of a fair first opportunity to lease the applicable space on terms on which landlord would indeed transact, the tenant should require the landlord to re-offer the space to the tenant on the same terms that the landlord offered the space to another party (after the tenant initially waived its ROFO), if those terms offered to another party were materially more tenant-favorable. In doing so, the landlord would be prohibited from proposing an artificially higher rent to the tenant and, after the tenant waives its ROFO, subsequently leasing the space to another party at a materially lower rent than offered to the tenant, without again giving the tenant an opportunity to lease the space on those offered terms. Landlords and tenants often negotiate what "material" means in comparing the rent and other terms offered to the tenant and to another party, with tenants seeking to define "materiality" as a very low percentage change in rental offer (e.g., 2 to 5 percent). Landlords usually do require some "cushion" to lower their rent proposal in order to transact with third parties once the tenant waives its opportunity to lease the applicable space.

Tenants should also seek to negotiate a time period (e.g., 180 days to a year) after which, if the tenant has waived its ROFO and the landlord did not subsequently lease that space to another party, the landlord must again re-offer the space to the tenant before the landlord can offer it to others. After all, the reasons for the tenant's waiver of a ROFO on a particular date may no longer apply after the passage of time, whether, for example, because the tenant's space needs or market economics have changed.

53.5 Standard Real Estate Board of New York Clause

None.

53.6 Comments on Standard Real Estate Board of New York Clause

None.

53.7 Litigation Issues

ROFOs are a creature of contract and their applicability and exercise depend on the specific language of the provision in question. As such, while various cases have considered ROFOs, it is difficult to distill general principles concerning how courts will interpret these provisions.

In *Vanlex Stores, Inc. v. BFP 300 Madison II, LLC*,[1] the lease contained a provision that, in the event the landlord chose to demolish the building, the lease would terminate and the tenant had a ROFO to lease space in the new building once it was built. According to the ROFO provision, in such event, the landlord was required to advise tenant of the terms and conditions upon which it was willing to lease space in the new building, and tenant would have "the option . . . to lease such . . . space . . . upon the terms . . . set forth in such offer." After the landlord demolished the existing building and built a new one, the landlord extended tenant an offer to lease space in the new building. However, the offered lease contained a use restriction prohibiting tenant from operating the same business that it had previously operated in the demolished building. The court found that the ROFO language—"is willing"—granted the landlord "discretion . . . to make an offer to [tenant] with whatever terms and conditions it is willing to provide at the time the offer is made." Thus, landlord's unilaterally imposed use restriction was permissible.

In *John Stuart, Inc. v. Diriro, Inc.*,[2] the tenant was granted a first option to lease contiguous space when and if the space "becomes available." The neighboring tenant assigned its lease to a third party after notifying the landlord of its intent to do so, and the tenant with the option sued the landlord. The court held that he ROFO language—"becomes available"—restricted the applicability of the clause to "when and if the space came under the landlord's control"; that is, when and if the neighbor surrendered the leased premises lease to the landlord, and did not apply if the neighbor assigned the lease.

In *Stellar Sutton LLC v. Dushey*,[3] the lease contained a clause titled "Right of First Offer," which provided that "upon the initial vacancy of any Terraced Units . . . , Landlord shall first offer by written notice [to the tenants] the opportunity to lease any such Terraced Units." In a suit concerning whether the ROFO provision was triggered, the landlord argued that it had not breached the provision because, while terraced units

---

1. Vanlex Stores, Inc. v. BFP 300 Madison II, LLC, 2008 N.Y. Misc. LEXIS 8190 (Sup. Ct. N.Y. Cnty. 2008), *aff'd*, Vanlex Stores, Inc. v. BFP 300 Madison II, LLC, 66 A.D.3d 580, 887 N.Y.S.2d 576 (1st Dep't 2009).

2. John Stuart, Inc. v. Diriro, Inc., 66 A.D.2d 682, 411 N.Y.S.2d 30 (1st Dep't 1978).

3. Stellar Sutton LLC v. Dushey, Judgment, Dkt. No. 54, Index No. 103215/2008 (Sup. Ct. Mar. 3, 2009) (unpublished).

were vacant, the landlord had not yet offered the space to a new prospective tenant. The court disagreed, holding that the language required the landlord to offer the space to the tenants "upon the initial vacancy," not before offering to lease the unit to a third party.

In *Amco Plastic Materials, Inc. v. Slone*,[4] the court also considered when a ROFO provision required the landlord to offer the space to the tenant. In that case, the lease provided that after a specific date, the tenant would have "the first option to rent all or part of the remaining space." During the period defined by this "first option" provision, a space became available and the tenant sued for specific performance. The appellate court found that the "key word 'first' preceding the word 'option'" granted "an option conditioned on the defendant's willingness to let the space in the first instance, or if the premises were sought by another, a first right to match a bona fide offer."

As a final note, the landlord in *Stellar Sutton*, *supra*, also argued that the ROFO provisions were invalid under the Rule Against Perpetuities (RAP).[5] While the court did not find this particular ROFO provision to be in violation of the RAP, parties should be mindful of RAP considerations when drafting a ROFO.

4. Amco Plastic Materials, Inc. v. Slone, 5 A.D.2d 817, 170 N.Y.S.2d 618 (1st Dep't 1958).
5. E.P.T.L. § 9-1.1(b).

CHAPTER 54

Leasehold Condominium for Nonprofits

54.1 General Purpose

As explained in Chapter 5 of this book, landlords generally pass the obligation to pay real property taxes through to the tenants of their buildings, which can result in significant monetary obligations for tenants in addition to the fixed rent they are required to pay.

Pursuant to section 420-a of the Real Property Tax Law (RPTL § 420), a nonprofit organization (NFP) is exempt from paying real property taxes in New York if it "owns" real property and is utilizing the property for religious, charitable, educational, or hospital purposes. Due to the requirement that NFPs "own" the real property they are utilizing, NFP tenants that "lease" their premises under traditional space leases cannot avail themselves of the RPTL § 420 exemption. However, in 2009, the New York City Department of Finance (DOF) ruled that ownership in fee simple of a leasehold condominium interest having a term of at least 30 years constitutes "ownership" of real property that qualifies for exemption under RPTL § 420. Based on this ruling, landlords and tenants have worked collaboratively to create "leasehold condominiums" that enable NFP tenants, in lieu of an ordinary space lease, to effectively "own" their demised premises for purposes of RPTL § 420 and thereby receive the real property tax exemption, resulting in significant monetary savings. The sole purpose of the leasehold condominium is to provide the NFP with ownership of a separate tax lot, and, as such, the property does not in actuality operate under a condominium regime (i.e., it is a "synthetic condominium").

The structure that was originally used to replace a traditional lease with a leasehold condominium was fairly complicated and entailed the following: (1) the fee owner ground leases the entire property to an affiliate landlord entity ("Affiliate Ground Lessee") for a term of 30 or more years, (2) Affiliate Ground Lessee subjects its leasehold estate to condominium ownership which (a) exists for the same term as the ground lease and (b) divides the building into separate taxable condominium units, (3) Affiliate Ground Lessee deeds the leasehold condominium unit or units comprising the NFP's premises (the "NFP Units") to the NFP, (4) the purchase price for the NFP Units is paid by the NFP on a monthly basis in amounts equivalent to what the fixed rent would have been under a lease, (5) Affiliate Ground Lessee and the NFP enter into a series of documents (including, typically, a purchase and sale agreement, a promissory note sometimes secured by a mortgage on the NFP Units, a negotiated condominium declaration and by-laws, and other agreements, all of which, in the aggregate, are intended to mimic the operative provisions that would otherwise appear in a typical space lease and (6) Affiliated Ground Lessee retains ownership of the other units and manages the entire property on behalf of itself and the condominium board, as if there were no condominium. The structure was expensive to document, and required a lot of explanation to existing or prospective mortgage lenders.

In late 2019, DOF issued guidance allowing for the first time creation of a so-called condominium within a condominium, which resulted in a simplified structure being available to achieve the same result for an NFP. Under this structure: (1) the fee owner unilaterally creates a fee condominium separating the building into separately taxable units, (2) the fee owner and the NFP enter into a typical lease of the NFP Units for a term of at least 30 years, and (3) the NFP unilaterally subjects its leasehold estate to a leasehold condominium regime.

54.2 Sample Clause

None.

54.3 Landlord Concerns

As mentioned, the time and cost associated with structuring and documenting these transactions is significant. Even under the newer simplified structure, a landlord will not want to undertake the effort except for an NFP taking a substantial amount of space. For example, in order to create a condominium, a landlord must have specialized architectural drawings of the entire building prepared and will require condominium counsel to shepherd the process through. Once a transaction is completed, however, the landlord has the added benefit of being able to utilize the structure for future NFPs and can use this as a marketing tool to NFPs.

In addition, creation of a condominium structure will certainly require consent of any mortgage lender and, if applicable, ground lessor, as well as partners. Lenders have generally been willing to accept these transactions, without additional financing cost, but the process of obtaining lender approval and documenting the necessary mortgage modifications is an added expense. The lender will have to enter into an agreement with the NFP, corresponding to an SNDA, in which the lender agrees that it will not collapse the condominium structure upon a foreclosure.

From a federal income tax perspective, synthetic leasehold mortgage transactions have been ignored and treated as ordinary leases, although there is no statutory authority for such treatment. It is therefore important to consult with tax counsel, particularly if the fee owner is a REIT, or has one or more REITs within its ownership structure, which require for federal income tax purposes that the income from the NFP be treated as rent.

A landlord should also anticipate the possibility that the NFP may be unable to obtain, or may later lose, the tax exemption (see Section 54.4, Tenant Concerns, for more information on this risk), and the NFP will be responsible for a substantial increase in rent payment because of the need to pay its full share of real estate taxes on a net basis. That could be a very significant hit to an NFP's budget.

Creation of a condominium regime in a building that has existing leases can create issues under those leases if they do not contain provisions anticipating condominium creation that allow for the adjustment of proportionate tax shares to reflect the separate taxable units.

54.4 Tenant Concerns

The exemption from payment of real estate taxes obtained by an NFP utilizing a leasehold condominium structure is, as just set forth, premised on a ruling issued by DOF and DOF's ongoing willingness to grant exemptions to NFPs utilizing the structure. There is no statutory basis for the exemption, and DOF is under no obligation to continue to recognize the exemption. NFPs, after obtaining the exemption, must reapply for the exemption each year. Should DOF change its policy, it could refuse to grant the exemption on a going forward basis. Retroactive loss of the exemption would be less likely but can't be ruled out.

Because availability of the exemption is not set in stone, NFPs have to bear the risk, should the exemption be lost, of having a substantial hit to their budgets should the cost of real estate taxes ever have to be borne by the NFP.

The original leasehold condominium structure resulted in less flexibility to the NFP, because it presented difficulties in the ability to have certain options, such as renewal rights and contraction and termination rights. The newer structure has eliminated most of such difficulties.

54.5 Standard Real Estate Board of New York Clause

None.

54.6 Comments on Standard Real Estate Board of New York Clause

None.

ABOUT THE AUTHORS

Lawrence D. Eisenberg is a partner at Katten Muchin Zavis Rosenman, where he concentrates his practice in real estate law. He is a member of the firm's Board of Directors.

Mr. Eisenberg has more than 30 years of experience in a wide range of complex real estate transactions. His skills have been utilized in the representation of numerous major institutional clients in connection with the relocation of their international headquarters facilities, with a special emphasis on facilities leasing and development.

In addition, he has represented public and private developers of shopping centers, museums, office buildings, residential projects, golf course facilities, hospitals and healthcare facilities, purchasers and sellers of large real estate portfolios, and lenders and borrowers in major construction and other real-estate-based financing, as well as in the workout of troubled loans. He has represented the state of New York in the privatization of several major facilities, including Stewart International Airport, the only commercial service airport privatization in the United States.

Mr. Eisenberg is a member of the American College of Real Estate Lawyers and an ongoing member of the Cornell University Real Estate Council.

Mr. Eisenberg has lectured at Columbia University in New York City and at the Urban Land Institute's headquarters. He received his undergraduate degree (BS, 1965) from Syracuse University and received his law degree (JD, 1968) from Cornell Law School, where he served as an editor of the law review.

Jonathan L. Mechanic is chairman of Fried Frank's Real Estate Department. Prior to joining Fried Frank as a partner, he was general counsel and a managing director of HRO International, a real estate development organization responsible for developing more than 2.5 million square feet of office space in Manhattan.

Mr. Mechanic routinely counsels developers, owners, investors, REITs, and lenders in all aspects of commercial real estate transactions. Notably, he represents JP Morgan in connection with its redevelopment of 270 Park Avenue into a new 2.5-million-square-foot headquarters building; Maefield Development in its approximately US$1.6 billion acquisition of 20 Times Square (aka 701 Seventh Avenue); and CWCapital Asset Management in its sale of Stuyvesant Town–Peter Cooper Village to Blackstone Group and Ivanhoé Cambridge. He also represents landlords and tenants in commercial leasing and ground lease transactions, including his recent representations of 21st Century Fox and News Corp. on their headquarters leases at 1211 Avenue of the Americas; Citigroup in its long-term lease of its global headquarters at 388–390 Greenwich Street and the exercise of its option to purchase the building; Coach in the sale-leaseback of its global headquarters at 10 Hudson Yards; Ernst & Young in its more than 600,000-square-foot lease for its new headquarters at One Manhattan West; Shiseido in its 225,000-square-foot lease at 390 Madison Avenue for its U.S. headquarters; and JP Morgan in its 437,000-square-foot lease at 390 Madison Avenue.

Mr. Mechanic has taught the real estate transactions course at Harvard Law School for more than ten years. He also lectures regularly for NYU Law School, the Real Estate Board of New York, and the Practising Law Institute and is a coauthor of *The Commercial Office Lease Handbook*, published by the American Bar Association.

Mr. Mechanic was awarded the 2016 Distinguished Alumnus Award from New York University and the 2016 Chambers USA Outstanding Contribution to the Legal Profession Award. For a decade, Mr. Mechanic has been recognized by Chambers USA as a "Star Individual" in real estate. He is consistently included on Commercial Observer's "Power 100" list of the most powerful people in New York real estate and was the only practicing attorney to make the list in 2015, 2016, 2017, and 2018. In 2019, Mr. Mechanic was joined by land use partner Melanie Meyers as the only two practicing attorneys on the list, and in 2020 he was one of three practicing attorneys recognized. In 2021 and 2022, Mr. Mechanic was recognized by City & State New York in its "Real Estate Power 100" list and its "Law Power 100" list. In addition, he was named "MVP Lawyer of the Year" by Law360 in 2019, 2013, and 2011. Fried Frank's Real Estate Department has been recognized as Law360's Real Estate Group of the Year, was recognized by Chambers USA as the 2019 Real Estate Law Firm of the Year, and was awarded the 2018 Real Estate Client Service Award and the 2009 Award for Excellence in Real Estate.

Mr. Mechanic is a member of the Executive Committee, Board of Governors for the Real Estate Board of New York and the Board of Trustees of NYU Law School. He is also Chairman of the Advisory Board of the NYU Furman Center for Real Estate and Urban Policy, a member of the Advisory Board of the NYU Schack Institute of Real Estate, a member of the Industrial Advisory Board for the Columbia University Center for Urban Real Estate, and a member of the American College of Real Estate Lawyers.

Mr. Mechanic received his JD from New York University School of Law in 1977, where he served as an editor of the law review and was elected to the Order of the Coif, and his BA, magna cum laude, from Brandeis University in 1974. He is admitted to practice in New York.

David Alan Richards is a graduate of Yale College (B.A. 1967, summa cum laude), Cambridge University (Keasbey Fellow, B.A. 1969 with First Class Honors, and M.A. 1971), and Yale Law School (J.D. 1972, awarded prizes for the best second-year essay and best paper on city planning). He retired from Steptoe & Johnson LLP as senior counsel in 2019, following partnerships in Coudert Brothers (where he founded its real estate department), Sidley & Austin (where he co-founded the firm's New York City office), and McCarter & English (where he managed its New York office). Throughout his career, for both domestic and foreign investors, he handled property acquisitions and dispositions, site assemblage and development and space leasing of or development rights transfers for office buildings (including 461 Fifth Avenue, 150 E. 52nd St., and 520 Park Avenue in New York City), design and construction agreements, and real estate financings. Among his transactions have been for Tiffany's the sale of its unused development rights to Trump Tower, for AT&T the net lease and purchase option for its Madison Avenue headquarters to Sony Corporation, for the Metropolitan Television Association the all-stations antenna lease for the new World Trade Center, and for Conrail and CSX the donation (taking 13 years) of the High Line elevated railway viaduct to the City of New York for a new public park.

He has published widely, particularly on the topics of foreign investment in U.S. real estate, development rights transfer in New York City, and commercial mortgage-backed securities, his articles appearing in *Yale Law Journal*; ABA *Real Property, Probate & Trust Journal*; *New York Law Journal*; *National Law Journal*; *Real Estate Law Journal*; *International Property Investment Journal*; *Anglo-American Real Property Institute Annual*; and *Taxes International*, as well as in coursebooks for the ALI-ABA Courses of Study, the Practicing Law Institute, and The Law Society of England and Wales. His articles have been reprinted in books by the Center for Urban Policy Research at Rutgers University, the University of St. Gall in Switzerland, and Little Brown's textbook *Modern Real Estate Financing: A Transactional Approach* by Madison and Zinman. By invitation he has spoken to the American Society of Planning Officials; the Association of the Bar of the City of New York; the International Council of Shopping Centers; the Mortgage Bankers Association of America; the state bar associations of New York, Virginia, Washington, Texas, and Florida; and foreign investor conferences in London, Berlin, Hong Kong, Zurich, Toronto, and Curacao.

Mr. Richards has served as chair of the 35,000-member ABA Section of Real Property, Trust and Estate Law; as chair of the 100-member Anglo-American Real Property Institute; and as board member of the American College of Real Estate Lawyers. He is admitted to practice in New York, the Second Circuit Court of Appeals, and the United States Supreme Court, and is a Life Member of the American Bar Foundation. He has been featured in *The Best Lawyers in America* (1983), *Who's Who in American Law* (1991), *Who's Who in the World* (1991), *Euromoney Guide to the World's Leading Real Estate Lawyers* (1996), *International Who's Who of Real Estate Lawyers* (1999), and *Legal Media Group Best of the Best* (2006, named one of the ten best real estate lawyers in the U.S., U.K., Canada, and France). In January 2020 he received the Wall Street Journal-Marquis Who's Who Lifetime Achievement Award.

His non-legal writings include *Rudyard Kipling: The Books I Leave Behind* (Yale University Press, 2007), *Rudyard Kipling: A Bibliography* (The British Library, 2010), *Skulls and Keys: The Hidden History of Yale's Secret Societies* (Pegasus Press, 2017), and *I Give These Books: The History of Yale University Library* (Oak Knoll Press, 2023), as well as numerous articles for the *Papers of the Bibliographical Society of America*, *Gazette of the Grolier Club*, *The Kipling Journal*, and the Baker Street

Irregulars' *Sherlock Holmes and the British Empire.* Mr. Richards serves as Chair of the Yale Library Associates, and as President of the London-based Kipling Society, has been a member of the Visiting Committee for Books and Manuscripts at the Morgan Library & Museum, and served as Secretary of the St. Bartholomew's Conservancy for the preservation of that Park Avenue church. In the 1996 presidential campaign he was co-chair of the New York Lawyers for Clinton-Gore.

Michael J. Werner is a partner in the Real Estate Department, resident in Fried Frank's New York office. He joined the firm in 2005 and became partner in 2015.

Mr. Werner's practice includes the representation of owners, developers, funds, real estate investment trusts (REITs), and other financial institutions in a broad range of commercial real estate transactions, concentrating in the acquisition, development, and disposition of office, hotel, retail, and multifamily properties; joint ventures; commercial mortgage, mezzanine, and construction financings; preferred equity investments and debt restructurings; ground leases; and commercial space leasing.

In addition, Mr. Werner is actively involved in real estate industry current affairs and is regularly asked to speak on industry topics. Most recently, he moderated a panel at the 2018 CREtech New York Venture Conference titled "Tech Savvy Landlords." Mr. Werner was also a panelist at the Realshare: New York Growth State of Mind conference discussing "Breaking Down NYC's Mega Deals" and lectured at Columbia University's Graduate School of Architecture, Planning, and Preservation. In addition, Mr. Werner authored a recent article titled "Representing the Borrower in a CMBS Loan," published by Lexis Practice Advisor.

Mr. Werner is recognized by *Legal 500* in Real Estate. In 2021, Mr. Werner was recognized in Crain's New York Business's 2021 Notable in Real Estate, which honors the individuals who have impacted the New York City real estate industry in major ways. In 2019, Mr. Werner was admitted as a member to the American College of Real Estate Lawyers (ACREL), a premier organization of U.S. real estate lawyers. In 2016, Mr. Werner was selected by Law360 as a 2016 "Rising Star" in real estate, an honor that recognizes top attorneys under the age of 40.

Mr. Werner is a member of the Board of Directors of Breaking Ground, a nonprofit organization focused on creating high-quality permanent and transitional housing for those who need it most. Mr. Werner previously served on Israel Bonds Real Estate New Leadership Division as Co-Chair and Vice-Chair of the cabinet. He serves as a member of the Attorney Development Committee of Fried Frank.

Mr. Werner received his JD, cum laude, from Fordham University School of Law in 2005 and his BA, cum laude, from Binghamton University in 2002. He is admitted to the bar in New York.

APPENDIX

7/04

STANDARD FORM OF OFFICE LEASE
The Real Estate Board of New York, Inc.

Agreement of Lease, made as of this day of in the year ,

between party of the first part, hereinafter referred to as OWNER, and

party of the second part, hereinafter referred to as TENANT,

Witnesseth: Owner hereby leases to Tenant and Tenant hereby hires from Owner

in the building known as
in the Borough of , City of New York, for the term of

(or until such term shall sooner cease and expire as hereinafter provided) to commence on the
day of in the year , and to end on the
day of in the year , and
both dates inclusive, at the annual rental rate of

which Tenant agrees to pay in lawful money of the United States, which shall be legal tender in payment of all debts and dues, public and private, at the time of payment, in equal monthly installments in advance on the first day of each month during said term, at the office of Owner or such other place as Owner may designate, without any setoff or deduction whatsoever, except that Tenant shall pay the first monthly installment(s) on the execution hereof (unless this lease be a renewal).

In the event that, at the commencement of the term of this lease, or thereafter, Tenant shall be in default in the payment of rent to Owner pursuant to the terms of another lease with Owner or with Owner's predecessor in interest, Owner may at Owner's option and without notice to Tenant add the amount of such arrears to any monthly installment of rent payable hereunder and the same shall be payable to Owner as additional rent.

The parties hereto, for themselves, their heirs, distributees, executors, administrators, legal representatives, successors and assigns, hereby covenant as follows:

Rent: **1.** Tenant shall pay the rent as above and as hereinafter provided.

Occupancy: **2.** Tenant shall use and occupy the demised premises for and for no other purpose.

Tenant Alterations: 3. Tenant shall make no changes in or to the demised premises of any nature without Owner's prior written consent. Subject to the prior written consent of Owner, and to the provisions of this article, Tenant, at Tenant's expense, may make alterations, installations, additions or improvements which are non-structural and which do not affect utility services or plumbing and electrical lines, in or to the interior of the demised premises, by using contractors or mechanics first approved in each instance by Owner. Tenant shall, before making any alterations, additions, installations or improvements, at its expense, obtain all permits, approvals and certificates required by any governmental or quasi-governmental bodies and (upon completion) certificates of final approval thereof, and shall deliver promptly duplicates of all such permits, approvals and certificates to Owner, and Tenant agrees to carry, and will cause Tenant's contractors and sub-contractors to carry, such worker's compensation, commercial general liability, personal and property damage insurance as Owner may require. If any mechanic's lien is filed against the demised premises, or the building of which the same forms a part, for work claimed to have been done for, or materials furnished to, Tenant, whether or not done pursuant to this article, the same shall be discharged by Tenant within thirty days thereafter, at Tenant's expense, by payment or filing a bond as permitted by law. All fixtures and all paneling, partitions, railings and like installations, installed in the demised premises at any time, either by Tenant or by Owner on Tenant's behalf, shall, upon installation, become the property of Owner and shall remain upon and be surrendered with the demised premises unless Owner, by notice to Tenant no later than twenty days prior to the date fixed as the termination of this lease, elects to relinquish Owner's right thereto and to have them removed by Tenant, in which event the same shall be removed from the demised premises by Tenant prior to the expiration of the lease, at Tenant's expense. Nothing in this article shall be construed to give Owner title to, or to prevent Tenant's removal of, trade fixtures, moveable office furniture and equipment, but upon removal of same from the demised premises or upon removal, of other installations as may be required by Owner, Tenant shall immediately, and at its expense, repair and restore the demised premises to the condition existing prior to any such installations, and repair any damage to the demised premises or the building due to such removal. All property permitted or required to be removed by Tenant at the end of the term remaining in the demised premises after Tenant's removal shall be deemed abandoned and may, at the election of Owner, either be retained as Owner's property or may be removed from the demised premises by Owner, at Tenant's expense.

Maintenance and Repairs: 4. Tenant shall, throughout the term of this lease, take good care of the demised premises and the fixtures and appurtenances therein. Tenant shall be responsible for all damage or injury to the demised premises or any other part of the building and the systems and equipment thereof, whether requiring structural or nonstructural repairs caused by, or resulting from, carelessness, omission, neglect or improper conduct of Tenant, Tenant's subtenants, agents, employees, invitees or licensees, or which arise out of any work, labor, service or equipment done for, or supplied to, Tenant or any subtenant, or arising out of the installation, use or operation of the property or equipment of Tenant or any subtenant. Tenant shall also repair all damage to the building and the demised premises caused by the moving of Tenant's fixtures, furniture and equipment. Tenant shall promptly make, at Tenant's expense, all repairs in and to the demised premises for which Tenant is responsible, using only the contractor for the trade or trades in question, selected from a list of at least two contractors per trade submitted by Owner. Any other repairs in or to the building or the facilities and systems thereof, for which Tenant is responsible, shall be performed by Owner at the Tenant's expense. Owner shall maintain in good working order and repair the exterior and the structural portions of the building, including the structural portions of the demised premises, and the public portions of the building interior and the building plumbing, electrical, heating and ventilating systems (to the extent such systems presently exist) serving the demised premises. Tenant agrees to give prompt notice of any defective condition in the demised premises for which Owner may be responsible hereunder. There shall be no allowance to Tenant for diminution of rental value and no liability on the part of Owner by reason of inconvenience, annoyance or injury to business arising from Owner or others making repairs, alterations, additions or improvements in or to any portion of the building or the demised premises, or in and to the fixtures, appurtenances or equipment thereof. It is specifically agreed that Tenant shall not be entitled to any setoff or reduction of rent by reason of any failure of Owner to comply with the covenants of this or any other article of this lease. Tenant agrees that Tenant's sole remedy at law in such instance will be by way of an action for damages for breach of contract. The provisions of this Article 4 shall not apply in the case of fire or other casualty, which are dealt with in Article 9 hereof.

Window Cleaning: **5.** Tenant will not clean nor require, permit, suffer or allow any window in the demised premises to be cleaned from the outside in violation of Section 202 of the Labor Law or any other applicable law, or of the Rules of the Board of Standards and Appeals, or of any other Board or body having or asserting jurisdiction.

Requirements of Law, Fire Insurance, Floor Loads: **6.** Prior to the commencement of the lease term, if Tenant is then in possession, and at all times thereafter, Tenant, at Tenant's sole cost and expense, shall promptly comply with all present and future laws, orders and regulations of all state, federal, municipal and local governments, departments, commissions and boards and any direction of any public officer pursuant to law, and all orders, rules and regulations of the New York Board of Fire Underwriters, Insurance Services Office, or any similar body which shall impose any violation, order or duty upon Owner or Tenant with respect to the demised premises, whether or not arising out of Tenant's use or manner of use thereof, (including Tenant's permitted use) or, with respect to the building if arising out of Tenant's use or manner of use of the demised premises or the building (including the use permitted under the lease). Nothing herein shall require Tenant to make structural repairs or alterations unless Tenant has, by its manner of use of the demised premises or method of operation therein, violated any such laws, ordinances, orders, rules, regulations or requirements with respect thereto. Tenant may, after securing Owner to Owner's satisfaction against all damages, interest, penalties and expenses, including, but not limited to, reasonable attorney's fees, by cash deposit or by surety bond in an amount and in a company satisfactory to Owner, contest and appeal any such laws, ordinances, orders, rules, regulations or requirements provided same is done with all reasonable promptness and provided such appeal shall not subject Owner to prosecution for a criminal offense, or constitute a default under any lease or mortgage under which Owner may be obligated, or cause the demised premises or any part thereof to be condemned or vacated. Tenant shall not do or permit any act or thing to be done in or to the demised premises which is contrary to law, or which will invalidate or be in conflict with public liability, fire or other policies of insurance at any time carried by or for the benefit of Owner with respect to the demised premises or the building of which the demised premises form a part, or which shall or might subject Owner to any liability or responsibility to any person, or for property damage. Tenant shall not keep anything in the demised premises, except as now or hereafter permitted by the Fire Department, Board of Fire Underwriters, Fire Insurance Rating Organization or other authority having jurisdiction, and then only in such manner and such quantity so as not to increase the rate for fire insurance applicable to the building, nor use the demised premises in a manner which will increase the insurance rate for the building or any property located therein over that in effect prior to the commencement of Tenant's occupancy. Tenant shall pay all costs, expenses, fines, penalties, or damages, which may be imposed upon Owner by reason of Tenant's failure to comply with the provisions of this article, and if by reason of such failure the fire insurance rate shall, at the beginning of this lease, or at any time thereafter, be higher than it otherwise would be, then, Tenant shall reimburse Owner, as additional rent hereunder, for that portion of all fire insurance premiums thereafter paid by Owner which shall have been charged because of such failure by Tenant. In any action or proceeding wherein Owner and Tenant are parties, a schedule or "make-up" of rate for the building or the demised premises issued by the New York Fire Insurance Exchange, or other body making fire insurance rates applicable to said premises shall be conclusive evidence of the facts therein stated and of the several items and charges in the fire insurance rates then applicable to said premises. Tenant shall not place a load upon any floor of the demised premises exceeding the floor load per square foot area which it was designed to carry and which is allowed by law. Owner reserves the right to prescribe the weight and position of all safes, business machines and mechanical equipment. Such installations shall be placed and maintained by Tenant, at Tenant's expense, in settings sufficient, in Owner's judgment, to absorb and prevent vibration, noise and annoyance.

Subordination: **7.** This lease is subject and subordinate to all ground or underlying leases and to all mortgages which may now or hereafter affect such leases or the real property of which the demised premises are a part, and to all renewals, modifications, consolidations, replacements and extensions of any such underlying leases and mortgages.

This clause shall be self-operative and no further instrument of subordination shall be required by any ground or underlying lessor or by any mortgagee, affecting any lease or the real property of which the demised premises are a part. In confirmation of such subordination, Tenant shall from time to time execute promptly any certificate that Owner may request.

Property Loss, Damage Reimbursement Indemnity: 8. Owner or its agents shall not be liable for any damage to property of Tenant or of others entrusted to employees of the building, nor for loss of or damage to any property of Tenant by theft or otherwise, nor for any injury or damage to persons or property resulting from any cause of whatsoever nature, unless caused by, or due to, the negligence of Owner, its agents, servants or employees. Owner or its agents will not be liable for any such damage caused by other tenants or persons in, upon or about said building, or caused by operations in construction of any private, public or quasi public work. If at any time any windows of the demised premises are temporarily closed, darkened or bricked up (or permanently closed, darkened or bricked up, if required by law) for any reason whatsoever including, but not limited to, Owner's own acts, Owner shall not be liable for any damage Tenant may sustain thereby, and Tenant shall not be entitled to any compensation therefore, nor abatement or diminution of rent, nor shall the same release Tenant from its obligations hereunder, nor constitute an eviction. Tenant shall indemnify and save harmless Owner against and from all liabilities, obligations, damages, penalties, claims, costs and expenses for which Owner shall not be reimbursed by insurance, including reasonable attorneys' fees, paid, suffered or incurred as a result of any breach by Tenant, Tenant's agents, contractors, employees, invitees, or licensees, of any covenant or condition of this lease, or the carelessness, negligence or improper conduct of the Tenant, Tenant's agents, contractors, employees, invitees or licensees. Tenant's liability under this lease extends to the acts and omissions of any subtenant, and any agent, contractor, employee, invitee or licensee of any subtenant. In case any action or proceeding is brought against Owner by reason of any such claim, Tenant, upon written notice from Owner, will, at Tenant's expense, resist or defend such action or proceeding by counsel approved by Owner in writing, such approval not to be unreasonably withheld.

Destruction, Fire and Other Casualty: 9. (a) If the demised premises or any part thereof shall be damaged by fire or other casualty, Tenant shall give immediate notice thereof to Owner, and this lease shall continue in full force and effect except as hereinafter set forth. (b) If the demised premises are partially damaged or rendered partially unusable by fire or other casualty, the damages thereto shall be repaired by, and at the expense of, Owner, and the rent and other items of additional rent, until such repair shall be substantially completed, shall be apportioned from the day following the casualty, according to the part of the demised premises which is usable. (c) If the demised premises are totally damaged or rendered wholly unusable by fire or other casualty, then the rent and other items of additional rent, as hereinafter expressly provided, shall be proportionately paid up to the time of the casualty, and thenceforth shall cease until the date when the demised premises shall have been repaired and restored by Owner (or if sooner reoccupied in part by the Tenant then rent shall be apportioned as provided in subsection (b) above), subject to Owner's right to elect not to restore the same as hereinafter provided. (d) If the demised premises are rendered wholly unusable or (whether or not the demised premises are damaged in whole or in part) if the building shall be so damaged that Owner shall decide to demolish it or to rebuild it, then, in any of such events, Owner may elect to terminate this lease by written notice to Tenant, given within ninety (90) days after such fire or casualty, or thirty (30) days after adjustment of the insurance claim for such fire or casualty, whichever is sooner, specifying a date for the expiration of the lease, which date shall not be more than sixty (60) days after the giving of such notice, and upon the date specified in such notice the term of this lease shall expire as fully and completely as if such date were the date set forth above for the termination of this lease, and Tenant shall forthwith quit, surrender and vacate the demised premises without prejudice however, to Landlord's rights and remedies against Tenant under the lease provisions in effect prior to such termination, and any rent owing shall be paid up to such date, and any payments of rent made by Tenant which were on account of any period subsequent to such date shall be returned to Tenant. Unless Owner shall serve a termination notice as provided for herein, Owner shall make the repairs and restorations under the conditions of (b) and (c) hereof, with all reasonable expedition, subject to delays due to adjustment of insurance claims, labor troubles and causes beyond Owner's control.

After any such casualty, Tenant shall cooperate with Owner's restoration by removing from the demised premises as promptly as reasonably possible, all of Tenant's salvageable inventory and movable equipment, furniture, and other property. Tenant's liability for rent shall resume five (5) days after written notice from Owner that the demised premises are substantially ready for Tenant's occupancy. (e) Nothing contained hereinabove shall relieve Tenant from liability that may exist as a result of damage from fire or other casualty. Notwithstanding anything contained to the contrary in subdivisions (a) through (e) hereof, including Owner's obligation to restore under subparagraph (b) above, each party shall look first to any insurance in its favor before making any claim against the other party for recovery for loss or damage resulting from fire or other casualty, and to the extent that such insurance is in force and collectible, and to the extent permitted by law, Owner and Tenant each hereby releases and waives all right of recovery with respect to subparagraphs (b), (d), and (e) above, against the other, or any one claiming through or under each of them by way of subrogation or otherwise. The release and waiver herein referred to shall be deemed to include any loss or damage to the demised premises and/or to any personal property, equipment, trade fixtures, goods and merchandise located therein. The foregoing release and waiver shall be in force only if both releasors' insurance policies contain a clause providing that such a release or waiver shall not invalidate the insurance. If, and to the extent, that such waiver can be obtained only by the payment of additional premiums, then the party benefiting from the waiver shall pay such premium within ten days after written demand or shall be deemed to have agreed that the party obtaining insurance coverage shall be free of any further obligation under the provisions hereof with respect to waiver of subrogation. Tenant acknowledges that Owner will not carry insurance on Tenant's furniture and/or furnishings or any fixtures or equipment, improvements, or appurtenances removable by Tenant, and agrees that Owner will not be obligated to repair any damage thereto or replace the same. (f) Tenant hereby waives the provisions of section 227 of the Real Property Law and agrees that the provisions of this article shall govern and control in lieu thereof.

Eminent Domain: 10. If the whole or any part of the demised premises shall be acquired or condemned by Eminent Domain for any public or quasi public use or purpose, then, and in that event, the term of this lease shall cease and terminate from the date of title vesting in such proceeding, and Tenant shall have no claim for the value of any unexpired term of said lease, and assigns to Owner, Tenant's entire interest in any such award. Tenant shall have the right to make an independent claim to the condemning authority for the value of Tenant's moving expenses and personal property, trade fixtures and equipment, provided Tenant is entitled pursuant to the terms of the lease to remove such property, trade fixtures and equipment at the end of the term, and provided further such claim does not reduce Owner's award.

Assignment, Mortgage, Etc.: 11. Tenant, for itself, its heirs, distributees, executors, administrators, legal representatives, successors and assigns, expressly covenants that it shall not assign, mortgage or encumber this agreement, nor underlet, or suffer or permit the demised premises or any part thereof to be used by others, without the prior written consent of Owner in each instance. Transfer of the majority of the stock of a corporate Tenant or the majority interest in any partnership or other legal entity which is Tenant shall be deemed an assignment. If this lease be assigned, or if the demised premises or any part thereof be underlet or occupied by anybody other than Tenant, Owner may, after default by Tenant, collect rent from the assignee, under-tenant or occupant, and apply the net amount collected to the rent herein reserved, but no such assignment, underletting, occupancy or collection shall be deemed a waiver of this covenant, or the acceptance of the assignee, undertenant or occupant as tenant, or a release of Tenant from the further performance by Tenant of covenants on the part of Tenant herein contained. The consent by Owner to an assignment or underletting shall not in any way be construed to relieve Tenant from obtaining the express consent in writing of Owner to any further assignment or underletting.

☞ **Electric Current: 12.** Rates and conditions in respect to submetering or rent inclusion, as the case may be, to be added in RIDER attached hereto. Tenant covenants and agrees that at all times its use of electric current shall not exceed the capacity of existing feeders to the building or the risers or wiring installation, and Tenant may not use any electrical equipment which, in Owner's opinion, reasonably exercised, will overload such installations or interfere with the use thereof by other tenants of the building. The

☞ Rider to be added if necessary

change at any time of the character of electric service shall in no way make Owner liable or responsible to Tenant, for any loss, damages or expenses which Tenant may sustain.

Access to Premises: 13. Owner or Owner's agents shall have the right (but shall not be obligated) to enter the demised premises in any emergency at any time, and, at other reasonable times, to examine the same and to make such repairs, replacements and improvements as Owner may deem necessary and reasonably desirable to the demised premises or to any other portion of the building or which Owner may elect to perform. Tenant shall permit Owner to use and maintain and replace pipes, ducts, and conduits in and through the demised premises and to erect new pipes, ducts, and conduits therein, provided they are concealed within the walls, floor, or ceiling. Owner may, during the progress of any work in the demised premises, take all necessary materials and equipment into said premises without the same constituting an eviction, nor shall the Tenant be entitled to any abatement of rent while such work is in progress, nor to any damages by reason of loss or interruption of business or otherwise. Throughout the term hereof, Owner shall have the right to enter the demised premises at reasonable hours for the purpose of showing the same to prospective purchasers or mortgagees of the building, and during the last six months of the term, for the purpose of showing the same to prospective tenants. If Tenant is not present to open and permit an entry into the demised premises, Owner or Owner's agents may enter the same whenever such entry may be necessary or permissible by master key or forcibly, and provided reasonable care is exercised to safeguard Tenant's property, such entry shall not render Owner or its agents liable therefore, nor in any event shall the obligations of Tenant hereunder be affected. If during the last month of the term Tenant shall have removed all or substantially all of Tenant's property therefrom, Owner may immediately enter, alter, renovate or redecorate the demised premises without limitation or abatement of rent, or incurring liability to Tenant for any compensation, and such act shall have no effect on this lease or Tenant's obligations hereunder.

Vault, Vault Space, Area: 14. No vaults, vault space or area, whether or not enclosed or covered, not within the property line of the building, is leased hereunder, anything contained in or indicated on any sketch, blue print or plan, or anything contained elsewhere in this lease to the contrary notwithstanding. Owner makes no representation as to the location of the property line of the building. All vaults and vault space and all such areas not within the property line of the building, which Tenant may be permitted to use and/or occupy, is to be used and/or occupied under a revocable license, and if any such license be revoked, or if the amount of such space or area be diminished or required by any federal, state or municipal authority or public utility, Owner shall not be subject to any liability, nor shall Tenant be entitled to any compensation or diminution or abatement of rent, nor shall such revocation, diminution or requisition be deemed constructive or actual eviction. Any tax, fee or charge of municipal authorities for such vault or area shall be paid by Tenant.

Occupancy: 15. Tenant will not at any time use or occupy the demised premises in violation of the certificate of occupancy issued for the building of which the demised premises are a part. Tenant has inspected the demised premises and accepts them as is, subject to the riders annexed hereto with respect to Owner's work, if any. In any event, Owner makes no representation as to the condition of the demised premises, and Tenant agrees to accept the same subject to violations, whether or not of record.

Bankruptcy: 16. (a) Anything elsewhere in this lease to the contrary notwithstanding, this lease may be cancelled by Owner by the sending of a written notice to Tenant within a reasonable time after the happening of any one or more of the following events: (1) the commencement of a case in bankruptcy or under the laws of any state naming Tenant (or a guarantor of any of Tenant's obligations under this lease) as the debtor; or (2) the making by Tenant (or a guarantor of any of Tenant's obligations under this lease) of an assignment or any other arrangement for the benefit of creditors under any state statute. Neither Tenant nor any person claiming through or under Tenant, or by reason of any statute or order of court, shall thereafter be entitled to possession of the premises demised but shall forthwith quit and surrender the demised premises. If this lease shall be assigned in accordance with its terms, the provisions of this Article 16 shall be applicable only to the party then owning Tenant's interest in this lease.

(b) It is stipulated and agreed that in the event of the termination of this lease pursuant to (a) hereof, Owner shall forthwith, notwithstanding any other provisions of this lease to the contrary, be entitled to recover from Tenant as and for liquidated damages, an amount equal to the difference between the rent reserved hereunder for the unexpired portion of the term demised and the fair and reasonable rental value of the demised premises for the same period. In the computation of such damages the difference between any installment of rent becoming due hereunder after the date of termination, and the fair and reasonable rental value of the demised premises for the period for which such installment was payable, shall be discounted to the date of termination at the rate of four percent (4%) per annum. If such demised premises or any part thereof be re-let by the Owner for the unexpired term of said lease, or any part thereof, before presentation of proof of such liquidated damages to any court, commission or tribunal, the amount of rent reserved upon such re-letting shall be deemed to be the fair and reasonable rental value for the part or the whole of the demised premises so re-let during the term of the re-letting. Nothing herein contained shall limit or prejudice the right of the Owner to prove for and obtain as liquidated damages, by reason of such termination, an amount equal to the maximum allowed by any statute or rule of law in effect at the time when, and governing the proceedings in which, such damages are to be proved, whether or not such amount be greater, equal to, or less than, the amount of the difference referred to above.

Default: **17.** (1) If Tenant defaults in fulfilling any of the covenants of this lease other than the covenants for the payment of rent or additional rent; or if the demised premises become vacant or deserted; or if any execution or attachment shall be issued against Tenant or any of Tenant's property, whereupon the demised premises shall be taken or occupied by someone other than Tenant; or if this lease be rejected under §365 of Title 11 of the U.S. Code (Bankruptcy Code); or if Tenant shall have failed, after five (5) days written notice, to redeposit with Owner any portion of the security deposit hereunder which Owner has applied to the payment of any rent and additional rent due and payable hereunder; or if Tenant shall be in default with respect to any other lease between Owner and Tenant; or if Tenant shall fail to move into or take possession of the demised premises within thirty (30) days after the commencement of the term of this lease, then, in any one or more of such events, upon Owner serving a written fifteen (15) days notice upon Tenant specifying the nature of said default, and upon the expiration of said fifteen (15) days, if Tenant shall have failed to comply with or remedy such default, or if the said default or omission complained of shall be of a nature that the same cannot be completely cured or remedied within said fifteen (15) day period, and if Tenant shall not have diligently commenced curing such default within such fifteen (15) day period, and shall not thereafter with reasonable diligence and in good faith, proceed to remedy or cure such default, then Owner may serve a written five (5) days notice of cancellation of this lease upon Tenant, and upon the expiration of said five (5) days this lease and the term thereunder shall end and expire as fully and completely as if the expiration of such five (5) day period were the day herein definitely fixed for the end and expiration of this lease and the term thereof, and Tenant shall then quit and surrender the demised premises to Owner, but Tenant shall remain liable as hereinafter provided.

(2) If the notice provided for in (1) hereof shall have been given, and the term shall expire as aforesaid; or if Tenant shall make default in the payment of the rent reserved herein, or any item of additional rent herein mentioned, or any part of either, or in making any other payment herein required; then, and in any of such events, Owner may without notice, re-enter the demised premises either by force or otherwise, and dispossess Tenant by summary proceedings or otherwise, and the legal representative of Tenant or other occupant of the demised premises, and remove their effects and hold the demised premises as if this lease had not been made, and Tenant hereby waives the service of notice of intention to re-enter or to institute legal proceedings to that end. If Tenant shall make default hereunder prior to the date fixed as the commencement of any renewal or extension of this lease, Owner may cancel and terminate such renewal or extension agreement by written notice.

Remedies of Owner and Waiver of Redemption: **18.** In case of any such default, re-entry, expiration and/or dispossess by summary proceedings or otherwise, (a) the rent shall become due thereupon and be paid up to the time of such re-entry, dispossess and/or expiration, (b) Owner may re-let the demised premises or any part or parts thereof, either in the name of Owner or otherwise, for a term or terms, which may at Owner's option be less than or exceed the period which would otherwise have constituted the balance of the term of this lease, and may grant concessions or free rent or charge a higher rental than that in this lease, and/or (c) Tenant or the legal representatives of Tenant shall also pay to Owner as liquidated damages for the failure of Tenant to observe and perform said Tenant's covenants herein contained, any deficiency between the rent hereby reserved and/or covenanted to be paid and the net amount, if any, of the rents collected on account of the lease or leases of the demised premises for each month of the period which would otherwise have constituted the balance of the term of this lease. The failure of Owner to re-let the demised premises, or any part or parts thereof, shall not release or affect Tenant's liability for damages. In computing such liquidated damages there shall be added to the said deficiency such expenses as Owner may incur in connection with re-letting, such as legal expenses, reasonable attorney's fees, brokerage, advertising and for keeping the demised premises in good order or for preparing the same for re-letting. Any such liquidated damages shall be paid in monthly installments by Tenant on the rent day specified in this lease, and any suit brought to collect the amount of the deficiency for any month shall not prejudice in any way the rights of Owner to collect the deficiency for any subsequent month by a similar proceeding. Owner, in putting the demised premises in good order or preparing the same for re-rental may, at Owner's option, make such alterations, repairs, replacements, and/or decorations in the demised premises as Owner, in Owner's sole judgment, considers advisable and necessary for the purpose of re-letting the demised premises, and the making of such alterations, repairs, replacements, and/or decorations shall not operate or be construed to release Tenant from liability hereunder as aforesaid. Owner shall in no event be liable in any way whatsoever for failure to re-let the demised premises, or in the event that the demised premises are re-let, for failure to collect the rent thereof under such re-letting, and in no event shall Tenant be entitled to receive any excess, if any, of such net rents collected over the sums payable by Tenant to Owner hereunder. In the event of a breach or threatened breach by Tenant of any of the covenants or provisions hereof, Owner shall have the right of injunction and the right to invoke any remedy allowed at law or in equity as if re-entry, summary proceedings and other remedies were not herein provided for. Mention in this lease of any particular remedy, shall not preclude Owner from any other remedy, in law or in equity. Tenant hereby expressly waives any and all rights of redemption granted by or under any present or future laws in the event of Tenant being evicted or dispossessed for any cause, or in the event of Owner obtaining possession of the demised premises, by reason of the violation by Tenant of any of the covenants and conditions of this lease, or otherwise.

Fees and Expenses: 19. If Tenant shall default in the observance or performance of any term or covenant on Tenant's part to be observed or performed under, or by virtue of, any of the terms or provisions in any article of this lease, after notice, if required, and upon expiration of any applicable grace period, if any, (except in an emergency), then, unless otherwise provided elsewhere in this lease, Owner may immediately, or at any time thereafter and without notice, perform the obligation of Tenant thereunder. If Owner, in connection with the foregoing, or in connection with any default by Tenant in the covenant to pay rent hereunder, makes any expenditures or incurs any obligations for the payment of money, including but not limited to reasonable attorneys' fees, in instituting, prosecuting or defending any action or proceeding, and prevails in any such action or proceeding, then Tenant will reimburse Owner for such sums so paid, or obligations incurred, with interest and costs. The foregoing expenses incurred by reason of Tenant's default shall be deemed to be additional rent hereunder, and shall be paid by Tenant to Owner within ten (10) days of rendition of any bill or statement to Tenant therefore. If Tenant's lease term shall have expired at the time of making of such expenditures or incurring of such obligations, such sums shall be recoverable by Owner, as damages.

Building Alterations and Management: 20. Owner shall have the right at any time without the same constituting an eviction and without incurring liability to Tenant therefore, to change the arrangement and/or location of public entrances, passageways, doors, doorways, corridors, elevators, stairs, toilets or other public parts of the building, and to change the name, number or designation by which the building may be known. There shall be no allowance to Tenant for diminution of rental value and no liability on the part of Owner by reason of inconvenience, annoyance or injury to business arising from Owner or other Tenants making any repairs in the building or any such alterations, additions and improvements. Furthermore, Tenant shall not have any claim against Owner by reason of Owner's imposition of such controls of the manner of access to the building by Tenant's social or business visitors as the Owner may deem necessary for the security of the building and its occupants.

No Representations Owner: 21. Neither Owner nor Owner's agents have made any representations or promises with respect to the physical condition of the building, the land upon which it is erected or the demised premises, the rents, leases, expenses of operation or any other matter or thing affecting or related to the demised premises, except as herein expressly set forth, and no rights, easements or licenses are acquired by Tenant by implication or otherwise, except as expressly set forth in the provisions of this lease. Tenant has inspected the building and the demised premises and is thoroughly acquainted with their condition and agrees to take the same "as-is", and acknowledges that the taking of possession of the demised premises by Tenant shall be conclusive evidence that the said premises and the building of which the same form a part were in good and satisfactory condition at the time such possession was so taken, except as to latent defects. All understandings and agreements heretofore made between the parties hereto are merged in this contract, which alone fully and completely expresses the agreement between Owner and Tenant, and any executory agreement hereafter made shall be ineffective to change, modify, discharge or effect an abandonment of it in whole or in part, unless such executory agreement is in writing and signed by the party against whom enforcement of the change, modification, discharge or abandonment is sought.

End of Term: 22. Upon the expiration or other termination of the term of this lease, Tenant shall quit and surrender to Owner the demised premises, "broom-clean", in good order and condition, ordinary wear and damages which Tenant is not required to repair as provided elsewhere in this lease excepted, and Tenant shall remove all its property. Tenant's obligation to observe or perform this covenant shall survive the expiration or other termination of this lease. If the last day of the term of this lease or any renewal thereof, falls on Sunday, this lease shall expire at noon on the preceding Saturday, unless it be a legal holiday, in which case it shall expire at noon on the preceding business day.

Quiet Enjoyment: 23. Owner covenants and agrees with Tenant that upon Tenant paying the rent and additional rent and observing and performing all the terms, covenants and conditions, on Tenant's part to be observed and performed, Tenant may peaceably and quietly enjoy the premises hereby demised, subject, nevertheless, to the terms and conditions of this lease including, but not limited to, Article 31 hereof, and to the ground leases, underlying leases and mortgages hereinbefore mentioned.

Failure to Give Possession: 24. If Owner is unable to give possession of the demised premises on the date of the commencement of the term hereof because of the holding-over or retention of possession of any tenant, undertenant or occupants, or if the demised premises are located in a building being constructed, because such building has not been sufficiently completed to make the demised premises ready for occupancy, or because of the fact that a certificate of occupancy has not been procured, or for any other reason, Owner shall not be subject to any liability for failure to give possession on said date and the validity of the lease shall not be impaired under such circumstances, nor shall the same be construed in any way to extend the term of this lease, but the rent payable hereunder shall be abated (provided Tenant is not responsible for Owner's inability to obtain possession or complete construction) until after Owner shall have given Tenant written notice that the Owner is able to deliver possession in condition required by this lease. If permission is given to Tenant to enter into possession of the demises premises, or to occupy premises other than the demised premises, prior to the date specified as the commencement of the term of this lease, Tenant covenants and agrees that such possession and/or occupancy shall be deemed to be under all the terms, covenants, conditions and provisions of this lease, except the obligation to pay the fixed annual rent set forth in the preamble to this lease. The provisions of this article are intended to constitute "an express provision to the contrary" within the meaning of Section 223-a of the New York Real Property Law.

No Waiver: 25. The failure of Owner to seek redress for violation of, or to insist upon the strict performance of, any covenant or condition of this lease or of any of the Rules or Regulations, set forth or hereafter adopted by Owner, shall not prevent a subsequent act which would have originally constituted a violation from having all the force and effect of an original violation. The receipt by Owner of rent and/or additional rent with knowledge of the breach of any covenant of this lease shall not be deemed a waiver of such breach, and no provision of this lease shall be deemed to have been waived by Owner unless such waiver be in writing signed by Owner. No payment by Tenant or receipt by Owner of a lesser amount than the monthly rent herein stipulated shall be deemed to be other than on account of the earliest stipulated rent, nor shall any endorsement or statement of any check or any letter accompanying any check or payment as rent be deemed an accord and satisfaction, and Owner may accept such check or payment without prejudice to Owner's right to recover the balance of such rent or pursue any other remedy in this lease provided. No act or thing done by Owner or Owner's agents during the term hereby demised shall be deemed an acceptance of a surrender of the demised premises, and no agreement to accept such surrender shall be valid unless in writing signed by Owner. No employee of Owner or Owner's agent shall have any power to accept the keys of said premises prior to the termination of the lease, and the delivery of keys to any such agent or employee shall not operate as a termination of the lease or a surrender of the demised premises.

Waiver of Trial by Jury: 26. It is mutually agreed by and between Owner and Tenant that the respective parties hereto shall, and they hereby do, waive trial by jury in any action proceeding or counterclaim brought by either of the parties hereto against the other (except for personal injury or property damage) on any matters whatsoever arising out of, or in any way connected with, this lease, the relationship of Owner and Tenant, Tenant's use of, or occupancy of, the demised premises, and any emergency statutory or any other statutory remedy. It is further mutually agreed that in the event Owner commences any proceeding or action for possession, including a summary proceeding for possession of the demised premises, Tenant will not interpose any counterclaim of whatever nature or description in any such proceeding, including a counterclaim under Article 4, except for statutory mandatory counterclaims.

Inability to Perform: 27. This lease and the obligation of Tenant to pay rent hereunder and perform all of the other covenants and agreements hereunder on part of Tenant to be performed shall in no way be affected, impaired or excused because Owner is unable to fulfill any of its obligations under this lease, or to supply, or is delayed in supplying, any service expressly or impliedly to be supplied, or is unable to make, or is delayed in making, any repair, additions, alterations, or decorations, or is unable to supply, or is delayed in supplying, any equipment, fixtures, or other materials, if Owner is prevented or delayed from so doing by reason of strike or labor troubles or any cause whatsoever including, but not limited to, government preemption or restrictions, or by reason of any rule, order or regulation of any department or subdivision thereof of any government agency, or by reason of the conditions which have been or are affected, either directly or indirectly, by war or other emergency.

Bills and Notices: 28. Except as otherwise in this lease provided, any notice, statement, demand or other communication required or permitted to be given, rendered or made by either party to the other, pursuant to this lease or pursuant to any applicable law or requirement of public authority, shall be in writing (whether or not so stated elsewhere in this lease) and shall be deemed to have been properly given, rendered or made, if sent by registered or certified mail (express mail, if available), return receipt requested, or by courier guaranteeing overnight delivery and furnishing a receipt in evidence thereof, addressed to the other party at the address hereinabove set forth (except that after the date specified as the commencement of the term of this lease, Tenant's address, unless Tenant shall give notice to the contrary, shall be the building), and shall be deemed to have been given, rendered or made (a) on the date delivered, if delivered to Tenant personally, (b) on the date delivered, if delivered by overnight courier or (c) on the date which is two (2) days after being mailed. Either party may, by notice as aforesaid, designate a different address or addresses for notices, statements, demand or other communications intended for it. Notices given by Owner's managing agent shall be deemed a valid notice if addressed and set in accordance with the provisions of this Article. At Owner's option, notices and bills to Tenant may be sent by hand delivery.

Services Provided by Owner: 29. As long as Tenant is not in default under any of the covenants of this lease beyond the applicable grace period provided in this lease for the curing of such defaults, Owner shall provide: (a) necessary elevator facilities on business days from 8 a.m. to 6 p.m. and have one elevator subject to call at all other times; (b) heat to the demised premises when and as required by law, on business days from 8 a.m. to 6 p.m.; (c) water for ordinary lavatory purposes, but if Tenant uses or consumes water for any other purposes or in unusual quantities (of which fact Owner shall be the sole judge), Owner may install a water meter at Tenant's expense, which Tenant shall thereafter maintain at Tenant's expense in good working order and repair, to register such water consumption, and Tenant shall pay for water consumed as shown on said meter as additional rent as and when bills are rendered; (d) cleaning service for the demised premises on business days at Owner's expense provided that the same are kept in order by Tenant. If, however, said premises are to be kept clean by Tenant, it shall be done at Tenant's sole expense, in a manner reasonably satisfactory to Owner, and no one other than persons approved by Owner shall be permitted to enter said premises or the building of which they are a part for such purpose. Tenant shall pay Owner the cost of removal of any of Tenant's refuse and rubbish from the building; (e) if the demised premises are serviced by Owner's air conditioning/cooling and ventilating system, air conditioning/cooling will be furnished to Tenant from May 15th through September 30th on business days (Mondays through Fridays, holidays excepted) from 8:00 a.m. to 6:00 p.m., and ventilation will be furnished on business days during the aforesaid hours except when air conditioning/cooling is being furnished as aforesaid. If Tenant requires air conditioning/ cooling or ventilation for more extended hours on Saturdays, Sundays or on holidays, as defined under Owner's contract with the applicable Operating Engineers contract, Owner will furnish the same at Tenant's expense. RIDER ☞ to be added in respect to rates and conditions for such additional service; (f) Owner reserves the right to stop services of the heating, elevators, plumbing, air-conditioning, electric, power systems or cleaning or other services, if any, when necessary by reason of accident, or for repairs, alterations, replacements or improvements necessary or desirable in the judgment of Owner, for as long as may be reasonably required by reason thereof. If the building of which the demised premises are a part supplies manually operated elevator service, Owner at any time may substitute automatic control elevator service and proceed diligently with alterations necessary therefor without in any way affecting this lease or the obligations of Tenant hereunder.

Captions: 30. The Captions are inserted only as a matter of convenience and for reference, and in no way define, limit or describe the scope of this lease nor the intent of any provisions thereof.

Definitions: 31. The term "office", or "offices", wherever used in this lease, shall not be construed to mean premises used as a store or stores, for the sale or display, at any time, of goods, wares or merchandise, of any kind, or as a restaurant, shop, booth, bootblack or other stand, barber shop, or for other similar purposes, or for manufacturing. The term "Owner" means a landlord or lessor, and as used in this lease means only the owner, or the mortgagee in possession for the time being, of the land and building (or the owner of a lease of the building or of the land and building) of which the demised premises form a part, so that in the event of any sale or sales or conveyance, assignment or transfer of said land and building, or of said lease, or in the event of a lease of said building, or of the land and building, the said Owner shall be, and hereby is, entirely freed and relieved of all covenants and obligations of Owner hereunder, and it shall be deemed and construed without further agreement between the parties or their successors in interest, or between the parties and the purchaser, at any such sale, or the said lessee of the building, or of the land and building, that the purchaser, grantee, assignee or transferee or the lessee of the building has assumed and agreed to carry out any and all covenants and obligations of Owner, hereunder. The words "re-enter" and "re-entry" as used in this lease are not restricted to their technical legal meaning. The term "business days" as used in this lease shall exclude Saturdays, Sundays and all days as observed by the State or Federal Government as legal holidays and those designated as holidays by the applicable building service union employees service contract, or by the applicable Operating Engineers contract with respect to HVAC service. Wherever it is expressly provided in this lease that consent shall not be unreasonably withheld, such consent shall not be unreasonably delayed.

Adjacent Excavation-Shoring: 32. If an excavation shall be made upon land adjacent to the demised premises, or shall be authorized to be made, Tenant shall afford to the person causing or authorized to cause such excavation, a license to enter upon the demised premises for the purpose of doing such work as said person shall deem necessary to preserve the wall or the building, of which demised premises form a part, from injury or damage, and to support the same by proper foundations, without any claim for damages or indemnity against Owner, or diminution or abatement of rent.

Rules and Regulations: 33. Tenant and Tenant's servants, employees, agents, visitors, and licensees shall observe faithfully, and comply strictly with, the Rules and Regulations and such other and further reasonable Rules and Regulations as Owner and Owner's agents may from time to time adopt. Notice of any additional Rules or Regulations shall be given in such manner as Owner may elect. In case Tenant disputes the reasonableness of any additional Rules or Regulations hereafter made or adopted by Owner or Owner's agents, the parties hereto agree to submit the question of

☞ Rider to be added if necessary

the reasonableness of such Rules or Regulations for decision to the New York office of the American Arbitration Association, whose determination shall be final and conclusive upon the parties hereto. The right to dispute the reasonableness of any additional Rules or Regulations upon Tenant's part shall be deemed waived unless the same shall be asserted by service of a notice, in writing, upon Owner, within fifteen (15) days after the giving of notice thereof. Nothing in this lease contained shall be construed to impose upon Owner any duty or obligation to enforce the Rules and Regulations or terms, covenants or conditions in any other lease, as against any other tenant, and Owner shall not be liable to Tenant for violation of the same by any other tenant, its servants, employees, agents, visitors or licensees.

Security: 34. Tenant has deposited with ☞ Owner the sum of $ as security for the faithful performance and observance by Tenant of the terms, provisions and conditions of this lease; it is agreed that in the event Tenant defaults in respect of any of the terms, provisions and conditions of this lease, including, but not limited to, the payment of rent and additional rent, Owner may use, apply or retain the whole or any part of the security so deposited to the extent required for the payment of any rent and additional rent, or any other sum as to which Tenant is in default, or for any sum which Owner may expend or may be required to expend by reason of Tenant's default in respect of any of the terms, covenants and conditions of this lease, including but not limited to, any damages or deficiency in the re-letting of the demised premises, whether such damages or deficiency accrued before or after summary proceedings or other re-entry by Owner. In the case of every such use, application or retention, Tenant shall, within five (5) days after demand, pay to Owner the sum so used, applied or retained which shall be added to the security deposit so that the same shall be replenished to its former amount. In the event that Tenant shall fully and faithfully comply with all of the terms, provisions, covenants and conditions of this lease, the security shall be returned to Tenant after the date fixed as the end of the lease and after delivery of entire possession of the demised premises to Owner. In the event of a sale of the land and building, or leasing of the building, of which the demised premises form a part, Owner shall have the right to transfer the security to the vendee or lessee, and Owner shall thereupon be released by Tenant from all liability for the return of such security; and Tenant agrees to look to the new Owner solely for the return of said security, and it is agreed that the provisions hereof shall apply to every transfer or assignment made of the security to a new Owner. Tenant further covenants that it will not assign or encumber, or attempt to assign or encumber, the monies deposited herein as security, and that neither Owner nor its successors or assigns shall be bound by any such assignment, encumbrance, attempted assignment or attempted encumbrance.

Estoppel Certificate: 35. Tenant, at any time, and from time to time, upon at least ten (10) days prior notice by Owner, shall execute, acknowledge and deliver to Owner, and/or to any other person, firm or corporation specified by Owner, a statement certifying that this lease is unmodified and in full force and effect (or, if there have been modifications, that the same is in full force and effect as modified and stating the modifications), stating the dates to which the rent and additional rent have been paid, and stating whether or not there exists any default by Owner under this lease, and, if so, specifying each such default and such other information as shall be required of Tenant.

Successors and Assigns: 36. The covenants, conditions and agreements contained in this lease shall bind and inure to the benefit of Owner and Tenant and their respective heirs, distributees, executors, administrators, successors, and except as otherwise provided in this lease, their assigns. Tenant shall look only to Owner's estate and interest in the land and building, for the satisfaction of Tenant's remedies for the collection of a judgment (or other judicial process) against Owner in the event of any default by Owner hereunder, and no other property or assets of such Owner (or any partner, member, officer or director thereof, disclosed or undisclosed), shall be subject to levy, execution or other enforcement procedure for the satisfaction of Tenant's remedies under, or with respect to, this lease, the relationship of Owner and Tenant hereunder, or Tenant's use and occupancy of the demised premises.

☞ Rider to be added if necessary

In Witness Whereof, Owner and Tenant have respectively signed and sealed this lease as of the day and year first above written.

Witness for Owner:

____

____________________________________ ____________________________________

Witness for Tenant:

____

____________________________________ ____________________________________

ACKNOWLEDGEMENT

STATE OF NEW YORK,

SS.:

COUNTY OF

On the ____________ day of ____________ in the year _____, before me, the undersigned, a Notary Public in and for said State, personally appeared ______________________, personally known to me or proved to me on the basis of satisfactory evidence to be the individual(s) whose name(s) is (are) subscribed to the within instrument and acknowledged to me that he/she/they executed the same in his/her/their capacity(ies), and that by his/her/their signature(s) on the instrument, the individual(s), or the person upon behalf of which the individual(s) acted, executed the instrument.

____

NOTARY PUBLIC

GUARANTY

FOR VALUE RECEIVED, and in consideration for, and as an inducement to Owner making the within lease with Tenant, the undersigned guarantees to Owner, Owner's successors and assigns, the full performance and observance of all the covenants, conditions and agreements, therein provided to be performed and observed by Tenant, including the "Rules and Regulations" as therein provided, without requiring any notice of non-payment, non-performance, or non-observance, or proof, or notice, or demand, whereby to charge the undersigned therefor, all of which the undersigned hereby expressly waives and expressly agrees that the validity of this agreement and the obligations of the guarantor hereunder shall in no way be terminated, affected or impaired by reason of the assertion by Owner against Tenant of any of the rights or remedies reserved to Owner pursuant to the provisions of the within lease. The undersigned further covenants and agrees that this guaranty shall remain and continue in full force and effect as to any renewal, modification or extension of this lease and during any period when Tenant is occupying the demised premises as a "statutory tenant." As a further inducement to Owner to make this lease, and in consideration thereof, Owner and the undersigned covenant and agree that in any action or proceeding brought by either Owner or the undersigned against the other on any matters whatsoever arising out of, under, or by virtue of, the terms of this lease or of this guarantee, that Owner and the undersigned shall and do hereby waive trial by jury.

Dated:. . . . . in the year . . . .

. . . .
Guarantor

. . . .
Witness

. . . .
Guarantor's Residence

. . . .
Business Address

. . . .
Firm Name

STATE OF NEW YORK) ss.:

COUNTY OF)

On the day of in the year before me, the undersigned, a Notary Public in and for said State, personally appeared , personally known to me or proved to me on the basis of satisfactory evidence to be the individual(s) whose name(s) is (are) subscribed to the within instrument and acknowledged to me that he/she/they executed the same in his/her/their capacity(ies), and that by his/her/their signature(s) on the instrument, the individual(s), or the person upon behalf of which the individual(s) acted, executed the instrument

. . . .
Notary Public

☞ IMPORTANT – PLEASE READ ☜

RULES AND REGULATIONS ATTACHED TO AND MADE A PART OF THIS LEASE IN ACCORDANCE WITH ARTICLE 33.

1. The sidewalks, entrances, driveways, passages, courts, elevators, vestibules, stairways, corridors or halls shall not be obstructed or encumbered by Tenant or used for any purpose other than for ingress or egress from the demised premises, and for delivery of merchandise and equipment in a prompt and efficient manner using elevators and passageways designated for such delivery by Owner. There shall not be used in any space, or in the public hall of the building, either by any tenant or by jobbers or others in the delivery or receipt of merchandise, any hand trucks, except those equipped with rubber tires and safeguards. If said premises are situated on the ground floor of the building, Tenant thereof shall further, at Tenant's expense, keep the sidewalk and curb in front of said premises clean and free from ice, snow, dirt and rubbish.

2. The water and wash closets and plumbing fixtures shall not be used for any purposes other than those for which they were designed or constructed, and no sweepings, rubbish, rags, acids or other substances shall be deposited therein, and the expense of any breakage, stoppage, or damage resulting from the violation of this rule shall be borne by the Tenant, whether or not caused by the Tenant, or its clerks, agents, employees or visitors.

3. No carpet, rug or other article shall be hung or shaken out of any window of the building and Tenant shall not sweep or throw, or permit to be swept or thrown, from the demised premises any dirt or other substances into any of the corridors or halls, elevators, or out of the doors or windows or stairways of the building, and Tenant shall not use, keep or permit to be used or kept, any foul or noxious gas or substance in the demised premises, or permit or suffer the demised premises to be occupied or used in a manner offensive or objectionable to Owner or other occupants of the building by reason of noise, odors, and/or vibrations, or interfere in any way with other tenants or those having business therein, nor shall any bicycles, vehicles, animals, fish, or birds be kept in or about the building. Smoking or carrying lighted cigars or cigarettes in the elevators of the building is prohibited.

4. No awnings or other projections shall be attached to the outside walls of the building without the prior written consent of Owner.

5. No sign, advertisement, notice or other lettering shall be exhibited, inscribed, painted or affixed by Tenant on any part of the outside of the demised premises or the building, or on the inside of the demised premise if the same is visible from the outside of the demised premises, without the prior written consent of Owner, except that the name of Tenant may appear on the entrance door of the demised premises. In the event of the violation of the foregoing by Tenant, Owner may remove same without any liability, and may charge the expense incurred by such removal to Tenant. Interior signs on door and directory tablet shall be inscribed, painted or affixed for Tenant by Owner at the expense of Tenant, and shall be of a size, color and style acceptable to Owner.

6. Tenant shall not mark, paint, drill into, or in any way deface, any part of the demised premises or the building of which they form a part. No boring, cutting or stringing of wires shall be permitted, except with the prior written consent of Owner, and as Owner may direct. Tenant shall not lay linoleum, or other similar floor covering, so that the same shall come in direct contact with the floor of the demised premises, and, if linoleum or other similar floor covering is desired to be used, an interlining of builder's deadening felt shall be first affixed to the floor, by a paste or other material, soluble in water, the use of cement or other similar adhesive material being expressly prohibited.

7. No additional locks or bolts of any kind shall be placed upon any of the doors or windows by Tenant, nor shall any changes be made in existing locks or mechanism thereof. Tenant must, upon the termination of his tenancy, restore to Owner all keys of stores, offices and toilet rooms, either furnished to, or otherwise procured by, Tenant, and in the event of the loss of any keys so furnished, Tenant shall pay to Owner the cost thereof.

8. Freight, furniture, business equipment, merchandise and bulky matter of any description shall be delivered to and removed from the demised premises only on the freight elevators and through the service entrances and corridors, and only during hours and in a manner approved by Owner. Owner reserves the right to inspect all freight to be brought into the building and to exclude from the building all freight which violates any of these Rules and Regulations of the lease, or which these Rules and Regulations are a part.

9. Canvassing, soliciting and peddling in the building is prohibited and Tenant shall cooperate to prevent the same.

10. Owner reserves the right to exclude from the building all persons who do not present a pass to the building signed by Owner. Owner will furnish passes to persons for whom Tenant requests same in writing. Tenant shall be responsible for all persons for whom he requests such pass, and shall be liable to Owner for all acts of such persons. Tenant shall not have a claim against Owner by reason of Owner excluding from the building any person who does not present such pass.

11. Owner shall have the right to prohibit any advertising by Tenant which in Owner's opinion, tends to impair the reputation of the building or its desirability as a building for offices, and upon written notice from Owner, Tenant shall refrain from or discontinue such advertising.

12. Tenant shall not bring or permit to be brought or kept in or on the demised premises, any inflammable, combustible, explosive, or hazardous fluid, material, chemical or substance, or cause or permit any odors of cooking or other processes, or any unusual or other objectionable odors, to permeate in, or emanate from, the demised premises.

13. If the building contains central air conditioning and ventilation, Tenant agrees to keep all windows closed at all times and to abide by all rules and regulations issued by Owner with respect to such services. If Tenant requires air conditioning or ventilation after the usual hours, Tenant shall give notice in writing to the building superintendent prior to 3:00 p.m. in the case of services required on weekdays, and prior to 3:00 p.m. on the day prior in case of after hours service required on weekends or on holidays. Tenant shall cooperate with Owner in obtaining maximum effectiveness of the cooling system by lowering and closing venetian blinds and/or drapes and curtains when the sun's rays fall directly on the windows of the demised premises.

14. Tenant shall not move any safe, heavy machinery, heavy equipment, bulky matter, or fixtures into or out of the building without Owner's prior written consent. If such safe, machinery, equipment, bulky matter or fixtures requires special handling, all work in connection therewith shall comply with the Administrative Code of the City of New York and all other laws and regulations applicable thereto, and shall be done during such hours as Owner may designate.

15. Refuse and Trash. (1) Compliance by Tenant. Tenant covenants and agrees, at its sole cost and expense, to comply with all present and future laws, orders, and regulations, of all state, federal, municipal, and local governments, departments, commissions and boards regarding the collection, sorting, separation and recycling of waste products, garbage, refuse and trash. Tenant shall sort and separate such waste products, garbage, refuse and trash into such categories as provided by law. Each separately sorted category of waste products, garbage, refuse and trash shall be placed in separate receptacles reasonably approved by Owner. Such separate receptacles may, at Owner's option, be removed from the demised premises in accordance with a collection schedule prescribed by law. Tenant shall remove, or cause to be removed by a contractor acceptable to Owner, at Owner's sole discretion, such items as Owner may expressly designate. (2) Owner's Rights in Event of Noncompliance. Owner has the option to refuse to collect or accept from Tenant waste products, garbage, refuse or trash (a) that is not separated and sorted as required by law or (b) which consists of such items as Owner may expressly designate for Tenant's removal, and to require Tenant to arrange for such collection at Tenant's sole cost and expense, utilizing a contractor satisfactory to Owner. Tenant shall pay all costs, expenses, fines, penalties, or damages that may be imposed on Owner or Tenant by reason of Tenant's failure to comply with the provisions of this Building Rule 15, and, at Tenant's sole cost and expense, shall indemnity, defend and hold Owner harmless (including reasonable legal fees and expenses) from and against any actions, claims and suits arising from such noncompliance, utilizing counsel reasonably satisfactory to Owner.

Address

Premises

TO

STANDARD FORM OF

Office Lease

The Real Estate Board of New York, Inc.

Dated **in the year**

Rent Per Year

Rent Per Month

Term
From
To

Drawn by ....

Checked by ....

Entered by..............................

Approved by ....

INDEX

S